OLIVER PARSONS

OFFICIAL (ISC)²®
GUIDE TO THE
ISSAP® CBK®

SECOND EDITION

OTHER BOOKS IN THE (ISC)²® PRESS SERIES

OFFICIAL (ISC)²®
GUIDE TO THE
ISSAP® CBK®

SECOND EDITION

Edited by
Adam Gordon - CISSP-ISSAP, ISSMP, SSCP

CRC Press
Taylor & Francis Group
Boca Raton London New York

CRC Press is an imprint of the
Taylor & Francis Group, an **informa** business

AN AUERBACH BOOK

CRC Press
Taylor & Francis Group
6000 Broken Sound Parkway NW, Suite 300
Boca Raton, FL 33487-2742

© 2014 by Taylor & Francis Group, LLC
CRC Press is an imprint of Taylor & Francis Group, an Informa business

No claim to original U.S. Government works

Printed on acid-free paper
Version Date: 20130806

International Standard Book Number-13: 978-1-4665-7900-2 (Hardback)

Visit the Taylor & Francis Web site at
http://www.taylorandfrancis.com

and the CRC Press Web site at
http://www.crcpress.com

Contents

Domain 2 - Communications & Network Security 131

Voice and Facsimile Communications 134

vii

Architecture

Foreword

CISSP-ISSAP® CBK Study Guide, *Second Edition*

As the complexity and vectors of security threats grow, professionals must concurrently acquire more advanced, specialized skills for prevention and mitigation in today's cyber world. Employers also recognize the increasing need for qualified professionals to demonstrate proven capabilities and subject-matter expertise beyond the requirements of the CISSP® credential.

The basis of any secure environment relies on a calculated architecture and design, involving a definition of strategic plans and tactical implementation for enterprise infrastructure. Those who specialize in security architecture need an understanding of multiple aspects of IT from a technical, developmental, and implementation perspective. They must also educate the C-suite and upper management on the beneficial business implications of applying appropriate security procedures – helping to meet goals and improve productivity, profitability, and efficiency.

As the only credential designed for the advanced security architecture professional that focuses on high-level security for enterprise-wide systems and infrastructure, the CISSP-ISSAP® is appropriate for system architects, business analysts, chief security officers, chief technology officers, and system and network designers. These credential holders report an impressive average annual salary of US$136,060*.

The second edition of the *Official Guide to the CISSP-ISSAP® CBK®* features expanded versions of the Communications and Security, Physical Security, and Technology Related Business Continuity Planning (BCP) & Disaster Recovery

Planning (DRP) Domains. Other enhancements include new tables and illustrations as well as updated and expanded references.

(ISC)² is pleased to offer the *Official (ISC)²* Guide to the ISSAP® CBK® – Second Edition*. This book will review and deepen your knowledge of security architecture, covering each of the six domains of the credential. I believe you will find this book helpful in your pursuit of the CISSP-ISSAP certification and as a reference guide throughout your security career.

We wish you success in your journey to adding ISSAP to your CISSP credential.

Sincerely,

W. Hord Tipton, CISSP-ISSEP, CAP
Executive Director
(ISC)²

* - Certification Magazine Salary Survey 2009

Architecture

Introduction

SECURITY ARCHITECTURE can be defined as the process of creating and maintaining the information security structure of an enterprise to ensure the confidentiality, integrity, and availability of critical and/or sensitive business systems. It follows, then, that the security architect is the individual that is qualified to perform the functions necessary to accomplish the security architecture goals of the organization. To be considered a professional security architect, it is necessary to delve much deeper into the elements that must be understood and employed to perform that role. The CISSP-ISSAP® certification is intended to measure and evaluate the ability of an individual to be accredited as a professional in this demanding field.

There are three requirements that must be met in order to achieve the status of CISSP-ISSAP; one must already be a CISSP in good standing, one must take and pass the CISSP-ISSAP certification exam, and be able to demonstrate a minimum of 2 years of direct full-time security work experience in one or more of the 6 domains of the (ISC)² CISSP-ISSAP CBK. A firm understanding of what the 6 domains of the CISSP-ISSAP CBK are, and how they relate to the landscape of business is a vital element in successfully being able to meet both requirements and claim the CISSP-ISSAP credential. The mapping of the 6 domains of theCISSP- ISSAP CBK to the job responsibilities of the Information Security architect in today's world can take many paths, based on a variety of factors such as industry vertical, regulatory oversight and compliance, geography, as well as public versus private versus military as the overarching framework for employment in the first place. In addition, considerations such as cultural practices and differences in language and meaning can also play a substantive role in the interpretation of what aspects of the CBK will mean, and how they will be implemented in any given workplace.

It is not the purpose of this book to attempt to address all of these issues or provide a definitive proscription as to what is "the" path forward in all areas. Rather, it is to provide the official guide to the CISSP-ISSAP CBK, and in so doing, to lay out the information necessary to understand what the CBK is, and how it is used to build the foundation for the CISSP-ISSAP and its role in business today. To that end, it is important to begin any successful project with a plan, specifically one that identifies where you are, and where you want to end up; and as a result, what tools you will need to have in order to make the journey comfortable and successful. The most important tool that the intrepid traveler can have at their disposal is a compass, that trusty device that always allows one to understand in what direction they are heading, and get their bearings when necessary. The compass of the Information Security professional is their knowledge, experience, and understanding of the world around them. The thing that is amazing about a compass is that no matter where you stand on Earth, you can hold one in your hand and it will point toward the North Pole. While we do not need to know where the North Pole always is in Information Security, as a CISSP-ISSAP, you are expected to be able to provide guidance and direction to the businesses and users that you are responsible for. Being able to map the CISSP-ISSAP CBK to your knowledge, experience, and understanding is the way that you will be able to provide that guidance, and to translate the CBK into actionable and tangible elements for both the business and its users that you represent.

1. The **Access Control Systems & Methodology** domain details the critical requirements to establish adequate and effective access controls for an organization.

Access Control key areas of knowledge include:

- Application of control concepts and principles (e.g., discretionary/mandatory, segregation/separation of duties, rule of least privilege).
- Account life cycle management (e.g., registration, enrollment, access control administration).
- Identification, authentication, authorization, and accounting methods such as centralized, decentralized and federation.
- Access Control Protocols and Technologies (e.g., RADIUS, Kerberos, EAP, SAML, XACML, LDAP).

These elements of Access Control Methodology are things that security architects interact with as they design systems for their organizations, as do the users of any systems that the business provides, such as Directory Services for logon authentication, File and Print systems that allow for the secure storage, retrieval, and manipulation of data in a variety of formats, as well as web services that expose data to front end interfaces for user consumption. Whenever a user attempts to access secured data from any legitimate or illegitimate interface, internal or external to the enterprise, the Access Control domain plays an active and indispensable part in the transactions that take place to ultimately either validate, or disqualify that user's access request. The ability to understand Identity Management, Data Access Controls, Information Classification, System Access Control Strategies, and Threats, are all key elements that go into the Access Control Domain. The security architect needs to be able to bridge the divide that is often present between the organization and the user with regards to Access Control, allowing the organization to secure the systems and information required to do business effectively, while also educating and informing users of their role in the system architecture and their responsibilities to operate securely and safely within the security frameworks that the architect has created.

2. The ***Communications & Network Security*** domain addresses the security concerns related to the critical role of communications and networks in today's computing environments.

Communications & Network Security key areas of knowledge include:

- Unified communications (e.g., convergence, collaboration, messaging)
- Communication topologies (e.g., centralized, distributed, cloud, mesh)
- Gateways, routers, switches and architecture (e.g., access control segmentation, out-of-band management, OSI layers)
- Monitoring (e.g., sensor placement, time reconciliation, span of control, record compatibility)

The Security Architecture Professional must understand the risks to communications networks whether they are data, voice or multimedia. This includes understanding of communications processes and protocols, threats and countermeasures, support for organizational growth and operations, and the ability to design, implement and monitor, secure architectures. The security architect needs to be comfortable designing architectures that are able to encompass the structures, techniques, transport protocols, and security measures used to provide integrity, availability, confidentiality and authentication for transmissions over private and public communication networks. The security architect is responsible for security at all levels of the business based on the system designs that they implement; whether it is with regards to a request to access controlled information, or the testing and deployment of an application, or the documentation for processes and procedures that are in place to safeguard mobile access to the business's data. Identification of threat and risk, and the implementation of mitigation techniques and strategies to counteract and minimize their impacts also play an important part in the list of activities that the security architect is responsible for carrying out and managing on a daily basis within the business. All of these things are part of the Communications & Network Security domain in one way or another.

3. The ***Cryptography*** domain addresses the principles, means, and methods of applying mathematical algorithms and data transformations to information to ensure its integrity, confidentiality and authenticity.

Cryptography key areas of knowledge include:

- Identifying Cryptographic Design Considerations and Constraints
- Defining the Key Management Lifecycle (e.g., creation, distribution, escrow, recovery)
- Designing integrated cryptographic solutions (e.g., Public Key Infrastructure (PKI), API selection, identity system integration)

While many of the physical elements of the Cryptography domain are used by business all the time to safeguard data and to ensure data integrity, security architects may not be aware of these functions and how they operate at the level of detail required to successfully create the security architecture that the organization relies on for protection of its information and sensitive data. Whether it is the use of Symmetric or Asymmetric Cryptography to protect data and ensure confidentiality, or the use of Hash Functions or Digital Signatures to ensure message integrity, or the practice of Encryption Management to ensure data availability on demand for authenticated users of a system, the security architect plays an active role in all aspects of the Cryptography domain, and its application to data security in the enterprise. The Security Architecture Professional should understand the responsibility involved in choosing, implementing and monitoring cryptographic products and adoption of corporate cryptographic standards and policy. This may include oversight of digital signatures and PKI implementations and a secure manner of addressing the issues and risks associated with management of cryptographic keys.

4. The ***Security Architecture Analysis*** domain is focused on the skills necessary to create diligence and attention to standards, awareness of threats, and identification of risks within the security architecture.

Security Architecture Analysis key areas of knowledge include:

- Identifying frameworks (e.g., Sherwood Applied Business Security Architecture (SABSA), Service-Oriented Modeling Framework (SOMF))
- Defining of business and functional needs (e.g., locations, jurisdictions, business sectors, cost, stakeholder preferences, quality attributes, capacity, manageability)
- Applying existing information security standards and guidelines (e.g., ISO/IEC, PCI, NIST) to the organization
- The Systems Development Life Cycle (SDLC) (e.g., requirements traceability matrix, security architecture documentation, secure coding)

The Security Architecture Professional should know and follow the best practices and standards for network and information systems design, and implement an architecture that will provide adequate security to accomplish the business goals of the enterprise. This requires the evaluation and choice of different architectures, and understanding the risks associated with each type of design. Security architectures that are designed and validated for the organization should contain the concepts, principles, structures, and standards used to design, implement, monitor, and secure, operating systems, equipment, networks, applications, and those controls used to enforce various levels of confidentiality, integrity, and availability.

5. The ***Technology Related Business Continuity Planning (BCP) & Disaster Recovery Planning (DRP)*** domain addresses the preservation of the business in the face of major disruptions to normal business operations. BCP and DRP involve the preparation, testing and updating of specific actions to protect critical business processes from the effect of major system and network failures.

Technology Related Business Continuity Planning (BCP) & Disaster Recovery Planning (DRP) key areas of knowledge include:

- Incorporation of the Business Impact Analysis (BIA) (e.g., legal, financial, stakeholders) into the security architecture
- Defining processing agreement requirements (e.g., reciprocal, mutual, cloud, outsourcing, virtualization)
- Ensuring availability of service provider/supplier support (e.g., cloud, SLAs)
- BCP/DRP Architecture Validation (e.g., test scenarios, requirements trace-ability matrix, trade-off matrices)

The security architect may or may not have direct experience with an actual disaster and the recovery actions that would be necessary to bring the business back to full functionality, while ensuring the safety and integrity of the business systems and information, as well as the safety and well- being of the users in the systems. A solid grounding in Project Management skills and the ability to interface with other risk management areas such as records management, regulatory compliance, vendor management, and physical security in the context of a Risk Management Framework that is used to help all areas of the business respond to and deal with risk effectively is a critical success factor for the security architect. The security architect should implement countermeasures to reduce the risk of incidents occurring that can lead to the necessity for a BCP/DRP plan to beactivated in the first place. Furthermore the Security Architecture Professional should play a key role in designing and developing business continuity plans that will meet the operational business requirements of the organization through planning for the provisioning of appropriate recovery solutions.

Business Continuity Planning (BCP) helps to identify the organization's exposure to internal and external threats. BCP counteracts interruptions to business activities and should be available to protect critical business processes from the effects of major failures or disasters. It deals with the natural and man-made events and the consequences, if not dealt with promptly and effectively.

Business Impact Analysis (BIA) determines the proportion of impact an individual business unit would sustain subsequent to a significant interruption of computing or telecommunication services. These impacts may be financial, in terms of monetary loss, or operational, in terms of inability to deliver.

Disaster Recovery Plans (DRP) contain procedures for emergency response, extended backup operation and post-disaster recovery, should a computer installation experience a partial or total loss of computer resources and physical facilities. The primary objective of the disaster recovery plan is to provide the capability to process mission-essential applications, in a degraded mode, and return to normal mode of operation within a reasonable amount of time.

6. The **Physical Security Considerations** domain recognizes the importance of physical security and personnel controls in a complete information systems security model.

Physical Security Considerations key areas of knowledge include:

- Policies and standards (e.g., export controls, escort policy, liaise with law enforcement and external media)
- Integrating physical security with identity management (e.g., wiring closet access, badge and enterprise identity management)
- Perimeter protection and internal zoning

Physical security describes measures that are designed to deny access to unauthorized personnel (including attackers) from physically accessing a building, facility, resource, or stored information; and guidance on how to design structures to resist potentially hostile acts.

The Security Architecture Professional should be able to demonstrate an understanding of the risks and tools used in providing physical security. These include secure management, administration and deployment of physical access controls, as well as whether to prevent, detect or react to suspicious activity. Designing architectures that seek to address the threats, vulnerabilities, and countermeasures that can be utilized to physically protect an enterprise's resources and sensitive information is the primary concern for the security architect. These resources include people, the facility in which they work, and the data, equipment, support systems, media, and supplies they utilize.

While many security architects will not be involved with the initial site and facility design criteria, and even the location choices for the organizations that they are a part of, that does not mean that they should not be aware of these factors with regards to their impact on security. Further, security architects need to play an active part in creating a focus within the business on the efficacy of its physical security posture, and if necessary, to be the agent that drives changes as required to ensure that security is maintained at appropriate levels given the threats and risks that are present in the operating environment.

Architecture

Editors

Adam Gordon - Lead Editor

With over 20 years of experience as both an educator and IT professional, Adam holds numerous Professional IT Certifications including CISA, CISSP, CRISC, CHFI, CEH, SCNA, VCP, and VCI. He is the author of several books and has achieved many awards, including EC-Council Instructor of Excellence for 2006-07 and Top Technical Instructor Worldwide, 2002-2003. Adam holds his Bachelor's Degree in International Relations and his Master's Degree in International Political Affairs from Florida International University.

Adam has held a number of positions during his professional career including CISO, CTO, Consultant, and Solutions Architect. He has worked on many large implementations involving multiple customer program teams for delivery.

Adam has been invited to lead projects for companies such as Microsoft, Citrix, Lloyds Bank TSB, Campus Management, US Southern Command (SOUTHCOM), Amadeus, World Fuel Services, and Seaboard Marine.

Steven Hernandez - Technical Editor

Steven Hernandez MBA, CISSP, CSSLP, SSCP, CAP, CISA is the Chief Information Security Officer and the Director of Information Assurance for the Office of Inspector General at the US Department of Health and Human Services. Hernandez has over seventeen years of information assurance experience in a variety of fields including international heavy manufacturing, large finance organizations, educational institutions, and Government agencies. Steven is affiliate faculty at the National Information Assurance Training and Education Center located at Idaho State University. Through his academic outreach, he has presented lectures over the past decade on numerous information assurance topics including risk management, information security investing, and the implications of privacy decisions to graduate and post graduate audiences. In addition to his credentials from (ISC)², Hernandez also holds six US Committee for National Security Systems certifications ranging from Systems Security to Organizational Risk Management. Steven also volunteers service to (ISC)²'s Government Advisory Board and Executive Writers Bureau. When not engaged in information assurance pursuits he enjoys relaxing with his family and their overly demanding dog.

Domain 1

Access Control Systems & Methodology

The Access Control Systems and Methodology domain details the critical requirements to establish adequate and effective access control restrictions for an organization. Access control protects systems, data, physical infrastructure, and personnel in order to maintain their integrity, availability, and confidentiality.

Failure to design, develop, maintain, and enforce access control will leave an organization vulnerable to security breaches. This applies to all types of breaches, whether they are locally or remotely initiated. It is imperative that you, as a security professional, understand the types of controls available, current technologies, and the principles of access control.

TOPICS

- Control access to systems and data through understanding

- Applying access control concepts, methodology, and techniques

- Control techniques and policies

- Access control administration

- Identification and authentication techniques

- Credentialing architecture

- Design validation

OBJECTIVES

The security professional architect is expected to:

- Apply both the hard and the soft aspects of access control
- Understand controls provided through:
  - Physical controls
  - Policy
  - Organizational structure
  - Technical means
- Demonstrate an awareness of the principles of best practices in designing access controls

Introduction

The implementation of access control in most environments has not changed much over the years. Access decisions are often left to the discretion of the information owner. Access control lists are used to distinguish which users will be granted access to a directory and / or a file within the directory, and what level of permissions these users will have in relation to the data being accessed. The availability of files stored on the network is ensured through backups. This represents the last line of defense against maliciously altered or deleted files. Automation of these previously manual controls does not entirely protect data from tampering or loss. Access controls must be properly set, otherwise information may be inappropriately copied or removed from a system, often without the knowledge of the information owner. Backups must be periodically checked to make sure that all target files were archived. Human interactions with these and other elements of a system can result in losses when activities are not conducted properly.

Automation of access control is also a double-edged sword. It does have benefits such as allowing a single individual to control access to a multitude of resources. However, the access and control an individual has can also be misused. Malicious code executing in the context of users can seriously impact the confidentiality, availability, and integrity of their resources. The design and implementation of access controls within a system must consider that the controls ultimately must be useable by humans, but also provide additional measure to detect, prevent, and correct undesirable resource access.

Access Control Concepts

Security architects should be interested in access control because it has desirable attributes that can preserve the critical information found in Line of Business systems. Systems with logical access controls watch over important information. These desirable attributes of logical access controls can:

- Protect resources from loss or exposure
- Provide accountability for those accessing the information or system

Arguably, the primary purpose of access control is to protect information from losses and exposure. This is accomplished through techniques that merge the attributes of actions between users and the information within a system. Access control occurs when rules are used to control the type of access a person has to a given resource. Essentially, access control is a way to discover the following:

Who is accessing the information? (the Subject doing the accessing)

What is being accessed? (the Object(s) being accessed)

How might the access occur? (the mechanism(s) used for access)

Being able to answer these questions creates the prerequisites for basic access control functionality. These questions are associated with a particular security policy governing actions within a system. This aids in the identification of a subject's actions on an object with respect to the permissions and rights granted according to a particular security policy. Some definitions follow:

Subject - The person, entity, or process in question.

Objects - A resource such as a file, device, or service.

Permissions - The type of access a subject is given. Common permissions include read, write, modify, delete, and execute.

Rights - Special abilities granted to a subject. For example, an administrator has the right to create accounts, while ordinary users do not. Rights have policy influences over the interactive *who*, *what*, and *how* questions of the access control mechanism.

The combined usage of subjects, objects, permissions, and rights forms the foundation of a system's access control. A security architect must strive to implement access control that conforms to the security policy of a system. *Figure 1.1* illustrates access control flow for subjects requesting specific objects. In the diagram, the access control system first determines if the subject has the appropriate rights to access the object. If the subject possesses the correct rights, then a subsequent check determines if the subject has sufficient permissions to view or manipulate the object.

Access control coupled with auditing establishes the basis for accountability. Auditing is the process of recording access control

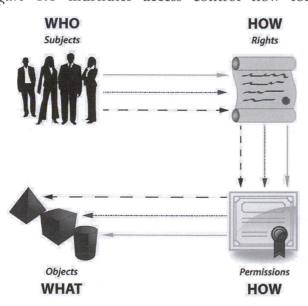

WHO
Subjects

HOW
Rights

Objects
WHAT

Permissions
HOW

Figure 1.1 - **Interaction between subjects, rights, permissions, and objects**

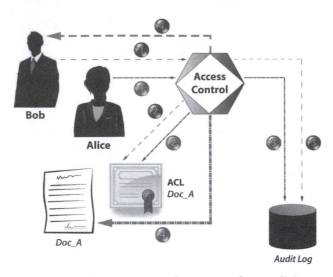

Figure 1.2 - **Access control support for auditing**

actions and is the principal method used to achieve accountability. Reviewing the actions of subjects on particular objects helps managers to determine if inappropriate activity occurred. *Figure 1.2* shows how an access control mechanism is used to audit successful and failed access. In the diagram, Alice makes a request to read Doc_A. The Access Control mechanism compares the request from Alice with the Access Control List (ACL) for Doc_A. The ACL indicates that Alice has the permission to read the document. The Access Control mechanism creates an entry in the Audit Log and allows Alice access to the document. Bob also requests access to Doc_A . The Access Control mechanism determines through the Doc_A ACL that Bob does not have permission for the document. The Access Control mechanism creates an audit log entry of Bob's failed request and informs him that access is denied.

Access control is the fundamental mechanism that provides for the confidentiality, integrity, and availability of information within an information technology (IT) system. Confidentiality is supported by only allowing access to a particular object for those entities that are explicitly authorized. Granular-level stipulations on how an entity can interact with a particular object can be used to ensure the object's integrity. The combined services of confidentiality and integrity help ensure that an object is only available to those who are authorized to access it. Access control thus enables

- **Confidentiality:** Through measures that protect objects from unauthorized disclosure
- **Integrity:** By preventing unauthorized modifications when properly implemented
- **Availability:** When integrity is properly enabled

The ability of an access control mechanism to provide the desired security services is predicated upon the correct implementation of a security policy. A system should be governed by a written standard that specifies the rules applicable to the system. These rules are derived from

- Laws
- Regulations
- Industry standards
- Organizational policies

The compilation of rules applicable to a particular IT system forms the security policy. The security policy addresses managerial, operational, and technical security requirements for a system. A system security policy can be viewed as a structure, such as the one depicted in *Figure 1.3*. Confidentiality, integrity, and availability establish the foundation of a security policy. Rules formed by laws, regulations, standards, and policy are the primary pillars supporting the policy. It is interesting to note that most rules exist for the purpose of establishing accountability for entry and activity within the system. The rules impart managerial, organizational, and technical controls that make up the foundation of the system security policy. More often than not, access control and auditing in an IT system represents the bulk of the technical security within the security policy. The interpretation of the correct access control implementation of the security policy is the responsibility of the security architect, based on the direction of the information owner.

Interpreting security policy is not a trivial matter. If the policy is written in terms that are too general, it might have multiple interpretations or at least give rise to implementation issues. Suppose a security policy contains the statement "Users are not allowed to access information for which they are not authorized." Does this mean if someone shares sensitive information with them that they are

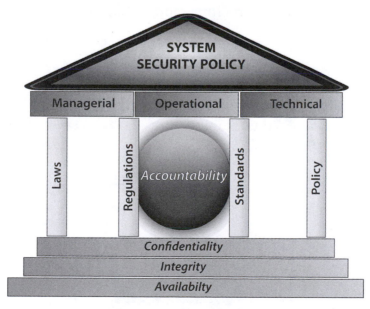

Figure 1.3 - **System security policy structure**

now authorized? The sharing might contradict some other part of the policy. If the sharing violates another part of the policy, does this mean that the system is flawed? What if someone saves sensitive information into a directory accessible by users not authorized to view the information? If some of these users view the sensitive information, does this mean they violated the policy or that the system failed to properly enforce the policy? Indeed, these issues arise on a daily basis and are not easily defined or enforced. However difficult these issues may be, a security policy is still one of the best ways to ensure adoption and enforcement of an organization's security requirments.

The main issue with access control implementation is interpreting security policy. A security architect needs to understand some of the science behind access control in order to integrate it with the world of abstract thought representative of security requirements. The art of implementing access controls involves the merging of a logical system, which is rigid in structure, with that of an organization, which is dynamic. Security architects must anticipate these issues and make interpretations based on their understanding of the organization, intent of the security policy, and the capabilities of the system for which the access control is being considered.

The process of interpreting security policy is at its core an attempt to balance requirements against available controls. Consider *Figure 1.4*, which shows the balancing task that a security architect faces to achieve the ideal security policy. The correct balance between requirements and controls is neither too weak nor too restrictive. On the one side, interpretation of requirements must consider the intent of policy. A literal interpretation of policy could be insufficient to

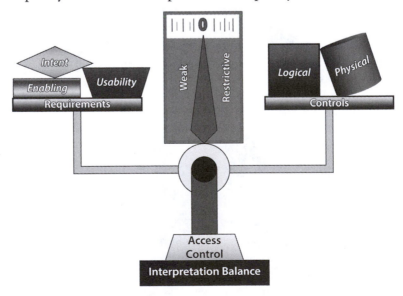

Figure 1.4 - **Balancing Access Control**

provide sufficient coverage or so pervasive as to be prohibitively expensive. The controls selected should not prevent the organization from accomplishing its mission. Rather, controls selected based on the requirements should enable the organization to continue routine operations. Finally, controls need to be usable otherwise they will likely be circumvented by system users.

The mechanisms of access control can be found in a variety of products and at multiple levels within an IT system. The more common products implementing access control include:

- **Network Devices** - Routers, switches, and firewalls
- **Operating Systems** - Linux, Unix, and Windows
- **Database Management Systems** - Oracle, MySQL, and SQL Server
- **Applications** - Certificate authorities, encryption software, and single sign-on products

Do certification authorities implement access control? Well, sort of. It is more correct to say that certification authorities *support* access control. What about encryption software? Actually, when an object is encrypted, unauthorized users are denied access to the cleartext information. This has the same effect as not being allowed permission to read an object. In reality, single sign-on products do not implement access control either. However, they do *facilitate* the integration of disjointed access control systems. This reduces the user and management headaches often experienced when switching between systems or components with different access control mechanisms.

Access control at the network level tends to be more connection oriented, such as allowing or disallowing ports and protocols associated with given IP addresses. Typically, an access control mechanism is limited to the box itself. Most operating systems provide some form of access control by default. At this level, an access control mechanism is sometimes shared among workstations and servers in a network. However, this is not always the case for every commercial operating system. Many databases provide capabilities to control access to the data they contain. In some cases, a database management system might also be able to distribute access control functionality among distributed systems, in much the same way as some operating systems.

Some applications contain their own access control mechanisms, which might be as simple as allowing or denying access based on presenting acceptable credentials or a robust access control mechanism similar to those found in an operating system or database. Unfortunately, these various access control mechanisms, more often than not, are proprietary and do not integrate easily with one another. This situation complicates the job of the security architect. Furthermore, the variety of access control mechanisms also compounds the problem of trying to determine at which layer or level in the network to enforce the security policy. For instance, if a security policy prohibits the use of unauthorized protocols, should this be enforced at the operating system only or should it also include all routers and switches? The security architect will need to make judgments about the depth and breadth of access control implementations to meet the security policy. *Figure 1.5* illustrates many different access control methods and techniques that can be applied to the various layers of the Open System Interconnectivity (OSI) model.

A variety of access control techniques and policy mechanisms exist. It is interesting to note that many of the access control techniques are designed to implement a particular type of policy. This means that a particular access control technique might not be the best choice in a given circumstance. Unfortunately, Commercial-Off-the-Shelf (COTS) products do not typically provide a method of selecting an access control technique that would be ideally suited for the system, or the particular environment in question. As a result, the security architect is often left to their own devices to make a particular type of access control mechanism fit as best it can when a more desirable mechanism is not available.

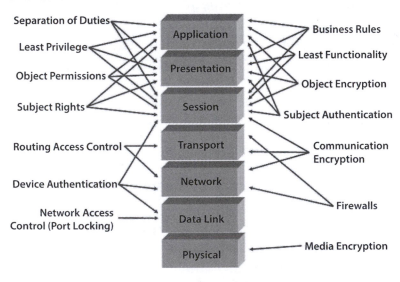

*Figure 1.5 - **Access control within the OSI model***

Two important features of access control mechanisms are the Access Control List (ACL) and the ACL repository. The ACL identifies the security attributes of a particular system object. Typically, this will include information about the object owner and other entities having authorized access associated with the rights granted to each entity. Each subject identified in an ACL is known as an Access Control Entry (ACE). The ACL repository is used to manage each ACL in the system. *Figure 1.6* illustrates these access control features.

Discretionary Access Control

Discretionary Access Control (DAC) is the predominant access control technique in use today. Most commodity systems implement some form of DAC. The underlying concept of DAC is to give an object owner the discretion to decide who is authorized access to an object and to what extent. In this regard, the policy is set or controlled by the owner of a particular object. At its most basic level, DAC implementations include the specific rights to read, append, modify, delete, and execute. The read permission allows a designated entity the ability to load the contents of an object into memory. The permission to append allows an entity to attach new information to the end of an object. Permission to modify an object means an entity can change any and all of the contents of an object. Entities with the permission to delete can destroy an object and cause it to be removed from volatile or nonvolatile memory. The execute permission gives an entity the ability to cause the system to create a new process or thread of execution based on the binary nature of the object.

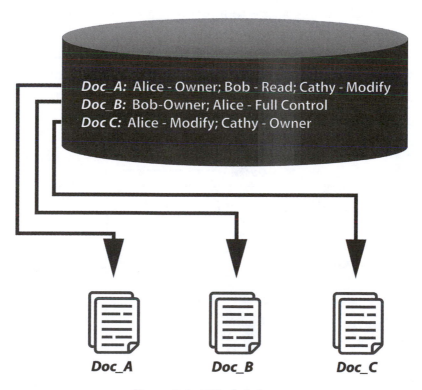

Figure 1.6 - **ACL database**

Implementing DAC can give rise to security problems if the mechanism is not well understood or if it is used contrary to its design. There are three important aspects of DAC that must be understood and questioned by the security architect:

- **Read** - What does it mean?
- **Write** - What are the implications?
- **Execute** - What is running on the box?

Although these aspects are essential elements of DAC, they can reveal apparent flaws in the access control mechanism.

It is essential to understand that the read permission does not mean read-only. It really means read-and-copy. Any subject with the permission to read a file can also make a copy of the same file. This frequently occurs during the reading process. When an application reads a data file, it makes a copy of the contents in memory. Because the user of the application owns the memory space where it is copied, the application user essentially creates a new copy of the data file. Thus, the entity provided with the permission to read a particular data file is now the owner of a copy of the same file. This functionality of DAC potentially empowers an attacker bent on information theft. Thus, read permission may complicate insider threat mitigation efforts.

The difficulty of limiting access to information is shown in *Figure 1.7*. In this illustration, Bob has permission to read Doc_A. Bob's ACE only allows him to read the document from the disk device that is owned by the system. When Bob reads the document, a copy of it is created on his local system in an area of memory over which he has full control. Bob is now the owner of the new document copy. At this point Bob can do what he wants with any portion of document. He could make copies of any section and send it to an output where he has the appropriate permission.

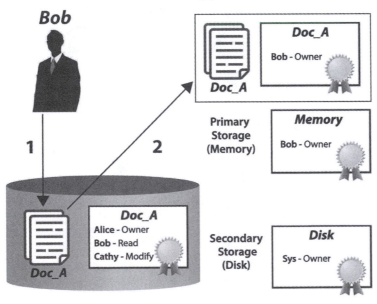

*Figure 1.7 - **Read permission challenge***

The next important aspect that must be considered is permission to write. Giving an entity the ability to write to a file object allows it to write anything to that object. "Anything" could include a virus, appended to the end. Another problem with this permission is that an entity could also replace all of the data in a file with one byte of information. Suppose a document file includes charts, graphs, and over a megabyte of text. The malicious entity could simply perform an overwrite, causing a multimegabyte file to shrink to one byte in a microsecond. This is similar to having the ability to delete a file. The implication of the permission to write is that object integrity can be affected. Inappropriate granting of the write permission has far-reaching and potentially devastating consequences.

Yet another troubling issue with the ability to write is when the object in question is a directory. Writing to a directory essentially means a subject is allowed to create a new object. In this case, entities with the ability to write to a directory can create any type of object in that directory, with ownership permissions on the newly created object. Consider the situation in *Figure 1.8*. In this example, Bob can create an exact copy of Doc_A in the same directory by using a new unique name, in this case Doc_D. As the new owner of the object, Bob could grant others access to the document, which may violate organizational policy.

A malicious entity may choose to write objects that are binary executables to any permitted directory, according to the subject's write permission. Even though an entity might not be given execute permissions for the directory object, this is not a hindrance because the object owner can change any inherited permissions on the new object from the directory to anything he or she likes.

The third significant DAC consideration is the execution permission. More specifically, it is essential to understand the concept of the context of an executing process. When an entity executes a process, that process typically has access to all objects available to the entity. A program

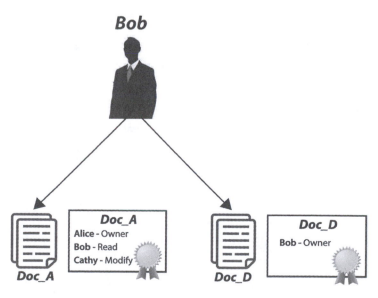

Figure 1.8 - **Write permission problem**

executed by the user has access to all files, interfaces, and other programs running in their context. Typically, an operating system does provide some memory separation between running processes. However, interprocess communications as well as graphical interfaces open avenues for one process to affect the execution of another. This feature of DAC is what gives a Trojan horse the ability to steal information or damage a system. This problem with DAC is well known and studied. Although researchers have proposed a variety of solutions to this problem, their solutions have not seen widespread commercial adoption.

Although the aforementioned problems seem to be flaws in the design of DAC, they are more essentially issues that arise due to implementation errors of the access control mechanism. The security architect should take proactive measures to overcome the shortcomings of DAC, which will reduce any risk that might be present. Some strategies for implementing DAC follow.

DAC Implementation Strategies

Overcoming the challenges of the read permission is a difficult task, but mitigations are possible. The efforts of a security architect will require technical and nontechnical techniques. The following are some approaches to consider:

- *Limit access to essential objects only.* Ensure user access to resources is restricted to only that which is needed for the performance of their duties. When we think of the concept of Least Privilege and combine it with the concept of "need to know", we have an effective mechanism for implementation from an architectural perspective.
- *Label sensitive data.* Use standardized file and folder-naming conventions, as well as headers and footers within documents that provide users with visual clues about the sensitivity of the information. Extended attributes of a file also provide an area to include label information of a file. For instance, the Summary Properties of a file within Windows include editable values such as Title, Subject, Category, Keywords, and Comments that can be used to store label information.
- *Filter information where possible.* Use filters to detect inappropriate transfers of sensitive information.
- *Promulgate guidance that prohibits unauthorized duplication of information.* Policies and procedures should inform users about the types of information that require protection, limited distribution, or replication. Provide users with periodic training and guidance reminders.
- *Conduct monitoring for noncompliance.* Use tools to search files containing sensitive information or labels in repositories where

they should not exist. The Windows Explorer Search tool and the grep utility in Unix are useful for finding particular words or phrases within a file.

Controlling write actions is essential to protect information and system integrity. Preventing unauthorized modification of resources is the primary means of controlling system integrity. Why do viruses often gain complete access to a system? Excessive permissions on configuration settings and files allow the virus to write to or delete critical files. Implementing the most restrictive permissions, such as read or no access, would prevent a virus from writing to important objects. Consider the access control list displayed in *Figure 1.9* for explorer.exe.

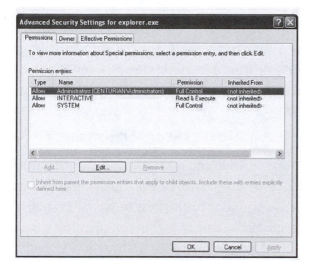

Figure 1.9 - **Commonly recommended permissions for explorer.exe**

This is a common security setting in many Windows systems. In fact, it is a recommended setting found in various security configuration publications. Is there a problem with this configuration? The trouble with this ACL is that the integrity of the file is not protected in the context of the System or any user in the Administrators group. Malicious processes executing in either context could either attach a virus to explorer.exe or associate a backdoor with the program.

Furthermore, the file could also be deleted altogether. The ACL should specify the Read permission for System and Administrators as well. So why would many publications recommend an ACL such as this? It is believed that the reason for this ACL recommendation is because it allows updates to binaries to be made on the fly. It supports the Windows Update process and simplifies life for administrators too. The weak ACL eases file level administration. This is a prime example of a trade-off between security and simplicity. It is challenging to meet both these goals simultaneously because there are so many executables in the average Windows based system. Does an alternative exist? Instead of living with the weak ACL, it is desirable that an automated process be instituted as a supportive measure. Assume that a file system is initially configured with a strong ACL (read permission for all subjects). Microsoft provides both the cacls.exe and icacls.exe tools, which can be scripted to handle ACL and ACE changes for any file. The cacls tool is officially listed as deprecated by Microsoft, but is still available in Windows 7 and Windows 8, as well as Server 2008/R2 and Server 2012. Microsoft also provides support for the same functionality through the use of PowerShell, although the knowledge required to use PowerShell for this task will be an order of magnitude higher than either cacls or icacls, as one must rely on Get-Acl and Set-Acl cmdlets to get, show and set permissions on a folder. However, since there are no cmdlets to help with the actual manipulation of the permissions, the security professional will need to use a few .NET classes and methods to get the job done.

With cacls, just before conducting a system update, run the following from the command line:

```
C:\cacls *.exe /t /e /p administrators:f system:f
```

This command instructs cacls.exe to edit the ACL for each executable in the C:\ drive, including subdirectories, and change the ACE for the Administrators group and the System account to full control. This will allow changes to any executable file on the C:\ drive. When the system update is complete, execute the following at the command line:

```
C:\cacls *.exe /t /e /p administrators:r system:r
```

This edits the ACL for each program on the drive and reduces the Administrators group and the System account to read, which restores the most appropriate settings. Consider using these commands on other important binary files such as ActiveX controls, libraries, drivers, screensavers, and applets. The primary caveat is that ACL changes must be coordinated with updates, whether via Microsoft Update or some other tool. It is important to note that this example of cacls.exe use disregards inheritable directory permissions. However, this tool does give the capability to accommodate those permission settings too. As with any new security management technique, it is important that testing be conducted first to ensure that the most appropriate configuration is achieved. The equivalent solution using icacls is below:

Step 1: (This command instructs icacls.exe to edit the ACL for each executable in the C:\drive, including subdirectories, and change the ACE for the Administrators group and the System account to full control.)

```
C:\icacls *.exe /grant administrators:F system:F
```

Step 2: (This edits the ACL for each program on the drive and reduces the Administrators group and the System account to read, which restores the most appropriate settings.)

```
C:\icacls *.exe /grant administrators:R system:R
```

To illustrate how this would be done with PowerShell, an object, Testfolder, will be created. Permissions will then be assigned to the object, and finally, the permissions that have been assigned will be verified by listing the ACL. **(The numbers denote a separate line of PowerShell commands, or code, and are in no way part of the example, and should not be entered when using PowerShell to create objects and assign permissions to them)**

```
1.  New-Item G:\Testfolder -Type Directory
2.  Get-Acl G:\Testfolder | Format-List
3.  $acl = Get-Acl G:\Testfolder
4.  $acl.SetAccessRuleProtection($True, $False)
5.  $rule = New-Object System.Security.AccessControl.
    eSystemAccessRule("Administrators","FullControl",
    "ContainerInherit, ObjectInherit", "None", "Allow")
6.  $acl.AddAccessRule($rule)
7.  $rule = New-Object System.Security.AccessControl.
    FileSystemAccessRule("Users","Read","ContainerInherit,
    ObjectInherit", "None", "Allow")
8.  $acl.AddAccessRule($rule)
9.  Set-Acl G:\Testfolder $acl
10. Get-Acl G:\Testfolder | Format-List
```

Encouraging users to make use of access control mechanisms can help limit loss of data due to malicious code. Owners of shared files, such as word processing documents, should set the ACE for all other subjects to read-only. Applying this philosophy will prevent other users from accidentally (or unwittingly, when compromised by malware) deleting a document shared by someone else.

Appropriate access control settings need to be established for all resources within a system. The following are a few more objects for which write permission should be restricted:

- **Configuration Files** - Any file used to store configuration information should be set to read-only where updates are not routine actions.

- **Windows Registry** - Lock down system registry keys to read-only. This is especially important for the Run keys, which designate software to execute at boot. Run keys are a primary target for malware.

- **Services** - If a service is not needed, it should be disabled. If particular users do not need a service, then they should be prevented through the ACL from interacting with it.

- **Data** - Follow the concepts of least privilege and separation of duties when assigning permissions to data files.

Solving the execute problem with DAC is by far the most important measure. The execution of unauthorized processes can threaten the integrity of user context, or worse, that of the entire system when the context is that of an administrator or the system itself. The best approach to this problem is to apply restrictive access controls to existing executables and monitor for unauthorized access instances. The following is a list of recommended approaches:

- *Set access control entries for all executable binary files to read-only.* This helps to protect their integrity. Examples of Windows-based executables, libraries, and other specialized binaries that should be set to read-only include those with the following extensions: com, exe, scr, dll, tlb, ocx, drv, sys, vxd, cpl, hlp, and msc.
- *Prevent execution from removable media.* Prevent applications from automatically running from removable media.
- *Use host-based firewalls.* Set the policy to explicitly identify which programs are allowed to connect to the network. Ensure that the associated policy file or registry entries are set to read-only using DAC.
- *Conduct software integrity inventories.* Use tools such as Tripwire (open source for Linux based systems, or Enterprise for Windows based systems),Cimtrak or splunk to identify unauthorized changes in programs, and validate the integrity of those that are authorized. [1]
- *Monitor executions.* Consider implementing specialized tools that can keep an audit of software running on a machine. This can be used to identify users violating policy or malware not detected by antivirus monitoring.

Nondiscretionary Access Control

Access control mechanisms that are neither DAC nor mandatory access control (MAC) are referred to as forms of nondiscretionary access control. These types of access control still rely on the fundamental concept of subjects, objects, and permissions. However, the association or specifications of these elements are different from DAC and MAC.

- **Role-Based Access Control (RBAC)** - It is desirable to limit individuals to only those resources that are needed to support their duties. Ideally, an access control mechanism would be able to ensure that the assignment of privileges to a particular resource does not introduce a conflict of interest or issue with separation

---

1   See the following for information on:

  A. Tripwire Open Source for Linux based systems: http://www.tripwire.org/

  B. Tripwire Enterprise for Windows based systems:
     http://www.tripwire.com/it-security-software/

  C. Cimtrak: http://www.fileintegritymonitoring.com/cimtrak/security

  D. splunk: http://www.splunk.com/

of duties. This can be achieved when user access is controlled according to assigned job function or role. RBAC is a specialized access control mechanism providing this capability. The unique quality of RBAC is that rights and permissions are ordered in a hierarchal manner. Privileges on resources are mapped to job functions. This prevents an object from being shared with those not authorized.

- **Originator Controlled (ORCON)** - An information owner may desire to control the life cycle of certain types of information. Some of the desired control might concern how long the information remains available or who is allowed to view it. The United States military makes use of ORCON 2 designations in paper documents that direct readers not to disseminate the information without the express consent of the originator (McCollum, Messing, Notargiacomo, 1990). 3

- **Digital Rights Management (DRM)** - Intellectual content such as music, movies, and books need methods to control who is authorized to access these types of content. Clearly, DAC is of no use in controlling the unauthorized distribution of these types of information. Additionally, DRM must have portability features because a user might want to access the protected content from different systems or platforms. DRM relies on cryptographic techniques to preserve the authenticity and access to protected information. Researchers are also investigating the use of multilevel security policies to improve DRM resistance to attackers (Popescu, Crispo, and Tanenbaum, 2004).

- **Usage Controlled (UCON)** - Another problem associated with protecting intellectual content involves frequency of access. Suppose a video store desires to rent access to its movies, but wants to limit the ability of consumers to only view each rental a maximum of three times. DRM techniques provide measures that attempt to control who can access the content, but they do not control how often. Addressing the "how often" issue will

---

2   The main reasons for ORCON classification codes include the following:
  a. Alert the holder that the item requires protection
  b. Advise the holder of the level of protection
  c. Show what is classified and what is not
  d. Show how long the information requires protection
  e. Give information about the origin of the classification
  f. Provide warnings about any special security requirements

3   For a historical review of the entire program of Information Classification by the United States Government, please see the following: http://www.fas.org/sgp/crs/secrecy/RL33494.pdf   (Relyea, Harold C. (2008), Security Classified and Controlled Information: History, Status, and Emerging Management Issues. Congressional Research Service Report for Congress, Order Code RL 33494.)

establish the ability to license the frequency of access to protected content. UCON 4 is one technique currently being investigated by researchers to control the frequency of access to protected content (Park and Sandhu, 2004).

■ *Rule-Based Access Control* - A number of different devices and applications provide their own type of access control mechanism in which decisions are made based on some predetermined criteria. These mechanisms use rules to decide if an action is permitted or denied. Rule-based access control is extensively used, but it is not scaleable. Firewalls, routers, virtual private network (VPN) devices, and switches are examples of products using rule-based access control.

Authentication is an important aspect of rule-based mechanisms. Subjects of a rule-based mechanism are usually identified as human users or system activity. People authenticated with rule-based access control often use passwords or cryptographic proofs such as a digital certificate. Authentication of system activity relies on operational aspects such as media and network addresses as well as cryptographic proofs. For example, a firewall enforces authentication decisions based on network addresses.

Rules developed for this type of access control can be complex. DAC makes determinations based on access control lists as opposed to rule-based access control, which evaluates activity. For example, a firewall may evaluate a network connection based on the address, port, and protocol used. This is a much more complicated evaluation than evaluating a subject's access to a particular object in DAC.

Permissions in rule-based access control are simplistic binary decisions. Either access is allowed or it is not. If the rule is met, then the action is allowed. This is in contrast to DAC, where a degree of access can be permitted, for example, read, write, or modify.

It is important to note that MAC is sometimes referred to as a rule-based access control (Bishop, 2003). It is differentiated within this text because the implementation and functionality of MAC contrasts significantly with other devices and applications that employ rule-based mechanisms.

---

4 UCON based access control systems are being proposed for a variety of areas such as social networks and cloud based computing systems as well. See the following for some examples of thinking in these areas:

 A. M.G. Jaatun, G. Zhao, and C. Rong (Eds.): CloudCom 2009, LNCS 5931, pp. 559–564, 2009. © Springer-Verlag Berlin Heidelberg 2009

 B. http://www.w3.org/2010/policy-ws/papers/17-Park-Sandhu-UTSA.pdf

Mandatory Access Control (MAC)

An organization may have many different types of information that need to be protected from disclosure. Many organizations around the world, both public and private, have employed a variety of mechanisms with regards to Mandatory Access Control solutions. Secure operating systems designed specifically with access control in mind, such as SELinux, have been examined and used as test beds for development of MAC solutions in many countries such as the United Kingdom. [5] Starting with Microsoft's Vista operating system, the use of Mandatory Integrity Control (MIC), which is a core security feature that adds Integrity Levels (IL)-based isolation to processes running in a login session has been used as another form of MAC. This mechanism 's goal is to selectively restrict the access permissions of certain programs or software components in contexts that are considered to be potentially less trustworthy, compared with other contexts running under the same user account that are more trusted. [6] The advent of Electronic Health Records, and the issues associated with the management of electronic patient data more broadly within the healthcare industry globally has become a key focus area for research and development of MAC models and systems to address the key concerns of Confidentiality and Integrity. Countries such as Australia have active research communities attempting to address issues in this area. [7]

The United States government has identified three particular classes of information that require integrity and unauthorized disclosure countermeasures

---

[5]   See the following for more information on SELinux:

A. SELinux overview:

http://selinuxproject.org/page/FAQ
http://www.nsa.gov/research/selinux/index.shtml
http://www.nsa.gov/research/selinux/related.shtml

B. Research overview of proposed implementation for a MAC system using SELinux in the UK:

http://publib.boulder.ibm.com/infocenter/lnxinfo/v3r0m0/topic/liaax/SELinux_White_Paper.pdf

[6]   See the following for more information on Mandatory Integrity Control (MIC) in Microsoft operating systems:

http://www.symantec.com/avcenter/reference/Windows_Vista_Security_Model_Analysis.pdf
http://blogs.technet.com/b/steriley/archive/2006/07/21/442870.aspx
http://blogs.adobe.com/asset/2010/07/introducing-adobe-reader-protected-mode.html

[7]   See the following for more info on Electronic Health Records and MAC systems:

http://dig.csail.mit.edu/2012/WWW-DUMW/papers/dumw2012_submission_2.pdf
http://eprints.qut.edu.au/14080/1/14080.pdf
http://eprints.qut.edu.au/10894/1/10894.pdf

due to the level of harm that their exposure might cause to the country. These classes in ascending hierarchal *sensitivity* are Confidential, Secret, and Top Secret. All other types of information are considered unclassified and must be protected according to other policies. Suppose an individual is granted a *clearance* to access Secret information. Such a person could view any Secret information, as well as Confidential information, when he has an appropriate need to know. However, he would not be allowed to access Top Secret information, because his clearance is lower than the sensitivity designation of the classified information. MAC was devised to support the concept of access based on a subject's clearance and the sensitivity of the information. The fundamental principles of MAC prevent a subject from reading up and writing down between classifications (Bertino and Sandhu, 2005).

MAC functions by associating a subject's clearance level with the sensitivity level of the target object. It is important to note that systems supporting MAC implement DAC as well. The key to the proper functioning of MAC is the use of specialized labels on each system object. The label specifies the highest classification for the particular object. The system protects the labels from alteration. A subject must have a clearance equal to or greater than the sensitivity of the target object. Furthermore, the system relies on DAC methods to determine if the subject has been granted the permission to interact with the

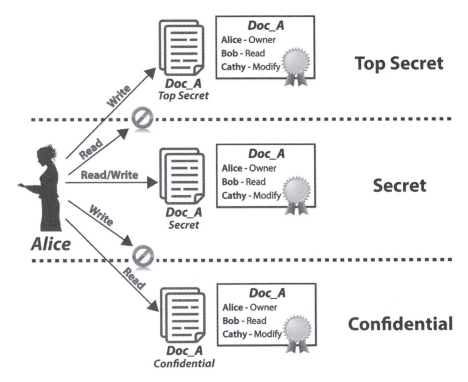

Figure 1.10 - **Classifications and sensitivity levels in MAC**

object. *Figure 1.10* illustrates the association between clearance, sensitivity levels, and the use of DAC. In the figure, Alice interacts with the system at the Secret level. Although she is the owner of a document within each sensitivity level, MAC prevents reading to higher levels and writing to lower. This aspect of MAC prevents the flow of information from a higher classification to one that is lower.

The important feature of MAC is its ability to control information flows. Subjects with higher clearances are permitted to read information at a lower classification level. Thus, a subject with a Secret clearance is permitted to access information at the Confidential level. However, MAC prevents a subject with a Secret clearance from writing information to an object at the Confidential level. This restriction of writing to a lower classification level prevents the accidental or intentional flow of information from a higher classification to a lower classification. This helps protect against policy violations or unauthorized exposures of the information to those without a need to know. Obviously, a subject with a lower clearance cannot read objects with a higher classification, but they are permitted to write information to a higher classification. This has the somewhat interesting consequence that a user can write information up, but will have no way to reread what was written. *Figure 1.11* is another way to view the read and write properties of MAC regarding clearance and sensitivity.

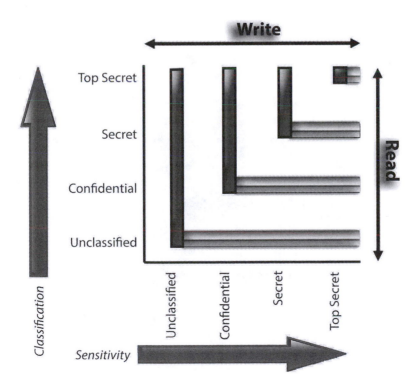

Figure 1.11 - **Sensitivity, Classification, reading, and writing matrix of MAC**

Suppose a manufacturing organization desires to use MAC as a way to protect its proprietary products. Manufacturing of proprietary products involves many people along the way, but not everyone needs to be aware of every step. Separate classifications are established based on the life cycle of a product based on materials used, fabrication techniques, and experimental improvements. Given these scenarios, three classifications for our hypothetical manufacturing company are proposed:

Development - Those involved in research and development of new products

Processing - Individuals involved in the proprietary assembly of the components

Components - Ordering and storage of the base components

Figure 1.12 describes the interaction between the classification levels and product life-cycle activity. In this example, subjects who order the base components have no idea about quantities used to create a particular product, because they write the quantity from their components classification to the processing classification. Similarly, they have no comprehension of the processing and development activities the components are involved in. Those involved in processing consume select components to create different products depending on

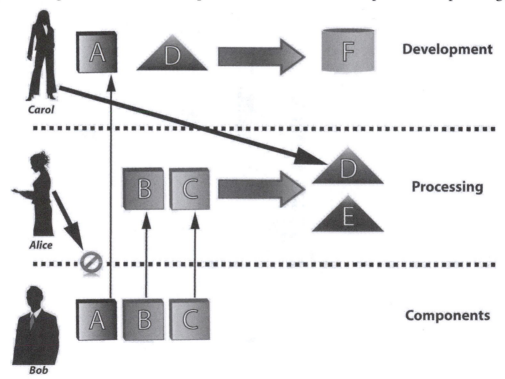

*Figure 1.12 - **Use of MAC in a business environment***

the particular process used. Processing is prevented from reading the quantities used for development. The output from processing is not accessible by those with a components clearance, but it is available to those with the development clearance. Workers in the development arena create experimental processes and consume various components to devise new products. The experimental output in the development classification is not accessible by those with a processing or components clearance.

Least Privilege

Consider an organization that does not restrict access to personnel records. Given a lack of access control, anyone browsing through the records could obtain privacy-protected information or information on compensation. What if compensation information is limited to only the people in the finance department? This is better, but is insufficient. Should the people who receive payments, also known as accounts receivable, from customers also have access to an individual's salary information? This is obviously unnecessary as the job function of people working in accounts receivable has nothing to do with payroll. As such, one would expect an appropriate use of the concept of least privilege to be implemented, preventing accounts receivable personnel from browsing payroll information. Limiting access to sensitive information is the crux of information security.

Implementing least privilege implies that an individual has access to only those resources that are absolutely necessary for the performance of their duties. In practice however, implementation is often fraught with difficulties. More commonly, the access granted is typical of what is seen in *Figure 1.13*. It is evident from the figure that the user is granted rights and permissions beyond what is needed to conduct his tasks. Why does this occur? Some of the reasons for this could be:

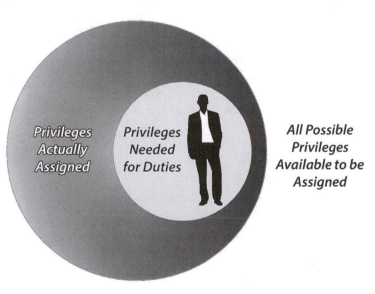

Figure 1.13 - **Common misallocation of privileges**

- *Lack of explicit definition of duties* - Neither the user nor manager has a clear grasp or definition of the duties assigned to the individual.
- *Weak internal controls* - Where explicit duties are known, changes in duties or access controls on the system may not be periodically reviewed for conflicts.
- *Complexities in administration* - In very large, distributed organizations, it is difficult to know the access limitations that should be imposed when access control is centralized.

Thus far, the complexities of least privilege, from the aspect of information access, have been considered, but are there considerations that extend beyond information? Assume that an organization has a centralized database containing sensitive information. Does it seem reasonable that each database user is allowed to have database administrator rights? This scenario would most likely violate least privilege because users would have the ability to easily access information outside of the scope of their duties. If the duty of a database user does not include administration functions, then following the concept of least privilege, a user would not be provided database administrative rights.

Another factor to be considered is access to system resources. Should a user be given access to all network resources? Suppose the sales team, as shown in *Figure 1.14*, has wireless access into the network. Assume that they require wireless access because they rely heavily on their laptops as their primary computing platform. The finance department is contemplating whether to connect its new

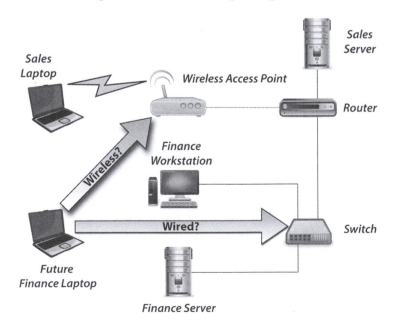

Figure 1.14 - **Least privilege dilemma in network resources**

laptops to the network using wired or wireless access. Does it seem reasonable that users in the finance department should also be allowed the ability to connect to the wireless access point? It is doubtful that the individuals in the finance department have a business need to connect to the wireless access point. Given this perspective, preventing their ability to connect to the wireless access point and reverting to wired access would follow the concept of least privilege.

Least Functionality: A Cousin of Least Privilege

Limiting access to resources is fairly straightforward. If an individual needs to run a tool, then access to the tool should be allowed. However, some tools contain *functionality* that can be damaging. In some cases, an acceptance of risk is necessary given the need to use the tool. When possible, the functionality of a tool should be reduced to mitigate actual or potential risk.

Consider the issue of phishing. A user receives an e-mail from what appears to be his or her personal banking institution. The message claims that the account password must be updated or access to the account will be lost. The "phishy" part is a hyperlink to the individual's bank. Protecting unsuspecting or uninitiated users from these types of attacks can be accomplished through simplistic measures. Many e-mail clients provide the capability to display plaintext information, excluding the rich or hypertext content. Configuring the e-mail client to display only plaintext exemplifies the application of least functionality. The sacrifice is a loss of aesthetically pleasing e-mails, but the gains in preventing individuals from unwittingly facilitating identify theft are substantial.

A security architect must consider design issues related to least privilege. Ideally, a system will provide technical methods for enforcing least privilege. The use of access control mechanisms will be the architect's primary method to design in the ability to implement least privilege. Consider the following techniques to implement least privilege:

- *Access Control Lists* - Use network- and system-based access controls to allow or deny access to network resources.

■ *Encryption* - Using cryptographic measures for network traffic prevents surreptitious gathering of information that a user is not authorized to access.

Nontechnical measures should also be implemented to support least privilege. Although an architect may not be responsible for these aspects, they should be promoted and considered nonetheless:

■ *Define data and associated roles* - Sensitive data requiring least privilege implementations should be identified. Information owners should explicitly identify the individuals or roles that are authorized access to the information.

■ *Sensitive data-handling procedures* - Rules on the use of data exiting the system should be explicitly identified. Data is commonly moved from systems through removable media, electronic sharing, and printing. Policies should establish acceptable circumstances and methods of transferring sensitive data. Ideally, procedures will also explicitly identify the best methods to securely transfer information.

■ *User education* - All users handling sensitive media should be made aware of the proper methods used to handle the information. They should be instructed on how to identify transfers of information that might violate least privilege. Obviously, the necessary tools used to facilitate secure transfer should be available for their use.

A security architect following the concept of least privilege designs a system that limits resources to only those subjects who require access in the performance of their duties. Resources of concern include files, devices, and services. Access control and encryption are two techniques that can be used to enforce least privilege. User role identification, data sensitivity, and user education are important factors supporting least privilege implementations.

Separation of Duties

One way to enforce accountability is through techniques that prevent a single individual from circumventing internal controls. Suppose Mr. Smith is allowed to make purchases for Rockit Enterprises. He orders 153 ACME widgets. Assume Mr. Smith is allowed to sign for the receipt of the products. Upon receipt, he modifies the paperwork to reflect an order and receipt of 100 ACME widgets. As a result of the modification, nobody is aware of the 53 widgets pocketed by Mr. Smith. This situation occurred due to a lack of separation of duty. Conceptually, separations of duties preclude an individual from perpetrating fraud. With sufficient separation, a single person should not have the ability to violate policy without colluding with at least one other individual. From a system security standpoint, separation of duty is necessary to ensure accountability for actions taken in the system. Weaknesses in separation of duties are identifiable by the excessive assignment of system privileges, which could allow an individual to perpetrate fraud and avoid detection.

Every person within an organization has at least one role. Ideally, all roles within an organization are discrete, which means that every role is unique. It is also desirable for every individual to be assigned to only one role. However, this is seldom the case, especially when there are staffing shortages. It is also common to see multiple people in the same role. The goal of separation of duties is to prevent the perpetration of fraud. To meet the goal of separation of duties requires confidence that the rights and permissions assigned to subjects are correct, without conflicting overlaps between roles.

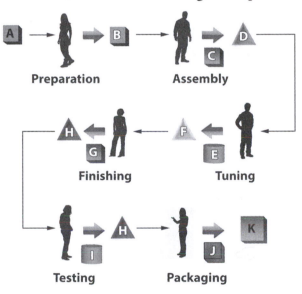

Figure 1.15 - **Assembly line work**

A role is nothing more than a job function within the organization. The duties assigned to individuals define their role. Ideally, they are assigned tasks that do not involve a separation of duties issue. An individual's role fits into the patterns of activity supporting the mission of the organization. Some of the patterns will involve workflows consisting of tasks that are linked together. An example of a workflow is the assembly line seen in *Figure 1.15*. Each station on the line adds components or makes modifications until a final product emerges at the end. The tasks and duties of each worker are naturally segregated by the workflow process of the assembly line. Thinking in these terms regarding security in information systems, the security architect can find ways to build segregation of duties into organizations as well.

Consider the work of an information systems auditor. A high-level overview of the job role entails

1. Enumeration of system requirements
2. System assessment against requirements
3. Report of findings and recommendations

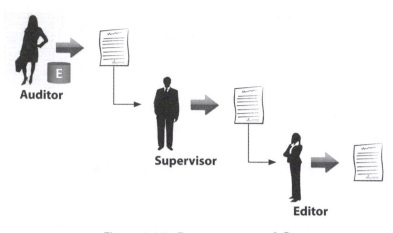

Auditor

Supervisor

Editor

Figure 1.16 - **Document workflow**

Think about what the reporting aspect of the role might involve. After assessing a system, auditors must compile a document for perusal by the management staff. A document workflow of this process is presented in *Figure 1.16*. Some organizations use tools that facilitate or even define the type of process seen in the figure.

The diagram depicts the auditor generating a report that is intended for review by a supervisor. The document is sent to a technical editor, who makes final adjustments for style and grammar. The final document is then delivered to the customer. This simplistic workflow involves three people with a single document. There are three very different roles - that of an auditor, supervisor, and technical editor - involved in the workflow. All three persons have access to the same data, but their duties are quite different. Therefore, following the paradigm of workflows in a system is helpful when defining individual user roles.

A system does not define the role of a person. Even when workflow tools are used, it is important to realize that people often have other tasks outside of a system. So how can job duties or roles be used to identify separation of duties within a system? This can be accomplished by establishing the necessary separation between the combined rights and permissions granted to subjects. In this regard, a role is composed of the following:

- **Rights** - The type of actions an individual is permitted to make in the system
- **Permissions** - Access granted to information shared or used in job-related workflows

The discussion thus far suggests that a role is the aggregate of a subject's rights and permissions. *Figure 1.17* presents an ideal situation, in which subject roles work together, but do not overlap. This example epitomizes the perfect separation of duties situation.

Reality is usually less than ideal however. In practice, it can be difficult to determine the exact rights and permissions an individual needs for the job.

Figure 1.17 - **Ideal role assignments**

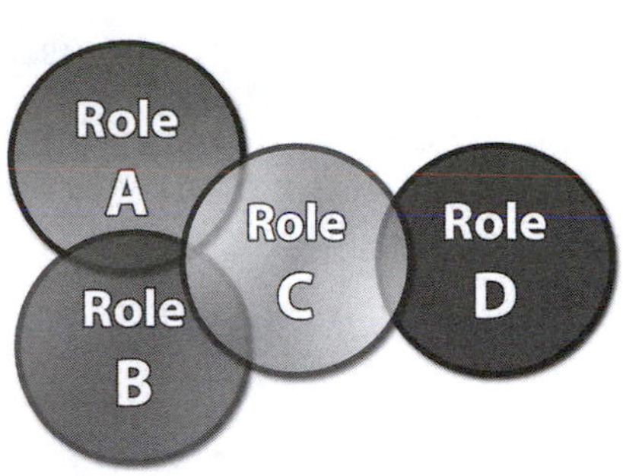

Figure 1.18 - **The challenge of role assignments in reality**

Ensuring separation of duties becomes a more difficult issue when people are assigned multiple roles, and as a result, when there is greater potential for conflict. *Figure 1.18* shows us the reality of separation of duties. The overlap between roles indicates that one role has excessive rights or permissions compared to those of another.

A broad observation can be made regarding the relation between rights and permissions. Those assigned elevated rights in a system should have less permission to data involved in workflows. This is necessary because those with elevated rights can potentially compromise confidentiality, integrity, and availability of workflows. Having this ability could enable an individual to perpetrate a fraud. Consider a scenario with the following roles:

■ *Developer* - Individuals within this role are responsible for developing or maintaining applications for organizational users. Their creativity enhances the usefulness of an information system. They should not have access to the production system.

■ *Administrator* - This role ensures the system is available for organizational use. Administrators are commonly tasked with managing user accounts and resources. Their duties do not ordinarily require access to or manipulation of sensitive organizational information. However, their powers of access into the system are such that they can be fairly characterized as having access to all system resources and data.

■ *Security Officer* - Monitors systems for misuse. Individuals in this role commonly review audit logs and the output from security tools such as those used for intrusion detection and vulnerability assessments. They are the information assurance sentinels tasked with protecting a system's security services.

■ *Ordinary User* - It is most likely that this role will span a plethora of subordinate roles where one type of user is separated from another. Users are the primary consumers and manipulators of organizational data. An information system exists primarily to connect ordinary users with the data they need to perform their assigned duties.

Assume that these roles are mutually exclusive; that is, a user in one role should not have the ability to perform the functions of another role. This represents an ideal implementation of separation of duties. Now, suppose that weaknesses in the assignment of separation of duties occur, as shown in the following tables.

As a general rule, developers should not have access to a production system. When this rule is followed, separation of duties is not an issue. However, when the conflicting roles shown in *Table 1.1* are coupled with a disregard of the aforementioned rule, problems can occur. If a developer is assigned conflicting roles, a situation is created in which data theft or system disruption becomes possible, and it will be difficult to track violations.

Conflicting Role	Potential Violation
Administrator	Can circumvent most, if not all, security controls through software changes such as the deployment of a malicious driver acting as a root kit.
Security Officer	Security events generated by malicious software deployed would be ignored. Developers in this capacity would be checking their own work and could easily cover up a fraud.
Ordinary User	With this level of access, a developer could create a covert channel allowing access to unauthorized information.

Table 1.1 - **Inappropriate Roles Assigned to a Developer**

By default, an administrator has the ability to access the most sensitive information within a system. A corrupt administrator has the potential to cause significant damage or expose a substantial amount of data. The substantial degree of access associated with this role necessitates a commensurate degree of monitoring. However, when this role is inappropriately merged with other roles seen in *Table 1.2*, it becomes possible for administrators to avoid critical monitoring.

Conflicting Role	Potential Violation
Developer	This has the same effect as a developer given administrator rights. It is absolutely the worst possible violation of the principle of separation of duties.
Security Officer	Administrators with this role would be checking their own work and could easily cover up security violations generated through monitoring activity.
Ordinary User	If granted ordinary user access, administrators might be able to bypass monitoring activity specifically designed to identify administrator abuse.

Table 1.2 - **Inappropriate Roles Assigned to an Administrator**

Security officers are concerned with monitoring and enforcement of a system security policy. In this regard, there should be little or no interaction with data workflows in the system outside the scope of their duties. Providing a security officer with additional abilities shown in *Table 1.3* would make it difficult to detect their fraudulent activity. Corrupt security officers given excessive privileges would most likely be able to hide their activity.

Conflicting Role	Potential Violation
Developer	Access violations due to malicious software developed by the security officer would be covered up.
Administrator	Changes in accounts or system policies might go unnoticed, and most likely unreported.
Ordinary User	Attempts to access unauthorized information would not be reported.

Table 1.3 - **Inappropriate Roles Assigned to the Security Officer**

The focus of the role of an ordinary user is to facilitate a job function as a workflow. The primary tasks involve the creation, manipulation, and consumption of system data. The assignment of conflicting roles as seen in *Table 1.4* would enable ordinary users to either perpetrate a fraud or prevent their malicious activities from being detected.

Conflicting Role	Potential Violation
Developer	A user could craft specialized code allowing backdoor access into the context of other system users.
Administrator	User could change workflow data with this level of privileged access.
Security Officer	Violations made by the user could be covered up or disregarded.

Table 1.4 - **Inappropriate Roles Assigned to an Ordinary User**

The previous scenario suggests an intuitive method of separating duties for individuals accessing a system. An initial separation determination based on the job function of an individual is possible with respect to the system. An individual with management or operational influence on the system should have reduced interaction with system data. In this regard, there are two broad categories that can be used as the initial basis for separation of duties:

■ *Individuals responsible for operational aspects of the system* - Within this area, duties are further decomposed according to their functions which might enable circumvention of accountability.

■ *Those primarily interacting with system data and information workflows* - Users are separated according to the type of data they interact with.

Security design efforts should consider various aspects that could affect separation of duties. At a minimum, it should be possible to enforce separation of duties through the user access control mechanisms whether the designation is manual or automated. A system should have sufficient administrative flexibility to accommodate the following aspects:

■ *Identify each explicit role* - Decompose all system use and management functions using a process similar to that shown in *Figure 1.19*. From there, examine each function and consider if further decomposition is needed to ensure appropriate separations to support workflow processes. Collect users into groups or roles according to the access control supported by the system. Attention should be given to disjoint access control. This occurs when multiple access control systems exist that do not share information. It is necessary that tracking of user grouping between the various access control systems be coordinated to avoid separation of duty issues. Document the process used to arrive at the segregations for repeatability purposes. The results of the segregations should also be documented.

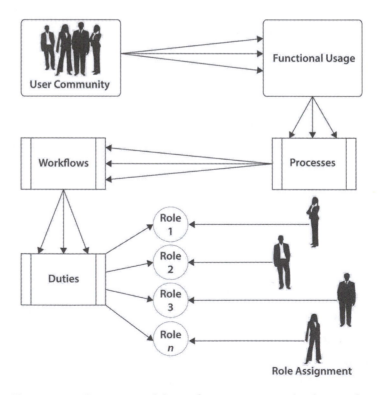

Figure 1.19 - **Decomposition of user community into roles**

- *Assign appropriate permissions* - Be aware of ways in which a role may violate segregation of duties (SoD). For each grouping, consider the rights necessary for users to accomplish their tasks. Within a system, rights may be cumulative. A user assigned multiple roles may end up with excessive rights. One way to counteract this scenario is to assign a user a specific account with properly separated rights.

- *Avoid unnecessary rights* - When privileges are cumulative, ensure excessive access is not inadvertently granted.

- *Mitigate workflow violation potentials* - Consider situations in which an identified role might be able to affect a workflow outside.

Organizations with constrained resources will find it difficult to fully achieve separation of duties. This is especially true in organizations with a small staff. In these cases, it is common to find that an individual is assigned to multiple roles. This situation makes separation of duties difficult to achieve. However, the following techniques can be of some assistance to help identify potential fraud:

- *Assign accounts on a per-role basis* - An individual should have a separate account for each role used. The rights corresponding to separate roles should be separated to the greatest extent possible.

- *Prevent those with multiple roles from reading and writing to the same storage area* - Where possible, prevent an individual with multiple roles from writing information with one role into an area that could be read by another role. Ideally, the permissions for the roles should be mutually exclusive.

- *Auditing is vital* - Consider implementing object-level auditing for individuals with multiple roles. Identify key areas where abuse might occur, and implement multiple methods to monitor for violations.

- *Conduct more frequent evaluations* - Use external system auditors and more frequent internal audits of the system to ensure that all controls are functioning properly. Audit workflows to assess any improper activity.

As stated earlier, the primary purpose of separation of duties is to ensure that an individual is unable to perpetrate fraud and simultaneously avoid accountability. However, separation of duties can also be a tool used to identify omitted job functions. Various system-related duties and organizational workflows require particular elements that must be filled by an individual to ensure a particular task is completed in its entirety. When a key element of a task is missing, it might cause a critical process to fail at an inopportune time. Missing task elements create a gap in separation of duties. Consider the following scenario depicted in *Figure 1.20*. In this situation, suppose one administrator is assigned to manage

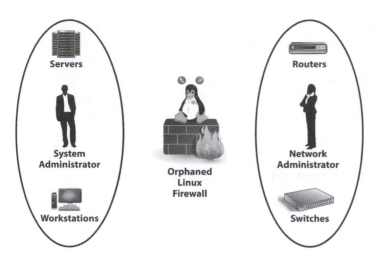

Figure 1.20 - **The orphaned Linux firewall**

operating systems, and another administrator is tasked with managing networking equipment. The system contains a Linux box running a firewall application at one of the network borders. The operating system administrator views the firewall as a network device because it is functioning as a network device. In contrast, the network administrator views the firewall as an operating system because it is built with commodity hardware and software. Neither has taken management responsibility of the firewall. This represents a gap in separation of duties.

Evaluating separation of duties involves identification of inappropriate and insufficient assignment of rights and permissions related to subject roles in a system. A security architect must consider all of the possible duties within a system and ensure that appropriate separations are identified and that capabilities exist for proper enforcement. An evaluation of separation of duties will look for

- *Overlaps* - The assignment of roles that conflict with one another. Overlaps can be identified by considering the rights and permissions assigned to any given account with that of another, where the two accounts should have distinct roles. Where it is possible for a fraud to be perpetrated, another role should exist that can detect abuse.

- *Gaps* - Roles should be designed to accommodate all operational aspects of the system and organizational workflows processed. Aspects of system management and workflows that orphan critical tasks represent gaps in separation of duties. Unassigned or abandoned tasks can potentially jeopardize the security services of a system.

It is interesting to note the complementary nature of least privilege and separation of duties. Much like the components of the bridge shown in *Figure 1.21*, the functional aspects of these security principles influence one another. Least privilege is necessary for the proper functioning of separation of duties. Without

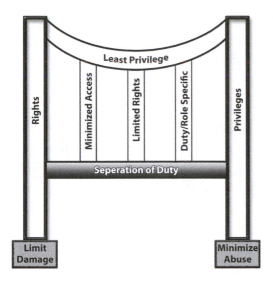

Figure 1.21 - **The mutual influence of least privilege and separation of duties**

least privilege, it is not possible to provide separation of duties. Excessive assignment of rights or permissions violates the concept of least privilege and can provide an avenue to exploit a weakness in separation of duties. The misalignment of duties, in the case of an overlap, suggests that one role is in possession of too many privileges. Overlaps in duties violate least privilege. Thus, harmony between least privilege and separation of duties is achieved when rights and permissions are properly balanced in support of the system security services.

Ideally, the design of a system allows easy implementation of separation of duties. However, this is often not the case, and the security architect must consider design aspects that will provide the necessary assignment of rights and permissions while preventing a role or individual from concealing a fraud. Assigning individuals to multiple roles is a common practice fraught with the possibility of inadvertent violation of separation of duties. The totality of a subject's access should be compared with all other subjects to identify overlaps and gaps. Overlaps violate separation of duties, while gaps represent orphaned aspects of critical tasks that may result in a security control weakness.

Architectures

The design of the security functions for a system should support its security policy. A well-designed system will be capable of making the necessary access decisions. Ideally, the system will fully support a defined security policy. In reality, access control systems are often capable of supporting a subset of the security policy. Nontechnical methods such as procedures and other operational aspects must be relied on to ensure that a security policy is met. To the greatest extent possible, the technical functions in a system should be designed to automate support for the security policy.

An architect must consider in what manner a subject should be allowed to access which objects in the system. A security kernel and the security reference monitor act as the electronic gatekeepers for the system by mediating a subject's access to authorized objects. The security monitor mediates object requests from the subject. Each request is provided to the reference monitor, which determines if the request is allowed and what degree of access should be permitted. Joint operations of the security kernel and reference monitor should be established to support the system security policy. In this way, a subject will be allowed or denied access according to the security policy enforced by the security kernel and reference monitor.

The security of an entire system depends on the joint properties of the controls implemented; that is, the security of a system is the sum of its collective security mechanisms. All of the technical security controls in a system are collectively referred to as the Trusted Computing Base (TCB). In this regard, the overall security of a system is no stronger than the most vulnerable components of the TCB. *Figure 1.22* provides an illustration of common components that comprise the TCB of most enterprise systems.

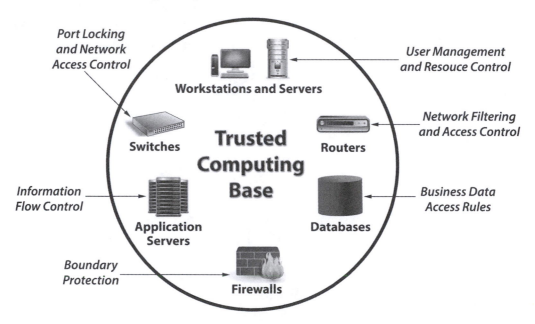

Figure 1.22 - **The trusted computing base**

A security kernel is the collection of components of a TCB that mediate all access within a system. It is important to note that a security kernel may be centralized or of a distributed nature. For instance, a router with access control capabilities has a self-contained security kernel. In contrast, a distributed system that implements a domain security model relies on the proper operation of different devices and operating systems. It is collectively recognized as a security kernel. Because it is responsible for mediating access requests, it is a choke point in the system. Any failure in the security kernel will affect the supported system. Ideally, components of a security kernel are not complicated and made up of a small amount of code. This allows for easier analysis to identify any flaws that might be present. The integrity of the security kernel's components is absolutely critical. The architect should make every effort possible to prevent unauthorized modifications to the kernel as well as provide mechanisms to monitor for any malicious changes.

The most common functions of the security kernel include authentication, auditing, and access control. The operational aspect of the security functions is referred to as the security reference monitor. Generally, the security reference monitor compares an access request against a listing that describes the allowed actions. *Figure 1.23* provides a brief overview of a security reference monitor. [8]

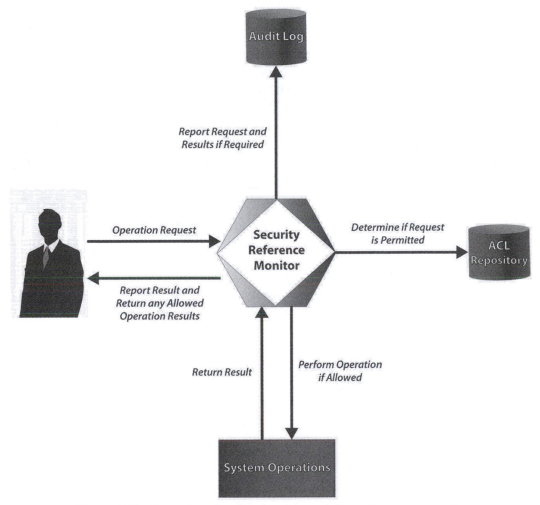

Figure 1.23 - **Functional aspects of a security reference monitor**

8　　For a discussion of the concepts inherent in a secure system architecture, and the associated parts that make it possible, see the following:　http://csrc.nist.gov/publications/history/ande72.pdf

Authentication, Authorization, and Accounting (AAA)

The acronym AAA refers to Authentication, Authorization, and Accounting. It is supported by RFC 2904,[9] which specifies an authorization framework for using AAA. The term is heavily used to discuss the access control mechanisms built into networking equipment and repeated to a large extent within many IETF RFC documents.

The design of access control within security architectures is driven by system usage and requirements. In some cases, it is necessary to retain tight centralized management of the access control mechanisms. In other cases, a distributed or decentralized technique is best employed to meet organizational needs. Enabling access control between systems from collaborating organizations requires y–et another approach, which is considered a type of federated access control. The differentiating factor among the potential architectures is the point where an access control decision is made.

Centralized Access Control

An access control system that is centralized relies on a single device as the security reference monitor. Authorization and access control decisions are made from the centralized device, which is referred to here as the access control server (ACS). This means that login as well as resource access requests are handled in one place. *Figure 1.24* describes the fundamental processes and decisions that centralized access control systems follow. There are three architectural approaches

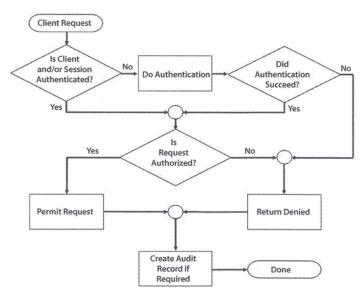

Figure 1.24 - **Flowchart of centralized access control**

9   See the complete RFC here: http://tools.ietf.org/html/rfc2904

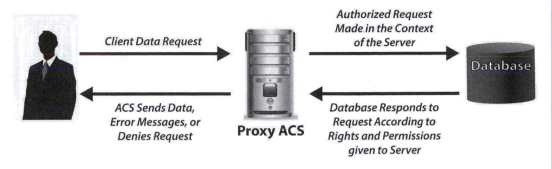

Figure 1.25 - **Proxy access control system**

to achieving centralized access control. Each method conforms to the generic concept of centralized access control as seen in Figure 1.24. However, the approaches are differentiated in the way each handles client resource requests.

One approach to centralized access control is for the ACS to proxy client resource requests. In this case, the ACS accesses resources on behalf of the client. *Figure 1.25* depicts centralized access control using a proxy methodology. This approach is commonly used in Web portals and database management systems (DBMSs). The front end to the portal or DBMS evaluates requests according to the permissions and rights of the subject and manipulates data based on the request. This approach tightly couples permissions on particular objects, but does not scale well. Permitting access via other protocols or to resources outside of the scope of the authentication server may involve substantial development effort.

The approach illustrated in *Figure 1.26* shows client resource requests by way of a gatekeeper mechanism. Conceptually, the ACS allows or disallows client access to network resources. Similar to a guard working a perimeter gate, it allows or denies traffic according to the rights and permissions allocated to the subject. A firewall with an integrated authentication mechanism is an example of a centralized access control device using the gatekeeper approach. This type of approach is primarily used to control access to resources and services at particular locations within the protected network. Generally, it lacks the ability to control granular-level access to resources. This is frequently the case when different proprietary solutions are used for access control and resource availability within the system. For instance, a firewall may allow externally authenticated individual access to a particular file server, but it might not be able to limit which directories are accessed.

The previous approaches to centralized access control exert communication dominance over the client. The ACS by proxy or traffic direction prevents the client from attempting to communicate with resources outside of the bounds established by its rule sets and permissions. A different concept is to allow clients to roam freely in a network, but requests for resources are validated with the

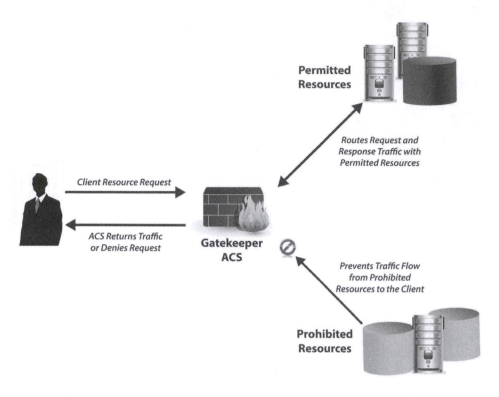

Figure 1.26 - **Centralized access control using a gatekeeper**

ACS before access is allowed. An authenticated subject is given a temporary credential that is used to identify him or her within the network. This approach, shown in *Figure 1.27*, has a scalability quality greater than that for the approaches previously mentioned. Subjects requesting a resource from a server submit their credential as a proof of who they are. The server with the requested resource verifies the requested access with the ACS. If the credential is authentic and the subjects have the appropriate permissions, then access to the resource is allowed.

Advantages of ACS include the following:

- *Single Point of Management* - Accounts, permissions, and rights are centrally managed. Having all of the security attributes in the same device simplifies access control management.
- *Audit log access* - A centralized access control mechanism also places the heart of the audit logging process in one location. This makes it easier for security and administrative personnel to access and manage the logs.
- *Physical security* - A device centralizing access control provides the opportunity to incorporate additional physical security measures promoting confidentiality and integrity. The access control device can be placed in a physically segregated area restricted to only those who are granted administrative access to the device.

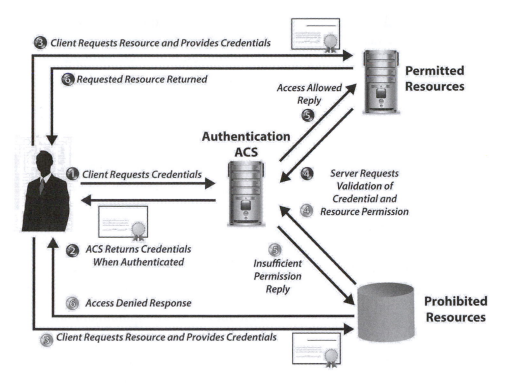

*Figure 1.27 - **Centralized access control with credentials***

Disadvantages of ACS to consider are the following:

- *Single point of failure* - The unavailability of a centralized access control mechanism would prevent access to authorized resources. Localized network and power disruptions may prevent geographically dispersed users from accessing resources. Software or hardware failures in the device itself could also disrupt operations.

- *Single point of compromise* - An attacker successfully compromising the device may be able to grant themselves access to all protected resources. Alternatively, an attacker might be able to compromise the authentication information and subsequently masquerade as the authorized users, thus hiding the nefarious activity.

- *Capacity* - The device itself can be a limiting factor in centralized access control. It might not have sufficient capacity to concurrently handle a large number of requests or connections, given the type of implementation. Locating the device in an area of the network with heavy traffic or bandwidth constraints may impede or disrupt user access to resources.

Common Implementations

A number of protocols exist that support centralized access control. TACACS, TACACS+, RADIUS, and EAP are just a few of the most common access control protocols that a security architect should be familiar with.

- **TACACS** - This older protocol was originally used for authenticating dial-up users. RFC 1492, "An Access Control Protocol, Sometimes Called TACACS" (Finseth, 1993), describes the protocol and suggests that the acronym is short for "Terminal Access Controller Access Control System." TACACS functions over UDP on port 49 or TCP on any locally defined port. This older protocol lacks many important features found in others that were more recently developed. A critical shortcoming in TACACS is the lack of encryption. All communication from a TACACS client to the server is in cleartext. Using this protocol through an untrusted or public network exposes the session and endpoints to a potential compromise.

- **TACACS+** - This proprietary protocol by Cisco is based on TACACS. It is primarily used with TCP on port 49. This protocol overcomes the security weaknesses of its predecessor by providing encryption for the packet payload. Authentication, Authorization, and Accounting (AAA) capabilities are built into the protocol, whereas it is missing from TACACS. However, the use of AAA capabilities is implementation specific. Therefore, a security architect must ensure that each TACACS+ implementation is consistent with the policy of the organization. An Internet-Draft memorandum describing TACACS+ is available through the IETF. [10]

- **RADIUS** - The Remote Authentication Dial In Service (RADIUS) also has AAA capabilities built into the protocol. RADIUS is a centralized access control protocol commonly used in the telecommunications industry as well as by Internet service providers. A network access server (NAS) acting as the gateway to a network passes client access requests to the RADIUS server. This enables RADIUS to be used in a variety of environments, such as dial-up or wireless. Callback and challenge response attributes are built into the protocol, supporting dial-up and other implementations that require additional security measures. According to the Internet Assigned Numbers Authority (IANA), which controls numbers for protocols, UDP is used to encapsulate RADIUS on ports 1812 for authentication and 1813 for accounting. However, some devices still implement RADIUS over ports 1645 and 1646, which were in use prior to the IANA decision. The user password is protected with MD5 and some additional XOR techniques when transmitted. No other aspects of the protocol implement cryptographic measures. As of this writing, RFC 2865 is the latest Internet Engineering Task

---

10   See the IETF TACAS+ memo here: http://tools.ietf.org/html/draft-grant-tacacs-02

Force (IETF) memo describing RADIUS. However, there are a multitude of other RFCs that describe other implementations and attributes of RADIUS. [11]

- *EAP* - The Extensible Authentication Protocol (EAP) is a protocol supporting multiple authentication methods. It operates above the data link layer and therefore does not rely on IP. This enables its use in a variety of wired and wireless implementations. EAP, defined in RFC 3748 (Aboda, Blunk, Vollbrecht, Carlson, and Levkowetz, 2004), is essentially a peer-to-peer protocol. The protocol relies on the lower layer to ensure packet ordering, but retransmissions are the responsibility of EAP. Its design as an authentication protocol prohibits its use for data transport, which would be inefficient. Request, response, success, and failure are the four main types of messages or codes in the protocol. EAP can pass through other authentication methods and protocols as long as they conform to the four types of codes. Both WPA and WPA2 require EAP as the supporting authentication methods. A number of methods of implementing EAP exist. For instance, EAP-TLS defined in RFC 5216 is one method that employs Public Key Infrastructure (PKI) to secure RADIUS in wireless environments.

Design Considerations

Protection of the device used for centralized access control is vital. Designs for this type of access control should include countermeasures that preserve the confidentiality, integrity, and availability of the implementation.

- *Reduce attack surface* - Remove unnecessary services from the device. Prevent the device from communicating on unauthorized ports. Consider the use of firewalls or packet-filtering routers between the device and the rest of the network. Only allow inbound and outbound connections according to those ports allocated to support management, authentication, and access control functionality.

- *Active monitoring* - Monitor network activity with the device. Dedicate an intrusion detection node at each physical network interface. Configure the intrusion detection node to monitor for known attacks as well as any activity outside the scope of the device. Enable internal auditing of the device. Each administrator provided access to the device should have their own unique credentials for access. Regularly review the audit logs for unauthorized changes or activity within the device.

---

11   See the latest IETF listing of RADIUS attribute types here: http://www.ietf.org/assign-ments/radius-types/radius-types.xml

■ *Device backup* - The database of users and authorized resources can be very large. Regular backups are needed for disaster recovery and contingency operations. The confidentiality and integrity of the backups must be preserved. Ideally, backups should be encrypted. In cases where encryption is not practical or possible, strong physical controls will be needed. Passwords or other secret keys would be retained on the backups; thus the confidentiality of the data contained within the backups must be protected from unauthorized disclosure or exposure. Integrity may be affected when a loss of physical control of backups is exploited by an attacker, who may allow for unauthorized access that could be subsequently granted during a restore process.

■ *Redundancy* - Ensure that sufficient redundancy is contained within the design to ensure continued availability when failures occur. External aspects to the device such as communications and power are normally addressed for other components of the system. However, these items become more important when distributed systems or remote clients depend on the centralized device to access resources unaffected by these types of disruptions. Where possible, implement a secondary access control device that can take over for failures in the primary.

Decentralized Access Control

A collection of nodes that individually make access control decisions through a replicated database characterizes a decentralized access control mechanism. The Microsoft Windows Domain model is a prime example of decentralized access control. *Figure 1.28* provides a view of decentralized access control. Note that while authentication information is distributed, access control is applies only to the local resource. This type of access control mechanism has the following qualities:

■ *Distributed* - Access control decisions are made from different nodes. Each node makes decisions independent of the others.

■ *Shared database* - Distributed nodes share the same database used to authenticate subjects. Changes to the database are communicated among the participating nodes. Ideally, the security policy is shared between nodes as well.

■ *Robust* - The access control mechanism continues to operate when an access control node fails or communications are severed.

■ *Scalable* - Access control nodes can be added or removed from the architecture with little impact on the rest of the architecture or the access control mechanism as a whole.

Although decentralized access control has advantages, it is not perfect. Some of the issues that need to be considered when implementing decentralized access control include

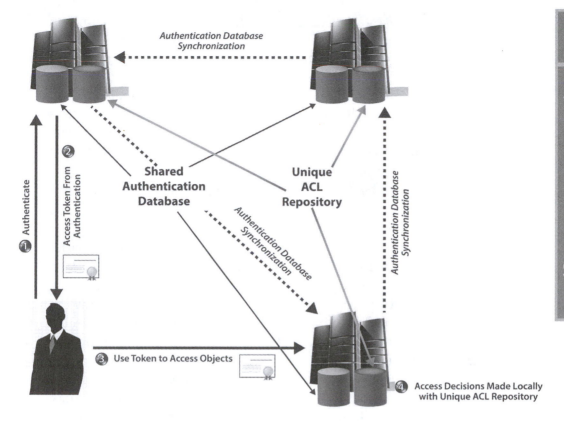

Figure 1.28 - **Decentralized access control**

- *Continuous synchronization considerations -* The access control mechanism is only as current as the last synchronization. Excessive gaps in the time between synchronizations may allow inappropriate access to the system or objects.

- *Bandwidth usage -* Synchronization events might consume a lot of bandwidth. Nodes joined through low-bandwidth connections may consume a disproportionate amount of bandwidth when synchronizing.

- *Physical and logical protection of each access control node -* A compromise of one access control node could propagate a compromise to all. Successful attacks against the centralized database in one location could provide the attacker with the ability to attack any node participating in the architecture.

Design Considerations

Inconsistencies in security countermeasures are a common issue with systems using decentralized access control. Servers providing access control services could be located in different facilities in the same region or in different parts of the world. Ensuring that the intended design is consistently applied for each instance can be quite challenging.

- *Physical security* - The integrity of the access control system can be globally impacted by a weakness in the physical security at just one site. Every site hosting a decentralized access control server must have sufficient physical security. Physical security is affected not only by the facility itself, but also by the individuals granted access to the areas housing the system. Physical security controls should be explicitly defined and periodically validated. Every site containing a decentralized access control server must adhere to a minimum baseline of controls.

- *Management coordination* - A decentralized access control system that is geographically distributed may have a multitude of individuals from various offices involved with system development, maintenance, and administration. The activities and duties of these individuals should be considered when assigning rights and privileges to their accounts. Furthermore, actions affecting the baseline of the system should only be permitted through appropriate change control processes. Ideally, the access control system is designed to facilitate separation of duties and least privilege. However, applying these concepts can make management coordination difficult. The design of the access controls should consider organizational structure, such as human resources, that will need to participate in the management of the decentralized access controls and the system in general.

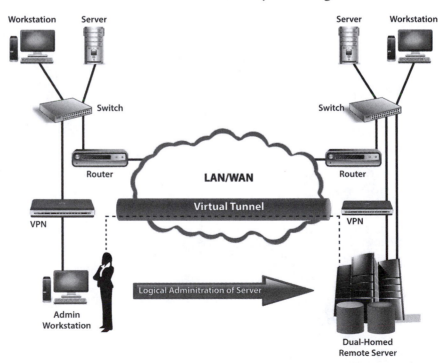

Figure 1.29 - **Remote maintenance with a VPN**

■ *Remote maintenance* - Organizations with decentralized access control often use remote management methods to maintain the distributed aspects of the system. Administrators conducting remote maintenance may iterate through a number of commands that could allow an attacker to compromise the access control system. The activities of the administrators must be protected with encryption during the communication session. Some devices might not directly support sufficient encryption of the entire session. In these cases, alternative methods, such as a VPN, should be used to ensure that administrator actions captured on the network could not be used to exploit the access control device. Where possible, connect the VPN device directly to an unused physical interface on the decentralized access control device. When this is not possible, use secondary network filtering such as a firewall or router to prevent propagation of the output from the VPN to other nodes in the subnet. Refer to *Figure 1.29* for an example.

■ *Exclude from Demilitarized Zone (DMZ)* - Decentralized access control devices share a common database allowing distributed AAA. An exploited vulnerability in one device, such as that seen in *Figure 1.30*, can result in compromise of resources dependent on the access control system. Given this situation, it is best to avoid placing a decentralized access control device within a DMZ. Servers and devices within a DMZ should not contain sensitive information. Rather, access to sensitive information by

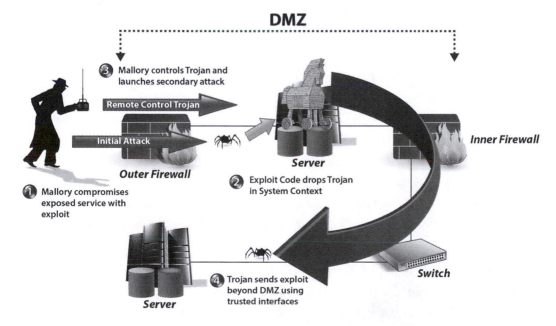

Figure 1.30 - **Problems with decentralized access control servers in a DMZ**

those outside of the trusted aspects of the organizational network should be handled by proxy servers that do not have rights or permissions outside of the DMZ. *Figure 1.31* illustrates this point. This design philosophy assumes that servers within the DMZ are at greater risk of exploitation than those that are inside the trusted area of the network. Decentralized access control servers require a high degree of protection and as such should not be placed directly inside the DMZ.

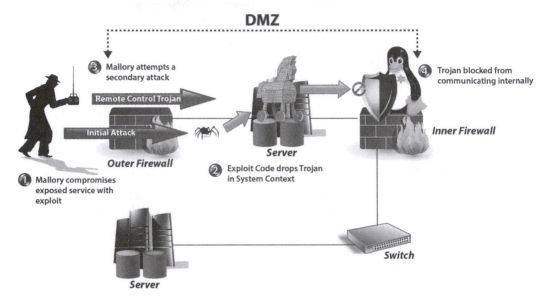

Figure 1.31 - **Using proxy servers in a DMZ to counter attacks**

Federated Access Control

Authentication is an essential part of any access control system. Each subject having access to organizational resources must be appropriately authenticated prior to being allowed access. This becomes problematic when an organization extends resource access to business partners and customers. Organizations with a large customer or partner population could potentially need to manage more accounts for external subjects than for those of its own employees. Recent efforts in the areas of Services Oriented Architecture (SOA) using Web 2.0 enabled organizational sharing of resources for individual subjects that are authenticated by an external organization. This is made possible through the establishment of a federation of organizations.

A federation consists of two or more organizational entities with access control systems that do not interoperate or functionally trust each other. At least one of the federation members has authenticated users that desire access to resources from another of the participating organizations. Members of the federation agree to recognize the claimed identity of a subject that has been fully authenticated by one of the members. Rather than require an individual to have a separate account in each organization, only one is required. This is the power of federated access, which is closely related to identity management and single sign-on, but crosses organizational boundaries. [12]

Federated access control occurs when an organization controlling access to a particular resource allows a subject access based on his or her identity, which is affirmed by the partner organization. The proof provided by a subject typically consists of a token or piece of information digitally signed by the authenticating organization, affirming the identity of the individual. Once the proof is verified, access is permitted to the subject. Access to resources can further be mediated using DAC, RBAC, or any other access control technique deemed appropriate by the organization. *Figure 1.32* illustrates an example of how a federated access control could be implemented.

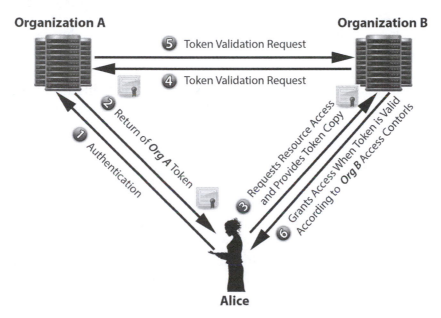

Figure 1.32 - **Federated access control**

Design Considerations

There are a number of issues that must be carefully considered when implementing federated access control. Given that an organization allows access to protected resources, great care must be given when providing access. This is a prudent precaution because the federation member providing access to a subject of another organization is required to extend a substantial amount of trust.

12   You can see an animated explanation of Federated ID management, as described by the UK Access Management Federation for UK higher (HE) and further (FE) education here: http://www. youtube.com/watch?feature=player_embedded&v=wBHiASr-pwk#!

- *Cooperative effort* - The federation is a joint effort that derives its ability to function based on the agreements of the participants. A written agreement should detail how individuals are authenticated and the handling of proofs used to confirm a subject's identity. This is minimally needed to ensure interoperability, but more importantly, an agreement should establish a set of security requirements that must be met by the participants.

- *Mutual risk* - Compromised subject accounts in one organization can impact other federation members. A security architect should consider this likelihood when designing controls to support participation in the federation. Nefarious activity could cause damage to both organizations and can even strain the trust of the participating members of the federation. In this regard, abuses and attacks must be considered ahead of time to ensure that appropriate countermeasures and responses are in place prior to accepting subject identities of external organizations within the federation.

- *Utilize a DMZ* - Externally authenticated subjects from a participating federation member should not be allowed direct access to internal resources. Just as in e-commerce, it is best to contain the activities of these types of customers and partners within a DMZ as well. Use proxy servers within the DMZ to retrieve information that is needed. Avoid storing sensitive information in the DMZ.

- *Exclude access control integration* - From the standpoint of a federation member, a previously authenticated subject from another organization should not be considered a subject in the primary access control system of the organization. In this regard, it is better to establish a centralized access control system dedicated to the support of a federated access control rather than mix outsiders with those on the inside. Keeping this type of barrier will prevent accidental or malicious escalation of privilege due to a weakness in the main access control system.

Directories and Access Control

In modern operating systems, information is stored and retrieved from directory structures. Data elements comprising information may be kept in a giant file, but generally, access to the information is in a hierarchal format that is managed either by the operating system or an application. Many commodity software products make use of proprietary formats to store information. This can inhibit the ability to share information between products of different vendors. Furthermore, proprietary formats might not have granular access control capabilities, do not interoperate with host-based access controls, or fail to function with those of other hosts.

The challenges of sharing information were recognized early on in the development of IT systems. The International Telecommunications Union–Telecommunications Standardization Sector (ITU-T) recognized this problem and developed X.500 Directory Specifications. This specification was subsequently adopted by the International Organization for Standardization (ISO) and International Electrotechnical Commission (IEC) as the ISO/IEC 9594 multipart standard.

The X.500 Directory Specification provides the framework to specify the attributes used to create a directory as well as the methods used to access its objects. An entry in the directory has its own Directory Information Tree comprising different types of objects. A directory schema describes how information is organized in a directory, while object classes indicate how each entry is to be structured. Access and management of X.500 information is conducted using the Directory Access Protocol (DAP), which requires an OSI-compliant protocol stack. In this regard, DAP is the X.500 standard.

Protecting the confidentiality of information transferred using DAP is not defined in X.500. However, protection of authentication factors, such as passwords, used to connect or *bind* to an X.500 directory are specified in the X.509 subset standard. This subset establishes the basis for Public Key Infrastructure (PKI) certificates. It also defines hashing techniques and the use of public-key encryption as methods to protect the confidentiality of bind requests.

The IETF has subsequently defined an alternative method to access an X.500-based directory over IP that is known as Lightweight Directory Access Protocol (LDAP). RFC 4510 (Zeilenga, 2006) provides a general overview of the specifications of LDAP and lists other applicable RFCs. Version 3 of the protocol (LDAPv3) is described in RFC 4511 and supports a limited number of DAP operations over TCP port 389. LDAPv3 also supports the use of TLS to secure directory access over TCP port 636. LDAP supports authenticated and unauthenticated access during the bind process. When authentication is desired, the credentials could be sent in plaintext using simple authentication or secured with Simple Authentication and Security Layer (SASL). Refer to RFC 4422 for a detailed explanation of SASL.

The concept of using directory access protocols is quite powerful. Vendors of network operating systems have embraced the concept and integrated directory access protocols into their products. For instance, the latest Microsoft servers rely extensively on their proprietary DAP implementation known as Active Directory (AD). The initial release of AD had limited support for LDAP. However, AD can now be extensively accessed using LDAP. This enables cross-domain and vendor product access to Windows resources. Security architects are advised to learn the intricacies of LDAP as it is likely to continue to increase in relevance and importance in the future.

Design Considerations

Directory specifications such as X.500 enable an organization to publish information in a way that supports hierarchical access to structured information. However, attention to security must be given when deploying a directory solution.

- *Access security* - Some directories may contain sensitive information. Ensure that directory access is protected with cryptographic measures in instances where an exposure of the information transiting a network would be unacceptable.

- *Protect authentication information* - A Simple Bind operation passes authentication information in cleartext over the network. This could be a default behavior in some implementations where a server accepts anonymous or unauthenticated bind operations. Verification of the correct functioning of the authentication mechanism should be conducted. Consider storing authentication information for publicly accessible servers within a DMZ in another location within the private network.

- *Leverage existing access control mechanisms* - According to RFC 2820, LDAP does not currently specify an access control model. Therefore, it is important that existing access control mechanisms on the host server be employed to protect directory access. In cases where anonymous or unauthenticated access to a directory is permitted, access to other files in the system should not be accessible by the service or daemon running the directory service. This is a prudent measure that can protect the rest of the system in the event a vulnerability in the service is found and exploited.

Identity Management

Identification is a token representation of a particular subject. In the physical realm, official documents such as a driver's license or a passport are representative of different token forms identifying the same person. Both types of identification have different levels of trust. For instance, a passport is a trusted form of identification when traveling internationally, while a driver's license is not normally given this level of trust. In contrast, within the United States, a passport is insufficient proof of an individual's ability to operate a motor vehicle. In this regard, one type of identification is not compatible with the purpose or trust of another even though they refer to the same person.

In the cyber realm, individuals frequently use multiple identities to access different services within the same system. Similar to Figure 1.33, an individual may have one account for network login and another for accessing a database. The most common form of identity is an account name, which is frequently nothing more than a string of characters. An account name, or identification, is the logical representation of a subject in most access control systems.

Individuals join and depart organizations. Assigned duties will also change, which might require extended or reduced access to system resources and services. In these situations, it is necessary to equate the identity of an individual with the totality of access needed to conduct their duties. Multiple identities and changes in access exemplify the need for identity management.

As previously mentioned, it is not uncommon for an individual to have multiple identities within an organizational system. Identities exist for a variety of IT products within any given system. Some of the more common instances include

- *Operating systems* - Microsoft, Unix, Linux, and mainframes are the most prevalent.
- *Directory services* - LDAP-enabled operating systems and applications may integrate with other products or deploy their own identity schemes.
- *Public Key Infrastructure (PKI)* - Each individual issued a public key certificate essentially has an identity within the PKI.
- *Network authentication* - Authentication of network devices makes use of a variety of protocols such as XACML [13], Kerberos, SSH, RADIUS, and SAML [14]. Each may have its own account identifier or integrate with an operating system.

---

13   eXtensible Access Control Markup Language (XACML) defines a declarative access control policy language implemented in XML and a processing model describing how to evaluate authorization requests according to the rules defined in policies.

XACML is primarily an Attribute Based Access Control system (ABAC), where attributes (bits of data) associated with a user or action or resource are inputs into the decision of whether a given user may access a given resource in a particular way. Role-based access control (RBAC) can also be implemented in XACML as a specialization of ABAC.

See the following for the Version 3 Standard Draft for XACML: http://docs.oasis-open.org/xacml/3.0/xacml-3.0-core-spec-cs-01-en.pdf

14   Security Assertion Markup Language 2.0 is a version of the SAML OASIS standard for exchanging authentication and authorization data between security domains. SAML 2.0 is an XML-based protocol that uses security tokens containing assertions to pass information about a principal (usually an end user) between a SAML authority, that is an identity provider, and a web service, that is a service provider. SAML 2.0 enables web-based authentication and authorization scenarios including single sign-on (SSO).

See the following for the Version 2 Standard Draft for SAML: https://www.oasis-open.org/committees/download.php/27819/sstc-saml-tech-overview-2.0-cd-02.pdf

- *Network management* - Simple Network Management Protocol (SNMP).

- *Database management systems* - Many popular databases have their own internal accounts for user access. Some integrate with the operating system for authentication purposes, but an account is still maintained in the database.

- *E-mail* - Most e-mail servers are integrated with the host operating system for identification purposes, but some are not. Access to an e-mail server from outside the organizational boundary may require a separate account in certain cases.

- *Smartcards* - These tokens represent the identification of the authorized holder. A separate list must be maintained matching a token to a particular user. Some smartcards contain multiple identities that can be used to accommodate multiple users.

- *Biometrics* - The identifier comprises features of an individual. Devices supporting biometrics collect the minutiae according to a particular template.

- *Network equipment* - Routers, switches, encryption devices, and printers commonly have console or remote management interfaces. These types of devices frequently have only one type of administrative account that is shared by those responsible for maintenance.

- *Networked applications* - Specialized software and services, such as financial accounting packages, may implement their own access control mechanism.

- *Web applications* - Many Web-based applications relay a user's account and password to a back-end database. However, some specialized Web applications have their own access control mechanism, which is separate from the underlying operating system or back-end database.

- *Encryption products* - Media encryption products such as those used for hard drive or file encryption may rely on the combined use of an identifier and authenticator. Other forms of identification, such as smartcards, might also be used.

Account identification is the fundamental identity for a system user. Within an access control mechanism, a subject is frequently equivalent to an account identifier. However, a user may have multiple accounts within a system. The identity of an individual user is therefore considered to encompass the totality of his or her access within a system.

Should standardized account-naming conventions be used within a system? The argument for standardization is that it simplifies account management. Using the same naming convention for system and application accounts expedites an administrator's ability to associate account actions, permissions, as well as manipulate account attributes for a given user. The counterargument is that a guessable naming convention gives attackers an advantage against a system. This may allow them to target particular users for phishing and spyware attacks or conduct focused attacks against system accounts. However, the ease of administration need not give rise to a weakness in the system. Consider the following:

E-mail Filtering - Malicious attachments and messages with mismatched header information should be discarded at the e-mail server.

Malware Scanning - Discovering and eliminating malware mitigates the threat.

Account Timeouts - Establishing low thresholds on the number of failed attempts mitigates guessing attacks.

User Awareness - Training is essential in any security program.

Process Validation - Knowing what is allowed to execute in the environment will enable countermeasures against and discovery of unauthorized software.

Intrusion Detection - Tune the network IDS to detect attacks against accounts. Use host-based IDS to identify malicious or abnormal activity.

Audit Log Review - Look for attempts to access an account from an unusual location. For instance, attempts to log on with service accounts from a workstation strongly indicate system misuse when it is contrary to a system policy.

A standard naming convention, when accompanied by other controls, will simplify account management without sacrificing the system's security posture.

The assignment of account identifications should be tightly coupled with the concepts of separation of duties and least privilege. This means if an individual does not require access to a particular database for his or her duties, then an associated account should not be given. The security design of a system should accommodate this type of granular access. Furthermore, manual or automated methods should be used to associate, track, and validate an individual with the rights and permissions granted. Manual methods could entail the use of spreadsheets or small databases. Automated management typically requires the use of specialized tools for single sign-on.

Some IT products have only one administrative account for management purposes. Linux, Unix, and many networking devices rely on a root or superuser account for management. It is quite common for IT departments to share the passwords associated with accounts among a group of individuals responsible for administrative support. Accountability is difficult to achieve when accounts are shared. Considerations for achieving some level of accountability for shared accounts include

- *Use of specialized protocols* - Consider the use of TACACS+ or RADIUS to manage access to network devices.
- *Manual tracking of account usage* - Implement a log to track the time and date of an individual's use of the privileged account. Change the password at short intervals where practical.
- *Verification of audit events* - Compare audit records for the device against those of manual logs or from specialized protocols.

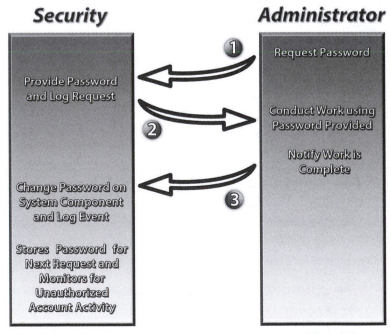

Figure 1.34 - **Simple method to control a shared account**

There exist some organizations that have sufficient resources to implement specialized software packages to manage shared accounts. Yet, there are many less well-funded organizations that must rely on manual techniques to control these shared accounts. A well-defined procedure or process implementing steps in a particular order is essentially a protocol. In *Figure 1.34*, a manual protocol that can be used to control access to a shared account is demonstrated.

The manual protocol described in Figure 1.34 is very simplistic, and has a significant drawback. The security person has access to the password as well as the audit records. This might enable persons in that capacity to conceal any nefarious activity they might pursue. Simply put, this simple method may not have sufficient separation of duties implemented in the protocol for some organizations. The situation could be improved if someone else is introduced who is involved with the audit records or manages the password. *Figure 1.35* describes an improvement where part of the password is split with a third party identified as a helper. This improved manual protocol also has a built-in feature that enables the security officer to evaluate the strength of the password while establishing better separation of duties as well.

Most devices have physical and logical addresses. The physical, or media access control address, should be unique for every device within a system.

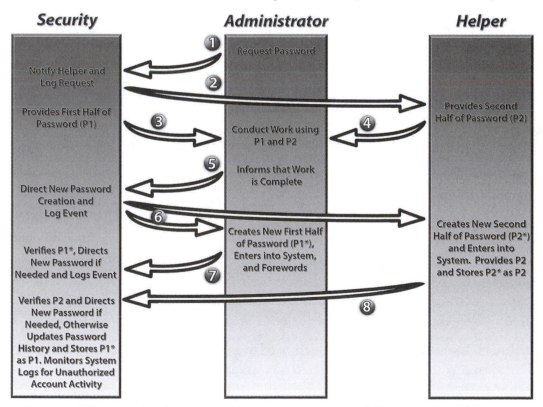

Figure 1.35 - **Password splitting to achieve greater accountability for a shared account**

Unfortunately, this may not always be the case. In the early days, physical addresses were hardwired into network interfaces from the manufacturer and could not be easily changed. Nowadays, some devices, and even operating systems, provide the ability to change the physical address. The most prevalent logical address is the Internet Protocol (IP) address. It is either manually assigned to a device or acquired through the Dynamic Host Configuration Protocol (DHCP). These attributes should be used to help uniquely identify each host connected to an organizational network. Due to the non-persistent nature of a device identity, it should not be relied upon exclusively as a means of authentication. Rather, device identity is a starting point that is useful to discover unauthorized devices connected to a system. Knowing what is connected to a network is an essential element in protecting a system. Use a scanning tool, such as Nmap, to discover unauthorized devices on a network. [15]

Some devices, such as those used for encryption, have the ability to participate in a PKI. Each device participating in the PKI has its own private key and public key certificate loaded on the system. This provides an enhanced means to identify participating devices. However, the integrity of those participating in the PKI is predicated on the physical security of the device. Any breakdown in the physical security affecting a device calls into question the authenticity of those affected by the weak controls. Use of a PKI to manage device identity is powerful, but it must be moderated with the appropriate physical controls as well.

The security architect should design systems to aid in the management of the complete identity of each subject. Properly designed identification management will help support the concepts of least privilege and separation of duties. Shared accounts present special challenges, and that must be accommodated. Device identification should also be a factor in a system's design.

Accounting

The initial concept of system accounting had a dual meaning. The term *accounting* evolved from the mainframe world. In the early days, computing time was very expensive. To recoup resources, system users or their departments were billed or charged back according to the amount of processing time consumed. In this respect, accounting literally meant financial accountability. However, it was also used in the traditional sense of security as in accounting for user actions.

Today, accounting is predominately used to established individual accountability. The term accounting goes by different names such as event logging, system logging,

---

[15]   Find a list of the most common Network Scanning tools and explanations about them here: http://sectools.org/

and auditing. Accounting records provide security personnel with the means to identify and investigate system misuse or anomalies. Ideally, all instances where accounts are used as means to identify subjects for access control purposes will have an auditing capability. The purpose of accounting is to minimally establish who accessed what. Recall that the who is the subject and what is the resource, or object. What should also include administrative activity such as policy changes and account management. To be more precise, it is also helpful to know from where and when the access occurred as well as the effect of the event. So accounting or auditing records should minimally include the following:

Who - The subject (device or user) conducting the action

What - Resources affected and administrative activity conducted

Where - Location of the subject and resource

When - Time and date of the attempt

Effect - Whether the action succeeded

Audit records are frequently used to identify anomalous or malicious activity. Investigators piece together information from audit logs into a time line of action to determine what happened. This effort can be more tedious when there is a difference between system clocks. The problem is best resolved by synchronizing the clocks of each device. Manual and automated methods can be used to synchronize system clocks. Regardless of the approach, a central clock must be chosen as the reference by which all other device clocks will be set. It is best to select a clock that is highly accurate and not affected by system activity. Manual methods are often necessary for those devices that lack automated means to update their time. Manual synchronization should be conducted at regular intervals. However, the best approach is to use automated techniques such as the Network Time Protocol (NTP). The protocol enables device clock synchronization from one host that acquires a time-base from another. *Figure 1.36* illustrates the use of NTP in a system.

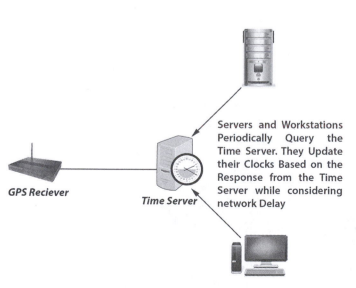

GPS Reciever

Time Server

Servers and Workstations Periodically Query the Time Server. They Update their Clocks Based on the Response from the Time Server while considering network Delay

Figure 1.36 - **Clock synchronization in a system**

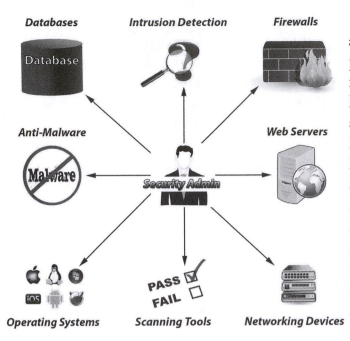

Databases   **Intrusion Detection**   **Firewalls**

Anti-Malware   **Web Servers**

Security Admin

Operating Systems   **Scanning Tools**   **Networking Devices**

PASS ☑
FAIL ☐

Figure 1.37 - **Sources of security events, information, and logs**

Log diversity abounds as vendors are free to proliferate their proprietary formats. Many systems have logs from numerous points and in a variety of formats. Fortunately, most vendors have settled on either syslog or integration with Microsoft Windows Event log as the audit recording method. The locations and types of services generating logs are substantial. *Figure 1.37* identifies just a few technologies that can be used to generate security events and information.

Audit records are most useful when they are analyzed. The most efficient way to analyze audit records and security events is when they are consolidated. Relevant audit records should be regularly collected into a centralized repository that enables their examination. *Figure 1.38* shows several methods commonly used to collect security logs and events. Further explanation of these popular methods used to collect audit and security information follows:

- *Listen* - Use a service that receives events as they are transmitted from network nodes. A syslog server is an example of this.

- *Polling* - A centralized server can be used to query other services to collect events periodically. It might also be used to copy log files from a shared directory.

- *Agents* - Autonomous process running on a node collects events as they are generated and sends them to a centralized collection point. Agents can be used to filter log messages and only transmit those that are the most important.

Traditionally, there have been two distinct approaches to Security Management: Security Event Management (SEM) and Security Information Management (SIM). Each of these approaches can be summarized at a high level as follows. Security Event Management evaluates collected information to identify security events, while Security Information Management collects information with some analysis of the information being done. While these systems have existed for some time as independent elements of many security

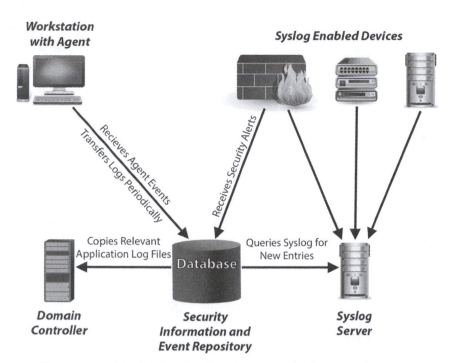

Figure 1.38 - **Methods of collecting security logs and events**

architectures, the combination of them into a single unified system, Security Information and Event Management (SIEM), allows for a more in depth look at the data collected, combining SIM and SEM plus additional capabilities. The additional capabilities of SIEM systems are listed below.

1. **Data Aggregation:** SIEM/LM (log management) solutions aggregate data from many sources, including network, security, servers, databases, applications, providing the ability to consolidate monitored data to help avoid missing crucial events.

2. **Correlation:** looks for common attributes, and links events together into meaningful bundles. This technology provides the ability to perform a variety of correlation techniques to integrate different sources, in order to turn data into useful information.

3. **Alerting:** the automated analysis of correlated events and production of alerts, to notify recipients of immediate issues.

4. **Dashboards:** SIEM/LM tools take event data and turn it into informational charts to assist in seeing patterns, or identifying activity that is not forming a standard pattern.

5. **Compliance:** SIEM applications can be employed to automate the gathering of compliance data, producing reports that adapt to existing security, governance and auditing processes.

6. **Retention:** SIEM/SIM solutions employ long-term storage of historical data to facilitate correlation of data over time, and to provide the retention necessary for compliance requirements.

63

Some security-related logs can become quite large, so the period used to collect them is important. File transfers of large logs can consume a substantial amount of network bandwidth. Similarly, an audit log source that automatically transmits events in near real time can affect bandwidth as well. Consideration for the timing of audit log collection should be weighed against operational needs of system users versus security requirements.

Two important considerations regarding audit log collection involve analysis and forensic value. Analysis requires logs to be consolidated in such a way that patterns of activity across multiple logs can be analyzed to detect violations and misuse. Inserting logs into a database is the most ideal way to accomplish this. Log records are decomposed into common elements and inserted into the database for query analysis. Unimportant records are commonly filtered out as they do not add value to the investigation. The decomposition and filtering helps an analyst discover security issues. It may also be necessary for the audit records to be preserved in their original state if they are to be presented as evidence in a court of law. In this case, unmodified logs are kept in a special archive where their integrity is assured. Cryptographic hashes of the logs should also be retained and protected to serve as evidence of the log's integrity. Accordingly, some logs are parsed for use, while others are retained as potential evidence.

A security architect must consider all of the possible locations where audit logs can be collected. Numerous devices, services, and applications produce a variety of useful logging information. At a minimum, audit logs should be collected from those devices where access control decisions are made. The collection process should be planned to consolidate the necessary logs in a timely manner, avoiding operational conflicts, providing the ability for detailed analysis, while guaranteeing their forensic value.

Access Control Administration and Management Concepts

Access Control Administration

Each type of access control architecture presents its own challenges for managing the fundamental aspects of subjects, objects, permissions, and rights. The security architect should consider the mechanisms that must be implemented to enable access control administration.

There are two principal entity types that are the subjects of access control. Ultimately, a subject is either a human or an automated feature of the system. The architect should ensure processes exist such that accounts assigned to each entity type are

- *Authorized* - Each account is approved and documented. This establishes its authenticity.
- *Monitored* - Accounts should be assessed for inactivity and abuse. Unused and unnecessary accounts are promptly removed. Employ specialized tools to identify abnormal use of accounts.
- *Validated* - The continued need for each account is reviewed on a periodic basis as established by the organization. This affirms the authenticity of each account.

Each person requiring access to a system should be individually identified. This enables accountability as well as the application of granular access controls. Limit the number of accounts assigned to each individual. Avoid the use of shared accounts as this will make accountability much more difficult.

Processes executing on a system do so within a security context; that is, every process has certain rights and permissions. An operating system that relies on an access control model, such as DAC, must regard human interactions and running processes within an appropriate security context. Human interaction occurs through an associated process. This might be a single process or more than one hundred processes. Regardless of the number, the actions taken by the process are forced to conform to the security context of the user. In this respect, processes are not permitted to take any actions beyond what the user is allowed. Processes not executing in the context of a user may have a security context of the system or their own unique context.

Some system processes have the special ability (right) to impersonate a user. When applied correctly, this technique allows the service to execute with the permissions and rights of the client. Processes with the ability to impersonate must be closely monitored. Vulnerabilities associated with impersonating processes may allow privilege escalation and system compromise.

Although permissions are commonly associated with objects within a system, a security architect must think in a broader perspective. A system is a collection of resources that may or may not be considered objects within a given access control mechanism. Each resource may contain many objects that can be managed by one or more access control techniques. Resources provide utility to the end user and may be consumable or enable system functionality. Diversity in resource types complicates the application of access control. Consider the following shortlist of resources common to many systems:

- *Web server* - Traditional Web servers enable access to Web-based content. Vendors are more frequently embedding Web servers into hardware products. In some cases, the access control mechanisms of embedded Web servers do not integrate with other security mechanisms, creating isolated islands that require security maintenance and configuration.

- *E-mail server* - This ubiquitous communication platform may be accessible inside as well as outside of an organization's security boundary. This resource is commonly abused by those peddling spam and launching phishing attacks.

- *Networked printer* - This device is loosely coupled to the access control mechanisms of a system. A printer is normally dependent on other security measures to protect it from abuse.

- *Network devices* - Switches, routers, and firewalls are resources that enable system functionality. Many have console or remote management ports that enable device configuration. The internal configuration features may not easily integrate with other access control mechanisms within a system. The loss of availability of one of these resources will likely impact the ability of users to access other resources.

- *Applications* - The most common applications are those installed locally on a system. However, advances in mobile code, and the continuing momentum of cloud based system solution architectures demand a broader perspective on what is considered an application and how it should be secured.

- *Removable media* - Removable-media devices such as USB, CD-ROM, tape, and disk drives provide users with access to resources beyond local or networked system storage. These resources enable sharing, backup, and transport of information.

- *Internet access* - Many organizations depend on Internet access as a core business resource. System users depend on the Internet for research, collaboration, and e-commerce. Internet use is similar to human use of fire. If used inappropriately, it can consume organizational resources in time and money. When used effectively, the Internet can be used to forge a wealth of opportunities to transact business and advance organizational objectives.

■ *File server* - This type of repository contains the bulk of an organization's information. A variety of networked storage is available for system consumption. Simple file servers functioning with commodity operating systems are the principal remote storage devices in any given system. Dedicated devices such as storage area networks and network attached storage are gaining in popularity as a means to enable massive storage capabilities for organizations of any size. Integrating these devices within an access control methodology for a system requires attention to detail on the part of a security architect.

■ *Databases* - Much of the business intelligence of an organization is kept in database repositories. Access to databases is often routed through a Web tier. But direct access through specialized tools or other databases is also a common practice. Database management systems often have their own access control mechanisms that are stand-alone, or, in some instances, integrate with those of other vendor products. As with file servers, a security architect should give special attention to database access control planning and implementation.

A system user is the principal subject of interest within an access control mechanism. Resource permissions are granted to users individually or collectively. The access control mechanism constrains user interaction with a resource object according to the permission granted. The possible exception to this statement is when a subject is identified as an object owner, such as within a DAC mechanism. In this case, the subject has full control over the permissions on the object. For instance, suppose an object owner only has read access to the object. This would prevent casual or unintentional modification of the object. However, as the object owner, a subject could modify his or her permissions on the object to perform any action desired. It is important to note that object owners have the ability to grant any permission to themselves or to others at their discretion when operating within the context of DAC.

Ideally, every object will be subject to an access control mechanism. This affords the ability to granularly control access to all aspects of a given resource. Unfortunately, this is not always the case. There are many technological resources that are not fully subject to an access control mechanism. For instance, network printers are commonly accessible to any device attached to a network. As long as the appropriate protocols are used, most printers will service any request received. Similarly, file permissions are not present on removable media. Aside from backups, most removable media are formatted using a file allocation table (FAT) or ISO 9660 for DVD and CD-ROM. This is understandable, considering that file-level access controls would not be useable from one access control system to another where a database of subjects is not held in common. Where granular access control is not possible, other methods are employed to control access to the entire resource. Although the all-or-nothing approach is less desirable, it is nevertheless a valid access control technique given security requirements and associated risk.

An effective access control mechanism is not easily bypassed. The mechanism should tightly couple permissions with protected objects. For any object protected, the permissions should be enforced; that is, a subject should not be able to circumvent an assigned permission by manipulating the object or permissions when not authorized. Any situation that allows a subject to exceed permissions represents a flaw in the access control mechanism. Vulnerabilities such as these are regularly discovered in commercial products. A security architect must be acutely aware of this situation when an organization develops proprietary applications with access control mechanisms. Testing of any homegrown security solution for access control weaknesses is critical.

The Power to Circumvent Security

Most systems do not encrypt stored data by default. When a system is powered down intentionally or not, the access control mechanism ceases operation. Data is vulnerable to physical attack when the system is without power. This could allow anyone with physical access to bypass access control and auditing mechanisms. To protect against this situation, a system should be designed with

1. Auditing of system restart, power on, and power off events

2. Sufficient physical security measures to prevent or detect unauthorized access to system hardware

3. Redundant or backup power

All unscheduled power-down or system restart events should be followed up with an investigation to determine the reason for the interruption and to detect if any malicious activity occurred.

File sharing occurs outside and within access control mechanisms. Transmitted e-mail attachments and files transported with removable media are examples of file sharing outside of an access control mechanism. Within a system's access control mechanism, it is common practice to make a file available to multiple users. A file is considered shared when it is accessible by more than one subject.

Assigning the appropriate permissions to a shared file is critical. A file with more than read access is subject to unintentional modification. Note that this is not to say that modification of the file is necessarily unauthorized. For instance, it is often necessary for people to make modifications to a file during collaboration activity. Modification of files used for collaboration is often expected. But this does not mean that every modification is intentional. Allowing modification of a collaboration file essentially authorizes changes to those who have access. Although this may not be an intended action, it is nonetheless authorized if not explicitly prohibited by policy. In contrast, it is almost never acceptable for ordinary users to modify binary files such as libraries and executables. Providing ordinary users with more than read access to a binary file is a risky proposition. Suppose a system policy prohibits users from modifying program files. In this case, it is reasonable to set permissions that prohibit a user from changing aspects of the file. Given the aforementioned policy, a system that does not restrict a user from making modifications to binary files is said to be noncompliant. Establishing the appropriate permission for shared files is an important consideration for any system.

Files such as word processing and spreadsheet documents are commonly shared during collaboration activities. It is not uncommon to find large directory structures with thousands of subdirectories and documents shared among users of certain groups. Typically, users are free to modify many of the documents within these directories. This is facilitated when permissions at the directory level are propagated to all its child objects. Each new object created in a directory inherits the permissions established for the parent. This situation is a disaster waiting to happen. Because users have read, write, and delete permissions in this scenario, the following situations may occur:

- User deletes files or whole directories by accident.
- Files or directories are accidentally moved.
- A user maliciously modifies, moves, or deletes files or directories.
- Malicious code is allowed to modify, move, or delete files or directories.

Each of these situations demonstrates an impact on information integrity and availability. Giving users the ability to modify file attributes, such as content and location, is not a best business practice. Users can make mistakes. Access controls on file shares should be established to prevent mistakes and malicious actions. Restricting users to only read access to resources is an effective method to control accidental or intentional modification to files used for collaboration (Price, 2007).

Peer-to-Peer (P2P): An Unintended Backdoor

Programs with the capability to allow file sharing represent a potential backdoor into an organization's system. A P2P program running in the context of the user has potential access to all the files that the user does. Normally, the program is configured to allow access to only specific file types or directories. When the program runs, it makes itself available to other systems outside of the protected network. Any flaw in the software or misconfiguration of the program parameters could allow

1. Compromise of the workstation in the context of the user

2. Access to sensitive information available to the user

3. Propagation of malicious software such as spyware, Trojans, viruses, and worms

Although P2P software is an interesting collaboration technology, it is fraught with substantial risk. Users who are not security experts may make poor judgments regarding the installation and configuration of this type of software. Security architects must carefully consider access control implementations to guard against misuse or flaws arising from authorized use of P2P applications.

Database Access

Many organizations use a Database Management System (DBMS) as a centralized information repository. Databases are ideal tools used to manage and share structured data. Some of the functional attributes of a DBMS can be used as mechanisms to support access control. Functionality such as views, triggers, and stored procedures can be leveraged to enhance access control within a DBMS.

■ *Views* - These virtual tables are named queries derived from a single or multiple tables. Although a view is virtual, it can be queried like a normal database table. A common use of views is to provide read-only data to the end user, which prevents the user from changing the data in the originating table. A well-constructed view enables granular access control over the database tables. Rather than giving database users the rights to a sensitive table, a view can be used to explicitly identify the attributes need for their duties. As such, users can be restricted to interact with specific columns, rows, or elements based on the attributes of the view's query.

- *Triggers* - Database events can be preceded or followed by a set of procedures. Triggers can be used to take an action according to database statements issued by the user or actions to interact with individual rows. This is useful to validate inputs from users or take actions based on the parameters or values in the SQL statement.

- *Stored procedures* - These subroutines enable performance of complex data manipulation tasks. Stored procedures enable programming languages, such as C or Java, to be used to conduct intricate actions on data that go beyond the capability of generic SQL. For instance, standard SQL returns an aggregate value based on a given query. Using stored procedures, it is possible to perform multiple unrelated queries and report the result individually or aggregately. Stored procedures are often used in conjunction with triggers to perform data validation or filtering actions.

Views, triggers, and stored procedures permit enforcement of business logic on data elements within a DBMS. These capabilities essentially allow the coding of business rules into database applications, which enables a level of access control that is more granular that the mechanism native to the DBMS. Using the power of these database extensions enables enhancements to security goals, such as separation of duties and least privilege, by restricting user access to only those data elements necessary for the performance of their assigned duties or tasks.

Access to information within a DBMS is enabled through a variety of authentication techniques. Users are identified individually or as a group. Permissions should be applied according to the method of access as well as business rules and the risk associated with the affected data. The various methods of access can be generally categorized as proxied anonymous, proxied access, direct access, and integrated authentication. Each category requires the security architect to consider the implications of the access type for potential data exposures that may occur.

The first category of access involves a logical grouping of all database requests. As seen in *Figure 1.39*, users are not individually identified, but rather, grouped

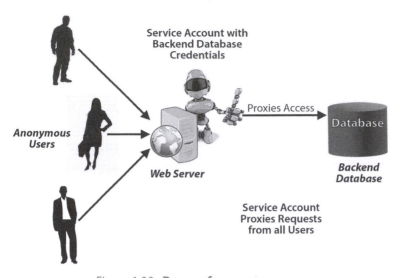

Figure 1.39 - **Proxy of anonymous users**

together. Individual accountability is difficult if no other authentication methods are used to associated connection events with actions in the database. In the figure, user requests for access to database items are proxied through a middle tier such as a Web server. This is a common scenario for public Web sites that provide search-related content to user requests. Instead of users possessing a particular account, the Web server uses database credentials to access data on behalf of the anonymous users. Given the lack of accountability in this scenario and the potential for abuse, it is best that database implementations such as these not include sensitive data in the repository. Segregating data in this regard will ensure that vulnerabilities associated with the database or Web server will not potentially expose sensitive information.

In many cases, it is desirable to individually identify users. A front-end application is commonly used to retrieve and format data for user consumption. Users submit credentials, such as an identifier and authenticator, to access protected resources. *Figure 1.40* illustrates this as proxied access. This three-tier application involves the client, a server layer, and the database tier. Perhaps the most common implementation of this architecture uses browsers at the client, Web servers

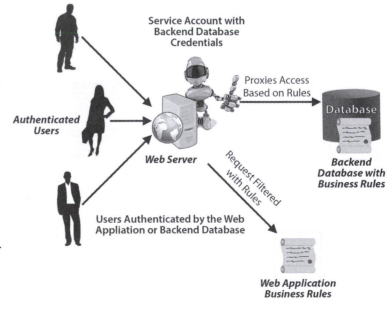

Figure 1.40 - **Proxy of authenticated users**

in the middle, and a database at the back end. The browser provides end users with the capability to view and interact with the underlying data. The server commonly implements business logic or rules that provide an intermediate access control capability for the backend data. The database may further implement business rules to further restrict data access.

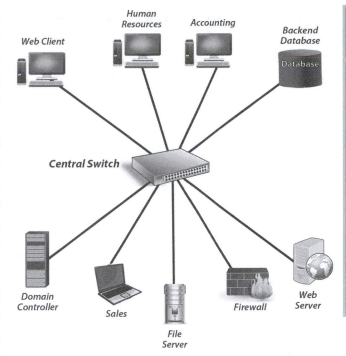

Central Switch

*Figure 1.41 -***Typical network with a central switch**

This multitier architecture design is a good way to enforce business rules and access control on elements within the database. *Figure 1.41* shows one way this type of architecture could be implemented in an actual system. Note that all components are mutually joined through a central switch. Each network component is physically linked to the other. If the network switch does not have access control capabilities, each node is considered logically connected. Although this represents an efficient design for the architecture, it does afford some opportunities for abuse. For instance, if no network-based access controls are implemented, an insider or a compromised workstation would be able to launch attacks directly at the database server. Given this

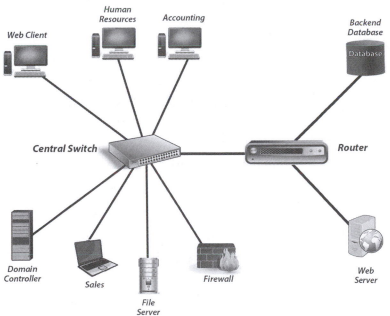

Figure 1.42 - **Improving security with router access control capabilities**

consideration, it becomes evident that the design lacks any defense in depth against these kinds of attacks. Furthermore, if the point of the design is to provide a layer of access control, then it seems reasonable that the logical abstraction from Figure 1.41 should implement physical and other logical access controls as well.

This situation can be improved through the use of network segregation. *Figure 1.42* demonstrates one way to accomplish this. In this diagram, a router is inserted to control the flow of network connections. Access controls within the router only allow traffic to flow from workstations to the server and from the server to the database. This effectively mitigates the potential for attacks focused directly on the database tier.

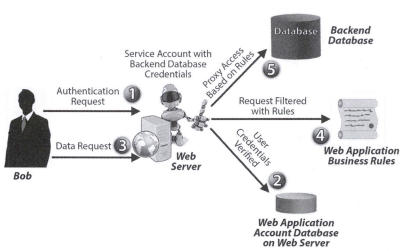

Figure 1.43 - **Database access through proxy controlled authentication**

Accounts used to access data through a three-tier solution are not always those that are integrated with the system. This is a common situation when data access through this type of architecture is provided to external users. One way to authenticate users is to rely on business logic at the server layer. Identifiers and authenticators submitted from the client layer are evaluated at the server layer. *Figure 1.43* provides a graphic of this concept. The server looks up the user identification and password either in a local file or from a database table. Users are granted access if their password matches an active account. Subsequent data requests from authenticated clients are frequently accessed through a common database account associated with the roles of the given user.

This approach provides a simple way of enabling a large number of users to access information within a database through a common account. There are some considerations when using this approach:

- *Password hashes* - Stored passwords will need to be hashed. It is best to implement logic that causes the password to be hashed on the client side.

- *Identity management* - A capability should exist to match accounts with active system users. Detailed management aspects such as password history, complexity, and lifetime will also need to be handled along with account dormancy.

- *Back-end database access* - Access control on the network and within the back-end database should be implemented as added layers of protection.

- *Protection of access control business logic* - Any compromise of the software implementing the business rules may compromise all data within the database. The integrity of the business logic must be ensured.

- *Auditing may be challenging* - A separate audit mechanism may need to be developed to support accountability.

A more integrated approach is to rely on the authentication mechanism inherent within the DBMS. *Figure 1.44* illustrates the use of a server that brokers access to the database by acting as an intermediary between user requests and database output. Here, the server

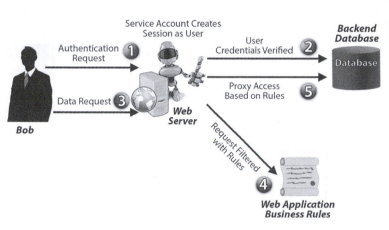

Figure 1.44 - **Proxy-facilitated database authentication and session**

proxies requests, but is not the primary access control mechanism. Database access control mechanisms, which include identification and authentication, are the mainline of defense for the data. Business logic built into the server has the potential to act as a secondary access control mechanism. This scenario has the following attributes:

Server:

- *Session management* - The server matches a user session with a DBMS session. This allows clients to communicate with the database using foreign protocols.

- *Information presentation* - The server provides query and other information in preformatted output for client consumption.

- *Business rule enforcement* - Additional security measures or business logic can be applied by the server as an access control layer.

Database:

- *Authenticates users* - Users connect to the database with accounts existing in the database.
- *Primary access control* - Access control mechanisms within the database such as views, triggers, stored procedures, and other privileges are required to control data access.

As previously mentioned, the server in this situation is a secondary access control mechanism. This is because users may still be able to circumvent the server altogether and access the data. Using protocols known to the DBMS such as Open Database Connectivity (ODBC), a user can access the data directly. In this case, access control is mostly dependent on the mechanism used within the DBMS. From a security perspective, ODBC has a significant drawback. All communications are conducted in cleartext, which means passwords used to log into the database as well as other sensitive data associated with a session could be captured on the network. This weakness in ODBC is affected by the underlying drivers of the protocol. Some database vendors provide confidentiality for the authentication session in some instances. However, in most cases, SQL commands using ODBC are sent in cleartext. However, the weakness can be reduced if the connection is physically or logically segregated from the rest of the network. Physical segregation can be effected through the use of dedicated hardware devices and interfaces. Logical segregation can be accomplished using VPN, IPSec, or a VLAN, which either encrypts the traffic flowing over common links or passes traffic through links which are not in common. The goal is to prevent the cleartext messages from being captured by rogue or compromised devices configured to capture network traffic.

Three-tier Web-based applications are a frequently used architecture to provide controlled access to organizational data. Implementing this type of architecture has its benefits and drawbacks. A security architect will need to weigh these aspects when evaluating new designs and consider countermeasures and monitoring aspects for existing implementations.

Advantages:

- *Data presentation* - A common application, the Web browser, provides universal access and presentation of the data. Deployments of proprietary applications are not needed.
- *Centralized access* - This type of design makes it easier to connect users to multiple databases.
- *Communication protection* - Some DBMSs do not have link encryption. A Web-based three-tier architecture can make use of Secure Socket Layer (SSL) to protect sensitive communications.

Disadvantages:

- *Increased complexity* - Organizations must carefully manage code developed to support the architecture. Business rules coded in server-side logic should be controlled by change management activities.
- *Cross-site scripting attacks* - Poorly coded or poorly protected Web-based applications are subject to cross-site scripting attacks. This essentially allows an attacker to redirect user requests to other servers of ill repute.
- *Middle-tier security* - Any breach in the server may compromise all data accessible through the server. Aggressive access controls and monitoring of the server are imperative to prevent and detect attacks.

Accountability may be difficult - Achieving the desired amount of accountability may require the development of an extensive access control mechanism. This may be fraught with challenges due to programming or implementation flaws. Although using accounts integrated within the database may be desirable, this is also not always practical and may not provide sufficient auditing.

Inherent Rights

All accounts will have a default set of rights assigned to it. The inherent rights are the core set of account attributes. Account types are necessary to constrain human and automated aspects according to a security policy. Assigning a user or process more rights than necessary increases risk. This occurs when a user or process acts maliciously or operates as a conduit for another threat agent. Managing assigned rights is an important aspect of a system's overall risk management. The three most basic types of accounts are ordinary, administrator, and system:

- **Ordinary** - Normally, these accounts have very few rights in the system. Most users should be assigned this type of account. Where practical, automated processes and services supporting users should also be assigned an ordinary account. Although ordinary accounts are constrained, they could also violate security policies by exploiting a flaw in the system.
- **Administrator** - Only those individuals tasked with the maintenance of the system should be assigned this type of account. Administrators have substantial rights in the system; anyone with such rights could circumvent security policies.
- **System** - This account type supports system functionality. System accounts have enormous powers similar to those of an administrator. Threat agents exploiting weaknesses associated with an account with system privileges may be able to compromise all aspects of a system.

It is important to note that some system components, such as networking devices, commonly provide only one administrator account for management.

In this situation, the account is typically shared among multiple individuals with system management responsibility. This can make accountability difficult. In cases like this, manual processes as well as physical and logical access control are needed to ensure appropriate device management. Secure such devices in a locked container or area. Implement processes that establish accountability for device access. This could be as simple as a key control log or as complex as an integrated facility access control system using two-factor authentication. In any case, where inherent rights cannot be separated and accountability is not automated, other processes will need to be implemented.

Granted Rights

Most accounts have the same rights granted to them even though they may have different resource permissions assigned. Accounts can ordinarily be grouped according to their type. Sometimes it is necessary to assign rights beyond those inherent for a given account by granting additional rights. This situation essentially creates an account with nonstandard rights. For instance, an ordinary user account may be granted additional rights so that it can be used as a system service. Altering the rights granted to a particular account can affect the overall security posture of the system. An attacker exploiting the properties of an account with nonstandard rights might be able to propagate an exploit more readily across a system. An account with nonstandard rights essentially establishes itself as a new type of account. The likelihood of a threat exploiting the new rights associated with the account should be properly assessed. Consider the following actions to manage the risk of creating accounts with nonstandard rights:

- *Document* - The rights of all accounts should be documented. When an account is given nonstandard rights, it is important that the reasons for the new rights be clearly enumerated. Risk associated with the changes should be documented as well. Documenting the reason and anticipated effects of the rights associated with the account will help future managers, administrators, and security personnel to understand the reasoning for the change and counter emerging threats when appropriate.

- *Authorize* - A change in account rights can pose new risks for the system. In this regard, management should authorize the change in writing. Ideally, alterations to account rights beyond what has been previously specified should be made using the system's change control process.

- *Monitor* - An account with nonstandard rights may end up an ideal target for an attacker. Actions of the account should be tracked to identify inappropriate activity or actions outside the scope of its intended use. Audit logs are an excellent resource that should be regularly reviewed for inappropriate account activity.

Just as rights can be granted for a particular account, they can be withdrawn as well. Reductions in rights support the concept of least privilege. There can be enormous security benefits to removing excessive or unused rights. This essentially helps eliminate or reduce possible attack vectors available to an authorized account. The trade-off comes with management overhead associated with reduced rights. If a selected right is removed for a security reason but is later restored to the account, then a previously mitigated weakness may reemerge on the system. Proper management steps should be followed whether rights are granted or curtailed. Following the previously mentioned steps of documenting, authorization, and monitoring will help manage any associated risk.

Change of Privilege Levels

Privileges are the combined rights and permissions allocated to interact with system resources. Altering object permissions and system rights for any given account has the potential to impact the overall security posture of the system. Changes in privileges should not be arbitrary and should only occur after consideration of the associated risk. Modification of permissions should include the involvement of resource managers or information owners. Similarly, altering account rights should only be done in coordination with the system owner or administrators. Inappropriate assignment of privileges can have undesirable consequences. When privileges are too lax, weaknesses may be introduced into the system that might expose sensitive information to abuse or compromise. Excessively rigid privileges can hamper operations, reduce system functionality, and frustrate users. A careful balance between usability and security is required to achieve the security goals of the system. Risk management is an important tool used by the security architect to strike the right balance.

Groups

Managing the security attributes for individual subjects and objects is an enormous undertaking. A system with hundreds of users and hundreds of thousands of objects is too difficult to manage individually. Thankfully, administrative tasks can be simplified when subjects and objects in common are manipulated simultaneously. Administrators make extensive use of groupings of subjects and objects to manage their vast numbers. Groups provide substantial advantages when managing large numbers of users and resources. This paradigm allows the convergence of management actions related to subjects and objects. The most common approach is to establish a group where membership is applied to particular objects or resources. Account membership in a group implies that different individuals have either a similar duty or need to access the same resource. Essentially, a group should be designed with the goal of accommodating accounts with

- Similar duties, but involving situations where they access different data. Here, a group is established to efficiently administer large numbers of accounts assigned permissions for a specific resource.
- Access to the same data, where each has different duties. This scenario is used to manage resource sharing among divergent types of users.
- Similar duties and data accesses. This type of group would essentially be the primary group used to manage a broad category of users such as Administrators or Ordinary users. However, more specific groups such as Accounting or Marketing could also be used.

Managing through the use of groups is indeed a double-edged sword. Although it provides substantial power to mitigate risk, when not properly managed it can cause other problems. Some issues facing a security architect when controls governing group management fail are the following:

- *Orphaned groups* - An excessive number of unused groups may appear on the system. Often, no one knows what the group was used for or if it should be retained. There is generally a reluctance to remove the group when no one is certain of the consequence.
- *Duplicated groups* - Often, multiple groups are created for the same purpose. They may have identical accounts and subgroups or nearly enough of the same members that the aggregate of different smaller groups equates to the sum of an existing group. Although particular members might be excluded from a given group, creating uniqueness, a lack of sufficient management reduces the advantages of the granularity provided.
- *Separation of duty violations* - It may occur that individuals included in the same group assigned to a given resource may ultimately violate separation of duties. Suppose a system administrator is included in a group of security officers managing audit logs. The administrator could potentially remove information in the logs associated with malicious activity. Adding members to groups without consideration of the use of the group can quickly result in unintended weaknesses.
- *Failures in least privilege* - Individuals might be given access to resources beyond the scope of their duties. Careless use of group assignments may result in the inclusion of individuals who should not have access to objects intended to be accessed by other members of the group. The haphazard or reckless addition of accounts may expose sensitive information to those who are not authorized or facilitate the introduction of malicious code such as a Trojan.

Administering group membership is an aspect of identity management. Processes should be implemented to control and monitor group assignments to prevent misuse or abuse. Some actions a security architect could take to establish management of group assignments include the following:

- *Identify purpose* - Record the reason for the group's existence. Indicate if the purpose is to group accounts according to function, data attribute, or both. Knowing the purpose for the existence of the group will help determine if future assignment to the group is appropriate for a given user.

- *Membership attributes* - Specify what types of members should be included in the group. Indicate if account types exist that would violate separation of duties or least privilege when included in the group.

- *Resource attributes* - List the various target resources that are to be associated with the group. Resource objects could be particular files, directories, or services. Indicate the permission levels to be assigned according to the type of object the group will be associated with.

- *Control changes* - Managing group memberships through a change control process is ideal, but may be difficult because changes may occur frequently. It is better to establish localized controls for changes. Assign one individual to approve changes and another to monitor compliance with the approvals. Coordinate changes with other information and system owners when a change impacts their area of responsibility.

- *Periodic review* - Establish a time frame to reexamine all groups in the system. Determine if an application of a group fails to meet its purpose. Consider each member and assess if they still should be included as a member. Determine if the group has any inappropriate resource assignments.

One way to think about the application of groups is through the relation of accounts with the activity of their owners. In this way, a group can be established according to the types of duties assigned to a user or a particular job function. Groups can be viewed from two perspectives: role based or task based.

Role Based

A role represents an organizational duty. It may be the totality of a job position or it could be a particular function within an organization. Managing account access control through the use of roles is an ideal way to assign rights and permissions. People can more readily identify with the concept of a role as opposed to a security group. When a role is aptly named, people are likely to anticipate what access and capabilities are associated with it. For example, one may correctly assume that the

Advertising role is associated with an organization's Marketing Department. We would further expect that this role would not have the same access as the Chief Financial Officer role. In this regard, access control based on roles may more likely appeal to those who are technical as well as those who are not.

Groups and roles are both a type of collection, but differ in their application. Groups are collections of users, while roles are collections of rights and permissions. In this regard, users are members of a group that can be assigned permissions for various resources. In contrast, a user assigned a role assumes a set of rights and permissions for designated resources. An RBAC implementation can be much more restrictive than those that rely on the use of groups.

An important aspect of an RBAC implementation is mutual exclusivity, which is the fundamental attribute used to establish separation of duties. Mutual exclusivity is a constraint in RBAC that specifies an incompatibility between roles; that is, two roles with mutual exclusivity have resource rights or permissions that must be kept apart to support separation of duties.

Assigning a single role to a user seems ideal, but it is difficult to do when using RBAC in a system or application with diverse types of resources. Limiting the number of roles in a system simply means more users must be assigned to the same role. This has the consequence of reducing the granularity of the access control implementation. Creating a role unique to each individual user seems like a good alternative. However, this has its problems as well. As the number of users and roles increases, it becomes more difficult to create new roles due to conflicts with existing roles. Furthermore, if mutual exclusivity is desired, then it can be difficult for users to even share data. Assigning a single role to a user in an RBAC implementation can work when the scope of the system or application is small. For instance, assigning a role to each user of a mobile or network device is reasonable. The limited functionality of the device and information that would be shared between users means there are fewer instances when sharing of rights or permissions is needed. Therefore, when mutual access to specific resources is uncommon, assignment of a single role to each user is less of a challenge. In cases where the number of rights and permissions is small, single roles may work well. However, assigning users a single role in a complex system with a diversity of data types will most likely result in a failed RBAC attempt.

Implementing an RBAC mechanism in a complex system will involve the creation and assignment of multiple roles. Rather than considering a role to match a particular individual or job function, we consider it to take on the attributes of the various activities associated with it. From this perspective, the organizational role of an individual is essentially the composition of many smaller roles. Suppose the organizational duty of a security officer is assigned the following roles:

A. Conduct a security assessment

B. Review audit logs

C. Advise the CIO

In this example, rights and permissions on resources associated with these activities are assigned to each of the prescribed roles. An individual who is a security officer is allowed to use those roles within the system. This is not to say that a role contains other roles, but rather, that the activity of an individual comprises many smaller, more discrete roles. Reducing the activities of individuals to more discrete roles enables separation of duties while preserving the ability for mutual access. Considering the prior example, a system administrator and security officer would both be assigned the role to *Review Audit Logs*, but a system administrator would not be allowed to *Conduct a Security Assessment* or *Advise the CIO*. This exemplifies the need to define roles at a granular level.

An RBAC implementation with a rich diversity of roles should provide sufficient granularity of resource usage. However, an important consideration is the number of roles a subject possesses at any one time. This raises a couple of questions:

1. Should a subject be allowed to hold multiple roles or only one role at a time?

2. What is the impact of access control layering?

Some RBAC implementations only allow one role at a time, while others permit more. The security architect must decide if one role at a time is sufficient from a usability perspective. If it is too difficult to use, then multiple roles will be needed. However, the assignment of multiple roles must consider the possibility of violating separation of duties. A user concurrently possessing multiple roles might allow a separation of duty violation, whereas using one role at a time would not. If the underlying RBAC mechanism supports the ability to specify mutual exclusivity constraints for conflicting roles, then it may be possible to securely use multiple roles concurrently.

A well-designed RBAC implementation with highly granular role assignments and constraints may be made inconsequential when combined with other access control systems. When the access control systems of diverse system components are of different types or do not communicate, the incompatibility may reduce the overall effectiveness of the design. This is a concern when products with an access control capability do not integrate well with those of other applications. This situation is even more problematic when the access control mechanisms are of different types. For instance, an RBAC instance within a DBMS may have ideal role assignments and constraints. Users connecting to the DBMS do so from an operating system implementing DAC. Further, suppose that two particular users are assigned mutually exclusive roles to satisfy separation of duties. A problem may arise when one user copies information from the database into an operating system directory accessible by the other. Although this action may be prohibited by policy, it demonstrates that the system is incapable of enforcing the policy of separation of duties due to the incompatibility of the access control mechanisms. An architect must consider the effect of layering access controls and determine if a reduction in the desired control may occur. The ease with which a control may be bypassed is as important a consideration as the cost associated with its implementation and management.

Ultimately, these questions can be answered by examining organizational policy and goals for the system. The RBAC implementation should support system policy and goals. A valid access control approach should not violate the rules and desired implementation of the system.

RBAC, similar to DAC, is not exactly the same from one vendor to the next. Some vendor products claiming to support RBAC simply allow the designation of a group of rights and permissions as a role, while others make an effort to implement most of its desirable aspects. Ideally, an RBAC-enabled product will allow the allocation of multiple roles and the ability to specify mutual exclusivity. The decision to select an RBAC-enabled product should be driven by business requirements and its suitability for the intended purpose to enforce a security policy.

A true implementation of RBAC is predicated on a mechanism that enforces its attributes. However, this may not be practical or feasible for resource-constrained organizations using commodity systems that desire this type of access control. In these cases, groups could be used to mimic role-based access. Because the term groups generally implies the use of DAC, it is important to note that designing groups to be used as roles:

A. Requires management discipline. Those creating groups and assigning membership will need to strictly adhere to group usage specifications.

B. Will not enforce separation of duties. DAC does not have an inherent capability to enforce separation of duties. However, proper use of groups can come close to achieving the same effect without the assurance of enforcement.

User accounts can be administered on a role basis when sufficient planning, management, and monitoring are implemented. The following guidance provides some recommendations regarding the use of groups as roles:

- *Create groups as if they were roles.* The mantra of fully documenting all aspects is essential here. A detailed listing of the attributes and uses of each group as a role is required. Inadequate or inconsistent specification for the design and use of groups as roles will yield less than desirable results.

- *Map the new roles (groups) to specific permissions and objects.* Identify which objects in the systems should have permissions associated with the roles.

- *Avoid assigning groups to groups.* This can quickly degrade the role-based effort. Assigning one role (group) to another will substantially add to the complexity needed and tracking required and should be avoided.

- *Refrain from assigning account permissions on objects.* Maintaining role-based access means that individual accounts should be assigned permissions only through the use of roles. This may be problematic for service and system accounts, but in most cases should not be too difficult for accounts assigned to people.

- *Issue users multiple accounts.* This is necessary if varying levels of rights are needed. This does not mean a user must have an account for each role, but rather, the inclusion of a member in a "role" must not create a situation where an account can easily circumvent its intended use. In this regard, a solid identity management methodology increases in importance.

- *Leverage system services.* Consider the implications of Web-based services, portals, databases, and other automation techniques that could act as intermediaries between subjects and objects. Designing services as a way to proxy access to objects without actually interacting with them can be used as a way to enforce role-based access for critical resources.

- *Limit object permissions.* Avoid giving subjects too much control over existing objects. Providing excessive permissions will make it more difficult to prevent inappropriate assignment of rights with the matching of roles and permissions. Furthermore, curtail the use of multiple roles for any object. This will help simplify verification of access. However, this may require the creation of more roles or those with broader assignment.

- *Monitor for inappropriate permissions.* Because object owners have full control over who can access their objects, it will be necessary to periodically check the permissions on all objects. Object permissions should match what has been documented for each role. An object should have a limited number of roles assigned to it. This will help ease role management and streamline its implementation.

■ *Audit for misuse.* Plan to use audit logs as a means to verify compliance. Look for events that indicate inappropriate assignment of rights or permissions. Use of rights capable of bypassing established permissions is another area worth monitoring.

Task Based

The output of an organization is a product, a service, or both. Either of these outputs is achieved by activity within the organization that transforms resources, such as raw materials or intellectual property, through effort exerted by its members. The activities associated with the resource conversions into outputs are called workflows. A task is a discrete activity in a workflow whereby people manipulate resources. A workflow may contain only one task or have multiple tasks. Some attributes of a task include time, sequence, and dependencies. A task may have to be conducted at specific times, but not necessarily in all cases. Most tasks will involve a series of steps and or events that may need to be accomplished in a particular order. An individual may not be able to conduct a task unless other tasks in the workflow are previously accomplished. For example, an editor cannot edit a document until the author has completed the drafting task. In this case, edit and drafting are tasks in the workflow of creating a document. Given the attributes of a task, an access control method supporting workflows is possible. These attributes can be specified as rules governing those aspects of the task. In this way, the rules can specify a subject, object, and permission in conjunction with a particular attribute. Task-based access control (TBAC) attributes consider

■ *Time* - This could be the amount of time allocated for a task as well as start and stop times. TBAC could specify a rule that requires a task to take no more than one hour, must be started between 6:00 AM and 8:00 AM, and is required to end by 9:00 AM. Days of a given week, month, or year could also be used as time parameters.

■ *Sequence* - A task may have elements that need to be performed in a certain order. If not, the task may produce erroneous output. The task sequence attribute of TBAC could specify the order of events or elements required to complete the task. A sequence can be enforced within a task by restricting access to elements until the ordering is correct.

■ *Dependencies* - Some tasks can only be performed after the work of a prior task in the workflow is completed. In this case, the task in question is dependent on the completion of the tasks before it. Similarly, subsequent tasks may also need to wait for the present task to complete. Like the previous example, a document editor cannot conduct the edit task until the author completes the drafting task. Edit has a dependency on drafting in this example. An obvious approach is to prevent the editor from accessing the draft before the author is finished. This may not work in all cases. Suppose the editor is required to periodically review the progress of the author. This may be a different task for the editor, but it is essentially part of the same overall workflow. By allocating permissions on objects according to their stage in a workflow, an editor could be given permission to read, but not write an object in the workflow given the requisite dependencies.

The concept of TBAC is still an emerging topic. 16 Presently, there are no accepted standards or definitions of what TBAC entails. However, this does not detract from the usefulness of implementing access control according to the attributes of a task in a workflow. Indeed, many organizations already implement types of access control in workflows. A number of document collaboration suites implement workflows and make use of TBAC enforcement attributes. A security architect should consider methods of leveraging TBAC attributes to enforce access controls on organization-specific workflows.

At first glance, TBAC appears to be closely related to RBAC. This is somewhat true. The important difference arises in the fact that the attributes specified for TBAC are more granular than those for RBAC. For example, a time attribute for RBAC is nondeterministic. This is to say that there is no specification within RBAC that requires the assignment of a role to begin or end at a specific point in time. In contrast, TBAC can have an assigned start and stop time as well as duration. RBAC also does not specify a sequence of events within a workflow, but rather broadly defines an activity indicative of a role. Finally, RBAC does not consider dependencies in a task, whereas TBAC may prevent an individual from starting a task before all of the necessary elements are in place.

Implementing TBAC has many advantages for an organization. It can reduce confusion and errors by automating manual processes that may otherwise be chaotic. The attributes of TBAC can be expressed in any number of ways to support the goals of the organization. Business rules can be created for each attribute, which can yield efficiencies and reduce errors. Standardization of workflows is an important consideration when safety is a concern. For instance, establishing TBAC for vulnerability scanning tasks may be important to some organizations. Suppose a health care organization needs to scan its network for vulnerabilities, but must exclude medical monitoring devices attached to the network. Furthermore, the scanning must be done at nonpeak times. One part

16   For an overview discussion of the conceptual framework of TBAC, please see the following: http://profsandhu.com/confrnc/ifip/i97tbac.pdf

of the task may require a preliminary scan to detect nonmedical monitoring devices. The result is fed into the actual scan, which limits the bounds of the vulnerability scan. The actual vulnerability scan has a dependency on the preliminary scan. Implementing an automated process governed by TBAC to control the preliminary scan, subsequent vulnerability scan, and the timing of these events supports the organization's safety goal and provides a higher level of assurance against mistakes.

Dual Control

Some organizational activities are so sensitive that it is absolutely critical that no single person be able to control an event or access the information. Access control requiring the cooperation of two individuals participating jointly in a process to access an object is called dual control. Within dual control, access is granted after two subjects with the proper permissions jointly agree and perform a rigid procedure to access the protected object. The implementation of dual control involves not only individuals, but a detailed protocol as well.

Dual control is commonly used as an assurance mechanism to prevent a catastrophic event. It is frequently used as a control mechanism for nuclear weapons, large financial transactions, and certificate authority management activities. In each of these cases, a rogue individual with the ability to commit a transaction could precipitate an event with significant consequences. Launching of nuclear weapons by a single individual is certainly chilling. Granting an individual the power to make billions of investment dollars vanish into secret accounts is a misguided reliance on trust. Providing a person with unfettered access to cryptographic keys or certificates used to support e-commerce or the identity of individuals is potentially devastating and irresponsible.

The premise of dual control is that inappropriate access to a sensitive resource will only happen with collusion. Dual control is a hard-core implementation of separation of duties. All individuals participating in the dual-control protocol should have sufficient separation to prevent the possibility of one person unduly influencing another in the process. To further reduce the opportunity for collusion, it is necessary to periodically rotate one or both of the individuals participating in the dual-control protocol. Job rotations are a common procedural control used to identify abuse of access or ongoing collusion. When dual control is implemented as an access control measure to protect against a serious event or loss, it must be accompanied by rotation of the individuals as well.

Usage of the term *dual control* is somewhat misleading. The term implies that access control requires only two individuals. In fact, a dual control protocol may involve many more participants. Other individuals may be responsible for witnessing the event while others might be assigned to monitor the activities. In some cases, the individuals participating in the dual-control process release the asset so that yet another individual may temporarily access it. One might argue that the involvement of more than two individuals clouds the definition. In a pure sense, that is not the case. Essentially, the protocol is truly dual control when two individuals are needed to unlock the asset. However, there must be at least one more individual participating in the protocol as an auditor. This individual is responsible for auditing the actions of the participants to ensure some level of accountability. The auditor would not have the authority to interact with the asset and would most likely not be allowed in the area when it is unlocked. Nevertheless, accountability is still essential to the integrity of the dual-control protocol and must be followed by someone on the periphery of the actions of those accessing the sensitive item.

Security requirements that point to the need for dual control must be accompanied by management commitment to provide the necessary resources. In uncommon cases when extensive resources are available, it is not ideal to design dual control with enormously complex countermeasures. Complexity can introduce more opportunities for weaknesses. The design of the dual-control implementation should be sufficient to meet the goals and objectives of protecting the sensitive resource. The security architect must bear in mind that elaborate designs are more difficult to implement and enforce. Therefore, the use and design of dual control should be concise, yet sufficient for its purpose. The following are some points to keep in mind when developing dual access control:

- *A rigid protocol* - A successful implementation of dual control is highly dependent on the manual and automated processes supporting it. The interactions between people and machines should be designed to work in harmony. This can only be achieved when the processes used to protect the resource, control access, and monitoring work together without error. All processes supporting protection, access, and monitoring should be well defined in a thoroughly documented protocol. The steps in the protocol should be clear and concise. It should not be possible to execute steps out of sequence without detection of the violation. All errors or violations encountered during the protocol should be met with responses to ensure the appropriate protection measures of the resource have not been compromised. In other words, the protocol should be self-checking and have defense-in-depth countermeasures integrated within.

- *Layering of physical and logical controls* - A variety of controls should be used in layers. Defense in depth is an important strategy for controls implemented. The strategy should call for controls that continue to operate when another fails. There should be little or no dependency from one control layer to the next; that is, a failure in one layer will not make it easier to compromise the next. For example, IT systems are highly dependent on physical security controls. This situation is augmented with other controls, such as media encryption, to protect the system when physical security cannot be ensured. Consider these types of controls for use inside facilities when systems used to protect critical assets must have strong assurances even if a breach occurs at the physical layer.

Power   Loss: The   Universal   Weakness

No matter how elaborate the complexity, redundancy, and failover measures planned by an organization are, they, like all modern systems, are vulnerable to a loss of electrical power. Organizations are heavily dependent on electrical grids for continuous power. Power disruptions occurring due to natural disaster are the most serious to deal with. Many sites plan for long-duration power outages by installing backup power generators. Most of these run off one fuel or another. However, during a natural disaster, fuel supplies may be disrupted. When the fuel dries up and the power goes off, the ability to monitor or control access to critical assets may be lost. Dual control may not even be possible to achieve in these instances. If access to a critical asset is necessary during such events, it is worth considering the use of manual methods to either supplement or replace electronic ones. Planning for the worst is imperative when the magnitude of harm from a loss of access control for a sensitive asset is significant.

- *Fail secure* - Ideally, the protocol and controls cannot be circumvented. Although it is not usually acceptable to rely on absolutes in the world of security, in the case of dual-control implementations, failing in a secure mode must be an important goal. Control failures are a reality. Nothing is perfect. Therefore, it is necessary to plan for imperfection. A failure in a control may indicate that an attack is under way and a breach is imminent. In this case, the protection of the asset is of paramount importance. The magnitude of harm that may occur due to its exposure should be met with a plan to prevent the catastrophic event. Fail-secure measures are alternative steps that further protect an asset from exposure. In the most critical cases, the asset is destroyed. A security architect implementing dual control should consider fail-secure measures that will deny unauthorized access to the resource when other controls fail.

- *Resource intensive* - It must be recognized and accepted that implementing dual control can be a costly endeavor. The involvement of multiple individuals, at a minimum, makes its usage inconvenient. Dual control is a form of access control that is best reserved for situations when the cost of a breach exceeds the cost of control by a large margin.

- *Frequency of use* - Use of the protocol should be kept to a minimum when possible. This will help keep adversaries who might be monitoring operations from analyzing the protocol and identifying weaknesses not previously considered. Ideally, the protocol will only be activated during special events that require access to the protected resource. Not only should use of the protocol be minimized, the timing of access should be varied as well. Vary the times and dates of initiating the protocol. This will help to further thwart adversarial activities. Unpredictability and randomness can increase the complexity of analysis by adversaries.

- *Keep protocol details confidential* - Centralize the entire documented protocol. Avoid distributing details of the entire protocol to its participants. Compartmentalize it to the greatest extent possible by only providing details to those who need to know what is necessary to execute their part.

- *Auditing* - Those assigned to audit or monitor activities should not be provided with the capability to manage access control layers or interact with the protected resource. Those responsible for monitoring will need to have full knowledge of the details of the protocol for those areas monitored. This provides the auditor with the ability to assess situations and make a determination if the protocol was violated. A protocol violation is an indication of an actual attack, human error, or control flaw. The auditor must have sufficient understanding of the protocol and controls to be capable of making this determination.

- *Key management* - To be certain, key management under dual control is not trivial. It is time consuming and should involve multiple participants to ensure integrity in the process. Nevertheless, keys should be periodically changed and must be controlled absolutely. Key management duties should be segregated outside of the scope of the individuals using the keys or managing any of the control layers.

Location

The physical attributes of system components provide yet another opportunity for the application of access controls. The locations of a subject versus the requested resource are often at different subnets, geographic locales, or devices. Access controls can be applied according to the location of the subject and the requested resource. Rule sets, policies, configurations, and network design can be implemented to dictate the extent of an access according to the origin and destination of the request. Locations have logical and physical attributes that can be used to enhance the granularity of other access control mechanisms.

Topology

Nodes in a distributed system are joined together through network topologies. The type of topology used in the network is influenced by the networking protocols and technology implemented. Regardless of the implementation, a common communication point will often be used that connects or routes network traffic between distant nodes. These junctures in the topology are the points in the network that are used to define locations. For instance, a router connecting the organizational network to the Internet defines internal and external locations. A wireless access point is another opportunity to define a location where trusted and untrusted traffic meet. The spans between the defining points are segments. The defining points that separate network subnets, geographical locales, or devices are where rules should be applied to establish location-based access controls.

Subnet

A subnet is used to logically segregate a network. In practice, a subnet is often associated with a particular grouping of users, devices, or areas within a network. The implementation of a subnet is commonly applied to a particular network segment or an entire local area network. This often results in a given location having the same subnet mask. In this regard, the logical address is frequently associated with a particular physical location. This is not exclusively the case, though. Organizations using a virtual LAN (VLAN) may mingle logical addresses with different subnets in the same network segment. Associating subnet masks with their locations can be leveraged to control access. For instance, suppose a policy stipulates that a Sales server can only be accessed from the Marketing group within the LAN. If each major group within the network is allocated its own subnet, then an internal router can be configured to deny connections to all but the Marketing group based on their subnet. *Figure 1.45* presents a diagram of this situation. A centralized router is configured to block subnet addresses that are not from Marketing. Because Accounting and Engineering

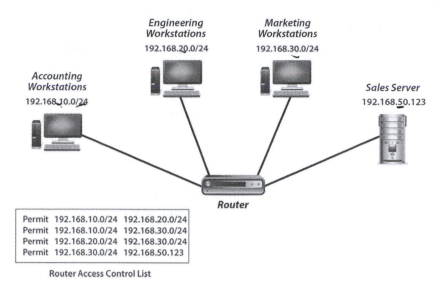

Engineering
Workstations
192.168.20.0/24

Marketing
Workstations
192.168.30.0/24

Accounting
Workstations
192.168.10.0/24

Sales Server
192.168.50.123

Router

Permit 192.168.10.0/24 192.168.20.0/24
Permit 192.168.10.0/24 192.168.30.0/24
Permit 192.168.20.0/24 192.168.30.0/24
Permit 192.168.30.0/24 192.168.50.123

Router Access Control List

Figure 1.45 - **Using a router to establish access control**

are in different subnets, the router prevents them from accessing the server. This demonstrates a method of implementing access control based on the logical location of a subject and the resource.

Using subnets as a way to enforce access control is helpful, but not perfect. Abuse can still occur, and this type of control can be bypassed. Furthermore, usability can also be difficult in some situations given the structure of the organization. Some issues with this implementation include

- *Stealing IP addresses* - Insiders may be able to reassign the network address on their workstation. This would allow them to bypass the controls on the router unless subsequent routers are used to counteract this situation.

- *DHCP* - If all DHCP requests are handled by the same server, then this type of access control would be difficult to implement. Alternatively, a DHCP server could be dedicated to the protected area to assign the protected range. This would also require the use of a router to block DHCP requests from traversing into or out of the protected subnet.

- *Logon from nonstandard location* - Users allowed to login from different locations may not be able to access the resource. This would be particularly difficult to accommodate when users must frequently use different workstations at various locations.

- *Network sniffing* - Sensitive-traffic-traversing network segments outside of the protected subnet range are vulnerable to capture. An insider might only need to record network traffic to obtain the information required rather than attacking the server itself.

Geographical Considerations

System nodes access resources from a given network segment. A node existing on a particular segment may access resources in the same segment or that of another. Each segment has a geographical location with respect to the organization's system. Consider a scenario where workstations, servers, and printers are physically joined to the network through switches. Nodes in a given area are clustered around a particular department within the organization. The switches joining the nodes in one department may connect to more switches or other networking devices, such as routers, enabling connectivity throughout the organization. The segments joining nodes and network devices are often contained in plenum areas such as ceilings, walls, and under floors, concealing their exact route. Although the exact path may not be known, the security architect and system engineers should know the area within a building serviced by a given segment. Knowing the approximate location serviced by a segment enables the application of access controls based on the physical location or a node. In this way, groupings of segments from a given networking device can be associated with a particular physical location. This could be used to control the types of traffic flows into and out of this area, based on the activities associated with the duties of those in the department.

Associating segments with node types is important, if only from an inventory perspective. However, this is less useful from a security standpoint if the types of activities in a segment are not known. For instance, security monitoring personnel may be tasked to conduct periodic port scans from their segment to the rest of the network. Given their duties, this is normal activity. However, port scanning would not be normal activity if it originated from the Accounting department segment. When the physical locations of nodes are associated with normal user activities, security policies can be applied accordingly. In this example, policy can be enforced for the Accounting department segment to prevent port scans from propagating across the network. Likewise, an intrusion detection sensor placed within the segment could be tuned to specifically look for activity that is known to be malicious, depending on the types of users within the segment.

Applying restrictions based on physical location involves the use of logical access controls. The idea is to designate logical access controls based on physical locations rather than logical addressing. The approach simply requires the designation of access controls for a network segment and those behind it having the same nodes or subjects. Consider mapping a network using a tree diagram such as the one shown in *Figure 1.46*. Mapping a network in this manner can aid in the identification of areas to best apply physical restrictions.

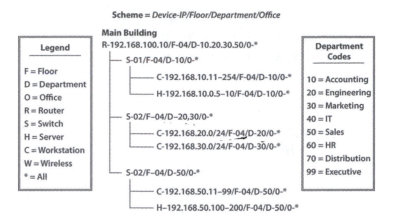

Figure 1.46 - **Network mapping using a tree diagram**

Logical addressing and subnets enable one to support physical restrictions while still permitting organizational communications. The routing node is configured to only pass traffic for a given subnet that is exclusively dedicated to a particular group of subjects. The routing access control list specifies subnets or addresses that are accessible from a segment. The critical point here is that different segments should be physically separated until they are connected to the node applying the logical access controls. This prevents an insider from spoofing an address in an alternate subnet and bypassing access controls based on physical location. The interface on the network node used to apply the access controls must be exclusively connected to the intended segment.

Establishing access controls for physical segments is complicated when users are not stationary. Users with roaming profiles or mobile users who are allowed to login from any segment in the network make it more difficult to establish behavior patterns. When the scope of network activity is too broad, then the application of access controls based on node location can be too restrictive for organizational purposes.

The idea of using access controls for network segments assumes that requests for resource access originate from a node within the segment. Unfortunately, this is not always the case. A node that has been compromised by malicious code, such as a bot or a Trojan, will access resources according to the commands given by someone outside of the network. In this regard, a compromised node extends the activity of an attacker within the context of an authorized subject on the network segment, which essentially bypasses the restrictions of access control based on physical location. Access controls on the network segment may be of little help if the activity of the malicious code is similar to that of an authorized user. However, many types of malicious code do launch subsequent attacks to further compromise the network. In these cases, access control based on physical location has its benefits, by restricting the propagation. If auditing is enabled for the access control device, the violations will be reported, which provides an opportunity to identify the offending node and eliminate the malicious code.

Device Type

Applying access controls based on the type of device connected to the network is a desirable goal. A variety of device types are regularly attached to networks. Some common types include wired networking equipment, wireless devices, servers, workstations, laptops, and smartphones. The granularity of identification of the device type is based on the security policies or goals of the organization. For instance, it may be desirable to distinguish workstations according to who normally uses them. In this case, a workstation device type might be further decomposed into subsets such as administrator, security, and ordinary user workstations. Enabling access controls according to device type is dependent on two important factors:

1. *Device recognition* - Each device type must be recognizable in some way by the access control mechanism.

2. *Policy enforcement* - Access control decisions are made according to the device type recognized. Devices that are not recognized should not be allowed to connect and pass traffic in the network.

There are generally three approaches to solving any problem in IT. These involve solutions that are ad hoc, standards based, and proprietary. With respect to the application of access controls for device types, an ad hoc approach involves the use of physical and logical addresses. The use of network-based access control is a standards-based approach worth exploring. Third-party software frequently represents a plethora of proprietary techniques that can be used to solve perplexing problems.

Physical and Logical Addresses

Prior to connecting a device, its physical address is registered. In cases where the logical address is static, this address would be recorded as well. The rules regarding what the device is allowed to communicate with would be encoded into Layer 2 devices, Layer 3 devices, and monitoring devices. Layer 2 devices are configured to lock a port to a given physical address. This is applied for every network port in the organization. Ideally, static logical addresses are used to strongly associate a given port with a unique device. However, this would be difficult to administer in a large organization. When dynamic addresses are used, an assigned range for a given area of the network must be used. This means multiple DHCP servers will be necessary to control which addresses are available in a given segment. Layer 3 devices are used to enforce policies for an explicit device when the logical address is known, or for a range when applied to a particular device type. Network monitoring will be necessary to capture network communication activity. A log of network activity containing logical and physical addresses allows the security team to detect violations to policy and take actions when suspicious activity is detected.

Advantages:

- *Easy to implement* - This approach makes use of devices common to many organizational networks.
- *Cost-effective* - The costs associated with the design and implementation are minimal. Some additional cost may be necessary to place a sufficient number of devices to control and monitor access. However, these need not necessarily be top-of-the-line models.

Disadvantages:

- *Manual registration* - Each device must be manually registered. A centralized database of what is allowed must be maintained. Furthermore, activity on the network will need to be periodically compared to the database to detect violations. This could be automated, but that requires software development, which also may be costly.
- *Lack of scalability* - The manual aspects of this approach will not scale well. Implementing this approach in an organization with a large network may be impractical.
- *Limited enforcement* - A lack of integration with monitoring and enforcement mechanisms reduces the ability of this approach to fully enforce a policy. Unless the monitoring activity is automated and can create Layer 3 changes on the fly, the ability to fully support the policy is diminished.
- *Spoofing* - Insiders could spoof their media access control and logical addresses and thereby circumvent the control all together.

Network-Based Access Control

Another approach is to implement the 802.1X standard as a means of authenticating each device attaching to the network. 17 As devices connect to the network, they are authenticated according to the certificate presented. A RADIUS server is used to support device authentication.

Advantages:

- *Standards based* - This approach relies on an existing protocol specifically designed to address the problem of device authentication.

---

17   For an overview of 802.1X standards support and implementation guidance on Microsoft networks see the following: http://technet.microsoft.com/en-us/network/bb545365.aspx

- *Policy enforcement* - Only authenticated devices are allowed to connect to the network.
- *Auditing support* - Connection attempts can be recorded to identify misuse and abuse.

Disadvantages:

■ *Not supported by all device types* - Some device classes such as PDAs may not support 802.1X. Existing network equipment internal to the organization also may not be capable of using the standard. Upgrading equipment to fully support this approach could be quite costly.

■ *Manual registration* - Each device will still need to be individually issued a certificate. Prior to deployment, it must be ensured that the correct device is issued the appropriate certificate. For many devices, this may require an administrator to manually load the certificate or visually determine that the target device is that which is intended.

■ *Certificate management* - The standard makes use of certificates that uniquely identify a given device. This implies the need to develop and maintain PKI to support 802.1X.

■ *Authentication only* - The policy enforcement is limited to device authentication. Applying permissions for access to other resources necessitates logical access controls via other devices such as Layer 2 and Layer 3 network equipment.

Third-Party Software

As the problem of identifying device types and applying granular access control continues, it is certain that vendors will develop proprietary solutions to mitigate the problem. The solutions could be as varied as the number of available products. It is difficult to determine the exact advantages and disadvantages of using third-party products because one product may be quite different from another. However, it is surmised that some potential advantages and disadvantages will be common to products that are developed to specifically address the issue of allocating access controls based on the device type.

Potential Advantages:

■ *Specialized* - A given technology may be uniquely designed to handle a given problem or task. In this regard, a vendor tool might prove quite useful and successful in enforcing organizational policy regarding device types in a network.

■ *Technical support* - Most products have some sort of support built into their purchasing agreement. The support provided may be sufficient to get the product deployed and staff adequately trained on its usage. Furthermore, vendor-supported products typically make updates available to address flaws or improve the native software.

- *Policy enforcement* - A tool that sufficiently supports the goals of the organization should support rule enforcement for a given device type.
- *Automated deployment* - Many products will have automated methods to deploy their tools to all intended targets. This can greatly simplify device management and expedite tool deployment.

Potential Disadvantages:

- *Cost* - Most tools may be too expensive for smaller organizations or departments with budgetary constraints. Reducing the scope of deployment to meet resource constraints may leave aspects of the policy unenforced.
- *Imaginary functionality* - The vendor marketing may be excellent, but the product could fail to live up to the hype. The vendor may overstate the actual capabilities of the product. The tool may not completely satisfy the intended security requirements specified by the acquiring organization.
- *May not support all device types* - A new product may not support all existing device types within an organization. Legacy operating systems and hardware may be outside the purview of the vendor's product. Furthermore, not all devices may be supported equally. The advertised functionality may not apply to all device types supported.

The aforementioned techniques to achieve location-based access control have various strengths and weaknesses. No individual technique is likely to be suitable for a moderate-sized organization or one that is geographically distributed. Location-based access control is best achieved through a combination of techniques. The design and implementation of location-based access control involves the following factors:

- *Join logical and physical* - Applying access controls based on location requires the use of logical and physical attributes of nodes and networking equipment. Identify all physical and logical characteristics that can be leveraged to achieve the desired level of access control.
- *Layer controls* - Use multiple techniques to achieve defense in depth.
- *Map and inventory the network* - Use scanning tools to identify all nodes in the network and the logical segments where they exist. Access controls in the network may prevent deep scanning. In

these cases, it may be necessary to conduct scans from multiple locations. Conduct an inventory of all devices connected to the network. At a minimum, the media access control address, device type, and physical location will need to be collected.

- *Conduct traffic pattern analysis* - Observe traffic patterns to assess normal activity. This information can be used to apply access controls to prohibit inappropriate connections from one area of the network to another. It can also constrain malicious code from propagating across the entire network.

- *Know where segments exist physically* - Conduct physical surveys to verify where the Ethernet cable connects to the networking device and in what area of a building it terminates. Some organizations may already have this information, but it is still advisable to verify their locations.

- *Implement rules on networking equipment* - Rely on networking equipment to enforce location-based rules. Ensure that the equipment is protected from logical tampering and located in physically controlled areas to prevent physical tampering. Trusting network nodes to enforce location-based access controls is less desirable unless it is integrated with network-based mechanisms such as 802.11X.

- *Monitor compliance* - Assess the location-based access control mechanisms by reviewing network device configurations and logs, and watching traffic connections.

Authentication

The basis of access control relies on the proper identification of a subject. This occurs when several elements are joined together in a process that validates a claimed identity. The necessary components of identity verification include

- **Entity** - A person or process claiming a particular identity.
- **Identity** - A unique designator for a given subject.
- **Authentication factor** - Proof of identity supplied by the entity. This element must be reproducible only by the entity.
- **Authenticator** - The mechanism to compare the identity and authentication factor against a database of authorized subjects.
- **Database** - A listing of identities and associated authentication factors. The database should be protected from tampering. Furthermore, the authenticator factors should also be protected from disclosure.

The act of an entity proving its identity is known as authentication. It is an exchange and validation of information that allows the entity further access into an environment. During authentication, an entity presents an identity and an authentication factor as proof that it is who it claims to be. The identity of the entity is verified by the authenticator comparing the authentication factor against a database of all identities. A successful match between the identity and authentication factor with an entry in the database supports the claim, and access is authorized. Once an entity is authenticated, it is recognized as a subject by the access control mechanism and is allowed access based on previously granted permissions and rights in the environment.

The Difference between an Entity and Subject

It is important to note that a distinction is made between an entity and a subject. An individual who is yet to be authenticated is referred to as an entity rather than a subject. This distinction is necessary because a subject represents someone or something with logical rights and permissions in a system. An entity has no logical rights before authentication. An entity graduates to a subject when successfully validated.

An authentication factor is essentially a key that opens a door into an environment. It is something tied to a specific identity and should only be reproducible by the entity. The three most common forms of authentication factors include something that is

A. Known only by the entity. Passwords and passphrases are the most common.

B. Held exclusively by the entity. An ATM card is an example of a token held by an owner.

C. A physical attribute of the entity. Fingerprints are one type of physical attribute.

The most important point of an authentication factor is its reproducibility. Only the entity should be able to present the correct authentication factor. It should not be trivial for an attacker to reproduce the authentication factor and masquerade as the intended subject. Three qualities emerge that can be used to evaluate the suitability of an authentication factor in a given authentication mechanism. An authentication factor meeting at least one of these qualities will provide sufficient confidence that an attacker will not be able to easily masquerade as the intended subject. These three qualities are as follows:

- *It is known only to the entity* - No other individuals have cleartext access to the secret. This means that other means must be employed to capture or persuade the entity to disclose the secret as opposed to its being easily guessed or known by others.

■ *Reproduction of it is infeasible* - It should be nearly impossible to create an illegitimate copy. Attributes of the authentication factor should be sufficiently complex or difficult to reproduce such that attempts to do so will have an extremely low likelihood of success.

■ *It is computationally impractical to replicate* - Mathematical shortcuts to guess or reproduce the authentication factor should not exist. Brute force attacks should be met with a sufficiently large search space and an extremely small probability of finding the authentication factor over a long period of time.

Sometimes, authentication factors are not used appropriately. On occasion, some authentication mechanisms use the authentication factor as a form of identity as well. The problem with this approach is that a compromised authentication factor may make it difficult to uniquely identify the subject in subsequent environments. This is not an advisable practice and should be avoided when possible.

Strengths and Weaknesses of Authentication Tools

Passwords have long been an authentication factor of choice for many systems. They are cheap and easy to deploy. Generally, users find a password easy to remember and use with a system. However, passwords are not necessarily the best authentication factor. Users tend to choose weak passwords that can be guessed in relatively short periods of time. To counter this situation, organizations require passwords to be sufficiently complex that they are not easily guessed. At this point, users begin to rebel. Passwords are now more difficult. Indeed, they can become so complex that users write them down to remember them. Fortunately, advances in technology have made other authentication factors available for use. Two types of authentication factors that have found their way into organizations are tokens and biometrics. Although some of these have strengths that may surpass fixed passwords, they each have their own unique issues that should be considered prior to rolling a new authentication system into an organization.

Token-Based Authentication Tools

A variety of devices are available that fall into the category of something held exclusively by the entity. These tokens rely on different types of technology to supply the authentication factor attribute.

Badges

These devices contain organization-specific designs, logos, and occasionally a picture of the authorized holder. Badges are most often used in conjunction with facility access control. Individuals posted at facility entry control points check the badge to ensure that it appears authentic, not expired, and is properly matched with the holder when an image is presented. Organizational staff should be trained to recognize badges to determine if an individual within the facility is authorized for facility access, a guest, or perhaps someone who inappropriately gained access. Plain badges are not used to interface with systems.

Strengths:

- *Low cost* - Badge blanks and the equipment used to print them are affordable.
- *Visually recognizable* - A unique design is recognizable by organizational members.

Weaknesses:

- *Easily spoofed* - The combined strengths are also a weakness. Attackers may be able to easily duplicate an organizational badge, which cannot be easily detected.
- *Relied upon as identification* - A badge lacking a feature or attribute permitting someone to verify its authenticity should not be used as an exclusive form of identification.

Considerations:

- *Mandate use of member pictures* - An individual's image ties the badge to the holder. Organizational members can at least determine that a badge is worn by the correct individual. Pictures also help validation at facility entry control points.
- *Manage badges like a credential* - Badges should be tracked and have a life cycle. Each badge should have a unique identifier tied to an individual. Those responsible for verifying identities at entry control points should be able to compare a badge number with an image of the holder. Periodically, change badge attributes to help visually detect frauds. Recover badges from those departing the organization.
- *Integrate machine-readable features* - Make the badge identifier machine readable using barcodes, magnetic strip, or proximity technologies.
- *Use different designs according to holder* - Use different colors and schemes to differentiate badge holders. Establish different badge holders by classes such as employees, contractors, visitors, maintenance crews, security personnel, escorts, and sensitive area access.

Magnetic Strip

This type of token normally has the same form factor as a credit card and has a magnetic tape stretching the length of the card. Magnetic strip cards are commonly used in facility access controls in a manner similar to that of door lock keys. In fact, the hotel industry makes extensive use of these tokens as room keys.

Strengths:

- *Cards are low cost* - Although the cards are relatively cheap, readers are moderately expensive.
- *Easy to use* - Most people have no problem using these cards.
- *Lock mechanism easily rekeyed* - Lock mechanisms are networked, so they can quickly be updated to reflect which magnetic strip cards can be used to gain entry.

Weaknesses:

- *Can be copied* - The magnetic strip is similar to the media used in audiocassette tapes. Readers can be easily procured to copy the magnetic information.
- *Vulnerable to magnetic fields* - Strong magnetic fields emanating from cell phones, cathode ray tube monitors and televisions, or permanent magnets can alter the information on the magnetic strip. Usually, the cards can be used after recoding.
- *Easily abused* - Magnetic strip cards are so easy to use that people often share them (whether voluntarily or involuntary). Many retail uses and facility access control implementations fail to employ techniques to detect masquerading or inappropriate use.

Considerations:

- *Use controls similar to those for badges* - Considerations listed earlier for badges apply to magnetic strip cards, given that the uses and form factors are similar.
- *Require two-factor authentication for sensitive areas* - A magnetic strip card alone represents a form of identification, but lacks an immediate way to authenticate without human intervention. Using another authentication factor, such as a PIN, strengthens the implementation, allows accountability, and increases the overall level of assurance.
- *Institute a challenge response process for card recoding* - Uses of the card in situations where the user is not immediately known to the issuer should be coupled with controls and processes that track and validate magnetic strip recoding.

Proximity Cards

Many organizations employ proximity or "prox" cards for facility access control. Proximity cards generally have the same form factor as a badge and use wireless techniques operating at either 125 kHz and 13.56 MHz. They provide a means to electronically identify a cardholder. Modern proximity cards operate at the 13.56

MHz range and comply with ISO 14443. Proximity card readers are capable of detecting a card up to several inches away. These cards contain no batteries, but are able to send their information in the presence of an electromagnetic field that powers the card, enabling transmission.

Strengths:

- *Double as ID badge* - The form factor of a proximity card allows it to easily be used as an ID badge as well.
- *Simple management* - Access control systems implementing proximity cards are relatively easy to use. Card activation and deactivation is a simple process.
- *Ease of use* - Proximity card use is relatively intuitive. They can generally be used not only in office environments, but in areas that are exposed to the elements as well.

Weaknesses:

- *Readers are costly* - Although the cards themselves are relatively low cost, readers can be hundreds of dollars and more.
- *Masquerading* - A card that is stolen or borrowed can be used to gain unauthorized access to areas granted to the intended cardholder.
- *Can be spoofed* - Most cards are not capable of using encryption to prevent spoofing. Rogue readers with high output fields and strong sensitivity can be used to capture card identities as people pass by. This information can be passed to specially constructed devices that retransmit card information, allowing access to protected areas.

Considerations:

- *Follow considerations given for magnetic strip cards* - Many of the same issues applicable to magnetic strip cards apply to proximity cards as well.
- *Periodically reaffirm access* - Ensure that cardholders continue to require access and have not left the organization.
- *Strategically deploy readers* - Proximity cards and readers provide an efficient mechanism to implement access control and auditing. They are useful for controlling access and primary entry points and are a more preferred choice than physical keys for protecting sensitive areas.
- *Protect controllers* - Central device controllers used with proximity card readers and electronic locks/strikes should be protected from unauthorized access. Restrict access to the controller to only those individuals delegated the duty of managing the proximity cards.

Common Issues with Token Management

Access control using physical tokens is a basic means of identifying a subject. However, they cannot always be relied upon to authenticate a subject according to something that is possessed. Security architects must consider several common factors when designing an access control system that uses tokens.

- *Loss of token* - A lost token can deny an authorized subject access to a system or facility. A supply of spare tokens and the availability of support personnel should be planned for. Users are bound to discover their tokens are lost while on business trips after hours. Staffing decisions to deal with these eventualities will need to be addressed and planned for.

- *Token damage* - An inoperative token may be apparent when it is presented to the security officer in multiple pieces. However, a malfunctioning token may not be physically evident and is bound to create some level of dissatisfaction and inconvenience for the subject attempting to use it; they will have difficulties accessing authorized resources or areas. Similar to the situation for lost tokens, the possibility that a token will become inoperative at the most inopportune time must be planned for. Further, the organization must have sufficient resources allocated to support end users.

- *Proprietary systems* - Tokens of the same type may not be able to interoperate with those of other vendors. This is especially true when tokens rely on proprietary protocols or form factors for proper operation. Locking into one vendor can prove expensive. Furthermore, vulnerabilities in one vendor product could affect an entire organization and be difficult and expensive to overcome.

- *Human resource management* - Tokens are issued to people who often move on to other opportunities. Those managing access control systems using tokens might not have been informed of the departure of the token owner. Timely revocation of the access provided by a token is a persistent problem in the real world. Security architects should seek ways to partner with human resource departments, payroll offices, and internal entities providing access to contractors and customers to identify when token holders depart the organization temporarily or permanently.

- *Binding tokens to owners* - Tokens without onboard microprocessors are not easily bound to the authorized individual. Most tokens are subject to theft and misuse. Unless the access control mechanism requires dual factor authentication, it is extremely difficult to ensure that a subject using a token is the authorized user. In this regard, tokens should be relied upon as a form of electronic identification, but not as a substitute for authentication.

Biometric Authentication Tools

The field of biometrics continues to grow and attract significant attention. Biometric authentication tools seek to uniquely identify an entity based on something they are. Regardless of the type of biometric targeted, a small amount of data is collected to form a template that describes the attributes of the individual measured with the biometric acquisition device.

Biometrics can be broadly categorized as either physical or behavioral. A physical biometric is a measurable attribute of an individual. It is something that is a tangible feature of a person. Fingerprints are an example of a physical biometric. In contrast, a behavioral biometric is something that is intangible about a person, but sufficiently unique that it can be used to identify an individual. For instance, the way each person uses a keyboard represents a biometric referred to as typing dynamics or keystroke dynamics. 18

Users are included in a biometric system through an enrollment process. During this period, users present their biometric for measurement. This may involve several attempts. The acquisition device collects various data elements about the patterns that make up the individual's biometric. The collected data points are referred to as minutiae, and are stored in a special template file. Multiple submissions during an enrollment are necessary to ensure that a sufficiently broad statistical representation of the biometric is collected. Minutiae templates can be as small as 9 bytes or up to several kilobytes, depending on the type of biometric collected and the algorithms used by the acquisition device. 19

Performance Characteristics

When comparing various biometric options, it is important to consider the aspects and performance characteristics associated with the type of biometric:

- *Accuracy* - This is the critical characteristic of a biometric. Accuracy is determined by the ability of a biometric acquisition device to correctly identify an enrolled individual and reject others who are not enrolled. This is arrived at through the use of statistical methods that look for error rates associated with

---

18   For background information on the mechanisms behind typing dynamics see the following:

Umphress, D., and Williams, G. Identity verification through keyboard characteristics, International Journal of Man-Machine Studies Vol 23, p263-273, September 1985

Monrose, F., Rubin, A., Authentication via Keystroke Dynamics, Proceedings of the 4th ACM Conference on Computer and Communications Security, p 48-56, April 1997

19   For background on Biometric system security and issues see the following: http://www.csee.wvu.edu/~ross/pubs/RossTemplateSecurity_EUSIPCO2005.pdf

incorrect associations made by the biometric system between the collected template and that held within its database. Type 2 errors, also known as false positives, occur when the biometric device incorrectly identifies an un-enrolled individual as legitimate. Type 1 errors, called false negatives, occur when the biometric system incorrectly prevents an authorized individual from accessing the system. Plotting Type 1 and Type 2 errors on a graph reveals a crossover error rate (CER) that represents the lowest possible trade-off between the two types of errors.

- *Enrollment time* - This is an estimate of the amount of time needed to initially collect the necessary attributes that identify a person. The enrollment time is almost always longer than the verification time. Enrollment in some types of biometrics is challenging and requires multiple attempts. This adds to the base enrollment time for a given biometric.

- *Response time* - This is the average amount of time needed for an acquisition device to collect the biometric and for the system to return a response to the user. In some cases acquisition can take a few seconds. Additionally, according to the type of biometric used, the search for a closely matching template could require more time as well.

- *Security* - Spoofing is the primary attack technique used against a biometric. An acquisition device should include countermeasures that increase its resistance to spoofing or abuse. For example, fingerprint readers should measure heat and pulse to ensure a real person is interacting with the device.

Implementation Considerations

Other factors affecting the use of biometric tools should also be included in any review by the security architect:

- *Cost* - To a large extent, biometric devices are expensive. Some types and technologies are substantially more expensive than others. For instance, fingerprint readers have good performance and are relatively low cost compared to retina scanners.

- *Acceptance* - The user community should not be largely resistant to the use of the biometric. Individuals commonly have health and privacy concerns regarding biometric devices. Their concerns should be tempered with an appropriate amount of education on the benefits and any perceived risk of using a particular biometric acquisition device.

- *Storage* - Biometric data storage should be thought out well in advance. Will the biometrics be stored on a central server or distributed? Perhaps smartcards will be used instead. Wherever the biometric template is stored, there must be sufficient controls in place to protect the data from unauthorized changes or exposure. Access controls over these authentication factors becomes critical.

■ *Changes* - People change due to behaviors, lifestyles, aging, injuries, and other medical conditions. These changes can affect the ability of the biometric system to accurately identify an individual.

Fingerprints

This type of biometric is the most well-known technical method of establishing an individual's identity. The uniqueness of a fingerprint is due to the differences in the ridges and furrows of a print. The characteristic differences commonly used as minutiae about a print include bifurcations, ridge endings, enclosures, and ridge dots. Other minutiae include pores, crossovers, and deltas, which are also used to further emphasize the uniqueness of an individual print. [20]

Fingerprint readers generally perform well, are low cost, and are generally accepted by the public. Enrollment time is generally quick, and the results are fairly accurate. Minutiae files are relatively small. Collecting a sample minutiae by a subject takes only a few seconds.

Although fingerprint recognition is one of the leading types of biometric authentication, it is not without its challenges. For instance, minutiae templates are not entirely standardized and, therefore, vendor products do not always interoperate. Widely deploying biometrics may require reliance on a particular vendor. This can be problematic if the vendor goes out of business. This might require a massive reenrollment for all users. Fingerprints can be also faked. Given the fact that fingerprints can be captured in an environment and spoofed, their use as a trusted authenticator is risky. The fingerprints of some individuals are difficult to collect due to aging or from exposure to abrasive activity, which could make the print difficult to capture during an enrollment process.

Hand Geometry

The physical attributes of an individual's hand are sufficiently unique to be usable as a biometric. Considering the finger length, width, and thickness combined with surface area of a hand, it is possible to create rather small template files enabling unique identification. Hand geometry biometrics appears to be quite accurate, with little to no resistance from users to data acquisition. However, cost, size of the device, and its proprietary nature inhibit wide adoption and deployment.

---

20   For background on the different aspects of minutiae based matching see the following: http://www.griaulebiometrics.com/en-us/book/understanding-biometrics/types/matching/minutiae

Iris

The patterns within the iris of each eye are quite unique. An iris has many attributes characterized as freckles, furrows, and rings that can be used as data points for a minutiae template. Eye color, the most obvious attribute, is not an element of iris detection technologies. The acquisition devices use black-and-white images to create the minutiae templates of the iris.

Iris-based technologies have proved themselves to be one of the best forms of biometrics (Chirillo and Blaul, 2003). They have very low error rates and are very accurate. These types of biometric devices have a moderate-to-low cost. It is likely that cost will continue to decrease as usage increases globally. Although these devices have good performance, there are issues. Users are still somewhat reluctant to participate in iris-based biometrics. It seems that people fear that the acquisition device could damage their eyes due to the use of infrared technology. Eye movement, proximity, and angle of the acquisition device, as well as lighting, affect the quality of the minutiae collected. These variations can hinder the enrollment process.

Retina

The vascular patterns at the back of an eye are used to form the retina template for this type of biometric. Retinal patterns are very consistent over time and not easily subject to surreptitious collection such as with fingerprint, facial recognition, and voiceprint. Retina templates have a higher minutiae data point count that substantially adds to their uniqueness.

Retina recognition systems are very accurate and very expensive. Spoofing a retina pattern is considered difficult. Aside from cost, the biggest drawback to retina-based biometrics is user acceptance. Enrollment and authentication with a retina recognition device requires an individual to place the eye very close to the input device. Many users fear damage to their eye by the device or contracting an eye disease from a prior user. Eye glasses and contacts also interfere with the proper operation of a retina detection device. Due to cost and acceptance considerations, retina-based biometrics should only be used when a high level of security is essential.

Facial Recognition

Although fingerprint biometrics is sometimes touted as the oldest form of biometrics, the simple truth is that this is not the case. Early systems of identification using fingerprints, although technical, were not automated. Humans have, however, relied on facial recognition as an absolute form of identification for many aeons. In fact, facial recognition through photographs, such as those used on a driver's license, has enjoyed a much broader deployment than the use of fingerprints. It is only recently that technology has advanced to the point that facial recognition can be sufficiently automated.

There are a number of techniques that can be used for facial recognition. Some of these techniques rely on grayscale image comparisons, thermal scanning to collect heat or blood vessel patterns, and local feature analysis based on differences in defined regions of a face.

Facial recognition technologies have acceptable performance, are low cost, and are not generally resisted by users. However, they do have some issues. Lighting, hairstyles, subject aging, cosmetics, accessories such as glasses or piercing, expressions, and facial hair can affect the accuracy of the detection process. Furthermore, some facial recognition techniques can be fooled with an image of the actual subject presented to the input device. Some facial recognition techniques also fail to distinguish between identical twins.

Authentication Tool Considerations

There is an important attribute of authentication factors that is sometimes overlooked. The strength attribute of an authentication factor lies in its ability to resist abuse; that is, a strong authentication factor is difficult to reproduce by anyone other than the owner. This is a major factor driving biometrics. Most people believe that something you are is superior to something you know or have. Indeed, this seems plausible. However, if something you are is reproducible or can be captured, then there is the risk of abuse. If authentication factors are considered in the context of cryptography, a different paradigm emerges. In cryptography, the algorithm is important, but the most critical aspect is key management. The key is what protects the confidentiality and integrity of the information. Protecting a cryptographic key is essential to the effective use of cryptography. With respect to cryptography, an authentication factor should be handled like a secret. No matter what authentication scheme or algorithm is used, the authentication factor must be protected from exposure. Given this line of thought, the use of authentication factors that can be publicly obtained undermines its strength. A difficult-to-capture or reproduced authentication factor is likely to be resistant to attack, which increases confidence in the authentication of a subject.

As time progresses, new attacks against biometrics will emerge. Spoofing of biometric features such as fake fingers or photographs of the victim will become more frequent. Countermeasures associated with biometric acquisition devices will be needed. Defense in depth involving people, processes, as well as technology will be necessary to help ensure biometrics uses are not abused. It is interesting to ponder the thought that biometrics has been hailed as an ideal replacement for weaker authentication factors such as fixed passwords. Time will tell if biometrics will prove more resistant to abuse than passwords.

However, there exists a more disturbing problem that will challenge biometric deployments. This problem is one that every security architect must carefully consider prior to recommending the acquisition or deployment of any biometric device. A threat that plagues passwords will likely have an equivalent counterpart affecting biometrics. Keystroke loggers are a particularly nasty threat to passwords. Those running within a system can capture all manner of authentication activity using a keyboard. Similarly, a Biometric Template Logger (BTL) could also be used to capture minutiae attributes before they are sent over a network. A carefully placed BTL running as a device driver could intercept the biometric data before the resident application or service has an opportunity to encrypt the data. An attacker could effectively replay this data at a future data and masquerade as a user when the biometric is the sole authentication method. Attacks against stolen passwords are recoverable by removing the offending malware and creating a new password. However, it is not necessarily this simple with biometrics. How do we recover from an attack that exposes biometric minutiae? A compromise to the database or interception of the minutiae template at the collection point would result in a permanent exposure of the biometric. It's not yet evident that reenrollment would be sufficient to exclude malicious use of the captured biometric template. This disturbing problem should be taken into account in the design considerations and risk assessments associated with any biometric usage.

Fortunately, there exists an architectural design that can improve on the weaknesses of tokens and biometrics-based authentication tools. Using dual factor authentication is one technique that can frustrate the ability of an attacker to masquerade or steal the identity of an authorized user. Where possible and necessary due to the level of risk, a security architect should design dual factor methods into authentication schemes. This approach is an effective way to mitigate known weaknesses and impending attack vectors that are likely to emerge against tokens and biometrics in the future.

Design Validation

Evaluating the design of a system is an important step to ensure that it meets all expectations. Design validation provides the security architect with the opportunity to ask questions and make determinations regarding the sufficiency of the implementation. Validation seeks to determine if the system is adequate, sufficient, and complete. Questions and testing presented by the security architect seek to identify inadequacies regarding any requirements, operations, functionality, and weaknesses in the implementation. A broad perspective of this approach seeks to answer questions in areas such as

- **Requirements** - Have all requirements been addressed?
- **Operations** - Are organizational needs met?
- **Functionality** - Does it work as desired?
- **Weaknesses** - Can it be circumvented?

Requirements specify the minimum attributes that must be supported by a system. With respect to access controls, requirements tend to be very broad and can have multiple interpretations. Requirements are derived from a variety of sources. The most common sources of security requirements are laws, regulations, industry standards, and organizational policies. An efficient way to determine if a system meets access control requirements is to list all applicable security requirements in a matrix. Cull all access control policy statements from applicable sources. Attempt to make each requirement as granular as possible. This may result in a single sentence from a policy statement spanning multiple requirement records in the matrix. Within the matrix, rows are used to identify individual requirement records, and columns specify the record and requirement attributes. Column headings useful in this regard include

- *Unique identifier* - Create a unique numeric or alphanumeric designator to distinguish the requirement record one from another. When discussing security issues, a unique identifier helps organizational members to be clear on which requirement is affected.
- *Sources* - Requirements from different sources may be worded differently, but are essentially the same. Combine similar policy statements from multiple sources to eliminate duplication among matrix requirements.
- *Requirement* - Create a statement that best describes the target requirement. Be as granular as possible regarding what must be implemented from an access control perspective.
- *Interpretation* - Because policy statements tend to be broad enough to have multiple interpretations, it is helpful to provide additional information clarifying the requirement. Identify in the interpretation the breadth and depth necessary for the implementation. For instance, indicate which type of hardware, software, or operations must implement the requirement.

A review of access controls should determine if the implementation meets the mission and operations of the organization. Access controls that are not related to operations or are excessive may be wasteful. There may also be aspects of operations that are unique and not covered by existing requirements. In these cases, a gap in access control coverage may exist. The security architect must strive to have access controls that are sufficient, but not excessive.

The proper operation of implemented controls is a fundamental expectation. Individuals using the system will anticipate that the access control mechanism works without too much difficulty on their part. The two elements of functionality that a security architect should bear in mind when reviewing an access control mechanism are

- *Operational* - The access control must work as intended with the desired results.
- *Usable* - A difficult-to-use access control mechanism will ultimately prove ineffective.

A failure or misconfiguration may prevent an access control mechanism from functioning properly. Similarly, an access control mechanism that is too difficult to use is in some cases just as worrisome as one that is not functioning properly. System users may seek methods to circumvent difficult-to-use access control mechanisms, rendering them ineffective. Therefore, it is necessary to test access control mechanisms through a battery of tests to ensure they are operating as intended and are usable as well. Testing should attempt to exercise controls and evaluate settings to ensure they are properly configured and are not too difficult to use.

A properly configured access control mechanism may meet requirements, operational expectations, and pass testing, and yet still have weaknesses. Flaws in software or hardware supporting the access control mechanism may allow unauthorized subjects or entities the ability to bypass a mechanism. Changes in the environment may also introduce weaknesses into the access control mechanism. Authorized software may inadvertently violate least privilege or separation of duties, nullifying existing access control implementations. This indirect weakness in access control nonetheless affects the mechanism. This illustrates the need to consider testing that extends beyond the mechanism itself. Other dependencies in the system can impact access controls and should also be reviewed for induced weaknesses.

Architecture Effectiveness Assurance

The overall goal of access control design validation is to ensure that the questions regarding requirements, operations, functionality, and weaknesses are not left unanswered. A common thread among these questions is the problem of something missing. Certain requirements may have been missed and not integrated into the system. Some operational aspects may have recently emerged that are not covered by the access control mechanism. A functional aspect of the access control mechanism may not be available to all system users. Insufficient access control coverage introduces a weakness into the system. One way to determine architecture effectiveness is to look for aspects of these questions that are missing from the access control implementation:

- *Identify access control gaps* - The effectiveness of access controls are impacted by gaps in their coverage. Access control gaps can occur for a variety of reasons. Incorrect configurations or missing software components can create areas in a system where access controls are missing. Recent installations may have inadvertently changed access controls, exposing sensitive resources to those who are not authorized. In some cases, a necessary control might be missing altogether. Periodic reviews of access controls should be conducted to identify gaps that may exist.

- *Policy deficiencies* - Insufficient access control coverage can occur due to problems with policies. Policies governing an organization may not adequately specify the requirements for access control. In this case, an organization may deploy ineffective access controls. This is a common problem for organizations that do not have access to seasoned information system security professionals. Another problem with policies involves their interpretation. A poorly worded policy that does not express the necessary access control depth and breadth may lead to weak implementations. In both of these cases, an incomplete policy can lead to poorly architected access controls.

- *Look for obvious ways to circumvent controls* - Security is imperfect. With this understanding, it is evident that no control will be 100% effective. Furthermore, some controls may be easier to bypass than others. Attackers will certainly look for ways to get around access controls in a system. The security architect should also search for obvious ways to bypass existing access control mechanisms. One prime example is unencrypted passwords sent over the network. A number of commonly used protocols such as Telnet, Open Database Connectivity (ODBC), and Post Office Protocol (POP) transmit passwords in the clear. An attacker sniffing the network could easily capture these passwords and masquerade as the authorized user, effectively bypassing the intended purpose of the access control mechanism. Adding point-to-point encryption is one way to overcome this type of weakness. IPSec could be used between clients and servers to protect the passwords and still enable the use of these protocols.

Weaknesses are likely to occur through errors, omissions, or flaws in the design. These issues can be accommodated by forward thinking in the design process. Two ways to plan for emergent problems are to create contingency countermeasures and exploit defense in depth:

■ *Identify countermeasure strategies for emergent vulnerabilities* - Flaws in software continue to plague the IT world. Although the problem with buffer overflows has been known for quite some time, they still occur. It is best to anticipate that flaws in critical areas will be discovered. A security architect can help mitigate the eventual emergence of flaws by devising methods that limit exposures to a newly discovered vulnerability. Evaluate different techniques that could be used to block or slow the exploitation of a flaw. Identify ways to incorporate control layers in the various protocols and resources within the network to limit the scope of a exploited vulnerability.

■ *Use defense in depth to counteract weaknesses* - Fully leverage people, policies, and technology to detect and defend against weaknesses in access controls. Design layers into access controls such that a failure in one layer will not compromise another layer. Implement redundant and backup controls to counteract failures. For example, a VLAN can be used to segregate user network traffic, limiting access to particular resources. Suppose a network has resources that should not be accessed by those who are not authorized. In a network with no traffic restrictions, shared resources are frequently protected with file-system-based access control lists. However, if the access control list is accidentally altered, allowing inappropriate read access to the protected resource, then a compromise may occur. A VLAN that excludes the protected resource from those not authorized represents an additional measure protecting the resource from an inadvertent compromise. This supplemental control acts as a defensive layer protecting network-accessible sensitive resources from failures in file system access controls. Integrating a defense in depth strategy can reduce compromises due to inadvertent or malicious changes.

Testing Strategies

The effectiveness and assurance of an access control mechanism is determined through testing. The goal of testing to is to conclude if the access controls adequately support or enforce security policies. Testing is essentially a validation that the policies are integrated into the system through the application of countermeasures. Security requirements form the standards by which the access controls are compared. Compliance with a requirement supports assurances that the controls within the system are effective.

Supporting versus Enforcing Security Policies

In the world of information security, a "system" is the entire collection of equipment, software, facilities, people, and processes interacting with organizational information in the electronic environment. A system supports a security policy when aspects minimally provide an ability to direct policy compliance and can also be used to detect deviations. A security policy is supported if methods exist to guide user behaviors along activities meeting security requirements. For example, a "Rules of Behavior" guide directing users to create complex passwords supports policies underscoring the need for passwords that cannot be easily guessed. The guide is a tool, and training is the process by which users are informed of the policy and correct behavior. A system with automated mechanisms that disallow noncomplex passwords is said to enforce the security policy. From this perspective, policy enforcement occurs when the system prevents (or at least obstructs) users from not complying with established security requirements.

Testing Objectives

Testing seeks to identify the extent to which access controls support security requirements. Assurance of architectural effectiveness is predicated on the comprehensive testing of these objectives. Access control testing objectives in the following list help the security architect determine if the controls are

- *Implemented correctly* - System controls should support all security requirements. The implementation of the control should be in accordance with the appropriate depth and breadth to support the security policy of the system. Where applicable, access controls should enforce the security policy too. This objective is used to draw a direct link between policy and system. A correct implementation supports or enforces a security requirement as directed by policy.

- *Operating as intended* - The implementation of the control should meet the intent of the requirement and its design. Controls should be properly configured to support the intended operation as identified in the system design and relevant security requirements. Access controls should work as designed. This access control objective is used to assess the adequacy of the control's functionality.

■ *Producing desired outcome* - Determining the degree to which access control supports operations and whether a weakness exists is the purpose of this objective. The implementation of a control alone, or in combination with others, satisfies the security requirements. Any gap within a control that is not supported by another control indicates that the control is not fully producing the desired outcome.

Testing Paradigms

Testing is conducted to evaluate to what extent an access control meets it objectives. Different testing paradigms are useful in determining the effectiveness of the control. Each type of testing approaches the control from a different angle. No single paradigm should be relied on exclusively. A security architect is encouraged to include aspects of each of the testing paradigms in the overall testing strategy to ensure that the objectives are met. The different testing paradigms include

■ *Exercise controls* - It is important to know if the control is working properly. This type of testing primarily verifies if the control works as intended, but it can also determine if the implementation is correct, with the appropriate output. A determination is made by running test cases and reviewing the results to ensure that the result is what was expected. Consider a test that determines if the access control enforces an account lockout policy for failed logon attempts. The test involves a successful login followed by subsequent logins with an incorrect authentication factor. When the number of intentionally unsuccessful logins equals those specified in the policy, a review of the account properties is made. If the account is locked out, the test passes. If not, then the control fails. This type of testing is especially important for in-house software, such as Web-based applications that do not have the benefit of beta testers, such as other commercial off-the-shelf (COTS) products.

■ *Penetration testing* - The testing paradigm seeks to discover if an access control can be bypassed or overcome. A control is bypassed when the penetration tester is able to circumvent the control by creating an alternate path to access the target. This may involve exploiting other flaws in the system. Another tactic of this paradigm is to crash through an existing control using brute force techniques that overcome the control. A successful brute force attack often indicates a flaw in the access control mechanism. The main thrust of penetration testing is to confirm that the outcome of the control is correct. However, if the testing is properly designed, the results can be used to indirectly determine if the control is configured and operating correctly.

- *Vulnerability assessment* - Identifying flaws in a system is a critical activity. This type of testing is essential to locate known software and configuration weaknesses that could be exploited. Vulnerabilities in software packages are discovered on a regular basis. The organization must regularly conduct vulnerability assessments to locate and correct flawed software. Some configurations in a system may also provide an attacker with avenues to compromise a system. Vulnerability assessments can be used to identify weak or inappropriate settings in the system, such as open file shares or weak ACL. This type of testing relies heavily on the use of automated tools. Manual methods can be used to identify vulnerabilities too, but are labor intensive.

Regardless of the testing paradigm followed, there must be sufficient testing conducted to determine if each of the testing objectives for each security requirement is met. A security architect is most likely to use all of the paradigms at one point or another to test an access control mechanism. Just as layering of security controls provides defense in depth, conducting an assessment from different perspectives can enhance test quality and results. Testing should be conducted using written test procedures that collectively evaluate the test objectives for each security requirement. Using a battery of paradigms will normally yield a comprehensive view of the control under test.

Repeatability

A hallmark of a quality-testing process is repeatability. This is a quality demonstrating that the testing process will provide the same or similar results when conducted by different individuals on a static system for a given standard. It is important to note that results may not always be identical. Minor changes on the system may yield slightly different results. So long as the results fall within the parameters of the standard specified by the security requirement, there is sufficient assurance that the testing methodology is sound. Test results that are substantially different on a static system indicate either a non-repeatable testing process or a flaw in the system.

Methodology

A standardized methodology is needed to allow others to duplicate the access control testing. This can be accomplished by creating a process that allows the explicit specification of testing parameters while incorporating result tracking. Once again, a matrix approach is a useful way to organize this information. Suggested columns for a testing matrix include these items:

- *Test number* - A unique identifier to distinguish one test step from another.

- *Requirement number* - Matches the unique identifier in a Requirements Matrix.
- *Requirement* - This should replicate the associated statement in the Requirements Matrix. It is the standard driving the expected result.
- *Assessors* - The name or identification and contact information of those involved in conducting the test.
- *Test date* - The time frame of the test. A particular test might take a minute or a month to complete.
- *Test procedure* - The explicit sequence of actions to be performed. It should be put together in such a way that it evaluates each of the test objectives. A detailed test procedure supports repeatability.
- *Expected result* - This is the outcome of a test given the requirement is met.
- *Actual result* - The result of the test performed. For brevity, it is suggested that a short statement such as "Compliant" be used when no failures are noted. Report as much detail as appropriate for noted failures. Minimally report which aspect of the test failed, as well as the identification of the device, process, document, or interviewee associated with the failure.
- *Corrective action* - A detailed explanation of mitigating controls, corrections, or acceptance of risk for the failed test. An initial report of the failure should include a recommendation. The details of this item should reflect system management's decision to implement the recommendation or some other course of action.
- *Validating agents* - The name or identification of the individuals confirming that the corrective action was successfully performed.
- *Validation date* - The final date when the validating agents confirm that the corrective action was in fact fully implemented or approved.

Developing Test Procedures

Overall, testing determines if the system sufficiently supports the security policy. The vagueness of security policies can make this a difficult task. The intent of the policy can be lost when applied at a granular level. A truly focused test may lose sight of the purpose of the security requirement when the relationships between the elements of access control are not fully considered. The security architect should bear in mind the relationships between access control attributes when developing test procedures. Consider the following relationships when developing access control tests:

- *Entities and authentication factors* - Subjects are allowed access to the system or resources based on their ability to successfully authenticate. Accountability also relies on the correct association between an entity and subject via the authentication factor. Exposure of the authentication factor destroys accountability and threatens the other security goals as well. Access control testing should ensure that the link between an entity and authentication factor is resistant to compromise and tampering.

- *Subjects and rights* - All subjects in a system have been granted some rights. These rights should closely match the roles or duties assigned to the user or process. Access control testing should consider whether the rights associated with subjects of the test are appropriate or not. A weakness in an access control mechanism may allow subjects to directly or indirectly increase their rights in the system. Testing should determine if subject interactions with the system could result in the ability to increase rights or not.

- *Objects and permissions* - Determining if a given object has the correct permission is simple in execution, but challenging from an assessment perspective. This is particularly true for information repositories such as file systems. Top-level directories may have the correct ACL, but files deep within the structure may have the wrong permissions or be contained in an inappropriate location. Access control tests should consider objects and permissions, but in some cases, obtaining a valid assessment result with a high degree of confidence may be quite difficult. At a minimum, those objects that are particularly critical, such as password files, should have their permissions checked.

Risk-Based Considerations

An evaluation of the effectiveness of the access controls within a security architecture may reveal a variety of weaknesses. Some of the weaknesses may have been known prior to the testing, while others may not have been evident. In an ideal world, sufficient resources exist to implement effective countermeasures when weaknesses are discovered. Sadly, this is not usually the case, and often, an action must be taken that is less than ideal to address the problem. A security architect will frequently face this type of dilemma. Resource constraints, although problematic, need not be viewed as a crisis. Risk-based decisions are an effective way for managers to designate temporary or permanent alternatives to the problem. Achieving an optimal solution that keeps risk as low as is practical requires careful contemplation of the options. The following list provides some options that can be used to support risk-based decisions:

- *Unconventional alternatives* - A security requirement may be met through a variety of methods. Identifying options to support risk-based decisions may call for some creative thinking. Solutions might involve the use of multiple tools or integration with manual methods to achieve the security requirement. Existing controls might be sufficient to mitigate the risk. Think about the different ways other controls could be used to achieve the same effect. This may simply necessitate enabling a software option or modifying an existing process or procedure.

■ *Enumerate risk* - Innovative options may incur new risk. Less than ideal solutions may be accompanied by new problems that were not previously considered. Any increase in risk associated with alternatives must be communicated to management for its consideration.

■ *Monitor weaker controls* - Insufficient controls can be bolstered with monitoring. An existing control that does not fully satisfy the testing objectives for a given requirement does not imply that it is flawed or useless. In some cases, monitoring combined with a weak control provides sufficient augmentation, allowing the requirement to be met. In instances when this is not the case, a carefully implemented monitoring scheme can still provide the ability to detect misuse and abuse. Monitoring can include automated or manual processes to support the weak control. The main point of the use of monitoring is to identify compromises that cannot be prevented through a weak control.

■ *Cost sensitivity* - Recommended control options for risk-based decisions should be practical from a resource perspective. The cost of a recommended tool or process should not exceed the value of the assets affected. When a tool is needed, compare costs and capabilities among various vendors. The most expensive tool might be ideal, but budget-conscious options may be suitable. It may be desirable to hire additional personnel to address the problem. This can also be an expensive alternative and is not always feasible. Automated mechanisms and alternatives must be leveraged to the greatest extent possible before requesting human resources.

■ *Manual processes* - Most automated processes can also be accomplished manually. Although automated processes are normally more efficient, their cost may be out of reach for an organization. Manual techniques may be sufficient when automation is not cost-effective. The implementation of manual access control methods must be supplemented with explicit documentation and sufficient end user training.

■ *Open source solutions* - The Internet is full of low-cost alternative tools. Open source tools, which are usually downloadable at no cost, are worth consideration. There are some excellent open source tools that can help augment or replace weak access controls. The downside to these solutions includes support and trust. An open source tool may not have any support and could conflict with other software in the organization's environment. Deployment and use of the tool may be complicated. Experimentation and learning may be a burden for the existing staff. Trust in the integrity of the tool is another consideration. Many open source organizations try to ensure their code does not contain backdoors or malicious aspects. When practical, an internal source code review of an open source tool should be conducted prior to compilation and deployment. Subsequent monitoring of the activity of the tool should be conducted when an internal source code review is not practical.

Summary

The automation of access control techniques appears to have evolved beyond tight-fisted control of a USB Flash Drive by incorporation of a rich variety of methods that support authentication, authorization, and accounting. The basic attributes of AAA can accompany a well-designed and well-implemented access control system. The essence of access control is to prevent information from falling into the wrong hands by controlling access to the data through techniques that allow accountability and verification of changes, or prevent tampering with our most precious information files. Possession of a USB Flash Drive seems to be the ultimate form of access control. In this case, the security policy is known and invoked by the owner of the disk. The physical handoff of the disk in a face-to-face exchange is a strong form of authentication and authorization. Subsequent retrieval of the drive enables verification that the data is intact. Modern access controls provide techniques that allow information to be shared on an unprecedented scale. Implementations of strong cryptography associated with authentication mechanisms and protocols seem sufficient to provide a high level of confidence that access to the information is secured. Yet, given all of the potential techniques and implementations to achieve AAA, assurances are tenuous. Insider threats, malware, and other abuses can circumvent the best access control mechanisms and not prevent a loss of data confidentiality in most systems. In this light, it may seem that controlling information on a USB Flash Drive is the best form of access control. However, it is not. The user borrowing the USB Flash Drive could just as easily make inappropriate copies of sensitive files too. Trojan horse applications could have been used on the shared machine to further capture sensitive files. The problem has always been with us. Access control is helpful, but knowing where information flows is a highly relevant aspect of a system's use that is insufficiently monitored. Indeed, access control can be harnessed by the tenacity and creativity of a security architect dedicated to the cause of defending organizational information against exposure. Wherever information resides, access controls must be used to control information flows.

References

Aboba, B., Blunk, L., Vollbrecht, J., Carlson, J., and Levkowetz, H. (2004). RFC3748—Extensible authentication protocol (EAP). Retrieved from http://www.faqs.org/rfcs/rfc3748.html.

Bertino. E., and Sandhu, R. (2005). Database security—concepts, approaches, and challenges. *IEEE Transactions on Dependable and Secure Computing, 2*(1), 2–19.

Bishop, M. (2003). *Computer Security: Art and Science.* Boston, MA: Pearson Education.

Chirillo, J., and Blaul, S. (2003). *Implementing Biometric Security.* Indianapolis, IN: Wiley.

Finseth, C. (1993). RFC1492—An access control protocol, sometimes called TACACS. Retrieved from http://www.faqs.org/rfcs/rfc1492.html.

McCollum, C. J., Messing, J. R., and Notargiacomo, L. (1990). Beyond the Pale of MAC and DAC: Defining new forms of access control. *Proceedings of the1990 IEEE Symposium on Research in Security and Privacy*, 190–200.

Melnikov, A., and Zeilenga, K. (2006). RFC4422—Simple authentication and security layer (SASL). Retrieved from http://www.faqs.org/rfcs/rfc4422.html.

Park, J. and Sandhu, R. (2004). The UCONABC usage control model. *ACM Transactions on Information and System Security, 7*(1), 128–174.

Price, S. M. (2007). Supporting resource-constrained collaboration environments. *Computer,* 40(6), 108, 106–107.

Popescu, B. C., Crispo, B., and Tanenbaum, A. S. (2004). Support for multi-level security policies in DRM architectures. *Proceedings of the 2004 Workshop on New Security Paradigms,* 3–9.

Relyea, Harold C. (2008), Security Classified and Controlled Information: History, Status, and Emerging Management Issues. Congressional Research Service Report for Congress, Order Code RL 33494.

Rigney, C., Willens, S., Livingston, Rubens, A., Merit, Simpson, W., and Daydreamer. (2000). RFC2865—Remote authentication dial in user servers (RADIUS). Retrieved from http://www.faqs.org/rfcs/rfc2865.html.

Sermersheim, J. (2006). RFC4511—Lightweight directory access protocol (LDAP): the pro. Retrieved from http://www.faqs.org/rfcs/rfc4511.html.

Stokes, E., Byrne, D., Blakley, B., and Behera, P. (2000). RFC2820—Access control requirements for LDAP. Retrieved from http://www.faqs.org/rfcs/rfc2820.html.

Zeilenga, K. (2006). RFC 4510—Lightweight directory access protocol (LDAP): Technic. Retrieved from http://www.faqs.org/rfcs/rfc4510.html.

 **Review Questions**

1. Which of the following represents the type of access given to a user?

    A. Permissions
    B. Subjects
    C. Objects
    D. Rights

2. The most widely adopted access control method is

    A. Discretionary access control.
    B. Mandatory access control.
    C. Rule-based access control.
    D. Role-based access control.

3. No read up and no write down are properties of

    A. Discretionary access control.
    B. Mandatory access control.
    C. Rule-based access control.
    D. Role-based access control.

4. Access control for proprietary distributable content is best protected using

    A. Discretionary access control.
    B. Digital rights management.
    C. Distributed access control.
    D. Originator controlled.

5. When designing a system that uses least privilege, a security architect should focus on

    A. Business requirements.
    B. Organizational mission.
    C. Affected usability.
    D. Disaster recovery.

6. Separation of duties is **BEST** implemented using

    A. roles.

    B. permissions.

    C. rights.

    D. workflows.

7. Which of the following is the **BEST** supplemental control for weak separation of duties?

    A. Intrusion detection

    B. Biometrics

    C. Auditing

    D. Training

8. Centralized access control

    A. Is only implemented in network equipment.

    B. Implements authentication, authorization, and accounting.

    C. Is implemented closest to the resources it is designed to protect.

    D. Is designed to consider and accept business partner authentication tokens.

9. Firewalls typically employ

    A. Centralized access control.

    B. Decentralized access control.

    C. Federated access control.

    D. Role-based access control.

10. A feature that distinguishes decentralized from centralized access control is its

    A. audit logging.

    B. proxy capability.

    C. security kernel.

    D. shared database.

11. Federated access control

    A. is implemented with RADIUS.

    B. is designed to be mutually exclusive with single sign-on.

C. is implemented closest to the resources it is designed to protect.

D. is designed to consider and accept business partner authentication tokens.

12. Lightweight Directory Access Control is specified in

A. X.509

B. X.500

C. RFC 4510

D. RFC 4422

13. This technique is commonly used to collect audit logs:

A. Polling

B. Triggers

C. Workflows

D. Aggregation

14. A word processing application, governed by Discretionary Access Control (DAC), executes in the security context of the

A. end user.

B. process itself.

C. administrator.

D. system kernel.

15. Peer-to-peer applications are problematic primarily because they

A. are prohibited by policy.

B. may be able to access all the user's files.

C. are a new technology that is difficult to evaluate.

D. may be derived from untrustworthy open source projects.

16. Business rules can **BEST** be enforced within a database through the use of

A. A proxy.

B. redundancy.

C. views.

D. authentication.

17. A well-designed demilitarized zone (DMZ) prevents

    A. direct access to the DMZ from the protected network.

    B. access to assets within the DMZ to unauthenticated users.

    C. insiders on the protected network from conducting attacks.

    D. uncontrolled access to the protected network from the DMZ.

18. Dual control is primarily implemented to

    A. complement resource-constrained separation of duties.

    B. distribute trust using a rigid protocol.

    C. support internal workflows.

    D. supplement least privilege.

19. A well-designed security test

    A. requires penetration testing.

    B. is documented and repeatable.

    C. relies exclusively on automated tools.

    D. foregoes the need for analysis of the results.

Domain 2

Communications & Network Security

THE 2012 VERIZON DATA BREACH INVESTIGATION REPORT found that over 97 percent of breaches were avoidable if security measures classified as simple or intermediate had been in place[1].

The communications and network security domain addresses the security concerns related to the critical role of telecommunications and networks in today's distributed computing environments. The security architect understands the risks to communications networks, whether they are data, voice, or multimedia networks. This includes an understanding of communications processes and protocols, threats and countermeasures, support for organizational growth and operations, and the ability to design, implement, and monitor secure network architectures.

---

1   See the following for the full *Verizon 2012 Data Breach Investigations Report*:   http://www.verizonbusiness.com/resources/reports/rp_data-breach-investigations-report-2012_en_xg.pdf

TOPICS

- Determine Communications Architecture
  - Unified communication (e.g., convergence, collaboration, messaging)
  - Content type (e.g., data, voice, video, facsimile)
  - Transport mechanisms (e.g., satellite, landlines, microwave, radio, fiber)
  - Communication topology (e.g., centralized, distributed, cloud, mesh)
- Determine Network Architecture
  - Network types (e.g., public, private, hybrid)
  - Protocols
  - Securing common services (e.g., wireless, e-mail, VoIP)
- Protect Communications and Networks
  - Communication and network policies
  - Boundary protection (e.g., firewalls, VPNs, airgaps)
  - Gateways, routers, switches and architecture (e.g., access control segmentation, out-of-band management, OSI layers)
  - Detection and response
  - Content monitoring, inspection and filtering (e.g., email, web, data)
  - Device control
- Identify Security Design Considerations and Associated Risks
  - Interoperability
  - Auditability (e.g., regulatory, legislative, forensic requirements, segregation,verifiability of high assurance systems)
  - Security configuration (e.g., baselines)
  - Remote access
  - Monitoring (e.g., sensor placement, time reconciliation, span of control,record compatibility)
  - Network configuration (e.g., physical, logical, high availability)
  - Operating environment (e.g., virtualization, cloud computing)
  - Secure sourcing strategy

OBJECTIVES

The security architect must be ever vigilant to recognize the threats and available countermeasures in order to ensure the provisioning of secure communications. Key areas of knowledge include:

- Secure voice and fax communications
- Data communications architecture
  - Network topologies
  - Network protocols
  - Network security devices
  - Accountability and monitoring
- Data and network protection
- Telecommunications security management and techniques
- Remote access protocols
- Network design validation

This chapter focuses on the interrelationship between telecommunications and network security. The term *telecommunications* can have several meanings based on the period in which the term was used. This chapter uses the most modern definition of the term telecommunications, which describes the transmission of voice and facsimile information over both circuit-switched and packet-switched networks.

After discussing voice and facsimile communications and the convergence of packet- and circuit-switched networks, the chapter moves to an overview of voice security, voice protocols, and the various hardware and software that contribute to protecting networks. In concluding this chapter, the focus is on a series of network design issues related to enhancing security and how organizations can configure and validate the security architect's efforts.

Voice and Facsimile Communications

Both voice and facsimile communications were originally developed to be transported via analog transmission. Although a typical person's voice has a range of 20 kHz, the frequency range of a communications channel was limited by the use of low-pass and high-pass filters to an approximate 3 kHz passband, with multiple conversations between two locations carried by analog multiplexing, which shifts conversations onto predefined channels of frequency division multiplexers (FDMs)[1]. The use of FDM was prone to frequency shifting, which required the use of guard bands, limiting the number of channels that could be transported by the technology. *Figure 2.1* illustrates a frequency division multiplexer, where multiple voice conversations are shifted up in frequency, with guard bands of a set frequency to minimize the effect of voice drift. The entire bandwidth is then output onto a trunk circuit, which enables multiple voice conversations to be carried on a common line between cities. The Y-axis of *Figure 2.1* is deliberately omitted as its values depend on the type of voice channel multiplexed. For example, a 3000 Hz voice channel typically has a 75 Hz guard band, while a 48 kHz wideband voice channel uses a much wider guard band of approximately 1 kHz. Although once commonly used in North America, due to the conversion of communications carriers to digital technology, FDMs are now obsolete[2].

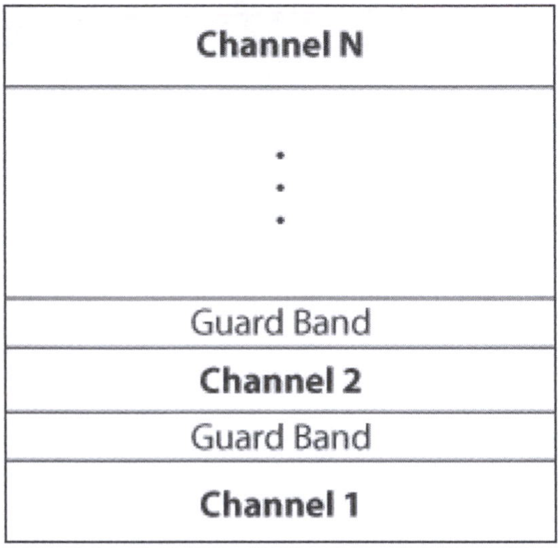

Channel N
. . .
Guard Band
Channel 2
Guard Band
Channel 1

Figure 2.1 - **Frequency Division Multiplexer (FDM)**

Similar to voice communications, facsimile transmission was initially an analog system. Due to the use of low-pass and high-pass filters by communications carriers, facsimile transmission was restricted to the use of an approximate 3 kHz channel, which represented the standard telephone analog bandwidth.

---

1   See the following for background information on low-pass and high-pass filtering:
Low-pass: http://www.allaboutcircuits.com/vol_2/chpt_8/2.html
High-pass: http://www.allaboutcircuits.com/vol_2/chpt_8/3.html

2   See the following for an overview of FDM and how it works: http://zone.ni.com/devzone/cda/ph/p/id/269

Pulse Code Modulation (PCM) [3]

With the development of the computer during World War II, technology started to become focused on the design of digital products. Within a short period of time, pulse code modulation (PCM) was used to encrypt voice by the Allies. PCM represents one of the earliest methods developed to digitize an analog signal, such as human voice or facsimile transmission. First, the analog signal is sampled at predefined time intervals. Next, each sample, which can have an infinite number of heights, is quantized into a predefined value that is closest to the height of the signal. Then, the resulting height is encoded into a series of bits. Early PCM systems used 7 bits per quantized value, with more modern systems using 8 bits. Using a sample rate of 8000 samples per second with 8 bits per sample, a voice conversation that is digitized using PCM results in a data rate of 64 kbps.

PCM was used by AT&T and other communications carriers to develop a digital highway for transportation calls between telephone company offices. First, 24 voice calls were sampled and encoded into 8 bits, and a framing bit was added to provide a pattern used for synchronization. This was the well-known T1 frame, which comprises 193 bits (8 × 24 + 1). Because sampling occurs 8000 times per second, the data rate of the now ubiquitous T1 line became 193 bits/frame × 8000 frames/second, or 1.544 Mbps. *Figure 2.2* illustrates the format of a T1 line. Note that when structured to hold 24 voice conversations, the T1 line is referred to as a "channelized" T1, while when used to transport data such as for Internet access, the T1 is referred to as a "nonchannelized" T1 line 4.

Figure 2.2 - **Forming a channelized T1 frame**

Moving up the initial digital highway are the T2 and T3 lines. A T2 consists of four T1 lines multiplexed with additional framing that is used between telephone company offices and operates at 6.312 Mbps, while a T3 consists of 28 T1

---

3   See the following for an overview article on Alec Reeves, the creator of PCM. The article profiles the work Reeves did to invent PCM and puts PCM into historical context, as well as describing the details of how the technology works.   http://www.todaysengineer.org/2012/Jun/history.asp

4   See the following for a complete overview of the T-Carrier solution: http://www.dcbnet.com/notes/9611t1.html

lines multiplexed with framing that is used for high-capacity communications and operates at 44.736 Mbps. *Table 2.1* provides a summary of the initially developed digital highway in North America 5. Note that the DS0 (pronounced digital signal level zero) signal level references the basic voice bandwidth data channel encoded via PCM.

Digital Signal Level/ Transmission Facility	Data Rate	Number of DS0s
DS0	64 kbps	1
T1	1.544 Mbps	24
T2	6.312 Mbps	96
T3	44.736 Mbps	672

Table 2.1 - **The Initial North American Digital Highway**

Circuit-Switched versus Packet-Switched Networks

Due to the relative high cost of long-distance communications prior to the 1980s, it was expensive to access remote computers. Both dial-up and leased lines were expensive, with dial-up long distance based on the time of day a call occurred, its duration, and the distance between the caller and called telephone numbers. Using dial-up resulted in the telephone company network establishing a series of switched network segments within their network infrastructure to connect the caller to the called party. Thus, the term switched or circuit-switched network resulted as a reference to a dialed call. Initially, frequency division multiplexing (FDM) was used to enable multiple calls to flow between telephone company offices. With the development of digital technology, time division multiplexing (TDM) replaced FDM, with signaling software allocating the routing of DS0s as 64 kbps PCM data streams onto and off various TDMs on a path that was established to link the caller to the called party. Once the circuit-switched path is set up, the digitized voice conversation flows over that path with no loss or interruptions[6].

5   See the following for some examples of more recent activity and investments around the building of digital highway infrastructure around the world:

http://www.unpan.org/PublicAdministrationNews/tabid/115/mctl/ArticleView/ModuleID/1467/articleId/34306/default.aspx
http://www.eso.org/public/announcements/ann12082/
http://www.booz.com/media/uploads/Digital_Highways_Role_of_Government.pdf
http://www.fas.org/sgp/crs/misc/RL30719.pdf
http://www.broadbandcommission.org/
http://ec.europa.eu/digital-agenda/en
6   See the following videos for overviews of TDM and how it works:
http://www.youtube.com/watch?v=Fjw_nj5UU64
http://www.youtube.com/watch?v=o8VBV6v2Tcs

The high cost associated with the use of the public switched telephone network resulted in the development of a new type of communications that was at first designed to transport data. Referred to as packet switching, vendors such as Telenet and Tymnet established networks consisting of modems in various cities, minicomputers located in those cities, and high-speed communications lines that connected the minicomputers to form a mesh-structured network. A customer would dial a Telenet or Tymnet telephone number to connect his terminal device to the network. He would then enter an authorization code, which the service provider would use to allow the customer the use of the network as well as for billing him or her. This would then be followed by an access code that would identify the resource connected to the network the customer wished to access. The minicomputer would packetize the data received from each customer in a particular city, placing a series of identifiers in each packet that indicated the source and destination address of the packet and its sequence number. This enabled packets from different customers to flow over the circuits that formed the backbone of the packet network.

Figure 2.3 illustrates a packet-switched network consisting of many nodes, shown as circles, where initially minicomputers were used for examining packet information and forwarding packets based on the contents of certain packet fields. Later, routers replaced the use of minicomputers in most packet networks.

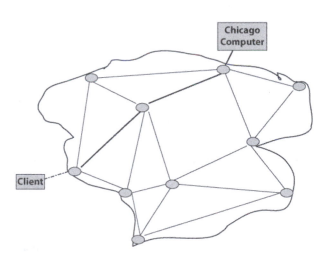

Figure 2.3 - **Using a packet network**

In examining Figure 2.3, note that a client is shown dialing into the network. After the client obtains authorization to use the network, packets are examined and a path is established through the packet network, which is indicated by heavy lines, to a destination computer located in Chicago and connected to the network via a leased line. Although the connection shown would be "taken down" once the client or computer completes the session, which is referred to as an "on demand" session, a connection can also be "permanent"; however, other users can have their data transmitted over most or all of the same connection paths as the permanent connection.

The use of packet-switched networks offered certain advantages over the use of the telephone network for transporting data [7]. First, numerous data sources could be routed over common high-speed circuits to either different or the same destination based on the connection desired by users. Second, each packet had its integrity checked via the use of a Cyclic Redundancy Check (CRC) character that was appended to each packet. The CRC was computed by treating the data in the packet as a long binary number, dividing that number by a fixed polynomial, discarding the integer, and keeping the remainder as the CRC. This CRC was referred to as the local CRC because it was computed locally. At the next minicomputer or router, the received packet was buffered and another CRC was computed, which was compared to the CRC in the packet. If they matched, the packet was forwarded toward its destination. If the two CRCs did not match, the packet was rejected, and the sender was requested to send another copy of the packet.

The use of CRCs for error checking on packet networks provides a higher level of data integrity than when asynchronous data is transmitted via the telephone network. This is because most asynchronous communications used parity checking, which cannot detect multiple bit errors commonly caused by machinery turning on or off, electric ballasts, and even sunspots. In comparison, the use of CRC checking reduces the probability of an undetected error to one in tens of millions of bits. Thus, packet networks offer a higher level of data integrity than the telephone network.

Other features common to early packet networks included reverse charges, which was similar to a collect call and alternate routing. Concerning the latter, if a packet network node that was typically a minicomputer failed or a circuit linking two nodes became inoperative, the network would use a series of predefined algorithms to route around the impediments. Once the problem was fixed, the alternate routing would terminate. Today, alternate routing is built into most of the routers on the Internet, enabling traffic to be moved around bottlenecks due to both line outages and high occupancy without the user being able to tell they are on an alternate route unless they use a traffic routing display program, such as traceroute, to determine the path from source to destination.

Although packet networks have significant advantages over circuit-switched networks, they also have many disadvantages. Foremost among the disadvantages was the delay resulting from the need to retransmit packets because of CRC mismatches caused by spurious hits on circuits resulting primarily from machinery and weather conditions. Fortunately, most impairments were due to the use of

---

7   See the following for an overview comparison between packet switched and circuit switched networks: http://voip.about.com/od/voipbasics/a/switchingtypes.htm

high-speed analog circuits by packet network operators during the 1970s. As fiber-optic cables began to interconnect cities, their use significantly reduced the error rate associated with older analog connections. Another problem associated with packet networks is data loss. Unlike circuit switching, which results in a dedicated connection between source and destination that prevents data loss, packet networks will drop data packets as they become overloaded. This is because network engineers size the transmission facilities to maximize revenues with minimum cost, knowing that dropped packets will result in the retransmission of the packet by the originator if a response (negative or positive acknowledgement) from the next node is not received within a predefined period of time.

The development of packet networks was based primarily on economics. In their prime, they could transport data from New York to San Francisco for the equivalent of 30 cents per minute while a long-distance call might cost well over $1 per minute. However, as the cost of telephone calls decreased, their reduction had a significant effect on the initial series of packet networks, with most of those networks shutting down in the late 1980s.

The packet networks previously described were based on the X.25 protocol, and were often referred to as X.25 networks [8]. Their development paved the way for the growth of a new type of packet network based on the TCP/IP protocol suite, which is now commonly referred to as the Internet protocol. Although originally developed to convey data between computers, advances in a series of technologies resulted in the transmission of digitized voice along with data, resulting in the convergence of voice and data on a common network.

VoIP Architecture Concerns

There are several key areas of concern in the development of a network architecture designed to move digitized voice over a packet network originally developed to transport data. Those concerns include the end-to-end delay associated with packets carrying digitized voice, jitter, the method of voice digitization used, the packet loss rate, and security.

End-to-End Delay

The end-to-end delay affects the ability of a user to know when the person at the other end of the connection has completed saying something. When the end-to-end delay is too long, a common conversational pause becomes so noticeable that the other party may begin to speak when the talker has merely paused in his or her conversation, resulting in a disjointed conversation. *Table 2.2* compares five important characteristics of circuit- switched and packet-switched networks.

---

8 See the following for a thorough discussion and overview of X.25 networking: http://www.farsite.com/X.25/X.25_info/X.25.htm

Characteristic	Circuit-Switched	Packet-Switched
Bandwidth allocation	Fixed slots	Variable
Traffic delay (jitter)	Minimal fixed	Variable, can be lengthy
Traffic support	Voice/video	Designed for data
Traffic type	Designed for constant	Designed for traffic bursts
Data loss	Not by design	Routers drop packets during periods of high traffic

Table 2.2 - **Comparing Circuit-Switched and Packet-Switched Network Characteristics**

Jitter

Jitter represents the variation in packet transit caused by queuing, contention, and the propagation of data through a network [9]. In general, the telephone network provides a fixed path for the transmission of data on an end-to-end basis, resulting in a near-uniform amount of jitter resulting primarily from transmission propagation. In comparison, on a packet network where multiple data sources can contend for transmission on a common backbone circuit, heavily congested links can result in variable jitter. This in turn can result in the reconstructed voice sounding awkward. To compensate for jitter, most VoIP devices employ a jitter buffer, allowing data arriving with different delays to be extracted uniformly with respect to time.

Method of Voice Digitization Used

Currently over ten voice digitization methods are used to encode a voice conversation. While it is fairly obvious that the decoding method must match the encoding method, less obvious but very important is the encoding method used. Currently, voice-encoding methods range in scope from the generation of a 64 kbps data stream developed via PCM encoding to more modern encoding methods that require as little as 2400 bps for the encoding of voice. While in general a lower encoding rate enables more voice conversations to be transported over a packet network, there is usually a reduction in the quality of a reconstructed voice conversation when an encoding method generates a lower digitization rate, especially when the digitization rate falls below 8000 bps.

Packet Loss Rate

A packet network experiences peaks and valleys with respect to packet flow, similar to a highway. However, instead of a traffic backup occurring on a highway

---

9   See the following for an overview of Jitter and Jitter Buffers: http://www. voiptroubleshooter.com/indepth/jittersources.html

when too many vehicles are entering the facility, on a modern packet network routers will drop packets. Although significant improvements have occurred in the type of packets dropped due to various expedited traffic flow methods, packets transporting voice will periodically be dropped along with data packets. While data packets can be retransmitted without adversely affecting data integrity, packets transporting digitized voice cannot be retransmitted if a real-time conversation is in effect. Thus, dropping too many packets transporting digitized voice will adversely affect a conversation.

Security

Perhaps an often-overlooked voice architecture concern is security. After all, many persons feel that if their voice conversation is somehow known to others, minimal harm will result. While this may be true, it may be possible for an unauthorized party to take control of a data PBX, router, or voice server; the unauthorized party can then take over a company's hardware, dial persons in international destinations, or other pay numbers and run up an expensive communications bill that could endanger the organization's financial health. While the preceding just touches the surface of voice security concerns, the following discuss some applicable policies and procedures.

Voice Security Policies and Procedures

There are several areas associated with voice that security architects must consider. Those areas include encryption, administrative change control, authentication, integrity, and availability.

Encryption

The use of encryption is significantly different when voice is transmitted via packets instead of being digitized and sent on a circuit-switched network. When voice is encrypted on a circuit-switched telephone network, the encryption and decryption process occurs on an analog waveform. Although the voice conversation is digitized, digitization occurs at the telephone company central office, and the subscriber line to the central office transports voice in analog form. To accomplish encryption, portions of the frequency spectrum are moved through the use of expensive filters. In comparison, when voice is transmitted over a packet network, there are two significant differences. First, each packet represents a digitized bit stream, so digital encryptors can be used. Second, encryption cannot occur on the full packet as each packet header contains one or more fields of routing information as well as other data that routers within the network must be able to examine and take action depending on their contents. Thus, this limits the type of encryption to hardware and software products specifically developed to operate with packet data.

Encryption

Data to be encrypted	11100100
Pseudo random key	10010101
Transmitted data	01110001

Decryption

Received data	01110001
Pseudo random key	10010101
Reconstructed data	11100100

Figure 2.4 - **Encryption and Decryption**

Figure 2.4 illustrates the ease with which digital data, to include digitized voice, can be encrypted via simple modulo 2 addition and modulo 2 subtraction. At the top of the referenced figure, the encryption process is shown. Here, the data to be encrypted is modulo 2 added with a pseudo-random key, resulting in the encrypted data being transmitted. In the lower portion of Figure 2.4, the decryption process is shown. Here, the same pseudo-random key is used; however, this time it is modulo 2 subtracted from the received encrypted data to produce the decrypted or reconstructed original data [10].

Through the use of encryption, it becomes very difficult for an unauthorized third party to hear different voice conversations. Thus, if someone was able to tap into a circuit connecting a business office to a packet network, the unauthorized party, for example, would normally not be able to ascertain that the company was able to bid up to $4 million on a project. However, if one had the resources of the NSA, it might be possible to decrypt the voice conversation and determine what was said, which explains why between the two Gulf wars, Iraq transferred most of its military communications onto fiber-optic lines, which were used in place of microwave towers that were relatively easy to monitor [11].

Authentication

Authentication represents the process of determining whether someone or something is, in fact, who or what it is declared to be. In voice communications, one can use Caller ID to authenticate the calling number and if known, the person's voice to authenticate the calling party. In the data world, authentication is commonly implemented through the use of logon passwords. Knowledge of

---

10   See the following for an overview of Modulo encryption: https://sites.google.com/site/dtcsinformation/encryption/modulo-encryption

11   See the following as examples of issues associated with the move from traditional communication platforms to fiber optics:
A. http://www.gwu.edu/~nsarchiv/NSAEBB/NSAEBB326/doc06.pdf
B. http://archive.newsmax.com/archives/articles/2001/2/22/213115.shtml

the password is assumed to guarantee that the user is authentic. Within the past few years, two-factor authentication has gained prominence. In this technique, a user has a key fob or similar display device which changes its numeric display every minute or so. The user must enter both the numeric displayed on the device and their "secret" password to gain access to the computer or network; hence, the term two-factor authentication.

Administrative Change Control

The process of administrative change control in a voice security environment refers to examining hardware and software to locate and modify default settings that control access to the product's administrative controls. Most security architects have used Wi-Fi in the home, office, or as a "road warrior." The transmission between the user's portable device and the Internet via an Internet Service Provider (ISP) occurs via a wireless router. That wireless router has a set of administrative controls that govern the type of data traffic permitted, hours when such traffic can flow to the Internet, and the key that governs encryption and other settings. All too often, routers have a default administrative password that is in the manual and never changed by the administrator. This allows a third party to simply gather a list of default passwords from different vendor manuals located on the Internet and try one after another to gain control of the router. Once control is achieved, the unauthorized person, depending on the router's capability, may be able to transfer a duplicate data stream of traffic flowing through the router to another location for analysis that is totally transparent to the users of the router. Similarly, in a voice environment and even for large Web servers and other types of computer and communications hardware, many products are shipped with default passwords that should be the first item the security architect changes when configuring such equipment.

Integrity

In a communications environment, it is important that what a person says be received correctly. Integrity refers to the ability of communications being received as sent. In a voice environment, there are several mechanisms that can result in a loss of integrity, including the recording and selective replay of a conversation, spoofing or someone pretending to be the person he or she claims to be, and the injection of speech into an existing conversation to distort the meaning of the conversation. Although integrity is rarely compromised, it represents a threat that must be considered by the security architect.

Availability

In the field of communications, the term *availability* refers to the period of time that a system, subsystem, or circuit is operable and can function to perform its mission. As an example of availability, consider a voice answering system that is operational 8750 hours in a year. Then, its availability becomes

$$A = \frac{Uptime}{Uptime + Downtime} = \frac{8750}{8750 + 10}$$

Voice Protocols

While there are numerous voice protocols that have attained a degree of prominence, this section will focus on an umbrella protocol and two signaling protocols. The umbrella protocol is referred to as the H.323 Recommendation, which defines a series of protocols to support audiovisual communications on packet networks. Session Initiation Protocol (SIP) defines the signaling required to establish and tear down communications, including voice and video calls flowing over a packet network. The third voice protocol discussed is Signaling System 7 (SS7), which represents a signaling system protocol originally used for establishing and tearing down calls made over the world's series of public switched telephone networks. However, to make a call over a packet network such as the Internet, SS7 information must be conveyed. This occurs by transporting SS7 over the Internet Protocol (IP).

The H.323 Protocol [12]

The H.323 standard can be considered to represent an umbrella recommendation from the International Telecommunications Union (ITU) that covers a variety of standards for audio, video, and data communications across packet-based networks and, more specifically, IP-based networks, such as the Internet and corporate intranets. The H.323 standard was specified within the ITU-Telecommunications organization by Study Group 16. The original standard was promulgated in 1996, and further enhancements have been developed in the intervening years [13].

One of the functions of H.323 is to define standards for multimedia communications over local area networks (LANs) that do not provide a guaranteed quality of service (QoS). Such networks represent a vast majority of connectivity for corporate desktops and include packet-switched TCP/IP, Fast Ethernet, Gigabit Ethernet, and the now-obsolete Token Ring network technologies. Thus, the H.323 standards represent important building blocks for a broad range of collaborative, LAN-based applications for multimedia communications. This umbrella standard includes parts of H.225.0—RAS

---

12   See the following for overview information about H.323:   http://www.packetizer.com/ipmc/h323/

13   See the following to access copies of all previous versions of the H.323Standards: http://www.packetizer.com/ipmc/h323/standards.html

(Registration and Administration Status), Q.931, H.245, and the RTP/RTCP (Real Time Transport Protocol/Real Time Control Protocol).

H.225 is a call signaling protocol for packet-based multimedia communication systems [14]. RAS, as its name implies, is concerned with registration, admission, and status. Q.931 is ISDN's connection control protocol, which is roughly comparable to TCP in the Internet protocol stack. Q.931 does not provide flow control or perform retransmission, because the underlying layers are assumed to be reliable and the circuit-oriented nature of ISDN allocates bandwidth in fixed increments of 64 kbps. However, Q.931 manages the connection setup and breakdown process [15].

H.245 represents a control signaling protocol in the H.323 multimedia communication architecture that is used for the exchange of end-to-end H.245 messages between communicating H.323 endpoints/terminals. H.245 control messages are carried over an H.245 control channel with logical channel 0 permanently open, unlike media channels. Messages carried include exchanging the capabilities of terminals as well as opening and closing logical channels. After a connection has been set up via the call signaling procedure, the H.245 call control protocol is used to resolve the call media type and establish the media flow [16].

RTP defines a standardized packet format for delivering audio and video over the Internet, while RTCP provides out-of-band control information for an RTP flow [17]. The RTP includes fields for carrying a sequence number, time stamp (which is useful in ensuring that playback at a receiver occurs correctly), a synchronization source field that identifies the synchronization source, and a field that can define up to 15 contributing sources, which enables a conference

---

14   See the following to download a copy for the current version of H.225.0 in force: http://www.itu.int/rec/T-REC-H.225.0-200912-I/en

15   See the following to download a copy for the current version of Q.931 in force: http://www.itu.int/rec/T-REC-Q.931/en

16   See the following to download a copy for the current version of H.245 in force: http://www.itu.int/rec/T-REC-H.245/en

17   See the following for the RTP RFC 3550 :   http://www.ietf.org/rfc/rfc3550.txt
See the following for updates to RFC 3550:
  A. Support for Reduced-Size Real-Time Transport Control Protocol (RTCP): Opportunities and Consequences: http://tools.ietf.org/html/rfc5506
  B. Multiplexing RTP Data and Control Packets on a Single Port: http://tools.ietf.org/html/rfc5761
  C. Rapid Synchronisation of RTP Flows: http://tools.ietf.org/html/rfc6051
  D. Guidelines for Choosing RTP Control Protocol (RTCP) Canonical Names (CNAMEs): http://tools.ietf.org/html/rfc6222

with many participants to be held. RTCP partners with RTP in the delivery and packaging of multimedia data, but does not transport any data itself. RTCP is used periodically to transmit control packets to participants in a streaming multimedia session. Thus, the primary function of RTCP is to provide feedback on the QoS provided by RTP. One of the key features of RTCP is its statistics-gathering capability. RTCP gathers statistics such as bytes sent, packets sent, lost packets, packet jitter, and round trip delay, which an application can use to perform different functions, such as increasing QoS by limiting data flow or selecting the use of a different codec. As previously mentioned, media streams are transported on RTP/RTCP. RTP carries the actual media, and RTCP carries status and control information. Signaling is transported reliably over TCP. The H.323 standard defines the following components:

- Terminal
- Gateway
- Gatekeeper
- MCU (multipoint control unit)
- Multipoint controller
- Multipoint processor
- H.323 proxy

Terminal

An H.323 terminal (client) represents an endpoint in a LAN that participates in real-time, two-way communications with another H.323 terminal, gateway, or multipoint control unit (MCU). Under the H.323 standard, a terminal must support audio communication and can also support audio with video, audio with data, or a combination of all three.

Gateway

An H.323 gateway (GW) provides the physical and logical connections from a packet-switched network to and from circuit-switched networks. The gateway can perform a variety of functions, such as translation between H.323 conferencing endpoints on a LAN and other compliant terminals on other ITU-compliant circuit-switched and packet-switched networks. Such services include a translation between transmission formats and communications procedures. A gateway may also be required to perform the translation between audio and video CODECs as well as perform call setup and call clearing operations.

Gatekeeper

Gatekeepers are optional devices within an H.323 network. When present they perform three important call control housekeeping functions, which assist in the preservation of the integrity of the packet network. Those functions are admission control, address translation, and bandwidth management. Address translation is used to associate LAN aliases with terminals and gateways and IP or IPX addresses. Under bandwidth management, the gatekeeper can be configured to enable a maximum number of simultaneous conferences on a LAN. Once that limit is reached, the gatekeeper would refuse additional connection requests. The result of this action limits the bandwidth of voice or video to a predefined fraction of the total bandwidth available, with the rest left for Web surfing, file transfers, e-mail and other data applications.

MCU

A Multipoint Control Unit (MCU) represents an endpoint on a LAN that provides the capability for three or more terminals and gateways to participate in a multipoint conference. It controls and mixes video, audio, and data from terminal devices to create a video conference. An MCU can also connect two terminals in a point-to-point conference that can later develop into a multipoint conference. The collection of all terminals, gateways, and multipoint control units managed by a single gatekeeper is known as an H.323 Zone.

Multipoint Controller

A multipoint controller that is H.323 compliant provides negotiation capacity with terminals to carry out different communications. The multipoint controller can also control conference resources, such as video multicasting.

Figure 2.5 illustrates an H.323 zone that is connected via a gateway to other LANs or terminal devices via the public switched telephone network.

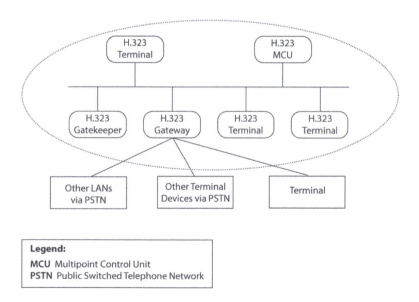

*Figure 2.5 - **An H.323 zone communicating with other devices.***

147

Network Calling

The various H.323 components illustrated in Figure 2.5 show three PCs with voice cards as H.323 terminal devices. All three are connected to a common Ethernet LAN. The LAN is in turn connected to the switched public telephone network, which enables call originating on the top network to be routed over the public switched telephone network to the client's other LANs or to other voice and video terminal devices.

SIP

The Session Initiation Protocol (SIP) represents an application layer signaling protocol that enables telephony and VoIP services to be delivered over a packet network. This protocol is used for establishing, manipulating, and tearing down sessions in an IP network. A session can vary from a simple two-way telephone call to a collaborative multimedia conference. The ability to establish a variety of calls allows a number of innovative services to be developed, such as Web page click-to-dial, instant messaging with buddy lists, and IP Centrex services. The major goal of SIP is to assist session originators to deliver invitations to potential session participants wherever they may be. SIP was modeled after the HyperText Transport Protocol (HTTP), using Uniform Resource Locators (URLs) for addressing and the Session Description Protocol (SDP) to convey session information.

SIP is a text-based protocol that uses UTF-8 encoding, transmitting on port 5060 both for UDP and TCP. SIP supports such common Internet Telephony features as calling, media transfer, multiuser conference calling, call holding, call transfer, and call end tasks.

SIP uses an "invite" message to create sessions that transport descriptions which allow participants to agree on a set of compatible media types. During the negotiation process, SIP recognizes that not all parties support the same features; thus, SIP negotiates a common set of features that all of the parties can support. In addition, SIP can issue a "reinvite" message to change an established session and a "cancel" message to cancel an invite.

SIP makes use of proxy servers to help route requests to a user's current location, authenticate and authorize users for services, implement provider call-routing policies, and provide numerous other features to users. SIP also provides a registration function that allows users to upload their current locations for use by proxy servers. This enables a call to reach a called party wherever he or she is located. Once a session is established, SIP can be used to terminate the session through the use of a "bye" message, which hangs up the session [18].

---

18   See the following for the web page of the IETF SIP Working group: http://datatracker.ietf.org/wg/sip/charter/

148

Comparing H.323 with SIP

A comparison of the H.323 protocol to SIP underscores the considerable difference between the two protocols. The H.323 protocol defines a unified system to support multimedia communications over IP networks, providing support for audio, video, and even data conferencing. Within the umbrella protocol, H.323 defines methods for handling device failures, such as using alternative gatekeepers and endpoints, and messages are encoded in binary. In comparison, SIP was developed to initiate a call, referred to as a *session*, between two devices and has no support for multimedia conferencing. In addition, SIP does not define procedures for handling device failures, and messages are encoded in ASCII text. The latter results in larger messages that are less suitable

See the following for the SIP RFC 3261:   http://tools.ietf.org/html/rfc3261

See the following for updates to RFC 3261:

A. Session Initiation Protocol (SIP)-Specific Event Notification: http://tools.ietf.org/html/rfc3265

B. S/MIME Advanced Encryption Standard (AES) Requirement for the Session Initiation Protocol (SIP):   http://tools.ietf.org/html/rfc3853

C. Actions Addressing Identified Issues with the Session Initiation Protocol's (SIP) Non-INVITE Transaction: http://tools.ietf.org/html/rfc4320

D. Connected Identity in the Session Initiation Protocol (SIP):   http://tools.ietf.org/html/rfc4916

E. Subscriptions to Request-Contained Resource Lists in the Session Initiation Protocol (SIP): http://tools.ietf.org/html/rfc5367

F. Addressing an Amplification Vulnerability in Session Initiation Protocol (SIP) Forking Proxies: http://tools.ietf.org/html/rfc5393

G. Message Body Handling in the Session Initiation Protocol (SIP):   http://tools.ietf.org/html/rfc5621

H. Managing Client-Initiated Connections in the Session Initiation Protocol (SIP):   http://tools.ietf.org/html/rfc5626

I. The Use of the SIPS URI Scheme in the Session Initiation Protocol (SIP):   http://tools.ietf.org/html/rfc5630

J. Change Process for the Session Initiation Protocol (SIP) and the Real-time Applications and Infrastructure Area: http://tools.ietf.org/html/rfc5727

K. Domain Certificates in the Session Initiation Protocol (SIP):   http://tools.ietf.org/html/rfc5922

L. Essential Correction for IPv6 ABNF and URI Comparison in RFC 3261:   http://tools.ietf.org/html/rfc5954

M. Correct Transaction Handling for 2xx Responses to Session Initiation Protocol (SIP) INVITE Requests: http://tools.ietf.org/html/rfc6026

N. Re-INVITE and Target-Refresh Request Handling in the Session Initiation Protocol (SIP): http://tools.ietf.org/html/rfc6141

O. Session Initiation Protocol (SIP) Event Notification Extension for Notification Rate Control: http://tools.ietf.org/html/rfc6446

for use on low-bandwidth circuits, but are easier to interpret than the binary messages associated with the H.323 protocol.

SS7 [19]

SS7, a mnemonic for Signaling System No. 7, represents a global telecommunications standard defined by the ITU. This standard defines the manner in which public switched telephone networks (PSTNs) perform call setup and breakdown, routing, and control by exchange signaling information over a digital signaling network that is separate from the network which actually transports calls. SS7 supports both landline or hardwired calls as well as cellular or mobile calls, with the latter including subscriber authentication and wireless roaming. Through the use of SS7, such enhanced features as call forwarding, caller identification, and three-way calling become possible. In addition, such products as toll-free calling via an 800, 888, or 878 and other prefixes, as well as toll services via the well-known 900 prefix, becomes possible.

Although the PSTN was at one time restricted to circuit-switched technology, over the past decade telephone companies have moved a considerable amount of traffic to their Internet, referred to as a corporate intranet. Using VoIP, telephone companies have saved considerable funds because the use of packet-switched technology and better voice digitization techniques permit more conversations to be transported per unit of bandwidth.

Because calls originated over the PSTN can be transported over IP, a method was required to transport signaling information over an IP network. That method is referred to as SS7-over-IP and employs protocols defined by the Signaling Transport (sigtran) working group of the Internet Engineering Task Force (IETF), the international organization responsible for recommending Internet standards. The actual conversion of SS7 signals to packets transported via IP is performed by a signaling gateway. The signaling gateway can perform such functions as terminating SS7 signaling or translating and relaying messages over the IP network to a media gateway, media gateway controller, or another signaling gateway. Due to its critical role in integrated voice networks, signaling gateways are often deployed in groups of two or more to ensure high availability.

The function of the media gateway is to terminate voice calls originating on interswitch trunks from the public switched telephone network, compress and packetize the voice data, and deliver compressed voice packets to the IP network.

---

19   See the following for overviews of SS7:
    A. http://www.aws.cit.ie/personnel/dpesch/notes/msc_sw/ss7_protocol_overview.pdf
    B. http://www.syrus.ru/files/docs/control/tech/Introduction%20to%20SS7.pdf
    C. http://www.informit.com/library/library.aspx?b=Signaling_System_No_7

For voice calls originating in an IP network, the media gateway performs these functions in reverse order. For ISDN calls from the PSTN, Q.931 signaling information is transported from the media gateway to the media gateway controller for call processing. In comparison, the media gateway controller handles registration and management of resources at the media gateways. A media gateway controller exchanges messages with the PSTN central office switches via a signaling gateway. Because media gateway controllers are often created on a computer platform through the use of off-the-shelf software, a media gateway controller is sometimes referred to as a softswitch.

Facsimile Security

When discussing modern facsimile transmission, the Group 3 Facsimile Protocol (G3) [20] is actually being discussed. G3 dates to 1980, when the International Telecommunications Union published its initial set of standards. Those standards included T.4, which specifies the image transfer protocol, and T.30, which specifies session management procedures that support the establishment of a fax transmission [21].

Because there are over 100 million facsimile G3-compatible devices in use around the world, the ability of one device to communicate with another is provided by the G3 protocol. While this provides worldwide compatibility, it also results in a number of security-related problems. Those can range from the lack of a policy defining the use of facsimile devices to the failure to use a coversheet that specifies who the sender and recipient are and the number of pages "faxed." Two of the major facsimile security-related problems are verifying the facsimile number dialed so the fax is not misdirected and the failure to enable the local facsimile device to print a confirmation of the delivery of the fax, which will include the number of pages transmitted and the receiving telephone number. Other facsimile security-related issues include having a secure location for a fax device and ensuring that incoming faxes are delivered to the correct recipient.

By itself, the G3 standard does not directly deal with security. Although a modified Huffman coding is employed to reduce transmission time of each scanned line, anyone who has the knowledge to tap a transmission can more than likely decode the transmission. Because the transmission of a fax is not secure,

---

20   The G3 Protocol standard was originally published in the following work: *International Telegraph and Telephone Consultative Committee (CCITT), Red Book, October, 1984.*

The Red Book is not available on line directly, but can be searched in its entirety here: http://catalog.hathitrust.org/Record/000592639

21   See the following to download a copy for the current versions in force:
  A. T.4 Standard: http://www.itu.int/rec/T-REC-T.4/en
  B. T.30 Standard: http://www.itu.int/rec/T-REC-T.30/en

	CRYPTO EQUIPMENT	UNSHIELDED SIGNAL AND TELEPHONE LINES	SHIELDED TELEPHONE LINES	POWER LINES
CRYPTO EQUIPMENT	0	3 ft	2 in	2 in
UNSHIELDED SIGNAL LINES	6 in	6 in	2 in	6 in
SHIELDED SIGNAL LINES	2 in	2 in	2 in	2 in
TEMPEST APPR. EQUIPMENT	2 in	6 in	2 in	NONE
NON-TEMPEST APPR EQUIPMENT	3 ft	3 ft	2 in	NONE

Table 2.3 - **TEMPEST Separation Matrix**

there are military standards that govern the encryption of fax transmission. In addition, because a fax machine radiates energy at certain frequencies that could be "read" by an unauthorized party, most military facsimile devices are "Tempest"-hardened by placing them in a secure area that is shielded from emitting frequencies that an uninvited third party sitting in a van in a parking lot might "read" [22]. *Table 2.3* provides a sample TEMPEST Separation Matrix.

Network Architecture

This section focuses on an examination of network architecture and terminology. Doing so will provide the security architect with the ability to better understand methods they can use to control and secure network facilities.

Redundancy and Availability

From a network engineering perspective, redundancy represents the duplication of circuits and equipments, with the goal of the additional components resulting in an increase in network availability. For example, an Internet service provider might connect its hub in one city to peering points at two different locations. Thus, if the connection to one peering point should become inoperative, data flow to and from the Internet could continue via the second peering point.

Internet versus Intranet

Most end users have little control over the network architecture of the Internet, with the exception of their access method. Concerning the latter, it is common for organizations to have multiple ISPs, because the failure of one vendor's network would usually not affect the second vendor. To take full advantage of redundant vendors, one would ensure that the connection from the organization to each

---

22   See the following for an overview of TEMPEST solutions: http://www.fas.org/irp/program/security/tempest.htm

See the following for a document from December of 1990, "*Engineering and Design - Electromagnetic Pulse (EMP) and Tempest Protection for Facilities Proponent: CEMP-ET*", detailing the specifications and requirements to build out a secure facility with TEMPEST shielding: http://www.fas.org/nuke/intro/nuke/emp/toc.htm

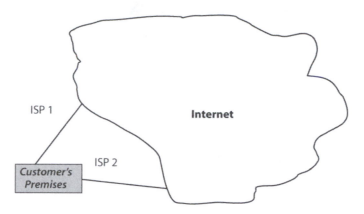

Figure 2.6 - **Using two ISPs for redundant access to the Internet**

vendor occurs over different communication facilities. *Figure 2.6* illustrates the use of two ISPs to provide redundant communications to the Internet from a customer premises.

Extranet

An extranet is a private network that while resembling an intranet extends the internal IP-based network of an organization to suppliers, vendors, and other types of business partners. Because an extranet is created by one or more organizations for their exclusive use, those vendors can control the network architecture of the extranet. Thus, they can order network circuits as well as equipment such as routers, DNS servers, and other devices to match the level of reliability and availability they both desire and can afford.

Network Types

The use of varied network architectures can benefit the security architect as they strive to create the appropriate balance for remote user connectivity, federation with one or more partner or vendor entities, as well as secure internal access to resources. The three main architectures traditionally identified are:

- Private Networks
- Public Networks
- Hybrid Networks

Private networks are usually associated with internal only access to data and resources for employees of a company. These networks are made available to physical endpoints through the use of private IP address schemes based on the Internet Assigned Numbers Authority (IANA) having reserved the following three blocks of the IPv4 address space for private internets: [23]

---

23   See the following for the Address Allocation for Private Internets RFC: http://tools.ietf.org/html/rfc1918

$$10.0.0.0 \quad - \quad 10.255.255.255 \ (10/8 \text{ prefix})$$
$$172.16.0.0 \quad - \quad 172.31.255.255 \ (172.16/12 \text{ prefix})$$
$$192.168.0.0 \quad - \quad 192.168.255.255 \ (192.168/16 \text{ prefix})$$

Internet Protocol Version 6 (IPv6) is the latest revision of the Internet Protocol (IP). It is intended to replace IPv4, which still carries the vast majority of Internet traffic as of 2013. IPv6 was developed by the Internet Engineering Task Force (IETF) to deal with the long-anticipated problem of IPv4 address exhaustion. IPv6 uses a 128-bit address, allowing for 2^{128}, or approximately 3.4×1038 addresses, or more than 7.9×1028 times as many as IPv4, which uses 32-bit addresses. IPv4 allows for only approximately 4.3 billion addresses.

IPv6 addresses consist of eight groups of four hexadecimal digits separated by colons, for example 2013:0db8:72b3:0082:1090:3c6h:0547:7264.

The hexadecimal digits are not case-sensitive; e.g., the groups 0DB8 and 0db8 are equivalent.

IPv6 is described in Internet standard document RFC 2460, published in December 1998 [24]. In addition to offering more addresses, IPv6 also implements features not present in IPv4. It simplifies aspects of address assignment (stateless address autoconfiguration), network renumbering and router announcements when changing network connectivity providers. It simplifies processing of packets by routers by placing the need for packet fragmentation into the end points. The IPv6 subnet size has been standardized by fixing the size of the host identifier portion of an address to 64 bits to facilitate an automatic mechanism for forming the host identifier from link-layer media addressing information (MAC address). Network security is also integrated into the design of the IPv6 architecture, including the option of IPsec.

An IPv6 address may be abbreviated by using one or more of the following rules: (Initial address: 2013:0db8:0000:0000:0000:ff00:0026:9734)

1. Remove one or more leading zeroes from one or more groups of hexadecimal digits; this is usually done to either all or none of the leading zeroes. (For example, convert the group 0026 to 26.)

2. Omit one or more consecutive sections of zeroes, using a double colon (::) to denote the omitted sections. The double colon may only be used once in any given address, as the address would be indeterminate if the double colon was used multiple times. (For example, 2013:db8::1:2 is valid, but 2013:db8::1::2 is not permitted.)

---

24   See the following for RFC 2460:   http://tools.ietf.org/html/rfc2460

The following are the text representations of these addresses: [25]

Initial address: 2013:0db8:0000:0000:0000:ff00:0026:9734

After removing all leading zeroes: 2013:db8:0:0:0:ff00:26:9734

After omitting consecutive sections of zeroes: 2013:0db8::ff00:0026:9734

After doing both: 2013:db8::ff00:26:9734

IPv6 addresses are classified by three types of networking methodologies: unicast addresses identify each network interface, anycast addresses identify a group of interfaces, usually at different locations of which the nearest one is automatically selected, and multicast addresses are used to deliver one packet to many interfaces. The broadcast method is not implemented in IPv6. Each IPv6 address has a scope, which specifies in which part of the network it is valid and unique. Some addresses are unique only on the local (sub-)network. Others are globally unique.

Some IPv6 addresses are reserved for special purposes, such as loopback, 6to4 tunneling, and Teredo tunneling, as outlined in RFC 5156 [26]. Also, some address ranges are considered special, such as link-local addresses for use on the local link only, Unique Local addresses (ULA), as described in RFC 4193 [27], and solicited-node multicast addresses used in the Neighbor Discovery Protocol.

Public networks are made up of computers that are connected to each other to create a network. These networks are often configured with "public" Internet Protocol (IP) addresses -- that is, the devices on the network are "visible" to devices outside the network (from the Internet or another network).

Computers on a public network have the advantage, and disadvantage, that they are completely visible to the Internet. As such, they have no boundaries between themselves and the rest of the Internet community. This advantage oftentimes becomes a distinct disadvantage since this visibility can lead to a computer vulnerability exploit if the devices on the public network have not been properly secured.

Hybrid networks use a combination of any two or more topologies to create a network design that leverages the best elements of the topologies being combined.

A newer architectural approach that security architects need to be able to address as well are the various Service architectures available through the "cloud". The most common ones discussed are:

---

25   See the following for RFC 5952, A Recommendation for IPv6 Address Text Representation: http://tools.ietf.org/html/rfc5952

26   See the following for RFC 5156:   http://tools.ietf.org/html/rfc5156

27   See the following for RFC 4193:   http://tools.ietf.org/html/rfc4193

- SaaS
- PaaS
- IaaS

The *Software-as-a-Service (SaaS)* service-model involves the cloud provider installing and maintaining software in the cloud and users running the software from their end point clients over the Internet. The users' client machines require no installation of any application-specific software - cloud applications run on servers in the cloud. In the SaaS model, cloud providers install and operate application software in the cloud and cloud users access the software from cloud clients. The cloud users do not manage the cloud infrastructure and platform on which the application is running. This eliminates the need to install and run the application on the cloud user's own computers simplifying maintenance and support.

Platform as a Service (PaaS) is a cloud computing service that provides end users with application platforms and databases as a service. This is the equivalent to middleware in the traditional (non-cloud computing) delivery of application platforms and databases. In the PaaS model, cloud providers deliver a computing platform typically including operating system, programming language execution environment, database, and web server.

Infrastructure as a Service (IaaS) takes the physical hardware and goes completely virtual. IaaS providers offer computers, as physical or more often as virtual machines, and other resources to customers on a fee based scheduled. To deploy their applications, cloud users install operating system images and their application software on the cloud infrastructure. In this model, it is the cloud user who is responsible for patching and maintaining the operating systems and application software.

Perimeter Controls

Products that can be used to control the flow of data at the entryway to the network are referred to as perimeter controls; devices that can be used include routers, firewalls, and special types of modems. The place at the network perimeter where such equipment is commonly installed is referred to as the network demilitarized zone (DMZ).

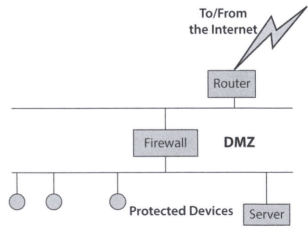

*Figure 2.7 - **Creating a DMZ***

Figure 2.7 illustrates a common architecture for a corporate DMZ. In this example, a router provides a connection to the Internet while the firewall, which is sometimes referred to as a corporate gateway, resides between two LANs, one of which has a router as its only device while the second LAN is populated by terminals, routers, various types of servers such as e-mail servers or gateways, Web servers and VPN servers, and other networking devices protected by the firewall. This architecture ensures that all data flow to and from the corporate network and Internet are examined by the firewall. Although the devices behind the firewall are protected from many types of attacks, this architecture does not protect devices from persons using USB memory devices to off-load corporate data from computers and servers. This is why many organizations prohibit the use of USB devices, and use special software to deactivate USB ports.

In *Figure 2.8*, a revised corporate DMZ is shown. In this example, a bank of security modems were added to the upper LAN, between the firewall and the corporate terminals, servers, and other devices on the protected network. To better understand how each device operates, let's review the operation of each of the three communications devices, with particular emphasis on their security role.

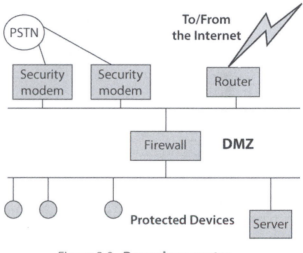

*Figure 2.8 - **Boundary router***

In addition to providing a communications capability that takes LAN frames and strips the header and trailer to convert them to IP datagrams for transport on the Internet, routers have a key role as the first line of defense in many organizations. Through the use of rule-based access lists, it becomes possible to filter packets based on a variety of data carried in the packet. Although most packet filtering occurs on the fields within a packet header, some boundary routers extend filtering into the packet, making it difficult to functionally separate the security features of a router from a firewall.

Figure 2.9 illustrates the delivery of TCP/IP application data onto a LAN. Note that as data delivery occurs, a string of headers is appended to the application data. Each header has a number of fields that can be examined by a router or firewall that can allow or deny the flow of data based on predefined criteria.

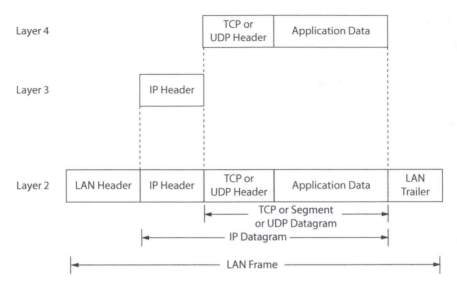

Figure 2.9 - **The delivery of TCP/IP application data onto a LAN**

Figure 2.10 illustrates the composition of the IPv4 header, which is appended to either a TCP header or UDP header to form an IP datagram. By looking into the IP header, the router can perform many security-related operations, such as accepting or rejecting datagrams based on the source or destination IP address within the IP header. Unfortunately, source addresses are not checked by devices on the Internet, so filtering on a source address can be problematic. For example, one could program their computer to send constant pings to www. whitehouse.gov and use the source address for the United States Federal Bureau of Investigation (FBI) gateway. Although not recommended, this would result in a stream of pings to the White House server that appeared to originate from the FBI.

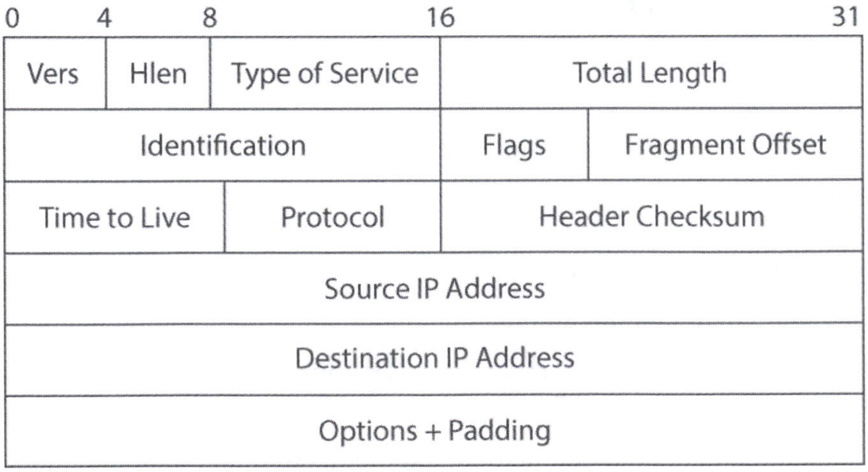

0	4	8	16	31
Vers	Hlen	Type of Service	Total Length	
Identification			Flags	Fragment Offset
Time to Live		Protocol	Header Checksum	
Source IP Address				
Destination IP Address				
Options + Padding				

Figure 2.10 - **The IPv4 header**

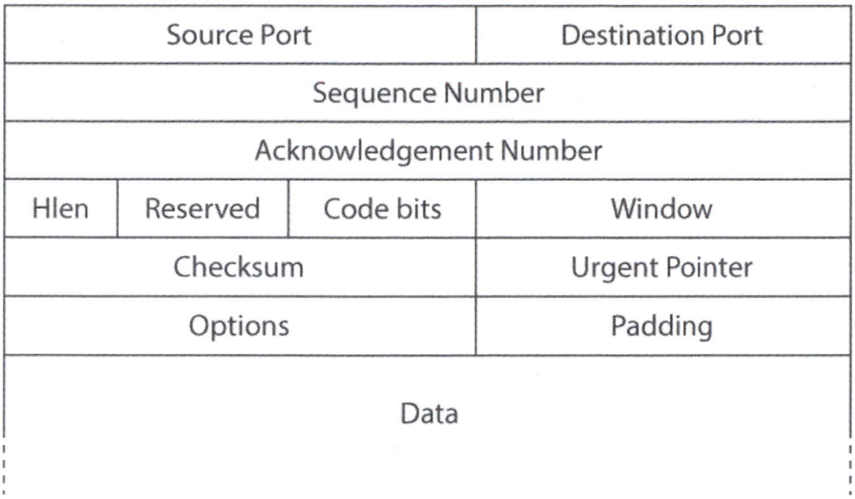

Source Port		Destination Port
Sequence Number		
Acknowledgement Number		
Hlen	Reserved	Code bits	Window
Checksum		Urgent Pointer
Options		Padding
Data		

Figure 2.11 - **The Transport Control Protocol.**

As previously mentioned, filtering based on the contents of packet headers, such as the headers in IP, TCP, and UDP, are commonly incorporated into firewalls. With applicable programming, the security architect can configure the router to reject packets either inbound, outbound, or both, based on source or destination address or type of packet or both. Concerning filtering based on packet type, this is accomplished by using port numbers to filter TCP or UDP packets.

Figure 2.11 illustrates the fields within the TCP header. Of particular importance—and used by both router access lists and firewalls for filtering purposes—are the source and destination port field values. TCP is used to transport connection-oriented, reliable data, such as control information. In comparison, UDP is used to transport connectionless data and reliability if an issue is provided by higher layers in the protocol stack. For example, setting up a VoIP call would require TCP data to convey the dialed number and other control information, while UDP would be used to transport digitized voice. By default, most router and firewall vendors disable the flow of data on all ports to each interface. Thus, because many applications use both TCP and UDP, it is quite common for routers and firewalls to be programmed to enable ports on both devices to allow corporate users to use certain types of Internet applications. In addition, many security devices can be programmed to support time-of-day functions, allowing the router and firewall administrators to open "holes" through their devices by equating data flow through certain ports on specific interfaces to the time of day. For example, a corporation could allow employees access to Amazon and eBay during lunch hour while blocking such access during the rest of the workday.

In addition to the previously mentioned types of filtering, many routers can be programmed to block all or certain types of Internet Control Message Protocol (ICMP) packets as well as some widely employed hacker attacks, such as the well-known SYN attack. Thus, many routers when programmed correctly can become an organization's first line of network defense.

Security Modems [28]

A security modem represents a special type of modem that allows remote access from trusted locations, may encrypt data, and may support Caller ID to verify the calling telephone number. When security modems first appeared on the market, they were configured with a list of allowable callback numbers and passwords. A remote user who wished to gain access to the corporate LAN would first dial the telephone number associated with the dial-in security modem. Upon establishing a connection, the person would be prompted to enter his or her callback number and a password associated with the callback phone number. If the password is correct, the security modem would disconnect the connection and dial back the callback number.

Modern security modems have considerably evolved from a simple list of authorized locations that would be dialed back upon the entry of an applicable password. Today, in addition to a callback feature, security modems may be capable of using Caller ID and passwords to authenticate a user and encrypt data based on the key entered by a verified user. In addition, some security modems provide the authenticated user with the ability to select an encryption algorithm from a series of supported algorithms, such as 3DES and various versions of the Advanced Encryption Standard (AES).

The rationale behind the use of a security modem is the fact that the PSTN assigns telephone numbers to fixed locations and cell phone numbers are assigned to known persons, with the exception of prepaid cell phones. Thus, an organization can decide the telephone numbers that can receive connections to the corporate network and then associate passwords with those numbers. This means that not only will the security modem call predefined numbers but, in

---

28   Secure modem solutions protect network assets from attacks by illegal users and malicious hackers. Secure Modem systems and products are designed with rigorous security solutions that meet the requirements of mission-critical network applications, such as service provisioning, banking and financial communication, transportation and governmental agencies. These solutions give security architects a suite of protection options for their large or small network environments, including Security, Authentication, Encryption and Disaster Recovery. Security modem solutions protect network assets by blocking disruption of service due to data theft, data corruption, illegal intrusions, shutdowns, line failure and component failure.

See the following for the General DataComm web site: http://www.gdc.com/products/prod_m_1.shtml

addition, to do so the person at that number must first call the security modem and enter an applicable password. Through the addition of encryption to security modems, it becomes possible to minimize potential threats while transmitting data over the public switched telephone network. Although the use of security modems as well as modems in general has to a large degree been replaced by the use of VPNs communicating over the Internet, certain applications continue to use security modems. For example, sales personnel, government investigators, and other travelers who must communicate securely and cannot use the Internet due to lack of availability or cost considerations frequently dial security modems at a corporate location [29]. While mobility can adversely affect the use of callback, the use of cell phones provides a fixed telephone number that avoids the problem of coordination and the reconfiguring of callback numbers as sales personnel move from motel to vendor location and need to quickly check the status of an order or the latest price of a product [30].

One of the major problems associated with the callback feature of security modems results from the use of Local Area Signaling Service (LASS) codes. LASS codes are numbers entered on a telephone touchpad to access special features of the telephone system. Two well-known LASS codes are 67, which toggles Caller-ID blocking, and 69 for Call Return. By knowing how to use LASS codes, a hacker may be able to exploit the configuration of the callback feature of a security modem [31].

Communications and Network Polices

On December 10, 2012, the Federal Communications Commission of the United States (FCC) chairman Julius Genachowski announced the formation of

---

29   Modems are also used for "Out of Band Management" (OBM) of systems as well. Traditional OBM solutions using non-secure modems are unsuitable for any application regarding sensitive information or mission integrity. The security of traditional OBM solutions typically contain the following weaknesses:

– There is no proper authentication, authorization and audit trail.
– A simple password is often used to block access to a cluster of remote devices.
– The user names, passwords, and stored telephone numbers are often widely published and distributed.

30   See the following for security guidance that is broadened to include securing the PBX that modems will be connected through from NIST. NIST developed a PBX vulnerability analysis that can be use to understand these systems. NIST SP 800-24 PBX Vulnerability Analysis: http://csrc.nist. gov/publications/nistpubs/800-24/sp800-24pbx.pdf

Also see the following from ATT. A checklist for securing a PBX system is provided by ATT's "ATT Security Statement" document. ATT PBS Security Checklist: http://images.bimedia.net/ documents/ATT_Security_Statement.doc

31   The Department of Homeland Security in the United States has developed the following guide: Recommended Practice for Securing Control System Modems, January 2008:   http://www. us-cert.gov/control_systems/practices/documents/SecuringModems.pdf

the 'Technology Transitions Policy Task Force' to deal with the task of creating policy for the next generation communications network, coordinating efforts on IP interconnection and the reliability and resiliency of the next generation networks, with a particular focus on voice services. According to the FCC, "the Task Force will conduct a data-driven review and provide recommendations to modernize the Commission's policies in a process that encourages the technological transition, empowers and protects consumers, promotes competition, and ensures network resiliency and reliability." [32]

Every security architect should have a good understanding of the importance of standards, policy, and procedure[33]. The need to be able to document all the information that is pertinent to the secure operation of the network is one of the most important responsibilities that the security architect has. Along with the responsibility to document, the security architect also has the obligation to strictly adhere to a change control regime that places all documentation, and system configurations under tight scrutiny and efficient control. The combination of complete documentation and change control systems to support the continued relevancy of that documentation is the foundation that the security architect builds on in order to create policy and procedures for the users of the network and systems. These policies and procedures need to be based on standards when and where appropriate to do so, such as NIST, CoBit, Payment Card Industry (PCI) Data Security Standard (PCI-DSS) or the ISO 27000 series. The policies and procedures then need to be communicated to all users within the organization that will be effected by them. This is typically carried out through security awareness training, and needs to be done at a minimum on a yearly basis, although the requirements for organizations will vary based on regulatory compliance concerns. The security architect should consider conducting on-going awareness training as needed to support any major revisions carried out through change management to policies and procedures.

Overview of Firewalls [34]

Firewalls have been available to the security architect in one form or another for many years now. There are multiple generations of firewalls that many security architects will have deployed into their networks over the last number of years

---

32   See the following for the official announcement press release from the FCC: http://www.fcc.gov/document/fcc-chairman-announces-technology-transitions-policy-task-force

33   See the following for the SANS Security Resources Information Security Policy Templates web site: http://www.sans.org/security-resources/policies/

34   For a dated, but very interesting review of the historical literature surrounding early firewall design and architecture up through 2001, see the following: http://www.cs.unm.edu/~treport/tr/02-12/firewall.pdf

as the technology has continued to evolve. Firewalls are devices or programs that control the flow of network traffic between networks or hosts that employ differing security postures. Organizations often need to use firewalls to meet security requirements from mandates such as PCI-DSS , which specifically requires firewalling [35].

The most basic feature of a firewall is the packet filter. Stateless inspection firewalls that were only packet filters were essentially routing devices that provided access control functionality for host addresses and communication sessions. These devices did not keep track of the state of each flow of traffic as it passed through the firewall. Unlike more advanced filters, packet filters are not concerned about the content of packets. Their access control functionality is governed by a set of directives referred to as a ruleset.

In their most basic form, firewalls with packet filters operate at the network layer. This provides network access control based on several pieces of information contained in a packet, including:

- The packet's source IP address—the address of the host from which the packet originated (such as 1.2.3.4)
- The packet's destination address—the address of the host the packet is trying to reach (e.g., 12.1.2.1)
- The network or transport protocol being used to communicate between source and destination hosts, such as TCP, UDP, or ICMP.
- Possibly some characteristics of the transport layer communications sessions, such as session source and destination ports.
- The interface being traversed by the packet, and its direction (inbound or outbound).

Stateful inspection improves on the functionality of packet filters by tracking the state of connections and blocking packets that deviate from the expected state. This is accomplished by incorporating greater awareness of the transport layer into the firewall. As with packet filtering, stateful inspection intercepts packets at the network layer and inspects them to see if they are permitted by an existing firewall rule, but unlike packet filtering, stateful inspection keeps track of each connection in a state table. While the details of state table entries vary by firewall product, they typically include source IP address, destination IP address, port numbers, and connection state information. Three major states exist for TCP traffic; connection establishment, usage, and termination. Stateful inspection in a firewall examines certain values in the TCP headers to monitor the state of each

---

35   See the following for the PCI DSS v2.0 Standard: https://www.pcisecuritystandards.org/ security_standards/documents.php

connection. Each new packet is compared by the firewall to the firewall's state table to determine if the packet's state contradicts its expected state.

The addition of a stateful protocol analysis capability creates deep packet inspection functionality in the application firewall. Stateful protocol analysis improves upon standard stateful inspection by adding basic intrusion detection technology via an inspection engine that analyzes protocols at the application layer to compare vendor-developed profiles of benign protocol activity against observed events to identify deviations. This allows a firewall to allow or deny access based on how an application is running over the network.

An application-proxy gateway is a feature of advanced firewalls that combines lower-layer access control with upper-layer functionality. These firewalls contain a proxy agent that acts as an intermediary between two hosts that wish to communicate with each other, and never allows a direct connection between them. Each successful connection attempt actually results in the creation of two separate connections; one between the client and the proxy server, and another between the proxy server and the true destination. The proxy is meant to be transparent to the two hosts. From their perspectives there is a direct connection. Like application firewalls, the proxy gateway operates at the application layer and can inspect the actual content of the traffic. These gateways also perform the TCP handshake with the source system and are able to protect against exploitations at each step of a communication. In addition, gateways can make decisions to permit or deny traffic based on information in the application protocol headers or payloads. Application-proxy gateways are quite different than application firewalls. First, an application-proxy gateway can offer a higher level of security for some applications because it prevents direct connections between two hosts and it inspects traffic content to identify policy violations. Another potential advantage is that some application-proxy gateways have the ability to decrypt packets (e.g., SSL-protected payloads), examine them, and re-encrypt them before sending them on to the destination host.

The term Unified Threat Management Gateway (UTM) was coined in 2004 by IDC; earlier in 2003 Internet Security Systems (ISS) launched a new product called Proventia, an "all-in-one protection product" which unified firewall, virtual private network (VPN), anti-virus, intrusion detection and prevention into one box. A UTM product typically will co-locate a stateful firewall and an IPS in one device, or use a limited DPI (just a stateful packet inspection firewall with some IDS/IPS signatures) which usually suffers from performance issues and limited visibility into network traffic. UTMs are a combination of network layer firewalls and application layer firewalls.

Web application firewalls are a relatively new technology, as compared to other firewall technologies, and the type of threats that they mitigate are still changing frequently. Because they are put in front of web servers to prevent attacks on the server, they are often considered to be very different than traditional firewalls.

Network activity that passes directly between virtualized operating systems within a host cannot be monitored by an external firewall. However, some virtualization systems offer built-in firewalls or allow third-party software firewalls to be added as plug-ins. Using firewalls to monitor virtualized networking is a relatively new area of firewall technology, and it is likely to change significantly as virtualization usage continues to increase.

Firewalls vs. Routers

The major difference between a router and firewall lies in three areas: the transfer of packets based on routing tables; the degree of packet inspection; and acting as an intermediate device by hiding the address of clients from users on the Internet, a technique referred to as acting as a proxy.

A router has routing tables that associate IP addresses with ports on the device. When a packet arrives at a router port, the device examines the destination address in the IP header. Then, through a table lookup process that associates IP addresses with router ports, the router forwards the packet onto and through the port listed in the routing table, with the packet then flowing onto a communications connection with the port. That communications connect depends on the type of router port, ranging from an Ethernet or Token Ring LAN to a serial port connected to a 56 kbps, T1, or even a T3 connection. In comparison, a firewall only performs one type of basic packet processing. That is, if a packet fails a test, it is discarded. Otherwise, the packet is forwarded through the firewall to its destination.

A second significant difference between a router and a firewall governs the degree of packet inspection. A router typically examines the headers in IP, TCP, and UDP. In comparison, a firewall looks deeper into packets, in some cases, examining the contents of the data transported within the packet, looking for repetitive potentially dangerous operations, such as attempted sign-ons to different IP addresses that might represent different corporate servers.

A third difference between a router and a firewall may result in the firewall performing proxy services. In doing so, the firewall services the requests of its clients by forwarding requests onto the Internet. In this situation, a client connects to the proxy service of the firewall, requesting some type of service, such as a file transfer (File Transfer Protocol (FTP)) operation or Web page

165

access. The proxy service of the firewall provides the resource by connecting to the specified IP address requesting the service on behalf of the client. In doing so, the proxy service of the firewall may use a single source IP address for all clients, keeping track of client sessions by using different port numbers to associate the client's real IP address with the common IP address used for all clients. Hiding the IP addresses of clients makes them more difficult to attack. If the proxy service passes all requests and replies in their original form, the service is usually referred to as a tunneling proxy service.

There are two basic types of firewall proxy services: circuit level and application. Previously, what is referred to as an application proxy service was discussed. In comparison, a circuit-level proxy is limited to a controlled network connection between internal and external systems. A circuit-level proxy results in a virtual "circuit" being established between the internal client and the proxy server. Internet requests are then routed through the circuit to the proxy server, and the proxy server forwards those requests to the Internet after changing the IP address of the internal client. Thus, external users are limited to denoting the IP address of the proxy server. In the reverse direction, responses are received by the proxy server and sent back through the circuit to the client. Although traffic is allowed to flow through the proxy, external systems never see the internal systems. This type of connection is often used to connect "trusted" internal users to the Internet.

Figure 2.12 illustrates an example of a proxy service. In this example, the highlighted middle computer acts as the proxy server between the other two devices.

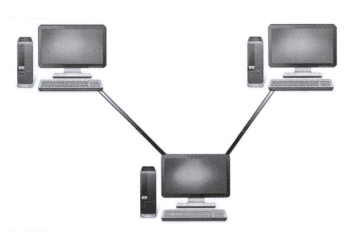

Figure 2.12 - **Example of a proxy service**

Demilitarized Zone's Perimeter Controls

The perimeter network represents an additional network between the protected network and the unprotected network, which provides an additional layer of security. By controlling access from the "untrusted" network through the perimeter network to a "trusted" network, security is enhanced. However, it is important to realize that the perimeter network also represents a vulnerability. Thus it is extremely important to ensure that equipment is correctly configured and that software operates at the latest release to provide an effective level of protection.

IDS/IPS [36]

An IDS represents hardware or software that is specifically designed to detect unwanted attempts at accessing, manipulating, and even disabling networking hardware and computers connected to a network. Such attempts can be made by hackers or even disgruntled existing or former employees. Here, the key to an IDS system is its ability to detect attacks. It is important to note however, that unless an IDS system has access to keys used for encryption, the IDS cannot directly detect attacks within properly encrypted traffic.

The capabilities of an IDS can significantly vary from vendor to vendor. Because the goal of an IDS is to detect malicious behavior that can adversely affect computer or communications hardware, at a minimum it should detect a variety of malware directed at computers, such as viruses, Trojans, and worms as well as denial of service (DoS) attacks, logon attempts that cycle through passwords and IDs against a host or set of computers, as well as attempts to use guest or other accounts to gain access to sensitive files, such as the corporate payroll.

IDS Architecture

A typical IDS consists of a console that monitors events reported by sensors, controls such sensors, and generates alerts. Alerts can range from simple messages displayed on a console to the transmission of an e-mail or pager message and prerecorded telephone or cell phone calls.

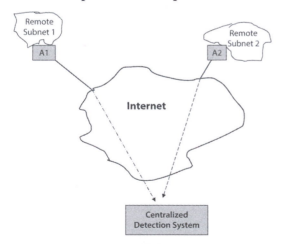

Figure 6.13 - **A centralized detection architecture**

Figure 2.13 illustrates a distributed IDS system with a centralized monitoring facility. In this example, agents designated by the letter A in boxes are placed at the entry point to remotely located subnets. Of course, one or more agents may also be located on the monitoring network, but they are not shown. This type of IDS represents a Network IDS

---

36   The most recent guidance on IDS/IPS solutions can be found in NIST Special Publication 800-94 Revision 1 (Draft): Guide to Intrusion Detection and Prevention Systems (IDPS) (Draft), July 2012:   http://csrc.nist.gov/publications/drafts/800-94-rev1/draft_sp800-94-rev1.pdf

(NIDS). Sensors or agents can be physical hardware or software that is designed to operate promiscuously and examine all traffic flowing on a network segment. This is comparable to a home alarm system. Windows and doors have sensors that can be considered to represent agents. Those agents are connected to a central panel in the home that broadcasts messages to control panels, typically located in a master bedroom and home entryways. When a door or window is open, a signal transmits to the control panel. The control panel examines the state of the alarm (off, at home, etc.) and generates a preplanned action, such as contacting a monitoring company. Similarly, when an intrusion is detected, the IDS will perform some predefined action based on its configuration. Most NIDS implementations use sensors located at choke points in the network to be monitored, such as the DMZ or at network borders. The sensors capture all network traffic, analyzing the contents of those packets for malicious traffic. Although many vendors market distributed NIDS systems, in less complex IDS implementations, all components are combined in a single device or network appliance.

There are numerous types of IDS systems that are designed to perform specific functions. For example, one common type of IDS is a protocol-based intrusion detection system that commonly is implemented in software and resides on servers, examining, for example, the HTTP data stream on a Web server. Another common type of IDS is a Host-based IDS (HIDS) that represents software tailored to operate on different types of computers, ranging from small Web servers to large IBM mainframes. A typical HIDS consists of an agent on a host that identifies intrusions by analyzing system calls, application logs, file-system modifications (such as password and access threshold files), and other host activities and state. These IDS types are commonly referred to as Network Behavior Analysis (NBA) IDS, which examines network traffic to identify threats that generate unusual traffic flows, such as Denial of Service (DoS) attacks, certain forms of malware, and policy violations (e.g., a client system providing network services to other systems).

Host-based IDS agents are most commonly deployed to critical hosts such as publicly accessible servers and servers containing sensitive information. Host-based IDSs typically perform extensive logging of data related to detected events. This data can be used to confirm the validity of alerts, to investigate incidents, and to correlate events between the host-based IDS and other logging sources. Data fields commonly logged by host-based IDSs include the following:

- Timestamp (usually date and time)
- Event or alert type
- Rating (e.g., priority, severity, impact, confidence)

■ Event details specific to the type of event, such as IP address and port information, application information, filenames and paths, and user IDs

■ Prevention action performed (if any)

NBA sensors are usually available only as appliances. Some sensors are similar to network-based IDS sensors in that they sniff packets to monitor network activity on one or a few network segments. Other NBA sensors do not monitor the networks directly, but instead rely on network flow information provided by routers and other networking devices. Flow refers to a particular communication session occurring between hosts. There are many standards for flow data formats, including NetFlow, sFlow, and IPFIX [37]. Typical flow data particularly relevant to intrusion detection and prevention includes the following:

■ Source and destination IP addresses

■ Source and destination TCP or UDP ports or ICMP types and codes

■ Number of packets and number of bytes transmitted in the session

■ Timestamps for the start and end of the session

NBA technologies typically perform extensive logging of data related to detected events. This data can be used to confirm the validity of alerts, to investigate incidents, and to correlate events between the NBA solution and other logging sources. Data fields commonly logged by NBA software include the following:

■ Timestamp (usually date and time)

■ Event or alert type

■ Rating (e.g., priority, severity, impact, confidence)

■ Network, transport, and application layer protocols

■ Source and destination IP addresses

■ Source and destination TCP or UDP ports, or ICMP types and codes

---

37

Netflow:

See the following for RFC 3954, Cisco Systems NetFlow Services Export Version 9: http://www.ietf.org/rfc/rfc3954.txt

The Cisco website for NetFlow Version 9:   http://www.cisco.com/en/US/products/ps6645/products_ios_protocol_option_home.html

sFlow:

The sFlow website:
http://www.sflow.org/

IPFIX:

See the following for RFC 5101, Specification of the IP Flow Information Export (IPFIX) Protocol for the Exchange of IP Traffic Flow Information: http://tools.ietf.org/html/rfc5101

- Additional packet header fields (e.g., IP time-to-live [TTL])
- Number of bytes and packets sent by the source and destination hosts for the connection
- Prevention action performed (if any)

Security architects also need to decide where the IDS sensors should be located. Sensors can be deployed in one of two modes:

Inline Sensor

An inline sensor is deployed so that the network traffic it is monitoring must pass through it, much like the traffic flow associated with a firewall. Inline sensors are typically placed where network firewalls and other network security devices would be placed—at the divisions between networks, such as connections with external networks and borders between different internal networks that should be segregated.

Passive Sensor

A passive sensor is deployed so that it monitors a copy of the actual network traffic; no traffic actually passes through the sensor. Passive sensors are typically deployed so that they can monitor key network locations, such as the divisions between networks, and key network segments, such as activity on a demilitarized zone (DMZ) subnet. Passive sensors can monitor traffic through various methods, including the following:

Spanning Port

Many switches have a spanning port, which is a port that can see all network traffic going through the switch. Connecting a sensor to a spanning port can allow it to monitor traffic going to and from many hosts.

Network Tap

A network tap is a direct connection between a sensor and the physical network media itself, such as a fiber optic cable. The tap provides the sensor with a copy of all network traffic being carried by the media.

IDS Load Balancer

An IDS load balancer is a device that aggregates and directs network traffic to monitoring systems, including IDS sensors. A load balancer can receive copies of network traffic from one or more spanning ports or network taps and aggregate traffic from different networks (e.g., reassemble a session that was split between two networks). The load balancer then distributes copies of the traffic to one or more listening devices, including IDS sensors, based on a set of rules configured by an administrator.

Network-based IDSs typically perform extensive logging of data related to detected events. This data can be used to confirm the validity of alerts, to investigate incidents, and to correlate events between the IDS and other logging sources. Data fields commonly logged by network-based IDSs include the following:

- Timestamp (usually date and time)
- Connection or session ID (typically a consecutive or unique number assigned to each TCP connection or to like groups of packets for connectionless protocols)
- Event or alert type
- Rating (e.g., priority, severity, impact, confidence)
- Network, transport, and application layer protocols
- Source and destination IP addresses
- Source and destination TCP or UDP ports, or ICMP types and codes
- Number of bytes transmitted over the connection
- Decoded payload data, such as application requests and responses
- State-related information (e.g., authenticated username)
- Prevention action performed (if any)

There are also Wireless IDSs (WIDS), which monitors wireless network traffic and analyzes it to identify suspicious activity involving the wireless networking protocols themselves. Unlike a network-based IDS, which can see all packets on the networks it monitors, a wireless IDS works by sampling traffic. There are two frequency bands to monitor (2.4 GHz and 5 GHz), and each band is separated into channels. Wireless sensors are available in multiple forms:

Dedicated

A dedicated sensor is a device that performs wireless IDS functions but does not pass network traffic from source to destination. Dedicated sensors are often completely passive, functioning in a Radio Frequency (RF) monitoring mode to sniff wireless network traffic. Some dedicated sensors perform analysis of the traffic they monitor, while other sensors forward the network traffic to a management server for analysis. The sensor is typically connected to the wired network (e.g., Ethernet cable between the sensor and a switch).

Bundled with an AP.

Several vendors have added IDS capabilities to APs. A bundled AP typically provides a less rigorous detection capability than a dedicated sensor because the AP needs to divide its time between providing network access and monitoring multiple channels or bands for malicious activity.

Wireless IDSs typically perform extensive logging of data related to detected events. This data can be used to confirm the validity of alerts, to investigate incidents, and to correlate events between the IDS and other logging sources. Data fields commonly logged by wireless IDSs include the following:

- Timestamp (usually date and time)
- Event or alert type
- Priority or severity rating
- Source MAC address (the vendor is often identified from the address)
- Channel number
- ID of the sensor that observed the event
- Prevention action performed (if any)

Intrusion Prevention System

Intrusion prevention systems (IPSs) can be considered to represent an evolution in security progress from IDS technology. Whereas an IDS represents a passive system, an IPS represents an active system that detects and responds to predefined events. Thus, the IPS represents technology built on an IDS system. This means that the ability of the IPS to prevent intrusions from occurring is highly dependent on the underlying IDS.

An IPS represents a software or a hardware appliance that monitors a network or system activities for malicious or unwanted behavior, such as repeated attempts to log onto a computer or gain access to a router's command interface and will in real time react to either block or prevent those activities. Of course, it will also issue one or more alarms via a console, e-mail, or dialing a predefined telephone number to alert applicable persons of the event. A network-based IPS, for example, will operate in-line to monitor all network traffic for malicious code or attacks. When an attack on a router's command port is detected, it can drop the offending packets while still allowing all other traffic to pass.

To operate effectively, an IPS must have an excellent intrusion detection capability. This also means that the software or hardware appliance itself should not become a liability by becoming subject to one or more types of network or computer attacks. Thus, some IPS products are designed to be installed without an IP network address. Instead, they operate promiscuously, examining each packet flowing on the network and responding to predefined attacks by dropping packets, changing equipment settings, and generating a variety of alerts. Thus, unlike a firewall that has an IP address, resides at the perimeter of a network, and will usually filter packets based on predefined packet addresses and packet content, the IPS can reside behind the firewall, has no IP address, and operates invisibly on the network.

In addition to identifying incidents and supporting incident response efforts, organizations have found other uses for IDS/IPSs, including the following [38]:

Identifying security policy problems. An IDS/IPS can provide some degree of quality control for security policy implementation, such as duplicating firewall rulesets and alerting when it sees network traffic that should have been blocked by the firewall but was not because of a firewall configuration error.

Documenting the existing threat to an organization. IDS/IPSs log information about the threats that they detect. Understanding the frequency and characteristics of attacks against an organization's computing resources is helpful in identifying the appropriate security measures for protecting the resources. The information can also be used to educate management about the threats that the organization faces.

Deterring individuals from violating security policies. If individuals are aware that their actions are being monitored by IDS/IPS technologies for security policy violations, they may be less likely to commit such violations because of the risk of detection.

Security Information & Event Management Considerations (SIEM)

Security Information and Event Management (SIEM) tools emerged right around 2000 - 2001. Historically, SIEM consisted of two distinct offerings: SEM (security event management), which collected, aggregated and acted upon security events; and SIM (security information management), which correlated, normalized and reported on the collected security event data.

SIEM technology is typically deployed to support three primary use cases:

- Compliance through log management and compliance reporting
- Threat management through real-time monitoring of user activity, data access, and application activity and incident management
- A deployment that provides a mix of compliance and threat management capabilities

Security Information and Event Management (SIEM) systems are designed to accept log event and flow information from a broad range of systems, including traditional security systems, management systems, or any other systems which provide a relevant data output that, when correlated and analyzed, is relevant for the enterprise. The SIEM system establishes an early warning capability to take preventative actions. An effective early warning system detects threats based on a holistic perspective and provides in-depth information about them. The

---

38   For information on establishing an effective incident response capability, see NIST Special Publication (SP) 800-61Revison 2, Computer Security Incident Handling Guide, August 2012: http://csrc.nist.gov/publications/nistpubs/800-61rev2/SP800-61rev2.pdf

information collected by the SIEM is typically aggregated or put into a single stream and translated into a standardized format, to reduce duplicates and to expedite subsequent analysis. It is then correlated between data sources and analyzed against a set of human defined rules, or vendor supplied or security analyst programmed correlation algorithms, to provide real-time reporting and alerting on incidents and events that may require intervention. The subsequent data is typically stored in a manner that prevents tampering to enable its use as evidence in any investigations or to meet compliance requirements.

The key features in SIEM systems include:

- *Log Aggregation* — Collection and aggregation of log records from the network, security, servers, databases, identity systems, and applications.
- *Correlation* — Attack identification by analyzing multiple data sets from multiple devices to identify patterns not obvious when looking at only one data source.
- *Alerting* — Defining rules and thresholds to display console alerts based on customer-defined prioritization of risk and/or asset value.
- *Dashboards* — An interface which presents key security indicators to identify problem areas and facilitate investigation.
- *Forensics* — The ability to investigate incidents by indexing and searching relevant events.
- *Reporting* — Documentation of control sets and other relevant security operations and compliance activities.

In order to deploy a SIEM system successfully, the first thing that the security architect needs to do is identify which systems will be forwarding events, typically all switches, routers, servers, application, and security systems (Network/Host Intrusion Prevention, Firewalls, anti-malware, etc). The number of devices forwarding events to the SIEM will depend on how much money an organization is willing to spend on event collectors that receive and normalize events, and the storage necessary to keep all of the data secured.

Deciding what events to send to the SIEM is often challenging. The security architect needs to be aware of two capacity limits that SIEM systems have:

1. *Storage.* How much space will the events take? To get a rough estimate go to every system that will be forwarding events and report on how much space they logged in a day then multiply that by the retention policy and add them all together. For instance take: (firewall logs for the day * 60 days) + (IPS logs for the day * 60 days) = required storage.

2. *Events per second.* It is recommended to go to all of the devices that will be forwarding events and report on how many they generated

in a day and divide that by 86,400 (number of seconds in a day). This will get an approximate number of total events per second which will determine the number and size of event collectors.

The other major area for the security architect to be aware of is rule sets. Due to the nature of SIEM systems, and the varied approaches that vendors take to rule creation, rules may need to be modified slightly to become effective. For example, a correlation rule monitoring for TCP port 31453 is going to trigger backdoor rules. Firewall events will trigger this occasionally because of an outbound connection. The reason for this is that when a computer initiates a connection to a web server on TCP port 80, it has to open a random port between 1024-65535 as well. This random port is what could trigger an alert. Modifying the rule to monitor for 31453 as a destination port would be a good way to tune this rule.

There are two specific areas that the security architect should begin to focus on as they look to deploy SEIM systems into the enterprise:

1. **Bandwidth Utilization**

   The most common way to get this data would be to use switch and router flow events. There may be other ways depending on the environment, such as forwarding Network Intrusion Prevention events to the SIEM. Regardless, this can take some time to benchmark and tune because bandwidth utilization is typically somewhat sporadic.

   To detect potential DDoS attacks a good place to start would be with monitoring for ingress traffic targeted to a handful of critical systems that would prevent the organization from functioning should they become inaccessible. The security architect would create a rule that would look something like "if the bandwidth directed to my web servers is greater than 40Mb/s for 10 minutes or more, trigger an alert."

2. **HTTP Tunneling**

   If a network is enforcing a least privilege architecture, the user network will be able to send HTTP and HTTPS traffic from the inside network out to the Internet. All of the SMTP traffic should go to the internal mail relay. If users are tunneling other protocols through HTTP they are likely attempting to evade controls, or it could be malware attempting to evade controls. The security architect will need to create a rule that monitors for TCP port 80 or 443 traffic that is NOT HTTP protocol based. On the SIEM, monitor for one of these events to be received to trigger the alert.

   This rule would require a Network Intrusion Detection/ Prevention System or Application Layer Firewall to be in place and feeding events to the SIEM system. The security architect should be aware of the need to tune the rule on the log generating device(s) and/or filter certain hosts from triggering the correlation rule in order to balance the system to the appropriate sensitivity level.

The deployment of a SIEM system needs to be carefully planned to meet clear and articulated requirements, and the architecture designed for the size and organization of the purchasing entity. Most of all, the security architect need to make sure that they are operationalizing the tool, which requires ongoing resources to keep the platform tuned, relevant, and complete. New devices and applications will be added, and those need to pump data into the SIEM system. New attacks will surface and new data types will emerge which must be integrated into the tool. SIEM is not a set-it-and-forget-it technology, and expecting the system to hum along without care and maintenance is a recipe for failure.

Wireless Considerations

No discussion of network security would be complete without discussing wireless networks.

Wireless LANs consist of computers with wireless adapters either built in or inserted into card slots, which collectively are referred to as stations, and one or more access points. An access point normally functions as a multiport bridge, with a wireless port and one or more wired ports. As data flows between wireless stations, from one wireless station to the Internet or from a wireless station onto the corporate LAN to a server, the access point operates as a bridge and broadcasts data onto all other ports, which makes it relatively easy for a person with a laptop with a promiscuous adapter to read traffic from or to other stations to include those stations residing on the LAN as they communicate with wireless stations.

Architectures

One or more stations and an access point are referred to as a Basic Service Set (BSS). To differentiate one BSS from another, each access point is assigned a Service Set identifier (SSID). The SSID is periodically broadcast by the access point, which enables a station to examine the names of networks within range and connect to the most appropriate one. One popular method to increase wireless security, which is not particularly practical when facing network-savvy hackers, is to turn off SSID broadcasting. While the network name is not shown, one can easily connect to the network by configuring their station to select the "unknown" network or configuring their station to use the network name "any." In addition, others can also capture the SSID in cleartext by observing association frames from legitimate clients.

Figure 2.14 illustrates the formation of an independent BSS. Wireless LANs can communicate is two different ways referred to as peer-to-peer and infrastructure. In peer-to-peer mode, stations communicate directly with one another. In the infrastructure mode of operation, stations communicate via the use of an access point. Thus, *Figure 2.14* shows how three stations can communicate with one another without an access point.

Figure 2.14 - **The Independent Basic Service Set**

The wireless access point, which is more popularly referred to as a wireless router when used in a home or small business, is the most common communications product used to connect wireless stations to a corporate LAN. In actuality, the basic access point is a two-port bridge, with one port representing the wireless interface while the second port is the wired interface. When functioning as a bridge, the access point operates according to the three-F rule, flooding, filtering, and forwarding, as it builds a table of MAC addresses associated with each port. As the access point evolved, many manufacturers added a routing capability to the device as well as several Ethernet switch ports, referring to the device as a wireless router. In actuality, most wireless routers perform limited routing capability at layer 3 and primarily operate at layer 2 to perform bridging among its wired and wireless ports. Unfortunately, this device is similar to other networking hardware with respect to a security loophole many

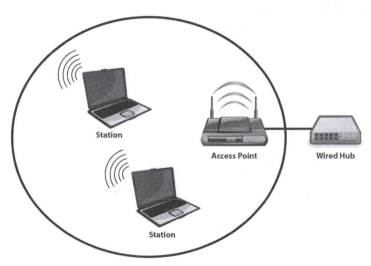

Figure 2.15 - **The Infrastructure Basic Service Set**

people fail to close. That is, it is configured at the factory with a default setting, such as "admin" or the name of the manufacturer for the password needed to access its configuration settings. Thus, the first thing a security architect should consider after the device is set up is to change the administrative password from its default setting.

Figure 2.15 illustrates an Infrastructure BSS, which is the most common type of BSS used. In this example two wireless stations are shown communicating via a common access point which is in turn cabled to a wired hub or switch, which provides connectivity to the corporate network. If default settings are not changed on the access point, not only can a hacker easily access the administrative functions of the access point, but, in addition, he or she can change the settings to either cause havoc to the organization or silently transmit a stream of data flowing through the device to a third party address for analysis.

When two BSSs are connected via a repeater or wired connection, they form an Extended Service Set (ESS). The ESS has an identifier or network name referred to as an Extended Service Set Identifier (ESSID). The ESSID can be considered as the network identifier for the wireless network. Devices may be set to "any" or to a specific ESSID. When set, they will only communicate with other devices using the same ESSID. *Figure 2.16* illustrates the relationship between the BSS and ESS for two BSSs linked via a wired LAN. In this example, each BSS could be located in different buildings on a campus, and the movement of a notebook

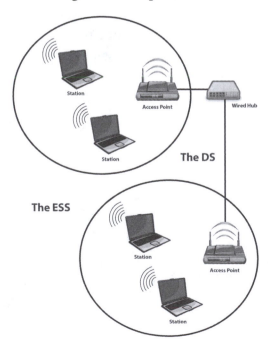

Figure 2.16 - **The Extended Service Set and the distribution system**

user from one building to another would occur similar to cell phone roaming. The connection between the two BSSs is referred to as a distribution system (DS). The DS can be a wired LAN, a leased line, or even a wireless LAN repeater to extend the range between the two service sets.

Security Issues

The original security for wireless LANs, referred to as Wired Equivalent Privacy (WEP), as its name implies, permits the equivalent of wired network privacy and nothing more. WEP was broken by several persons many years ago, and many improvements were made to the security technology to include rotating WEP keys and the use of RADIUS servers to strengthen wireless security. Other security enhancements include permitting only predefined MAC addresses via filtering, the use of better encryption beyond WEP, and level-3 security measures associated with Web browsing[39]. While these security techniques made it a bit more difficult for hackers to recover the WEP key in use, they still represented security vulnerabilities.

In an attempt to minimize the vulnerability of wireless transmissions, several additional security-related techniques were developed. These techniques included two versions of Wi-Fi Protected Access (WPA and WPA2), and two new wireless-security-related standards from the IEEE referred to as the 802.11i and 802.1X. Concerning the latter, this standard includes a security protocol referred to as the Temporal Key Integrity Protocol (TKIP).

WPA and WPA2

Both WPA and WPA2 represent security protocols created by the Wi-Fi Alliance to secure wireless transmission, and resulted from the security weakness of WEP. The protocols implement a large portion of the IEEE wireless security standard referred to as 802.11i, and WPA included the use of TKIP to enhance data encryption. TKIP was designed to add a level of security beyond that provided by WEP. To do so, TKIP added a key mixing function, a sequence counter that protects against replay attacks, and a 64-bit message integrity check to eliminate the potential of a man-in-the-middle attack. TKIP was launched during 2002 and has been superseded by more robust encryption methods, such as AES and CCMP [40].

---

39   See the following for an overview of the various security issues uncovered with WEP: http://www.isaac.cs.berkeley.edu/isaac/wep-faq.html

40   While TKIP has not been broken, it has known vulnerabilities, such as a susceptibility to dictionary-based attacks for short keys (eight characters), and some very clever ways to insert packets through manipulating a flaw in the packet integrity protocol. TKIP and WEP are not being allowed in new devices with the Wi-Fi stamp in a staged elimination over three years starting in 2011, and scheduled to be completed by 2014.

Under WPA2, two modes of operation are supported: Personal mode and Enterprise mode. Personal mode was developed to support wireless security in the home and small office environment that lacked access to an authentication server. This mode of operation is referred to as Pre-shared key (PSK), and its use requires wireless network devices to encrypt traffic using a 256-bit key. That key can be entered as a passphrase of 8 to 63 printable ASCII characters or as a string of 64 hex digits. Because WPA-PSK automatically changes encryption keys, a technique referred to as rekeying, it provides a level of security significantly beyond that of WEP.

It is important to note that although WPA and WPA2 are not IEEE standards, they implement the majority of the IEEE 802.11i standard, with WPA2 supporting the Advanced Encryption Standard (AES). AES supports three block ciphers; AES-128, AES-192, and AES-256. While each block size is 128 bits, the keys can be 128, 192, or 256 bits, resulting in the terms used to reference each portion of the standard. Today, most wireless products sold for use in the home or small office support WPA2. Because setup involves a few clicks within the operating system to enter a passphrase or string of hex digits, the major difficulty reported by users typically involves the failure to use the same passphrase or hex code on each wireless device.

IEEE 802.11i and 802.1X

While WPA and WPA2 represent a majority of the 802.11i standard, they are not fully compatible with it. While 802.11i makes use of the AES block cipher, both the original WEP and WPA use the RC4 stream cipher. Another difference is the fact that the 802.11i architecture includes support for the 802.1X standard as an authentication mechanism based on the use of the Extensible Authentication Protocol (EAP) and an authentication server as well the use of AES-based Counter Mode with Cipher Block Chaining Message Authentication Code Protocol (CCMP), the latter an encryption protocol based on AES that provides confidentiality, integrity, and origin authentication. These additions in the 802.11i standard are well suited for the enterprise.

802.1X [41]

The IEEE 802.1X standard provides port-based authentication, requiring a wireless device to be authenticated prior to gaining access to a LAN and its resources. Under this standard, the client node is referred to as a supplicant, while the authenticator is usually an access point or a wired Ethernet switch. By default, the authenticator bars the supplicant's access to the network. The authenticator

---

[41]   See the following to download a copy of the current 802.1x -2010 Standard: http://standards.ieee.org/getieee802/download/802.1X-2010.pdf

passes the supplicant's request to access the network to an authentication server. Assuming the authentication server accepts the supplicant's request, the authenticator opens the port to the supplicant's traffic, otherwise it is blocked. Messages from the supplicant authenticator and server are transported via EAP.

In addition to the previously mentioned wireless enhancements, another technique commonly used to provide a high level of security is the use of a layer 3 VPN. Because this will be described through use of VPNs later in this chapter, a detailed discussion is not warranted however, it is worth mentioning that they provide an alternative security mechanism that can be valuable when users are traveling or their organization does not fully support the 802.1X standard.

Zones of Control

Through the use of virtual LANs, it becomes possible to partition switch-based networks into zones of control. Not only does this restrict who can access devices attached to specific switch ports, but in addition, this can enhance throughput by limiting broadcast traffic.

Figure 2.17 illustrates an 8-port LAN switch subdivided into two networks based on port associations. In this example, ports 1, 2, 3, and 4 are assigned as VLAN 1, while the other ports are assigned to VLAN2. Note that traffic in VLAN1 is never seen by users in VLAN2 and vice versa, which provides a degree of both administrative control and security. Concerning the former, all accounting personnel could be assigned to VLAN1, while all engineering personnel could be assigned to VLAN2. Concerning security, the partition of

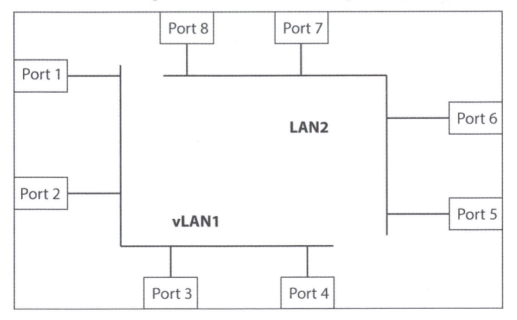

Figure 2.17 - **VLAN switch partitioned by ports.**

the switch into two VLANs would then preclude accountants from accessing the engineering server, and vice versa. Also note that the segmentation of a switch into two or more VLANs can enhance performance. This results from the fact that broadcasts are restricted to each VLAN. VLANs can be further strengthened by adding encryption endpoints that encrypt all traffic across a VLAN.

Network Security

This section will examine some specific network security measures. In doing the use of generic products as well as different types of tunneling and endpoint security measures the security architect needs to be familiar with will be discussed.

Content Filtering

Content filtering represents a technique whereby the contents of packets are either blocked or allowed based on an analysis of its content, rather than its IP address or other criteria. The most prominent use of content filtering is in programs that operate as add-ons to Web browsers or at a corporate gateway, blocking unacceptable messages that might be pornographic or racist. In an e-mail environment, the use of content filtering is designed to place e-mail advertisements and similar types of junk mail based on subject, content, or both in a spam folder that most persons ignore.

Anti-Malware

Anti-malware software can be considered as a special type of content filter. However, instead of examining the content of packets for pornography, racist remarks, and similar content, this software is focused on detecting viruses, worms, Trojans, and other potentially harmful software. Once detected, the antimalware software will, based on its configuration, either block the packets or quarantine them. Often, antimalware is sold as a virus-checking system that operates on a separate e-mail server in a corporate environment and checks for a variety of potentially malicious software.

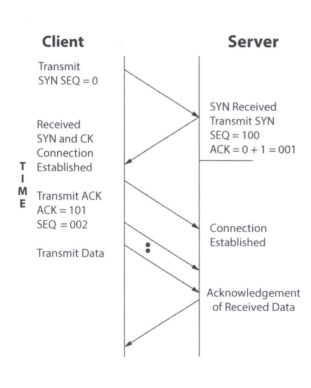

Figure 2.18 - **The three-way handshake.**

182

One special type of software product that is incorporated into many routers is designed to block DoS attacks. One type of DoS attack occurs due to the manner in which TCP operates, which results in a three-way handshake. *Figure 2.18* illustrates an example of the TCP three-way handshake process, which results in the exchange of SYN, SYN/ACK, and ACK messages. First, a client accessing a server transmits a SYN message to the server. The server responds with a SYN/ACK message, to which the client would normally respond with an ACK. However, if a hacker spoofs the IP source address, the SYN/ACK message will not receive an ACK. Although the server will eventually time out the connection, during the period it remains open it takes resources away from the server. When a hacker floods the server with spoofed IP addresses in a series of connection requests, the result is a DoS attack, which limits the ability of real clients to access the server.

Through the use of DoS prevention, most routers can be configured to restrict the number of open connections at a specific time or from a specific address.

Anti-Spam

Content filtering is the building block upon which anti-spam products operate. For example, an e-mail spam filter could examine the originator, subject, or content of e-mails to decide whether to pass the mail to the recipient or place it in his or her spam folder. *Figure 2.19* illustrates a portion of a spam folder on Yahoo mail. Note that the "From" column has names instead of e-mail addresses,

Spam   Upgrade to the all-new Yahoo! Mail

SpamGuard is ON: [Edit Settings]
SpamGuard ensures that suspected spam is delivered to the **Spam** folder, and is deleted after one month.

View: **All** | Unread | Flagged | From Connections   Messages 1-25 of 1179   First | Previous | Next | Last

| Delete | Mark ▾ | Move... ▾ |

	⚑	From	🖉 Subject	Date	▾ Size
☐	*	Cash Locator	Lenders waiting to loan you money !	Mon, 1/18/38	4KB
☐	*	The Fun Cards	Send Christmas eCards to Family and Friends for Free ...	Mon, 1/18/38	3KB
☐	*	Josefina	Hurry...High-quality Medications! Don't miss the chance !	Mon, 1/18/38	2KB
☐	*	Need Cash Quick	Get up to $1500 in 1 hour- Fast Approval for !	Mon, 1/18/38	4KB
☐	*	eBay Profit Machine	Retire Early: Ebay Needs New Workers Gilbert Held	Mon, 1/18/38	4KB
☐	*	Real Visa	Get A REAL Visa. Right Away Gilbert Held today!	Mon, 1/18/38	4KB
☐	*	Jesus Kennedy	Can't find high-quality medications?	Mon, 1/18/38	2KB
☐	*	Henry Otto	Quality medications all over the world	Mon, 1/18/38	2KB
☐	*	Henry Otto	Quality medications all over the world	Mon, 1/18/38	2KB
☐	*	Dillard Rocky	Find the Huge Selection of Replicas	Mon, 1/18/38	2KB
☐	*	Mary johnson	Hurry.. CHEAP CIALIS,Viagra ONLINE - LOWEST NET P...	Mon, 1/18/38	2KB
☐	*	Google Business	Let Google Make You Money While You Sleep Gilbert ...	Mon, 1/18/38	4KB

*Figure 2.19 - **Examining a Yahoo spam folder.***

which makes it easy to differentiate span from genuine e-mail. Note that at the time this author's spam file was captured, spam e-mailers were using improper dates, which represents another way to filter their junk mail. Between the two columns is the column labeled Subject, which can also be used to filter junk mail. Here, such keywords as *lenders*, *free*, and *medication* can be used to place e-mail in the spam filter.

Outbound Traffic Filtering

There are several types of communications devices that can be used to perform outbound traffic filtering. Such devices are primarily used to control the use of e-mail and Web access. The security architect should be familiar with the issues that this can create with regards to the deployment of secure gateway and proxy solutions, and the advanced deep inspection capabilities that these products may have to "look into" encrypted traffic, such as HTTPS, as it transits the network [42].

When filtering outbound e-mail, some organizations use a special server to encrypt messages to certain third parties, forcing the recipient to register to receive mail as well as to either set up a user ID and password to access the mail server or to use a private key to decrypt the message encrypted with a public key.

42   By encrypting HTTP communication with SSL a client can establish a secure and private communication channel with a web server. Using HTTPS the security architect can provide essential protection for passing authentication credentials and prevent the disclosure of sensitive information.

While the end-to-end secure encrypted channel provided by HTTPS enables important security and privacy protection, the protocol is often abused. The root of the problem is that most firewalls are unable to inspect HTTPS communication because the application-layer data is encrypted with SSL. Knowing this, attackers frequently leverage HTTPS to deliver malicious payloads to a user confident that even the most intelligent application-layer firewalls are completely blind to HTTPS and must simply relay HTTPS communication between hosts. Frequently end users will leverage HTTPS to bypass access controls enforced by their corporate firewalls and proxy servers, using it to connect to public proxies and for tunneling non-HTTP protocols through the firewall that might otherwise be blocked by policy.

HTTPS inspection allows a firewall to terminate outbound HTTPS sessions at the firewall. Essentially it provides a true proxy for HTTPS, instead of simply just tunneling HTTPS communication blindly. This is accomplished by acting as a trusted man-in-the-middle. When a request is made of the firewall for an HTTPS protected resource, the firewall will establish a new connection to the destination server and retrieve its SSL certificate. The firewall then copies the information from the certificate and creates its own certificate using these details and provides that to the client. As long as the client trusts the root certificate of the firewall the process is completely transparent to the end user.

By enabling forward (outbound) HTTPS inspection the firewall can now provide complete protection for all web-based protocols. With the firewall terminating outbound SSL sessions, the firewall can now decrypt and inspection HTTPS communication, allowing for the enforcement of HTTP policy, more accurate application of URL filtering, and inspection of files transferred over HTTPS.

In other situations, an organization may configure a mail server to block mail sent to certain addresses, such as those with the domain .xxx.

The filtering of outbound Web traffic is commonly employed by several well-known security programs. Although the primary goal of Web outbound traffic filtering is to block users from accessing predefined URLs, such as phishing sites or sites considered racist, sites offering gambling or pornography, a secondary goal is to enhance employee productivity by limiting the time that workers can access the Internet.

The ability to restrict outbound Web traffic to certain periods of time is commonly incorporated into routers, firewalls, and certain network appliances. For example, an organization might restrict outbound Web traffic to all locations other than servers at different organizational locations, with the exception of lunch hour, when employees are allowed to pay bills, shop, or perform other Internet-related chores.

Mobile Code

Another type of outbound traffic filtering involves blocking mobile code. This type of code is software obtained from remote system or systems, transmitted over a network, and then downloaded and executed on a local system, all without the computer operator being aware of the activity taking place. Some common examples of mobile code include code developed using script languages such as JavaScript and VBScript, Java applets, ActiveX controls, Flash animations, and even macros embedded within Microsoft Office documents such as Excel and Word documents. Mobile code can occur by a hacker scanning a network for holes in the perimeter and sending mobile code to specific addresses or using e-mail attachments that activate when clicked, executing code.

Some mobile code can be harmful, consisting of Distributed Denial of Service (DDoS) agents designed to attack a target or list of targets at specific times, viruses, worms, and other harmful software. By examining the content of outbound packets, the spread of malware may be contained; however, it does not rid the computer of the problematic software. To do so, a virus checker or the alert message of the device performing the outbound traffic filtering must be examined.

Policy Enforcement Design

Content-aware Data Loss Prevention (DLP) tools enable the dynamic application of policy based on the classification of content determined at the time of an operation. Content-aware DLP describes a set of technologies and inspection techniques used to classify information content contained within an object such as a file, email, packet, application or data store while at rest (in storage), in use (during an operation) or in transit (across a network); and the ability to dynamically apply a policy such as log, report, classify, relocate, tag and encrypt and/or apply enterprise data rights management protections. DLP technologies help organizations develop, educate and enforce better business practices concerning the handling and transmission of sensitive data. There are three broad categories of DLP that the security architect needs to be familiar with as they plan the deployment of a solution:

- *Enterprise DLP* solutions, which provide organizations with advanced content-aware inspection capabilities and robust management consoles.

- *Channel DLP*, which consists of content-aware DLP capabilities that are integrated within an existing application — typically email.

- *DLP-lite*, a new subcategory of offerings that group a specific set of capabilities in a way that addresses a niche market typically by requirement, such as discovery only, or for a specific use case, such as small or midsize business (SMB), where a need may exist to monitor only a few protocols and provide a simplified management console or workflow.

Gartner inquiry data through 2011 indicates several major observations that should help security architects to develop appropriate requirements and select the right technology for their needs [43]:

- About 30% of enterprises led their content-aware DLP deployments with network requirements — 30% began with discovery requirements, and 40% started with endpoint requirements. Enterprises that began with network or endpoint capabilities nearly always deploy data discovery functions next. The majority of large enterprises purchase at least two of the three primary channels (network, endpoint and discovery) in an initial purchase, but few deploy all of them simultaneously.

- Many enterprises struggle to define their strategic content-aware DLP needs clearly and comprehensively.

- The primary appeal of endpoint technologies continues to be the protection of IP and other valuable enterprise data from insider theft and accidental leakage (full disk encryption mitigates the external theft and compliance issues). The value of network and discovery solutions, by contrast, lies in helping management to identify and correct faulty business processes, in identifying and preventing accidental disclosures of sensitive data, and in providing a mechanism for supporting compliance and audit activities.

---

43   See the following for the Gartner Research Magic Quadrant for Content-Aware Data Loss Prevention Study, ID Number G00213871, Publication Date, 10 August 2011:   http://www.aptsecure.com/wp-content/uploads/2011/08/Gartner_DLP_MQ_2011.pdf

- DLP solution providers continue to focus on text-based data in their analysis of content. Although a few vendors are making inroads into identifying non-text data, such as images, video, audio and other media, these remain in the early stage.

- Many DLP deployments are sold on the basis of being a tool to assist in risk management activities; however, most DLP solution reporting capabilities do not provide dashboard or feedback relevant for this function.

It is imperative that the security architect continue to be aware of the absolute need to involve non-IT stakeholders in the planning and operationalization of DLP. Although IT/IT security can play a role in ensuring the day-to-day operation of a DLP system, ultimately, the business needs to decide when an event is a policy violation and what the appropriate remedies for the incident are. The security architect needs to then be able to act as a bridge for those conversations, and link the outputs directly back to the security architecture as required, incorporating the feedback from the organization in an ongoing way.

Application and Transport Layer Security

The TCP/IP protocol suite in effect combines the upper three layers of the OSI model (application, presentation, and session), as shown in *Figure 2.20*, into a single layer that is commonly referenced as a TCP/IP application. Over the past two decades, several application protocols were developed to support secure e-commerce and in turn safe browsing and purchasing from different Web sites. This section briefly discusses social media technologies, and describes and

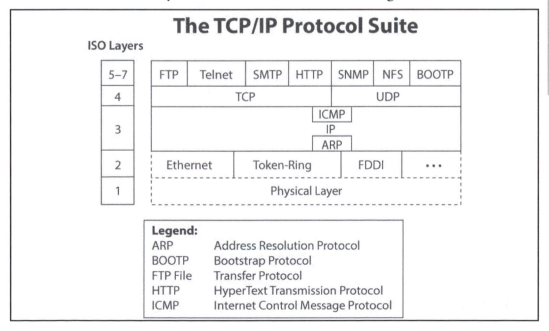

Figure 2.20 - **Comparing the TCP/IP protocol suite to the ISO reference model**

discusses some security-related protocols that enable safe credit card transactions and deposits and withdrawals from checking accounts.

Social Media

Social media is defined as online content created by people using highly accessible and scalable publishing technologies. Twitter, Facebook, LinkedIn, MySpace, YouTube and even Wikis are all great examples of social media. Other sub categories of social media include social networking, blogging, micro-blogging and more. Social networking sites, which provide users the ability to connect, communicate, and share with others, also serve as a platform for the advertising industry. They allow businesses to become known globally with ease since the social networking sites users are distributed in different geographical locations. They also allow business owners to have a "personal" connection with customers and a place to find and to get to know potential employees.

One of the main challenges for the security architect with regards to social media and more broadly, social networking technologies in the enterprise, comes from the intersection of the tremendous increase in smart device capabilities and the Bring Your Own Device (BYOD) phenomenon that has become prevalent in recent years [44]. The increased capabilities that smart devices offer to end users are proving to be a boon for productivity in many cases. However, these gains are coming at the expense of security and access control to sensitive data. As more and more unregulated end points are allowed to connect to a network, the

---

44   There is a trend in the BYOD security arena that security architects need to be aware of. As of late 2012, and into 2013, there are apps making there way into Smartphones and mobile platforms that present a significant potential challenge to the security architect's ability to successfully integrate Mobile Device Management (MDM) into their overall security architecture.

The deployment and use of applications that allow users to send messages to each other and to others outside the organization that are deleted by default, as well as applications that allow users to send voice, text and audio messages, all of which delete themselves after a period of time presents some very interesting and unique challenges.

Snapchat allows users to text self-destructing photos in real time, as well as being able to update the sender if the recipient takes a screen capture of the content prior to deletion from the system.

A similar app called Wickr takes the concept to the next level. Wickr lets users share more than just photos -- they can send encrypted multimedia messages that self-destruct after a set amount of time. Wickr encrypts everything and it also scrubs content from the file system, making it hard for anybody to know what was sent or if anything was sent. Wickr employs military-grade encryption of text, picture, audio and video messages relying on both the Advanced Encryption Standard (AES) symmetric block cipher implemented with random 256-bit keys and the asymmetric RSA-4096 algorithm. Wickr deletes all metadata from your pictures, video and audio files, like your device info, your location, and any personal information captured during the creation of those files via a process that while running, works continuously to wipe areas of main memory and device storage recently used to display text or multimedia content. The Wickr app does not require you to tie an email address to your account, allowing you to be as private and discreet as needed.

Snapchat can be found here: http://www.snapchat.com/
Wickr can be found here: https://www.mywickr.com/en/index.php

ability for the security architect to enforce access control policy and information security governance continues to erode.

For cybercriminals, the shift from desktop-based applications to Web-based ones, particularly those on social networking sites, presents a new vector for abuse. As more and more people communicate through social networks, the more viable social networks become malware distribution platforms. An example of the issues that the security architect faces from social network based communication in the enterprise is KOOBFACE, which is a revolutionary piece of malware, being the first to have a successful and continuous run propagating through social networks.

"KOOBFACE is composed of various components, each with specific functionalities. While most malware cram their functionalities into one file, KOOBFACE divides each capability into different files that work together to form the KOOBFACE botnet. A typical KOOBFACE infection starts with spam sent through Facebook, Twitter, MySpace, or other social networking sites containing a catchy message with a link to a "video." KOOBFACE can also send messages to the inbox of a user's social network friends. Clicking the link will redirect the user to a website designed to mimic YouTube (but is actually named YuoTube), which asks the user to install an executable (.EXE) file to be able to watch the video. The .EXE file is, however, not the actual KOOBFACE malware but a downloader of KOOBFACE components. The components may be subdivided into the following:

- KOOBFACE downloader
- Social network propagation components
- Web server component
- Ads pusher and rogue antivirus (AV) installer
- CAPTCHA breaker
- Data stealer
- Web search hijackers
- Rogue Domain Name System (DNS) changer

The KOOBFACE downloader is also known as the fake "Adobe Flash component" or video codec the fake YouTube site claims the user needs to view a video that turns out to be nonexistent. The downloader's actual purpose includes the following:

- Determine what social networks the affected user is a member of.
- Connect to the KOOBFACE Command & Control (C&C).
- Download the KOOBFACE components the C&C instructs it to download.

189

In order to determine what social networks the affected user is a member of, the KOOBFACE downloader checks the Internet cookies in the user's machine. The KOOBFACE downloader checks the cookies for the following social networking sites:

- Facebook
- Tagged
- MySpace
- Bebo
- Hi5
- Netlog
- Friendster
- fubar
- myYearbook
- Twitter

The presence of cookies means the user has logged in to any of the above-mentioned social networking sites. The KOOBFACE downloader then reports all found social networking site cookies to the KOOBFACE C&C. Apart from the necessary social network propagation components, the KOOBFACE C&C may also instruct the KOOBFACE downloader to download and install other KOOBFACE malware that act as Web servers, ads pushers, rogue AV installers, CAPTCHA breakers, data stealers, Web search hijackers, and rogue DNS changers." [45]

The social network propagation components of KOOBFACE may be referred to as the actual KOOBFACE worm since these are responsible for sending out messages in social networking sites that eventually lead to the KOOBFACE downloader. The components of the KOOBFACE botnet owed their continued proliferation to gratuitous link-sharing behaviors seen commonly on social networking sites. It is this link sharing behavior that is the most problematic for the security architect with regards to access control and information security governance. Because most of the content that individuals share links to will be hosted outside of the security boundaries of the organization, the security architect has no direct control over the content, and as a result, cannot apply access control mechanisms, content filtering, malware and virus scanning, packet inspection, and / or any forms of screening and policy based content controls that would normally be applied to data as it transits through the organizations network and infrastructure. Finding ways to address these issues through the separation of social and work related activities via physical and logical controls,

---

45   See the following for the TREND MICRO whitepaper, The Real Face of KOOBFACE: The Largest Web 2.0 Botnet Explained: http://www.trendmicro.com/cloud-content/us/pdfs/security-intelligence/white-papers/wp_the-real-face-of-koobface.pdf

down to the device level, is one of the key challenges that security architects face in the area of social media today.

Secure E-Commerce Protocols

A protocol represents a set of rules that govern communication between two network entities. Some of the most widely used protocols are members of the TCP/IP family, such as the Internet Protocol (IP), the Transmission Control Protocol (TCP), the User Datagram Protocol (UDP), and the Internet Control Message Protocol (ICMP). A security protocol is a communication protocol that is specifically designed to provide secure communications. Several security protocols are either in use or being developed for use on the Internet. Such security protocols are designed for different applications ranging from the use of credit cards to spending micro dollars, which add up cumulatively to a large amount spread over hundreds to thousands of Web sites. In addition, each security protocol may provide different benefits, depending on where it is positioned in the TCP/IP protocol suite.

The most widely used security protocol is the Secure Socket Layer (SSL) because it is built into every popular Web server and browser. As its name implies, SSL does not secure a transaction directly; instead, it provides a secure connection for any information flowing between a browser and server via the HyperText Transmission Protocol (HTTP). SSL has been used over the past few years to migrate to a derivative IETF standard referred to as Transport Layer Security (TLS) that is very similar to SSL Version 3.0; these standards will be referred to interchangeably in this chapter. SSL resides just above TCP but below the application it protects and is transported by underlying protocols, so it does not require modification to the operating system's networking software and does not affect data or document structures. *Figure 2.21* illustrates the relationship of SSL to other layers in the TCP protocol stack.

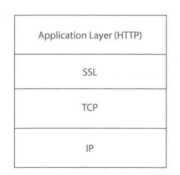

Figure 2.21 - **SSL and the TCP/IP protocol stack**

SSL/TSL and the TCP/IP Protocol Stack

As the name Secure Sockets Layer indicates, SSL connections act like sockets connected by TCP. Therefore, one can think of SSL connections as secure TCP connections because the place for SSL in the protocol stack is right above TCP. It is important to note, however, that SSL does not support some TCP features, such as out-of-band data.

The SSL protocol was developed by Netscape Communications Corporation in 1994. SSL allows clients, such as Web browsers and HTTP servers, to communicate over a secure communications connection. To accomplish this, SSL supports encryption, source authentication, and data integrity as key mechanisms that are used to protect information exchanged over insecure public networks such as the Internet. There are several versions of SSL, with SSL 3.0 being the latest version, which is universally supported. A newer "version" of SSL known as the Transport Layer Security (TLS) is an improvement over SSL 3.0, was promulgated as an Internet standard, and is supported by just about all recent software.

After building a TCP connection, the SSL handshake is started by the client. The client which can be a browser as well as any other program such as Windows Update or PuTTY sends a number of specifications: which version of SSL/TLS it is running, what ciphersuites it wants to use, and what compression methods it wants to use. The server checks what the highest SSL/TLS version is that is supported by them both, picks a ciphersuite from one of the client's options (if it supports one), and optionally picks a compression method.

After this the basic setup is done, the server sends its certificate. This certificate must be trusted by either the client itself or a party that the client trusts. For example if the client trusts ABC, then the client can trust the certificate from 123.com, because ABC cryptographically signed 123's certificate.

Having verified the certificate and being certain this server really is who he claims to be (and not a man in the middle), a key is exchanged. This can be a public key, a PresharedSecret, or simply nothing, depending on the chosen ciphersuite. Both the server and the client can now compute the key for the symmetric encryption. The client tells the server that from now on, all communication will be encrypted, and sends an encrypted and authenticated message to the server.

The server verifies that the MAC (used for authentication) is correct, and that the message can be correctly decrypted. It then returns a message, which the client verifies as well.

The handshake is now finished, and the two hosts can communicate securely. To close the connection, a close_notify 'alert' is used. If an attacker tries to terminate the connection by finishing the TCP connection (injecting a FIN packet), both sides will know the connection was improperly terminated. The connection cannot be compromised by this though, merely interrupted.

Encryption

Encryption is used to protect data from observation and potential use by converting it to an apparently meaningless form prior to transmission. The data is encrypted by one side (either the client or the server), transmitted, and then decrypted by the other side prior to being processed.

Authentication

Authentication represents a method of verifying the identity of the other party in a communications session. In e-commerce, this enables the client accessing a server to verify its identity and the server to verify the identity of the client.

There are several ways of configuring authentication. First, if an authentication method is not configured, no authentication will occur. Basic server authentication can also be enabled, which provides authentication of the server accessed by a client. A third authentication method is referred to as mutual authentication, which results in the server authenticating the client while the client authenticates the server.

The first time a browser or other client attempts to communicate with a Web server over a secure connection, the server presents the client with a set of credentials. Those credentials are in the form of a certificate.

Certificates and Certificate Authorities [46]

Certificates are issued and validated by trusted authorities referred to as certification authorities (CAs). A certificate represents the public-key identity of a person. It is a signed document that in effect says: "I certify that the public key in this document belongs to the entity named in this document." One of the most widely used CAs are certificates issued by VeriSign.

Data Integrity

The function of data integrity is to ensure that data has not been modified. Implementing data integrity can include monitoring and modification detection of key files, regardless of whether the modification was malicious, or accidental. In a Windows environment, this can include looking for changes to the registry, changes to files' security access permissions, changes to services, as well as changes to the contents of files.

---

46   See the following for an example of one of the potential issues associated with the use of Certificates and Certificate Authorities based on incorrect issuance of certificates by a CA to a third party:
  A. http://googleonlinesecurity.blogspot.com/2013/01/enhancing-digital-certificate-security.html
  B. http://www.networkworld.com/community/blog/chrome-firefox-ie-block-fraudulent-digital-certificate?source=NWWNLE_nlt_security_2013-01-07
  C. http://www.networkworld.com/news/2013/010313-google-finds-unauthorized-certificate-for-265479.html?source=NWWNLE_nlt_security_2013-01-04
  D. http://technet.microsoft.com/en-us/security/advisory/2798897
  E. http://blog.mozilla.org/security/2013/01/03/revoking-trust-in-two-turktrust-certfcates/
  F. https://freedom-to-tinker.com/blog/sjs/turktrust-certificate-authority-errors-demonstrate-the-risk-of-subordinate-certificates/

SSL/TLS Features

The original design of SSL and its subsequent reincarnation as TLS were well thought out and resulted in the two protocols being used for secure e-commerce transactions. SSL represents a de facto standard, while TLS represents a formal standard promulgated by the IETF. At the very beginning, the designers of SSL were aware of the fact that not all parties would use the same client software. In addition, due to different hardware platform processing, clients would not embrace a single encryption algorithm. This is because an encryption algorithm suitable for one hardware platform might be unsuitable for another. The same was true for servers. Thus, under SSL and TLS, the client and server at the two ends of a connection negotiate the encryption and decryption algorithms (cipher suites) during their initial handshake.

Although SSL permits both the client and the server to authenticate each other, typically only the server is authenticated in the SSL layer. Clients are primarily authenticated in the application layer, through passwords sent over an SSL-protected communications link between client and server

Figure 2.22 illustrates the beginning of an SSL session when this author used a browser to access the Smith Barney Web site. In the background, note the lock in the upper right that is used to indicate a secure connection. Depending on the browser and version used, the lock can be at different locations on the Web page. In general, SSL- or TLS-enabled Web sites are recognizable by the lock or key icon displayed at the top or bottom of a browser window when visiting a site that supports transmission security.

Figure 2.22 - **Accessing a secure Web site**

Limitations of SSL/TLS

A key limitation of SSL/TLS is the fact that information passed over a secure connection becomes nonsecure when the server being accessed stores the received data on a hard drive. In fact, this major limitation allowed hackers to obtain millions of credit card numbers and other information by hacking into an organization's server and downloading the contents of various server files. Unfortunately, that server held account information for several brands, resulting in the credit card information of over a million persons who purchased items at over a thousand stores being compromised. Thus, for additional safety, SSL should be supplemented by the encryption of data stored on e-commerce servers.

In addition to its use for securing access to Web servers, SSL can be used to secure communications with mail servers via POP3 (Post Office Protocol Version 3), IMAP (Internet Message Access Protocol), and SMTP (Simple Mail Transfer Protocol), directory servers via LDAP (Lightweight Directory Assistance Protocol), CA servers, FTP servers, and many custom applications.

Other Security Protocols

Some additional security-related protocols include Secure Multimedia Internet Mail Extensions (S/MIME), used for securing e-mail; iKP, which represents a family of protocols that provides a model for secure credit card transactions; Millicent, which was developed as a method for micropayments; and Netcash and Digicash, the latter two developed for anonymous transactions.

S/MIME is an application-layer protocol that was developed to provide security for e-mail documents. It accomplishes this by securing the transmission of e-mail through store-and-forward processing and even during storage on a destination hard drive. S/MIME can be used to create signed orders and other types of e-commerce records. Currently, several popular e-mail programs support S/MIME; however, the requirement for a full Public Key Infrastructure (PKI) to deploy digital identities to users has hindered its widespread adoption

The iKP family of protocols was designed at IBM-Zürich to provide secure credit card payments over an insecure network, such as the Internet [47]. Millicent was designed by Digital Equipment's Systems Research Center at Palo Alto, California, to enable secure micropayments, enabling transactions that cost a fraction of a cent to occur on the Internet [48]. Because the cost associated with a typical security protocol can exceed a micropayment, Millicent addresses this

---

47   See the following for overview information on the iKP family of protocols: http://www.zurich.ibm.com/security/past-projects/ecommerce/iKP_overview.html

48   See the following for overview information on Millicent: http://sellitontheweb.com/blog/millicent-micropayment-product-review/

2

economic problem by providing lightweight secure transactions more suitable for micropayment transactions. Another series of security-related protocols such as IPSec, L2TP, and SOCKS are used for constructing virtual private networks (VPNs).

Secure Remote Procedure Calls

Prior to discussing the securing of Remote Procedure Calls (RPCs), it is important to understand what it is and how it is used [49]. An RPC represents a technique for building client–server-based applications. An RPC can be considered to be similar to a function call, with calling arguments passed to the remote procedure while the calling software waits for a response from the remote procedure operating on a server. At the client, the software thread that initiated the RPC is blocked from further processing until either a response is received from the server or a timeout occurs. At the server, a routine is initiated that performs the requested service and transmits a response to the client.

To secure RPCs, several steps are required. First, the client software must create an association with a server. The client then invokes appropriate security services to compute a checksum of the previously created checksum. Finally, the client initializes two 32-bit sequence numbers that are used to establish pairwise credentials between the client and server. At the server, upon receipt of an association request, the computer stores the association checksum. Next, the server creates two 32-bit sequence numbers. Although client and server sequence numbers are not transmitted, they are used to compute a variety of security checks, such as ensuring that data is transmitted and received in the same order.

The programming of the RPC permits various security options, such as defining a desired protection level and the algorithm used to protect data via an authentication service. Because some options are more CPU intensive than others, a distinction can be made between intranet and Internet RPCs. That is, in an intranet environment where the threat is substantially reduced, processing may be enhanced by reducing security. In comparison, when used over the Internet, RPCs should be configured for maximum security.

Network Layer Security and VPNs

VPN technology is based on a technique referred to as tunneling. Under VPN tunneling, a logical connection is established and maintained between two locations connected via a packet network. Over this connection, packets are formed and transmitted via a client according to a specific VPN protocol being

---

49   See the following for the RPC: remote Procedure Call Protocol Specification Version 2 RFC 5531:   http://tools.ietf.org/html/rfc5531

used. The client typically places a header and possibly a trailer around each packet, which encapsulates each packet and, depending on the protocol used, may encrypt and add authentication to the packet. At its destination, the packet is stripped of its header and optional trailer, and may be authenticated and decrypted based on the protocol in use.

The primary purpose of a VPN is to enable clients to access servers via a public packet network such as the Internet in a secure manner. Another reason for the use of VPNs is economics. That is, a VPN enables two or more locations to use the Internet as a transmission facility, enabling companies to avoid the cost of expensive leased lines or dial charges. One key application of VPNs is to link or interconnect networks in two or more distributed locations to one another via the Internet. In fact, over the years, VPNs have progressed from being client–server tunneling protocols to developing network-to-network protocol capability; the introduction of network appliances that support VPNs enables network operators to purchase off-the-shelf hardware that facilitates interconnecting networks at multiple locations via the Internet in a secure manner.

Other reasons for the use of VPNs include securing wireless transmission from hot spots in airports and coffee shops back to a corporate server, perhaps reducing the need for third-party support, network scalability and, sometimes, ease of use. Concerning network scalability, while the cost associated with constructing a network using dial-up and leased lines may appear reasonable at first, as the need to add more branch offices expands, so does the cost. By using a VPN, all that is required to add additional locations is a line connecting the office to the Internet, making the Internet's vast collection of interconnected lines and routers available to an organization both domestically and overseas.

Figure 2.23 illustrates the use of the Internet to interconnect four geographically distributed branch offices. Note that only four connections to the Internet are required, one from each location. In comparison, 6 leased lines would be required to interconnect the offices without the use of the Internet. If the organization expanded its branches by two, it would need six Internet connections; however, the number of leased lines would increase to 15 to provide a similar interconnectivity capability. In addition, the mesh structure of the Internet provides a high degree of alternate routing capability, which routes data around impairments such as network outages or traffic bottlenecks; this capability would be very costly to duplicate on an individual organizational basis. Thus, for some organizations, the ability to add branch connections at a nominal cost makes economics and scalability an important driver for the use of VPNs.

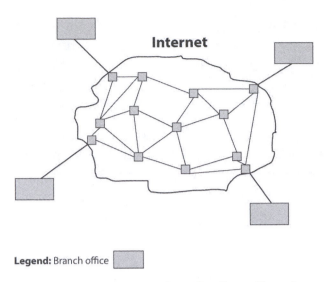

Figure 2.23 - **Using the Internet to connect four distributed locations to one another**

Types of VPN Tunneling

A VPN interconnects two or more locations via tunneling. There are two basic types of VPN tunneling: voluntary and compulsory. Both types of tunneling are commonly used in different VPN protocols. In addition, depending on the VPN protocol used, additional differences may exist.

Under voluntary tunneling, the VPN client manages the connection setup process. The client first initiates a connection to the communications carrier, which is an Internet service provider (ISP), when establishing an Internet VPN. Then, the VPN client application creates the tunnel to a VPN server over the connection.

Under compulsory tunneling, the communications carrier network provider is responsible for managing the VPN connection setup process. Thus, when the client initiates a connection to the carrier, the carrier in turn immediately initiates a VPN connection between that client and a designated VPN server. As viewed by the client, the VPN connection is set up in just one step compared to the two-step procedure required for voluntary tunnels. Compulsory VPN tunneling automatically authenticates clients and associates them with specific VPN servers by using predefined programming in the carrier network. The predefined programming is commonly referred to as a VPN Front End Processor (FEP), Network Access Server (NAS), or Point of Presence Server. Note that compulsory tunneling hides the details of VPN server connectivity from VPN clients and transfers management control over the tunnels from clients to the ISP. In return, service providers become responsible for the installation and maintenance of VPN hardware and software in their network.

VPN Tunneling Protocols

Since the early 1980s, several computer network protocols were developed to support VPN tunnels. Some of the more popular VPN tunneling protocols include the Point-to-Point Tunneling Protocol (PPTP), Layer 2 Tunneling Protocol (L2TP), IP Security (IPSec), a combination of L2TP and IPSec referred to as L2TP/IPSec, and TCP Wrappers.

Point-to-Point Tunneling Protocol (PPTP)

Although PPTP was bundled with most versions of Windows beginning with Windows 95, its actual development resulted from a joint effort between Microsoft Corporation and several other vendors, including Ascend Communications, a router manufacturer. The initial version of PPTP for Windows was for dial-up access, with later versions supporting tunneling via the Internet. Encryption is based on the RC4 algorithm, which Microsoft refers to as Microsoft Point-to-Point Encryption (MPPE) and is not part of the PPTP specification [50]. Instead, it is performed by the RAS server and is not supported by all vendors.

Operation

PPTP is built on top of the Point-to-Point Protocol (PPP), which is commonly used as the login protocol for dial-up Internet access. PPTP stores data within PPP packets, then encapsulates the PPP packets within IP datagrams for transmission through an Internet-based VPN tunnel. PPTP supports data encryption and compression and uses a form of General Routing Encapsulation (GRE) to get data to and from its final destination. PPTP VPN tunnels are

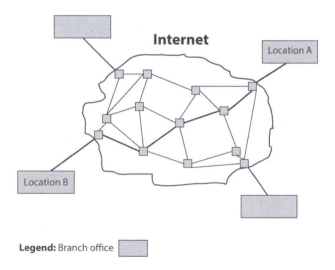

Figure 2.24 - **Using the Internet to create a PPTP tunnel from one location to another**

50   See the following for the Microsoft Point-To-Point Encryption (MPPE) Protocol RFC: http://www.ietf.org/rfc/rfc3078.txt

created via the following two-step process. First, the PPTP clients connect to their ISP using PPP dial-up networking, typically via a modem or ISDN connection. Next, PPTP creates a TCP control connection between the VPN client and the destination VPN server to establish a tunnel. PPTP uses TCP port 1723 for these connections. PPTP also supports VPN connectivity via a LAN. If the VPN is localized to the LAN, then ISP connections are not required, allowing PPTP tunnels to be created directly, because PPTP will create a TCP control connection between the VPN client and the destination VPN server.

A common security method implemented in routers is to employ access lists to allow IP datagrams containing a specified source and destination address that transports TCP with a destination port of 1723. In effect, this action creates a PPTP tunnel. *Figure 2.24* illustrates the use of the Internet to create a tunnel between locations A and B. Assuming for simplicity that the IP address of the client at location A is 1.2.3.4 and the IP address of the VPN server at location B is 4.3.2.1, then the generic statements in an access list for the router at location B to allow PPTP datagrams from the VPN tunnel established by a client at location A becomes

Allow IP 1.2.3.4 4.3.2.1 TCP any 1723

This assumes that the access list format requires specifying a protocol (IP) followed by source and destination IP addresses followed by another protocol (TCP) and source and destination ports.

PPTP Security
PPTP supports authentication, encryption, and packet filtering. PPTP authentication uses PPP-based protocols such as the Password Authentication Protocol (PAP), the Challenge-Handshake Authentication Protocol (CHAP), and the Extensible Authentication Protocol EAP. PPTP supports packet filtering on VPN servers. Intermediate routers and other firewalls can also be configured to selectively filter PPTP traffic.

PPTP Advantages and Disadvantages
A key advantage of PPTP is its inclusion in just about every version of Windows. Thus, Windows servers also can function as PPTP-based VPN servers without having an organization bear any additional cost.

Unfortunately, PPTP has several vulnerabilities. First, it is vulnerable to man-in-the-middle attacks. Second, and perhaps most important, PPTP supports only single-factor, password-based authentication. As a result, if a hacker steals or guesses an employee's password, that intruder can access the company's network. It is quite common to walk through a floor in an organization and see sticky messages with passwords posted on cubicle walls or monitors; obviously, any simple password-based system represents a risk.

Another disadvantage of PPTP is its failure to embrace a single standard for authentication and encryption. Thus, two products that both fully comply with the PPTP specification can be totally incompatible with each other if they encrypt data differently. In addition, numerous concerns have arisen over the level of security PPTP provides compared to alternative VPN protocols. As a result of questions regarding its security, PPTP has been made obsolete by Layer 2 Tunneling Protocol and IPSec.

Layer 2 Tunneling Protocol (L2TP)

When PPTP was being developed for VPN tunneling by Microsoft and Ascend Communication, Cisco Corporation was supporting the development of an alternative VPN, referred to as Layer 2 Forwarding (L2F)[51]. L2F was primarily used in Cisco products and did not provide either encryption or authentication, relying on the protocol being tunneled to provide either or both. While L2F was specifically designed to tunnel PPP traffic, it was capable of carrying many other protocols. In an attempt to improve on L2F, the best features of it and PPTP were combined to create new standard called the Layer 2 Tunneling Protocol (L2TP).

Similar to PPTP, L2TP exists at the data link layer (Layer 2) in the OSI reference model; hence, the origin of its name. However, in actuality, L2TP is a Layer 5 protocol and operates at the session layer of the OSI model using UDP Port 1701.

L2TP does not actually provide encryption or authentication, relying on the protocol that passes within the tunnel it provides for this capability. The protocol was originally published in 1999 as proposed standard RFC 2661[52]. A more recent version of L2TPv3 was published as proposed standard RFC 3931 in 2005[53]. The key difference between the latter and earlier version is the fact that L2TPv3 provides additional security features, improved encapsulation, and the ability to transport data links such as Frame Relay, Ethernet, and ATM over an IP network, whereas the original L2TP was restricted to supporting PPP.

Operation

L2TP uses the User Datagram Protocol (UDP). In doing so, the entire L2TP packet, including payload and L2TP header, is sent within a UDP datagram.

---

51   See the following for the Cisco Layer Two Forwarding (Protocol) "L2F" RFC: http://tools.ietf.org/html/rfc2341

52   See the following: https://tools.ietf.org/html/rfc2661

53   See the following: https://tools.ietf.org/html/rfc3931

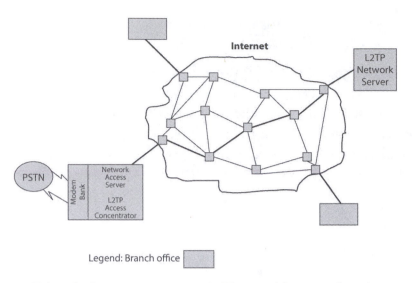

Figure 2.25 - Using the Internet to create a L2TP tunnel from one location to another

Although PPP sessions are commonly transported within an L2TP tunnel, as previously mentioned, Ethernet, Frame Relay, and other types of data can be transported under L2TPv3.

The two endpoints of an L2TP tunnel are called the LAC (L2TP Access Concentrator) and the LNS (L2TP Network Server). The LAC is the initiator of the tunnel, while the LNS is the server, which waits for new tunnels to be established. Once a tunnel is established, network traffic is bidirectional. When higher-level protocols are then run through an L2TP tunnel, an L2TP session is established within the tunnel for each higher-level protocol, such as PPP, Frame Relay, or Ethernet. Either the LAC or LNS may initiate sessions. The traffic for each session is isolated by L2TP, so it becomes possible to set up multiple virtual networks across a single tunnel.

The packets exchanged within an L2TP tunnel can be categorized as either control packets or data packets. L2TP provides reliability features for the control packets, but no reliability for data packets. If reliability is required for data packets, it must be provided by protocols running within each session of the L2TP tunnel.

Figure 2.25 illustrates the equipment required to provide multiple tunnels from one location to another via the Internet. In the lower-left corner, a modem bank terminates calls from the PSTN and passes them to a network access server (NAS), which is normally combined with an L2TP Access Concentrator (LAC). The L2TP Access Concentrator encapsulates PPP frames with L2TP headers and transmits them over the Internet as UDP packets. Or, as previously mentioned, the LAC can transmit over an ATM, Frame Relay, or X.25 network.

At the destination, the L2TP Network Server (LNS) terminates the PPP session and passes the IP packets to the LAN. Because L2TP software can execute in a PC, the tunnel can extend from a remote user dialing the modem bank through the NAS and LAC to the LNS and destination LAN.

Today, most L2TP deployments are used to support the creation of VPNs via LAN connections over the Internet. Because such use is primarily by businesses, such PPP authentication protocols as CHAP, PAP, and EAP are employed for corporate access authentication. To support such authentication methods, L2TP creates a tunnel between the client and the corporate network. Then, the users' identification is verified, and they can proceed as if they were directly connected to the distant network.

There are two basic types of tunneling: compulsory and voluntary. Under L2TP, compulsory tunneling is ideal for a business environment. This is because the tunnel is created from the LAC via the Internet to the LNS on a distant corporate network, and neither remote client has knowledge of the tunnel nor needs L2TP client software. Instead, each remote client creates a PPP connection to the LAC and is then tunneled to the LNS. Another advantage of compulsory L2TP tunneling is the fact that remote clients need to access the LAC to gain access to the distant corporate network. Thus, network managers can configure a single point, the LAC, to control permissions to include the authentication of remote clients.

The major problem associated with compulsory L2TP tunneling is its difficulty to support mobility away from a remote LAN. Thus, in an L2TP environment, an individual client to LNS tunneling method is required to support mobility. This method of tunneling is referred to as voluntary L2TP tunneling.

L2TP does not provide any encryption. In addition, by itself, it lacks authentication and data integrity methods because it was designed primarily as a mechanism to extend a PPP tunnel. To overcome the previously mentioned security deficiencies, it is common to combine IPSec with L2TP. Using IPSec, the L2TP tunnel can be secured, either from the LAC to LNS under compulsory tunneling or from a remote client to the LNS under voluntary tunneling.

Under L2TP, authentication occurs via PPP at the LAC or the LNS. Authentication can occur using PPP authentication protocols such as CHAP, PAP, or EAP. When the PPP connection process is encrypted by IPSec, any PPP authentication method can be used, with mutual authentication occurring if EAP or CHAPv2 is used.

The type of encryption used is determined during the establishment of the IPSec security association. Available encryption algorithms include the original 56-bit Digital Encryption Standard (DES), 3DES, and certain versions of Advanced Encryption Standard (AES). Data authentication and integrity are accomplished by the use of a hash message authentication code, such as Message Digest 5 (MD5), which is a hash algorithm that generates a 128-bit hash of the authenticated payload or the Secure Hash Algorithm (SHA), which produces a 160-bit hash of the authenticated payload. Thus, the use of IPSec with L2TP can considerably strengthen the tunneling protocol.

L2TP Packet Exchange

The setup of an L2TP connection results in the exchange of a series of control packets between clients and servers to establish tunnels and sessions in each direction. During the setup process, a specific tunnel and session ID is assigned. Through the use of the assigned tunnel and session ID numbers, multiple tunnels can be established on the same path with data packets exchanged using compressed PPP frames as the payload. Because L2TP does not include encryption (as does PPTP), it is often used in combination with IPSec to provide VPN connections from remote users to the corporate LAN.

IPSec [54]

IP Security (IPSec) represents a family of security protocols promulgated as RFCs from the IETF that provides both authentication and encryption over the Internet [55]. Unlike SSL, which provides services at Layer 4 and secures two

54   See the following for a thorough overview of IPSec: http://www.unixwiz.net/techtips/iguide-ipsec.html

55   See the following list for the RFC's pertaining to IPSec:

   A. Security Architecture for Ipsec: http://tools.ietf.org/html/rfc4301

   B. AH: Authentication Header: http://tools.ietf.org/html/rfc4302

   C. Use of HMAC-MD5-96 within ESP and AH: http://tools.ietf.org/html/rfc2403

   D. Use of HMAC-SHA-1-96 within ESP and AH: http://tools.ietf.org/html/rfc2404

   E. HMAC: Keyed-Hashing for Message Authentication: http://tools.ietf.org/html/rfc2104

   F. The ESP DES-CBC Cipher Algorithm With Explicit IV: http://tools.ietf.org/html/rfc2405

   G. ESP: Encapsulating Security Payload: http://tools.ietf.org/html/rfc4303

   H. The Internet IP Security Domain of Interpretation for ISAKMP: http://tools.ietf.org/html/rfc2407

   I. Internet Security Association and Key Management Protocol (ISAKMP):   http://tools.ietf.org/html/rfc2408

   J. The Internet Key Exchange (IKE) Protocol: http://tools.ietf.org/html/rfc4306

   K. The NULL Encryption Algorithm and Its Use With IPsec: http://tools.ietf.org/html/rfc2410

   L. IP Security Document Roadmap: http://tools.ietf.org/html/rfc2411

   M. The OAKLEY Key Determination Protocol: http://tools.ietf.org/html/rfc2412

applications, IPSec operates at Layer 3 and secures everything in the network. Also, unlike SSL, which is typically built into every Web browser, IPSec requires a client installation. IPSec can provide security for both Web and non-Web applications, whereas SSL is primarily used for Web access, but with additional effort can be used to secure such applications as file sharing and e-mail.

The primary use of IPSec is for building VPNs. IPSec secures individual packets flowing between any two computers connected to an IP network. IPSec includes the ability to establish mutual authentication between computers at the beginning of the session and supports the negotiation of encryption keys to be used during the session. In addition to securing data flows between a pair of computers, IPSec can be used to secure communications to routers, firewalls, and other devices that are IPSec compliant.

Operation

IPSec operates at the IP layer (Layer 3) of the Internet Protocol Suite. The operation of IPSec at Layer 3 makes this security protocol more flexible than SSL/TLS and higher-layer protocols. This results from the fact that IPSec can be used for protecting all the higher-level protocols. This enables applications to avoid having to be designed to use IPSec, whereas the use of TLS/SSL or other higher-layer protocols must be incorporated into the design of an application.

IPSec represents a family of security-related protocols. Each protocol was designed to perform different security-related functions. Those protocols and their functions include:

1. ***Authentication Header (AH):*** Provides authentication for IP datagrams as well as protection against replay attacks.

2. ***Encapsulating Security Payload (ESP):*** Provides authentication, data integrity, and confidentiality of packets transmitted. While ESP supports encryption-only and authentication-only modes of operation, note that using encryption without authentication is strongly discouraged because it is insecure.

3. ***Internet Key Exchange (IKE):*** It is an IPSec protocol that is used to set up a Security Association (SA) by handling negotiation of the encryption and authentication keys to be used by IPSec.

Security Association

The IP security architecture uses the concept of a security association as the basis for building security functions into IP. A security association represents the

N. Use of IPsec Transport Mode for Dynamic Routing: http://tools.ietf.org/html/rfc3884

O. Cryptographic Algorithm Implementation Requirements for Encapsulating Security Payload (ESP) and Authentication Header (AH):   http://tools.ietf.org/html/rfc4835

P. Securing L2TP Using IPSEC: http://tools.ietf.org/html/rfc3193

bundling of algorithms and parameters that are used to encrypt and authenticate a particular flow in one direction. Because data traffic is normal bidirectional traffic, the flows are secured by a pair of security associations. The actual choice of encryption and authentication algorithms can be selected from a predefined list by the IPSec administrator.

IPSec uses a Security Parameter Index (SPI), which points to a location in a Security Association Database (SADB), along with the destination address in a packet header, which together uniquely identify a security association for that packet. A similar procedure is performed for an outgoing packet, where IPSec gathers decryption and verification keys from the security association database.

Authentication Header (AH)

AH operates directly above IP, using IP protocol number of 51. AH is employed to authenticate the origin of data as well as provide for the data integrity of IP datagrams. In addition, it can optionally protect against replay attacks through the use of a sliding window technique and discarding old packets. AH protects the IP payload and all header fields of an IP datagram except for fields that might be altered in routing, such as router fields that are changed when data flows through the device.

Figure 2.26 illustrates where an AH packet resides within an IP datagram and the fields within the header.

The Next Header is an 8-bit field that identifies the type of the next payload after the Authentication Header. The value of this field is chosen from the set of IP Protocol Numbers defined in the most recent "Assigned Numbers" RFC from the Internet Assigned Numbers Authority (IANA). For example, hex 6 is used for TCP, whereas hex 11 designates UDP. The following field, Length, defines the size of the AH packet. The third field, shown padded to zero, represents a "Reserved" field that is currently not used. The fourth field, Security parameters index (SPI), identifies the security parameters, which, in combination with the IP address, identifies the security association (SA). The SA represents a simplex or one-way channel and logical connection that provides a secure data connection between network devices implemented with this packet. The fifth field, Sequence number, represents an increasing number that is used to prevent replay attacks. The sixth field is the Authentication Data field. This field contains the integrity check value (ICV) necessary to authenticate the packet.

Modes of Operation

There are two "modes" of operation that are supported by AH and ESP: tunnel mode and transport mode. Transport mode provides a secure connection between

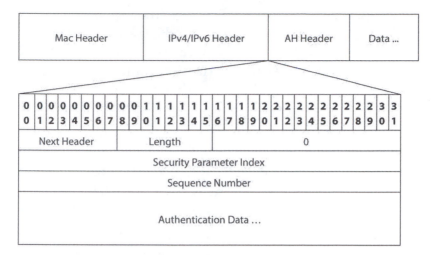

Figure 2.26 - **The AH header provides authentication and data integrity**

two endpoints as it encapsulates IP's payload, while tunnel mode encapsulates the *entire* IP packet to provide a virtual "secure hop" between two gateways. Tunnel mode is used to form a traditional VPN, where the tunnel generally creates a secure "tunneled" path across a packet network, such as the Internet or extranet.

■ *Transport Mode* - Transport mode is used to protect end-to-end communications between two hosts. This protection can be either authentication or encryption or both, but it is not a tunneling protocol. Thus, it has nothing to do with a traditional VPN as it simply represents a secured IP connection. In AH transport mode, the IP packet is modified only slightly to include the new AH header placed between the IP header and the protocol payload, such as TCP, UDP, or another payload. In addition, there is a shuffling of the protocol code that links the various headers together, which allows the original IP packet to be reconstituted at the other end. At the destination, assuming the packet passes the authentication check, the AH header is removed and once again some protocol field values are shuffled, which results in the IP datagram reverting to its original state.

■ *Tunnel Mode* - Tunnel mode provides a more familiar VPN type of functionality, where entire IP packets are encapsulated inside another and delivered to their destination. Similar to transport mode, each packet is sealed with a hash message authentication code (HMAC) that is usually created via the use of Message Digest 5 (MD5) or SHA1 (Secure Hash Algorithm 1). The HMAC is used to both authenticate the sender as well as to prevent the modification of data from occurring as it flows between source and destination. Under AH tunnel mode, the full IP header as well as payload data is encapsulated, which enables source and destination addresses to be different from those of the original packet. This encapsulation permits the packet to flow between two intermediary devices that form the tunnel, such as IPSec-compatible routers. At the destination router, an authentication check is performed, and packets that pass the check have their entire IP and AH readers removed, resulting in the recreation of the original datagram. That datagram is then routed to its original source IP address.

Figure 2.27 illustrates the manner by which an IP datagram is encapsulated within another IP header when AH is used in tunnel mode. Note that the wrapped or new header usually had the destination IP address of a network appliance representing a hardware box. That box is typically a computer with multiple fast processors that can rapidly compute integrity check values and different types of encryption and thus support AH, ESP, and iKey.

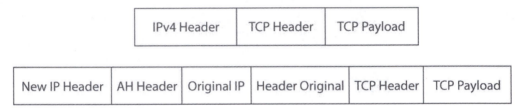

Figure 2.27 - **IPSec in an AH tunnel mode**

Encapsulating Security Payload (ESP)

ESP represents the portion of IPSec that provides origin authentication, data integrity, and confidentiality of packets. ESP also supports encryption-only and authentication-only configurations, but using encryption without authentication is strongly discouraged because it is insecure.

Unlike AH, ESP does not protect the IP packet header. However, in tunnel mode, where the entire original IP packet is encapsulated with a new packet header added, ESP protection is afforded to the whole inner IP packet to include the inner header, while the outer header remains unprotected because it provides the unencrypted address information necessary for routing. ESP operates directly on top of IP, using IP protocol number 50.

Similar to AH, ESP can operate in transport or tunnel mode. In transport mode, the datagram's payload is encrypted and transported via a new IPv4 header, which is essentially the same as the old header but has a few field values shifted while source and destination IP addresses are unchanged. Thus, similar to AH, ESP in transport mode is designed for host-to-host communications. In tunnel mode, ESP is similar to AH, where the encapsulation covers the original datagram, enabling the original IP header, TCP header, and payload to be encrypted. Thus, ESP in tunnel mode would be similar to Figure 2.27, with the AH replaced by an ESP header. Concerning that header, it is much simpler having just two fields: a security parameters index (SPI) and a sequence number. The SPI identifies the security parameters in combination with an IP address, while the sequence number represents a monotonically increasing number that is used to prevent replay attacks. Although replacing the AH with an ESP header shown in Figure 2.27 represents a majority of ESP tunnel mode connections, it should be mentioned a real VPN supporting both encryption and authentication can be constructed by adding authentication data to ESP in tunnel mode. This option is frequently used, with authentication data being added to a tunneled packet after the encryption of the IP header, TCP header, and payload. Another method is to use ESP+AH instead of AH+ESP. The reason ESP is not wrapped inside of AH is that most networks have routers that perform Network Address Translation (NAT), and by using AH+ESP, this tunnel becomes incapable of traversing a NAT device. Thus, ESP+AH is primarily used in tunnel mode to completely encapsulate and encrypt datagrams, adding authentication to protect the data and ensure its integrity as it flows across an untrusted network.

Cryptographic Algorithms

There are several cryptographic algorithms presently defined for use with IPSec. Some of the more popular algorithms include the Hash Message Authentication Code Secure Hash Algorithm (HMAC-SHA1) for data integrity protection and 3DES and AES for confidentiality. A list of algorithms is included in RFC 4835 [56].

L2TP/IPSec

Due to the lack of encryption and authentication in the L2TP protocol, it is often implemented along with IPSec; the result is referred to as L2TP/IPSec, and is standardized as RFC 3193 [57]. The process of setting up an L2TP/IPSec VPN is a three-step process. First, a negotiation of the IPSec Security Association (SA) occurs, typically performed through the use of the Internet Key Exchange (IKE). This exchange occurs over UDP port 500, and commonly uses either a shared password (so-called "pre-shared keys"), public keys, or X.509 certificates on both ends, although other keying methods exist. Next, the establishment of an ESP transport mode occurs with the IP Protocol number for ESP inserted as 50. Once this occurs, a secure channel has been established, but no tunneling is taking place. Thus, the third step involves the negotiation and establishment of an L2TP tunnel between the SA endpoints. The actual negotiation of parameters

---

[56]   See the following for RFC 4835:   http://tools.ietf.org/html/rfc4835

[57]   See the following for RC 3193:   http://tools.ietf.org/html/rfc3193

takes place over the SA's secure channel, within the IPSec encryption, with L2TP using UDP port 1701. This action results in L2TP packets between the endpoints being encapsulated by IPSec. Because the L2TP packet is both wrapped and hidden within the IPSec packet, no information about the content of the packet can be obtained from the encrypted packet. In addition, a side benefit is the fact that it is not necessary to open UDP port 1701 on firewalls between the endpoints, because the inner packets are not acted upon until after IPSec data has been decrypted, which only occurs at the endpoints of the connections.

Authentication Using EAP

An additional benefit from the use of IPSec with L2TP is the ability to enhance authentication via the use of EAP. Created as an extension of PPP, EAP is used when PPP peers negotiate to perform this authentication method during the connection authentication process. Technically, the negotiation of EAP is referred to as an EAP method, resulting in an exchange of messages between the client (referred to as the supplicant) and the authentication server, which is commonly a RADIUS server. Once an EAP method is agreed upon, an exchange of messages will occur between the supplicant and authentication server based on requests for authentication information.

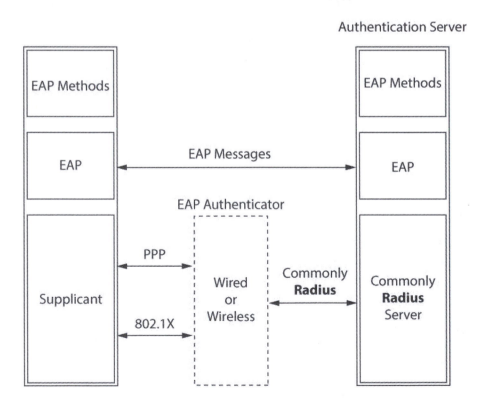

Figure 2.28 - **Selecting the use of EAP**

Figure 2.28 illustrates the selection and operation of EAP. In this example, a client is shown using PPP initially to communicate with an access point or network access server (NAS) to obtain EAP authentication prior to obtaining access to a network. Both wired and wireless devices can operate as the EAP authenticator, with the IEEE 802.1X standard defining how EAP operates when used for authentication by 802 devices, such as wireless access points and wired Ethernet switches. In this example, the NAS is shown communicating with a Remote Authentication Dial-In User Service (RADIUS) authentication server to negotiate the specific EAP method to use, with EAP messages flowing between the client and server.

TCP Wrapper [58]

TCP wrappers represent a host-based networking access control list (ACL) system that can also be considered as a filtering method. Through the use of ACLs, network access to Internet Protocol servers on (UNIX-like) operating systems such as Linux or BSD can be controlled. By filtering on destination or source IP address, one can control access to hosts, subnets, and query replies [59].

The original code was written by Wietse Venema at the Eindhoven University of Technology, The Netherlands, between 1990 and 1995. As of June 1, 2001, the program was released under its own BSD-style license.

SOCKS [60]

SOCKS represents an abbreviation for "sockets," which provides a reference to the Berkeley socket interface used in UNBIX. The protocol was originally developed by David Koblas, a system administrator at MIPS Computer Systems.

The SOCKS protocol is designed to route packets between client-server applications via a proxy server. The protocol operates at Layer 5, the Session Layer of the OSI reference model, between the presentation layer and the transport layer. Clients behind a firewall have to connect to a SOCKS proxy server to access external services provided by the server. The proxy server controls the ability of the client to access the external server in the client-server access attempt. If the client is approved by the proxy server, the latter will then pass the request on to the destination server. SOCKS is bidirectional; thus, it can also be used in the opposite way, allowing the clients outside the firewall to connect to servers inside the firewall.

---

58   See the following for a collection of work by Wietse Venema, including the original paper on TCP Wrappers, presented at The 3rd UNIX Security Symposium in Baltimore, September 1992: ftp://ftp.porcupine.org/pub/security/index.html

59   See the following for an overview of TCP Wrappers functionality and configuration: http://www.freebsd.org/doc/handbook/tcpwrappers.html

60   See the following for the SOCKS Protocol Version 5 RFC: http://bit.ly/19yERRq

Currently, the latest version of SOCKS is V.5. Under V.5, SOCKS supports several authentication methods to include EAP, one-time passwords, MD5-challenge, and token cards. Through additions to SOCKS V.5, several vendors now offer modules that work with Windows, intercepting WinSock communications requests issued by application programs and processing those requests based on a previous set of configurations. This enables network managers to specify the use of different types of authentication and encryption for different applications or the use of fixed methods.

Comparing SOCKS and HTTP Proxies

SOCKS employs a handshake protocol to inform the proxy software about the connection that a client initiated. The SOCKS protocol supports any form of TCP or UDP socket connection. In comparison, an HTTP proxy will analyze HTTP headers to determine the address of the destination server, which restricts its support to HTTP traffic.

VPN Technical Considerations
Topology supported
Authentication support
Encryption supported
Scalability
Management
VPN client software
Operating system and browser support
Performance

Table 2.4 - **Technical features to consider when selecting a VPN**

VPN Selection

The selection of an appropriate VPN can include a variety of factors ranging from technical issues to cost, with the latter including personnel and maintenance. *Table 2.4* lists eight technical features readers should examine when considering the selection of a VPN.

Topology Supported

Many organizations that need to interconnect sites via a site-to-site topology will opt for a VPN that supports compulsory tunneling. In comparison, the need to support mobile workers in a secure environment will result in a requirement for voluntary tunneling. Fortunately, most, but not all VPN methods support both; however, the personnel cost associated with voluntary tunneling will increase as the number of remote users increases.

Authentication Supported

There are numerous authentication methods supported by different types of VPNs. Those methods can range from the simple use of passwords to digital certificates and two-factor authentication employing key fobs with numeric displays that change the digits periodically. While the latter two methods, for example, are considerably more viable than a simple password, the security architect needs to consider the cost of certificates and key fobs as well as maintenance issues.

Encryption Supported

Some VPNs by themselves do not perform encryption, which results in the ability of a third party to easily observe the contents of tunneled packets. If the organization requires encryption, then the security architect will need to consider either the use of a VPN protocol that natively supports encryption or a protocol that can be added to a VPN to provide encryption, such as adding IPSec to L2TP.

Scalability

As organizations add staff at different locations, the need for a VPN that provides scalability assumes importance. Thus, most organizations need to consider the scalability of different types of VPNs under consideration.

Management

The ease of configuration as well as the ability to generate reports are two key areas that the security architect should examine. In addition, the type of reports provided by a VPN management system can enhance the ability of the security architect to denote potential bottlenecks and take action before users complain about a sluggish network.

VPN Client Software

Certain types of VPNs, such as L2TP used in compulsory tunneling, do not require any additional client software. In addition to obvious cost saving, this also simplifies the configuration of the VPN in a site-to-site environment. Thus, the security architect needs to consider the role of client software when selecting a VPN.

Operating System and Browser Support

Often easily overlooked, both operating system and browser support are important criteria for the selection of a VPN. While there are many VPNs that support Windows, this is a generic term and does not mean that support for a specific version of Windows is available. Similarly, if an organization has a large base of Firefox users or uses Opera or another browser, the security architect needs to carefully check the support of the VPN for the type and versions of the browsers used or anticipated to be used.

Performance

As features are added to a VPN, additional processing can be expected. While the additional processing may not be noticeable on a new computer, users with

2

Communications
& Network Security

legacy platforms may receive sluggish responses. Thus, a benchmark on various types of computers may provide important information concerning the ability of VPNs to appropriately operate on different hardware platforms used by the organization.

Endpoint Security

One of the more modern security problems security architects face is controlling the termination of endpoint locations within a network. In a modern computer, the floppy drive has been replaced by a variety of USB and sometimes FireWire ports. Thus, instead of having to contend with deactivating floppy drives with limited storage, security architects now have to consider disabling USB ports as well as preventing Zipped files being transferred via e-mail. Concerning USB ports, it becomes possible for an employee to make off with a significant amount of corporate data at an insignificant cost. In fact, because most smart phones include an SD or micro SD slot, even an employee who wants to set up his computer–phone relationship at work can now copy documents onto the memory card in his or her smart phone. Along with the previously mentioned threats, the availability of WinZip and similar programs makes it very easy for an employee to "zip" a number of documents and mail the zipped file as an attachment addressed to themselves at an alternate e-mail address or to the address of a third party. Due to these potential security breaches, many organizations use software to block the use of USB ports and automatically drop zip files from outbound e-mail.

Encryption

One of the chief means of enhancing endpoint security is encrypting traffic. Depending on the manner in which data is being transmitted from an endpoint, encryption may be built into the transmission method, such as with the use of several types of VPNs, or encryption can be added to enhance security. With the latter, the sender can select an encryption method from a variety of sources as long as the recipient uses the same encryption method and, when required, has the same key so that decryption occurs correctly. Encryption sources vary widely, from the addition of hardware-based datacryptors that can be used with both dial-up and dedicated circuits to various software add-ons, such as Pretty Good Privacy (PGP). PGP encryption uses public-key cryptography and includes a system that binds the public keys to a user name or an e-mail address, which results in both encryption and authentication being performed.

Network Security Design Considerations

This section focuses on a series of network security design considerations, including cross-domain attacks and methods to minimize such attacks, device and data flow interoperability, audits, monitoring, and remote network access.

Interoperability and Associated Risks

Interoperability in a networking environment references the ability of diverse systems to work together or interoperate. In a modern network environment where routers, firewalls, virus checkers, and other devices are employed, it becomes a relatively easy process for the security architect to overlook one or more coding or configuration settings. In doing so, the end result may be that a hole is opened in the network defense, or a legitimate opening necessary for an approved application to work properly may be closed. Thus, the use of security audits and monitoring can be an effective tool to determine risks associated with the configurations and parameter settings of various devices that need to interoperate with one another.

Cross-Domain Risks and Solutions

There are a variety of cross-domain attacks that can adversely affect the end user and his or her organization. Some of the more popular attack methods include cross-site request forgery, cross-site scripting, DNS rebinding, time of check/time of use, and wildcarding attack methods. This section focuses on each attack method as well as potential solutions to mitigate their effect.

A Cross-Site Request Forgery (CSRF) represents an attack method developed to fool a victim into loading a Web page that contains a malicious request. The page to be loaded is malicious because it inherits the identity and privileges of the victim, enabling the attacker to assume the victim's identity. Examples of malicious actions can include changing the victim's e-mail address, home page address, or even purchasing something. Most popular virus-checking software recognizes the potential of a CSRF attack and warns users before they arrive at a site where CSRF software is known to exist[61].

A second type of popular Web-based attack is referred to as a cross-site scripting attack. This type of attack exploits the trust most users place in accessing a Web-site. Cross-site scripting attacks commonly occur in two basic forms, such as when an attacker embeds a script in data pushed to the user as a result of a GET or POST request (first order) or when the script is retained in long-term

---

61   See the following for the Dynamic Cross-Site Request Forgery: A Per-request Approach to Session Riding paper by Shawn Moyer and Nathan Hamiel, presented at Defcon 17:   http://voices. washingtonpost.com/securityfix/Moyer-Hamiel-DC17-Dynamic-CSRF.pdf

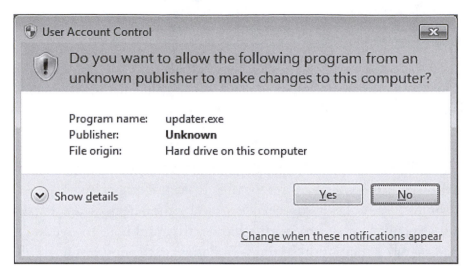

Figure 2.29 - **User Account Control dialog in Windows 7 when the user attempts to load unsigned code**

storage before being activated (second order). Similar to CSRF prevention, most modern comprehensive virus-checking software provides protection against cross-scripting attacks. In addition, under Windows Vista, Windows 7, Windows 8, Windows Server 2008, and Windows Server 2012 the operating system will prompt users to allow or deny the operation of programs, providing a mechanism to disable the program through the use of User Account Control (UAC). *Figure 2.29* shows the User Account Control dialog in Windows 7 when the user attempts to load unsigned code. *Figure 2.30* shows the User Account Control dialog in Windows 7 when the user attempts to load signed code.

Figure 2.30 - **User Account Control dialog in Windows 7 when the user attempts to load signed code**

DNS rebinding represents an attack on the insecure binding between DNS host names and network addresses. During a DNS rebinding attack, the attacker manipulates DNS records for a Web site he or she controls. The attack can at times use the host name at a server under his or her control, while at other times the host name can be used to point to a victim server or device, such as a router. Through a DNS rebinding attack, the attacker is able to bypass a same-origin-policy restriction because both the victim and attacker have the same host name, albeit at different points in time. This attack technique can also result in the circumvention of a firewall, as a victim server behind an organizational firewall is normally reachable by a browser operated by an employee of the organization. One solution to nullify the potential effect of DNS rebinding is to strengthen the client's binding between a DNS host name and the network address. In addition, the use of HTTPS and verification of the host header on inbound requests can also be used to minimize the threat of DNS rebinding.

Time of Check/Time of Use (TOC/TOU) represents two types of attacks that are based on changes in principals or permissions. Such attacks occur in requests where principals or permissions have changed between the time of permission checking and the time of actual use of the permissions. Most such attacks result from the failure of server software to remove cached permissions after a reconfiguration that changes client permissions. Over the years, both SUN Microsystems and Microsoft have issued several patches to their server software designed to block such attacks. However, an organization either has to enable automatic software updates or manually apply such software patches to close such security-related holes.

Another attack that warrants attention is the wildcarding attack. This attack occurs when access controls are set in error and open a security hole for unintended access. For example, if access control rules are set to *.edu, any .edu site can access the user's resources. Wildcard mistakes can occur due to typographical errors, when organizations merge, when contractors or employees make simple mistakes, and for numerous other reasons. As access-control rules become more complex, the likelihood of configuration errors increases. Thus, the use of configuration checking of software products may be justified for some organizations that operate a variety of communications equipment that perform access control.

Audits and Assessments

It is important to understand that routers, firewalls, and virus checkers as well as IDS and intrusion protection systems can together have hundreds to thousands of possible settings. While it is possible to perform a manual audit of equipment used within a small organization, as the organization expands and its network complexity increases, it becomes much harder to perform auditing without the use of software. Today, several vendors provide software designed to do the following: perform auditing as well as reporting, enable the changing of equipment configurations from a central management platform, employ a third-party database management system to track both hardware and software, etc. Such software typically includes a Simple Network Management Protocol (SNMP) and Remote MONitoring (RMON) capability, enabling the software to collect information on up to tens of thousands of assets, security, and configuration settings into a configuration database for reporting, auditing, baselining, and change tracking.

Monitoring

An SNMP-compatible system consists of one or more central monitoring systems and distributed agents operating on various types of hardware and even embedded into software. Today, most hardware and software products include a built-in RMON-compatible agent, allowing a central site SNMP system to monitor network activity, change device permissions and configurations as well as to gather statistics. For example, in a Cisco router environment, each router port can be enabled for SNMP monitoring, providing the network manager with detailed information about the use of router ports as well as denoting potential or actual bottlenecks. Through the use of SNMP systems available from many vendors, software overlaying the SNMP capability can even issue projections as to when, for example, a router port can be expected to operate at 75% of utilization or drop a certain percentage of packets.

Operating Environment

In an operational environment, it is quite common for security architects to create a "protected bench network" of equipment prior to its actual use. Here, the term *protected bench network* references a network of devices to be used that are not connected to an operational network. This then provides the security architect with the ability to perform penetration testing to uncover any inadvertent holes in the security architecture without compromising actual live data. Here, the term *penetration test* represents a method of evaluating the security of the networkand if desired the computers attached to the network— by simulating different types of attacks and observing the ability of the network and computers to fight those attacks. The penetration test is one of several components that make up a security audit. The other major components include monitoring traffic and certain logs available on both network hardware products and computers.

It has become possible for the security architect to set up both testing and production environments using virtualization technologies[62]. The use of virtualization technology is a very important element in the security architects design for the organizations infrastructure. Virtualization technologies are available from a number of vendors such as VMware, Microsoft, Citrix, and Oracle. Many organizations are moving aggressively to virtualize up and down their infrastructure stacks wherever and whenever possible[63].

According to the *2012 State of the Data Center* report, June 2012, by Information Week, "No technology in recent years has enabled IT to do more in a fixed hardware and data center footprint than server virtualization. When asking respondents what best describes their overall data center strategy, 33% say they seek to virtualize most applications, with an additional 25% standardizing on either discrete (14%) or integrated blade/network/storage (11%) systems running virtualized servers. IT's commitment to VMs as the new standard application platform is readily apparent when looking at the degree of workload virtualization. Half of respondents report that half or more of their production servers will be virtualized by the end of 2013." [64]

There are 3 main areas that the security architect needs to consider regarding security in the virtualized infrastructure that they manage.

1. ***Oversight*** - One of the grey areas that virtualization has created is that of server oversight. Who's ultimately responsible for virtual servers is not always clearly defined. While physical servers are, as a matter of course, under the direct purview of the data center, it's not always as straightforward for virtual servers.

2. ***Maintenance*** - Virtual servers tend to be launched and then their image is archived, and it may or may not be recreated when patches or configuration changes take place. Placing virtualized servers under the same change management controls as physical infrastructure is necessary to ensure uniformity fro configurations and patch management.

3. ***Visibility*** - One of the risks involved with having significant virtualized infrastructure is that those network controls that are used to segment specific applications off due to reasons of

---

62   See the following for the NIST Special Publication 800-125, January 2011, Guide to Security for Full Virtualization Technologies: http://csrc.nist.gov/publications/nistpubs/800-125/SP800-125-final.pdf

63   Christofer Hoff, chief security architect at Juniper, has been exploring the frontiers of computer and network security for a couple of decades now; see the following for his blog: http://www.rationalsurvivability.com/blog/

64   See the following for the full report (Report ID: R5000612):   http://reports.informationweek.com/

compliance and security often are not virtualized. This, of course, can lead to issues with HIPPA and other security regulations and IT Governance compliance regimes.

Christopher Hoff sounded the alarm about the unintended consequences of virtualization and cloud computing in 2008 in a slide (slide # 23) he presented in his deck titled "*The Four Horsemen of the Virtualization Security Apocalypse*" [65] In his deck, Hoff outlined the many and varied potential vulnerabilities of virtualized systems and identified the various attack surfaces and threat avenues they face. " He categorizes seven modes of attack:

1. Guest OS to guest
2. Guest to host or hypervisor
3. Guest OS to self
4. External to host or hypervisor
5. External to guest OS
6. Host or hypervisor to others
7. Hardware to hypervisor

These vulnerabilities are addressed by new virtualized security products operating in three domains: *intra-VM* (within the hypervisor), *inter-VM* (between virtualized hosts) and *guest OS* (running on the hypervisor). Intra-VM or -hypervisor security products address threats 1, 2 and 5. Inter-VM or -hypervisor (sometimes known as edge) products address threats 4, 5 and 6, while guest/client endpoint products primarily address threat 3, but also assist in combatting threats 1, 2 and 5. Threat 7, in which the server hardware itself is compromised and used to attack the baremetal hypervisor or host VMs, is really the domain of hardware-based protection schemes. Perhaps the best known of these are Intel's vPro and Trusted Execution Technology (TXT). " [66]

In the Interagency Report 7904 (Draft), December 2012, *Trusted Geolocation in the Cloud: Proof of Concept Implementation (Draft)*, NIST has moved to address some of the issues discussed above by outlining a use case Proof of Concept that seeks to use Intel Trusted Execution Technology (Intel TXT), which provides a mechanism to enable visibility, trust, and control in the cloud. Intel TXT is a set of enhanced hardware components designed to protect sensitive information from software-based attacks. Intel TXT features include capabilities in the microprocessor, chipset, I/O subsystems, and other platform

---

65   See the following for the full PDF, The Four Horsemen of the Virtualization Security Apocalypse: http://www.packetfilter.com/presentations/FHOTVA-SecTor.pdf

66   See the following for the Next-Generation VM Security, Kurt Marko, InformationWeek Report, June 2012 (ReportID:S5200612):   http://reports.informationweek.com/

components. When coupled with an enabled operating system, hypervisor, and enabled applications, these capabilities provide confidentiality and integrity of data in the face of increasingly hostile environments.

According to the NIST Draft, "the motivation behind this use case is to improve the security of cloud computing and accelerate the adoption of cloud computing technologies by establishing an automated hardware root of trust method for enforcing and monitoring geolocation restrictions for cloud servers. A hardware root of trust is an inherently trusted combination of hardware and firmware that maintains the integrity of the geolocation information and the platform. The hardware root of trust is seeded by the organization, with the host's unique identifier and platform metadata stored in tamperproof hardware. This information is accessed using secure protocols to assert the integrity of the platform and confirm the location of the host"[67].

Intel has also presented their vision of where virtualization, the cloud and security merge, in the white paper, *Intel® Cloud Builders Guide to Cloud Design and Deployment on Intel® Platforms: Power Management & Security within the Open Source Private Cloud with Intel & OpenStack*, September 2011 [68]. In the white paper, Intel seeks to describe the concept of a trusted compute pool (TCP), which is a collection of physical platforms known to be trustworthy, using Intel® Trusted Execution Technology (Intel® TXT) available with Intel® Xeon® processors.

According to Intel, in order to minimize security risks, it is essential to protect and validate the integrity of the infrastructure on an ongoing basis. One approach is to establish a "root of trust" – where each server must have a component that will reliably behave in the expected manner, and contain a minimum set of functions enabling a description of the platform characteristics, and its trustworthiness.

The value of Intel TXT is in the establishment of this root of trust, which provides the necessary underpinnings for reliable evaluation of the computing platform and the platform's level of protection. This root is optimally compact, extremely difficult to defeat or subvert, and allows for flexibility and extensibility to measure platform components during the boot and launch of the environment including BIOS, operating system loader, and virtual machine managers (VMM). Given the current nature of malicious threats prevalent in today's environment

---

67   See the following for NIST draft 7904:   http://csrc.nist.gov/publications/drafts/ir7904/draft_nistir_7904.pdf

68   See the following for the Intel white paper: http://www.intel.com/content/dam/www/public/us/en/documents/guides/cloud-builders-xeon-5500-5600-openstack-power-mgmt-security-guide.pdf

and the stringent security requirements many organizations employ, a system cannot blindly trust its execution environment. The security architect needs to keep up with the most current developments in the area of virtualization security so that they are able to assess the organizations security posture against the latest threats and vulnerabilities at all times.

Remote Access

Before setting up a new application for remote access, the security architect should consider testing it with respect to various network security issues. Such testing can include configuring authentication and encryption methods as well as planning for the establishment of firewall and router configuration changes to enable the application to take effect.

Monitoring

The security architect can monitor both network traffic as well as logs maintained by communications devices and computers to validate the architectural design of the network as well as to ensure that any potential holes that could present a security risk are closed. For example, most modern computer operating systems, including Microsoft Windows, SUN's Solaris, and various versions of Linux, support audit event logging, which provides a variety of valuable information. In the area of network equipment, routers, firewalls, virus checkers, IDS, and intrusion protection systems have a similar logging capability. In addition, such devices can be programmed to generate alerts upon the occurrence of predefined conditions.

Design Validation

When designing or modifying a network, it is extremely important to ensure that the design will work as expected. The process used to verify that the network will operate correctly is referred to as design validation. In a security environment, there are several methods that can be employed to ensure that the network design will perform correctly. Those methods include penetration testing, vulnerability assessments, and network monitoring.

Penetration Testing

Penetration testing is a critical method used to validate the security associated with a network. This type of testing literally can involve throwing the preverbal kitchen sink at a network, trying every known type of malicious software in an attempt to break into a system. Because most security architects do not have the resources to assemble a collection of such software, third-party products are commonly used. Such products perform an analysis of the network, including checking for the latest software releases designed to plug security holes as well as examining router, firewall, and even DNS configurations. Any security issues are reported usually with an assessment of the criticality of each issue.

Vulnerability Assessment

Penetration testing can be considered as the predecessor to a vulnerability assessment. That is, until the security architect determines what weaknesses exist in the network, it will not be possible to determine the vulnerability due to those weaknesses. For example, penetration testing could result in a report showing that a firewall was misconfigured, allowing all employees instead of just engineers to access the Internet at lunch time and that a server operating system does not have a patch to negate a well-known vulnerability. Here, the second vulnerability would be more critical to fix for most organizations, and they would prioritize their efforts by placing the server patch at the top of their list of fixes.

Monitoring and Network Attacks

Because nothing is static in the world of communications, security architects need to continuously monitor network traffic. Doing so may provide the opportunity to recognize that the network is being scanned for open ports, a hacker is attempting to run a password checker against a server, or some other security-related issue. Sometimes, a reconfiguration of a firewall to block a hacker from further attacks may suffice, while the apparent recognition of a new type of attack may require the security architect to contact a security organization for assistance.

Risk-Based Architecture

In concluding the examination of communications and network security, the next section will discuss the network as an enterprise where data flows on an end-to-end basis. In attempting to minimize network attacks, the security architect needs to minimize the risk of an attack.

The security architect can minimize the risk of an attack by identifying risk elements, risk metrics, and network controls and assessing the vulnerability level of the network. In addition, the security architect needs to verify that equipment such as routers and firewalls are correctly configured and both clients and servers are operating with the latest patches. By performing these functions as well as staying abreast of the latest security vulnerabilities and corrections, the security architect can develop and maintain a network architecture that minimizes threats to the enterprise.

Secure Sourcing Strategy

According to Gartner, the definition of IT Outsourcing is:

> "The use of external service providers to effectively deliver IT-enabled business process, application service and infrastructure solutions for business outcomes.
>
> Outsourcing, which also includes utility services, software as a service and cloud-enabled outsourcing, helps clients to develop the right sourcing strategies and vision, select the right IT service providers, structure the best possible contracts, and govern deals for sustainable win-win relationships with external providers.
>
> Outsourcing can enable enterprises to reduce costs, accelerate time to market, and take advantage of external expertise, assets and/or intellectual property." [69]
>
> There is also the concept of rightsourcing, which is selecting the best way to procure a service and deciding whether an organization is best served by performing a business requirement in-house (insourcing) or contracting it out to a third-part service provider (outsourcing). Rightsourcing literally means "choosing the correct source."

The security architect needs to be concerned with all aspects of the security posture of the organization. The need to identify risks and threats is as important as the need to identify solutions to mitigate them, as well as to improve the overall security architecture whenever possible. One area that is sometimes overlooked by the security architect is the need to know who they are doing business with, or more correctly, who the organization is doing business with. Given the continued drive towards virtualized computing environments, as well as the continued focus on the cloud that many organizations have, it becomes harder and harder for the security architect and the organizations that they represent to truly know who is on the other end of the service, or connection, that they are negotiating for.

Outsourcing strategies are rarely the same from one company to the next, as each organization has different needs to address through rightsourcing. The security architect needs to be able to ask a series of questions that will allow them to gain the insight necessary to pursue the right sourcing strategy for the organization. The following questions should be the starting point for the security architect's discussion:

---

69   See the following for the Gartner IT Glossary: http://www.gartner.com/it-glossary/it-outsourcing/

1. Can the function be performed according to a set of rules and procedures?
2. Is the application slated to be retired or moved to a SaaS provider?
3. Is the application or infrastructure unstable?
4. Is there a documented history for the change control and change management for the application or infrastructure?
5. Does the organization have strong vendor management skills?

These questions will allow the security architect to begin to develop an accurate picture of the pros and cons involved in a potential outsourcing of the application, service, or infrastructure in question, versus keeping it in house. In addition, making sure that an outsourcing strategy is designed to address these key issues is also important to the success of the solution, and the smooth integration into the security architecture:

- The organizational culture.
- Making sure to use a competitive bid process (not using a sole sourcing solution).
- Being wary of a focus on cost as the primary factor driving the decision to award a contract.
- Too much information disclosed to a potential vendor vis-à-vis performance metrics and IT costs.
- The financial health of the potential outsource partner (how does the organization operationalize risk, and take into account the negative impact that poor financial health may have on an outsourced service or application with regards to availability and disaster recovery).
- Internal competition from IT for the service dollars that may be outsourced.
- The balance and risks associated with a public vs. a private cloud outsourcing solution.
- What are the public cloud provider's liability limits for the outsourced solution.

If the security architect decides that outsourcing will be the best approach for the organization, then the following issues need to be considered with regards to the outsource partner:

- *Access to confidential data* – How much access will the service provider have to the organization's data?
- *Compliance with regulations* – Where will the organization's data reside, and what are the legal and regulatory issues that have to be addressed based on geolocation of the data?

- *Constant churn and suitability or clearance of service provider staff* – What standards are in place on the service providers side to assure stability and continuity of operations and data security?
- *Lack of a comprehensive security program* – The organization needs to create a "culture of security" and ensure that all users are educated with regards to responsible use and due care for all data that is hosted externally

The security architect will need to use a multiple step approach, as noted below, to ensure that the organization is as prepared as it can be for the outsourcing to occur successfully:

1. Refine the enterprise IT architecture to improve security through:
   a. Data classification and masking
   b. Role classification
   c. Define enterprise security standards
2. Carry out a detailed pre-assessment of each provider and its delivery site that includes these steps:
   a. Review service provider security policies for corporate information and for physical and facility security to ensure that all key risks are covered.
   b. Ensure that network security controls exist and the delivery site is certified, per industry standard security policies, which satisfy internationally recognized security compliance standards, including ISO 27001, BS17799 and others as applicable.
   c. Check that an SAS 70 (or equivalent third party audit) Type I and II assessment has been done for the delivery location [70]. (Now an SSAE 16, see footnote below)

---

[70] Statement on Auditing Standards No.70 (SAS 70) is an internationally recognized auditing standard developed by the American Institute of Certified Public Accountants (AICPA) in 1992. It is used to report on the "processing of transactions by service organizations". A SAS 70 Type I is known as "report on controls placed in operation", while a SAS 70 Type II is known as "report on controls placed in operation" and "tests of operating effectiveness".

To adopt to the globally accepted changes in accounting principles certain amendments were required to be made in SAS 70. This led to the introduction of SSAE 16 by the Auditing Standards Board (ASB) of American Institute of Certified Public Accountants (AICPA). These changes helped in aligning companies with the new international service organization reporting standards – ISAE 3402.

SSAE 16 stands for Statement of Standards for Attestation Engagements No. 16. It is the new attestation and auditing standard. It addresses the engagements conducted by service providers on service organization for reporting design control and operational effectiveness. It requires the companies to report the description of the system along with an Assertion from the Management. These are the two major changes from SAS 70 in this standard. For the reporting period ending on or after 15 June 2011 it has become the new standard for control reporting at service organizations.

Germany
The German standard report in this section is called IDW PS 951. It is similar to SAS 70 Type II. IDW PS 951 is released by Institut der Wirtschaftsprüfer.

    d. Carry out or review a detailed risk assessment for individual delivery locations followed by an onsite audit of each delivery site before "signoff."

3. Set up a regular audit and assessment program. This program should include:

    a. A review and audit of the remote service provider's security policies, which must occur at least once a year.

    b. An on-site review of the specific site and area used to conduct client business, which should be conducted biannually or as project requirements and risks dictate.

4. Build security obligations into the outsourcing contract. Clients should include all security-related controls in the contract. The contract should provide for:

    a. Non-disclosure agreements (NDA).

    b. Personal background checks.

    c. The understanding that service provider staff cannot work for a direct competitor until a specified amount of time elapses.

    d. Security assessments.

    e. Definitions of security breach and related liabilities.

    f. If required, the contract should insist that the service provider take insurance to cover liabilities arising from a security breach.

    g. Contract termination provisions, which a client can invoke as a last resort if a material security breach arises.

    h. Unilateral data portability. The organization must release information on demand and in a specified format and media.

The security architect will also need to ensure that there is a strong focus on IT Governance within the organization to help shape and guide the outsourcing strategy. The current ISO standard originated as AS8015-2005, which was published in January 2005. AS8015-2005, The Australian Standard

United Kingdom

A SAS 70 is similar to the United Kingdom guidance provided by the Audit and Assurance Faculty of the Institute of Chartered Accountants in England and Wales. The technical release is titled AAF 01/06 which supersedes the earlier FRAG 21/94 guidance.

Canada

In Canada, a similar report known as a Section 5970 report may be issued by a service organization auditor. It usually gives two separate audit opinions on the controls in place. Furthermore, it may also give an opinion on the operating effectiveness over a period. These reports tend to be quite long, with descriptions of the controls in place.

India

Similar to the SAS 70 Report in the United States of America, reporting requirements are defined in India's Audit and Assurance Standards 24 "Audit Consideration Relating to Entities Using Service Organizations". The AAS 24 is issued by the Institute of Chartered Accountants of India, and is operative for all audits relating to periods beginning on or after 1 April 2003.

2

Communications & Network Security

for Corporate Governance of Information and Communication Technology was submitted for fast-track ISO adoption, and it was published as ISO/IEC 38500:2008 Corporate Governance of Information Technology in May 2008, largely unchanged[71].

The standard for the Governance of IT provides a framework through which "Directors", those to whom they turn to for advice or those to whom they delegate responsibilities for managing the operations of the organization, such as Senior managers, technical specialists, vendors and service providers, can understand their obligations and work more effectively to maximize the return and minimize the cost of using ICT in their organizations.

There are many other standards, by country, which may also be of interest to the security architect, such as King I, II, and III from South Africa. The revised Code of and Report on Governance Principles for South Africa (King III) were released on 1 September 2009, with an effective date of 1 March 2010. The Chapters of King III are[72]:

- Ethical leadership and corporate citizenship
- Boards and directors
- Audit committees
- The governance of risk
- The governance of information technology
- Compliance with laws, rules , codes and standards
- Internal audit
- Governing stakeholder relationships
- Integrated reporting and disclosure

The Organization for Economic Co-operation and Development (OECD) has published the OECD Principles of Corporate Governance, 2004[73]. Following on these, corporate governance has been adopted as one of twelve core best-practice standards by the international financial community. The World Bank is the assessor for the application of the OECD Principles of Corporate Governance. Its assessments are part of the World Bank and International Monetary Fund (IMF) program on Reports on the Observance of Standards and Codes (ROSC).

---

71   See the following for the ISO/IEC 38500:2008 Corporate Governance of Information Technology Standard: http://www.iso.org/iso/catalogue_detail?csnumber=51639

72   See the following for overview information and the full text of King III: https://www.saica.co.za/TechnicalInformation/LegalandGovernance/King/tabid/626/language/en-ZA/Default.aspx

73   See the following for the OECD principles: http://www.oecd.org/corporate/corporateaffairs/corporategovernanceprinciples/31557724.pdf

The goal of the ROSC initiative is to identify weaknesses that may contribute to a country's economic and financial vulnerability. Each Corporate Governance ROSC assessment benchmarks a country's legal and regulatory framework, practices and compliance of listed firms, and enforcement capacity vis-à-vis the OECD Principles.

The assessments are standardized and systematic, and include policy recommendations and a model country action plan. In response, many countries have initiated legal, regulatory, and institutional corporate governance reforms.

The assessments focus on the corporate governance of companies listed on stock exchanges. At the request of policymakers, the World Bank can also carry-out special policy reviews that focus on specific sectors, in particular for banks and state-owned enterprises. Assessments can be updated to measure progress over time.

By the end of October 2010, 75 assessments had been completed in 59 countries around the world[74].

It is important for the security architect to become familiar with the appropriate Standards and specific compliance requirements, based on geography and business vertical or mission, that may impact the organization and its drive to securely outsource.

2

Communications
& Network Security

---

[74]   See the following web site for a list of participating countries, and their ROSC reports: http://www.worldbank.org/ifa/rosc_cg.html

Summary

The Communications and Network Security domain requires the security architect to bring together all of the knowledge and theory from all other domains and examine the practical implications of networking designs from the ground up. The security architect needs to be able to apply all of the theoretical insights and knowledge gained from the BIA and the Risk Assessments done for the organization in order to be able to create secure designs that will both address and support the strategic goals of the organization while also mitigating as many risks as possible. At the same time, this design needs to also be functional for the end users, allowing them to be able to be productive and carry out their required activities on a daily basis with a minimal impact on performance and productivity. This domain, more than any other, highlights the need to use all of the knowledge that the security architect has access to from all other domains, as well as understanding where the potential gaps may be in their knowledge base with regards to certain areas, and seeking out the appropriate third party, or industry specific actor as required in order to create a secure and viable security architecture.

Review Questions

1. Compare the frequency range of a person's voice to the size of the passband in a voice communications channel obtained over the telephone. Which of the following accounts for the difference between the two?

    A. The telephone company uses Gaussian filters to remove frequencies below 300 Hz and above 3300 Hz because the primary information of a voice conversation occurs in the passband.

    B. The telephone company uses low-pass and high-pass filters to remove frequencies below 300 Hz and above 3300 Hz because the primary information of a voice conversation occurs in the passband.

    C. The telephone company uses packet filters to remove frequencies below 500 Hz and above 4400 Hz because the primary information of a voice conversation occurs in the passband.

    D. The telephone company uses low-pass and high-pass filters to remove frequencies below 500 Hz and above 4400 Hz because the primary information of a voice conversation occurs in the passband.

2. What is the data rate of a PCM-encoded voice conversation?

    A. 128 kbps

    B. 64 kbps

    C. 256 kbps

    D. 512 kbps

3. How many digitized voice channels can be transported on a T1 line?

    A. Up to 48

    B. Up to 12

    C. Up to 60

    D. Up to 24

4. How many T1 lines can be transported on a T3 circuit?

    A. 12

    B. 18

    C. 24

    D. 36

5. The three advantages accruing from the use of a packet network in comparison to the use of the switched telephone network are a potential lower cost of use, a lower error rate as packet network nodes perform error checking and correction, and

   A. the ability of packet networks to automatically reserve resources.
   B. the greater security of packet networks.
   C. the ability of packet networks to automatically reroute data calls.
   D. packet networks establish a direct link between sender and receiver.

6. Five VoIP architecture concerns include

   A. the end-to-end delay associated with packets carrying digitized voice, jitter, the method of voice digitization used, the packet loss rate, and security.
   B. the end-to-end delay associated with packets carrying digitized voice, jitter, attenuation, the packet loss rate, and security.
   C. the end-to-end delay associated with packets carrying digitized voice, jitter, the amount of fiber in the network, the packet loss rate, and security.
   D. the end-to-end delay associated with packets carrying digitized voice, jitter, the method of voice digitization used, attenuation, and security.

7. What is the major difference between encrypting analog and digitized voice conversations?

   A. Analog voice is encrypted by shifting portions of frequency, making the conversation unintelligible.
   B. Digitized voice is generated by the matrix addition of a fixed key to each digitized bit of the voice conversation.
   C. Analog voice is encrypted by shifting portions of amplitude to make the conversation unintelligible.
   D. Digitized voice is encrypted by the modulo-2 addition of a fixed key to each digitized bit of the voice conversation.

8. In communications, what is the purpose of authentication?

   A. Establishing a link between parties in a conversation or transaction.
   B. Ensuring that data received has not been altered.
   C. Securing wireless transmission.
   D. Verifying the other party in a conversation or transaction.

9. What is the purpose of integrity?

   A. Integrity is a process that ensures data received has not been altered.
   B. Integrity is a process that ensures a person stands by his beliefs.

C. Integrity is a process that ensures that the amount of data sent equals the amount of data received.

D. Integrity is a process that ensures data received has been encrypted.

10. The key purpose of the Session Initiation Protocol (SIP) is to

A. define the protocol required to establish and tear down communications, including voice and video calls flowing over a packet network.

B. define the signaling required to establish and tear down communications, including voice and video calls flowing over a PSTN.

C. define the protocol required to establish and tear down communications, including voice and video calls flowing over a circuit-switched network.

D. define the signaling required to establish and tear down communications, including voice and video calls flowing over a packet network.

11. Briefly describe the H.323 protocol.

A. It represents an umbrella recommendation from the ITU that covers a variety of standards for audio, video, and data communications across circuit-switched networks.

B. It provides port-based authentication, requiring a wireless device to be authenticated prior to its gaining access to a LAN and its resources.

C. It defines the protocol required to establish and tear down communications, including voice and video calls flowing over a packet network.

D. It represents an umbrella recommendation from the ITU that covers a variety of standards for audio, video, and data communications across packet-based networks and, more specifically, IP-based networks.

12. What is the difference between RTP and RTCP?

A. RTP defines a standardized port for delivering audio and video over the Internet, while the RTCP provides out-of-band control information for an RTP port.

B. RTP defines the protocol required to establish and tear down communications, including voice and video calls flowing over a packet network, while the RTCP provides out-of-band control information for an RTP port.

C. RTP defines a standardized packet format for delivering audio and video over the Internet, while the RTCP provides out-of-band control information for an RTP flow.

D. RTP defines a standardized port for delivering audio and video over the Internet, while the RTCP defines the protocol required to establish and tear down communications, including voice and video calls flowing over a packet network.

2

Communications
& Network Security

233

13. List the components defined by the H.323 standard.

    A. Terminal, gateway, gatekeeper, multipoint control unit (MCU), multipoint controller, multipoint processor, and H.323 proxy

    B. Path, gateway, gatekeeper, multipoint control unit (MCU), multipoint controller, multipoint processor, and H.323 proxy

    C. Terminal, gateway, gatekeeper, multipoint control unit (MCU), multipoint transmitter, multipoint receiver, and H.323 proxy

    D. Protocol, terminal, gatekeeper, multipoint control unit (MCU), multipoint controller, multipoint processor, and H.323 proxy

14. What are some of the major functions performed by a security modem?

    A. Allows remote access to occur from trusted locations, may encrypt data, and may support Caller ID to verify the calling telephone number.

    B. Allows remote access to occur from any location, may encrypt data, and may support Caller ID to verify the calling telephone number.

    C. Allows remote access to occur from a mobile location, may encrypt data, and may support Caller ID to verify the calling telephone number.

    D. Allows remote access to occur from trusted locations, may encrypt data, and may identify the calling telephone number.

15. The major difference between a router and firewall lies in three areas:

    A. The transfer of packets based on routing tables, the degree of packet inspection, and ensuring that the header data is correct.

    B. The transfer of packets based on absolute addresses, the degree of packet inspection, and acting as an intermediate device by hiding the address of clients from users on the Internet.

    C. The transfer of packets based on routing tables, the degree of packet inspection, and acting as an intermediate device by hiding the address of clients from users on the Internet.

    D. The transfer of packets based on routing tables, the degree of packet inspection, and creating a DMZ behind Internet-facing applications.

16. What is the purpose of an intrusion detection system (IDS)?

    A. To hide the address of clients from users on the Internet.

    B. To detect unwanted attempts to access, manipulate, and even disable networking hardware and computers connected to a network.

    C. To detect and respond to predefined events.

    D. To prevent unauthorized access to controlled areas within a site or a building.

17. What are the two methods that can be used for wireless LAN communications?

    A. Peer-to-peer and infrastructure

    B. Peer-to-peer and cloud

    C. Cloud and infrastructure

    D. Peer-to-peer and remote

18. What is the benefit of WPA over WEP for enhancing wireless LAN security?

    A. WPA permits the equivalent of wired network privacy and includes the use of TKIP to enhance data encryption.

    B. WPA implements a large portion of the IEEE 802.11i and includes the use of TKIP to enhance data encryption.

    C. WPA implements a large portion of the IEEE 802.11i and includes the use of IKE to enhance data encryption.

    D. WPA implements IEEE 802.11a and g and includes the use of IKE to enhance data encryption.

19. What is the purpose of the IEEE 802.1X standard?

    A. To provide port-based authentication.

    B. To provide port-based authorization.

    C. To detect and respond to predefined events.

    D. To secure wireless transmission.

2

Communications & Network Security

Domain 3

Cryptography

THE CRYPTOGRAPHY DOMAIN requires security architects to understand cryptographic methodologies and the use of cryptography to protect an organization's data storage and communications from compromise or misuse. This includes awareness of the threats to an organization's cryptographic infrastructure. The security architect must understand the importance of choosing, implementing, and monitoring cryptographic products and adoption of corporate cryptographic standards and policy. This may include oversight of digital signatures and PKI implementations and a secure manner of addressing the issues and risks associated with management of cryptographic keys.

TOPICS

- Identify Requirements (e.g., confidentiality integrity, non-repudiation)
- Determine Usage (i.e.. in transit, at rest)
- Identify Cryptographic Design Considerations and Constraints
  - Vetting of proprietary cryptography
  - Computational overhead
  - Useful life
  - Design testable cryptographic system
- Define Key Management Lifecycle (e.g., creation, distribution, escrow, recovery)
- Design integrated cryptographic solutions (e.g., Public Key Infrastructure (PKI), API selection, identity system integration)

OBJECTIVES

Key areas of knowledge include:

- The application and use of cryptographic solutions
  - Interoperability of devices
  - Strength of cryptographic algorithms
- Cryptographic methodologies and methods
- Addressing key management issues
- Public Key Infrastructure
- Application-level encryption
- Design validation
- Defining cryptanalysis methods and threats
- Cryptanalytic attacks

3

Cryptography

Cryptographic Principles

Cryptography provides the bedrock for a multitude of security controls. The wide variety of applications where cryptography can be applied offers plenty of opportunity for security controls that provide an overall benefit. Its wide range of applications and uses also means there is more chance for a security control to be the weakest link in a chain. If cryptography is to be used effectively, the methodology and principles behind cryptography must be fully understood by the security architect.

Applications of Cryptography

Benefits

While cryptography may not directly benefit the *availability* of information, the encryption of data is the most straightforward means of protecting its *confidentiality*. Hash functions such as MD5, SHA-256, and the new SHA-3 are used for *integrity* to protect against unauthorized modification of data and are cryptography's workhorses[1]. The use of public key certificates and digital signatures are but two examples of cryptography providing a means of *Authentication*. This can include user authentication, data authentication, and data origin authentication—which is verification that a message received from a sender also originated from that sender. By binding a public key to its owner using a Public Key Infrastructure (PKI), a *non-repudiation* service can also be provided[2]. Non-repudiation offers protection from either the sender or the receiver of a message, denying that the message has been sent or received. Non-repudiation can be used to prove to a third party that a particular event took place and can prove to a third party that a particular event did or did not occur.

---

1   NIST announced a public competition in a Federal Register Notice on November 2, 2007 to develop a new cryptographic hash algorithm called SHA-3. The competition was NIST's response to advances made in the cryptanalysis of hash algorithms.

NIST received sixty-four entries from cryptographers around the world by October 31, 2008, and selected fifty-one first-round candidates in December 2008, and fourteen second-round candidates in July 2009. On December 9, 2010, NIST announced five third-round candidates – BLAKE, Grøstl, JH, Keccak and Skein, to enter the final round of the competition.

The winning algorithm, Keccak (pronounced "catch-ack"), was created by Guido Bertoni, Joan Daemen and Gilles Van Assche of STMicroelectronics and Michaël Peeters of NXP Semiconductors. Keccak will now become NIST's SHA-3 hash algorithm.

See the following for full information on the entire 5 year process to pick the new SHA-3 algorithm: http://csrc.nist.gov/groups/ST/hash/sha-3/index.html

See the following for the original Federal Register Notice, November 2, 2007, announcing the NIST competition to develop a new cryptographic hash algorithm: http://csrc.nist.gov/groups/ST/hash/documents/FR_Notice_Nov07.pdf

These benefits form four fundamental goals from which all the major benefits of cryptography are derived:

Confidentiality means the secrecy and privacy of information must be protected from unauthorized disclosure or access. Personal information, intellectual property, diplomatic and military communications, and credit card numbers are a few examples of such data. Protection methods can utilize public-key/private-key pairs (asymmetric encryption) or secret-keys (symmetric encryption).

Integrity is concerned with guaranteeing data is not accidentally or maliciously changed. Integrity also relates to ensuring that the methods used for processing information perform with accuracy and completeness. One-way hash functions, while not necessarily the most effective, are the most common means used to ensure integrity.

Authentication is the broad goal of verifying that data is of undisputed origin and includes verifying the positive identity of users or other entities such as network devices. Passwords, PINs, and tokens can also be used. Digital signatures are used to provide data origin authentication.

Non-repudiation involves preventing denial by one of the entities involved in a communication of having participated in all or part of the communication. It is also used to prove to a third party that some kind of event or action did or did not occur. PKI certificates, where a digital signature binds together a public key with an individual's identity during a valid time period, can be used to provide a measure of cryptographic non-repudiation.

Uses

The need to use cryptography depends in part on the level of criticality of data being protected. While financial transaction data, such as credit card information or personal data and privacy information, could have a strong requirement for confidentiality provided by encryption, inventory data or public reference

---

2   The ISO/IEC 13888-1, -2 and -3 standards provide for a series of non-repudiation services as follows:

- *Non-repudiation of Origin:* This service will verify a signed message's originator and content through a data validity check.
- *Non-repudiation of Delivery:* This service will digitally sign an X.400 proof of delivery message.
- *Non-repudiation of Submission:* This service will digitally sign an X.400 proof of submission message.
- *Non-repudiation of Transport:* This service will provide proof that a delivery authority has delivered the message to the intended recipient.

3

Cryptography

files in a central data store may have low confidentiality needs. The rationale for spending money on encryption controls depends on the data protection required. At the same time, technological improvements are lowering the costs of hardware and software encryption and making the controls provided by encryption ubiquitous. For example, at rest encryption for data stored within portable devices and in flight encryption for remote access VPNs have become common.

Cryptography remains at the heart of many logical information security controls. Cryptography is used in security controls that protect data during transmission over a network (data in flight), data residing in a storage medium (data at rest), data being processed within an application, user authentication, and device authentication [3].

---

3   See the following for the historical documents that establish the United States Government's guidance on Data at Rest encryption:

A. Office of Management and Budget – Memo M-06-16 – "*Protection of Sensitive Agency Information*" http://www.whitehouse.gov/sites/default/files/omb/memoranda/fy2006/m06-16.pdf
B. DoD Policy Memo, July 03, 2007 Encryption of Sensitive Unclassified Data at rest on Mobile Computing Devices and Removable Storage Media: http://www.dod.gov/pubs/foi/privacy/docs/dod_dar_tpm_decree07_03_071.pdf
C. DON CIO – Message DTG 091256Z OCT 07 - "DON Encryption of Unclassified Data at Rest Guidance"

See the following for the NIST definitions of different data states:
I. The first citation comes from the Federal Register / Vol. 74, No. 79 / Monday, April 27, 2009 / Rules and Regulations, page 19008

DEPARTMENT OF HEALTH AND HUMAN SERVICES
45 CFR Parts 160 and 164
Guidance Specifying the Technologies and Methodologies That Render Protected Health Information Unusable, Unreadable, or Indecipherable to Unauthorized Individuals for Purposes of the Breach Notification Requirements Under Section 13402 of Title XIII (Health Information Technology for Economic and Clinical Health Act) of the American Recovery and Reinvestment Act of 2009; Request for Information   Supplementary Information: II. Guidance Specifying the Technologies and Methodologies That Render Protected Health Information Unusable, Unreadable, or Indecipherable to Unauthorized Individuals

http://www.hhs.gov/ocr/privacy/hipaa/understanding/coveredentities/federalregisterbreachrfi.pdf

The second citation comes from the Federal Register / Vol. 74, No. 162 / Monday, August 24, 2009 / Rules and Regulations, page 42742

DEPARTMENT OF HEALTH AND HUMAN SERVICES
45 CFR Parts 160 and 164
RIN 0991–AB56
Breach Notification for Unsecured Protected Health Information   Supplementary Information: II. Guidance Specifying the Technologies and Methodologies That Render Protected Health Information Unusable, Unreadable, or Indecipherable to Unauthorized Individuals

http://www.gpo.gov/fdsys/pkg/FR-2009-08-24/pdf/E9-20169.pdf

Cryptography is not limited to uses in access control and telecommunications security. Business continuity planning lends itself to cryptographic uses for protecting data transferred to a hot site. A recovery site service provider may need to be one of the trusted parties having access to encryption keys for storage data, for instance.

Cryptography can depend on physical security as well. One example is the physical security of the master key in a media encryption system. Storage of the key may leverage physical security by splitting it into key shares (known as split knowledge; see section titled "Key Management"), with portions of the encryption key stored on separate smart cards in different safes, thereby limiting physical access to the master encryption key. To expound on this example further, the same key can reside within a hardware component of a cryptographic system, requiring specialized physical protection of the computing device itself. The US National Institute of Standards and Technology (NIST) FIPS 140-2 defines standards for both hardware and software components of cryptographic modules. The specialized physical protection of cryptographic modules required by FIPS 140-2 may include tamper-proof enclosures and means of destroying or zeroizing keys upon physical opening [4].

In addition, many ISO standards also provide guidance for the security architect in this area. ISO/IEC 18033-2:2006 specifies encryption systems (ciphers) for the purpose of data confidentiality. ISO/IEC 18033-2:2006 specifies the functional interface of such a scheme, and in addition specifies a number of particular schemes that appear to be secure against chosen ciphertext attack. The different schemes offer different trade-offs between security properties and efficiency [5]. ISO/IEC 11770-1:2010 defines a general model of key management that is independent of the use of any particular cryptographic algorithm [6]. ISO/IEC 11770-1:2010 addresses both the automated and manual aspects of key management, including outlines of data elements and sequences of operations that are used to obtain key management services [7]. Examples of the use of key management mechanisms are included in the ISO 11568 series, which specifies the principles for the management of keys used in cryptosystems

---

4   See the following for FIPS PUB 140-2 Security Requirements for Cryptographic Modules: http://csrc.nist.gov/publications/fips/fips140-2/fips1402.pdf

5   See the following for ISO/IEC 18033-2:2006: http://www.iso.org/iso/home/store/catalogue_tc/catalogue_detail.htm?csnumber=37971

6   See the following for ISO/IEC 11770-1:2010: http://www.iso.org/iso/home/store/catalogue_ics/catalogue_detail_ics.htm?ics1=35&ics2=040&ics3=&csnumber=53456

3

Cryptography

implemented within the retail-banking environment [8]. If non-repudiation is required for key management, ISO/IEC 13888 is applicable [9]. The fundamental problem is to establish keying material whose origin, integrity, timeliness and (in the case of secret keys) confidentiality can be guaranteed to both direct and indirect users. Key management includes functions such as the generation, storage, distribution, deletion and archiving of keying material in accordance with a security policy (ISO 7498-2) [10].

The core areas that benefit from cryptography deal with keeping data confidential, maintaining its integrity, guaranteeing authenticity not only of data but of those accessing the data as well as those from whom the data originates, and of ensuring non-repudiation for data originators.

Message Encryption

Secure communication of messages is a traditional use of cryptography. Military communications have employed cryptography since at least the time of the Greco-Persian wars, with techniques such as hiding messages within wax tablets. Commercial messaging systems transmitting across untrusted networks also require encryption for privacy of messages. Corporate e-mail traffic may contain various types of sensitive information including financial data, personal information, intellectual property, or trade secrets. In addition to needing confidentiality for messages, e-mail can require authentication of the message recipient to the message, integrity of the message content, and non-repudiation of the message being sent or received.

---

7   There are several other ISO/IEC 11770 sub standards that the security architect will want to become familiar with in this context:
ISO/IEC 11770-2:2008 Security Techniques – Key Management – Part 2: Mechanisms using symmetric techniques
ISO/IEC 11770-3:2008 Security Techniques – Key Management – Part 3: Mechanisms using asymmetric techniques
ISO/IEC 11770-5:2011 Security Techniques – Key Management – Part 5: Group Key Management

8   See the following for ISO/IEC 11568-1:2005 Banking- Key Management(retail) – Part 1: Principles: http://www.iso.org/iso/home/store/catalogue_tc/catalogue_detail.htm?csnumber=34937

9   See the following for ISO/IEC 13888-1:2009 Security Techniques – Non-repudiation – Part 1: General: http://www.iso.org/iso/home/store/catalogue_ics/catalogue_detail_ics.htm?ics1=35&ics2=040&ics3=&csnumber=50432

There are two other ISO/IEC 13888 sub standards that the security architect will want to become familiar with in this context:
   A. ISO/IEC 13888-2:2010 Security Techniques – Non-repudiation – Part 2: Mechanisms using symmetric techniques
   B. ISO/IEC 13888-3:2009 Security Techniques – Non-repudiation – Part 3: Mechanisms using asymmetric techniques

10   See the following for ISO/IEC 7498-2:1989 Information processing systems – Open Systems Interconnection – Basic Reference Model – Part 2: Security Architecture: http://www.iso.org/iso/home/store/catalogue_tc/catalogue_detail.htm?csnumber=14256

Messaging security standards include:

- *Secure Multi-Purpose Internet Mail Extensions (S/MIME)*: This extension of the MIME standards that specify e-mail formatting and encapsulation adds encryption of message content. S/MIME also uses a hashing algorithm for message integrity, public key certificates for message authentication, and digital signatures to provide non-repudiation of origin[11].

- *Privacy-Enhanced Mail (PEM)*: An early Internet Engineering Task Force (IETF)-proposed standard for securing e-mail using public-key cryptography with trusted distribution of public keys via PKI, PEM was never widely used for securing e-mail[12].

- Only PEM's definition of header field format (PEM format) has found use as a common means of representing digital certificates in ASCII form.

- *Pretty Good Privacy (PGP)*: Originally developed by Phil Zimmermann in 1991, PGP is a cryptosystem utilizing symmetric key, asymmetric key, and message digest algorithms. When applied to securing e-mail, PGP provides message authentication by binding a public key to an e-mail address where the public key is distributed to a community of users who trust each other, commonly known as a web of trust. PGP with e-mail also provides message encryption, uses a hashing algorithm for message integrity, and digital signatures for non-repudiation[13].

Secure IP Communication

TCP/IP is a standard communication protocol for information systems today. Various cryptographic protections are provided for data traveling over IP networks by the IPSec suite of open standards developed by the Internet Engineering Task Force (IETF)[14]. The IPSec set of standard protocols provides cryptographic security services at Layer 3, the Network layer of the OSI model.

IPSec includes two protocols: Authentication Header (AH) and Encapsulating Security Protocol (ESP). The cryptographic benefits provided by them are:

---

11   See the following for information on S/MIME and the current state of the S/MIME working group: http://datatracker.ietf.org/wg/smime/charter/

12   See the following for historical information on PEM: http://www.csee.umbc.edu/~woodcock/cmsc482/proj1/pem.html

13   See the following for an overview of PGP and how it works: http://www.pgpi.org/doc/pgpintro/

14   See the following for information on IPSEC: http://datatracker.ietf.org/wg/ipsec/charter/

See the following for a good overview and detailed descriptions of how IPSEC works and all of the parts that make up IPSEC: http://www.unixwiz.net/techtips/iguide-ipsec.html

3

Cryptography

- **AH:** Authentication Header provides data origin authentication and data integrity but does not provide confidentiality for the IP payload and header that it protects.
- **ESP:** Encapsulating Security Protocol also provides data origin authentication and data integrity, and also offers confidentiality for the IP payload it protects.

IPSec operates in one of two modes:

- *Transport mode*: In transport mode, only the IP payload is protected by the AH or ESP protections. Transport mode is used for end-to-end security between two systems, such as between a client and a server.
- *Tunnel mode*: In tunnel mode, both the IP payload and the header are protected, and a combination of AH and ESP protections can be used. Tunnel mode sets up a virtual tunnel where multiple intermediaries may exist and is used for protecting traffic between hosts and network devices such as gateways or firewalls, routers, and VPN appliances.

Secure TCP/IP communication is not limited to IPSec. Transport Layer Security (TLS) and its predecessor, Secure Sockets Layer (SSL), are additional cryptographic protocols that provide communications security for TCP/IP[15]. TLS/SSL provides confidentiality, integrity, and authentication for securing data traveling over IP networks. Authentication in TLS/SSL is commonly provided when an HTTP server proves to a client such as a browser that the server is authentic, and may also be used for mutual or server-to-server authentication. TLS/SSL is often used to provide secure HTTP (HTTPS), and is also used for securing data communicating over other application level protocols, such as File Transfer Protocol (FTP), Lightweight Directory Access Protocol (LDAP), and Simple Mail Transfer Protocol (SMTP).

Remote Access

Cryptographic controls are used when remote access is necessary. Examples include the need for integrity protection to prevent man-in-the-middle spoofing and hijacking attacks and vendor remote network access to a customer's data center, where the authentication and confidentiality of the network access are important. Likewise, remote access by telecommuting employees commonly uses virtual private networks (VPNs), which provide encryption and user authentication. Often, remote access means crossing boundaries where untrusted networks are present. In such cases, the need for confidentiality increases.

---

15   See the following for the TLS v1.2 RFC: http://tools.ietf.org/html/rfc5246

A VPN provides confidentiality by encrypting IP traffic and offering authentication between VPN endpoints. Because VPNs are often based on IPSec or SSL, the security benefits of the underlying protocols are provided. VPNs are implemented in the following architectures:

- *Remote Access VPN*: A remote access VPN provides security for remote users connecting to a central location via IP.
- *Site-to-Site VPN*: A site-to-site VPN provides communications security for separate locations in an organization that can connect over IP.
- *Extranet VPN*: An extranet or trading partner VPN provides an organization with communications security when one or more separate organizations are connecting to that organization over IP.

Point-to-Point Protocol (PPP) is another means of establishing remote connectivity. PPP, operating at the data link layer of the OSI model, was designed to be used with network layer protocols such as IP or IPX. By default, PPP does not provide any security or rely on any cryptographic controls. However, PPP does include an optional authentication phase and an optional encryption feature, *PPP Encryption Control Protocol (ECP)* [16].

A common protocol for remote access that involves cryptographic controls is Secure Shell (SSH), which operates at the application layer of the OSI model. SSH can be used in a client-server model for remote administration of servers, and in combination with other protocols such as Secure File Transfer Protocol (SFTP) or Secure Copy (SCP). SSH encrypts the data it transfers, and provides authentication using password- or public-key based methods. SSH also uses a keyed hash for integrity protection.

Secure Wireless Communication

Wireless networks are commonly used for enhancing user mobility and extending or even replacing wired IP networks. Their transmission is easily intercepted, so confidentiality is a must. Wireless transmissions can be more susceptible to man-in-the-middle attack than wired communication, so authentication is very important.

The most commonly used family of standards for Wireless Local Area Networks (WLANs) is Institute of Electrical and Electronics Engineers (IEEE) 802.11[17]. 802.11 originally relied on the Wired Equivalent Privacy (WEP)

---

16   See the following for the PPP Encryption Control Protocol RFC 1968:   http://tools.ietf.org/html/rfc1968

17   See the following to download the IEEE 802.11-2012 copy of the standards: http://standards.ieee.org/getieee802/download/802.11-2012.pdf

security method to provide confidentiality and integrity. WEP has been proved insecure due to the way it implements its RC4 stream cipher algorithm; thus, WLANs using WEP are often vulnerable to eavesdropping and unauthorized access.

As a result, IEEE introduced a range of new security features designed to overcome the shortcomings of WEP in the IEEE 802.11i amendment. 802.11i introduces the concept of a Robust Security Network (RSN), an element of the protocol that allows a variety of encryption algorithms and techniques to be used for providing confidentiality and authentication[18]. Prior to the introduction of 802.11i, the Wi-Fi Alliance, a global nonprofit industry association, created a protocol and certification program for wireless network components known as Wi-Fi Protected Access (WPA). WPA, based on a draft of IEEE 802.11i, securely implements the RC4 stream cipher for more effective confidentiality and authentication. The biggest difference between WPA and the draft is that WPA does not require support for the Advanced Encryption Standard (AES) strong encryption algorithm. WPA allows many existing IEEE 802.11 hardware components that cannot support the computationally intensive AES encryption.

At the same time the IEEE 802.11i amendment was ratified, the Wi-Fi Alliance introduced WPA2, its term for interoperable equipment that is capable of supporting IEEE 802.11i requirements. WPA2 certification is based on the mandatory elements of the IEEE 802.11i standard, but there are some differences. WPA2 extends its certification program to include interoperability with a set of common Extensible Authentication Protocol (EAP) methods. For example, WPA2 adds EAP-TLS, which is not a component of the 802.11i standard. WPA2 also excludes support for ad hoc networks, an 802.11i feature that allows peer-to-peer network device communication.

A short-range wireless protocol commonly used by many types of business and consumer devices such as mobile phones, smart phones, personal computer peripherals, cameras, and video game consoles is Bluetooth. The Bluetooth specification was developed, and is managed, by the Bluetooth Special Interest Group, a privately held trade association[19]. By creating wireless Personal Area Networks (PANs), Bluetooth enables ad hoc communication between multiple wireless devices. Bluetooth optionally encrypts, but does not provide integrity protection for the transmitted data. It is possible to easily modify a transmitted

---

18   See the following for NIST Special Publication 800-97 Establishing Wireless Robust Security Networks: A Guide to IEEE 802.11i: http://csrc.nist.gov/publications/nistpubs/800-97/SP800-97.pdf

19   See the following for the Bluetooth Special Interest Group's web site: https://www.bluetooth.org/About/bluetooth_sig.htm

Bluetooth packet without being detected because only a simple cyclic redundancy check (CRC) is appended to each packet, and no message authentication code is used. Another security weakness with Bluetooth involves device pairing, the initial exchange of keying material that occurs when two Bluetooth-enabled devices agree to communicate with one another. In version 2.0 and earlier of the Bluetooth specification, pairing is performed over a nonencrypted channel, allowing a passive eavesdropper to compute the link key used for encryption. Version 2.1 introduced the use of Elliptic Curve Diffie–Hellman (ECDH) public key cryptography, which can be utilized by Bluetooth device developers for protection against a passive eavesdropping attack. The Bluetooth specification defines its own stream cipher called E0. Several weaknesses have been identified in Bluetooth's E0 stream cipher, which is not a Federal Information Processing Standards (FIPS)-approved algorithm and can be considered nonstandard [SP800-121][20][21].

Version 3.0 + High Speed (HS) of the Bluetooth Core Specification was adopted by the Bluetooth SIG on 21 April 2009. The Bluetooth SIG completed the Bluetooth Core Specification version 4.0 and it has been adopted as of 30 June 2010. It includes Classic Bluetooth, Bluetooth high speed and Bluetooth low energy protocols. Bluetooth high speed is based on Wi-Fi, and Classic Bluetooth consists of legacy Bluetooth protocols. General improvements in version 4.0 include the changes necessary to facilitate BLE modes, as well the Generic Attribute Profile (GATT) and Security Manager (SM) services with AES Encryption.

The Security Manager (SM) is responsible for device pairing and key distribution. The Security Manager Protocol (SMP) is defined as how the device's SM communicates with its counterpart on the other device. The SM provides additional cryptographic functions that may be used by other components of the stack.

Other Types of Secure Communication

Secure communication is not limited to IP networks. Plain Old Telephone Service (POTS), including voice as well as data, needs encryption for ensuring confidentiality. Encrypted telephones are no longer the domain of military communications. Portable/wireless telephone headsets that include encrypted

---

20   See the following for an overview of security weaknesses with Bluetooth: http://www.yuuhaw.com/bluesec.pdf

See the following for a detailed explanation of the Correlation Attack on Bluetooth Keystream Generator E0:   http://lasecwww.epfl.ch/pub/lasec/doc/YV04a.pdf

21   See the following for the NIST Special Publication 800-121 Revision 1: Guide to Bluetooth Security: http://csrc.nist.gov/publications/nistpubs/800-121-rev1/sp800-121_rev1.pdf

transmission and reception are available in office supply stores for commercial use. Sensitive data, including personally identifiable information, trade secrets, and intellectual property, are routinely shared over telephone networks with limited protections.

While Storage Area Networks (SANs) utilizing protocols such as FICON and Fibre Channel (FC) are thought to be less exposed and thus need less protection than the common TCP/IP networks, cryptographic controls are still necessary. A service provider hosting multiple clients in a data center may use encryption for privacy of data within a SAN. This can be done using Fibre Channel Security Protocol (FC-SP), a security framework that includes protocols to enhance FC security in several areas, including authentication of Fibre Channel devices, cryptographically secure key exchange, and cryptographically secure communication between FC devices[22].

Depending on the criticality of the data, radio frequency communications of all types can require some measure of protection. Communication satellites, for instance, will require encryption, which may be in the form of hardware modules for securing telemetry, tracking, and control. Radio Frequency Identification (RFID) sensors and tags used for tracking and identification purposes can benefit from short transmission encryption to guarantee that the information they deliver is confidential, authentic, and unchanged.

Identification and Authentication

Cryptography is used for identification as well as user, device, and data origin authentication. An early use of cryptographic identification for distinguishing friendly aircraft was developed during WWII with the Identification, Friend or Foe (IFF) system using coded radar signals to trigger a transponder on the aircraft. Modern military IFF transponders encrypt challenge and response messages, and include the use of key codes to prevent unauthorized use.

Similar to IFF, RFID relies on use of a transponder, or an RFID tag, to identify physical assets such as warehouse inventory when queried with a reader. RFID tags are finding their way into a wide range of applications such as libraries, transportation toll collection, and passports. Use of cryptography with RFID may become a necessity for privacy or to ensure authenticity.

Securely identifying physical items can prevent counterfeiting of bank notes, pharmaceuticals, computer parts, and a host of other products. While use of bar

---

22   See the following for the INCITS xxx-200x T11/Project 1570-D/Rev 1.74 Fibre Channel Security-Protocols (FC-SP) draft: http://www.t10.org/ftp/t11/document.06/06-157v0.pdf

See the following for the T11 FC-SP-2 overview for the Fibre Channel Security Protocols v2 project: http://www.t11.org/t11/stat.nsf/
0704e303a54f2e42852566cf007ac45d/00720b2204288f8e8525713700668728?OpenDocument

codes, holographic labels, and watermarks or signets is common, these methods often involve use of a simple code versus a cryptographic key and algorithm. Newer methods of applying cryptographic means include use of digital certificates, embedded encryption processing chips, and Hardware Security Modules (HSMs) to securely identify components. One such application could involve use of a cryptographic component identification system to protect automotive components from theft, counterfeiting, or manipulation.

Securely identifying persons is necessary for user authentication and for access to information resources and processing systems. Authentication systems based on a user entering a password or a PIN are widely deployed and provide a low-cost but easily compromised means of authenticating users. A common method for user authentication involves comparing the results of a one-way hash operation performed on the password a user enters with the hash value stored in the authentication system.

User authentication can also be done with a software token. A software token can involve a user presenting a secret key during authentication, or may involve a system based on public key cryptography. Symmetric encryption is used in Kerberos, the MIT-developed authentication protocol commonly used for providing users single-sign on access to computing resources[23].

Using cryptographic hardware tokens for user authentication can provide increased security at a higher cost. Hardware tokens combined with passwords are commonly used for providing two-factor authentication. Hardware tokens may be able to generate and store private keys, support use of one-time passwords, and often contain cryptographic processing capabilities along with tamper resistance. Examples of hardware-token-based technologies include smart cards, Universal Serial Bus (USB) tokens, and special-purpose interfaces such as the NSA-developed Crypto Ignition Key (CIK) used in the STU-III family of secure telephones [CIK].

Authentication protocols used by Point-to-Point Protocol (PPP) include Password Authentication Protocol (PAP) and Challenge-Handshake Authentication Protocol (CHAP). PAP is a weak authentication method, transmitting a cleartext password and static identifier that does not protect against replay attack. CHAP transmits a hash that is computed based on a random challenge value and shared secret, providing replay protection and a stronger level of authentication. Another protocol originally developed to provide authentication services for PPP and commonly found in wireless

---

23   See the following for information on Kerberos:

  A. History and background: http://web.mit.edu/kerberos/

  B. Current activities and information on cross platform development: http://www.kerberos.org/

3

Cryptography

network communication is Extensible Authentication Protocol (EAP). EAP is an authentication framework that supports a number of authentication mechanisms such as pre-shared keys, digital certificates, Kerberos, and others[24]. These authentication mechanisms are implemented in a number of ways called EAP methods, for example, EAP-MD5 and EAP-TLS.

Storage Encryption

Storage encryption is typically known as encryption at rest. This includes file-level, file-system-level, and entire disk encryption. Storage encryption provides confidentiality of data, but it also requires authentication. For instance, a SAN may store its data in encrypted form, but the authorized hosts and devices that can access the data must be identified for the encryption to be effective. Cryptographic controls also provide integrity for storage media. For instance, Content Addressable Storage (CAS) provides file integrity via cryptographic methods.

Storage media encryption can be an excellent means of ensuring that removable media is protected during transit. Portable tape media, USB devices or "thumb drives," and notebook computers must be encrypted if they contain data that is not public. While secure data erasure should be depended upon to destroy data from disk drives that are decommissioned or that fail, disk encryption can also provide a degree of protection in those situations.

Storage encryption has a great reliance on proper encryption key management. Magnetic tape media must be encrypted when the criticality of the data warrants it, and especially when the tape is physically moved, such as via third-party carriers. Key management comes into play when the encrypted tapes must be read by a third party requiring access to a symmetric key that was used to encrypt the data. It should also be noted that using unique keys when encrypting multiple tape volumes provides greater protection than using a common key for a set of tapes, should the encryption key be compromised. Solutions being developed for managing keys for disk and tape encryption should take into account the OASIS Key Management Interoperability Protocol (KMIP)[25]. KMIP is an architecture specification for managing keys that defines a low-level protocol

---

24   Extensible Authentication Protocol, or EAP, is an authentication framework frequently used in wireless networks and Point-to-Point connections. It is defined in RFC 3748, which made RFC 2284 obsolete, and was updated by RFC 5247.

See the following for RFC 5247:   http://tools.ietf.org/html/rfc5247
25   See the following for the OASIS KMIP Technical Committee charter: https://www.oasis-open.org/committees/kmip/charter.php

See the following for the main home page for the KMIP TC: https://www.oasis-open.org/committees/tc_home.php?wg_abbrev=kmip

that can be used to request and deliver keys between any key manager and any encryption system.

Other standards produced by the IEEE Standards Association are applicable to disk and tape encryption products. The approved standard IEEE P1619 addresses data storage on disk drives, and the approved standard IEEE P1619.1 is for data encryption on tape drives. An additional standard in progress is P1619.2 for encrypting whole disk sectors [P1619][26].

While tape and disk encryption may be provided by software methods, appliances that perform encryption at hardware speed offer better performance, often with increased cost. Such specialized encryption appliances may continue to have a place; however, the trend is for tape, disk and network devices to provide the encryption functionality within the device itself.

Electronic Commerce (E-Commerce)

E-commerce consists of two or more parties using information technology infrastructures to execute financial transactions, and often involves the buying and selling of goods or services over networks such as the World Wide Web. Examples include consumers accessing online services over the World Wide Web or trading partners processing orders via an extranet. E-commerce includes the integration of Web-based IT applications in activities that do not directly involve buying and selling, such as in advertising, sharing production capacity information, or servicing warranties.

E-commerce business models are normally defined as:

- Business to Business (B2B)
- Business to Consumer (B2C)
- Consumer to Consumer (C2C)

A common infrastructure supporting e-commerce includes the following elements:

- Client: may be a web browser or customer's back-office network.
- Front-end systems: may consist of one or more Web servers connected to the Internet and to back-end systems.
- Back-end systems: may include application servers and databases necessary for supplying information to front-end systems (such as product information) and for receiving data from them (such as payment information).

---

26   See the following for the IEEE 1619 SISWG P1619.2 Wide-Block Encryption working group home page: http://siswg.net/index.php?option=com_content&task=view&id=36&Itemid=75

For transactions to occur, there must be a level of trust between the trading parties and a level of assurance in the security of the transacting environment. The security requirements of the expansive and technologically entrenched use of e-commerce are supported by all the basic goals of cryptography: *confidentiality*, *integrity*, *authentication*, and *non-repudiation*. Cryptography also supports a number of detailed security requirements of e-commerce, including:

- *Auditing*: Accountability in financial transactions depends on secure audit logging records, and cryptographic methods such as hash functions and digital signing can ensure that records are not modified.

- *Authorization*: E-commerce depends on being able to authorize transactions based on pre-associated policies for a given user or other entity that is successfully authenticated. The access control mechanisms involved in authorization may involve cryptographic components such as digital certificates.

- *Privacy*: Web-based transactions may include personal information. If this information is to be stored, cryptography can provide access control and secure storage.

B2B e-commerce still widely uses Electronic Data Interchange (EDI), the decades-old set of standards for exchanging data between trading partners[27]. EDI transmissions often occur using a value-added network (VAN), which acts as a gateway and clearinghouse for supporting the transmission. EDI can also be transmitted by a variety of methods including modems, FTP, e-mail, and HTTP. EDI transmission methods must include appropriate security methods, such as encryption for confidentiality or digital signing for authentication. One specification for protecting EDI transmitted over the Internet is Applicability Statement 2 (AS2), found in RFC 4130 [28]. AS2 specifies use of existing security methods including Secure/Multipurpose Internet Mail Extensions (S/MIME), Cryptographic Message Syntax (CMS), and cryptographic hash algorithms in order to provide confidentiality, data authentication, and non-repudiation for EDI.

B2B, B2C, and C2C e-commerce often require Web Services Security (WS-Security) as part of the server-to-server protection mechanism involved in IP communications between front-end and back-end systems. WS-Security is an OASIS standard that builds a security layer to the Simple Object Access Protocol (SOAP). SOAP is used for exchanging XML-based messages over HTTP.

---

27   See the following for a good general review of EDI information and solutions: http://www.edibasics.co.uk/

28   See the following for RCF 4130:   http://tools.ietf.org/html/rfc4130

WS-Security allows SOAP messages to be signed and encrypted, and adds Kerberos tickets or X.509 certificates as tokens for authentication [WS-Security].

Software Code Signing

While WS-Security uses digital signatures to ensure that an XML-based message is not altered during server-to-server transactions, client browser to Web server based transactions may require downloading a piece of code such as a Java applet, browser plug-in, or Microsoft ActiveX control. To ensure integrity of the code, digital certificates and cryptographic hash functions may be used, such as with the Microsoft Authenticode protocol.

One-way hash functions such as MD5 or SHA-1 are also commonly used for ensuring integrity when software such as source code or executables is distributed. While using a hash-function alone can provide integrity, unless the recipient knows the hash value is the same one supplied by the software provider, authentication of the software cannot be guaranteed. The software's authenticity is often protected by publishing the hash value separately.

Interoperability

Cryptographic interoperability means that the suite of cryptographic algorithms available is used in a manner that meets industry and governmental standards.

One example of a cryptographic interoperability objective is the United States National Security Agency (NSA) Suite B cryptography [NSA Suite B Cryptography] [29]. NSA Suite B is a subset of cryptographic algorithms approved by NIST including those for hashing, digital signatures, and key exchange.

Suite B includes the following:

- **Encryption:** Advanced Encryption Standard (AES)—FIPS 197 (with key sizes of 128 and 256 bits) [30]
- **Digital Signature:** Elliptic Curve Digital Signature Algorithm (ECDSA) - FIPS PUB 186-3 (using the curves with 256 and 384-bit prime moduli) [31]

---

29   See the following for the NSA Suite B Cryptography home page: http://www.nsa.gov/ia/programs/suiteb_cryptography/

Suite B Cryptography is formalized in CNSSP-15, National Information Assurance Policy on the Use of Public Standards for the Secure Sharing of Information Among National Security Systems, dated March 2010.

See the following for a fact sheet on NSA Suite B: http://www.cas.mcmaster.ca/~soltys/math5440-w08/NSA_Suite_B.pdf

30   See the following for FIPS-197:   http://csrc.nist.gov/publications/fips/fips197/fips-197.pdf

31   See the following for FIPS-186-3:   http://csrc.nist.gov/publications/fips/fips186-3/fips_186-3.pdf

3

Cryptography

- **Key Exchange:** The Ephemeral Unified Model and the One-Pass Diffie Hellman (referred to as ECDH) - NIST Special Publication 800-56A (using the curves with 256 and 384- bit prime moduli) [32]

- **Hashing:** Secure Hash Algorithm (SHA) - FIPS PUB 180-4 (using SHA-256 and SHA-384) [33]

The goals of Suite B are to provide a common set of cryptographic algorithms that the commercial industry can use for creating products that are compatible in the United States as well as internationally[34].

Methods of Cryptography

A cryptosystem contains the algorithm used as well as the key, and can include the plaintext and ciphertext. Because the algorithm or cipher is a mathematical function that produces a predictable result, using a key provides the ability to control the algorithm and limit predictability of the ciphertext. These elements are reflected in *Figure 3.1*.

A simple way to represent an encryption function is the following, where ciphertext "C" results from message "M" being encrypted by an algorithm together with a key denoted by "E_k":

$$E_k(M) = C$$

Symmetric Cryptosystems

Suppose the same key is used to decrypt the ciphertext. In the following decryption function, an algorithm together with the same key in our previous

---

32   See the following for NIST SP 800-56A: http://csrc.nist.gov/groups/ST/toolkit/documents/SP800-56Arev1_3-8-07.pdf

33   See the following for FIPS-180-4:   http://csrc.nist.gov/publications/fips/fips180-4/fips-180-4.pdf

34   The following documents provide guidance for using Suite B cryptography with internet protocols:

- IPsec using the Internet Key Exchange (IKE) or IKEv2: "Suite B Cryptographic Suites for IPsec," RFC 6379   http://tools.ietf.org/html/rfc6379
- "Suite B Profile for Internet Protocol Security (IPsec)," RFC 6380   http://tools.ietf.org/html/rfc6380
- TLS: "Suite B Profile for TLS," RFC 6460   http://tools.ietf.org/html/rfc6460
- "TLS Elliptic Curve Cipher Suites with SHA-256/384 and AES Galois Counter Mode (GCM)" RFC 5289   http://tools.ietf.org/html/rfc5289
- S/MIME: "Suite B in Secure/Multipurpose Internet Mail Extensions (S/MIME)," RFC 6318 http://tools.ietf.org/html/rfc6318
- SSH: "AES Galois Counter Mode for the Secure Shell Transport Layer Protocol," RFC 5647 http://tools.ietf.org/html/rfc5647
- "Suite B Cryptographic Suites for SSH, "RFC 6239   http://tools.ietf.org/html/rfc6239

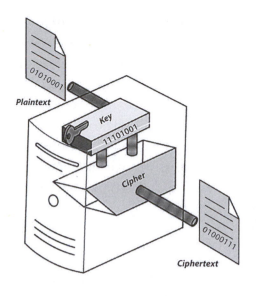

function, denoted by D_k, produces the original message M when the previous ciphertext is decrypted:

$$D_k(C) = M$$

These are the elements of a symmetric cryptosystem, the primary element being use of the same secret key (see *Figure 3.2*).

In symmetric cryptosystems, the secret key used for decryption by the message recipient was also used for encryption by the sender. Confidentiality of the secret key becomes paramount, because knowledge of the key allows an unintended individual the ability

*Figure 3.1 - **Elements of a cryptosystem***

to see the message. With the secret key in hand, all the individual needs is the ciphertext and cipher to read the message. Thus, transport and protection of the secret key are important factors to consider in architectures using symmetric cryptosystems.

In a symmetric cryptosystem, management of keys can also become a problem. When a sender wishes to communicate with individual secrecy to multiple receivers, a symmetric cryptosystem requires the sender to distribute unique keys to each receiver. If the receiving parties share the same secret key, then the receiving parties would be able to access each other's messages from the

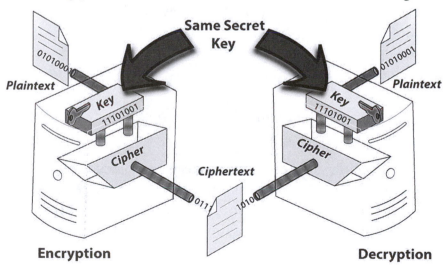

*Figure 3.2 - **Elements of a symmetric cryptosystem.***

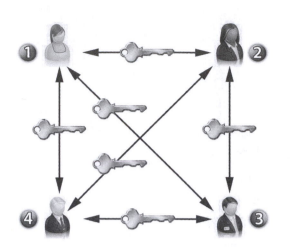

Figure 3.3 - **Management of secret keys problem**

sender, which the sender does not want. In such a case, where confidentiality is required between the sender and each receiver, the number of secret keys required becomes larger than the number of individuals. This is shown in *Figure 3.3*, where four individuals require six keys.

The number of keys is based on the number of communication channels, and increases dramatically. It is possible to determine the number of secret keys required for a given number of individual communication channels. In order to ensure secure communication between everyone in a group of *n* members, the number of keys is given by the following:

$$\textbf{Keys} = [n \times (n-1)]/2$$

Thus, while a group of 2 requires 1 secret key, a group of 100 requires 4950 keys.

While taking into account the problems inherent in management and distribution of secret keys, cryptographic solution development should be aware of the performance characteristics of symmetric algorithms. Symmetric key algorithms perform faster than asymmetric key algorithms. A few common examples of symmetric algorithms are the following:

- Advanced Encryption Standard (AES)
- Blowfish
- Data Encryption Standard (DES)
- IDEA
- RC2, RC4, RC5, and RC6
- Triple-DES (3DES)

Symmetric algorithms fall into two categories: block ciphers and stream ciphers. In block ciphers, plaintext is encrypted using the secret key in blocks of a certain size, for example, 128-bit block size. In stream ciphers, plaintext is encrypted one bit, byte, or word at a time using a rotating stream of bits from the key.

Block Cipher Modes

Symmetric key algorithms that operate as block ciphers are used in one or more modes of operation. Each block cipher mode provides a different level of security, efficiency, fault tolerance, or in some cases, provides a specific protection benefit such as confidentiality or authentication.

Block ciphers operate on blocks of plaintext of a certain size (often 64 or 128 bits) to produce ciphertext in blocks of the same size. The block size affects security (larger is better), at the cost of increased complexity. Secret key size also affects security, as larger keys increase the randomness of the keyspace. Block ciphers typically include an Initialization Vector (IV), a block of bits added to ensure that identical plaintext messages encrypt to different ciphertext messages.

There are several common block cipher modes of operation [Modes]. The following offer various degrees of security, a range of performance characteristics, and different levels of implementation complexity:

- *Electronic Code Book (ECB) Mode*: The least complex mode; each block is operated on independently, and an IV is not used. Because identical plaintext blocks result in identical ciphertext, this mode is not useful for providing message confidentiality. ECB may be useful for short transmissions such as key exchange. ECB is commonly, and erroneously, implemented by vendors for bulk data encryption. This contradicts NIST guidance and puts customer data at grave risk.

- *Cipher Block Chaining (CBC) Mode*: Adds an IV and uses a chaining method such that results of the encryption of previous blocks are fed back into the encryption of the current block. This makes CBC useful for message confidentiality.

- *Cipher Feedback (CFB), Output Feedback (OFB), and Counter (CTR) Mode*: These modes are capable of producing unique ciphertext given identical plaintext blocks, and are useful for message confidentiality. Because these modes employ a block cipher as a keystream generator, they can operate as a stream cipher. This may be desirable in applications that require low latency between the arrival of plaintext and the output of the corresponding ciphertext.

The previous modes do not provide integrity protection; thus, an attacker may be able to undetectably modify the data stream. Additional security benefits are provided by the following block cipher modes:

- *Cipher-Based Message Authentication Code (CMAC) Mode*: This mode provides data integrity and data origin authentication with respect to the original message source, allowing a block cipher to operate as a Message Authentication Code (MAC). The CMAC algorithm addresses security deficiencies found in the Cipher Block Chaining MAC algorithm (CBC-MAC), which has been shown to be insecure when using messages of varying lengths such as the type found in typical IP datagrams. The CMAC algorithm thus offers an improved means of using a block cipher as a MAC.

■ *Counter with Cipher Block Chaining-Message Authentication Code (CCM) Mode*: This mode can provide assurance of both confidentiality and authenticity of data by combining a counter mode with CBC-MAC.

■ *Galois/Counter Mode (GCM)*: This mode also can provide assurance of both confidentiality and authenticity of data, and combines the counter mode with a universal hash function. GCM is suitable for implementation in hardware for high-throughput applications.

■ The following are some of the block ciphers currently in use, or that have been popular at one time:

■ *Advanced Encryption Standard (AES) [FIPS197]*: Adopted as a standard by the United States in NIST FIPS PUB 197, AES is one of the most popular block ciphers. AES supports a fixed block size of 128 bits and a key size of 128, 192, or 256 bits [35].

■ *CAST [RFC2144]*: The popular CAST family of block ciphers uses a 64-bit block size and key sizes of between 40 and 128 bits. CAST-128 is a strong cryptosystem suitable for general-purpose use [36].

■ *Cellular Message Encryption Algorithm (CMEA) [CMEA]*: Designed for encrypting the control channel for mobile phones in the United States, CMEA is a deeply flawed encryption algorithm. The simple CMEA block cipher employs a block size of 16–64 bits and a 64-bit key [37].

■ *Data Encryption Standard (DES) [SCHNEIER]*: This once highly popular 64-bit block cipher, derived from Lucifer and modified to use a 56-bit key size, was called the Data Encryption Algorithm (DEA) in the FIPS 46-1 adopted in 1977. DEA is also defined as ANSI Standard X3.92. With the availability of increasing computing power, DES with its 56-bit key size was found to be insufficient at protecting against brute force attack. DES is more

---

35   See the following for FIPS 197:   http://csrc.nist.gov/publications/fips/fips197/fips-197.pdf

36   See the following for RFC2144:   http://www.ietf.org/rfc/rfc2144.txt

37   See the following for CMEA: http://www.schneier.com/paper-cmea.pdf

commonly implemented as Triple DES (3DES or TDES and also known as TDEA), offering a simple way to enlarge the key space without throwing away the algorithm. 3DES uses multiple keys in a block mode, allowing a key size of 168 bits. 3DES is specified in ANSI X9.52 and replaces DES as a FIPS-approved algorithm. 3DES is gradually being replaced by AES as an encryption standard [38].

- *GOST 28147-89 [GOST]*: GOST is a strong 64-bit block size cipher using a 256-bit key in addition to 512 bits of additional secret keying material in the form of optional Substitution-boxes (S-box). GOST 28147-89 is the name of a government standard of the former Soviet Union, where the cipher was developed. GOST is now freely available, and used in software and hardware implementations in the former Soviet republics and elsewhere[39].

- *International Data Encryption Algorithm (IDEA) [SCHNEIER]*: This 64-bit block cipher with 128-bit keys is used in the popular encryption software, Pretty Good Privacy (PGP). Commercial use of IDEA requires licensing from a Swiss company. Thus far IDEA has stood up to attack from the academic community[40].

- *LOKI [SCHNEIER]*: The LOKI family of ciphers originated in Australia with LOKI89 and LOKI91, which use a 64-bit block and 64-bit key. LOKI91 is a redesign of LOKI89, which was shown to be especially vulnerable to brute force attack. The LOKI97 evolution has a 128-bit block size and offers a choice of 128, 192, or 256-bit key length. LOKI97 was rejected as a candidate for the AES standard, and was shown to be susceptible to cryptanalytic attack[41].

- *Lucifer [SCHNEIER]*: Some of the earliest block ciphers originated at IBM by the early 1970s with the name Lucifer. Early variants

---

38   DES was approved as a federal standard in November 1976, and published on 15 January 1977 as FIPS PUB 46, authorized for use on all unclassified data. It was subsequently reaffirmed as the standard in 1983, 1988 (revised as FIPS-46-1), 1993 (FIPS-46-2), and again in 1999 (FIPS-46-3), the latter prescribing Triple DES. On 26 May 2002, DES was finally superseded by the Advanced Encryption Standard (AES), following a public competition. On 19 May 2005, FIPS 46-3 was officially withdrawn, but NIST has approved Triple DES (3DES) through the year 2030 for sensitive government information. The algorithm is also specified in ANSI X3.92, NIST SP 800-67 and ISO/IEC 18033-3 as a component of TDEA.

39   See the following for GOST: http://tools.ietf.org/html/rfc5830

40   See the following for an overview of IDEA: http://www.rsa.com/rsalabs/node.asp?id=2254

41   See the following for an overview of LOKI 97:   http://www.unsw.adfa.edu.au/~lpb/research/loki97/

See the following for the design details of LOKI 97:   http://www.unsw.adfa.edu.au/~lpb/papers/ssp97/loki97b.html

operated on a 48-bit block using a 48-bit key, and a later version used 128-bit blocks with a 128-bit key. Even with a longer key length, Lucifer has been found vulnerable to cryptanalytic attack[42].

■ *RC2, RC5, RC6*: The RC algorithms, invented by Ron Rivest, are proprietary and largely unrelated to one another. RC2 is a variable key-size 64-bit block cipher intended as a replacement for DES. RC2 was found vulnerable to a related-key attack [RC2]. RC5 is a fast cipher with a variable block size (32, 64, 128-bit) and employs a variable key size (0 to 2040 bits). Brute force attack against RC5 is possible using distributed computing, and the level of security provided by RC5 is dependent upon how it is implemented [RC5]. RC6 was designed as a candidate for the AES standard, and is based on RC5 with improved performance, security, and a 128-bit block size and key sizes of 128, 192, or 256-bits. RC6 is a strong cipher with excellent performance characteristics [RC6].

■ *Skipjack [SCHNEIER]*: Invented by NSA, the now-declassified Skipjack algorithm uses a 64-bit block size with 80-bit key length. Skipjack was intended for implementation in tamperproof hardware using the Clipper chip as part of a now-defunct key escrow program that would allow U.S. government agency decryption of telecommunications. Skipjack is considered a strong cipher[43].

■ *Tiny Encryption Algorithm (TEA)*: Designed at Cambridge University in England and first presented in 1994, TEA operates on 64-bit blocks and uses a 128-bit key. Corrected Block TEA (referred to as XXTEA) corrects weaknesses in the original version. Because TEA can be implemented in a few lines of code, it may be suitable for resource-constrained hardware implementations[44].

■ *Twofish*: A freely available 128-bit block cipher using key sizes up to 128 bits, Twofish was one of the finalists that were not selected for the AES standard. Cryptanalysis of Twofish continues to reveal that it is secure[45].

---

42   See the following citation for the original article by A. Sorkin on Lucifer: A. Sorkin, (1984). LUCIFER: a cryptographic algorithm. Cryptologia, **8**(1), 22–35, 1984.

43   See the following for the NIST SKIPJACK and KEA Algorithm Specifications Version 2.0 document: http://csrc.nist.gov/groups/ST/toolkit/documents/skipjack/skipjack.pdf

44   See the following for the original research paper that defined TEA and its implementation: http://www.cl.cam.ac.uk/techreports/UCAM-CL-TR-355.pdf

45   See the following for the paper Twofish: A 128-Bit Block Cipher: http://www.schneier.com/paper-twofish-paper.pdf

Stream Ciphers

In contrast to block ciphers, stream-based algorithms operate on a message flow (usually bits or characters) and use a keystream. Stream ciphers are applied where buffering may be limited or where data must be processed as it is received. While the case may exist for block ciphers to function as stream ciphers, and for block ciphers to be implemented in hardware, stream ciphers are generally less complex than block ciphers. Thus, stream ciphers may traditionally be found in hardware implementations of encryption.

Stream ciphers may be viewed as approximating the function of a one-time pad or Vernam cipher, which uses a random keystream of the same length as the plaintext. Due to the size of the keystream, a Vernam cipher is cumbersome and impractical for most applications. Traditional stream ciphers approximate the randomness of a keystream with a much smaller and more convenient key size (128 bits, for example). Encryption is accomplished by combining the plaintext with the keystream using the exclusive or (XOR) binary operation (see *Figure 3.4*).

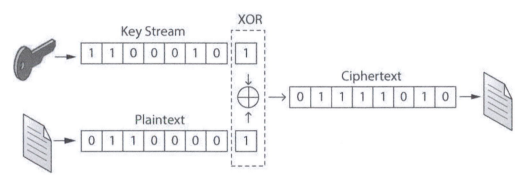

Figure 3.4 - **High-level view of stream cipher encryption**

Stream ciphers that operate in this fashion require sender and receiver to be in step during operations and are called synchronous stream ciphers for that reason. A benefit to using synchronous stream ciphers when the data transmission error rate is high is that if a digit of ciphertext is corrupted, only a single digit of plaintext is affected. However, this property is a disadvantage to security, because an attacker may be able to introduce a predictable error. Examples of synchronous stream ciphers are RC4 and HC-128.

Self-synchronizing or asynchronous stream ciphers overcome this security limitation by generating keystreams based on a set of former ciphertext bits. This allows resynchronization if ciphertext bits are corrupted, with loss of usually only a few characters. From a security standpoint, asynchronous stream

3

Cryptography

ciphers are less susceptible to attack by attempting to introduce predictable error. Examples of asynchronous stream ciphers are ciphertext autokey (CTAK) and stream ciphers based on block ciphers in cipher feedback mode (CFB).

Asymmetric Cryptosystems

While the same key is used to decrypt the ciphertext in symmetric cryptosystems, asymmetric cryptosystems require use of a different key for decryption. In the following, the encryption key K1 is different from the corresponding decryption key, K2:

$$\textit{Encryption: } E_{K1}(M) = C$$

$$\textit{Decryption: } D_{K2}(C) = M$$

Use of a different key to encrypt the message than the key used to decrypt and the fact that it is infeasible to generate one key from the other are what distinguishes an asymmetric or public key cryptosystem (see *Figure 3.5*).

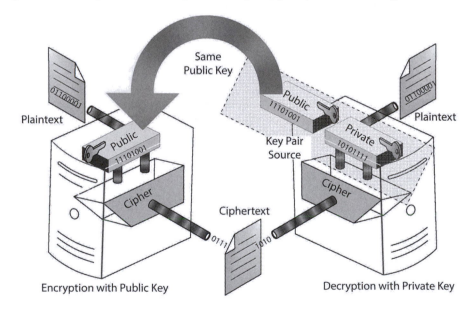

Figure 3.5 - **Asymmetric cryptosystem.**

Asymmetric cryptosystems rely heavily on mathematical functions known as trapdoor functions. Such functions are easy to apply in one direction but extremely difficult to apply in the reverse.

Public key encryption can provide the benefits of confidentiality of message data, provide authenticity and data origin integrity of message data, and non-repudiation of data. Using public key encryption for the secure distribution of a secret key with a recipient is also possible, as long as a mechanism is used to authenticate the recipient and to ensure that the public key is authentic.

To review how confidentiality can easily be produced, let us ask Bob to send a secret message to Alice. We want Alice to be the only person who can read Bob's message. For this to occur, Alice must first generate a public/private key pair, and publish her public key for Bob to read in the local newspaper. Bob meticulously enters the public key into his asymmetric cryptosystem, and encrypts his plaintext message, "Hello this is Bob!"

When Alice uses the private key she generated earlier, she finds she can read the message. Because Alice has kept her private key secure, she is assured no one else was able to read Bob's message. However, Alice is not sure the message is really from Bob, because the public key is available to any newspaper subscriber.

So, to see how authenticity can be produced with an asymmetric cryptosystem, Bob's private key, not Alice's public key, must be used to encrypt the message. Bob generates a public/private key pair and publishes the public key. Bob uses his private key to encrypt the message "This message is from Bob!" Anyone, including Alice, can now obtain a copy of Bob's public key and decrypt the message. While there is no confidentiality of the message, using Bob's public key provides assurance the messages decrypted with it are from Bob. Thus, asymmetric cryptosystems can also be used for signing.

Because asymmetric cryptosystems tend to perform slower than symmetric cryptosystems, Alice and Bob can use their public/private key system to exchange the secret keys of a faster symmetric cryptosystem, using it for future communications.

The idea that separate keys for encryption and decryption could be used was presented in 1976 by Whitfield Diffie and Martin Hellman [DH]. This is the basis for the Diffie–Hellman (DH) key agreement protocol, also called exponential key agreement, which is a method of exchanging secret keys over a nonsecure medium without exposing the keys. The DH protocol is based on the difficulty of calculating discrete logarithms in a finite field.

While DH provides confidentiality for key distribution, the protocol does not provide authentication of the communicating parties. Thus, a means of authentication such as digital signatures must be used to protect against a man-in-the-middle attack.

The idea of a public-key cryptosystem and its use in digital signing was presented by Ron Rivest, Adi Shamir, and Leonard Adleman in 1977 [RSA]. RSA public and private keys are functions of a pair of large prime numbers. Recovering the plaintext from RSA encryption without the key would require factoring the product of two large primes, forming the basis for the security

3

Cryptography

provided by the RSA algorithm. The keys must be generated in such a way that it is computationally infeasible to factor them; thus, proper creation of random prime numbers is a factor in how secure the cryptosystem is. An additional factor is the size of the key. Typically, key size of 1024 bits is required; however, 2048 or even 4096 bits may be used to provide additional security at the cost of performance.

Cryptosystems employ cryptographic primitives, which are the basic mathematical operations on which the encryption procedure is built. Primitives by themselves do not provide security. A particular security goal is achieved by employing the cryptographic primitives in what is known as a cryptographic scheme. Cryptosystems built using RSA schemes may be used for confidentiality, signing to provide authenticity, or key exchange.

Use of a different scheme can also provide a different level of security, including resistance to attack. The RSA Cryptography Specifications Version 2.1 combines the RSA Encryption Primitive (RSAEP) and RSA Decryption Primitive (RSADP) with particular encoding methods to define schemes for providing encryption for confidentiality and for digital signatures for providing authenticity of messages. While the current specification allows for use of earlier RSA schemes for compatibility reasons, it is highly recommended that the newer schemes be used for improved security. For instance, while the version 2.1 RSA Cryptography specification allows use of the version 1.5 scheme known as "RSAES-PKCS1-v1_5" for cryptographic applications requiring backward compatibility, if possible, the newer "RSAES-OAEP" scheme based on a more secure optimal asymmetric encryption padding encoding method should be used [PKCS #1] [46]. Cryptosystems must consider not only the algorithm but the scheme to use for a given application.

While RSA and DH enjoy widespread use in applications such as for IPSec or for protecting AES private keys, their continued use will require improvements to the level of security they provide. Even if newer methods for attack against the fundamental problem of factoring large prime numbers or discrete logarithms are not created, computing power continues to increase significantly over time. As a result, implementing existing attack methods using special-purpose ultra-high-speed computers poses a theoretical threat to RSA and DH. To counter the threat, key size may be increased, which also requires additional computing power. Another option is to use a different asymmetric encryption algorithm altogether.

---

46   See the following for RFC 3447 :   http://tools.ietf.org/html/rfc3447

Another popular approach to public-key cryptography, which is more computationally efficient than either RSA or DH, is elliptic curve cryptography (ECC). For instance, recommendations by the National Institute of Standards and Technology (NIST) for protecting AES 128-bit private keys is to use RSA and DH key sizes of 3072 bits, or elliptic curve key size of 256 bits [NISTSP800-57-1]. Although ECC is slightly more complex than either RSA or DH, ECC has been shown to offer more security per bit increase in key size.

ECC schemes are based on the mathematical problem of computing discrete logarithms of elliptic curves. Because the algorithm is very efficient, ECC can be very useful in applications requiring limited processing power such as in small wireless devices and mobile phones.

Other asymmetric cryptosystems include El Gamal and Cramer–Shoup. El Gamal is based on the problem of computing discrete logarithms, and makes use of the Diffie–Hellman key exchange protocol. Cramer–Shoup is an extension of El Gamal.

Asymmetric cryptosystems that have been proved insecure and should not be used are those based on the knapsack algorithm. The first of these to be developed was the Merkle–Hellman Knapsack cryptosystem [Merkle–Hellman Knapsack]. The knapsack algorithm is based on having a set of items with fixed weights and needing to know which items can be combined to obtain a given weight.

Public key cryptosystems will continue to be necessary when secret key exchange is required. Common software protocols and applications where they are used include IPSec, SSL/TLS, SSH, and PGP.

Hash Functions and Message Authentication Codes

Hash functions are cryptographic algorithms that provide message integrity by producing a condensed representation of a message, called a message digest. Message Authentication Codes (MACs) are cryptographic schemes that also provide message authenticity along with message integrity by using a secret key as part of message input.

At a minimum, the following properties are present in a hash function:

- *Compression*: The hash function H transforms a variable-length input M to a fixed-length hash value h. This is represented by

  $$H(M) = h$$

- *Ease of computation*: Given a hash function H and an input M, the hash value h is easy to compute.

3

Cryptography

In addition, the following properties of cryptographic hash functions exist:

- *Preimage resistance*: Given a hash function *h*, it is computationally infeasible to compute what the input *M* was. This is known as the "one-way" property of hash functions.

- *Second preimage resistance*: For a given input *M*, is computationally infeasible to find any second input which has the same hash value *h*.

- *Collision resistance*: For hash function *h*, it is computationally infeasible to find any two distinct inputs that produce the same hash value.

Hash functions may be built from one-way compression functions, algorithms that exhibit the property of collision resistance. One-way functions are limited in their ability to provide collision resistance, however. A popular means of constructing the hash function and strengthen its collision resistance is the Merkle–Damgård technique, which involves breaking the message input up into a series of smaller blocks. A compression function is performed taking the first message block and an initial fixed value as inputs. The output is fed along with the next message block into the compression function being used. Successive outputs combine with respective message blocks as input to the collision-resistant compression function in an iterative fashion. This results in a fixed-length message digest. A simplified typical Merkle–Damgård construction is shown in *Figure 3.6*.

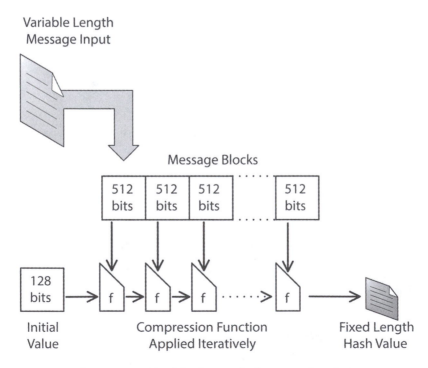

Figure 3.6 - **Merkle-Damgård strengthening**

MD5 (Message Digest algorithm 5), designed by Ron Rivest in 1991, is one such hash function based on a one-way algorithm and utilizing Merkle–Damgård construction. While MD5 has been widely used, it has been found to be prone to collision weakness and is thus insecure [Tunnels].

A common replacement recommended for MD5, and which is also widely used, is SHA-1 (Secure Hash Algorithm), designed by the United States National Security Agency (NSA). SHA-1 is also based on a one-way function utilizing Merkle–Damgård, and produces a 160-bit message digest. It has been found possible to derive a collision (determine a pair of different inputs that produce the same hash value) with 2^{63} hash operations, which is less than the brute force strength of 2^{80} steps that would be necessary [SHA-1 Collisions]. To determine a collision in SHA-1 would still require significant computational resources, such as those provided by distributed computing.

An alternative to SHA-1 is RIPEMD-160, designed by Hans Dobbertin, Antoon Bosselaers, and Bart Preneel and which also produces a 160-bit message digest. RIPEMD-160 also replaces RIPEMD, which has been found to be prone to collision weakness [Collisions].

A summary of hashing functions based on one-way algorithms, along with their susceptibility to collision weakness, is summarized in *Table 3.1*.

Another means of creating a hash function is by using a block cipher algorithm. Thus, it is possible to use AES to create a cryptographic hash function. Block ciphers operate by encrypting plaintext using a private key to produce ciphertext. The ciphertext cannot be used by itself to recreate the plaintext, which resembles the one-way property of a hash function. However, because the block cipher's secret key and decryption algorithm would allow reconstruction of the plaintext, some additional operations must be added to a block cipher to turn it into a secure cryptographic hash function.

An example of a block cipher hash function is MDC-2 (Modification Detection Code 2, sometimes called Meyer-Schilling), developed by IBM, which produces a 128-bit hash. Another example is Whirlpool, which produces a 512-bit hash; it was adopted by the International Organization for Standardization (ISO) in the ISO/IEC 10118-3:2004 standard [Dedicated Hash].

Another use of a block cipher is in a MAC, which is a key-dependent hash function. A MAC adds to the input message the secret key used by the symmetric block cipher, and the resulting output is a fixed-length string called the MAC. Adding the secret key to the message produces *origin authentication*, showing that the message must have been constructed by someone with knowledge of

Algorithm	Message Digest Output Size (bits)	Message Input Block Size (bits)	Collision Possible?
HAVAL	128/160/192/224/256	1024	Yes
MD4	128	512	Yes
MD5	128	512	Yes
RIPEMD	128	512	Yes
RIPEMD-128/256	128/256	512	Not yet
RIPEMD-160/320	160/320	512	160 - Yes 320 - Not Yet
SHA-1	160	512	Yes
SHA-224/256	224/256	512	Yes
SHA-384/512	384/512	1024	Yes
Tiger	128/160/192	512	Yes

Table 3.1 - **Hashing Functions Based on One-Way Algorithms**

the secret key. MACs also provide *integrity*, because any change to the message would result in a different MAC value. The most common form of MAC algorithm based on a block cipher employs cipher block chaining, and is known as a CBC-MAC.

A MAC may also be derived using a hash function, where the hash function is modified to incorporate use of a secret key to provide *origin authentication* and *integrity*. This is known as an MDx-MAC scheme, and can be based on a RIPEMD-128, RIPEMD-160, or SHA-1 hash function.

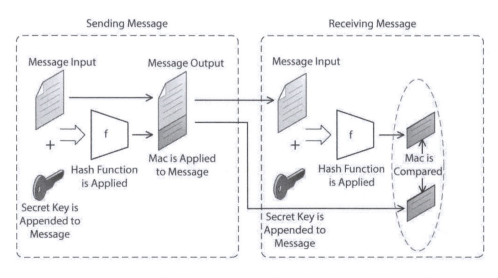

Figure 3.7 - **A Hashed Message Authentication Code (HMAC)**

A Hashed Message Authentication Code (HMAC) is another case of a MAC derived using a hash function. In an HMAC, the underlying hash function is not modified, but is treated as a "black box." HMAC uses any iterative hash function and adds a secret key to the input message in order to obtain *origin authentication* and *integrity*. See *Figure 3.7* for a simplified view of HMAC.

HMAC is used in a variety of applications from mobile phones to network-attached storage devices and in IPSec. The construction of HMAC was published in IETF RFC 2104. The use of HMACs is standardized in NIST FIPS PUB 180, the Secure Hash Standard, and in ISO/IEC 9797-2.

Digital Signatures

MACs depend on use of a symmetric key that must be securely transmitted from the sender to the receiver. A digital signature may be thought of as a MAC that uses asymmetric cryptography, because a digital signature uses a private signing key and a public verification key. A digital signature scheme operates in the following manner:

1. A message digest is generated using a hash function.

2. The message digest is encrypted with the sender's private key and attached to the cleartext message, signing it (note that a digital signature does not provide confidentiality).

3. The attached message digest is decrypted by the receiver, using the sender's public key. The receiver also compares this message digest with the message digest produced by hashing the cleartext message, to ensure that the message was not altered.

Figure 3.8 depicts digital signing and verifying.

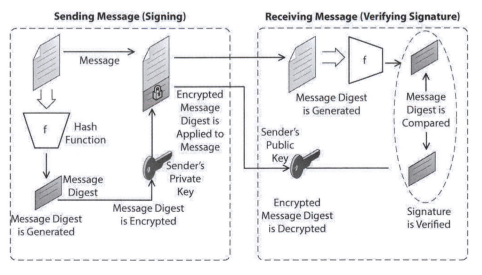

Figure 3.8 - **Digital Signing and Verifying**

A digital signature can provide *origin authentication*, *non-repudiation*, and *integrity*. By using a public/private key pair, the message is bound to the originator who used the private key. The originator can be bound to an individual using a mutual certification authority such as a PKI, thus assuring some measure of *non-repudiation* for the sender. *Integrity* is provided by using the cryptographic hashing function to make certain any alteration of the message can be detected.

A digital signature scheme contains the following elements:

- *Cryptographic hash function*: Hashing is done by the sending and receiving parties to determine integrity of the message.

- *Key generation algorithm*: Key generation produces a private key for signing and a public key for distribution to parties who will verify the digital signature.

- *Signing algorithm*: Signing produces a digital signature output using the private key and message.

- *Verification algorithm*: Verification uses the public key and digital signature to determine authenticity of the message.

Public key cryptosystems that are used to implement digital signature schemes include ECC, El Gamal, DSA, and RSA.

Standards that specify various schemes for digital signature algorithms exist. Digital Signature Algorithm (DSA) is a NIST standard specified for use in the Digital Signature Standard (DSS). DSS is defined in FIPS PUB 186. ISO/IEC 9696 and ISO/IEC 14888 specify a portfolio of digital signature schemes. Additional international standards specifying digital signature standards include ANSI X9.30.1, ANSI X9.62, and IEEE 1363.

Vet Proprietary Cryptography & Design Testable Cryptographic Systems

When it comes to the design and implementation of cryptographic systems, the main school of thought is that if the system is going to be designed for use commercially, then it cannot be a proprietary system, as the ability to test it and probe for weaknesses would be a problem. There are many issues associated with the ability to successfully vet proprietary cryptographic systems and the requirements inherent in designing testable cryptographic systems. The main issue is that the algorithm(s) used must be made available publically so that they can be tested by cryptanalysis, to establish a benchmark for the relative security of the system. There is no specific series of tests that can be performed against an algorithm to accurately evaluate its security per se; instead, what has to be done is that the algorithm needs to be vetted publically for an extended period of time through the rigorous application of cryptanalysis by experts in order to potentially discover any flaws or vulnerabilities inherent in the cryptography. If an algorithm is kept secret, then there is no vetting of it by experts, and as a result, its true strength, or potential weakness, is unknown by its users, which presents many issues for the security architect.

A practical example of this thought process can be seen by looking at some of the history surrounding DES, the unusual circumstances of its creation and the uniqueness of one architectural element of its implementation. DES was created as the result of a partnership between the NSA and IBM in the 1970's. Due to the involvement of the NSA in the creation of DES, there have always been rumors of some sort of backdoor, or hidden element(s) within DES that could be exploited by the NSA if it needed to break the confidentiality of the data encrypted with DES. There has never been any proof of this found, despite glaring scrutiny of the algorithm for years, with one exception. The interesting thing that was found regarding DES was the unique way that the algorithm implemented S-Boxes, which are used to break up the plaintext as input in order to encrypt it as it is run through the algorithm. When the new attack methods discovered through differential cryptanalysis were applied to DES over 20 years after it was first released, the version built by NSA and IBM was found to be immune to these attack methods due to the unique bit shift that the S-Boxes utilized. The fact that DES was able to withstand an attack that had not even been invented until more than 20 years after its release has served to perpetuate the myths and legends surrounding the NSA's involvement with DES, but it also serves to illustrate another important lesson, which is that no amount of vetting and scrutiny of an algorithm can discover all potential vulnerabilities, nor can it expose all potential defense mechanisms either. The need to allow algorithms to be vetted by communities of experts is a critical success factor in the construction of testable cryptographic systems.

There have been many more recent examples of the use of proprietary, or hidden, architectural elements to carry out attacks against infrastructure all over the world. The creation, deployment, and use of malware such as Flame, Stuxnet, and Duqu among others should focus the attention of security architects on the potential impact of the Advanced Persistent Threat (APT) category of attack vectors and their potential impact[47]. The issue, which is at the heart of these

---

47   See the following for overviews of the APT phenomenon and its impact:

   A. http://static.usenix.org/event/lisa09/tech/slides/daly.pdf

   B. http://go.secureworks.com/advancedthreats

   C. http://www.mcafee.com/us/resources/white-papers/wp-operation-shady-rat.pdf

   D. http://www.reuters.com/article/2011/08/03/us-cyberattacks-idUSTRE7720HU20110803

   E. http://googleblog.blogspot.com/2010/01/new-approach-to-china.html#!/2010/01/new-approach-to-china.html

3

Cryptography

specific APT attacks, is the proprietary nature of their architecture and design, and their ability to operate undetected for years in some cases. This is just an extension of the same issues faced by the security architect with regards to the use of proprietary cryptographic systems and algorithms, and the inability to properly vet and understand the risks associated with operating them.

Computational Overhead & Useful Life

The computational overhead of encryption systems and algorithms is an issue that is not well understood by many security architects. We have always been told that encryption imposes computational overhead on a system, and that this overhead, or "crypto-tax ", is just the price of using the encryption in the first place. The challenge that most security architects, and indeed most IT professionals at large, face with regards to an issue such as computational overhead is that it is not something that is explained by those who understand it in such a way that it can be addressed easily. In the area of cryptography for instance, the discussions with regards to computational overhead are highly technical affairs that involve complex mathematics and cutting edge research by leading experts in the fields of mathematics and systems engineering and design [48]. A good example of one of the more approachable research papers on this subject is *"A generic characterization of the overheads imposed by IPsec and associated cryptographic algorithms"*[49]. This paper presents an assessment of the communication overheads of IPsec and evaluates the feasibility of deploying it on handheld devices for the UMTS architecture. A wide range of different cryptographic algorithms are used in conjunction with IPsec, such as Data Encryption Standard (DES), Advanced Encryption Standard (AES), Message Digest (MD5) and Secure Hash Algorithm 1 (SHA-1). The paper considers the processing and packetization overheads introduced by these algorithms and quantifies their impact in terms of communication quality (added delay for the end-user) and resource consumption (additional bandwidth on the radio interface).

The security architect needs to be aware of these solutions and the research that supports them in order to be able to make informed decisions with regards to implementation of the best possible elements within the security architecture to align the needs of the business with the architecture. It is hard however for the

---

48   See the following for some examples of research in this area:

   A. http://eprint.iacr.org/2010/106.pdf

   B. http://hal.archives-ouvertes.fr/docs/00/74/79/47/PDF/81.pdf

   C. http://hal-ujm.ccsd.cnrs.fr/docs/00/69/96/14/PDF/2012_Cosade_Fischer.pdf

   D. http://jestec.taylors.edu.my/Vol%206%20Issue%204%20August%2011/Vol_6_4_411_428_AL%20JAMMAS.pdf

   E. http://www.cryptography.com/public/pdf/leakage-resistant-encryption-and-decryption.pdf

49   See the following for the full paper: http://www.cse.msstate.edu/~ramkumar/ipsec_overheads.pdf

security architect to stay informed about this kind of research and to consume and utilize it in an effective manner, as it is often presented in academic journals, and does not always make its way out to the security community in ways that allow for it to be readily available to practitioners.

The security architect also needs to stay informed regarding useful life concepts in their security architectures. The algorithms that the security architect chooses to deploy all have a useful life, and just like any other metric that indicates something of importance with regards to the health of a system under management, monitoring is the key to successful usage and consumption. Publically available algorithms are all subject to constant scrutiny and cryptanalysis in order to ensure that weaknesses and vulnerabilities are discovered before they can lead to compromise and data loss if at all possible. One of the key outcomes of this exhaustive vetting process is an eventual end of life milestone for the algorithm, if it is found to be vulnerable for any number of reasons.

For instance, the announcement by NIST with regards to the approval of the withdrawal of DES in 2005, and the subsequent announcement just over one year later by the MIT Kerberos Team to end of life Kerberos Version 4 as a result of the issues associated with DES that NIST reacted to, as well as serious protocol flaws with the implementation of Kerberos v4, are both examples of algorithms and protocols that reached the end of their useful life. The security architect that had deployed either DES, or DES in support of a Kerberos v4 implementation would need to change the effected elements of the systems in question to address the loss of DES and Kerberos.

Security architects need to ensure that they stay informed with regards to useful life concerns in all areas of their system architectures in order to ensure that they are not operating systems past their useful life, and in so doing, putting the users of those systems, and the data in those systems at unnecessary risk.

3

Cryptography

Key Management

Historically, a lot of efforts in the field of cryptography have been devoted to the development and implementation of secure algorithms and protocols. They have been put through scrutiny at all levels. There are a lot of publications that give an estimation of an algorithm's strength. But it is very unlikely that a real attacker will prefer brute force to lower-hanging fruit in order to break a code. A real vulnerability can most likely be found in the key management methods. Key management in the real world is the most difficult part of cryptography [SCHNEIER]. It is much easier to find a flaw in one of the key management processes than to expend resources on sophisticated crypto attacks. It is not easy to design and implement a well-thought-out key management system. That is why the most successful crypto attacks have exploited poor key management. Moreover, the fact of using strong crypto algorithms and long keys very often creates a false sense of security that results in overlooking more mundane chores related to key management. Key management should provide the foundation for the secure generation, storage, distribution, and destruction of keys [NISTSP800-57-1]. Modern key management is usually an automated process, which helps to minimize human errors in the process of key generation, distribution and update, and also increases the key's secrecy. One of the principles of modern cryptography requires that keys not appear in cleartext outside the crypto module (except public keys, which are usually distributed within public key certificates).

The subject of key management is multidimensional because of different types of cryptography and the purposes they serve. Thus, asymmetric (public and private) keys are managed differently from symmetric keys. Likewise, data encryption keys are managed differently from signing keys. One of the goals of this section is to address these specifics.

Although the main purposes of cryptography have been reviewed from an application perspective earlier in this chapter, let us look at the main purpose from a key management perspective.

Purpose of the Keys and Key Types

Either as a stand-alone service or as a supporting part of another system, cryptography supports one or several security services or properties: *confidentiality, authentication, integrity, non-repudiation,* and *authorization.* The important characteristics of the cryptographic keys, such as key size and life span, are defined by the security services and type of cryptography these keys should support. One of the cryptographic principles is a preferred use of each key type for one designated purpose, although issuing and using a multipurpose key in real life is common.

Confidentiality

Confidentiality is protection of information against unauthorized disclosure, and it is achieved by data encryption. Data to be protected may be either a human-readable text, or any type of binary, including other crypto keys. Both symmetric and asymmetric cryptography can be used. An unauthorized party should not be able to deduce or obtain the key for decryption. Keys for data at rest encryption may have a long crypto period; thus, they need to have a sufficient length and to be supported by a sophisticated and robust key management system (KMS). On the other hand, the keys for data in transit encryption may have a short life span, sometimes limited to one session. Their key length may be shorter and, thus, the KMS for this purpose may need to simply include a key generating and distributing mechanism.

The following key types support confidentiality:

- Symmetric data encryption key
- Symmetric key wrapping key; aka key encrypting key
- Public and private key transport keys
- Symmetric key agreement key
- Public and private static key agreement keys
- Public and private ephemeral key agreement keys

Authentication

Broadly, authentication is a way to verify the origin of information. If the information is just data or an executable, authentication would verify its integrity as well as the identity of the person or system that created the information. If authentication is part of an access control system and the information consists of user or system identity, authentication will verify that identity in order to allow authorization services to make access control decisions. Both symmetric and asymmetric cryptography techniques may be used, such as digital signature and MAC. The main idea is that possession of the key proves the authenticity of an information originator. Both data at rest and in transit may employ key-based authentication.

The following key types support authentication:

- Private signature key
- Public signature verification key
- Symmetric authentication key
- Public and private authentication keys

Data Integrity

Data integrity is a security feature that protects data against unauthorized alteration either in transmission or in storage. An unauthorized alteration may include substitution, insertion, or deletion and may be intentional or unintentional. None of these can happen unnoticed if data integrity control is in place. Both symmetric and asymmetric cryptography techniques, such as digital signature and MAC, may be used. The following key types support data integrity:

- Private signature key
- Public signature verification key
- Symmetric authentication key
- Public and private authentication keys

Non-Repudiation

Non-repudiation is concerned with providing data integrity and authentication in a special way that allows a third party to verify and prove it. It is provided by asymmetric key cryptography and a digital signature relying on a signer's private key. This security feature requires an especially rigid control of the keys, because it should prevent a signing party from successfully denying its signature. The following keys may be found when non-repudiation is supported:

- Private signature key
- Public signature verification key

Authorization

Authorization is the component of access control that is responsible for granting an object access to a particular resource after that object has already proved its identity (authenticated). A Kerberos ticket-granting service is a typical example of a key used for authorization. In more general terms, the following keys may be used for authorization:

- Symmetric authorization key
- Private authorization key
- Public authorization (verification) key

Cryptographic Strength and Key Size

The strength of cryptography depends on the strength of the algorithms, protocols, and keys and the strength of the security around the keys. In cryptographic applications that require key generation, key distribution, and encryption, whole suites of algorithms are used. For example, the first phases of IPSec and SSL include key negotiation and exchange, which may employ RSA cryptography. The following phases include generating a symmetric session key and using that key for encrypting data in transit with 3DES or AES. The strength of cryptography in this case is defined by the weakest link in this chain, so if in this example the key exchange employs very short public and private keys, the symmetric encryption key can be successfully intercepted and the transmitted data can be decrypted. Many factors should be considered, including the data and key's life span, volume of the data to be encrypted with the same key, the key size, and the way the keys are generated. For example, if a key is generated straight from a password, the entropy in the key is significantly reduced, because a smart brute force attack can generate just the keys deriving from ASCII characters that meet password policy requirements.

The difficulty of breaking a key using brute force grows exponentially with key length (i.e., number of bits), because each bit doubles a number of possible combinations for brute force. A long key gives better security but worse performance, so figuring an optimal key size is important. It should also depend on the projected key's lifetime. Temporary, or so-called ephemeral, keys generated for one session or one connection, may be shorter. The long-life keys protecting data at rest for years should be as long as possible.

One of the important characteristics of the keys is a crypto period. It is defined [NISTSP800-57-1] as the time span during which a specific key is authorized for use by legitimate entities, or during which the keys for a given system will remain in effect [50]. Duration of a crypto period limits a "window of opportunity" for successful cryptanalytic or any other attacks and volume of information that can be exposed if the keys are compromised. Generally, the shorter the crypto period, the better security, although more frequent key generation, revocation, and replacement may be costly and may create additional risk. Many factors should be taken into consideration when the crypto period for each key type is defined. NIST recommendations [NISTSP800-57-1] regarding crypto period, which assume usage of the environment with the goal of achieving better operational efficiency, are in *Table 3.2*.

Originator Usage Period (OUP) is a period of time in the crypto period of a symmetric key during which cryptographic protection may be applied to data.

As was mentioned earlier in this chapter, both the continuous progress in cryptanalysis techniques and increasing computer power available for breaking the keys, should be considered. By Moore's law, computer speed doubles every 18 months, so the key size should be selected accordingly to protect the encrypted

3

Cryptography

---

50   See the following for NIST SP 800-57 Recommendation for Key Management – Part 1: General (Revision 3), July 2012:   http://csrc.nist.gov/publications/nistpubs/800-57/sp800-57_part1_rev3_general.pdf

Key Type	Originator Usage Period (OUP)	Recipient Usage Period
Private Signature Key	1–3 years	1–3 years
Public Signature Key	Several years	Several years
Symmetric Authentication Key	< = 1–2 years	< = OUP + 3 years
Private Authentication Key	1–2 years	1–2 years
Public Authentication Key	1–2 years	1–2 years
Symmetric Data Encryption Key	< = 1 month	< = OUP + 3 years
Symmetric Key Wrapping Key	< = 1 month	< = OUP + 3 years
Symmetric Master Key	1 year	N/A
Private Key Transport Key	1–2 years	1–2 years
Public Key Transport Key	< = 2 years	< = 2 years
Symmetric Key Agreement Key	1–2 years	1–2 years
Private Static Key Agreement	1–2 years	1–2 years
Public Static Key Agreement	1–2 years	1–2 years
Private Ephemeral Key Agreement Key	One key agreement transaction	One key agreement transaction
Public Ephemeral Key Agreement Key	One key agreement transaction	One key agreement transaction
Symmetric Authorization Key	< = 2 years	< = 2 years
Public Authorization Key	< = 2 years	< = 2 years
Private Authorization Key	< = 2 years	< = 2 years

Table 3.2 - **Recommended Crypto Periods for the Key Types**

data against a brute force attack[51]. If a computer is N time faster, the key size should increase by $\log_2 N$ bits.

A successful brute force attack on a symmetric key algorithm, which in the case of perfect key entropy essentially consists of an exhaustive search of all the keys, would require on 2^N, divided by 2, where N is a size of the key in bits cycles. In addition to the key length, there is an effective key length factor. In the case of 3DES, which assumes total $3 * 56 = 168$ bit key encryption, the effective

---

51   Moore's Law specifically stated that the number of transistors on an affordable CPU would double approximately every two years. In 2000 the number of transistors in the CPU numbered 37.5 million, while in 2009 the number went up to 904 million.

See the following for information on Moore's Law: http://www.intel.com/content/www/us/en/silicon-innovations/moores-law-technology.html

key size is 80 bits if the first and third encryption rounds are performed using the same 56-bit key, and it is 112 bits if all three rounds employ unique 56-bit keys. As already discussed in the example of the keys derived from an ASCII or EBCDIC password, and as will be demonstrated in the example of asymmetric key strength, there is another factor which impacts the strength in addition to the effective key length. This factor is a key space.

Breaking asymmetric key cryptography may need much less resources than breaking symmetric key cryptography. This stems from the nature of asymmetric key cryptography. For example, an RSA private key, which is a target of asymmetric cryptography attack, should be generated to meet certain RSA criteria. When this key is generated, as well as its counterpart public key, it is being derived from the space of large prime numbers. It means the key space for an exhaustive search is much smaller. Also, some advances in research of factoring large numbers indicates that increasing the size of public/private keys is required. RSA indicated that if an easy solution to the factoring problem is found and further increase of RSA key size beyond 2048 bits is required, then using the RSA algorithm may become impractical. Elliptic curve cryptography (ECC) is based on the elliptic curve discrete logarithm problem, which may take a full exponential time to solve. It is comparable with symmetric encryption strength. That is why ECC is considered the most likely successor of the RSA algorithm in the asymmetric cryptography area.

Comparison of symmetric, RSA, and ECC asymmetric cryptography and the corresponding key lengths are shown in *Table 3.3* [NISTSP800-57-1].

Bits of Security	Symmetric Key Algorithms	FFC (e.g., DSA, D-H)	IFC (e.g., RSA)	ECC (e.g., ECDSA)
80	2TDEA	L = 1024; N = 160	k = 1024	f = 160–223
112	3TDEA	L = 2048; N = 224	k = 2048	f = 224–255
128	AES-128	L = 3072; N = 256	k = 3072	f = 256–383
192	AES-192	L = 7680; N = 384	k = 7680	f = 384–511
256	AES-256	L = 5360; N = 512	k = 15360	f = 512+

Table 3.3 - **Comparable Key Strength**

Some observations regarding comments in this table [NISTSP800-57-1]

1. Column 1 indicates the number of bits of security provided by the algorithms and key sizes in a particular row. Note that the bits of security are not necessarily the same as the key sizes for the algorithms in the other columns, due to attacks on those

algorithms that provide computational advantages. Because some combinations of 0 and 1 for 2TDES and 3TDES keys can be predicted, it takes less computational power to guess the key value, which is equivalent to a shorter key.

2. Column 2 identifies the symmetric key algorithms that provide the indicated level of security (at a minimum), where 2TDEA and 3TDEA are specified in [SP800-67], and AES is specified in [FIPS197]. 2TDEA is TDEA with two different keys; 3TDEA is TDEA with three different keys.

3. Column 3 indicates the minimum size of the parameters associated with the standards that use finite field cryptography (FFC). Examples of such algorithms include DSA as defined in [FIPS186-3] for digital signatures, and Diffie–Hellman (DH) and MQV key agreement as defined in [SP800-56A]), where L is the size of the public key, and N is the size of the private key.

4. Column 4 indicates the value for k (the size of the modulus n) for algorithms based on integer factorization cryptography (IFC). The predominant algorithm of this type is the RSA algorithm. RSA is specified in [ANSX9.31] and [RSA PKCS#1]. These specifications are referenced in [FIPS186] for digital signatures. The value of k is commonly considered to be the key size.

5. Column 5 indicates the size of the key for algorithms based on elliptic curve cryptography (ECC)

Key Life Cycle

Key life cycle should be analyzed for each key type in a crypto system in order to build a secure, cost-effective cryptographic architecture. Four major phases should be considered:

- *Preoperational phase*: The key is not generated yet, but preactivation processes are taking place. It may include registering a user's attributes with the key management system, installing the key policies, and selecting algorithms and key parameters, and initial installation or update of the software or hardware cryptographic module with initial key material, which should be used just for testing and then replaced for production operation. Finally, the key material will be generated and optionally (depending on the application) distributed in a secure manner to other entities. For a more detailed description of these processes, see the sections "Key Creation" and "Key Distribution" of this chapter. The keys must be registered, which essentially includes binding them to the subject's identity. For PKI, it is implemented in the X509 certificate, which binds a public key with subject's name (usually DN), alternative name (usually e-mail) and some other attributes, and signs this binding by a digital signature of a trusted CA. For symmetric keys, it may be another mechanism, for example, implemented in a Kerberos Key Distribution Center (KDC).

- *Operational phase:* Key material is ready for normal operational use (encryption, decryption, signing, etc.). In many cases, the key is stored in the crypto module hardware or disk storage that meets certain requirements; for example, FIPS 140-2 [FIPS 140-2]. Key material availability is important, and backup and recovery mechanisms should be used to support this requirement. However, if a key may be recovered by means other than backup/restore methods, such as regenerating or rederiving it, it reduces the probability of compromising the key's backups. Even if the key is not lost, it may need to be updated or changed during the operational phase. The main reasons are either the key policy regarding crypto period expiration or suspected or real key compromise. The key change may be accomplished either by simple rekeying, or replacing the old key with a completely independent new key, or updating the old key. The former method is used usually when a key is compromised, and it requires key redistribution. In the latter case, a new key is produced from the previous one, based on the protocol known to all parties, so no key redistribution is required. According to their policies, encryption/decryption and signing/verification key pairs have their own lifetime (crypto period). PKI applications automatically start trying to update the keys that enter into the transition period after a particular time interval, which is normally a percentage of the key lifetime.

■ *Postoperational phase:* Key material is not in operation, but access to the keys still may be needed. This need may be associated, for example, with the need to decrypt a document or verify a signature on the document after expiry of the crypto period. The keys for this purpose are stored in an archive in encrypted form, with access and integrity control. There is a special recovery process in place, usually available for designated administrators, to obtain the keys from archive. It is a good practice to have on-site and off-site (backup) archives. Not all the key types may, and should, be archived. Further destruction of the keys stored in the archive may be warranted by the applicable policies. More details about archiving, revocation, and destruction of the keys is in one of the following sections of this chapter.

■ *Key destruction* is performed either when the key is compromised or when its crypto period and retention in the archive have expired, according to the policy.

Key Creation

A key generation process is a part of the key establishment function of the key management preoperation phase [NISTSP800-57-1].

The security of cryptography is based on the secrecy of the keys and the virtual impossibility of deducing the keys from the cipher or other sources. Another principle of cryptography that relates specifically to key generation is to avoid weak keys and make a key space "flat," deriving from random numbers. Theoretically, any n-bit key's key space, based on the random number generator, is a 2^N. In reality, in many cases, it is significantly smaller, which translates into lower resources required to break the key by specialized brute force. The older basic encryption tools generated keys from ASCII characters [SCHNEIER], which reduced the key space at least by half and also invited dictionary attacks. In 1995, two PhD students found that a release of Netscape's SSL implementation chose the key from a recognizable subspace (bound to the clock) of the total key space. It significantly simplified attacks on SSL traffic. Another key generation weakness was discovered in one open source system that used a "predictable random" number generator [TECHREV-OPENSSL]. Originating the keys only from true random numbers may help to avoid this flaw. Another potential weakness of keys stems from a specific algorithm and its implementation, when knowledge of just one portion of a key is enough to decrypt a cipher and deduce the whole key. As in the previous discussion about key size, we need to look at the process of key generation in context: type of the keys, purpose of the keys, crypto application, and operation environment. It may be difficult to evaluate these factors because some of them may be proprietary. For crypto systems that support applications for the federal government, the FIPS 140-2 [FIPS 140-2] and the second draft of FIPS 140-3 [FIPS 140-3] are clearly defining requirements for key generation [52]. These standards give a good benchmark for commercial systems as well and help to avoid the crypto system design flaws as described earlier. As FIPS 140-2 defines [FIPS 140-2]:

Random Number Generators (RNGs) used for cryptographic applications typically produce a sequence of zero and one bits that may be combined into sub-sequences or blocks of random numbers. There are two basic classes: deterministic and nondeterministic. A deterministic RNG consists of an algorithm that produces a sequence of bits from an initial value called a seed. A nondeterministic RNG produces output that is dependent on some unpredictable physical source that is outside human control.

A seed key, in its turn, is defined as "a secret value used to initialize a cryptographic function or operation." NIST has documented approved methods of producing random numbers [ANNEXC-FIPS 140-2]. It also has certain criteria of entering the seed during a key generation process, both for the case when the keys are generated inside a crypto module or outside. Entering the keys into the crypto module may be manual (e.g., keyboard) or electronic (e.g., smart cards, tokens, etc.). A seed key, if entered during key generation, may be entered in the same manner as cryptographic keys. Physical security requirements for the crypto modules that generate the keys are also described in FIPS 140-2 and 140-3 (draft) and include temper-resistant measures.

Although crypto key generation both for symmetric and asymmetric cryptography is based on RNG, the process is different for generating symmetric keys and asymmetric key pairs.

- *For asymmetric cryptography*, the key pairs are generated according to the approved algorithms and standards. A static key pair can be generated by the end entity or by a facility that securely distributes the key pairs or by both the end entity and the facility in concert. A private signing key supporting the non-repudiation property should be generated on the end entity site and never leave that site. Ephemeral asymmetric keys are usually generated for the establishment of other

---

[52]   See the following for information on the current status of the efforts around the FIPS 140-3 drafting process: http://csrc.nist.gov/groups/ST/FIPS140_3/

keys, have a short life, and may be generated by the end entities and key distribution facilities. The following is a brief description of the RSA key pair, as one of the asymmetric key pair generation processes.

■ *An RSA key pair* consists of an RSA private key, which in digital signature applications is used to compute a digital signature, and an RSA public key, which in the digital signature applications is used to verify the digital signature. In encryption and decryption applications, the RSA private key is used to decrypt data and the RSA public key is used to encrypt the data. As described in [FIPS 186-3] [53]:

An RSA public key consists of a modulus n, which is the product of two positive prime integers p and q (i.e., $n = pq$), and a public key exponent e. Thus, the RSA public key is the pair of values (n, e) and is used to verify digital signatures. The size of an RSA key pair is commonly considered to be the length of the modulus n in bits (nlen). The corresponding RSA private key consists of the same modulus n and a private key exponent d that depends on n and the public key exponent e. Thus, the RSA private key is the pair of values (n, d) and is used to generate digital signatures. Note that an alternative method for representing (n, d) using the Chinese Remainder Theorem (CRT) is allowed as specified in PKCS #1. In order to provide security for the digital signature process, the two integers p and q, and the private key exponent d shall be kept secret. The modulus n and the public key exponent e may be made known to anyone. Guidance on the protection of these values is provided in SP 800-57. This Standard specifies three choices for the length of the modulus (i.e., nlen): 1024, 2048 and 3072 bits.

A CA for signing certificates should use a modulus whose length nlen is equal to or greater than the moduli used by its subscribers. For example, if the subscribers are using an nlen = 2048, then the CA should use nlen ≥ 2048. RSA keys shall be generated with respect to a security strength S.

Parameters p and q are randomly generated and should be produced from seeds from a random or pseudorandom generator [NIST SP 800-90]. These prime numbers' seeds should be kept secret or destroyed after the modulus n is computed.

■ *For symmetric cryptography*, the keys may be generated from a random number generation method or regenerated from the previous key during a key update procedure. Another way is to derive the key from a master key using approved FIPS140-2

---

53   See the following for FIPS 186-3:   http://csrc.nist.gov/publications/fips/fips186-3/ fips_186-3.pdf

derivation functions, but eventually they are also coming from a random number. For secure key distribution purposes, split knowledge procedures can be used, and in that case, different components of the key may be generated in different locations, or may be created at one location and then split into components. Each key component will provide no knowledge of the entire key value (e.g., each key component must appear to be generated randomly). The principle of split knowledge is that if knowledge of k (where n is a total number of components and k is less than or equal to n) components is required to construct the original key, then knowledge of any $k - 1$ key components will not provide any information about the original key other than, possibly, its length. In addition, a simple concatenation of key components should not produce a key.

Key Distribution and Crypto Information in Transit

Key distribution mainly belongs to the key establishment function of the preproduction phase of key life cycle. By the NIST definition [NISTSP800-57-1], "it is the process of transporting a key and other keying material from an entity that either owns the key or generates the key to another entity that is intended to use the key." In many cases, it is a hard problem, which is solved differently for different types of keys. For example, data encryption keys are originated and distributed differently compared with signature verification keys, and public keys are distributed differently from secret keys. This problem is more difficult for symmetric key applications, which need to protect the keys from disclosure. In any case, key distribution should use certain protection mechanisms to meet the following requirements, either the business dictates manual distribution or automated or a combination of both:

1. Availability of the keys for a recipient after transmission by a sender (redundant channels, "store and forward" systems, and retransmission as a last resort).

2. Integrity, which should detect modification of keys in transit. MAC, CRC, and digital signature can be used. Physical protection is required as well.

3. Confidentiality. It may be achieved by key encryption or by splitting the key and distributing its components via separate channels ("split knowledge"). Physical protection should apply as well.

4. Association of the keys with the intended application usage and related information may be achieved by appropriate configuration of the distribution process.

3

Cryptography

Symmetric Keys Distribution

Symmetric keys may be distributed manually or electronically, by using a public key transport mechanism, or they may be previously distributed for transport using other encryption keys. Keys used only for encrypting data in storage should not be distributed at all, except for backup or other specially authorized entities. A description of methods of symmetric keys distribution follows.

Splitting the keys. It is formally defined in FIPS 140-2 as a process by which a cryptographic key is split into multiple key components that individually share no knowledge of the original key. These components can be subsequently input into, or output from, a cryptographic module by separate entities and combined to recreate the original cryptographic key. Thus, FIPS 140-2 Level 3 requires

- A cryptographic module that separately authenticates the operator entering or outputting each key component.
- Cryptographic key components must be directly entered into or output from the cryptographic module without traveling through any enclosing or intervening systems where the key components may inadvertently be stored, combined, or otherwise processed.
- At least two key components must be required to reconstruct the original cryptographic key.

In practical examples, several components of the key can be stored on devices with different ports and network connections, as well as on different crypto tokens that require individual authentication by designated security officers.

Manual Key Distribution

The process should ensure that the keys are coming from an authorized source and are received by the intended recipient. Also, the entity delivering the key should be trusted by both the sender and the receiver. A key in transit should be encrypted with a key intended for key wrapping.

Electronic Distribution of Wrapped Keys (Key Transport)

It requires a preliminary distribution of key-wrapping keys. In many implementations, a public key of an asymmetric key pair is used as a key-wrapping key; therefore, a recipient in possession of the private key will be able to "unwrap" the symmetric key. If symmetric cryptography is used for wrapping the keys, those key-wrapping keys should be distributed via a separate channel of communication.

Public and Private Keys Distribution

As was discussed in the review of the methods of cryptography, one of the main advantages of using public and private key cryptography is easier key distribution of public keys. A party in possession of private keys can sign its message, and any receiving party who obtains the sender's public key can verify the signature. Likewise, any sender can obtain an encryption public key of a recipient, and only the recipient in possession of the counterpart private key can decrypt the encrypted data. While confidentiality of the public key is not needed, authenticity is. That is why public keys are usually distributed wrapped in public key certificates, issued and signed by a trusted certificate authority. The certificate, along with a public key, contains the subject's name and other attributes that indicate how the public key can be used. For easy access by relying parties, the certificates are either delivered with a signed message or made available in the directories and other publicly accessible distribution points.

Private keys are managed and distributed differently. If a signing private key must support non-repudiation, it should be generated and remain only in possession of the owner of this key, so no distribution applies. Although generating of public/private key pairs often takes place on a subject's node and the keys are placed in the crypto store on its hard drive or a hardware module, in some applications this is not the case. As described in the "Key Creation" section of this chapter, sometimes asymmetric key pairs, which do not have to support digital signatures with non-repudiation, may be generated on one of the servers of the public key infrastructure (either registration or distribution server), in cooperation between the servers and the subscriber, who is the owner of the keys. In such applications, private keys should be delivered to a subscriber via a secure encrypted channel with mutual authentication. Depending on policy, private decryption keys are also put in escrow, so that data may be decrypted if a subscriber leaves the organization or loses access to the keys.

When the public/private key pair is generated on the subscriber's site, there is no need to distribute the private key—it stays where it was generated and where it belongs.

A private key of a key pair generated on a central facility will be distributed only to the intended owner of that key, using either secure manual distribution or electronic distribution with security measures similar to those for symmetric key distribution, for example, authentication, encrypted channel, split knowledge, etc.

As was mentioned earlier, distributing static public keys does not require encrypted channels or split knowledge techniques, but it has its own specifics. A relying party, who obtains the keys either for verifying an owner's signature or for encrypting a message for the key owner, should have a high level of assurance that,

1. The key really belongs to the subject.
2. The key is associated with certain attributes belonging to the subject.
3. The key is valid.
4. The key is allowed by its policy to be used for the intended purpose.

All of these issues are addressed by using Public Key Infrastructure (PKI) and issuing X.509 certificates containing the subject's public keys and attributes. The certificates are digitally signed by a PKI Certificate Authority and can be distributed via open channels, manually, or via e-mail or published by LDAP, HTTP, and FTP servers. Because each subject's certificate is signed by a CA, a relying party should treat that CA's certificate itself as an anchor of trust. Distribution of the trusted CA's certificate is usually done via other channels. It can be preinstalled by a software manufacturer or obtained from other distribution points. More details about asymmetric key management are provided in a separate PKI section later in this chapter.

Key Storage

The ultimate goal of key management is to prevent any unsanctioned access without impeding legitimate use of the keys by crypto applications and service and key life cycle management processes. Key storage should meet several requirements, which may be different for different type of keys [NISTSP800-57-1]. Generally, these requirements are broken into several categories.

Keys may be maintained within a crypto module when they are in active use, or they may be stored externally under proper protection and recalled when needed. The protection of the keys in storage should provide

- *Integrity* (by CRC, MAC, digital signature, checksums, parity check, etc.): In addition to logical integrity, the keys stored in HSM may be physically protected by the storage mechanism itself. For example, a crypto store may be designed so that once the key is installed, it cannot be observed from outside. Some key-storage devices (specifically those that meet FIPS 140-2 level 3) are designed to self-destruct when threatened with key disclosure or when there is evidence that the key device is being tampered with.
- *Confidentiality* (by encryption, wrapping, and logical access control). Also, physical security is important (see earlier comments related to integrity).
- *Association with Application and Objects* (making sure that the key belongs to a designated object; e. g., encapsulating public keys with the object DN in a signed certificate or storing private signing keys in the object's protected key store).
- *Assurance of Domain Parameters* (making sure that domain parameters used in the PKI keys exchange are correct). Domain parameters are used in conjunction with some public key algorithms such as DSA and ECDSA (called p, g, and q parameter) to generate key pairs, to create digital signatures, or when generating shared secrets that are subsequently used to derive keying material.

Key Type	Security Service (Key Usage)	Required Security Protection	Required Association Protection	Period of Protection
Private signature key	Authentication; Integrity; Non-repudiation	Integrity; Confidentiality	Usage or application; domain parameters; public signature verification key	From generation until the end of the crypto period
Public signature verification key	Authentication; Integrity; Non-repudiation	Integrity	Usage or application; key pair owner; domain parameters; private signature key; signed data	From generation until no protected data needs to be verified
Symmetric authentication key	Authentication; Integrity	Integrity; Confidentiality	Usage or application; other authorized entities; authenticated data	From generation until no protected data needs to be verified
Private authentication key	Authentication; Integrity	Integrity; Confidentiality	Usage or application; public authentication key; domain parameters	From generation until the end of the crypto period
Public authentication key	Authentication; Integrity	Integrity	Usage or application; key pair owner; domain parameters; private authentication key; authenticated data	From generation until no protected data needs to be authenticated
Symmetric data encryption/ decryption key	Confidentiality	Integrity; Confidentiality	Usage or application; owner authorized entities; plaintext/ encrypted data	From generation until the end of the lifetime of the data or the end of the crypto period (whichever comes later)
Symmetric key wrapping key	Support	Integrity; Confidentiality	Usage or application; other authorized entities; encrypted keys	From generation until the end of the crypto period or no wrapped keys require protection (whichever comes later)
Symmetric and asymmetric RNG keys	Support	Integrity; Confidentiality	Usage or application	From generation until replaced
Symmetric master key	Support	Integrity; Confidentiality	Usage or application; other authorized entities; derived keys	From generation until the end of the crypto period or the end of the lifetime of the derived keys (whichever comes later)
Private key transport key	Support	Integrity; Confidentiality	Usage or application; encrypted keys; public key transport key	From generation until the end of the period of protection for all transported keys
Public key transport key	Support	Integrity	Usage or application; key pair owner; private key transport key	From generation until the end of the crypto period
Symmetric key agreement key	Support	Integrity; Confidentiality	Usage or application; other authorized entities	From generation until the end of the crypto period or until it is no longer necessary to determine key (whichever is later)
Private static key agreement key	Support	Integrity; Confidentiality	Usage or application; domain parameters; public static key agreement key	From generation until the end of the crypto period or until it is no longer necessary to determine key (whichever is later)
Public static key agreement key	Support	Integrity	Usage or application; domain parameters; key pair owner; private static key agreement key	From generation until the end of the crypto period or until it is no longer necessary to determine key (whichever is later)
Private ephemeral key agreement key	Support	Integrity; Confidentiality	Usage or application; domain parameters; public ephemeral key agreement key	From generation until the end of the key agreement process. After the end of the process, the key should be destroyed
Public ephemeral key agreement key	Support	Integrity	Usage or application; domain parameters; private ephemeral key agreement key; key pair owner	From generation until the end of the key agreement process.
Symmetric authorization key	Authorization	Integrity; Confidentiality	Usage or application; Other authorized entities	From generation until the end of the crypto period of the key
Private authorization key	Authorization	Integrity; Confidentiality	Usage or application; domain parameters; public authorization key	From generation until the end of the crypto period of the key
Public authorization key	Authorization	Integrity	Usage or application; key pair owner; private authorization key; domain parameters	From generation until the end of the crypto period of the key

Table 3.4 - **Protection requirements by key types [NIST SP 800-57-1]**

3

Cryptography

In addition to key protection, the key store should also provide availability. Keys should be available for authorized users and applications for as long as data is protected by these keys. A secure key and escrow is usually used for this. After the crypto period expires, the keys should be placed in an archive, which can be combined with backup storage.

Overall security requirements and business reasons may define the type of crypto store. Keys stored in the computer files may be more easily accessible than those that are stored in the hardware such as smart cards, external token devices, or PCMCIA. Usually the vendors of crypto applications such as PKI CA or application gateways, which perform signing and decrypting of SOAP messages, provide the users with the choice, so the implementer may decide to either use a hardware security module as a key store or to store the keys in the files. An application's independence from hardware crypto device vendors is achieved by using standard RSA PKCS#11 compliant interfaces [54]. A key file store is usually protected with an additional level of access control, so even a root user may not be able to access the key database if he or she does not have permissions and credentials for it.

Symmetric and private keys must be destroyed if they have been compromised or when their archive period (according to the policy) expires. Through the crypto period, when copies of the keys are made, these events should be documented; therefore, the keys' destruction should apply to all the copies. Specific methods used for key destruction are warranted by application and business requirements and acceptable risk. There are no specific requirements for destroying public keys. More specifically, processes for key destruction are described in NIST SP800-57 Part 2 [("Recommendation for Key Management—Part 2: Best Practices for Key Management Organization")] [55]. *Zeroization* is a technical term for destroying the keys by causing the storage medium to reset to all zeroes [NIST SP800-21] [56]. Automatic zeroization is required when an attempt is made to access the maintenance interface or tamper with a device meeting FIPS 140-2 level 3 requirements [FIPS 140-2]. The key management policy should describe in detail the process of zeroization in a specific key management system.

---

54   See the following for information on the RSA PKCS #11 Cryptographic Token Interface Standard: http://www.rsa.com/rsalabs/node.asp?id=2133

See the following for the PKCS #11 Base Functionality v2.30: Cryptoki – Draft 4:   ftp://ftp. rsasecurity.com/pub/pkcs/pkcs-11/v2-30/pkcs-11v2-30b-d6.pdf

55   See the following for NIST SP800-57 Part 2 Recommendation for Key Management— Part 2: Best Practices for Key Management Organization: http://csrc.nist.gov/publications/ nistpubs/800-57/SP800-57-Part2.pdf

56   See the following for NIST SP 800-21 [second edition], Guideline for Implementing Cryptography in the Federal Government: http://csrc.nist.gov/publications/nistpubs/800-21-1/ sp800-21-1_Dec2005.pdf

If it is believed that an encryption key of data at rest was compromised, this data should be reencrypted with a new key. This whole process is called key rotation, and it includes decrypting data with the old encryption key (which is believed to be compromised) and rekeying this data with the new encryption key. With large volumes of data, data availability may be affected. That is why a lot of efforts are made to limit the need to rekey data. It is achieved by using a randomly generated value as an encryption key and making it unavailable directly for any user, including administrators. The application administrator may control encryption and decryption processes, but the key contents will never be disclosed.

Key Update

Modern key management is highly automated. For most phases of the key life cycle, manual steps are not required. Although creating a seed sometimes may require users to move a mouse or enter a long sequence of random key strokes, users do not manually select, communicate, or transcribe real crypto keys. Modern key management makes a periodic key update in accordance with key policies easier. One example is an automatic key and certificates rollover in the PKI. When a key or certificate is approaching the "valid to" date and time, an automated key update will kick off. Another example is session encryption keys. When an encrypted connection just starts, an initial key is negotiated and exchanged between parties using the key encryption key. When a session duration or volume of transferred data exceeds the limits, a new session is established between the same parties, and a new session key will be renegotiated and used for transactions. More frequent key updates will reduce the chance of a successful cryptoanalytic attack and the volume of confidential data at risk. On the other hand, it may reduce system performance and increase the chance of key compromise in the case of misconfiguration. All the pros and cons should be evaluated, and keys' life span and frequency of key updates should be reflected in the policy.

Change of keys in the operational phase of the key life cycle may be caused by several reasons, as was alluded to earlier: key compromise, crypto period approaching the expiration date, or just a desire to reduce the volume of data encrypted with the same key.

A new key may be produced by auto rekeying or by an automated function updating an existing key. Rekeying is producing a key that is completely independent on the key it replaces. Rekeying is applicable when an old key is compromised, the key approaches its expiration date, or a new session key must be established according to the requirements.

3

Cryptography

Another way of changing the keys is by applying a nonreversible function to an existing key. Updating an old key in this manner does not require new key distribution or exchange between parties, so it may be less expensive. Parties may agree to exchange the keys on a particular day and time or upon exchanging a certain volume of encrypted data or on other conditions. This method does not apply in the case of key compromise.

Key Revocation

Whenever a key is compromised, it cannot be trusted to provide required security, cannot serve its purpose, and should be revoked. Generally, the key is considered to be compromised if it is released to or discovered by an unauthorized entity or this event is suspected to have happened. A key may enter the compromised state from any state except the destroyed state. Although the compromised key cannot be used for protection, in some cases it still may be used to process cryptographically protected information, with reasonable caution and suspicion. For example, a digital signature may be validated if it can be proved that the data was signed before the signing key was compromised and that the signed data has been adequately protected.

Key revocation applies both to symmetric and asymmetric keys and the process should be formally described in the Key Management Policy. In the asymmetric key management systems and PKI, technically, a public key is revoked (or most often, a public key certificate, containing that key), but as a result, its counterpart private key is also getting automatically revoked.

Information about key revocation may be sent as a notification to the involved parties, which would indicate that the continued use of the key is not recommended. This notification should include complete information about the revoked key, the date and time of revocation, and the reason. Based on the revocation information provided, other entities could then make a determination of how they would treat information protected by the revoked keying material.

Another method is to provide the participating entities (i.e., relying parties) with the access point for obtaining the status of the key material. For example, if a signature verification public key is revoked because an entity left the company, the information may be published in the Certificate Revocation List (CRL). But an application may still honor the signature if it was created before the certificate was published in the CRL [57]. At the same time, if a signing private key was compromised in an unknown time frame, but eventually the public

---

[57] Another problem is that many applications do not check CRLs by default e.g., most Web browsers
.

key certificate was revoked, the situation should be assessed more carefully. Certificate revocation in more detail will be reviewed in the section titled "Public Key Infrastructure."

A symmetric key that is used to generate a MAC may be revoked so that it is not used to generate a new MAC for new information. However, the key may be retained so that archived documents can be verified.

The recommended approach to the key revocation policy is to reflect it in the life cycle for each particular key. Thus, when a key is used in communication between just two parties, the entity revoking the key just informs another entity. On the other hand, if the key is used within an infrastructure with multiple relying parties, the revoking entity should inform the infrastructure, which should make the information about key revocation available to all relying parties.

Key Escrow

Generally, *escrow* is defined as something delivered to a third person (usually called an "escrow agent") to keep, and to be returned to the delivering entity under certain proof and conditions. This "something" may be a document, money, or a key.

In cryptography applications, a key escrow system operates with two components of one key, and these two components are entrusted to two independent escrow agents. For government applications [FIPS 185], these key components will be presented by the escrow agent to a requester, which may be an entity related to the owner of the key or a law enforcement organization, upon certain conditions, authorizations, and authentication [58].

This approach is implemented in electronic surveillance of encrypted telecommunications involving specific electronic devices. The key components obtained by the requester are entered into this device and enable decryption. Neither of the escrow agents can perform decryption, because it has just one component of the key. In applications for the private sector, the key components may be kept by two officers; therefore, if a key owner entity is not available, its encrypted information may be decrypted upon directions to the escrow officers from a higher official. Two types of risk exist in this schema: (1) collusion and (2) failure of reassembling and using the key for its intended purpose.

In order to support escrow capabilities in telecommunication, the U.S. government adopted the symmetric encryption algorithm SKIPJACK and a Law Enforcement Access Field (LEAF) method, which presents one part of a key

---

58   See the following for FIPS-185:   http://www.itl.nist.gov/fipspubs/fip185.htm

escrow system enabling decryption of encrypted telecommunications. Both the SKIPJACK and the LEAF creation method are implemented in electronic devices. The devices may be incorporated in security equipment used to encrypt (and decrypt) telecommunications data [59].

Decryption of lawfully intercepted telecommunications may be achieved through the acquisition and use of the LEAF, the decryption algorithm, and the two escrowed key components.

Backup and Recovery

Backup

According to 800-57-2 [NISTSP800-57-2], key recovery is a stage in the life cycle of keying material; mechanisms and processes that allow authorized entities to retrieve keying material from key backup or archive [60]. Key backup and recovery is a part of the KMS contingency plan, which according to 800-57-1 [NISTSP800-57-1],… "is a plan that is maintained for disaster response, backup operations, and post-disaster recovery to ensure the availability of critical resources and to facilitate the continuity of operations in an emergency situation."

As in the life cycle of any system, data can become unusable because of many reasons such as file corruption, hardware failure, configuration errors, etc. But in the case of cryptosystems management, backup should be considered only if there are no other ways (such as rekeying or key derivation) to provide continuity. These specific recommendations apply because of the risk associated with key backup, and the fact that key and other crypto information backup compromise is detrimental to the KMS operations. When planning key backup, the following questions should be answered: what key material needs to be backed up, where and how will the backup be stored, how will the backup and recovery procedures be performed, and who is responsible.

Not all the keys and cryptographic information should be backed up. For

---

59   See the following for RFC 4949, Internet Security Glossary, Version 2, [page 122], which is the basis of the definition of Law Enforcement Access Field (LEAF):   http://tools.ietf.org/html/rfc4949

See the following for a discussion of what LEAF is in relation to the Clipper Chip and its application: http://www.rsa.com/rsalabs/node.asp?id=2349

See the following for a discussion of what the Clipper Chip is: http://www.rsa.com/rsalabs/node.asp?id=2318

See the following for a discussion of Project Capstone and the SKIPJACK algorithm (commonly referred to as CLIPPER):   http://www.rsa.com/rsalabs/node.asp?id=2317

60   See the following for NIST SP800-57-2:   http://csrc.nist.gov/publications/nistpubs/800-57/SP800-57-Part2.pdf

instance, private signing keys should not be backed up, to avoid any questionable situation with non-repudiation. However, in the specific case of the CA's signing key, this does not apply, because unrecoverable loss of this key would prevent new certificates from being issued until the CA was rekeyed. Special security measures apply for the backup of this key, such as storing it on a removable hardware crypto token protected by multiple keys and passwords that is stored in a safe under administrative control. Separation of duties in this schema prevents collusions and key compromise. Ephemeral keys and shared secrets, which are generated during key negotiations and used for one session for data in transit, do not need to be backed up. An RNG seed should not be backed up either, because it is not used immediately for data encryption and is needed only for key generation.

It is important to mention that the life span of the key backup should be equal to or longer than the life span of the encrypted or signed data. Another specific feature that makes key backup and recovery different compared with similar processes for other data is the criticality of a key's availability and, thus, backup redundancy. Both competing requirements for minimizing risk of the backed-up keys' disclosure and redundant storage for robust key recovery should be considered.

Key Recovery

Keys may not be available for cryptographic operations when the key material stored as a file in the system or on a hardware device/token is corrupted, the key owner either loses access to the key material (i.e., forgotten/lost password) or is not available when the organization needs access to the data, and some other situations. Keys may need to be recovered to enable decryption of data previously encrypted with a lost key or to verify the integrity and authenticity of previously signed data if a signature verification key is lost. The key recovery process acquires a key from backup storage and makes it available for the decryption or verification process.

Public Key Infrastructure

At this point, the security architect should have fundamental knowledge about asymmetric cryptography, public key certificates, and PKI. The following will provide additional in-depth information regarding PKI and associated subjects. Before delving into the subjects in the following subsections, several points should be noted that will influence the context of those subsections:

- The most important aspects of certificates, their life cycle, purpose, restrictions, and the way these certificates are supposed to be managed should be documented in the Certificate Policy (CP) and

3

Cryptography

Certificate Practice Framework (CPF) [RFC 3647] [61]. CPF includes one or more Certificate Practice Statements (CPSs) that address "… the practices that a certification authority employs in issuing, managing, revoking, and renewing or rekeying certificates."

■ There are two categories of end entities that use PKI services: subscribers and relying parties. Subscribers are getting registered with PKI and subsequently generating or receiving private and public key pairs and receiving their certificates from a certificate authority (CA). Relying parties have access to the subscribers' public certificates, which they use for secure exchanges with subscribers. They trust the Certificate Authority, which is the heart of the PKI; hence, they rely on the PKI, which issues and supports certificates issued to subscribers.

■ Depending on the policies that rule PKI and the need for relying applications, there may be one-key two-key, and sometimes multikey pair implementations. A single key pair PKI application uses one public/private key pair for all applications needs, chiefly for data decryption/encryption and signing/verification.

■ Interoperability and integration of PKI with other IT infrastructure components and both client and server applications are very important issues for successful implementation and deployment. Although many relevant standards exist and are widely adopted, it should not be taken for granted that in the process of PKI enrollment, the keys will be placed in the right location on the client (subscriber) part and the certificate will be stored and published in a location that every relying party is aware of.

Key Distribution

The main reason why asymmetric cryptography and public certificates gained popularity is the manner in which they address the key distribution problem. In order to support authentication and confidentiality, each party needs to have its own symmetric keys dedicated for data exchange with one correspondent. If A is going to encrypt for B, C, and D, it would have to have individual keys for B, C, and D and send the keys to those parties in a secure manner. Each of B, C, and D would have to do the same. In sum, the two main problems of symmetric cryptography are the number of the required keys and the problem of their secure distribution. Public key cryptography solves both problems because of its nature. Keys come in pairs, and only the private key should be kept secret and should not be distributed. Its counterpart public key may be available to all parties, and hence may be published for public access on any server; that is, file server, LDAP, or Web server.

---

61   See the following for RFC 3647:   http://www.ietf.org/rfc/rfc3647.txt

For encryption, a recipient's public key may be used by any party wanting to encrypt data for that recipient, who is in possession of the counterpart private key. It guarantees that only this recipient in possession of that private key will be able to decrypt the data.

For digital signature verification, each recipient may obtain a public verification key of the sender and be confident in the authenticity of the signature, because only the sender holds the private key that is used to produce the digital signature being verified.

The main problem that exists with public key distribution is to guarantee the key's integrity and binding to the identifier of the holder of the counterpart private key. This problem is solved by using X.509 public key certificates, which bind the subject name to a public key, and this binding is sealed by the signature of the PKI Certificate Authority. Because the CA signature is trusted by all parties, the integrity of the public key and its binding with the subject are trusted too.

Public key distribution, which is implemented via certificate distribution, boils down to publishing these certificates on a server accessible by relying parties or just attaching the certificate to an encrypted or signed message. Private keys should not be distributed at all.

Certificate and Key Storage

When talking about PKI certificates and the keys, we should always remember the guidance provided in CP and CPS documents. The purpose of the certificates and their keys will dictate how they should be handled and stored.

For two-key-pair applications, where the encryption key pair and the corresponding public key certificate are created by the CA, the encryption public key certificates are most often placed in the subscriber's Directory entry and also in the PKI/CA database. Copies of the decryption private key and the encryption public key certificate will be securely sent to the subscriber and will be stored on the subscriber's machine on the disk or HSM. Decryption private keys should never be published, but they should be backed up. In a two-key-pair PKI, the subscriber generates the signing key on its machine and securely stores the signing private key on the disk or HSM. It sends only the verification public key to the CA in a secure manner. The signing private key is not sent to the CA, and it is never backed up in the CA's database. When the CA receives the verification public key, it generates a verification public key certificate. A copy of this certificate is stored in the CA database, and is also sent to the subscriber. Often, when the PKI subscriber sends a signed message to

3

Cryptography

any recipient, it attaches the verification certificate to it. So, a relying party does not have to access the directory to retrieve this certificate, which is required for signature verification.

For one-key-pair applications, a dual-usage key pair is generated on the subscriber's machine and stored on the disk or HSM. A copy of the dual-usage private and public key will be sent to the CA. The private key will be stored in the CA database. The CA will use the public key to generate a dual-usage public key certificate and will put it in the user's Directory entry. A copy of this certificate will be stored in the CA database. It will be also sent to the subscriber and will be stored on its machine on the disk or HSM.

In summary, there are several places where certificates and public and private keys are stored: PKI/CA database, Directory server, and subscriber's machine. The specifics are highly dependent on PKI implementation and CPS directives.

PKI Registration

PKI consists of many components: Technical Infrastructure, Policies, Procedures, and People [PKIREGAG]. Initial registration of subscribers (either users, or organizations, or hardware, or software) for a PKI service has many facets, pertaining to almost every one of the PKI components. There are many steps between the moment when a subscriber applies for a PKI certificate and the final state, when keys have been generated and certificates have been signed and placed in the appropriate locations in the system. These steps are described either explicitly or implicitly in the PKI CPS.

Reference to the CP and CPS associated with a certificate may be presented in the X.509.V3 certificates extension called "Certificate Policies." This extension may give to a relying party a great deal of information, identified by attributes "Policy Identifier" and "Policy Qualifier" in the form of Abstract Syntax Notation One object IDs (ASN.1 OID).

One type of Policy Qualifier is a reference to CPF, which describes the practice employed by the issuer when registering the subscriber (the subject of the certificate). Here we focus on the following:

1. How the subject proves its organizational entity.
2. How the person, acting on behalf of the subject, authenticates himself in the process of requesting a certificate.
3. How the certificate issuer can be sure that the subject, whose name is in the certificate request, is really in possession of the private key, to which the public key is presented in the certificate request along with the subject's name.

How the Subject Proves Its Organizational Entity

Authentication requirements in the process of registration with PKI depend on relations between the CA and the organization, the nature of an applying End Entity (EE) and CP, which is stating the purpose of the certificate. Thus, the organization may have its internal CA or may use a commercial CA to serve its all certificates needs. It may issue certificates of low assurance, which support just internal e-mail digital signature, or issue high assurance certificates, which encrypt and authenticate high value transactions between the organization and external financial institutions. Among end entities, there can be individuals, organizations, applications, elements of infrastructure, etc.

Organizational certificates are usually issued to the subscribing organization's devices, services, or individuals within the organization. These certificates support authentication, encryption, data integrity, and other PKI-enabled functionality when relying parties communicate. Among organizational devices and services may be,

- Web servers with enabled TLS, which support the server's authentication and encryption
- Web services security gateways, which support SOAP messages' authentication and signatures' verification, encryption, and decryption
- Services and devices, signing content (software codes, documents, etc.) on behalf of the organization
- VPN gateways
- Devices, services, and applications supporting authentication, integrity, and encryption of Electronic Data Interchange (EDI), B2B, or B2C transactions
- Smart cards for end user authentication

Among procedures enforced within applying organizations (before a certificate request to an external CA is issued) are the following:

- An authority inside the organization should approve the certificate request.
- The authority should verify that the subject is who he or she claims to be.
- After that, an authorized person (authorized submitter) within the organization will submit a certificate application on behalf of the organization.
- The organizational certificate application will be submitted for authentication of the organizational identity.
- Depending on the purpose of the certificate, an external certificate issuer will try to authenticate the applying organization, which

may include some but not all of the following steps, as in the following example [VeriSignCPS]:

- ¤ Verify that the organization exists.
- ¤ Verify that the certificate applicant is the owner of the domain name, which is the subject of the certificate.
- Verify employment of the certificate applicant and if the organization authorized the applicant to represent the organization.

A correlation between the level of assurance provided by the certificate and the strength of the process of validation and authentication of the EE registering with PKI and obtaining that certificate is always taking place.

How a Person, Acting on Behalf of the Subject, Authenticates to Request a Certificate (Case Studies)

Individual certificates may serve different purposes, for example: for e-mail signing and encryption, and for user authentication when they are connecting to servers (Web, directory, etc.) to obtain information or for establishing a VPN encryption channel. These kinds of certificates, according to their policy, may be issued to anybody who is listed as a member of a group (for example, an employee of an organization) in the group's directory and who can authenticate itself. An additional authorization for an organizational person may or may not be required for PKI registration.

An individual who does not belong to any organization can register with some commercial CAs with or without direct authentication and with or without presenting personal information. As a result, an individual receives his or her general use certificates. Different cases are now briefly described.

Online Certificate Request without Explicit Authentication

As in the example with VeriSign certificate of Class 1, a CA can issue an individual certificate (aka Digital ID) to any EE with an unambiguous name and e-mail address. In the process of submitting the certificate request to the CA, the keys are generated on the user's computer, and initial data for a certificate request, entered by the user (user name and e-mail address) is encrypted with a newly generated private key. It is all sent to the CA. Soon the user receives by e-mail his or her PIN number and the URL of a secure Web page to enter that PIN in order to complete the process of issuing the user's certificate. As a consequence, the person's e-mail address and ability to log into this e-mail account may serve as an indirect minimal proof of authenticity. However, nothing prevents person A from registering in the public Internet e-mail as person B and requesting, receiving, and using person B's certificate.

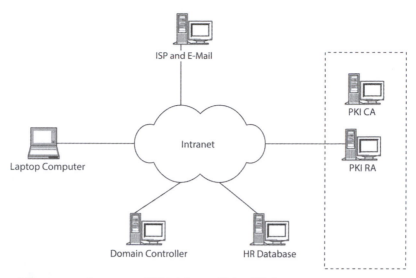

1. User enters to the corporate PKI/RA via intranet Web or GUI client.
2. User enters his name, e-mail address and other information pertaining to his authentication within corporate network.
3. PKI RA is using the data to authenticate the user against a corporate data IAW CPS policy
4. In the case of successful authentication an initialization request is forwarded to PKI CA
5. PKI/CA initiates the process of the user registration and issues authentication codes, bound to the user's distinguished name.
6. User receives the code, initiates key generation, sends to its certificate data to PKI/CA to complete the certificate issuing.

Figure 3.9 - **Authentication of an Organizational Person**

Authentication of an Organizational Person

The ability of the EE to authenticate in the organization's network (e.g., e-mail, domain) or with an organization's authentication databases may provide an acceptable level of authentication for PKI registration. Even just the person's organizational e-mail authentication is much stronger from a PKI registration perspective than authentication with public e-mail. In this case, user authentication for PKI registration is basically delegated to e-mail or domain user authentication. In addition to corporate e-mail and domain controllers, an organization's HR database, directory servers, or databases can be used for the user's authentication and authorization for PKI registration. In each case, an integration of the PKI registration process and the process of user authentication with corporate resources needs to be done (see *Figure 3.9*).

A simplified case occurs when a certificate request is initiated by a Registration Authority upon management authorization. In this case, no initial user authentication is involved.

Individual Authentication

In the broader case, a PKI registration will require a person to authenticate potentially with any authentication databases defined in accordance with CPS. For example, to obtain a purchasing certificate from the CA, which is

3

Cryptography

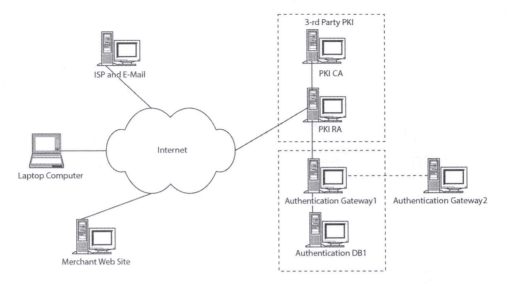

1. User enters to the 3-rd party PKI/RA via intranet Web or GUI client.
2. User enters his credentials to authenticate with his financial/payment institutions.
3. 3-rd party PKI RA is using the data to auhenticate the user with those institutions via authentication gateways IAW CP and CPS policy.
4. In the case of successful authentication an initialization request is forwarded to 3-rd party PKI CA
5. 3-rd party PKI/CA initiates the process of the user registration and issues authentication codes, bound to the user's distinguished name.
6. User receives the code, initiates key generation, sends to its certificate data to 3-rd party PKI/CA to complete the certificate issuing.
7. In the later transactions with merchant web site the user uses his certificate as credential.

Figure 3.10 - **Authentication of an Organizational Person**

integrated into a B2C system, a person will have to authenticate with financial institutions, which participate in the Internet purchasing transactions. In many cases, an authentication gateway or server will do it, using a user's credentials (see *Figure 3.10*).

Dedicated Authentication Bases

In rare cases, when a PKI CPS requires user authentication that cannot be satisfied by the existing authentication bases, a dedicated authentication database may be created to meet all CPS requirements. For example, for this purpose a prepopulated PKI Directory may be created, where each person eligible for PKI registration will be challenged with his or her password or personal data attributes. Among possible authentication schemes with dedicated or existing authentication databases may be a password with additional personal challenge-response data, such as mother's maiden name, make and year of a first car, biometrics, and others.

Face-to-Face

The most reliable, but most expensive method to authenticate an EE for PKI registration is face-to-face authentication. It is applied when the issued certificate will secure either high risk and responsibility transactions (certificates for VPN gateways, CA and RA administrators) or transactions of high value, especially when the subscriber will authenticate and sign transactions on behalf of an organization. To obtain this type of certificate, the individual must personally present and show his or her government-issued ID or badge and other valid identifications to the dedicated corporate registration security office and sign a document, obliging use of the certificate only for assigned purposes. All the procedures and sets of ID and documents that must be presented before an authentication authority are described in CPS.

Proof of Possession

A group of the key PKIX-CMP messages, sent by the EE in the process of initial registration, includes "Initialization Request," "Certification Request," and "PKCS10 Certification Request" messages. The full structure of these messages is described in [CRMF] [62] and [PKCS10] [63]. Certificate request messages, among other information, include "Public Key" and "Subject" name attributes.

The EE has authenticated itself out-of-band with the registration authority (RA) on the initialization phase of initial registration. Now an additional proof, that the EE, or the "subject," is in possession of a private key, which is a counterpart of the "public key" in the certificate request message, is required. It is a proof of binding, or so-called "Proof of Possession", or POP, which the EE submits to the RA.

Depending on the types of requested certificates and public/private key pairs, different POP mechanisms may be implemented:

- For encryption certificates, the EE can just provide a private key to RA/CA, or the EE can be required to decrypt with its private key a value of the following data, which is sent back by RA/CA:

  - In the direct method, it will be a challenge value, generated and encrypted and sent to the EE by the RA. The EE is expected to decrypt and send the value back.

  - In the indirect method, the CA will issue the certificate, encrypt it with the given public encryption key, and send it to the EE. The subsequent use of the certificate by the EE will demonstrate its ability to decrypt it, and hence the possession of the private key.

---

62   See the following for RFC 2511 Internet X.509 Certificate Request Message Format: http://www.ietf.org/rfc/rfc2511.txt

63   See the following for the current version of the PKCS#10 Standard: http://www.rsa.com/rsalabs/node.asp?id=2132

See the following for RFC 2986 PKCS #10: Certification Request Syntax Specification Version 1.7: http://tools.ietf.org/html/rfc2986

3

Cryptography

■ For signing certificates, the EE just signs a value with its private key and sends it to RA/CA.

Certificate Issuance

A certificate can be looked at as an electronic equivalent of a subject's ID document, which is issued for particular purposes in accordance with the organization's policy. Technically, the sanctioned and expected usage of the certificate is represented in the X.509 certificate "Key Usage" attribute. A relying party application is capable of verifying this attribute; therefore, the certificate will be used only within the scope of its key usage. For example, encryption certificates are issued for encrypting data for a recipient whose name is in the certificate, and verification certificates are issued to verify a signature of the sender who signed the message. Very often, one certificate is issued to serve many purposes. In any case, a relying party has information to help decide how much security the certificate can support, provided that the issuance and management of this certificate is trustworthy. Two main issues relating to this question are: Is an issuing CA trustworthy and how is the information in the certificate secured?

■ A certificate is digitally signed by an issuing CA, and it can be trusted only if the CA is trusted. A guard verifying a person's ID first looks to see what organization or country issued that ID and if the issuing authority is in the trusted list. In the same way, a relying party that verifies a certificate will verify if an issuing CA is in the trusted list. Technically, the application checks if that CA's certificate is installed in a designated storage and if it is not in the revocation list.

Information in the certificate is secured by a digital signature of the issuing CA. Anybody can view and browse the certificate and each of its attributes, including the subscriber ("subject") name with its public key and the CA ("issuer") name with its key identifier and the thumbprint. The certificate binds together all the attributes, including the most important: the subject's name and its public key. The integrity of this binding is preserved by the signature of the trusted issuing CA. Some details of this process already have been mentioned in the previous section, "PKI Registration." Before signing that binding, the CA has to receive evidence that a subscriber public key is associated with the subscriber. One of the ways to obtain it is a proof of possession of the private key. The subscriber, who generated a key pair, signs a message containing its public key and its common name with its private key. The message is sent to the CA directly or via the registration authority (RA) and is used as material for the public certificate. Other certificate attributes and extensions are defined

Public Key Certificate

Version
Certificate Serial Number
Signature algorithm ID
Issuer DN
Validity Perion
Subject DN
Subject Public Key Info
Issuer Unique ID
Subject Unique ID
Extentions
Signature

Figure 3.11 - **Format of X509.V3 certificate**

by certificates' templates. The format of the X509.V3 certificate is presented in *Figure 3.11*.

■ Once all the attributes are filled in, the certificate is digitally signed by the CA and sent to the subscriber or published in the Directory.

Trust Models

One fundamental purpose of PKI is to represent the trust relationship between participating parties. When a verifying party verifies another participant's certificate, generally it verifies a chain of trust between that participant's certificate and the verifier's anchor of trust. If that party's certificate was issued by a CA that is directly trusted by the verifier, then that CA is an anchor of trust. Otherwise, there are one or more intermediate CAs that constitutes a chain between the anchor of trust and the party's certificate to be verified. In both cases, the anchor of trust is based on a preconfigured certificate, in most cases provided out of band or as a configuration process. Several models described in the following text are available to provide chains of trust for PKI applications supporting multiple communities.

Subordinate Hierarchy

Very often, the current and long-term business reasons suggest putting two or more CAs into a hierarchical trust relationship. The CA hierarchy contains one root CA on top of the hierarchical tree and one or more levels of CA hierarchy of subordinate CAs (*Figure 3.12*). Each of the subordinate CAs has one immediate superior and may have one or more subordinates (the root CA is a top superior). A superior CA issues and signs CA certificates for its immediate subordinates. Only the root CA can issue and sign its own certificate. For crypto application operations, a subordinate issuing CA does not need to certify its superior. Each participant should know and trust a root CA, which establishes an anchor of trust. A relying party that trusts the root CA needs to validate a path from the root CA to the sender's certificate.

This model is good for internal enterprise applications, but the hierarchy may be hard to implement between enterprises because it must have in place the

3

Cryptography

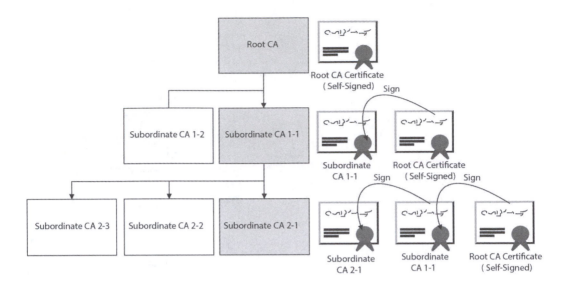

Figure 3.12 - **Hierarchical PKI CAs.**

shared cross-enterprise certificate policies and one shared root of trust. For more details about certificate chains issued by hierarchical PKI, see the section titled "Certificate Chains" later in this chapter.

Cross-Certified Mesh

Cross-certified mesh is probably the most general model of trust between CAs and participating PKIs. The hierarchical model described earlier may be interpreted as a mesh with some constraints. The mesh model is good for intercommunity and dynamically changing enterprise PKI applications, especially for nonhierarchical organizations. When organizations need to establish trust relations, they cross-certify their CAs, which does not require a change of anchors of trust or other elements of existing PKIs. This model is also good for merging previously implemented PKIs into one PKI. Cross-certification includes an exchange of participating PKIs' public verification keys and having each participating PKI sign the received key by its internal root CA. When more than two PKIs participate in the mesh, they create a web of trust by mutually cross-certifying each to each. Although no changes to each participating PKI are required, certificate verification in this model of trust is more difficult to implement because there may be multiple certificate paths. More details are given in the section titled "Cross-Certification" later in the chapter.

Bridge CA

When a cross-certified mesh is too dynamic and grows too fast to include n CAs, it may not scale well because it is supposed to include and support $n(n-1)$ cross-certifications and also because of potentially ambiguous verification paths. A bridge CA model may be helpful in this case. A large and very comprehensive implementation of this model is Federal Bridge Certification Authority (FBCA), which is well described in [FBCACP] and [FPKIATO][64]. As in the FBCA example, any bridge CA issues and manages cross-certificates for participating PKIs. By creating a mesh of participating root CAs, the bridge CA model allows participating parties to mutually validate each other's certificate paths. More details are given in the section titled "Cross-Certification" later in this chapter.

Trusted List

The most well-known example of a Trusted List model is a set of publicly trusted root certificates embedded in the Internet browsers. When a client system verifies another party's certificate, it tries to chain that certificate to one of the certificates in the list of trusted roots. A fundamental difference between this model and the previously discussed hierarchical, mesh, and bridge models is in the fact that the parties to be verified have to accommodate the relying parties' trusted roots. It moves management overheads from PKI CAs to the clients and in an environment with many CAs, may require a large number of root certificates to be included in the list of trusted CAs.

Certificate Chains

Each CA's certificate is located in the certificate chain, which starts at the root CA certificate and includes the certificates of all superior subordinate CAs. Certificates of the issuing CAs that issue certificates for end entities are at the end of this chain (see Figure 3.12). Several considerations should be taken into account:

- The validity of an issuing CA's certificate depends on the validity and life span of the whole certificate chain. If a root or an intermediate certificate at a higher level of hierarchy expires, validation of the end entity certificate issued by the issuing CA down the hierarchy should show negative. If any certificate in the chain is revoked, validation should show negative also. That is why the higher CA's certificates and certificate revocation lists (CRLs) usually have a life span that is significantly longer. The decreasing life span of the certificates in the chain is presented in *Figure 3.13*.

---

64   See the following for an overview of the IDManagement.GOV web site, specifically, the Federal PKI Management Authority documents section: http://www.idmanagement.gov/pages.cfm/page/Federal-PKI-Management-Authority-documents

The FBCACP and the FPKIATO documents can be found here:

FBCACP Certificate Policy for Federal Bridge Certification Authority Version 2.25, December 9, 2011.
 http://www.idmanagement.gov/fpkipa/documents/fbca_cp_rfc3647.pdf

FPKIATO Federal Public Key Infrastructure (FPKI) Architecture Technical Overview 2005.
http://www.idmanagement.gov/fpkima/documents/FPKIAtechnicalOverview.pdf

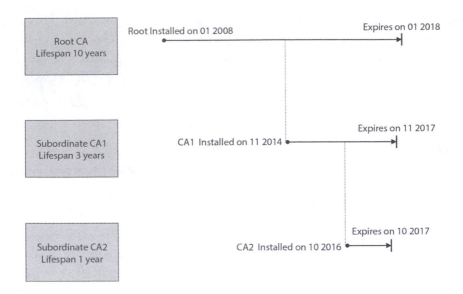

Figure 3.13 - **Hierarchical PKI certificate life span**

- The higher hierarchical CAs require higher security, because a compromise means revoking of all the subordinate and issuing CAs on lower levels as well as all the end entities' certificates. As a result, more certificates will be compromised and will require revocation. It is a common practice in PKI to take a root CA offline and lock its key storing medium in a secured safe store. It needs to be returned online only when its root certificate and immediate subordinate CA's certificates are approaching the end of life and need to be reissued to maintain validity of all subordinate chains or when a new immediate subordinate CA certificate should be issued or when one of the existing subordinate CAs is compromised and its certificate must be revoked. Another reason to put the root CA online is to let it update and publish the CRL when approaching the CRL expiration or when the CRL must be updated.

- The main purpose of the CA hierarchy and the use of certificate chains is to establish an anchor of trust (based on the root CA) and create a hierarchical model of trust. Distributing only a root CA certificate among all the relying parties is easier than distributing multiple CA's certificates. A relying party that needs to validate a certificate issued by an issuing CA in the hierarchical PKI starts walking up the chain until it reaches a root certificate, which is expected to be installed as a trusted CA certificate.

Certificate Revocation

When the private key of a subscriber is compromised or is suspected to be compromised, when an attribute of the certificate (e.g., rank) changes, or when trust between the CA and the subscriber is changed (for example, the employee holder of the certificate leaves the company), the issued certificate should be revoked immediately. The revocation process, from its origination to execution, should be described in the CPS. To inform relying parties, the revoked certificate is placed on a CRL, and the CA reissues, signs, and publishes the updated CRL. Regularly, or immediately after the revocation event, the latest CRL is published in a commonly available space (such as the directory server).

When a relying party (an application) receives a signed message, it should try to verify the signature. First, it checks to make sure the associated certificate has not expired, and second, it checks to make sure the certificate is still valid. Depending on business requirements, there can be two scenarios:

- A relying party is required to validate the certificate with the instantaneous revocation data. This is a real-time validation, and the relying party does not use any cache CRL.
- A relying party is only required to use a valid nonexpired CRL. A CRL is considered valid if a trusted CA has signed it and the current time is between the "this Update" and "next Update" CRL attributes. So any caching mechanisms can be used to store the CRL on the validating site.

Traditional CRL Model
A relying party checks a certificate against the latest published CRL. If the certificate is not in the CRL, it is assumed valid. Two cases are possible when the application is making this check:

- It does *not* have the current CRL in cache and has to retrieve it from a directory or other repository. This may also be the case if the real instantaneous certificate status is required. Requesting the CRL, the application will try to obtain the most current one.
- It *does* have the current CRL in cache. In this case, no instantaneous status is required, and, therefore, certificate validation can be done without retrieving the CRL from a repository.

In applications with a large number of subscribers and relying parties and with a high revocation rate, the CRL request rate can be very high, and CRLs themselves can be very long. This may introduce network and CRL-repository performance problems.

Modified CRL-Based Models

Several methods described in [CRMOD] and in [DCRL] attempt to address the aforementioned problems [65].

Overissued CRLs Reduce Peak Request Rate

Importantly, when the cache CRL is acceptable, the CRL requests' distribution peaks exponentially at the moment when all relying parties try to request the CRL the first time or when they try to do it after their cached CRLs expire.

As described in [CRMOD], one remedy for reducing the peak of CRL requests may be to issue the CRLs before they expire or to overissue CRLs. Because the CRL validity time remains the same, new overissued CRLs will have a shifted "next update" expiration time. Hence, relying parties will request replacement of their expired CRLs at different times. In other words, this method will spread out CRL requests. As shown in [CRMOD], if a CRL is valid for 24 hours and is reissued every 6 hours instead of every 24 hours, the peak request rate is reduced almost four times. This method can be recommended for applications that allow CRL cache and for which the expected revocation rate is low.

Segmented CRLs Reduce CRL Size

The idea is to reduce the size of the CRL or the portion of the CRL that a relying party needs to download, although this measure cannot reduce the peak request rate. Certificates may be allocated to different CRLs, based on some criteria or at random. This method was implemented in CRL distribution points (CRLDP), as in [RFC2459] [66]. X.509v3 certificates have a standard extension attribute called "CRLDistributionPoints" that provides the URI for the CRL, which is designated to the certificate if this certificate is revoked. When a relying party needs to validate the certificate, it requests this particular CRL. Designation of a particular CRL segment (CRLDP) to certificates is supported by CAs.

This method is recommended for applications that allow CRL caching and that have a high certificate-revocation rate. If instantaneous revocation data is required, it is also better than the method suggested earlier in traditional CRL

---

65   See the following for discussions of CRMOD and DCRL:

CRMOD -- Cooper, D. A Model of Certificate Revocation. Proceedings of the Fifteenth Annual Computer Security Applications Conference. December 1999.

Can be downloaded here: http://csrc.nist.gov/groups/ST/crypto_apps_infra/documents/acsac99.pdf

DCRL -- Cooper, D. A More Efficient Use of Delta-CRL. Proceedings of the 2000 Symposium on security and privacy.

Can be downloaded here: http://csrc.nist.gov/groups/ST/crypto_apps_infra/documents/sliding_window.pdf

A good overview of PKI and research such as the papers cited above through NIST can be found here: http://csrc.nist.gov/groups/ST/crypto_apps_infra/pki/pkiresearch.html

66   See the following for RFC 2459:   http://www.ietf.org/rfc/rfc2459.txt

or in the earlier section of this chapter titled "Over-Issued CRLs Reduce Peak Request Rate."

Delta CRLs

As was described earlier DCRL, the idea of using delta CRL was introduced to reduce the peak bandwidth in PKI applications, allowing caching but also requiring fresh certificate revocation information. A delta CRL provides only certificate revocation information changes since the full base CRL was issued. Base CRL is a traditional CRL containing all nonexpired revoked certificates. Its validity is much longer-lived than delta CRL, and a relying party does not request it frequently. Delta CRL validity is short. Hence, a relying party has to request it often. Because it contains only certificates revoked since the latest base CRL was issued, its size is supposed to be small. With delta CRL, an average request rate for the base CRL drops significantly, although the peak rate does not.

In DCRL, Cooper describes a further modification of delta CRL, which should allow a significant reduction of the base CRL request peak rate as well. It is a so-called sliding window delta CRL, which combines delta CRL with the CRL over-issuing method. Every time a delta CRL is issued, a full CRL is reissued as well. As described in the section titled "Over-Issued CRLs Reduce Peak Request Rate," it spreads out CRL requests from relying parties and reduces peak base CRL requests.

This sliding window delta CRL method promises the ability to supply very fresh CRL data combined with relatively low values for CRL-based validation methods, peak request rate, and bandwidth. Choosing an optimal window size is crucial.

Online Certificate Status Protocol

The Online Certificate Status Protocol (OCSP) is presented in [OCSP][67]. A relying party sends to the validation server its request on the status of the certificate in question. The server returns its signed response. The request/respond formats are presented in the following text. Because the OCSP request and response data chunks are significantly smaller than with all CRL-based ones, the bandwidth required for OCSP is lower compared with the CRL models for the same validation rate. On the other hand, the need to sign all OCSP responses implies higher power requirements on the validation server.

The following three items are data structures. These represent OCSP transactions.

3

Cryptography

---

67   See the following for RFC 2560:   http://www.ietf.org/rfc/rfc2560.txt

OCSP Request
- Protocol version
- Service request
- Target certificate identifier
- Optional extensions

OCSP Response
- Version of the response syntax
  - Name of the responder
  - Responses for each certificate in a request
  - Optional extensions
  - Signature algorithm OID
  - Signature computed across hash of the response
- Response for Each Certificate in a Request
  - Certificate identifier
  - Certificate status value (GOOD, REVOKED, UNKNOWN)
  - Response validity interval
  - Optional extensions

Unlike CRL-based models, an OCSP model is designed to provide instantaneous certificate status upon the certificate status request. Also, unlike CRL-based models, OCSP provides only the status of requested certificates, and it cannot be used by offline clients; for example, wireless devices wishing to authenticate the network to which they are attaching.

Cross-Certification

Cross-certification is a way of establishing trust between entities that are subscribers for different PKI certificates services and which have been issued certificates by different nonrelated CAs. In other words, it is a way of establishing a third-party trust. To make this happen, two CAs need to establish trust between each other, which is implemented via CA cross-certification. Cross-certification has a lot of implications. Complete understanding of Certificate Policy and Practice of each CA is required, because each party needs to know how much it can trust to the certificates issued by another CA, what are the enrollment, issuing, and revocation procedures of another CA, and what is the liability. Legal agreements and documents may be required as well.

How Applications Use Cross-Certification

If company A wants to trust company B, it should receive from company B its verification key, then issue a cross-certificate containing this verification key, and sign this certificate with company A's signing key. If an entity in company

A receives a message signed by company B, it will trust the signature because A certified its verification key with its signature. Trust does not necessarily have to be mutual. If company B does not want to trust A, it does not have to cross-certify A, although A cross-certified B; that is why we should also be specific if cross-certification is one-way or two-way (or mutual) trust. In addition to cross-certification, the companies should provide each other access to the end users' certificates.

Consider two cases when users of two companies that cross-certified their CAs will exchange secure messages (see *Figure 3.14*).

- An employee of A is going to send a signed and encrypted message to an employee of company B. He needs to find that employee and his certificate in the search base or through directory lookup.
- The employee of A verifies the cross-certificate issued by company A, to make sure that company B is still trusted. This is done by verification of its signature and validity dates and also checking if that certificate is not in the authority revocation list (ARL) of company A.
- Now the employee of A can verify if the encryption certificate of the recipient in company B is valid. It is done by checking integrity, validity dates, and presence in the CRL of company B. Also, the certificate should be signed by a key associated with the public key of the CA of company B, which is available in the cross-certificate.

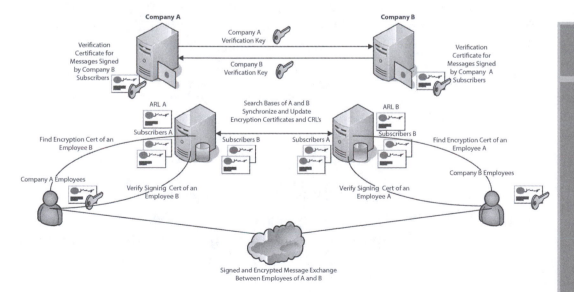

Figure 3.14 - **Cross-certified sites' exchange**

- If all the foregoing verifications are successful, then a user in company A will send the message with its signature and will encrypt this message with the public key from the certificate of the user of company B.
- Recipient B, after decrypting the message, will try to verify the signature of sender A.
- It validates the issuer of the verification certificate attached to the message by comparing the signature with a public key of the CA of company A, which is available in the cross-certificate issued by company B. It also verifies if the cross-certificate is valid and is not in company B's ARL.
- The user of company B also validates the verification certificate's integrity, its validity dates, and presence in company A's CRL.

How Cross-Certification Is Set Up

With all the considerations mentioned at the beginning of this section, both mutual and unilateral cross-certification may be done online and offline.

Online Cross-Certification

Online cross-certification requires TCP/IP connectivity between both CAs as well as their Directories. A company A, which wants to trust company B, has to give company B special access credentials (one time password, generated by CA A) to access A. A CA administrator of company B enters these credentials and connects to A to complete cross-certification. It securely sends online the CA B verification public key. CA A generates and signs a cross-certificate containing the public key of B. Depending on implementation and the PKI vendor, the process may be automated, and the new cross-certificate issued by A may be sent over to B and imported into its database and Directory.

Offline Cross-Certification

Offline cross-certification is the only method for CAs that does not have network connectivity. Nevertheless, the Directories should have connectivity for cross-certification as well as for online cross-certification. As in the case of online cross-certification, we assume that CA A wants to trust CA B, and CA B wants to be trusted by A. However, unlike in the online case, the offline cross-certification process is started by B generating its PKCS#10 certificate request with its verification public key and sending it to company A. After A verifies the request, it issues and signs the cross-certificate, stores it, and also sends it to B. The administrator of trusted CA B will import the cross-certificate issued by CA A into its database and Directory.

Once unilateral cross-certification is complete, the process may be repeated in the opposite direction if mutual cross-certification is required for business needs.

Cross-Certificates' Revocation

In order to break the trust between CAs, the cross-certified parties revoke the cross-certificates they issued. For example, if company A revokes the cross-certificate for company B, users of A will not be able to verify messages signed by users of B and will not be able to encrypt messages for users of B. Cross-certificates may need to be revoked for one of the following reasons:

- Partnership between companies A and B is terminated and their users do not need to use each other's certificates.
- The cross-certified CA is not trusted anymore.
- The cross-certified CA reissued its certificate and regenerated keys; thus, a new public key should be used for the cross-certificate.

Revoked cross-certificates are added to the ARL, which is used for any certificate verification as was mentioned earlier.

How Cross-Certification with a Bridge CA Is Implemented in Practice

The preceding example just described how cross-certification between two CAs works. With more than two CAs participating in this model and the CAs' mesh growing, certificate verification difficulties will start increasing. The bridge CA model helps to resolve these problems. Diagrams representing a cross-certified mesh and bridge CA are presented in *Figure 3.15*. Let us use FBCA [FBCACP] as an example for the Bridge CA case study:

- FBCA can be looked at as a nonhierarchical hub that would allow trust paths between participating PKIs to be created.

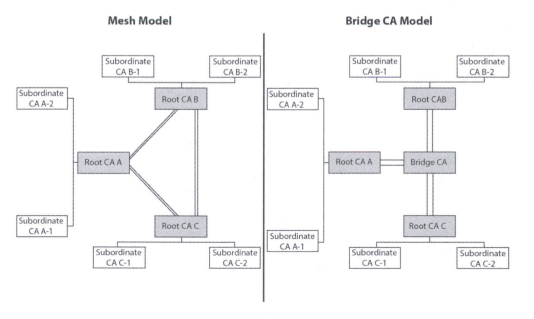

Figure 3.15 - **Cross-certified mesh and bridge CA models.**

- The FBCA would issue certificates to Principal CAs, which are CAs within participating PKIs, designated to cross-certify those PKIs directly with FBCA through the exchange of cross-certificates. The number of cross-certificates to support *n* PKIs is n * 2.
- Each PKI participating in FBCA, should be represented to FBCA by a single Principal CA. If a participating PKI is a hierarchical PKI, the Principal CA is typically its root CA. If a participating PKI is a mesh PKI, the Principal CA may be any designated CA within that PKI.
- The issued certificate will be posted in the FBCA directory. All cross-certified entities are notified by FBCA when the certificates are issued.
- Now, the subscribers of PKIs registered with FBCA may exchange signed and encrypted messages. The certificate's verification path will span FBCA and a sender's certificates.
- The certificate trust path between one participating PKI and all others can be discontinued by revoking its FBCA cross-certificate. A new CRL will be published in the FBCA directory.

Design Validation

Review of Cryptanalytic Attacks

Attacking a cryptosystem reveals its weaknesses and flaws. Cryptanalysis can be used to improve the design of a cryptosystem and may result in the discarding of a cryptographic algorithm altogether. The security architect should understand how cryptanalytic attacks can be used in validating cryptographic design as part of an architecture.

Attack Models

The following basic types of attacks are based on having some knowledge of the algorithm used. These attacks are characterized by the degree of plaintext and ciphertext the cryptanalyst has access to:

- *Ciphertext-only attack*: A sample of ciphertext, and preferably a large volume of ciphertext encrypted with the same algorithm, is required. While this is one of the most difficult attacks to execute, a successful attack reveals plaintext, and if completely successful, the key. This type of attack can reveal flaws in the algorithm. While cryptographic algorithms used in real-world applications must be vetted for weaknesses against ciphertext-only attacks, some protocols such as WEP have been found vulnerable to this type of attack.
- *Known-plaintext attack*: Having some plaintext and the corresponding ciphertext is necessary. An objective of this type

of attack is to determine the key and decipher all messages encrypted by it. This type of attack can be very practical when the corresponding plaintext is discoverable or can be deduced. Users of ZIP file archive encryption are very susceptible to this type of attack when a small portion of their archive is decrypted and becomes available for use in a known-plaintext attack.

■ *Chosen-plaintext attack*: This attack involves choosing the plaintext with the corresponding ciphertext.

■ *Chosen-ciphertext attack*: This attack involves choosing the ciphertext to be decrypted and gaining access to the resulting plaintext.

Symmetric Attacks

Variations on the attack models can be used in a controlled environment to reveal weaknesses in a cryptosystem and analyze an algorithm's strength. Two common attacks applied to the testing of symmetric ciphers are the techniques of differential cryptanalysis and linear cryptanalysis:

■ *Differential cryptanalysis*: These techniques involve a chosen plaintext attack with the aim of recovering the secret key. The basic method of differential cryptanalysis involves investigating the differences in ciphertext produced from pairs of chosen plaintext having specific differences. While this type of attack was used for determining a theoretical weakness in DES, the amount of chosen plaintext necessary (in excess of 10^{15} bytes) makes it impractical. DES was designed to resist differential cryptanalysis [Coppersmith].

■ *Linear cryptanalysis*: These techniques are based on a known-plaintext attack using pairs of known block-cipher plaintext and corresponding ciphertext in order to generate a linear approximation of a portion of the key. Instead of trying to keep track of differences propagated by chosen plaintext, linear cryptanalysis seeks to keep track of Boolean information in pairs of known plaintext and corresponding ciphertext to generate a probability in the confidence level of a specific key value. This method of attack is also commonly used to test block algorithms. While a theoretical attack against DES using linear cryptanalysis exists, it is considered impractical due to the amount of known plaintext–ciphertext required (2^{43} plaintexts) [Matsui].

Asymmetric Attacks

The algorithm in asymmetric cryptosystems is often based on solving some sort of mathematical problem such as the difficulty of integer factorization. As a result, applying the attack models to asymmetric cryptosystems can involve

3

Cryptography

319

finding improved or faster methods of solving the various mathematical problems. Designing or integrating with a particular asymmetric scheme must take into account mathematical discoveries such as more efficient methods of finding discrete logarithms or integer factorization.

Hash Function Attacks

The principle applied in determining the collision resistance of hash functions is based on the birthday problem in probability theory. This type of attack is known as the *Birthday attack*. The term *birthday* pertains to the probability that in a set of randomly chosen people some pair of them will have the same birthday [68].

Many cryptographic hash algorithms such as MD5 and SHA-1 are built from one-way functions, which are limited in their ability to provide collision resistance. When validating security in cryptosystems, one must consider that hash functions are applied in digital signature schemes and used as building blocks in MAC construction.

Network-Based Cryptanalytic Attacks

Cryptanalytic attacks can be facilitated by network communications such as protocols involved in the transmission of data or in operations such as key exchange. The following network-based attacks target more than just the cryptographic algorithm and exploit weaknesses in areas such as communication protocols or transmission methods:

- *Man-in-the-Middle attack*: This technique involves intercepting and forwarding a modified version of a transmission between two parties. In this type of attack, the transmission is modified before it arrives at the receiving party. Safeguarding a protocol against this attack usually involves making sure authentication occurs at each endpoint in the communication. For example, in a Web service design, it may be necessary to require mutual SSL authentication involving use of a mutually trusted certification authority.

- *Replay attack*: This attack involves capturing and retransmitting a legitimate transmission between two parties. Using this technique, impersonation or key compromise and unauthorized access to information assets may be possible. Protecting a protocol against this attack usually involves use of session tokens, time-stamping of data, or synchronization of transmission. For instance, IPSec provides an antireplay service using verification of sequence numbers, and the AH protocol in IPSec employs one-way hash functions to protect against impersonation.

---

68   See the following for a discussion of the Birthday Attack problem [page 66]:   http://www.rsa.com/rsalabs/faq/files/rsalabs_faq41.pdf

■ *Traffic Analysis attacks*: Observing traffic flow in encrypted communications can reveal information based on message volume or communication patterns, or show which parties are communicating. Protection against traffic analysis is a concern not only in the design of military signals intelligence systems, but in the design of commercial systems as well. For instance, SSH, when operating in interactive mode, transmits every key stroke as a packet. Packet analysis can therefore reveal information about the password lengths. A general countermeasure to protect against traffic analysis is to use traffic padding where feasible. Another approach to protecting messages traversing untrusted networks from traffic analysis involves anonymizing the message sender. This can be done by using a chain of proxy servers where the message is encrypted separately at each proxy in order to make the source and destination of the communicating parties more difficult to determine.

Attacks against Keys

An ideal goal for cryptanalysis is to extract the secret key. Observing how keys are used is important in validating a cryptographic design. Using the same key to encrypt larger volumes of data increases the success of a cryptanalytic attack. Also, the use of an appropriate key length is important, as noted earlier in the chapter.

Testing for weak keys during generation is another basic element of validating a cryptosystem. Understanding the ability of a random number generator to introduce entropy during key generation is an important factor in this, because greater randomness makes determining the key more difficult.

Secret keys must also be protected from unauthorized access and should remain encrypted when stored. In a cryptographic system where multiple secret keys are necessary, for example, with a tape encryption appliance device, it is common to encrypt individual working keys with a top-level master key. The storage of the top-level secret key used in such a cryptosystem can be done using key shares, a technique also known as split-knowledge. This involves splitting the key into multiple pieces and granting access to each share to separate individuals. This ensures that no one individual has access to the stored master key. To ensure security of this master secret key when it is in use within the cryptosystem, logical access controls and physical controls such as tamper-proof enclosures are used. In validating cryptosystems, it is essential to check that the subsystem components and processes that protect the secret key are functioning as intended. The following attacks against keys are variations on the cryptanalytic attack models and are also important in validating cryptosystems:

3

Cryptography

■ *Meet-in-the-Middle attack*: This attack applies to double encryption schemes such as 2DES and 3DES; it works by encrypting known plaintext using each possible key and comparing results obtained "in the middle" from decrypting the corresponding ciphertext using each possible key. This known plaintext attack was used against DES to show that encrypting plaintext with one DES key followed by encrypting it with a second DES key is no more secure than using a single DES key, and it reduces the strength of 3DES to only 112 bits.

■ *Related-Key attacks*: These forms of attack involve relationships between keys that become known or are chosen while observing differences in plaintext and ciphertext when a different key is used. For instance, two keys that transform all plaintexts identically can be considered equivalent, a simple relation. It is beneficial to employ a related-key attack against stream ciphers because they typically employ a common key in combination with some varying nonsecret initialization vector (IV). An example of using a *related-key attack* to demonstrate that an encryption scheme is insecure is with WEP, in which the RC4 stream cipher uses a keystream comprising a WEP secret key and an exposed IV.

Brute Force Attacks

For a cryptosystem to be considered secure, a successful brute force attack must be computationally infeasible. For symmetric key ciphers, this involves an exhaustive search of the key space in order to determine plaintext. The result of the brute force is the secret key used for encrypting the ciphertext. Besides providing an indication of the security of the cryptosystem, a successful brute force attack involving a particular secret key would mean that any ciphertext encrypted with that particular key and potentially all future derived keys would become readable via the attack.

A brute force attack against asymmetric key ciphers involves applying computing resources to solving the underlying mathematical problem the algorithm is based on, such as in factoring large integers for RSA public-key encryption. The computational feasibility of solving a particular problem such as factoring an integer of a particular size gives an indication of the strength of the algorithm.

Side-Channel Cryptanalysis

Side-channel attacks are based on information gained from the physical implementation of the cryptosystem. These attacks mainly deal with obtaining and analyzing information that originates from the cryptosystem hardware rather than weaknesses in the cryptographic algorithm. Side-channel attacks can be based on the execution time of a cryptographic algorithm, power consumption within a cryptographic module, or electromagnetic emanations from a computer. Side-channel cryptanalysis requires substantial technical knowledge of the underlying hardware.

Susceptibility to side-channel cryptanalytic attack is an important consideration for any architecture where cryptography is applied. The following are some of these types of attacks:

- *Timing attacks*: This attack requires the ability to accurately measure the time required to perform a particular operation within a cryptosystem. Timing attacks are based on detailed hardware performance characteristics such as memory cache hits and CPU instruction time for a given key and input data (plaintext or ciphertext). By using the baseline performance characteristics for a specific piece of hardware where the cryptosystem is implemented, successful attacks against protocols and algorithms such as Diffie–Hellman, RSA, DSS, and others can be executed [Kocher].

- *Differential Fault Analysis*: This method involves introducing hardware faults into the cryptosystem in order to determine the state of internal data. This type of attack can be used to read the state of memory in order to determine a secret key. The technique can be applied to various types of semiconductor memory, including integrated circuits that are frozen and removed or to smart card memory that is read nondestructively [Samyde et al.].

- *Differential Power Analysis*: In this method, power consumption measurements in a hardware device such as a smart card are made during encryption operations while ciphertext is recorded. The attack can be used to reveal a secret key [Kocher et al.].

Risk-Based Cryptographic Architecture

Computing power, which grows by Moore's law; new developments in cryptanalysis; virtually borderless enterprise network topologies; wider than ever exposure to targeted attacks from different domestic and foreign entities—all these factors are constantly moving cryptographic standards higher. At the same time, the main purpose of cryptography—supporting confidentiality, integrity, and availability—should be served in the most productive and cost-effective manner. We move from DES to AES, from a key size of 56 bits to 256 bits, but as was stated in the section titled "Key Management," the strength of any crypto system or application is more than just strength of the algorithms and key size.

More often, crypto systems are compromised because of weaknesses in key management and processes around it. A risk-based approach to the crypto

3

Cryptography

systems and applications design should help to architect a balanced and cost-effective solution that meets business requirements. Many areas of cryptographic architecture for government agencies are driven by regulatory compliance with appropriate prescriptive guidance documented in the NIST FIPS publications referred to earlier. Designing cryptography for private sector industries, where regulatory compliance is less strict or not required at all, leaves more room for the security architect making design decisions. But it may still be a good idea to follow a risk-based approach. The security architect can use either qualitative or quantitative measures when assessing the risk. If quantitative risk assessment data is available, each design option may be assessed based on the cost, benefits, and the risk. Otherwise, qualitative methods should be used. Risk is assessed to determine the impact of given losses and the probability that these losses will occur.

The process of designing a cryptographic system is similar to the process used for any other IT system. The architecture should include appropriate crypto modules, components, and methods, and should be integrated with the surrounding infrastructure and supported applications in order to address the organization's needs and meet the requirements. Based on the requirements, several cryptographic methods may be needed. For example, both symmetric and asymmetric cryptography may be needed in a system, each performing different functions (e.g., symmetric encryption, asymmetric digital signature, and key establishment). It is important to be able to demonstrate traceability from the requirements back to the policies, goals, and risks to be mitigated. The following areas may be considered for a cryptographic system high-level design:

- Hardware- and software-based components
- Security of cryptographic modules
- What cryptography should be used for a network environment
- What approved algorithms will be used, and key lengths
- Key management infrastructure
- Integration with hosting infrastructure and supported applications
- Interoperation with external organizations
- User interface
- User acceptance
- User training

It is important for the security architect to develop confidentiality, integrity, and availability objectives. These objectives are at a high level and should address security, in general, and cryptography, specifically. The design should include software and hardware, procedures, physical security considerations, environmental requirements, etc.

After preliminary high-level and requirements-based architecture design is done, a preliminary risk assessment should be performed, and specific unique requirements associated with each component should be finalized. After the risk assessment has been performed, policies should be developed regarding the use of evaluated systems and cryptographic modules operating within the designed system.

Identifying Risk and Requirements by Cryptographic Areas

Risk management includes two components: assessing the risk and selecting and implementing appropriate countermeasures. The largest areas of risk addressed by cryptography are unauthorized disclosure and data modification, or confidentiality and integrity. Although the risks cannot be completely eliminated, they can be reduced to an acceptable level by using cryptographic controls. The risk management process ensures that the threats are known, as well as their impact, and that cost-effective countermeasures are applied. Risk assessment includes assessment of the assets and current protecting mechanisms, identification and assessment of the threats, assessment of potential losses and their likelihood, and their classification by criticality and sensitivity, and, finally, identification of potential mitigating controls and cost-benefit analysis.

Most often, the type of risk assessment that is performed is a qualitative analysis, rather than a formal quantitative analysis, and the results are used in developing the system requirements and specifications. The scope of risk analysis varies depending on the sensitivity of the information and the number and types of risks that need to be addressed. The next task is to identify categories of cryptographic methods and techniques that meet the requirements and mitigate the specific risks. There may be more than one method that can mitigate each risk.

Traceability from the requirements back to the policies and associated risk assessment is important. The following table is based on the data presented in the NIST SP800-21-1 [SP800-21-1] and demonstrates logical dependencies between risk and requirements for different cryptographic areas.

3

Cryptography

	Cryptographic Area	Risk	Technical and Assurance Requirements
1	Cryptographic Module Specification: Specify cryptographic boundary; specify cryptographic algorithms; diagram configuration; specify security policy; describe operational and error states	Incorrect implementation	Cryptographic requirements addressed in overall system/product requirements.
			Security policy (including security rules), configuration block diagram
2	Cryptographic Algorithms (identify FIPS-approved algorithms and other cryptographic algorithms): Encryption	1. Unauthorized disclosure of data or undetected modification of data (intentional and accidental) during transmission or while in storage	1. FIPS-approved AES algorithm or three key TDEA algorithm; conformance tests
		2. Denial of service	
		3. Session capture	
		4. Man-in-the- middle attack	
3	Cryptographic Algorithms: Block Cipher Modes of Operation	Same as above	
4	Cryptographic Algorithms: Cryptographic Modules	Same as above	FIPS-approved cryptographic algorithms; conformance testing
5	Cryptographic Algorithms: Hash Functions	Same as above	Secure Hash Algorithm, message digest; conformance tests
6	Cryptographic Algorithms: Digital Signatures		Digital Signature Algorithm (DSA), RSA, ECDSA, digital signature generation/verification; message digest; random/pseudorandom number generation; hash function
			Algorithms for generating primes p and q; private key generation; conformance tests
			Cryptographic requirements addressed in overall system/product requirements
7	Cryptographic Algorithms: Random Number Generation		Algorithms for generating deterministic random bit generators; conformance tests
8	Cryptographic Module Ports and Interfaces: physical and logical input and output data paths	Unintentional output of plaintext data	Physical/logical separation of data input /output ports, control input, status output, data input, data output; documentation of the interfaces and input and output data paths
		Design error	
9	Roles, Services, and Authentication: Roles and associated services; authorization and access control mechanisms	1. Unauthorized access by authorized/unauthorized individuals	1. Role-based authentication mechanisms
		2. Masquerade	2. Identity-based authentication mechanisms, maintenance-access interface; documentation of the authorized roles, services, operations, and functions
		3. Password compromise	1. Token-based authentication
		4. Replay attacks	2. Biometrics-based authentication
			3. Cryptographic authentication protocols (secret key and public key cryptosystems)
			1. Digital signature algorithm
			2. Digital signatures
			3. Random/pseudorandom number generator
			4. Unilateral authentication protocol
			5. Mutual authentication protocol
			Cryptographic requirements addressed in overall system/product requirements

	Cryptographic Area	Risk	Technical and Assurance Requirements
10	Physical Security: Specify physical security configuration and mechanisms; specify features or testing procedures (includes EFP/EFT)	1. Unauthorized physical access to the contents	1. Production grade enclosures
		2. Unauthorized use or modification, e.g., module substitution	2. Tamper evidence, or tamper resistance
		3. Unusual environmental conditions or fluctuations that results in disclosures of critical security parameters	3, 4. Tamper response of shutdown of the module; zeroization of plaintext security keys and other unprotected critical security parameters (CSPs)
		4. Unauthorized disclosure of plaintext critical security parameters	1, 2, 3. Specification of the physical embodiment, description of the applicable physical security mechanisms
			4. Specification of the environmental failure protection features, documentation of the environmental failure tests performed and the results
11	Operational Environment: Specify access, authorization, audit controls; identify critical security parameters (CSPs) and cryptographic data	1. Unauthorized access by authorized/unauthorized individuals	Level 1: Single operator, executable code, approved integrity technique
		2. Undetected modification of cryptographic component	Level 2: Referenced PPs evaluated at EAL2 with specified discretionary access control mechanisms and auditing
		3. Unauthorized modification, substitution, insertion, and deletion of cryptographic keys and other CSPs	Level 3: Referenced PPs plus trusted path evaluated at EAL3 plus security policy modeling
			Level 4: Referenced PPs plus trusted path evaluated at EAL4
12	Cryptographic Key Management: Specify random number generation, key generation, key establishment, key entry and output, key storage, and key destruction	1. Unauthorized disclosure, modification, and substitution of secret/private keys	Key entry/output: Levels 1, 2. plaintext. Levels 3, 4. encrypted keys or split knowledge for manual-distribution
		2. Unauthorized substitution and modification of public keys	Key destruction: Zeroize all plaintext cryptographic keys and other unprotected CSPs
			Specification of the FIPS-approved key generation algorithm; documentation of the key distribution techniques
			1. NIST-approved key generation algorithms
			2. Use of error detection code (message authentication code)
			1. Encrypted IVs
			2. Key naming
			3. Key encrypting key pairs
			4. Random number generation
			Cryptographic requirements addressed in overall system/product requirements
13	EMI/EMC: identify FCC conformance requirements	Emanations	Conformance to FCC requirements
			Cryptographic requirements addressed in overall system/product requirements
14	Self-Tests: Identify power-up and conditional tests	1. Module malfunction	Cryptographic requirements addressed in overall system/product requirements
		2. Unauthorized disclosure of sensitive data	Documentation on error conditions and actions to clear the errors;
			1. Cryptographic algorithm test
			2. Critical functions test.
			3. Pair-wise consistency test (for public and private keys)
			5. Software/firmware load test
			6. Manual key entry test
15	Design Assurance: Describe the design of the software/hardware/firmware; explain the correspondence between the design and the security policy	Incorrect/invalid operation of the module	Cryptographic requirements addressed in overall system/product requirements
			Level 4. Formal model, informal proof

3

Cryptography

Note that the risk of each cryptographic area should be assessed for each individual system and application. If the risk is higher than an acceptable level, technical requirements should be strengthened.

Case Study

To clarify how all this information fits together, walk through the following use case and the process of defining requirements, identifying risks, and then proposing cryptographic methods that meet those requirements and mitigate the risks.

The use case involves secure communications for a device management function. Cryptography for communication between a management console and management server and between the management server and managed devices should support confidentiality, authentication, authorization, and integrity. In this scenario, the business function being performed is firewall rule changes. So the management console will be a firewall administrator's workstation, the management server will be the system that affects firewall rulebase changes, and the managed devices will be firewalls. For simplicity's sake, the scope will exclude firewall monitoring, audit logging, and device network configuration functions, and the design will be vendor neutral (refer to *Figure 3.16*).

Information flow in this use case is represented by flow "1" between the management console and management server, and by flow "2" between the management server and the managed devices. For the rulebase management scenario:

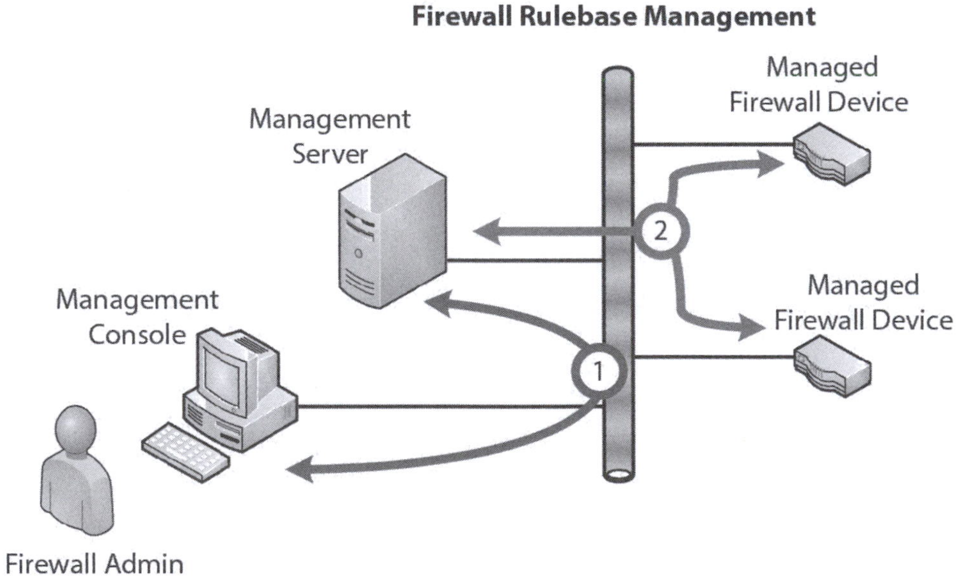

Figure 3.16 - **Cryptography for communication between a management console and management server and between the management server and managed devices**

- Managed devices may receive and store very sensitive configuration and corporate information, and its unauthorized disclosure may be detrimental.
- Integrity of the management data in transit and in store is crucial.
- Availability of these encrypted communication channels is important, but lost connectivity for a short time will not lead to major losses.

The functional requirements will be:

- Provide secure communication between the manager's console and the management server.
- Provide secure communication between the management server and managed devices.

The following risks are defined:

- Unauthorized disclosure of data in transit between the console and server and server and managed devices.
- Unauthorized and undetected modification of data in transit between the console and server and server and managed devices.
- An unauthenticated or unauthorized console gets access to the server.
- An unauthenticated or unauthorized server gets access to a managed device.
- Data in transit is modified in a nonauthorized manner (man-in-the-middle attack).
- Unauthorized disclosure, modification, and substitution of secret/private keys.
- Unauthorized substitution and modification of public keys.

The intent is to apply cryptography as the means to meet the requirements and address the risks. For the use case, a security architect would recommend the following:

1. The management server includes an internal CA, which issues certificates for every console and managed device.
2. Key pairs are generated on each new console and device added to the system. After that, the keys are sent to the management server's CA for issuing certificates.
3. TLS tunnels with Mutual Authentication (MTLS) between the management server, and devices and console provide required access control, integrity, and confidentiality of the data in transit.
4. A FIPS 140-2-compliant hardware cryptographic module provides required physical and logical security, including protection of the private and secret keys, RNG, and AES 128 encryption for TLS

3

Cryptography

sessions. Keys never appear in cleartext. These measures ensure mandatory key management.

5. Access to the consoles and management server with an internal CA requires 2-factor authentication. All data flows between the management server and console and devices goes encrypted via MTLS tunnels.

The recommendations we propose for our scenario fall into the following cryptographic areas. For a sound design, they should meet the following requirements:

Cryptographic Area:

- Cryptographic algorithms (identify FIPS-approved algorithms and other cryptographic algorithms): Encryption.
- Cryptographic algorithms: Digital signatures.
- Cryptographic key management: Specify random number generation, key generation, key establishment, key entry and output, key storage, and key destruction.

Technical and Assurance Requirement:

- FIPS-approved AES algorithm or three key TDEA algorithm; conformance tests.
- Digital Signature Algorithm (DSA), RSA, ECDSA, digital signature generation/verification; message digest; random/pseudorandom number generation; hash function. Algorithms for generating primes p and q; private key generation; conformance tests. Cryptographic requirements addressed in overall system/product requirements.
- Key entry/output: Levels 1, 2—plaintext. Levels 3, 4—encrypted keys or split knowledge for manual distribution.
- Key Destruction: Zeroize all plaintext cryptographic keys and other unprotected CSPs.
- Specification of the FIPS-approved key generation algorithm; documentation of the key distribution techniques.
- NIST-approved key generation algorithms.
- Use of error detection code (message authentication code).
- Encrypted IVs.
- Key naming.
- Key encrypting key pairs.
- Random number generation.
- Cryptographic requirements addressed in overall system/product requirements.

It is important to look at the cryptographic areas and requirements both individually and as a whole. The following are some common design flaws that might be found in this or other scenarios:

1. Using a strong cryptographic algorithm when the RNG supporting key generation is weak does not protect against key weaknesses and potential compromise.

2. The RNG may be very strong, but key management has a flaw and does not provide sufficient protection for private and secret keys.

3. Remote access control to the system incorporates strong two-factor authentication, but local access and physical access control are very weak.

4. Bulk data encryption is performed on the management server data store using the wrong block cipher mode; for example, ECB for bulk data encryption.

5. Encryption is implemented without any integrity checking; for example, HMAC.

6. Key exchange is performed with weak or no authentication.

7. Faulty key distribution methods; for example, sending the key in cleartext!

8. Symmetric key is not changed when the IV or the counter space is exhausted.

An unbalanced architecture design will produce a weak crypto system in which properly selected and designed components cannot compensate for the weak ones that introduce additional risks.

Cryptographic Compliance Monitoring

A risk-based cryptographic architecture will employ components in a manner that meets business requirements while allowing for a business-defined acceptable level of risk. To manage this risk effectively, there must be control over the risk-impacting factors in designs of solutions employing cryptography. For instance, a digital signature scheme must employ an acceptable cryptographic hashing function, such as those specified in NIST FIPS 180-4, the Secure Hash Standard [FIPS 180-4][69]. So, cryptographic compliance monitoring in the context of design of a cryptosystem would mean assessing conformity to cryptographic standards.

Security requirements for an IT solution can include *confidentiality*, *integrity*, or one of the other benefits of cryptography. The source of these requirements can be regulations or standards specified by legal frameworks, corporate governance,

---

69 See the following for FIPS PUB 180-4 Secure Hash Standard (SHS), March 2012: http://csrc.nist.gov/publications/fips/fips180-4/fips-180-4.pdf

or policies. For instance, corporate standards requiring confidentiality of personal information may require encrypting the information. So, cryptographic compliance monitoring in the design of an IT solution would mean measuring adherence to regulations in a larger context, where cryptographic controls are used to satisfy a regulatory requirement.

Cryptographic Standards Compliance

Cryptographic standards provide for assurance that a particular security level that is required can be maintained. An example is NSA Suite B, which includes FIPS-197 (AES) and complements encryption algorithms for hashing, digital signature, and key exchange that U.S. federal agencies must adhere to. Making certain that products follow the same standards such as NSA Suite B will also help ensure compatibility.

The Computer Security Division at NIST coordinates test suites for many of the NIST cryptographic standards. The Cryptographic Algorithm Validation Program (CAVP)[70], established by NIST and the Communications Security Establishment Canada (CSEC)[71], provide validation testing via accredited third-party laboratories for a number of cryptographic algorithms. CAVP validation of an algorithm used in a cryptosystem is a prerequisite for another validation program established by NIST, the Cryptographic Module Validation Program (CMVP)[72]. CMVP validates adherence of cryptographic modules to Federal Information Processing Standards (FIPS)140-2 Security Requirements for Cryptographic Modules, and other FIPS cryptography-based standards. CAVP and CMVP programs maintain and publish validation lists for algorithms and cryptographic modules. The CAVP list provides validated implementations of cryptographic algorithms showing vendor, validation date and certification number, operational environment, and other information such as key sizes and block cipher mode. The CMVP list shows FIPS-140-2 validated modules by vendor, validation date and certification number, and other details related to FIPS-140-2.

Cryptographic standards will also appear in corporate security policies and standards such as those indicating when to use encryption or specifying the level and strength of encryption to use, including key lengths and crypto periods.

---

70   See the following for an overview of the NIST CAVP: http://csrc.nist.gov/groups/STM/cavp/index.html

71   See the following for the CSEC web site: http://www.cse-cst.gc.ca/index-eng.html

72   See the following for an overview of the NIST CMVP: http://csrc.nist.gov/groups/STM/cmvp/index.html

Determining if cryptographic controls meet governmental or corporate standards is a function of compliance monitoring. Determining compliance with such cryptographic standards should be performed as part of an assessment of an IT system's design. It is important that this be completed during the requirements phase of an IT project, so that a given solution is developed to meet these standards.

Compliance with security standards for cryptography can also occur at the user level. For example, an organization may require that its personnel use encryption when sending certain types of data via e-mail. It should be noted that monitoring user-level actions such as these may be difficult, and require specialized services such as those provided by data leak protection solutions.

An additional area where compliance is associated with a cryptosystem is the notion of a compliance defect that may exist within a cryptosystem. A compliance defect may be thought of as the inability of a cryptosystem to securely perform one of its functions, and is a noncompliance in a more general sense. Don Davis defines a compliance defect in a cryptosystem as a rule of operation that is both difficult to follow and unenforceable [Davis]. According to Davis, public key cryptography has five unrealistic rules of use corresponding with the crucial moments in a key pair's life cycle. Davis calls these compliance defects and specifies them as follows:

1. Authenticating the user (issuance): How does a CA authenticate a distant user when issuing an initial certificate?
2. Authenticating the CA (validation): Public key cryptography cannot secure the distribution and validation of the root CA's public key.
3. Certificate revocation lists (revocation): Timely and secure revocation presents enormous scaling and performance problems. As a result, public key deployment is proceeding without a revocation infrastructure.
4. Private key management (single-sign on): The user must keep his long-lived private key in memory throughout his login session.
5. Passphrase quality (PW-Change): There is no way to force a public key user to choose a good passphrase.

Industry- and Application-Specific Cryptographic Standards Compliance

It is important that cryptographic controls themselves be compliant with standards. It is likewise important to satisfy the requirements of standards that specify how a cryptographic benefit must be employed. For instance, the California Information Practice Act (SB1386) [73] specifies that if customer information is encrypted when it is stored and transmitted, it is exempt from costly notification procedures in the event of a breach. Regulations applying to information systems that include cryptographic requirements will often specify use of a cryptographic control in a general sense, such as needing "encryption" or requiring a "key management system."

Payment Card Industry Data Security Standard

One industry standard involving encryption is the Payment Card Industry Data Security Standard (PCI DSS), which requires protection and encryption of cardholder data. In the PCI standard, the essential requirement in protecting cardholder data is to not store it at all if possible. When it must be stored, the PCI standard specifies general attributes for cryptographic controls while enumerating the operational methods that must be employed. For instance, hash functions, cryptography, and key generation must be "strong." In relation to cryptographic requirements, PCI focuses on operational procedures and administrative controls such as key-custodian acceptance of responsibilities.

So, auditing a system for PCI compliance will include these types of cryptographic requirements. To see the PCI DSS 2.0 requirements relating specifically to encryption, refer to the portions of the standard that describe key management as well as protection and encryption of cardholder data at the PCI Security Standards Council Web site: https://www.pcisecuritystandards.org/security_standards/index.php

Health Insurance Portability and Accountability Act

A governmental regulation that includes requirements for the benefits that cryptography can provide are the provisions of the Health Insurance Portability and Accountability Act of 1996 (HIPAA) enacted by the U.S. Congress. These requirements are found in the Administrative Simplification provisions of the act (HIPAA, Title II), which among other things addresses the security and privacy of health data.

Requirements relating to cryptography are found in the Final Rule on Security Standards [Final Rule]. The Final Rule is where the U.S. Department of Health and Human Services stipulates three types of security safeguards required for compliance: administrative, physical, and technical. Within the technical safeguards, the Final Rule provides a set of security standards as follows:

- Access Control
- Audit Controls

---

73   See the following for the full text of SB1386:   http://leginfo.ca.gov/pub/01-02/bill/sen/sb_1351-1400/sb_1386_bill_20020926_chaptered.html

- Integrity
- Person or Entity Authentication
- Transmission Security

These standards support the Final Rule by providing a minimum security baseline intended to help prevent unauthorized use and disclosure of Protected Health Information (PHI). Within each standard, policies, procedures, and technologies are either required and must be adopted, or are subject to individual evaluation (known as "addressable implementation specifications").

Encryption for data at rest falls under the Access Control standard, because encryption used with an appropriate key management scheme can be used to deny access to PHI, except for authorized individuals. The standards in the Final Rule state that encryption of data at rest is an addressable implementation specification, leaving it up to the system owner to determine whether it is required.

While the use of specific cryptographic technologies is not stipulated in the Audit Controls and the Integrity standards, meeting these standards is required by HIPAA. Thus, cryptographic hashing algorithms and digital signatures can be used as a basis for supporting the Integrity standard. The same cryptographic controls can support Audit Controls by ensuring that a change to a transaction log's integrity can be detected.

The Final Rule makes person or entity authentication a mandatory requirement without providing specifics. The Person or Entity Authentication standard does not specify use of any particular technology, allowing "covered entities to use whatever is reasonable and appropriate."

Transmission Security is required in the Final Rule, which stipulates

> The covered entity must implement technical security mechanisms to guard against unauthorized access to electronic protected health information that is transmitted over an electronic communication network.

The Transmission Security standard includes integrity controls to ensure that electronically transmitted PHI is not improperly modified. The standard also specifies encryption as a mechanism to protect electronic PHI being transmitted over open network such as the Internet. Both of these controls, integrity and encryption, are addressable implementation specifications and hence can be optional.

3

Cryptography

So, when considering HIPAA compliance, one will certainly need to address whether or not cryptographic controls are required [74]. Auditing a system for HIPAA compliance must take into account the basis for a decision when cryptographic controls are deemed unnecessary in meeting a HIPAA standard. In order to monitor cryptographic compliance for a system that processes, transmits, or stores data subject to HIPAA standards, these system-specific cryptography requirements must be defined.

International Privacy Laws

Not all industry or government regulations explicitly stipulate use of particular cryptographic controls such as encryption or digital signatures. Privacy laws, in particular, deal with confidentiality of data but generally do not stipulate that encryption be used as the means of control. Use of encryption to protect confidentiality is left to the detailed security requirements defined for a particular solution, based on the security risk present.

An example of a privacy law where confidentiality is required is Article 17 of the European Union Data Protection Directive [EU Data Protection] which states:

> Member States shall provide that the controller must implement appropriate technical and organizational measures to protect personal data against accidental or unlawful destruction or accidental loss, alteration, unauthorized disclosure or access, in particular where the processing involves the transmission of data over a network, and against all other unlawful forms of processing[75].

Audit Readiness and Compliance

Audit readiness and compliance oversight must take into account the requirements for cryptographic controls when addressing cryptographic compliance. In general, the need for cryptographic compliance with industry and government regulations is dependent upon criticality of data and security risk. For a given

---

74   On January 2, 2013, the United States Department of Health & Human Services announced that losing a single laptop containing sensitive personal information about 441 patients will cost a non-profit Idaho hospice center $50,000, marking the first such penalty involving fewer than 500 data-breach victims. The patient data was unencrypted at the time of the laptop loss.

See the following for the official HHS News Release announcing the settlement: http://www.hhs.gov/news/press/2013pres/01/20130102a.html

75   See the following for the full text of the Directive 95/46/EC of the European Parliament and of the Council of 24 October 1995 on the protection of individuals with regard to the processing of personal data and on the free movement of such data: http://eur-lex.europa.eu/LexUriServ/LexUriServ.do?uri=CELEX:31995L0046:en:HTML

solution, the business requirements, type of data, and how the data will be accessed stored and transmitted all contribute to the need for compliance with such standards. The security architect should be prepared to engage in an audit and explain complex systems, such as an organization's implementation of PKI, and why specific design decisions were chosen.

Summary

There are many moving parts in a well- constructed security architecture. These parts have to be managed and monitored, pulling together infor-mation, business needs, risks, threats, vulnerabilities, and users into a dynamic solution that can be volatile. The security architect needs to provide solutions to the business that will safeguard data as well as ensuring that it remains available for use by authorized users on demand. The cryptography domain illustrates for the security architect the many options that are available for them to create systems that provide for data confidentiality, integrity and availability. The challenge that the security architect has is in finding the right balance in their designs, allowing for users to create, store, consume, and manage data over time, while also ensuring that the needs of the business are met, and risks are mitigated.

3

Cryptography

References

SHA-3 NIST. Announcing Request for Candidate Algorithm Nominations for a New Cryptographic Hash Algorithm (SHA–3) Family, Office of the Federal Register. National Archives and Records Administration. Available at http://csrc.nist.gov/groups/ST/hash/federal_register.html.

S/MIME IETF S/MIME Working Group. Internet Draft. Secure/Multipurpose Internet Mail Extensions (S/MIME) Version 3.2 Message Specification. Expires March 18, 2009.

PEM IETF Privacy-Enhanced Electronic Mail Working Group. RFC 1421, RFC1422, RFC 1423, RFC 1424. Proposed Standards. February 1993.

PGP Copyright © 1990-2001 Network Associates, Inc. and its Affiliated Companies. All Rights Reserved., *PGP Freeware for Windows 95, Windows 98, Windows NT, Windows 2000 & Windows Millennium User's Guide Version 7.0*. January 2001.

802.11 IEEE Std 802.11™-2007 (Revision of IEEE Std 802.11-1999). IEEE Computer Society. June 12, 2007.

WEP ibid.

802.11i IEEE Std 802.11i™-2004 (Amendment to IEEE Std 802.11™, 1999). IEEE Computer Society. July 23, 2004.

WPA B. Bing (Ed.). Understanding and achieving next-generation wireless security. *Emerging Technologies in Wireless LANs: Theory, Design, and Deployment*. Cambridge University Press, New York, 2008.

WPA2 ibid.

SP800-121 NIST Special Publication 800-121. Guide to Bluetooth Security. September 2008.

FC-SP H. Dwivedi. *SANs: Fibre Channel Security*. Securing Storage: A Practical Guide to SAN and NAS Security. 2005.

CIK Department of Defense Security Institute. *STU-III Handbook for Industry*. February 1997.

P1619 https://siswg.net/.

EDI NIST. Federal Information Processing Standards Publication 161-2. April 29, 1996.

CMS IETF Network Working Group. *Cryptographic Message Syntax (CMS)*. RFC 3852. Proposed Standard. July 2004.

WS-Security M. O'Neill et al. *Introduction to WS-Security*. Web Services Security. 2003.

NSA Suite B Cryptography http://www.nsa.gov/ia/industry/crypto_suite_b.cfm.

Modes A. Menezes, P. van Oorschot, and S. Vanstone. *Block Ciphers*. Handbook of Applied Cryptography. 1996.

RFC2144 C. Adams, Entrust Technologies. *The CAST-128 Encryption Algorithm*. RFC2144. Informational Memo. May 1997.

CMEA D. Wagner, B. Schneier, J. Kelsey. 17th Annual International Cryptology Conference. *Cryptanalysis of the Cellular Message Encryption Algorithm.* August 1997.

GOST State Standards Committee of the USSR. *Cryptographic Protection for Data Processing Systems, Cryptographic Transformation Algorithm, GOST 28147-89.* Government Standard of the U.S.S.R. July 1, 1990.

RC2 D. Wagner, B. Schneier, J. Kelsey. ICICS '97. *Related-Key Cryptanalysis of 3-WAY, Biham-DES, CAST, DES-X, NewDES, RC2, and TEA.* November 1997.

RC5 A. Biryukov, E. Kushilevitz. Advances in Cryptology—EUROCRYPT '98. *Improved Cryptanalysis of RC5.* June 1998.

RC6 R. Rivest, M.J.B. Robshaw, R. Sidney, Y.L. Yin. RSA Laboratories. *The RC6 Block Cipher.* August 20, 1998.

TEA http://143.53.36.235:8080/tea.htm.

Twofish http://www.schneier.com/twofish.html.

DH W. Diffie, M. Hellman. *New Directions in Cryptography. IEEE Trans. Information Theory.* Vol. 22, No. 6, pp. 644–654, November 1976.

RSA R.L. Rivest, A. Shamir, and L. Adleman. A method for obtaining digital signatures and public-key cryptosystems. *Commun. ACM.* Vol. 21, Issue 2, pp. 120–126, February 1978.

PKCS #1 B. Kaliski, J. Staddon, RSA Laboratories. *PKCS #1: RSA Cryptography Specifications Version 2.0.* RFC 2437. Informational Memo. October 1998.

Merkle-Hellman Knapsack A. Menezes, P. van Oorschot, and S. Vanstone. Public-key encryption. *Handbook of Applied Cryptography.* CRC Press, Boca Raton, FL. 1996.

Tunnels V. Klima. IACR ePrint archive Report 2006/105. *Tunnels in Hash Functions: MD5 Collisions within a Minute.* Version 2. April 2006.

SHA-1 Collisions X. Wang, Y.L. Yin, and H. Yu. *Finding Collisions in the Full SHA-1.* Advances in Cryptology, Crypto'05. 2005.

Collisions X. Wang, D. Feng, X. Lai, and H. Yu. IACR ePrint archive Report 2004/199. Collisions for Hash Functions MD4, MD5, HAVAL-128 and RIPEMD. August 17, 2004.

Dedicated Hash ISO/IEC 10118-3:2004. *Information technology—Security techniques—Hash-functions—Part 3: Dedicated hash-functions.* March 1, 2004.

SCHNEIER Bruce Schneier. *Applied Cryptography.* Second edition, John Wiley & Sons, New York, 1996.

NISTSP800-57-1 NIST Special Publication 800-57. Recommendation for Key Management—Part 1: General (Revision 3). NIST July 2012.

SP800-67 NIST Special Publication 800-67. Recommendation for the Triple Data Encryption Algorithm (TDEA) Block Cipher. Revised May 19, 2008.

FIPS197 Federal Information Processing Standards Publication 197. Announcing the ADVANCED ENCRYPTION STANDARD (AES). November 26, 2001.

SP800-56 NIST Special Publication 800-56A. Recommendation for Pair-Wise Key Establishment Schemes Using Discrete Logarithm Cryptography (Revised). March 2007.

RSA PKCS#1 PKCS #1 v2.1: RSA Cryptography Standard. *RSA Laboratories.* June 14, 2002.

3

Cryptography

339

FIPS 140-2 Federal Information Processing Standards Publication 140-2. Security Requirements for Cryptographic Modules. May 25, 2001.

TECHREV-OPENSSL Technology Review. Alarming Open-Source Security http://www.technologyreview.com/news/410159/alarming-open-source-security-holes/.

FIPS 140-3 Federal Information Processing Standards Publication 140-3 (DRAFT). (Will Supersede FIPS PUB 140-2, May 25, 2001).

ANNEX C-FIPS 140-2 Annex C Approved Random Number Generators For FIPS PUB 140-2. Draft. October 2007.

FIPS 186-3 Federal Information Processing Standards Publication. FIPS 186-3. Digital Signature Standard (DSS). June 2009.

SP800-90 NIST Special Publication 800-90. Recommendation for Random Number Generation Using Deterministic Random Bit Generators (Revised). March 2007.

NIST SP800-21 NIST Special Publication 800-21. Guideline for Implementing Cryptography in the Federal Government. November 1999.

FIPS 185 Federal Information Processing Standards Publication 185. Escrowed Encryption Standard. November 1994.

NIST SP800-56, 56A, 57 part 1 and 57 part 2.

FIPS186-3 FEDERAL INFORMATION PROCESSING STANDARDS PUBLICATION. Digital Signature Standard (DSS). March 2006.

ANS X9.42-2003 (Public Key Cryptography for the Financial Services Industry: Agreement of Symmetric Keys Using Discrete Logarithm Cryptography).

ANS X9.63-2001 (Public Key Cryptography for the Financial Services Industry: Key Agreement and Key Management Using Elliptic Curve Cryptography).

RFC 3647 IETF Network Working Group. RFC 3647. Internet X.509 Public Key Infrastructure Certificate Policy and Certification Practices Framework. November 2003.

PKIREGAG A. Golod, PKI registration. *Information Security Management Handbook*. 4th Ed., Auerbach Publications, Boca Raton, FL, 2003.

VeriSignCPS Verisign Certificate Practice Statement, version 2.0. 2001.

CRMF IETF Network Working Group. RFC 2511. Certificate Request Message Format. March 1999.

CRMOD Cooper, D. *A Model of Certificate Revocation*. Proceedings of the Fifteenth Annual Computer Security Applications Conference. December 1999.

DCRL Cooper, D. *A More Efficient Use of Delta-CRL*. Proceedings of the 2000 Symposium on security and privacy.

RFC2459 Housley, R., W. Ford, W. Polk, D. Solo, *Internet X.509 Public Key Infrastructure Certificate and CRL Profile*. RFC2459. January 1999.

OCSP M. Myers, R. Ankney, A. Malpani, S. Galperin, C. Adams, *X.509 Internet Public Key Infrastructure. Online Certificate Status Protocol—OCSP*. RFC2560. June 1999.

Coppersmith D. Coppersmith. The DES Encryption Standard (DES) and its strength against attacks. *IBM J. Res. Develop.*, Vol. 38 No. 3. May 1994.

Matsui M. Matsui, Advances in Cryptology—CRYPTO '94. The First Experimental Cryptanalysis of the Data Encryption Standard. 1994.

Kocher P. Kocher. *Timing Attacks on Implementations of Diffie–Hellman, RSA, DSS, and Other Systems*. Proceedings of the 16th Annual International Cryptology Conference on Advances in Cryptology , LNCS, Vol. 1109, pp 104–113, August 1996.

Samyde et al D. Samyde, S. Skorobogatov, R. Anderson, and J. Quisquater. *On a New Way to Read Data from Memory*. Proceedings of the First International IEEE Security in Storage Workshop, pp 65-69, December 2002.

Kocher, et al P. Kocher, J. Jaffe, and B. Jun. *Differential Power Analysis*. Proceedings of the 19th Annual International Cryptology Conference on Advances in Cryptology, LNCS, Vol. 1666, pp 388-397, August 1999.

FIPS 180-4 Federal Information Processing Standards Publication. FIPS 180-4. Secure Hash Standard (SHS). March, 2012.

[Davis] D. Davis. *Compliance Defects in Public-Key Cryptography*. Proceedings of the 6th USENIX Security Symposium. July 1996.

[Final Rule] Department of Health and Human Services HIPAA Security Rule, Office of the Federal Register, National Archives and Records Administration, available at http://www.cms.hhs.gov/SecurityStandard/Downloads/securityfinalrule.pdf.

[EU Data Protection] Directive 95/46/EC of the European Parliament and of the Council of 24 October 1995 available at http://eur-lex.europa.eu/LexUriServ/LexUriServ.do?uri=CELEX:31995L0046:en:HTML

[RIPEMD-160] http://homes.esat.kuleuven.be/~bosselae/ripemd160.html.

[RFC4301] S. Kent, K. Seo, BBN Technologies. Network Working Group. Proposed Standard. *Security Architecture for the Internet Protocol*. RFC 4301. December 2005.

[RFC2404] C. Madson, Cisco Systems Inc., R. Glenn, NIST. Network Working Group. *The Use of HMAC-SHA-1-96 within ESP and AH*. RFC2404. November 1998.

[RFC 2406] S. Kent, BBN Corp, R. Atkinson, @Home Network. Network Working Group. *IP Encapsulating Security Payload (ESP)*. RFC2406. November 1998.

RFC4650 M. Euchner. Network Working Group. *HMAC-Authenticated Diffie–Hellman for Multimedia Internet KEYing (MIKEY)*. RFC4650. September 2006.

FBCACP Certificate Policy for Federal Bridge Certification Authority Version 2.25, December 9, 2011.

http://www.idmanagement.gov/fpkipa/documents/fbca_cp_rfc3647.pdf

FPKIATO Federal Public Key Infrastructure (FPKI) Architecture. Technical Overview. 2005.

http://www.idmanagement.gov/fpkima/documents/FPKIAtechnicalOverview.pdf

3

Cryptography

 **Review Questions**

1. What cryptographic hash function would be the acceptable replacement for MD4?

    A. MD5

    B. RIPEMD

    C. RIPEMD-160

    D. SHA-1

2. An IPSec Security Association (SA) is a relationship between two or more entities that describes how they will use security services to communicate. Which values can be used in an SA to provide greater security through confidentiality protection of the data payload?

    A. Use of AES within AH

    B. SHA-1 combined with HMAC

    C. Using ESP

    D. AH and ESP together

3. Suppose a secure extranet connection is required to allow an application in an external trusted entity's network to securely access server resources in a corporate DMZ. Assuming IPSec is being configured to use ESP in tunnel mode, which of the following is the most accurate?

    A. Encryption of data packets and data origin authentication for the packets sent over the tunnel can both be provided.

    B. ESP must be used in transport mode in order to encrypt both the packets sent as well as encrypt source and destination IP Addresses of the external entity's network and of the corporate DMZ network.

    C. Use of AH is necessary in order to provide data origin authentication for the packets sent over the tunnel.

    D. Source and destination IP Addresses of the external entity's network and of the corporate DMZ network are not encrypted.

4. What is the **BEST** reason a network device manufacturer might include the RC4 encryption algorithm within an IEEE 802.11 wireless component?

    A. They would like to use AES, but they require compatibility with IEEE 802.11i.

    B. Their product must support the encryption algorithm WPA2 uses.

    C. RC4 is a stream cipher with an improved key-scheduling algorithm that provides stronger protection than other ciphers.

    D. Their release strategy planning includes maintaining some degree of backward compatibility with earlier protocols.

5. What is true about the Diffie–Hellman (DH) key agreement protocol?

    A. The protocol requires initial exchange of a shared secret.

    B. The protocol depends on a secure communication channel for key exchange.

    C. The protocol needs other mechanisms such as digital signatures to provide authentication of the communicating parties.

    D. The protocol is based on a symmetric cryptosystem.

6. What is the main security service a cryptographic hash function provides, and what is the main security property a cryptographic hash function must exhibit?

    A. Integrity and ease of computation

    B. Integrity and collision resistance

    C. Message authenticity and collision resistance

    D. Integrity and computational infeasibility

7. What is necessary on the receiving side in order to verify a digital signature?

    A. The message, message digest, and the sender's private key

    B. The message, message digest, and the sender's public key

    C. The message, the MAC, and the sender's public key

    D. The message, the MAC, and the sender's private key

8. What is a known plaintext attack used against DES to show that encrypting plaintext with one DES key followed by encrypting it with a second DES key is no more secure than using a single DES key?

    A. Meet-in-the-middle attack

    B. Man-in-the-middle attack

    C. Replay attack

    D. Related-key attack

9. What is among the most important factors in validating the cryptographic key design in a public key cryptosystem?

    A. Ability of a random number generator to introduce entropy during key generation

    B. Preimage resistance

    C. Confidentiality of key exchange protocol

    D. Crypto period

10. What factor would be most important in the design of a solution that is required to provide at-rest encryption in order to protect financial data in a restricted-access file sharing server?

    A. Encryption algorithm used

    B. Cryptographic key length

3

Cryptography

    C. Ability to encrypt the entire storage array or file system versus ability to encrypt individual files

    D. Individual user access and file-level authorization controls

11. A large bank with a more than one million customer base implements PKI to support authentication and encryption for online Internet transactions. What is the best method to validate certificates in a timely manner?

    A. CRL over LDAP

    B. CRLDP over LDAP

    C. OCSP over HTTP

    D. CRLDP over ODBC

12. A car rental company is planning to implement wireless communication between the cars and rental support centers. Customers will be able to use these centers as concierge services, and rental centers will be able to check the car's status if necessary. PKI certificates will be used to support authentication, non-repudiation, and confidentiality of transactions. Which asymmetric cryptography is a better fit?

    A. RSA 1024

    B. AES 256

    C. RSA 4096

    D. ECC 160

13. A key management system of a government agency's PKI includes a backup and recovery (BR) module. PKI issues and manages separate certificates for encryption and verification. What is the right BR strategy?

    A. Back up all certificates and private keys

    B. Back up all private keys and verification certificates

    C. Back up decryption keys and all certificates

    D. Back up signing keys and all certificates

14. A company needs to comply with FIPS 140-2 level 3, and decided to use split knowledge for managing storage encryption keys. What is the right method for storing and using the key?

    A. Store the key components on the encrypted media.

    B. Create a master key and store it on external media owned by the first security officer.

    C. Store key components on separate external media owned by a different security officer.

    D. Publish key components on an LDAP server and protect them by officers' asymmetric keys encryption.

15. An agency is using symmetric AES 128 cryptography for distributing confidential data. Because of its growth and key distribution problems, the agency decided to move to asymmetric cryptography and X.509 certificates. Which of the

following is the **BEST** strength asymmetric cryptography to match the strength of the current symmetric cryptography?

   A. RSA 2048
   B. ECC 160
   C. ECC 256
   D. RSA 7680

16. One very large company created a business partnership with another, much smaller company. Both companies have their own PKI in-house. Employees need to use secure messaging and secure file transfer for their business transactions. What is the **BEST** strategy to implement this?

   A. The larger company creates a PKI hierarchical branch for the smaller company, so all parties have a common root of trust.
   B. The larger company enrolls all employees of the smaller company and issues their certificates, so all parties have a common root of trust.
   C. Companies should review each other's CP and CPS, cross-certify each other, and let each other access each other's search database.
   D. Employ an external third-party CA and have both company's employees register and use their new certificates for secure transactions.

17. When applications of cross-certified PKI subscribers validate each other's digitally signed messages, they have to perform the following steps:

   A. The signature is cryptographically correct, and sender's validation certificate and sender's CA cross-certificate are valid.
   B. Validate CRL and ARL.
   C. Validate sender's encryption certificate, ARL, and CRL.
   D. The signature is cryptographically correct, and sender's CA certificate is valid.

18. A company implements three-tier PKI, which will include a root CA, several sub-CAs, and a number of regional issuing CAs under each sub-CA. How should the life span of the CA's certificates be related?

   A. Root CA = 10 years; sub-CA = 5 years; issuing CA = 1 year
   B. Root CA = sub-CA = issuing CAs = 5 years
   C. Root CA = 1 year; sub-CA = 5 years; issuing CA = 10 years
   D. Root CA = 5 years; sub-CA = 10 years; issuing CA = 1 year

3

Cryptography

19. Management and storage of symmetric data encryption keys most importantly must provide

    A. Integrity, confidentiality, and archiving for the time period from key generation through the life span of the data they protect or the duration of the crypto period, whichever is longer.

    B. Confidentiality for the time period from key generation through the life span of the data they protect or duration of crypto period, whichever is longer.

    C. Integrity, confidentiality, and archiving for the duration of the key's crypto period.

    D. Integrity, confidentiality, non-repudiation and archiving for the time period from key generation through the life span of the data they protect or duration of crypto period, whichever is longer.

20. Management and storage of public signature verification keys most importantly must provide

    A. Integrity, confidentiality, and archiving for the time period from key generation until no protected data needs to be verified.

    B. Integrity and archiving for the time period from key generation until no protected data needs to be verified.

    C. Integrity, confidentiality and archiving for the time period from key generation through the life span of the data they protect or the duration of crypto period, whichever is longer.

    D. Integrity and confidentiality for the time period from key generation until no protected data needs to be verified.

Domain 4

Security Architecture Analysis

INFORMATION SYSTEMS ARCHITECTURE depends on many factors such as awareness of threats, the identification of risk, and the value of data, as well as attention to standards and best practices as they apply to the systems being de-signed and operated. The security architect should apply the best practices and standards for network and infor-mation systems design and implement an architecture that will provide an appropriate level of security and reliability for the enterprise given the requirements and constraints that they have to operate within. This requires the evaluation and selection of different architectures as well as an understanding of the risk(s) associated with each type of design. Key areas of knowledge include:

1. Analysis of design requirements
2. Valuation of data
3. Design architecture
4. Understanding information systems security standards and guidelines
5. Assessment of the information systems security design effectiveness
6. Attack vectors

The system can be defined as an integrated collection of people, products, and processes that provide the capabilities to satisfy the stated needs or objectives of the design.

Requirements analysis begins with understanding what the customer's goals and needs are for the system. This is done through the process of gathering requirements that are designated by the customer. Various items such as Statements of Work (SOW), contract documents, system specifications, Service Level Agreements (SLA), Requests for Proposals (RFP), legal and regulatory documents, interviews with designated representatives of the business such as stakeholders and power users, and / or any other types of information that will bear on system design and as a result, need to be taken into account in the design phase.

Functional requirements come in the form of business or mission needs of the customer, who is looking to automate a particular set of capabilities and functionality. These requirements reflect those needs and desires. They are also driven by the need to satisfy business policy and regulatory compliance.

Security requirements complement system functional requirements by addressing the needs to provide protection of the information systems, its data, and its users. Security requirements flow down from the functional requirements. They are typically addressed separately from functional requirements, but at the same time, act to complement the functional requirements by addressing concerns regarding the confidentiality, integrity, availability, and accountability of the information system, and the system protection needs.

Requirements analysis is critical to the success of a project. In systems design, requirements analysis encompasses those tasks that go into determining the conditions that must be met by new or altered products, taking into account any conflicting requirements from various stakeholders. It is sometimes referred to as requirements gathering, requirements capture, or requirements specification. Requirements must be actionable, measurable, testable, related to identified business needs or opportunities, and defined to a level of detail sufficient for system design. Requirements analysis is used to develop functional and performance requirements. Customer requirements are translated into a set of requirements that define what the system must do and how well it must perform.

The goal is to ensure that the requirements are understandable, unambiguous, complete, and concise. Require-ments analysis must clarify and define functional requirements and design constraints. Functional requirements define quantity (how many), quality (how good), coverage (how far), time lines (when and how long), and availability (how often). Design constraints define those factors that limit design flexibility, such as environmental conditions, defense against internal or external threats, and contract, customer or regulatory standards.

Requirements are captured in a variety of ways. Usually, they are captured in a table, spreadsheet, or database. There are many software packages available today that not only allow for the capture of requirements, but also contain features that allow the requirements to be traced to the solution, develop test cases, and contain pointers back to the requirement to ensure validation.

Security requirements typically come from two sources: best practices that are industry standards for safety and security, and regulatory requirements that are mandated by federal, state, local, or international law. Additional requirements are sometimes included that may be considered unnecessary but may be forward looking for future growth. In the absence of functional, legal, or regulatory requirements levied on the system, at a minimum, the security architect should recommend and insist on implementing industry best practices as a measure of due diligence and ethics.

TOPICS

- Identify Security Architecture Approach
  - Types and scope (e.g., enterprise, neiwork, SOA)
  - Frameworks (e.g., Sherwood Applied Business Security Architecture (SABSA), Service-Oriented Modeling Framework (SOMF))
  - Supervisory Control and Data Acquisilion (SCADA) (e.g., process automation networks, work interdependencies, monitoring requirements)
- Perform Requirements Analysis
  - Business and functional needs (e.g., locations, jurisdictions, business sectors, cost, stakeholder preferences, quality attributes, capacity, manageability)
  - Threat modeling
  - Evaluate use cases (e.g., business rules and control objectives, misuse, abuse)
  - Gap analysis
  - Assess risk
  - Apply maturity models
- Design Security Architecture
  - Apply existing information security standards and guidelines (e.g., ISO/IEC, PCI, NIST)
  - Systems Development Life Cycle (SDLC) (e.g., requirements traceability matrix, security architecture documentation, secure coding)
  - Application Security (e.g., Commercial Off-the-Shelf (COTS) integration)
- Verify and Validate Design
  - Validate threat model (e.g., access control attacks, cryptanalytic attacks, network attacks)
  - Evaluate controls against threats and vulnerabilities
  - Remediafe gaps
  - Independent verification and validation

OBJECTIVES

Security Architecture Analysis depends on diligence and attention to standards, awareness of threats, and identification of risks. The Security Architecture Professional should:

- Know and follow the best practices and standards for network and information systems design
- Implement an architecture that will provide adequate security to accomplish the business goals of the enterprise.
- Evaluate and select appropriate architectures
- Understand the risks associated with each type of design.

Risk Analysis [1]

A risk analysis should be conducted to determine the requirements and any risk to the system or data processed, stored, or transmitted. Risks should be mitigated to an acceptable level. There are numerous risk analysis methods including Operationally Critical Threat, Asset, and Vulnerability Evaluation (OCTAVE)[2], National Institute of Standards and Technology (NIST) Special Publication 800-30[3], and ISO/IEC 27005[4]. Broadly, risk analysis can be categorized as either Quantitative or Qualitative in approach.

Quantitative Risk Analysis

This approach employs two fundamental elements; the probability of an event occurring and a value or measure for the loss should it occur.

Quantitative risk analysis makes use of a single figure produced from these elements. This is called the 'Annual Loss Expectancy (ALE)' or the 'Estimated Annual Cost (EAC)'. This is calculated for an event by multiplying the potential

---

1   There are many different methodologies for risk analysis that exist, and that could potentially be used to examine risk within the context of the enterprise. While small and narrowly defined subsets are discussed in this conversation, some additional examples not discussed are listed here for reference:

Qualitative Methodologies
-    Preliminary Risk Analysis
-    Hazard and Operability studies(HAZOP)
-    Failure Mode and Effects Analysis(FMEA/FMECA)

Tree Based Techniques
-    Fault tree analysis
-    Event tree analysis
-    Cause-Consequence Analysis
-    Management Oversight Risk Tree
-    Safety Management Organization Review Technique

Techniques for Dynamic system
-    Go Method
-    Digraph/Fault Graph
-    Markov Modeling
-    Dynamic Event Logic Analytical Methodology
-    Dynamic Event Tree Analysis Method

2   See the following for an overview of the OCTAVE methodology: http://www.cert.org/octave/

3   See the following for the NIST Special Publications on 800-30: (original through revision 1)
   a. Original NIST SP 800-30 (July 2002): http://csrc.nist.gov/publications/nistpubs/800-30/sp800-30.pdf
   b. NIST SP 800-30 initial public draft for revision 1 (September 2011): http://csrc.nist.gov/publications/nistpubs/800-30/sp800-30.pdf
   c. NIST SP 800-30 revision 1(September 2012): http://csrc.nist.gov/publications/nistpubs/800-30-rev1/sp800_30_r1.pdf

4   See the following for an overview of the ISO/IEC 27005 standard: http://www.27000.org/iso-27005.htm

loss from a single event occurrence by the estimated occurrence rate for a period of time, which is one year. The formula for this is as follows:

$$ALE = SLE * ARO$$

Qualitative Risk Analysis

This is by far the most widely used approach to risk analysis. Probability data is not required and only estimated potential loss is used.

Most qualitative risk analysis methodologies make use of a number of interrelated elements:

THREATS

These are things that can go wrong or that can 'attack' the system. Examples might include fire, fraud or hacking. Threats are present for every system.

VULNERABILITIES

These weaknesses make a system more prone to attack by a threat or make an attack more likely to have some success or impact.

CONTROLS

These are the countermeasures for vulnerabilities. There are four types:

a. Deterrent controls reduce the likelihood of a deliberate attack.

b. Preventative controls protect vulnerabilities and make an attack unsuccessful or reduce its impact.

c. Corrective controls reduce the effect of an attack.

d. Detective controls discover attacks and trigger preventative or corrective controls.

Risk Theory

It is unrealistic to think that 100% protection against all possible threats, at all times, is attainable or even desirable. Organizations require a risk-based management process that weighs potential impacts or losses, which may be expected to occur in the presence of a given vulnerability (with a particular threat likely), against the business resource cost of mitigating or eliminating the risk. The qualitative expression of this approach is as follows:

$$R_{(risk)} = \frac{V_{(vulnerability)} \times T_{(threat)} \times I_{(impact)}}{C_{(countermeasures)}}$$

Risk assessments evaluate the sensitivity and criticality of the system or application data to the vulnerabilities, threats, impacts, and potential countermeasures that may exist in its environment. A risk analysis includes the following activities:

- Develop a business case
- Perform system characterization
- Conduct threat analysis
- Perform impact analysis
- Perform vulnerability and control analysis
- Develop a risk mitigation strategy
- Determine the risk level
- Report the residual risk

By conducting these risk assessment activities, the security architect can focus security countermeasures where they provide the most protection for the system and data.

No matter what the size of the enterprise may be, the following steps should be completed when defining the security requirements:

Step 1 - Identify requirements - Requirements come from formal proposals, statements of work, specifications, industry best practices, and other sources to form a baseline. Also included are user needs discussions with managers, and review of existing documentation for the operational system. The results should be presented and discussed with the business owners and stakeholders.

Step 2 - Verify and validate requirements - Before finalizing the baseline requirements, they should be verified and validated with the stakeholders to gain consensus. This is crucial because stakeholders' understanding of the requirements and the vetting process will help avoid scope creep, schedule delays, and general confusion.

Step 3 - Document the requirements - Requirements documentation provides a basis for architecting and designing the solution. Key personnel who are present at the beginning of the project may not be there throughout the development life cycle. Therefore, it is an excellent idea to get the requirements signed off by the stakeholders.

In defining requirements, careful consideration should be given to how a requirement is crafted. It is worth the extra time to develop and vet good requirements. Why is this so important? Well, experience has shown that incomplete or missing requirements are the major reasons for unsuccessful projects, resulting in a greater number of system defects [5]. These defects eventually surface late in the development phase or after delivery to the users and end up as

---

5   For a further discussion of this topic, as well as an overview of the literature in this area that supports the assertion that incomplete or missing requirements are the major reasons for unsuccessful projects, please see the following: http://proceedings.informingscience.org/InSITE2008/IISITv5p543-551Davey466.pdf

punch list items that must be addressed before final sign-off. System defects are very time consuming and expensive to correct. Poorly written requirements can also lead to a continuous stream of new requirements designed to fill the gaps and inadequacies found throughout the project. New requirements cause a great deal of rework and extend development time and costs. This is a form of scope creep that should be avoided.

Requirements that are ambiguous, untestable, and not capable of fully satisfying the identified needs of the users can cause higher development costs, schedule slippage, and unhappy customers. Therefore, organizations must emphasize the importance of requirements definition to ensure that they are clear, meaningful, effective, and efficient.

Table 4.1 provides an example of two requirements that are analyzed to interpret the meaning of the requirement: what it takes to satisfy the requirement and the validation of the requirement. In this case, identification and authentication and access control is reviewed. Extensive details are given to explain and understand the requirement and a number of ways it can be satisfied and validated.

Attack Vectors

The security architect should be intimately familiar with the most common types of attacks in order to select countermeasures that will be able to successfully combat them. An attack vector is a path or means by which an attacker can gain access to a computer or network server in order to deliver a payload, resulting in a malicious outcome. Attack vectors enable hackers to exploit system vulnerabilities, including the human element. Attack vectors can include viruses, e-mail attachments, Web pages, pop-up windows, instant messages, chat rooms, and deception. All of these methods involve programming or, in a few cases, hardware, except deception, in which a human operator is fooled into removing or weakening system defenses.

To some extent, firewalls and antivirus software can block attack vectors. But no protection method is totally attack proof. An effective defense method today may not remain so for long, because hackers are constantly updating attack vectors and seeking new ones, in their quest to gain unauthorized access to networks and computer systems. Some of the most common malicious payloads are viruses, Trojan horses, malware, and rootkits.

Methods of "Vector" Attack

Attack "vector" refers to the method of attack: the attacker's choice of weapon to infiltrate a system, with the end goal of gaining control and / or causing the normal operations of the system to become compromised in a variety of ways.

Requirement	Requirement Meaning and Comments	Review and Validation: Details
An Identification and Authentication (I&A) management mechanism that ensures a unique identifier for each user and that associates that identifier with all auditable actions taken by the user. The following must be specified:* [*Alternative controls, such as biometrics or smart cards, may be used. These alternative methods may have similar requirements. For example, the electronically stored version of biometric authentication patterns needs to be protected, as do password authenticators.] • Initial authenticator content and administrative procedures for initial authenticator distribution.	To meet this requirement you must: • Provide an I&A management mechanism that: • Provides a unique identifier for each user. • Provides an association of all auditable actions taken by a given user. • System documentation must describe the mechanism used to ensure that every user can be uniquely identified and authenticated and that the identity is associated with all auditable actions. • System documentation must describe how the initial authenticator is delivered to the user.	Documentation Inspection Required: • System documentation must describe the identification and authentication management mechanism used to ensure that every user can be uniquely identified and authenticated and that the identity is associated with all auditable actions in an immutable way. • System documentation must describe the type of authenticator(s) that are being utilized. • System documentation must describe the management mechanism used to distribute the initial authenticator (must be delivered to a unique user). • System documentation must describe how the initial authenticators are delivered to the user.
Individual and Group authenticators. (Group authenticators may only be used in conjunction with an individual/unique authenticator, that is, individuals must be authenticated with an individual authenticator prior to use of a group authenticator). • Length, composition, and generation of authenticators. • Change Processes (periodic and in case of compromise). • Aging of static authenticators (i.e., not one-time passwords or biometric patterns). • History of authenticator changes, with assurance of non-replication of individual authenticators, per direction in approved System documentation. • Protection of authenticators to preserve confidentiality and integrity.	• System documentation must describe any/all appropriate authenticator change process(es). • System documentation must describe appropriate mechanism or process designed to disable the authenticator after a certain period of time. • System documentation must describe how changes to the authenticator content is tracked and configured to prevent the reuse of authenticators. • System documentation must describe how authenticators are protected to preserve confidentiality and integrity.	• System documentation must describe the use of any group authenticators utilized by the system, and how the system is configured to prevent direct login with a group authenticator. • System documentation must fully describe the type of authenticator(s) used within a system (their length, composition, and generation). • System documentation must describe the authenticator change process, both periodic and in case of compromise. • System documentation must describe authenticator aging, reuse preclusion (generation checking/history). • System documentation must provide detailed description regarding how authenticator history is tracked by the system and configured to prevent its reuse from compromising the non-replication of individual authenticators.
		• System documentation must describe how authenticators and their corresponding content are protected at rest and in transit over the network. • Demonstration or Test Required: • Demonstrate/Verify IA management mechanism works as described. • Demonstrate/Verify that each user has a unique identification and that identification must be directly attributable to all auditable actions taken by that user. • Demonstrate how dissemination of authenticators (i.e. passwords, SecureID, etc.) is handled • Demonstrate that if Group authenticators are being utilized, that one cannot log in directly with a group authenticator. • Demonstrate how password strength is enforced (review password management within the system): • Review system configuration files, mechanisms, etc. that control the generation of authenticators.

Requirement	Requirement Meaning and Comments	Review and Validation: Details
		• Demonstrate/Verify that a "weak" authenticator cannot be generated by the system. • Demonstrate how password aging is implemented (review password management within the system). • Demonstrate how Authenticator Histories are tracked. • Capture and Review network data and storage locations for passwords that are stored or transmitted in an unsecured open manner that would offer simple compromise.
Access control, including: • Denial of physical access by unauthorized individuals unless under constant supervision of technically qualified, authorized personnel. • Procedures controlling access by users and maintainers to IS resources, including those that are at remote locations.	To meet this requirement you must: • Deny physical access to unauthorized individuals. • Supervise any unauthorized individuals with authorized personnel if the unauthorized individual ever needs physical access. • Have procedures that control authorized access to IS resources.	Documentation Inspection Required: • How-To: • System documentation must address and include a physical construct of the space where all components of the IS are located.

	Apply same protections/procedures to any users, maintainers, and IS resources at remote locations.	• System documentation must provide description of physical protection measures employed to prohibit unauthorized access (unless escorted properly).
		• System documentation must describe procedures that are utilized to control access to IS resources.
		• Demonstration or Test Required: (Site Inspection)
		• How-to:
		• Demonstrate/Verify how IS resources are physically protected by unauthorized personnel (including any IS resources at remote locations), examples:
		  • Badge/Card Reader access to room(s) containing IS resources.
		  • Approved combination locks on door(s) to rooms containing IS resources.
		  • Locked cabinets, equipment racks, etc.
		• Demonstrate/Verify that procedures for access control (as defined in the System documentation) are in use at the facilities.

Table 4.1 - **Requirements Analysis and Validation**

E-mail attachments are a prime example. It is often easy to get them past the firewall, or screening device. In most cases, the human element is the end target. Users are often THE weakest link in the system, and as a result, once they click to open attachments, they actively carry out the required action to make this form of attack popular and successful.

Do not confuse attack vectors with the attack payload however. Historically, worms, for example, would always count on some vector to grant them access to a system. They usually would carry malware, a virus, or a Trojan as their payload. The term "Worm" alluded to the nature of their behavior and replication mechanism. Worms would gain access to a computer, self-replicate, and then crawl out over a network (LAN or WAN) to infect other computers, with no help, or additional support from a human, or any other system in order to spread. Trojan horses, spyware, malware, keyloggers, hijackers, etc., are the kinds of payloads worms are capable of delivering. All attacks against systems will combine a payload with a vector.

While ordinary virus based attacks have been declining, Trojan horses and malware attacks have been on the rise, as hostile software developers move to more damaging types of attacks [6]. The number of overall attacks launched against enterprise systems has been increasing dramatically as a result. The attack vectors described below are how most of these attacks are being launched today.

Attack by E-Mail

E-mail messages themselves have become vectors, even though attacks using attachments are still more common. The hostile content is either embedded in the message, or linked to the message in some way. Sometimes, attacks combine the two vectors, so that if the message does not infect the client, the attachment will. E-mail provides a convenient delivery vehicle for deceptions of all kinds.

---

6   The most commonly seen types of attacks in enterprise networks can be grouped into the following categories and types:
- Keyloggers and the use of stolen credentials
- Backdoors and command control
- Tampering
- Pretexting
- Phishing
- Brute force
- SQL injection

For supporting data regarding the rise in attack payload categories pertaining to malware, please see the following

http://www.verizonbusiness.com/resources/reports/rp_data-breach-investigations-report-2012_en_xg.pdf

http://www.verizonbusiness.com/resources/reports/rp_data-breach-investigations-report-2011_en_xg.pdf

http://www.verizonbusiness.com/resources/reports/rp_2010-data-breach-report_en_xg.pdf

The weak point is the ignorance or imprudence of the computer user, not the computer itself. E-mail attacks continue to advance in sophistication. Criminals are combining their tricks with the techniques of spammers to make these attacks more effective. Millions of messages can be sent out in the hope that a large number of people will be duped.

Spam is almost always a carrier for scams, fraud, dirty tricks, or malicious actions of some kind. Any link that offers something "free" or tempting is to be considered suspect. A user acting on a spam message will usually lead to an outcome that is negative. Attachments (and other malicious files) are one of the most powerful ways to attack a PC. They are a simple way to deliver a highly effective payload. They are being overtaken by Web page trickery, but attachments still pose a major threat to the enterprise systems security architecture due to the rising prevalence of the "Bring Your Own Device" (BYOD) phenomena, and its associated implications for the security architect[7].

Attack by Deception

Social engineering in the form of deception is aimed at the user/operator of a computer or a system as the vulnerable entry point. It is not just malicious computer code that organizations need to watch out for. Fraud, scams, hoaxes, and to some extent spam, not to mention viruses, worms, and such, require the unwitting cooperation of the computer user to succeed. Social engineering is the art of convincing people to do something they would not ordinarily do, such as giving up a valuable secret, or exposing a secure system to unauthorized access. Malware developers use social engineering techniques in spam to con people into doing careless things, such as opening attachments that carry viruses and worms or using the telephone to get passwords or other sensitive information.

Hoaxes

Hoaxes are another form of deception that is often an attack vector. Ignorance and gullibility is the target that attackers will seek to take advantage of. Hoaxes can result in an exponentially growing number of messages that can easily swamp an e-mail system. Other hoaxes trick people into damaging their own PC by deleting necessary files.

Hackers

Originally, *hacker* was a term of respect for experts who could do "cool" things with computers. Some hackers crossed over to the dark side. These villains

---

7   For a general overview of BYOD issues, and data points regarding the advent of the phenomena and its impacts on enterprise system security, see the following:

   A. http://www.juniper.net/us/en/local/pdf/additional-resources/jnpr-2011-mobile-threats-report.pdf#search=%22Juniper%20Mobile%20Security%20Report%202011%22

   B. http://www.sans.org/reading_room/analysts_program/mobility-sec-survey.pdf

are more properly known as *crackers*. The distinction is not often made in the popular press. That annoys hackers, who like to think of themselves as white-hats, aka, good guys. Hackers are a formidable attack vector because, unlike ordinary malicious code, people are flexible, and they can improvise when faced with a dynamic landscape. They use a variety of hacking tools, heuristics, and "social engineering" mechanisms to gain access to computers and online accounts. They often install a Trojan horse so that they can commandeer the computer for their own use at a later time, or repeatedly over a period of time, as needed, to execute the initial breach, and any subsequent follow up access to gain advantage and control within one or more systems.

Web Page Attack

Counterfeit Web sites are often used to extract personal information from people. They look very much like the genuine Web sites that they seek to imitate. Organizations and individuals think they are doing business with someone they trust, but they are really giving personal and business information, such as name, address, and credit card numbers to a scam artist. They are often used in conjunction with spam, which provides the delivery mechanism that gets the user there in the first place.

Pop-up Web pages can install spyware, adware, hijackers, Trojans, or other scamware. They may even close Internet connections, and then make *very* expensive phones call using an organization's VOIP system, or PBX. All of these activities are malicious.

Attack of the Worms

Many worms are delivered as attachments via e-mail, but network worms use holes in network protocols to directly propagate themselves between hosts. The Window's DCOM vulnerability was a prime example of this type of behavior[8]. Any remote access service, such as file sharing, was vulnerable to this sort of worm. These worms propagate without relying on victims to open attachments. In most cases, a firewall will block system worms, or vulnerable services can be disabled to prevent spread to unaffected systems.

Many worms install Trojan horses. Some can disable ordinary antimalware software, and then install the worm's payload. Next, they begin scanning the Internet from the computer they have just infected, looking for other computers to infect. If the worm is successful, it propagates rapidly. The worm owner soon has thousands of "zombie" computers, or bots to use for more mischief[9]. One

---

8   For the original CERT vulnerability listing for the Microsoft Windows DCOM/RPC vulnerability, listed in October 2003, see the following: http://www.kb.cert.org/vuls/id/547820

9   For a good historical overview of worms, and their specific behaviors, see the following: http://lyle.smu.edu/~tchen/papers/network-worms.pdf

4

of the latest trends in worm based attacks is the use of a worm to spread a ransomware payload to multiple systems. Ransomware is a form of malware that is used to infect a targeted PC or system, and then prevent normal system operation and usage until a " ransom " has been paid or somehow provided to the controlling agent behind the attack[10].

Malicious Macros

Many documents such as those generated by Microsoft Word and Excel, for example, allow the use of macros. A macro can be used to automate spreadsheets, forms, or document templates, for example. The problem is that macros can also be used for malicious purposes, as they can be used to attack a computer directly[11]. A malicious macro may come from anybody. If they have picked one up, their documents will contain a copy of the malicious macro. Ensuring that the most secure settings possible for macro usage are being deployed and used within the enterprise is the best way for the security architect to have a positive impact in this area. See *Figure 4.1* for an illustration of the macro settings available in Microsoft Office 2010.

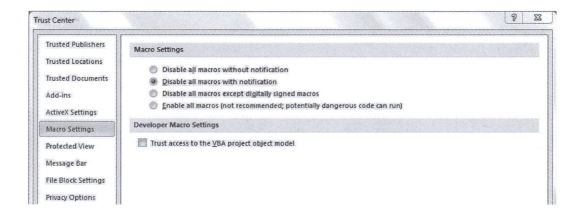

Figure 4.1 - **Trust Center Macro Settings in Microsoft Office 2010**

---

10   For a discussion of the anatomy of ransomware attacks at a high level, see the following: http://www.slate.com/articles/technology/technology/2012/10/ransomware_hackers_new_trick_to_take_over_your_computer_and_blackmail_you_for_cash_.html

For a discussion of the specifics of the ransomware attack involving GoDaddy and DNS server record manipulation, see the following: http://nakedsecurity.sophos.com/2012/11/23/hacked-go-daddy-ransomware/

11   For instance, the metasploit framework, and associated toolkits, could easily be used to carry out something such as the following macro based attack. Create a malicious .docx file which will spawn a tcp shell on any port specified, 12345 for instance, upon simply opening the file.

See the following for an overview of Metasploit: http://www.metasploit.com/about/choose-right-edition/

Instant Messaging, IRC, and P2P File-Sharing Networks

These three Internet services rely on connections between a host computer and other computers on the Internet. When using them, the special peer-to-peer (P2P) software installed makes the host machine more vulnerable to hostile exploits. Just as with e-mail, the most important things to be wary of are attachments and Web site links provided either as part of the installation of this software in the first place, or as a result of information exchange through the software once it is installed and configured for use.

Spyware is software that adds hidden components to a system on the sly. It is often bundled with some attractive software or other bait. The stealth process is installed without the knowledge of the end user and then will be used by an external control mechanism to execute remote control over the PC or system.

Viruses

Viruses are malicious computer code that hitches a ride as an attachment or through some other form of transmission such as infection of a file. This behavior makes them the "payload". The original virus vector, floppy disks, would carry the infected files from machine to machine, as the floppy disk was exchanged between users to transfer one or more files. Now, virus vectors include e-mail attachments, downloaded files, worms, USB drives and more [Happy Trails 2009].

Asset and Data Valuation

In the world of data protection, prevailing practices imply that every piece of an organization's data is equal to every other piece. This also holds true for all other company assets. Companies do not always see the same value in intangible assets that they do in tangible ones. They tend to use a "one-size-fits-all" approach in both cases, for instance, ensuring that hardware, software, and data are included in the recovery plan for backup, redundancy, business continuance, and other data protection. As a result, priceless data may be poorly protected, whereas relatively unimportant files consume disproportionate amounts of time and resources. What is missing is the concept of asset and data valuation as part of the initial business assessment[12].

This assessment should take into account the physical infrastructure, information systems (hardware), people, facilities, and the like. Architecting the system depends on more than just protecting the data. Consider the defense-in-depth approach. It calls for policies, procedures, technology, and personnel

---

12   For an overview discussion of the guidelines for information asset valuation see the following: http://www.iso27001security.com/ISO27k_Guideline_on_information_asset_valuation.pdf

to be considered in the system security development process. The customer requirements as well as the regulatory and statutory requirements must also be satisfied within the design functions of the system architecture. Classification of information into categories will be necessary to help identify a framework for evaluating the information's relative value and the appropriate controls required to ensure its value to the organization.

Different types of data have different values when placed in the context of their business use. One way of determining the value of specific information is in conducting a Business Impact Analysis (BIA) based on how individual departments or business units would be affected if their systems were compromised under a denial-of-service attack, or the data was lost or deleted [13]. How quickly could the system be brought back into service? How long would it take to restore the data in the event of such a loss? Only then can the individual or the enterprise determine the appropriate data protection, storage services, and redundancy required for each type of data.

Context and Data Value

Let us take a look at the concept of data valuation in more detail, beginning with an examination of the importance of organizational data. What data merits the greatest data protection investment? According to common practices, core company databases and mission-critical data files are the most obvious choices. As these are typically housed on central servers, Information Technology (IT) departments tend to devote their energies to backing up these files at specific periods (often on a daily or weekly basis), while also providing redundancy through Redundant Array of Inexpensive/Independent Disks (RAID) systems or server replication and other advanced means of data protection. While this approach is certainly better than leaving everything to fate, it neglects the concept of value. For instance, just how impacted would the organization be if it suffered a catastrophic failure of corporate systems? Perhaps all the database records are immediately recoverable, but what about the operating system and applications harnessing that database? Without those, the database is useless. For example, what is the Maximum Time to Repair (MTTR) access to the data or system in question? If the organization can survive a few days without its information systems while operating systems and applications are reinstalled and database files restored, then it may not need to invest in high-availability redundant data storage or protection methods to continue doing business. However, if the company would effectively "die" due to such an event, or would suffer massive

---

13   For an overview of the Business Impact Analysis (BIA) methodology, see the following: http://www.ready.gov/business-impact-analysis

losses, then investment in a high-availability redundant system should be a high priority to mitigate such threats. According to David Paulison, a former executive director of the United States' Federal Emergency Management Agency, 40-60 percent of small businesses do not open their doors after a disaster.[14] It is the security architects responsibility to drive this dialog with the business, and ensure that the proper outcomes from the BIA are being derived by the business, and as a result, that the right design choices and architectures are being implemented to mitigate any reasonable issues that the BIA has uncovered.

Corporate versus Departmental: Valuation

Another aspect of context is relative position on the organizational chart. From the standpoint of the enterprise, perhaps only key database files deserve the highest priority in data protection. While that may be correct for the company as a whole, departments or remote offices may require different priorities. Thus, each echelon of management should consider its own data protection needs and take actions accordingly.

In Company X, for example, the sales and marketing database may be assigned the greatest importance. However, at a local level, a software engineering department would probably have a completely different set of priorities and, therefore, different data protection needs. While the corporate IT department may be taking care of database backup and protection, local IT personnel management needs to ensure that their critical information is safeguarded, either by handling storage management locally or by justifying the need to protect that data to the corporate IT department.

Business, Legal, and Regulatory Requirements

Business requirements vary depending on the type of business or enterprise being examined. Parts of the U.S. healthcare industry must comply with Health Insurance Portability and Accountability Act (HIPAA) [15]. Other U.S. organizations that handle personal/privacy data may have Sarbanes–Oxley Act of 2002 compliance requirements [16]. Organizations that process credit card information must comply with Payment Card Industry Data Security Standard

---

14   http://www.propertycasualty360.com/2009/11/11/experts-say-small-firms-lag-in-disaster-planning

15   For an overview of the Health Insurance Portability and Accountability Act of 1996 (HIPAA) see the following: http://www.hhs.gov/ocr/privacy/index.html

16   For an overview of the Sarbanes-Oxley Act of 2002 (SARBOX) see the following: http://www.soxlaw.com/

(PCI DSS) [17]. Other U.S. businesses or government agencies requirements include compliance with Gramm–Leach–Bliley Act (GLBA) [18] and FISMA [19].

Most European countries' data protection laws follow principles detailed in two EU directives, whether or not these countries are part of the European Union. These directives are

1. *Directive 95/46/EC* of the European Parliament on the Protection of Individuals with Regard to the Processing of Personal Data and on the Free Movement of Such Data (commonly called the Data Protection Directive) [20] and

2. *Directive 2002/58/EC* Concerning the Processing of Personal Data and the Protection of Privacy in the Electronic Communications Sector [21]. The first directive applies to the collection, storage, disclosure, and other uses of personal data. The second directive

---

17   For an overview of the Payment Card Industry Data Security Standard (PCI DSS) see the following: https://www.pcisecuritystandards.org/security_standards/documents.php

To download the PCI DSS v2 standard see the following: https://www.pcisecuritystandards.org/documents/pci_dss_v2.pdf

18   For the original text of the Gramm-Leach-Bliley Act of the 106th US Congress, enacted on November 12 1999, see the following: http://www.gpo.gov/fdsys/pkg/PLAW-106publ102/html/PLAW-106publ102.htm

19   For information on the Federal Information Security Act of 2002 (FISMA) see the following links:

a. For the overarching Act that enables FISMA as a subset of the broader E-Government Act of 2002 see: http://csrc.nist.gov/drivers/documents/HR2458-final.pdf

b. For the FISMA specific section of the broader E-Government Act of 2002, commonly referred to as Title III, see: http://csrc.nist.gov/drivers/documents/FISMA-final.pdf

c. For general information on FISMA and all FISMA related activities, see: http://csrc.nist.gov/groups/SMA/fisma/overview.html

20   For the original text of Directive 95/46/EC of the European Parliament on the Protection of Individuals with Regard to the Processing of Personal Data and on the Free Movement of Such Data (commonly called the Data Protection Directive), see the following:

http://eur-lex.europa.eu/LexUriServ/LexUriServ.do?uri=CELEX:31995L0046:en:HTML

21   For an overview of Directive 2002/58/EC Concerning the Processing of Personal Data and the Protection of Privacy in the Electronic Communications Sector, see the following: http://europa.eu/legislation_summaries/information_society/legislative_framework/l24120_en.htm

For the original text of Directive 2002/58/EC Concerning the Processing of Personal Data and the Protection of Privacy in the Electronic Communications Sector, see the following:

http://eur-lex.europa.eu/LexUriServ/LexUriServ.do?uri=CELEX:32002L0058:EN:NOT

addresses the use of "cookies" and places restrictions on spam, telemarketing, and interception of communications and traffic data [22] [IT Law Group].

As stated earlier, the security architect needs to understand what is specifically called out in national and international policies that affect any systems that they are responsible for. Further, the trends that have been moving data and its supporting infrastructures and services into the cloud, and as a result, into a "boundless" as opposed to a specifically defined "boundary based" architecture that organizations have been used to within traditional IT models for many years is causing tremendous shifts in this area of responsibility for security architects as well as IT professionals more broadly today. The knowledge that is now required for a security architect to address cloud based system designs and usage, as well as security and disaster recovery and business continuity planning has grown to encompass areas such as transitory data pathways for data as it moves between and among cloud based storage endpoints over third party networks, in addition to virtualization of both the end users' desktop (VDI) as well as the infrastructure operating systems and application loads that create, process, store, and access data.

For instance, privacy laws in one country differ from those of another. Interconnection agreements between other countries must be considered as well as some ground rules that express an understanding of how these countries can operate effectively across international borders. Typically, the most stringent policy prevails because it covers the more loosely coupled policy. But what if there is a disagreement among international parties? How does it get resolved? Memorandums of agreement or memorandums of understanding can help identify a mutually acceptable solution.

Product Assurance Evaluation Criteria

The Common Criteria (CC) was born out of the necessity to expand product security assurance programs in the United States, Canada, United Kingdom, France, and Germany. The goal of the program was to establish a high degree of assurance that products would consistently perform the security function safely and securely when handling data and that failure would not result in

---

22   On January 25, 2012, the EU Commission published drafts of two documents that are the main pillars of the proposed reform taking place around the EU data protection regime: (i) a Regulation "on the protection of individuals with regard to the processing of personal data and on the free movement of such data" ("Regulation") and (ii) a Directive "on the processing of certain criminal data by competent authorities" ("Directive on Processing Criminal Data by Authorities"). These reforms are not due to go into effect before the Spring of 2015 at the earliest. For a summary of the proposed changes and a high level discussion of their possible impact see the following:

http://www.orrick.com/publications/item.asp?action=article&articleID=4489

the compromise of sensitive information. The expansion of the program also provided a broader market for those products completing the evaluation process by allowing international sales to the nations participating in the program. Some participating nations mandate the use of these products in their information systems. This mandate has translated into requirements for the system under development.

Product evaluations began in the United States with the Orange Book (TCSEC), which was the criterion for evaluating secure systems and vendor products. The Orange Book had an assurance range from D2 up to A-3. The D class had the least amount of rigorous testing, and A class consisted of more formal evaluation methods.

The Orange Book only addressed confidentiality. It was part of the Rainbow series, a set of security guidance named after its colorful covers. Each colored cover addressed a different security topic. The Orange Book and the Rainbow series were developed by the United States' National Security Agency (NSA), and all certified products were tested by them[23]. Over time, a backlog of evaluations made the delay in product evaluation less cost-effective. By the time the product reached evaluation, it may have already been at the end of the life cycle. Businesses began to lose interest in this process because there was little return on investment in time and money. They were interested in selling their secure products in the international market as well.

The next evaluation criteria, the ITSEC, was created by Canada, the United Kingdom, France, Spain, and Germany. The United States adopted and participated in the ITSEC. This evaluation criteria addressed integrity as well as confidentiality and was a step in the right direction. ITSEC had classes of assurance products, but the process did not go far enough. So, discussions began to develop a common set of standards that could be agreed to by a consortium of countries and the Common Criteria was established as a direct result of these efforts.

Using these evaluated products is mandated by law for all countries that have signed the arrangement discussed in the following text. For instance, a device such as a firewall seeking an Evaluation Assurance Level (EAL) 4 certification must meet all the requirements set in the criteria for that level of assurance. While conducting a requirements analysis, the security architect must include the functional requirements for that device as identified in the Common Criteria [Common Criteria, 2006].

---

23   For a complete overview of each book in the Rainbow Series, as well as for the actual text of each book in the series, see the following: https://www.fas.org/irp/nsa/rainbow.htm

Common Criteria (CC) Part 1

The Common Criteria philosophy is to provide assurance based on an evaluation (active investigation) of the IT product that is to be trusted. Evaluation is the traditional means of providing assurance and is the basis for prior evaluation criteria documents. The Common Criteria proposes to use expert evaluators to measure the validity of the documentation and the resulting IT product with increasing emphasis on scope, depth, and rigor. It does not comment on the relative merits of other means of gaining assurance. Researchers continue looking for alternative ways of gaining assurance. As mature alternative approaches emerge from these research activities, they will be considered for inclusion in the Common Criteria.

The Common Criteria provides a common set of requirements for the security functionality of IT products and for assurance measures applied to the IT products during a security evaluation. These IT products may be implemented in hardware, firmware, or software. The evaluation process establishes a level of confidence that the security function of IT products as well as the assurance measures applied to these IT products meet these requirements. The evaluation results may help the security architect and the consumers determine whether these IT products fulfill the security needs of the system.

The Common Criteria is useful as a guide for the development, evaluation, or procurement of IT products with security functionality. It addresses protection of assets from unauthorized disclosure, modification, or loss of use. The categories of protection relating to these three types of failure of security are commonly called confidentiality, integrity, and availability, respectively. The Common Criteria may apply to risks arising from human activities (malicious or otherwise) and to risks arising from nonhuman activities. It may also be applied in other areas of IT depending on the nation's security policies, but makes no claim of applicability in these areas [Common Criteria 2006].

The latest version of the Common Criteria is version 3.1R4. It is based on version 2.3, with updates that include a number of interpretations and editorial changes with no impact on the technical content. These standards have also been published as International Organization for Standardization (ISO) and the International Electrotechnical Commission (IEC) 15408:2005 and ISO/IEC 18045:2005. The Common Criteria consists of three parts:

> ***Part 1 - Introduction and General Model*** is the introduction to the Common Criteria. It defines general concepts and principles of IT security evaluation and presents a general model of evaluation. Part 1 also presents constructs for expressing IT security objectives, for selecting and defining IT security requirements, and for writing

high-level specifications for products and systems. In addition, the usefulness of each part of the Common Criteria is described in terms of each of the target audiences.

Part 2 - Security Functional Requirements establish a set of functional components as a standard way of expressing the functional requirements for the Target of Evaluation (TOE). Part 2 catalogs the set of functional components, families, and classes.

Part 3 - Security Assurance Requirements establish a set of assurance components as a standard way of expressing the assurance requirements for the TOE. Part 3 catalogs the set of assurance components, families, and classes. Part 3 also defines the evaluation criteria for Protection Profile (PP) and Security Target (ST) and presents evaluation assurance levels that define the predefined Common Criteria scale for rating assurance for the TOE, which is called the Evaluation Assurance Level (EAL).

The purpose of this arrangement is to advance those objectives by bringing about a situation in which IT products and protection profiles that earn a Common Criteria certificate can be procured or used without the need for further evaluation. It seeks to provide grounds for confidence in the reliability of the judgments on which the original certificate was based, by requiring that a Certification/Validation Body (CB) issuing Common Criteria certificates meet high and consistent standards [Common Criteria Part 1, 2006].

A management committee, composed of senior representatives from each signatory's country, was established to implement the arrangement and provide guidance to the respective national schemes conducting evaluation and validation activities. The list of current arrangement members is discussed in the following text.

In October 1998, after 2 years of intense negotiations, government organizations from the United States, Canada, France, Germany, and the United Kingdom signed the historic recognition arrangement for Common Criteria-based IT security evaluations. The arrangement officially known as the *Arrangement on the Mutual Recognition of Common Criteria Certificates in the Field of IT Security* was a significant step forward for government and industry in IT product and protection profile security evaluations. The U.S. Government and its foreign partners in the arrangement share the following objectives with regard to evaluations of IT products and protection profiles:

1. Ensure that evaluations of IT products and protection profiles are performed to high and consistent standards and are seen to contribute significantly to confidence in the security of those products and profiles.

2. Increase the availability of evaluated, security-enhanced IT products and protection profiles for national use.

3. Eliminate duplicate evaluations of IT products and protection profiles.

4. Continuously improve the efficiency and cost-effectiveness of security evaluations and the certification/validation process for IT products and protection profiles.

In October 1999, Australia and New Zealand joined the Mutual Recognition Arrangement, increasing the total number of participating nations to 7. Following a brief revision of the original arrangement to allow for the participation of both certificate-consuming and certificate-producing nations, an expanded Recognition Arrangement was signed in May 2000 at the 1st International Common Criteria Conference by Government organizations from 13 nations. These included the United States, Canada, France, Germany, the United Kingdom, Australia, New Zealand, Italy, Spain, the Netherlands, Norway, Finland, and Greece.

The State of Israel became the 14th nation to sign the Recognition Arrangement in November 2000. As of December 2012, 26 countries are currently part of the Common Criteria Recognition Agreement (CCRA). Sixteen countries (Australia, Canada, France, Germany, Italy, Japan, Malaysia, Netherlands, New Zealand, Norway, South Korea, Spain, Sweden, Turkey, the United Kingdom, and the United States) are Certificate Producers, and ten countries (Austria, Czech Republic, Denmark, Finland, Greece, Hungary, India, Israel, Pakistan, and Singapore) are Certificate Consumers [24].

The Common Criteria evaluated products begin the process by being evaluated in a certified laboratory[25]. These commercial laboratories agree to use stringent principles and test methods that are approved by the National Information Assurance Partnership (NIAP) members[26]. The National Voluntary Laboratory Accreditation Program (NVLAP) provides third-party accreditation to testing and calibration laboratories[27]. The NVLAP is established in response to Congressional mandates or administrative actions by the federal government or from requests by private-sector organizations[28].

---

24   For the most up to date information on the make-up of the membership of the CCRA, see the following: http://www.commoncriteriaportal.org/ccra/members/

25   For the most up to date information on the list of certified laboratories worldwide see the following: http://www.commoncriteriaportal.org/labs/

26   For information and an overview on NIAP see the following: http://www.niap-ccevs.org/cc-scheme/

27   For information on the NVLAP see the following: http://www.nist.gov/nvlap/

28   For the most up to date information on NVLAP accredited laboratories see the following: http://ts.nist.gov/standards/scopes/programs.htm

The NVLAP must be in full conformance with the standards of the ISO/IEC, including ISO/IEC 17025 and Guide 58. NVLAP is required before becoming a Common Criteria Testing Laboratory. The accreditation ensures that the Common Criteria laboratories meet the requirements of ISO/IEC Guide 25, General Requirement for Competence of Calibration and Testing Laboratories, and specific Common Criteria Evaluation and Validation Scheme requirements for IT security evaluations [Common Criteria, 2006].

Common Criteria (CC) Part 2

Part 2 of the Common Criteria defines the Security functional components. It is really the heart of the Common Criteria process. The security functional requirements are expressed in a PP or ST. These requirements describe the security behavior the TOE is expected to meet. The requirements describe security properties that users can detect by direct interaction (i.e., inputs, outputs) with the TOE or by the IT response to stimulus. Security functional components express security requirements intended to counter threats in the assumed operating environment of the TOE and cover any identified organizational security policies and assumptions.

This part of the Common Criteria and the associated security functional requirements are not meant to be a definitive answer to all the problems of IT security. Instead, it offers a set of well-understood security functional requirements used to create trusted products reflecting the needs of the market. These security functional requirements are presented as the current state of the art in requirements specification and evaluation [Common Criteria, 2012].

This part of the Common Criteria contains a catalog of security functional requirements that may be specified for a TOE. A TOE is a set of software, firmware, or hardware possibly accompanied by user and administrator guidance documentation. A TOE may contain resources such as electronic storage media (e.g., main memory, disk space), peripheral devices (e.g., printers), and computing capacity (e.g., CPU time) that can be used for processing and storing information and is the subject of an evaluation. The TOE evaluation is concerned primarily with ensuring that a defined set of Security Functional Requirements (SFR) are enforced over the TOE resources. The SFR defines the rules by which the TOE governs access to and use of its resources, and thus information and services controlled by the TOE.

The SFR may also include one or more Security Functions Policies (SFP). Each SFP has a scope of control that defines the subjects, objects, resources, or information, and operations controlled under it. All SFP's are implemented by the TOE Security Functionality (TSF), whose mechanisms enforce the rules defined in the SFR and provide necessary capabilities.

Those portions of a TOE that must be relied on for the correct enforcement of the SFR are collectively referred to as the TSF. The TSF consists of all hardware, software, and firmware of a TOE that is either directly or indirectly relied upon for security enforcement.

The Target of Evaluation (TOE)

The Common Criteria is flexible in what to evaluate and is, therefore, not tied to the boundaries of IT products. Instead of the term *IT product*, the Common Criteria uses the term *TOE (Target of Evaluation)*. While there are cases where a TOE consists of an IT product, this need not be the case. The TOE may be an IT product, a part of an IT product, a set of IT products, a unique technology that may never be made into a product, or a combination of these. The precise relation between the TOE and any IT product is only important in one respect: the evaluation of a TOE containing only a part of an IT product should not be misrepresented as the evaluation of the entire IT product. Examples of a TOE include:

    a. A software application

    b. An operating system

    c. A software application in combination with an operating system

    d. A software application in combination with an operating system and a workstation

    e. An operating system in combination with a workstation

    f. A smart card integrated circuit

    g. The cryptographic coprocessor of a smart card integrated circuit

    h. A local area network including all terminals, servers, network equipment, and software

    i. A database application excluding the remote client software normally associated with that database application [Common Criteria Part 2, 2006]

Table 4.2 lists the primary classes of the security functional requirements. Note that the abbreviations for the classes for the security functions begin with an "F" - this denotes its reference to the functional requirements. (Assurance class acronyms begin with an A.) This can be helpful if a security architect only sees the acronym, such as FPR. Drop the F, and PR makes sense as an acronym for privacy. FAU would indicate Functional (F) and Audit (AU). The functional class description is spelled out in the Security Functional Class column. [29]

---

[29]   The complete Common Criteria document set for the September 2012 V3.1 R4 release can be accessed for download here: http://www.commoncriteriaportal.org/cc/

Evaluation Assurance Level (EAL) Overview

Table 4.3 represents a summary of the EALs. The columns represent a hierarchically ordered set of EALs, while the rows represent assurance families. Each number in the resulting matrix identifies a specific assurance component where applicable. As outlined in the next section, seven hierarchically ordered evaluation assurance levels are defined in the Common Criteria for the rating of a TOE's assurance. They are hierarchically ordered inasmuch as each EAL represents more assurance than all lower EALs. The increase in assurance from EAL to EAL is accomplished by the substitution of a hierarchically higher assurance component from the same assurance family (i.e., increasing rigor, scope, or depth) and from the addition of assurance components from other assurance families (i.e., adding new requirements).

These EALs consist of an appropriate combination of assurance components as described in Chapter 7 of the Common Criteria Part 3 [30]. More precisely, each EAL includes no more than one component of each assurance family, and all assurance dependencies of every component are addressed. While the EALs are defined in the Common Criteria, it is possible to represent other combinations of assurance. Specifically, the notion of "augmentation" allows the addition of assurance components (from assurance families not already included in the EAL) or the substitution of assurance components (with another hierarchically higher assurance component in the same assurance family) to an EAL. Of the assurance constructs defined in the Common Criteria, only EALs may be augmented. The notion of an "EAL minus a constituent assurance component" is not recognized by the standard as a valid claim. Augmentation carries with it the obligation on the part of the claimant to justify the utility and added value of the added assurance component to the EAL. An EAL may also be augmented with extended assurance requirements.

EALs are augmented to show increased assurance capabilities or functionality. The additional functions are added from the next higher EAL and show compliance with parts of that level placing emphasis on certain functions. The augmented function should be listed as part of evaluation so that stakeholders will understand what additional capabilities were tested.

The next section contains a list of the EALs followed by a more detailed description of each EAL. The list of EALs and its short title is as follows:

---

30   The full citation is as follows: Common Criteria for Information Security Technology Evaluation | Part 3: Security assurance components, September 2012 Version 3.1 Revision 4.

Security Function Class (Fxx)	Description
Audit (FAU)	Security auditing involves recognizing, recording, storing, and analyzing information related to security relevant activities (i.e. activities controlled by the TSF). The resulting audit records can be examined to determine which security relevant activities took place and whom (which user) is responsible for them.
Communications (FCO)	This class provides two families specifically concerned with assuring the identity of a party participating in a data exchange. These families are related to assuring the identity of the originator of transmitted information (proof of origin) and assuring the identity of the recipient of transmitted information (proof of receipt). These families ensure that an originator cannot deny having sent the message, nor can the recipient deny having received it.
Cryptographic support (FCS)	The TSF may employ cryptographic functionality to help satisfy several high-level security objectives. These include (but are not limited to): identification and authentication, non-repudiation, trusted path, trusted channel and data separation. This class is used when the TOE implements cryptographic functions, the implementation of which could be in hardware, firmware and/or software.

The FCS: Cryptographic support class is composed of two families: Cryptographic key management (FCS_CKM) and Cryptographic operation (FCS_COP). The Cryptographic key management (FCS_CKM) family addresses the management aspects of cryptographic keys, while the Cryptographic operation (FCS_COP) family is concerned with the operational use of those cryptographic keys. |
| **User data protection (FDP)** | This class contains families specifying requirements related to protecting user data. FDP: User data protection is split into four groups of families that address user data within a TOE, during import, export, and storage as well as security attributes directly related to user data. |
| **Identification and authentication (FIA)** | Families in this class address the requirements for functions to establish and verify a claimed user identity.

Identification and Authentication is required to ensure that users are associated with the proper security attributes (e.g. identity, groups, roles, security or integrity levels).

The unambiguous identification of authorized users and the correct association of security attributes with users and subjects is critical to the enforcement of the intended security policies. The families in this class deal with determining and verifying the identity of users, determining their authority to interact with the TOE, and with the correct association of security attributes for each authorized user. Other classes of requirements (e.g. User Data Protection, Security Audit) are dependent upon correct identification and authentication of users in order to be effective. |
| **Security management (FMT)** | This class is intended to specify the management of several aspects of the TSF: security attributes, TSF data and functions. The different management roles and their interaction, such as separation of capability, can be specified.

This class has several objectives:

a) management of TSF data, which include, for example, banners;

b) management of security attributes, which include, for example, the Access Control Lists, and Capability Lists;

c) management of functions of the TSF, which includes, for example, the selection of functions, and rules or conditions influencing the behavior of the TSF;

d) definition of security roles. |
| **Privacy (FPR)** | This class contains privacy requirements. These requirements provide a user protection against discovery and misuse of identity by other users. |

Security Function Class (Fxx)	Description
Protection of the TOE security functions (FPT)	This class contains families of functional requirements that relate to the integrity and management of the mechanisms that constitute the TSF and to the integrity of TSF data. In some sense, families in this class may appear to duplicate components in the FDP: User data protection class; they may even
	be implemented using the same mechanisms. However, FDP: User data protection focuses on user data protection, while FPT: Protection of the TSF focuses on TSF data protection. In fact, components from the FPT:
	Protection of the TSF class are necessary to provide requirements that the SFPs in the TOE cannot be tampered with or bypassed.
	From the point of view of this class, regarding to the TSF there are three significant elements:
	a) The TSF's implementation, which executes and implements the mechanisms that enforce the SFRs.
	b) The TSF's data, which are the administrative databases that guide the enforcement of the SFRs.
	c) The external entities that the TSF may interact with in order to enforce the SFRs.
Resource utilization (FRU)	This class provides three families that support the availability of required resources such as processing capability and/or storage capacity. The family Fault Tolerance provides protection against unavailability of capabilities caused by failure of the TOE. The family Priority of Service ensures that the resources will be allocated to the more important or time-critical tasks and cannot be monopolized by lower priority tasks. The family Resource Allocation provides limits on the use of available resources, therefore preventing users from monopolizing the resources.
TOE access (FTA)	This family specifies functional requirements for controlling the establishment of a user's session.
Trusted path/channels (FTP)	Families in this class provide requirements for a trusted communication path between users and the TSF, and for a trusted communication channel between the TSF and other trusted IT products. Trusted paths and channels have the following general characteristics:
	- The communications path is constructed using internal and external communications channels (as appropriate for the component) that isolate an identified subset of TSF data and commands from the remainder of the TSF and user data.
	- Use of the communications path may be initiated by the user and/or the TSF (as appropriate for the component).
	- The communications path is capable of providing assurance that the user is communicating with the correct TSF, and that the TSF is communicating with the correct user (as appropriate for the component).
	In this paradigm, a trusted channel is a communication channel that may be initiated by either side of the channel, and provides non-repudiation characteristics with respect to the identity of the sides of the channel.
	A trusted path provides a means for users to perform functions through an assured direct interaction with the TSF. Trusted path is usually desired for user actions such as initial identification and/or authentication, but may also be desired at other times during a user's session. Trusted path exchanges may be initiated by a user or the TSF. User responses via the trusted path are guaranteed to be protected from modification by or disclosure to untrusted applications.

Source: Common Criteria, *Common Criteria for Information Technology Security Evaluation*, Part 2: Security functional components. September 2012. Version 3.1 Revision 4.

Table 4.2 - **Security Function Requirement Classes**

Assurance Class	Assurance Family	Assurance Components by Evaluation Assurance Level						
		EAL1	EAL2	EAL3	EAL4	EAL5	EAL6	EAL7
Development	ADV_ARC		1	1	1	1	1	1
	ADV_FSP	1	2	3	4	5	5	6
	ADV_IMP				1	1	2	2
	ADV_INT					2	3	3
	ADV_SPM						1	1
	ADV_TDS		1	2	3	4	5	6
Guidance Documents	AGD_OPE	1	1	1	1	1	1	1
	AGD_PRE	1	1	1	1	1	1	1
Life-Cycle Support	ALC_CMC	1	2	3	4	4	5	5
	ALC_CMS	1	2	3	4	5	5	5
	ALC_DEL		1	1	1	1	1	1
	ALC_DVS			1	1	1	2	2
	ALC_FLR							
	ALC_LCD			1	1	1	1	2
	ALC_TAT				1	2	3	3
Security Target Evaluation	ASE_CCL	1	1	1	1	1	1	1
	ASE_ECD	1	1	1	1	1	1	1
	ASE_INT	1	1	1	1	1	1	1
	ASE_OBJ	1	2	2	2	2	2	2
	ASE_REQ	1	2	2	2	2	2	2
	ASE_SPD		1	1	1	1	1	1
	ASE_TSS	1	1	1	1	1	1	1
Tests	ATE_COV		1	2	2	2	3	3
	ATE_DPT			1	1	3	3	4
	ATE_FUN		1	1	1	1	2	2
	ATE_IND	1	2	2	2	2	2	3
Vulnerability Assessment	AVA_VAN	1	2	2	3	4	5	5

Table 4.3 - **Evaluation Assurance Level Summary**

Evaluation Assurance Level 1 (EAL1) - functionally tested

Evaluation Assurance Level 2 (EAL2) - structurally tested

Evaluation Assurance Level 3 (EAL3) - methodically tested and checked

Evaluation Assurance Level 4 (EAL4) - methodically designed, tested, and reviewed

Evaluation Assurance Level 5 (EAL5) - semiformally designed and tested

Evaluation Assurance Level 6 (EAL6) - semiformally verified design and tested

Evaluation Assurance Level 7 (EAL7) - formally verified design and tested

4

Evaluation Assurance Level 1 (EAL1) - Functionally Tested

EAL1 is applicable where some confidence in correct operation is required, but the threats to security are not viewed as serious. It will be of value where independent assurance is required to support the contention that due care has been exercised with respect to the protection of personal or similar information. EAL1 requires only a limited security target. It is sufficient to simply state the SFRs that the TOE must meet, rather than deriving them from threats, Organizational Security Policy (OSP)'s, and assumptions through security objectives. EAL1 provides an evaluation of the TOE as made available to the customer, including independent testing against a specification and an examination of the guidance documentation provided. The goal is for an EAL1 evaluation to be successfully conducted without assistance from the developer of the TOE, and for minimal investment. An evaluation at this level should provide evidence that the TOE functions in a manner consistent with its documentation.

Evaluation Assurance Level 2 (EAL2) - Structurally Tested

EAL2 requires the cooperation of the developer in terms of the delivery of design information and test results, but should not demand more effort on the part of the developer than is consistent with good commercial practice. As such, it should not require a substantially increased investment of cost or time. EAL2 is, therefore, applicable in those circumstances where developers or users require a low to moderate level of independently assured security in the absence of ready availability of the complete development record. Such a situation may arise when securing legacy systems, or where access to the developer may be limited.

Evaluation Assurance Level 3 (EAL3) - Methodically Tested and Checked

EAL3 permits a conscientious developer to gain maximum assurance from positive security engineering at the design stage without substantial alteration of existing sound development practices. It is applicable in those circumstances where developers or users require a moderate level of independently assured security, and require a thorough investigation of the TOE and its development without substantial reengineering. EAL3 provides assurance by a full security target and an analysis of the SFRs in that ST, using a functional and interface specification, guidance documentation, and an architectural description of the design of the TOE, to understand the security behavior.

The analysis is supported by independent testing of the TSF, evidence of developer testing based on the functional specification and TOE design, selective independent confirmation of the developer test results, and a vulnerability analysis (based on the functional specification, TOE design, architectural design, and guidance evidence provided) demonstrating resistance to penetration attackers with a basic attack potential.

Evaluation Assurance Level 4 (EAL4) - Methodically Designed, Tested, and Reviewed

EAL4 permits a developer to gain maximum assurance from positive security engineering based on good commercial development practices that, though rigorous, do not require substantial specialist knowledge, skills, and other resources. It is the highest level at which it is likely to be economically feasible to retrofit to an existing product line. It is, therefore, applicable in those circumstances where developers or users require a moderate to high level of independently assured security in conventional commodity TOEs and are prepared to incur additional security-specific engineering costs.

EAL4 provides assurance by a full security target and an analysis of the SFRs in that ST, using a functional and complete interface specification, guidance documentation, a description of the basic modular design of the TOE, and a subset of the implementation, to understand the security behavior.

Evaluation Assurance Level 5 (EAL5) - Semiformally Designed and Tested

EAL5 permits a developer to gain maximum assurance from security engineering based on rigorous commercial development practices supported by moderate application of specialist security engineering techniques. Such a TOE will most likely be designed and developed with the intent of achieving EAL5 assurance. It requires additional costs attributable to the EAL5 requirements, relative to rigorous development without the application of specialized techniques.

EAL5 is applicable in circumstances where developers or users require a high level of independently assured security in a planned development and require a rigorous development approach without incurring unreasonable costs attributable to specialist security engineering techniques. It provides assurance by a full security target and an analysis of the SFRs in that ST, using a functional and complete interface specification, guidance documentation, a description of the design of the TOE, and the implementation, to understand the security behavior. A modular TSF design is also required [Common Criteria Part 2, 2012].

Evaluation Assurance Level 6 (EAL6) - Semiformally Verified Design and Tested

EAL6 permits developers to gain high assurance from application of security engineering techniques to a rigorous development environment in order to produce a premium TOE for protecting high-value assets against significant risks. It is, therefore, applicable to the development of security TOEs for application in high-risk situations where the value of the protected assets justifies the additional costs [Common Criteria Part 2, 2012].

EAL6 provides assurance by a full security target and an analysis of the SFRs in that ST, using a functional and complete interface specification, guidance documentation, the design of the TOE, and the implementation, to understand the security behavior. Assurance is additionally gained through a formal model of select TOE security policies and a semiformal presentation of the functional specification and TOE design. A modular and layered TSF design is also required.

The analysis is supported by independent testing of the TSF, evidence of developer testing based on the functional specification, TOE design, selective independent confirmation of the developer test results, and an independent vulnerability analysis demonstrating resistance to penetration attackers with a high attack potential.

EAL6 also provides assurance through the use of a structured development process, development environment controls, and comprehensive TOE configuration management, including complete automation and evidence of secure delivery procedures. This represents a meaningful increase in assurance from EAL5 by requiring more comprehensive analysis, a structured representation of the implementation, more architectural structure (e.g., layering), more comprehensive independent vulnerability analysis, and improved configuration management and development environment controls.

Evaluation Assurance Level 7 (EAL7) –
Formally Verified Design and Tested

EAL7 is applicable to the development of security TOEs for application in extremely high-risk situations or where the high value of the assets justifies the higher costs. Practical application of EAL7 is currently limited to TOEs with tightly focused security functionality that is amenable to extensive formal analysis. EAL7 provides assurance by a full security target and an analysis of the SFRs in that ST, using a functional and complete interface specification, guidance documentation, the design of the TOE, and a structured presentation of the implementation, to understand the security behavior. Assurance is additionally gained through a formal model of select TOE security policies and a semiformal presentation of the functional specification and TOE design. A modular, layered, and simple TSF design is also required.

The analysis is supported by independent testing of the TSF, evidence of developer testing based on the functional specification, TOE design and implementation representation, complete independent confirmation of the developer test results, and an independent vulnerability analysis demonstrating resistance to penetration attackers with a high attack potential. EAL7 also provides assurance through the use of a structured development process, development environment controls, and comprehensive TOE configuration management, including complete automation and evidence of secure delivery procedures. This EAL represents a meaningful increase in assurance from EAL6 by requiring more comprehensive analysis using formal representations and formal correspondence, and comprehensive testing.

Common Criteria (CC) Part 3: Assurance Paradigm

The Common Criteria Part 3 begins with a philosophy of the approach to assurance that will permit the reader to understand the rationale behind the assurance requirements. This philosophy is that the threats to security and organizational security policy commitments should be clearly articulated and the proposed security measures be deemed sufficient for their intended purpose.

Measures should be adopted that reduce the likelihood of vulnerabilities, the ability to exercise (i.e., intentionally exploit or unintentionally trigger) a vulnerability, and the extent of the damage that could occur from a vulnerability being exploited. Additionally, measures should be taken to facilitate the subsequent identification of vulnerabilities and to eliminate, mitigate, or provide notification that a vulnerability has been exploited or triggered.

Significance of Vulnerabilities

There are threat agents that will continue to actively seek to exploit opportunities to violate security policies for illicit gains. These threat agents may also accidentally trigger security vulnerabilities, causing harm to the organization. Because of the need to process sensitive information and the lack of trusted products, there is significant security risk to IT systems that is likely to cause security breaches resulting in significant loss.

IT security breaches come from the intentional exploitation or unintentional triggering of vulnerabilities in the application of IT within business concerns. Steps should be taken to prevent vulnerabilities in IT products. To the extent feasible, vulnerabilities should be:

1. *Eliminated*, by taking steps to expose, remove, or neutralize all exercisable vulnerabilities.
2. *Minimized*, by taking steps to reduce to an acceptable level residual potential impact of any risks or vulnerability.
3. *Monitored*, by taking steps to ensure that any attempt to exercise a residual vulnerability will be detected so that steps can be taken to limit the damage.

The Causes of Vulnerabilities

Vulnerabilities are attributable to a variety of things, including inadequate requirements definition, defects in hardware or software, or misconfigured equipment security settings. The system developer or customer may not adequately define the security requirements, which can lead to inadequate security countermeasures. Vulnerabilities may be introduced into the system as a result of poor development standards or incorrect design choices. An IT product may possess all the functions and features required of it and still contain vulnerabilities that render it unsuitable or ineffective with respect to security. IT products placed in operation may have been configured according to the correct specification, but vulnerabilities may have been introduced as a result of inadequate controls upon the operation. This is not an exhaustive list of all possible reasons for vulnerabilities, but rather, a general overview of the types of causes that may affect the security of the system.

Common Criteria Assurance

Assurance is the foundation for confidence that an IT product meets its security objectives. It can be derived from a reference to sources, such as unsubstantiated assertions, prior relevant experience, or specific experience. However, the Common Criteria provides assurance through active investigation. Active investigation is an evaluation of the IT product in order to determine its security properties [Common Criteria Part 3, 2012].

Assurance through Evaluation

Evaluation is the traditional way of gaining assurance. It serves as the basis of the Common Criteria approach. Evaluation techniques can include, but are not limited to:

a. Analysis and checking of processes and procedures

b. Checking that processes and procedures are being applied

c. Analysis of the correspondence between TOE design representations

d. Analysis of the TOE design representation against the requirements

e. Verification of proofs

f. Analysis of guidance documents

g. Analysis of functional tests developed and the results provided

h. Independent functional testing

i. Analysis for vulnerabilities, including flaw hypothesis

j. Penetration testing

The Common Criteria Evaluation Assurance Scale

The Common Criteria philosophy asserts that greater assurance results from the application of greater evaluation effort, and that the goal is to apply the minimum effort required to provide the necessary level of assurance. The increasing level of effort is based on:

Scope - That is, the effort is greater because a larger portion of the IT product is included.

Depth - That is, the effort is greater because it is deployed to a finer level of design and implementation detail.

Rigor - That is, the effort is greater because it is applied in a more structured, formal manner.

The security architect should understand the basic EAL structure and levels as well as where to find evaluated products. Currently, a list of these evaluated products can be found on the National Information Assurance Partnership (NIAP) Web site[31]. This site contains the following types of information:

1. List of evaluated products currently on the market, evaluating country, and the EAL level
2. List of products in the test cycle
3. List of products no longer on the active products list
4. List of available protection profiles
5. The Common Criteria Parts 1–3
6. Other useful information about Common Criteria EAL and assurance

ISO/IEC 27000 Series

ISO/IEC 27000 is part of a growing family of ISO/IEC ISMS standards[32]. This series is the number reserved for a new international standard, which is titled: *"Information technology - Security techniques - Information security management systems - Overview and vocabulary."* The standard is known informally as "ISO 27000." The 27000 series of standards is being developed by a subcommittee of the Joint Technical Committee (JTC1) of the International Organization for Standardization and the International Electrotechnical Commission. ISO 27000 provides an overview of standards related to the ISO/IEC 27000 Information Security Management Systems (ISMS) family of standards that provide uniformity and consistency of fundamental terms and definitions (vocabulary) used throughout the ISMS family. Information security, similar to so many technical subjects, continues to develop a complex web of terminology. Relatively few authors take the trouble to define precisely what they mean, an approach that is unacceptable in the standards arena as it potentially leads to

---

31   The NIAP web site can be found here: http://www.niap-ccevs.org/

32   See the following for the entire ISO/IEC ISMS standards body: http://www.iso.org/iso/home/store/catalogue_ics.htm

confusion and devalues formal assessment and certification. As with ISO 9000 and ISO 14000, the base "000" standard is intended to address this.

Although ISO/IEC 27001:2005 does not specifically address requirements analysis, organizations may require compliance with this document from the standpoint of implementing best security practices, which in turn may be interpreted as a requirement. Meeting ISO standards is generally good for business as they lend credibility to the company's commitment to quality and excellence. Customers may seek out organizations that meet the ISO standards and may require compliance for their information systems.

ISO/IEC 27001:2005 covers a variety of organizations including commercial enterprises, government agencies, and nonprofit organizations. If compliance with this standard is made mandatory by the contract or statement of work, the security architect will need to evaluate the contents of this code of practice to ensure that they are adequately addressed. ISO/IEC 27001:2005 specifies the requirements for establishing, implementing, operating, monitoring, reviewing, maintaining, and improving a documented Information Security Management System within the context of the organization's overall business risks. It specifies requirements for the implementation of security controls customized to the needs of individual organizations or parts thereof.

ISO/IEC 27001:2005 is designed to ensure the selection of adequate and proportionate security controls that protect information assets and give confidence to stakeholders. ISO/IEC 27001:2005 is intended to be suitable for:[33]

- Use within organizations to formulate security requirements and objectives.
- Use within organizations as a way to ensure that security risks are cost-effectively managed.
- Use within organizations to ensure compliance with laws and regulations.
- Use within an organization as a process framework for the implementation and management of controls to ensure that the specific security objectives of an organization are met.
- The definition of new information security management and governance processes.
- The identification and clarification of existing information security management processes.
- Use by the management of organizations to determine the status of information security management activities.

---

33   See the following for the abstract of the ISO/IEC 27001:2005 Standard: http://www.iso.org/iso/home/store/catalogue_tc/catalogue_detail.htm?csnumber=42103

- Use by the internal and external auditors of organizations to determine the degree of compliance with the policies, directives, and standards adopted by an organization.
- Use by organizations to provide relevant information about information security policies, directives, standards, and procedures to trading partners and other organizations with whom they interact for operational or commercial reasons.
- The implementation of business-enabling information security.
- Use by organizations to provide relevant information about information security to customers.

Software Engineering Institute -
Capability Maturity Model (CMMI-DEV) Key Practices Version 1.3

Introducing the Capability Maturity Model

The Capability Maturity Model (CMM) for Development is a framework that describes the key elements that make up a comprehensive integrated set of guidelines for developing products and services. The CMM describes an evolutionary improvement path from an ad hoc, immature process to a mature, disciplined process. The CMMI-DEV model provides guidance for applying Capability Maturity Model best practices in a development organization. Best practices in the model focus on activities for developing quality products and services to meet the needs of customers and end users. The CMMI-DEV, V1.3 model is a collection of development best practices from government and industry that is generated from the CMMI V1.3 Architecture and Framework. CMMI-DEV is based on the CMMI Model Foundation or CMF (i.e., model components common to all CMMI models and constellations). When followed, these key practices improve the ability of organizations to meet goals for cost, schedule, functionality, and product quality. It establishes a yardstick against which it is possible to judge, in a repeatable way, the maturity of an organization's processes and compare it to the state of the practice of the industry [Paulk et al., 1993a]. The Capability Maturity Model may also be used by organizations and the security architect to plan improvements to its processes.

Sources of the Capability Maturity Model (CMM)

The Software Engineering Institute (SEI) developed an initial version of a maturity model and maturity questionnaire at the request of the government and with the assistance of the MITRE Corporation. Throughout the development of the model and the questionnaire, the SEI paid attention to advice from practitioners who are involved in developing and improving software processes. The objectives were to provide a model that:

- Is based on actual practices
- Reflects the best of the state of the practice
- Reflects the needs of individuals performing software process improvement, software process assessments, or software capability evaluations
- Is documented
- Is publicly available

Additional knowledge and insight into software process maturity has been gained since the earlier versions of the maturity model. This insight has been gained by:

- Performing and observing software process assessments and software capability evaluations
- Studying non software organizations
- Participating in meetings and workshops with industry and government representatives
- Soliciting and analyzing change requests to the model
- Soliciting feedback from industry and government reviewers

Generally, CMMs focus on improving processes in an organization. They contain the essential elements of effective processes for one or more disciplines and describe an evolutionary improvement path from ad hoc, immature processes to disciplined, mature processes with improved quality and effectiveness. Combining this general thought process regarding CMMs with the additional knowledge garnered from continuous examination and improvement of prior models, the CMM and its practices have been revised, creating CMM v1.3. *Figure 4.2* illustrates the historical evolution of CMMs.

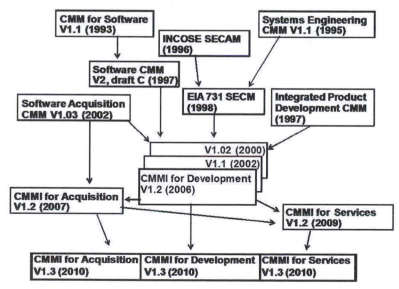

Figure 4.2 - **History of CMMs**

Structure of the CMMI-DEV V1.3[34]

CMMI® for Development (CMMI-DEV) consists of best practices that address development activities applied to products and services. It addresses practices that cover the product's lifecycle from conception through delivery and maintenance. The emphasis is on the work necessary to build and maintain the total product.

CMMI-DEV contains 22 process areas. Of those process areas, 16 are core process areas, 1 is a shared process area, and 5 are development specific process areas.

All CMMI-DEV model practices focus on the activities of the developer organization. Five process areas focus on practices specific to development: addressing requirements development, technical solution, product integration, verification, and validation.

All CMMI models are produced from the CMMI Framework. This framework contains all of the goals and practices that are used to produce CMMI models that belong to CMMI constellations.

All CMMI models contain 16 core process areas. These process areas cover basic concepts that are fundamental to process improvement in any area of interest (i.e., acquisition, development, services).

Model components are grouped into three categories - required, expected, and informative.

Required components are essential to achieving process improvement in a given process area. This achievement must be visibly implemented in an organization's processes. The required components in CMMI are the specific and generic goals. [CMMI-DEV, 2010].

Expected components describe the activities that are important in achieving a required CMMI component. Expected components guide those who implement improvements or perform appraisals. The expected components in CMMI are the specific and generic practices. Before goals can be considered to be satisfied, either their practices as described, or acceptable alternatives to them, must be present in the planned and implemented processes of the organization. [CMMI-DEV, 2010].

Informative components help model users understand CMMI required and expected components. These components can be example boxes, detailed explanations, or other helpful information. Subpractices, notes, references, goal titles, practice titles, sources, example work products, and generic practice

---

34   See the following for complete information on the Software Engineering Institute and the CMMI for Development V1.3 model: http://www.sei.cmu.edu/library/abstracts/reports/10tr033.cfm

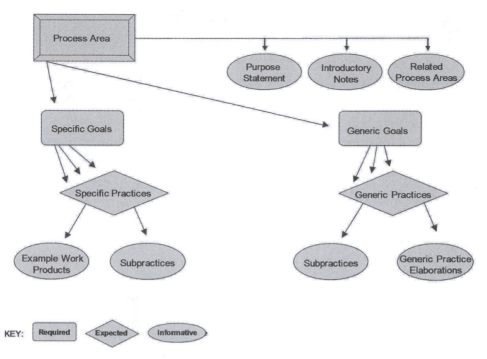

Figure 4.3 - **CMMI Model Components**

elaborations are informative model components. The informative material plays an important role in understanding the model. It is often impossible to adequately describe the behavior required or expected of an organization using only a single goal or practice statement. The model's informative material provides information necessary to achieve the correct understanding of goals and practices. [CMMI-DEV, 2010]. This structure of the CMMI is illustrated in *Figure 4.3*.

Developing reliable and usable products and services that are delivered on time and within budget is a difficult endeavor for many organizations. Products that are late, over budget, or that do not work as expected also cause problems for the organization's customers. As projects continue to increase in size and importance, these problems are amplified. They can be overcome through a focused and sustained effort at building a process infrastructure of effective engineering and management practices.

To build this process infrastructure, organizations producing products and services, such as software, need ways to appraise their ability to execute their process successfully. They also need guidance to improve their process capability. Customers, such as the United States' Department of Defense (DoD), need ways to effectively evaluate an organization's capability to perform successfully on engineering contracts. Prime contractors need ways to evaluate the capability of potential subcontractors.

To help organizations and customers such as the DoD and prime contractors, the Software Engineering Institute (SEI) developed the CMMI for Development, which delineates the characteristics of a mature, capable software process. The progression from an immature, unrepeatable software process to a mature, well-managed software process also is described in terms of maturity levels in the model. The CMMI for Development may be put to the following uses:

- Software process improvement, in which an organization plans, develops, and implements changes to its software process.
- Software process assessments, in which a trained team of software professionals determines the state of an organization's current software process, determines the high-priority software process-related issues facing the organization, and obtains organizational support for software process improvement.
- Software capability evaluations, in which a trained team of professionals identifies contractors who are qualified to perform the software work or monitor the state of the software process used in an existing software effort.

The Software Engineering Institute's CMMI for Development V1.3 document describes the key practices that correspond to each maturity level in the Capability Maturity Model. It provides detailed elaboration of what is meant by maturity at each level of the Capability Maturity Model and a guide that can be used for software process improvement, software process assessments, and software capability evaluations.

The key practices of the Capability Maturity Model are expressed in terms of what is expected to be the normal practices of organizations that work on large government contracts. In any context in which the CMMI-DEV model is applied, a reasonable interpretation of how the practices would be applied should be used.

Specifically, Chapter 4 of the CMMI for Development V1.3 document, Relationships Among Process Areas, provides insight into the meaning and interactions among the CMMI-DEV process areas, while Chapter 5, Using CMMI Models, describes paths to adoption and the use of CMMI for process improvement and benchmarking of practices in a development organization.

CMMI-DEV does not specify that a project or organization must follow a particular process flow or that a certain number of products be developed per day or specific performance targets be achieved. The model does specify that a project or organization should have processes that address development related practices. To determine whether these processes are in place, a project or organization maps its processes to the process areas in this model.

Continuous Representation

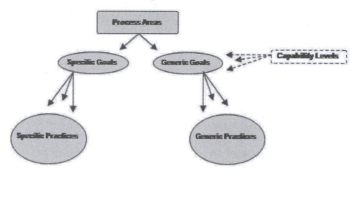

Staged Representation

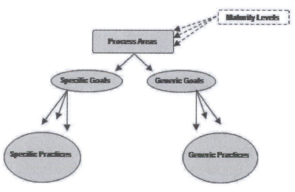

Figure 4.4 - **Structure of the Continuous and Staged Representations**

The mapping of processes to process areas enables the organization to track its progress against the CMMI-DEV model as it updates or creates processes.

Levels are used in CMMI-DEV to describe an evolutionary path recommended for an organization that wants to improve the processes it uses to develop products or services. Levels can also be the outcome of the rating activity in appraisals. Appraisals can apply to entire organizations or to smaller groups such as a group of projects or a division. CMMI supports two improvement paths using levels. One path enables organizations to incrementally improve processes corresponding to an individual process area (or group of process areas) selected by the organization. The other path enables organizations to improve a set of related processes by incrementally addressing successive sets of process areas. These two improvement paths are associated with the two types of levels: *capability levels and maturity levels.*

389

These levels correspond to two approaches to process improvement called "representations." The two representations are called "continuous" and "staged." Using the continuous representation enables an organization to achieve "capability levels." Using the staged representation enables an organization to achieve "maturity levels." To reach a particular level, an organization must satisfy all of the goals of the process area or set of process areas that are targeted for improvement, regardless of whether it is a capability or a maturity level. *Figure 4.4* represents the structures of the Continuous and Staged Representations.

Capability levels apply to an organization's process improvement achievement in individual process areas. These levels are a means for incrementally improving the processes corresponding to a given process area. The four capability levels are numbered 0 through 3.

Maturity levels apply to an organization's process improvement achievement across multiple process areas. These levels are a means of improving the processes corresponding to a given set of process areas (i.e., maturity level). The five maturity levels are numbered 1 through 5. *Table 4.4* represents a comparison between the 4 Capability Levels and the 5 Maturity Levels.

Level	Continuous Representation Capability Levels	Staged Representation Maturity Levels
Level 0	Incomplete	(N/A)
Level 1	Performed	Initial
Level 2	Managed	Managed
Level 3	Defined	Defined
Level 4	(N/A)	Quantitatively Managed
Level 5	(N/A)	Optimizing

Table 4.4 - **Comparison of Capability and Maturity Levels**

Capability Levels 0 – 3 are discussed below.

Capability Level 0: *Incomplete*

An incomplete process is a process that either is not performed or is partially performed. One or more of the specific goals of the process area are not satisfied and no generic goals exist for this level since there is no reason to institutionalize a partially performed process. [CMMI-DEV, 2010].

Capability Level 1: *Performed*

A capability level 1 process is characterized as a performed process. A performed process is a process that accomplishes the needed work to produce work products; the specific goals of the process area are satisfied.

Although capability level 1 results in important improvements, those improvements can be lost over time if they are not institutionalized. The application of institutionalization (the CMMI generic practices at capability levels 2 and 3) helps to ensure that improvements are maintained. [CMMI-DEV, 2010].

Capability Level 2: *Managed*

A capability level 2 process is characterized as a managed process. A managed process is a performed process that is planned and executed in accordance with policy; employs skilled people having adequate resources to produce controlled outputs; involves relevant stakeholders; is monitored, controlled, and reviewed; and is evaluated for adherence to its process description.

The process discipline reflected by capability level 2 helps to ensure that existing practices are retained during times of stress. [CMMI-DEV, 2010].

Capability Level 3: *Defined*

A capability level 3 process is characterized as a defined process. A defined process is a managed process that is tailored from the organization's set of standard processes according to the organization's tailoring guidelines; has a maintained process description; and contributes process related experiences to the organizational process assets. [CMMI-DEV, 2010].

A critical distinction between capability levels 2 and 3 is the scope of standards, process descriptions, and procedures. At capability level 2, the standards, process descriptions, and procedures can be quite different in each specific instance of the process (e.g., on a particular project). At capability level 3, the standards, process descriptions, and procedures for a project are tailored from the organization's set of standard processes to suit a particular project or organizational unit and therefore are more consistent, except for the differences allowed by the tailoring guidelines. [CMMI-DEV, 2010].

Another critical distinction is that at capability level 3 processes are typically described more rigorously than at capability level 2. A defined process clearly states the purpose, inputs, entry criteria, activities, roles, measures, verification steps, outputs, and exit criteria. At capability level 3, processes are managed more proactively using an understanding of the interrelationships of the process activities and detailed measures of the process and its work products. [CMMI-DEV, 2010]. Maturity Levels 1 – 5 are discussed below.

Maturity Level 1: *Initial*

At maturity level 1, processes are usually ad hoc and chaotic. In spite of this chaos, maturity level 1 organizations often produce products and services that work, but they frequently exceed the budget and schedule documented in their plans.

391

Maturity level 1 organizations are characterized by a tendency to overcommit, abandon their processes in a time of crisis, and be unable to repeat their successes. [CMMI-DEV, 2010].

Maturity Level 2: *Managed*

At maturity level 2, the projects have ensured that processes are planned and executed in accordance with policy; the projects employ skilled people who have adequate resources to produce controlled outputs; involve relevant stakeholders; are monitored, controlled, and reviewed; and are evaluated for adherence to their process descriptions. The process discipline reflected by maturity level 2 helps to ensure that existing practices are retained during times of stress. When these practices are in place, projects are performed and managed according to their documented plans.

At maturity level 2, the status of the work products are visible to management at defined points (e.g., at major milestones, at the completion of major tasks). Commitments are established among relevant stakeholders and are revised as needed. Work products are appropriately controlled. The work products and services satisfy their specified process descriptions, standards, and procedures. [CMMI-DEV, 2010].

Maturity Level 3: *Defined*

At maturity level 3, processes are well characterized and understood, and are described in standards, procedures, tools, and methods. The organization's set of standard processes, which is the basis for maturity level 3, is established and improved over time. These standard processes are used to establish consistency across the organization.

A critical distinction between maturity levels 2 and 3 is the scope of standards, process descriptions, and procedures. At maturity level 2, the standards, process descriptions, and procedures can be quite different in each specific instance of the process (e.g., on a particular project). At maturity level 3, the standards, process descriptions, and procedures for a project are tailored from the organization's set of standard processes to suit a particular project or organizational unit and therefore are more consistent except for the differences allowed by the tailoring guidelines.

Another critical distinction is that at maturity level 3, processes are typically described more rigorously than at maturity level 2. A defined process clearly states the purpose, inputs, entry criteria, activities, roles, measures, verification steps, outputs, and exit criteria.

At maturity level 3, the organization further improves its processes that are related to the maturity level 2 process areas. [CMMI-DEV, 2010].

Maturity Level 4: *Quantitatively Managed*

At maturity level 4, the organization and projects establish quantitative objectives for quality and process performance and use them as criteria in managing projects. Quantitative objectives are based on the needs of the customer, end users, organization, and process implementers. Quality and process performance is understood in statistical terms and is managed throughout the life of projects. For selected subprocesses, specific measures of process performance are collected and statistically analyzed. When selecting subprocesses for analyses, it is critical to understand the relationships between different subprocesses and their impact on achieving the objectives for quality and process performance.

A critical distinction between maturity levels 3 and 4 is the predictability of process performance. At maturity level 4, the performance of projects and selected subprocesses is controlled using statistical and other quantitative techniques, and predictions are based, in part, on a statistical analysis of fine-grained process data. [CMMI-DEV, 2010].

Maturity Level 5: *Optimizing*

At maturity level 5, an organization continually improves its processes based on a quantitative understanding of its business objectives and performance needs. The organization uses a quantitative approach to understand the variation inherent in the process and the causes of process outcomes.

Maturity level 5 focuses on continually improving process performance through incremental and innovative process and technological improvements. The organization's quality and process performance objectives are established, continually revised to reflect changing business objectives and organizational performance, and used as criteria in managing process improvement. The effects of deployed process improvements are measured using statistical and other quantitative techniques and compared to quality and process performance objectives. The project's defined processes, the organization's set of standard processes, and supporting technology are targets of measurable improvement activities.

A critical distinction between maturity levels 4 and 5 is the focus on managing and improving organizational performance. At maturity level 4, the organization and projects focus on understanding and controlling performance at the subprocess level and using the results to manage projects. At maturity level 5, the organization is concerned with overall organizational performance using data collected from multiple projects. Analysis of the data identifies shortfalls or gaps in performance. These gaps are used to drive organizational process improvement that generates measureable improvement in performance. [CMMI-DEV, 2010].

The Capability Maturity Model must be appropriately interpreted when the business environment of the organization differs significantly from that of a large contracting organization. The role of professional judgment in making informed use of the Capability Maturity Model must be recognized. The Software Engineering Institute's CMMI for Development should be used by

- Organizations wanting to understand and improve their capability to develop software effectively
- Professionals wanting to understand the key practices that are part of effective processes for developing or maintaining software
- Anyone wanting to identify the key practices that are needed to achieve the next maturity level in the CMM
- Acquisition organizations or prime contractors wanting to identify the risks of having a particular organization perform the work of a contract
- Instructors preparing teams to perform software process assessments or software capability evaluations

Taking a sample project, such as a software engineering solution, and examining it through the lens of the Maturity Levels of the model as listed above, the specific activities and requirements by level will become clear. Begin at Maturity Level 2, as Level 1 is found to be in a chaotic state, and at best, luck is often the deciding factor between successful deployment and completion of a project and failure. Projects are often delivered over budget and late within Maturity Level 1 organizations, and it is almost impossible to recreate a successful deployment using the same methods and processes, as they are not documented and standardized.

Beginning at Maturity Level 2, processes must be repeatable in the areas of project planning, tracking, oversight, contracts management, QA, configuration management, process definition, and training. Requirements Management is established to foster a common understanding between the software project requirements and the customer. This involves establishing and maintaining an agreement with the customer on the requirements for the software project. The agreement covers both the technical and nontechnical requirements. It forms the basis for estimating, planning, performing, and tracking the software project's activities throughout the software life cycle [Paulk93a].

The purpose of Software Project Planning is to establish reasonable plans for performing the software engineering and for managing the software project. Software Project Planning involves developing estimates for the work to be performed, establishing the necessary commitments, and defining the plan to perform the work.

The software planning begins with a statement of the work to be performed and other constraints and goals that define the software project. The software planning process includes steps to estimate the size of the software work products and the resources needed, produce a schedule, identify and assess software risks, and negotiate commitments. This plan provides the basis for performing and managing the software project's activities and addresses the commitments to the software project's customer according to the resources, constraints, and capabilities of the software project [Paulk93a].

Software Project Tracking and Oversight provides visibility into actual progress so that management can take effective actions when the software project's performance deviates significantly from the plans. Project Tracking and Oversight involves tracking and reviewing the software accomplishments and results against documented estimates, commitments, and plans, and adjusting these plans based on the actual accomplishments and results.

A documented plan for the software project is used as the basis for tracking the software activities, communicating status, and revising plans. These activities are monitored by the management. Progress is determined by comparing the actual software size, effort, cost, and schedule to the plan when selected work products are completed and at selected milestones. Other Maturity Level 2 activities can include:

- *Software Subcontract Management*, which selects qualified software subcontractors and manage them effectively in cases where these activities are monitored and managed as if the work was done in-house.
- *Software Quality Assurance*, which involves reviewing and auditing the software products and activities to verify that they comply with the applicable procedures and standards as well as providing the project managers with the results of these reviews and audits.
- *Software Configuration Management*, which involves identifying the configuration of the software at given points in time, systematically controlling changes to the configuration, and maintaining the integrity and traceability of the configuration throughout the software life cycle.

A software baseline library is established containing the software baselines as they are developed. Changes to baselines and the release of software products built from the software baseline library are systematically controlled via the change control and configuration auditing functions of software configuration management. The practice of performing the software configuration management function identifies specific configuration items/units that are contained in the key process areas.

At Maturity Level 3, the process must be repeatable in all the Level 2 task areas and have defined processes for organizational process focus, process definition, training, integrated software management, intergroup coordination, and peer reviews. (Most medium to large organizations reach Level 3 with relative ease once they decide that CMM is a value worth the investment.)

Process definition involves developing and maintaining the organization's standard software process, along with related process assets, such as descriptions of software life cycles, process tailoring guidelines and criteria, the organization's software process database, and a library of software process-related documentation [Paulk93a].

These assets may be collected in many ways. For example, the descriptions of the software life cycles may be an integral part of the organization's standard software process or parts of the library of software-process-related documentation that may be stored in the organization's software process database. The organization's software process assets are available for use in developing, implementing, and maintaining the projects' defined software processes.

The training program is a key process area for developing the skills and knowledge of individuals so that they can perform their roles more effectively. Building training programs involves first identifying the training needed by the organization, projects, and individuals, and then developing or procuring training to address the identified needs.

The purpose of integrated software management is to integrate the software engineering and management activities into a coherent, defined software process that is tailored from the organization's standard software process and related process assets, which are described in the organization process definition. The project's defined software process is tailored from the organization's standard software process to address the specific characteristics of the project. The software development plan is based on the project's defined software process and describes how the activities of the project's defined software process will be implemented and managed. The management of the software project's size, effort, cost, schedule, staffing, and other resources is tied to the tasks of the project's defined software process.

Because the projects' defined software processes are all tailored from the organization's standard software process, the software projects can share process data and lessons learned. The basic practices for estimating, planning, and tracking a software project are described in the Software Project Planning and Software Project Tracking and Oversight key process areas. They focus on recognizing problems when they occur and adjusting the plans or performance to address the problems. The practices of this key process area build on, and are in addition to, the practices of those two key process areas. The emphasis of Integrated Software Management shifts to anticipating problems and acting to prevent or minimize the effects of these problems.

Software Product Engineering should consistently execute a well-defined engineering process that integrates all the software engineering activities to produce correct, consistent software products effectively and efficiently. Software Product Engineering involves performing the engineering tasks to build and maintain the software using the project-defined software processes, methods, and tools. The software engineering tasks include:

1. Analyzing the system requirements allocated to software
2. Developing the software requirements
3. Developing the software architecture
4. Designing the software
5. Implementing the software in the code
6. Integrating the software components
7. Testing the software to verify that it satisfies the specified requirements

Documentation needed to perform the software engineering tasks include the software requirements document, software design document, test plan, and test procedures. They are developed and reviewed to ensure that each task addresses the results of predecessor tasks, and that the results produced are appropriate for the subsequent tasks [Paulk93a].

Intergroup Coordination

Intergroup coordination establishes a means for the software engineering group to participate actively with the other engineering groups, so that the project is better able to satisfy the customer's needs effectively and efficiently. It involves the software engineering group's participation with other project engineering groups to address system-level requirements, objectives, and issues. Representatives of the project's engineering groups participate in establishing the system-level requirements, objectives, and plans by working with the customer and end users, as appropriate. These requirements, objectives, and plans become the basis for all engineering activities.

The technical working interfaces and interactions between groups are planned and managed to ensure the quality and integrity of the entire system. Technical reviews and interchanges are regularly conducted with representatives of the project's engineering groups to ensure that all engineering groups are aware of the status and plans of all the groups, and that system and intergroup issues receive appropriate attention.

Peer Reviews

Peer reviews are designed to remove defects from the software work products early and efficiently. An important corollary effect is to develop a better understanding of the software work products and of defects that might be prevented.

The specific products that will undergo a peer review are identified in the project's defined software process and scheduled as part of the software project planning activities, as described in the Integrated Software Management key process area. This key process area covers the practices for performing peer reviews. The practices identifying the specific software work products that undergo peer review are contained in the key process areas that describe the development and maintenance of each software work product.

Maturity Level 4 processes must be managed. This level includes all the attributes of Level 2 and 3 and also includes quantitative process management and software quality management.

Quantitative Process Management involves establishing goals for the performance of the project's defined software process, which is described in the Integrated Software Management key process area; taking measurements of the process performance; analyzing these measurements; and making adjustments to maintain process performance within acceptable limits. When the process performance is stabilized within acceptable limits, the project's defined software process, the associated measurements, and the acceptable limits for the measurements are established as a baseline and used to control process performance quantitatively.

The organization collects process performance data from the software projects and uses these data to characterize the process capability (i.e., the process performance a new project can expect to attain) of the organization's standard software process, which is described in the Organization Process Definition key process area. Process capability describes the range of expected results from following a software process (i.e., the most likely outcomes that are expected from the next software project the organization undertakes). This process capability data is, in turn, used by the software projects to establish and revise their process performance goals and to analyze the performance of the projects' defined software processes.

Software Quality Management involves defining quality goals for the software products, establishing plans to achieve these goals, and monitoring and adjusting the software plans, software work products, activities, and quality goals to satisfy the needs and desires of the customer and end user for high-quality products.

This practice builds on the Integrated Software Management and Software Product Engineering key process areas, which establish and implement the project's defined software process, and the Quantitative Process Management key process area. It establishes a quantitative understanding of the ability of the project's defined software process to achieve the desired results. The goals are to establish software products based on the needs of the organization, the customer, and the end users. They are achieved by developing strategies and plans that address these goals.

Maturity Level 5 processes must optimize all of the Level 2 through 4 attributes as well as identifying the cause of defects and preventing them from occurring. The purpose of Technology Change Management is to identify new technologies (i.e., tools, methods, and processes) and track them into the organization in an orderly manner. It involves identifying, selecting, and evaluating new technologies, and incorporating effective technologies into the organization. The objective is to improve software quality, increase productivity, and decrease the cycle time for product development.

By maintaining an awareness of software-related technology innovations and systematically evaluating and experimenting with them, the organization selects appropriate technologies to improve the quality of its software and the productivity of its software activities. With appropriate sponsorship by the organization's management, the selected technologies are incorporated into the organization's standard software process and current projects, as appropriate, using pilot programs to assess new technologies. Other Level 5 activities include imparting Process Change Management and training to the organization's standard software process (as described in the Organization Process Definition key process area); the projects' defined software processes (as described in the Integrated Software Management key process area) resulting from these technology changes are handled as described in the Process Change Management key process area [Paulk93a].

Process Change Management involves defining process improvement goals and, with senior management sponsorship, proactively and systematically identifying, evaluating, and implementing improvements to the organization's standard software process and the projects' defined software processes on a continuous basis. Training and incentive programs are established to enable and encourage everyone in the organization to participate in process improvement activities. Improvement opportunities are identified and evaluated for potential payback to the organization. Pilot efforts are performed to assess process changes before they are incorporated into normal practice.

399

The review of the Maturity Levels of the CMMI for Development helps to put into perspective the necessary actions and structures that the security architect will need to contemplate and build as the enterprise strives to mature over time. In addition to the CMMI for Development, another of the SEI's models, the CMMI for Services V1.3 will also be of interest to the security architect in this area, and should be investigated as part of a thorough planning solution to build out the enterprise architectures necessary to maintain and sustain directed growth and maturity over time, with an emphasis on secure, documented processes that are consistent and reproducible[35].

ISO 7498[36]

The purpose of this reference model of Open Systems Interconnection is to provide a common basis for the coordination of standards development for the purpose of systems interconnection, while allowing existing standards to be placed into perspective within the overall reference model. The term *Open Systems Interconnection* (OSI) qualifies standards for the exchange of information among systems that are "open" to one another for this purpose by virtue of their mutual use of the applicable standards.

This ISO standard does not specifically address requirements analysis, but the security architect should be familiar with its content when designing information systems. The fact that a system is open does not imply any particular systems implementation, technology, or means of interconnection, but refers to the mutual recognition and support of the applicable standards.

It is also the purpose of this reference model to identify areas for developing or improving standards, and to provide a common reference for maintaining consistency of all related standards. It is not the intent of this reference model to serve as an implementation specification. Nor is it a basis for appraising the conformance of actual implementations, or to provide a sufficient level of detail to precisely define the services and protocols of the interconnection architecture. Rather, this reference model provides a conceptual and functional framework that allows international teams of experts to work productively and independently on the development of standards for each layer of the OSI reference model.

The reference model has sufficient flexibility to accommodate advances in technology and expansion in user demands. This flexibility is also intended to allow the phased transition from existing implementations to OSI standards.

---

35   See the following for the Software Engineering Institutes CMMI for Services V1.3:   http://www.sei.cmu.edu/library/abstracts/reports/10tr034.cfm

36   See the following for the ISO 7498 Standard: http://www.iso.org/iso/home/store/catalogue_tc/catalogue_detail.htm?csnumber=20269

While the scope of the general architectural principles required for OSI is very broad, the reference model is primarily concerned with systems comprising terminals, computers, and associated devices and the means for transferring information between such devices. Other aspects of OSI requiring attention are described briefly. The description of the Basic Reference Model of OSI is developed in the following stages:

- *Clause 4* - establishes the reasons for Open Systems Interconnection, defines what is being connected, the scope of the interconnection, and describes the modeling principles used in OSI.

- *Clause 5* - describes the general nature of the architecture of the reference model; namely, that it is layered, what layering means, and the principles used to describe layers.

- *Clause 6* - names and introduces the specific layers of the architecture.

- *Clause 7* - provides the description of the specific layers.

- *Clause 8* - provides the description of management aspects of OSI.

- *Clause 9* - specifies compliance and consistency with the OSI reference model.

An indication of how the layers were chosen is given in Annex A to the Basic Reference Model. Additional aspects of this reference model beyond the basic aspects are described in several parts. The first part describes the Basic Reference Model. The second part describes the architecture for OSI Security. The third part describes OSI Naming and Addressing. The fourth describes OSI System Management.

The Basic Reference Model serves as a framework for the definition of services and protocols that fit within the boundaries established by the reference model. In those few cases where a feature is explicitly marked (optional) in the Basic Reference Model, it should remain optional in the corresponding service or protocol (even if at a given instant the two cases of the option are not yet documented).

The reference model does not specify services or protocols for OSI. It is neither implementation specific for systems nor a basis for appraising the conformance of implementations. For standards that meet the OSI requirements, a small number of practical subsets are defined from optional functions to facilitate implementation and compatibility.

Concepts of a Layered Architecture

Clause 5 sets forth the architectural concepts that are applied in the development of the reference model of OSI. First, the concept of a layered architecture (with layers, entities, service access points, protocols, connections, etc.) is described. Second, identifiers are introduced for entities, service access points, and connections. Third, service access points and data units are described. Fourth, elements of layer operation are described, including connections, transmission of data, and error functions. Then, routing aspects are introduced and, finally, management aspects are discussed.

The concepts described in clause 5 are those required to describe the reference model of Open Systems Interconnection. However, not all of the concepts described are employed in each layer of the reference model. There are four basic elements to the reference model:

1. Open systems
2. The application entities that exist within the OSI environment
3. The associations that join the application entities and permit them to exchange information
4. The physical media for OSI

Clause 6 states that when referring to these layers by name, the (N)-, (N + 1)-, and (N − 1)-prefixes are replaced by the names of the layers, for example, transport protocol, session entity, and network service.

Payment Card Industry Data Security Standard (PCI-DSS)

Payment Card Industry Data Security Standard (PCI-DSS) was developed by the major credit card companies as a guideline to help organizations that process card payments prevent credit card fraud, cracking, and various other security vulnerabilities and threats. A company processing, storing, or transmitting payment card data must be PCI-DSS compliant or risk losing their ability to process credit card payments and being audited or fined. Merchants and payment card service providers must validate their compliance periodically. This validation gets conducted by auditors (i.e., persons who are the PCI-DSS Qualified Security Assessor [QSAs]). Although individuals receive QSA status reports, compliance can only be signed off by an individual QSA on behalf of a PCI council-approved consultancy. Smaller companies, processing *fewer* than about 80,000 transactions a year, are allowed to perform a self-assessment questionnaire. The current version of the standard (2.0) specifies 12 requirements for compliance, organized into six logically related groups, which are called "Control Objectives."

The control objectives and their requirements are the following:

Build and Maintain a Secure Network

Requirement 1: Install and maintain a firewall configuration to protect cardholder data.

Requirement 2: Do not use vendor-supplied defaults for system password and other security parameters.

Protect Cardholder Data

Requirement 3: Protect stored cardholder data.

Requirement 4: Encrypt transmission of cardholder data across open, public networks.

Maintain a Vulnerability Management Program

Requirement 5: Use and regularly update antivirus software or programs.

Requirement 6: Develop and maintain secure systems and applications.

Implement Strong Access Control Measures

Requirement 7: Restrict access to cardholder data by business need to know.

Requirement 8: Assign a unique ID to each person with computer access.

Requirement 9: Restrict physical access to cardholder data.

Regularly Monitor and Test Networks

Requirement 10: Track and monitor all access to network resources and cardholder data.

Requirement 11: Regularly test security systems and processes.

Maintain an Information Security Policy

Requirement 12: Maintain a policy that addresses information security for all personnel.

PCI-DSS originally began as five different programs: Visa Information Security Program, MasterCard Site Data Protection, American Express Data Security Operating Policy, Discover Information and Compliance, and the JCB Data Security Program. Each company's intentions were roughly the same: to create an additional level of protection for customers by ensuring that merchants meet minimum levels of security when they store, process, and transmit cardholder data. The Payment Card Industry Security Standards Council (PCI-SSC) was formed and, on December 15, 2004, these companies aligned their individual policies and released the PCI-DSS.

In September 2006, the PCI standard was updated to version 1.1 to provide clarification and minor revisions to version 1.0. PCI is one of multiple data security standards that have emerged over the past decade: Basel II, Gramm–Leach–Bliley Act (GLBA), Health Insurance Portability and Accountability Act (HIPAA), Sarbanes–Oxley Act of 2002, and California Senate Bill 1386. Version 1.2 was released in October 2008. Standards derived from the PCI-DSS include Payment Application Best Practices (PABP), which was renamed Payment Application Data Security Standards (PA-DSS). The current version of the PCI standard, Version 2, was released in October of 2010[37].

Architectural Solutions

The security architect should be familiar with current architectures such as Service Oriented Architecture (SOA), Client Server Architecture, distributed centralized architectures, or database architectures. The functional architectures describe the types of data that need to be processed and transmitted as well as the bandwidth needed and whether or not the topology is hub and spoke, Ethernet, Star, FDDI, wireless, and so on. The security architect will need to develop a security architecture that complements and supports the functional architecture. The architecture must provide security mechanisms that implement the appropriate levels of security to ensure the confidentiality, integrity, availability, and accountability of the system.

The security architecture hardware and software may require an evaluation under the Common Criteria. A discussion on this type of evaluation is included in the next section. Security architectures include hardware and software people processes and environment as part of the overall information systems and security.

Best security practices should include an architecture that provides defense in depth where layers of technology are designed and implemented to provide data protection. These layers include people, technology, and operations (including processes and procedures). Defense in depth includes:

- **Protect** - preventative controls and mechanisms
- **Detect** - identify attacks, expect attacks
- **React** - respond to attacks, recover

Three primary elements of defense in depth include the following:

- **People** - They can defeat the most complex security at times due to a lack of knowledge of the policies. By nature, humans would rather trust than distrust others, but when excessive regulations are put in place, it looks as if there is a lack of trust. People are considered part of the defense-in-depth strategy because they are users of the system and must be able to use it safely and securely. People must be aware of policies, procedures, and safe security

---

37   See footnote 16 for detailed information on the current PCI version 2 Standard.

404

Defense-In-Depth

Layers of security that ensure that a failure in any single countermeasure does not compromise the entire system

People

Technology

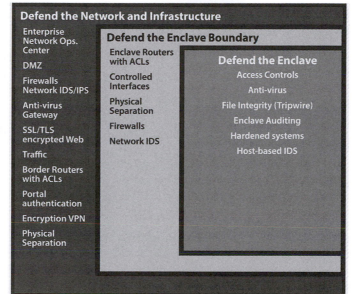

Defend the Network and Infrastructure

Enterprise
Network Ops.
Center

DMZ

Firewalls
Network IDS/IPS

Anti-virus
Gateway

SSL/TLS
encrypted Web

Traffic

Border Routers
with ACLs

Portal
authentication

Encryption VPN

Physical
Separation

Defend the Enclave Boundary

Enclave Routers
with ACLs

Controlled
Interfaces

Physical
Separation

Firewalls

Network IDS

Defend the Enclave

Access Controls

Anti-virus

File Integrity (Tripwire)

Enclave Auditing

Hardened systems

Host-based IDS

Operations

Figure 4.5 - **illustrates the components of a Defense-in-Depth solution**

practices. Training the users in these aspects of the system can prevent inadvertent compromise of data and potential harm to the operational systems. Security awareness training can help prevent users from attempting to circumvent security on the system for convenience. Users should be part of the systems design and development team to give input and feedback on decisions that affect their access, operation, and use.

- *Technology* - Evaluation of products, Information Assurance (IA) architecture and standards, validation by a reputable third party, as well as configuration standards and guidance are all elements of implementing IT security technology. The security architect must keep abreast of current technology, and its capabilities to ensure the right security services and protections are included in the design. Within the defense-in-depth (DiD) technology framework, layered protection should be considered. The security architect can work from the desktop to the security perimeter or from the perimeter to the desktop. Security mechanisms such as access controls (i.e., userID and password, authentication mechanisms, virus protection, operating systems lockdown or systems hardening, intrusion detection systems, firewall, and various types of encryption mechanisms) are technologies to be considered.

■ **Operations** - Security Policy, Certificate Authority (CA), Security Management, Key Management, Respond quickly, and restore critical services. The systems should be under configuration management controls to ensure that changes made to the operational system are authorized. Other considerations for operations are backup and recovery as well as incident response, awareness training, and management of encryption mechanisms and keys.

The effectiveness of information protection is based on the value of the information. In that way, decisions are based on risk analysis and aligned with the operational objectives of the organization. Key elements of the people side of the defense-in-depth equation are:

■ Awareness training - ongoing
■ Clearly written policy - that users can understand
■ Consequences to the organization and individual - liability for management
■ Incentive/reward

Table 4.5 illustrates the types of mechanisms that are required to defend the computing environment.

Defend	Mechanism or Process
Defend the computing environment	Access control
Defend the enclave boundaries	Firewalls and IDS
Defend the network and infrastructure	Protection from denial of service (DOS), inbound and outbound traffic protection
Defend the supporting infrastructures	Key management and other infrastructures

Table 4.5 - **Information Management Tool**

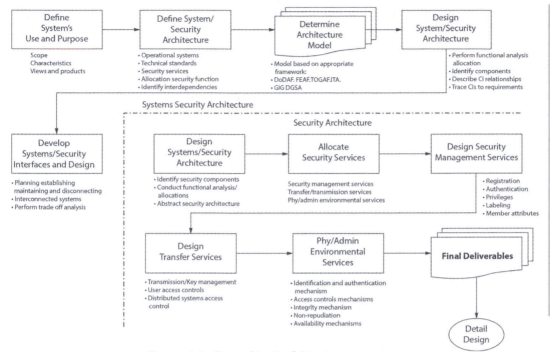

Figure 4.6 - **Security Architecture process**

(From Hansche, S. *The Official Guide to the CISSP-ISSEP CBK*, New York: Auerbach Publications, 2005.)

There are many architectures to keep track of in modern IT systems. For example, let's begin by looking at the outer perimeter of the network where security mechanisms, such as firewalls and intrusion detection systems are in place to provide filtering and monitoring to defend the network perimeter. Firewall devices filter incoming and outgoing IP traffic to permit or deny access based on a rule set or policy settings that are enabled or disabled within the device. These settings should be documented and protected to ensure that they can be duplicated should the need arise.

Encryption solutions such as Secure Socket Layer (SSL) or Transport Layer Security (TLS) may be used to protect the confidentiality of data being transmitted over the Internet. If the network is physically connected with dedicated leased lines, then other encryption appliances will be used to encrypt the point-to-point connections. These types of connections require network encryption devices as opposed to IP encryption devices.

The security architecture process depicted in *Figure 4.6* shows the steps that should be taken to develop the systems and security architecture. The security architecture is closely integrated with the system functional architecture and supports those functional mechanisms based on a set of defined threats, vulnerabilities, customer and regulatory requirements, and best practices.

During the design process, countermeasure selections are made based on the results of a thorough functional and security analysis of the baseline requirements established during the early phases of the design. Countermeasure selection is a collaborative activity between the security architect and the security engineer. The architect defines the security features and conducts the analysis review. The security engineer develops and applies the detailed analysis to support the countermeasures selected. If an architecture framework was used to develop the architecture, such as U.S. Department of Defense (DoD) Architecture Framework (DoDAF), then a systems view Level 5A SV-5a might be used to show what services are being provided and how they are being secured. If the architects and engineers are not using a framework or model, then a matrix can be developed to serve the same purpose.

Determining whether the systems require redundant architecture elements depends on the data requirement, performance, and criticality of the data where the single points of failure in the architecture are located. For instance, if all the data is stored in a single database and this data is critical to the success of the organization, it would be wise to have backups and perhaps an alternate database that is updated frequently with the date. If the architecture calls for heavy use of the Internet or transmission of data to other sites, then redundant communications equipment and transmission paths might be necessary.

Enterprise Information Security architecture is a key component of the information security technology governance process at any organization of significant size. More and more companies are implementing a formal enterprise security architecture process to support the governance and management of IT. However, as noted in the opening paragraph of this article, it ideally relates more broadly to the practice of business optimization in that it addresses business security architecture, performance management, and process security architecture as well. Enterprise Information Security architecture is also related to IT security portfolio management and Metadata in the enterprise IT sense.

Architecture Frameworks

The enterprise architecture frameworks shown in *Figure 4.7* are high-level depictions of the frameworks. There are numerous architecture frameworks, and the list continues to grow. They include architectural frameworks such as those listed in the following text as well as a number of reference architectures designed to provide fast development of typical network architectures for specific projects. The list provides a general idea of the type of architecture frameworks the security architect may want to become more familiar with as they engage in various projects based on customer needs and requirements. The frameworks include the following:

- The U.S. Department of Defense (DoD) Architecture Framework (DoDAF)[38]
- Zachman Framework[39]
- U.S. Government Federal Enterprise Architecture Framework (FEAF) [40]
- The Open Group Architecture Framework (TOGAF) [41]
- Capgemini's Integrated Architecture Framework[42]
- The U.K. Ministry of Defense (MoD) Architecture Framework (MoDAF)[43]
- National Institute of Health Enterprise Architecture Framework[44]
- Open Security Architecture[45]
- Sherwood Applied Business Security Architecture (SABSA) Framework and Methodology[46]
- Service-Oriented Modeling Framework (SOMF)[47]

The Zachman Framework, the U.S. Department of Defense (DoD) Architecture Framework (DoDAF), and the U.S. Government Federal Enterprise Architecture Framework (FEAF) provide good examples for discussion. If the conceptual abstraction of Enterprise Information Security Architecture were simplified within a generic framework, each would be acceptable as a high-level conceptual architecture framework.

Figure 4.8 represents the information that links the operational view, systems and services view, and technical standards view. The three views and their interrelationships are driven by common architecture data elements that provide the basis for deriving measures such as interoperability or performance and for measuring the impact of the values of these metrics on operational mission and task effectiveness.

---

38   See the following for information on the current version of DoDAf, Version 2.02: http://dodcio.defense.gov/dodaf20.aspx
39   See the following for information on the current version of the Zachman Framework, Version 3.0: http://www.zachman.com/about-the-zachman-framework
40   See the following for information on the current version of the Federal Enterprise Architecture and its associated reference models: http://www.whitehouse.gov/omb/e-gov/fea
41   See the following for information on the current version of TOGAF, Version 9.1:   http://www.opengroup.org/togaf/
42   See the following for information on Capgemini and the Integrated Architecture Framework: http://www.us.capgemini.com/services-and-solutions/technology/soa/soa-solutions/ent_architecture/iaf/
43   See the following for information on the current version of MoDAF, Version 1.2.004: http://www.mod.uk/defenceinternet/aboutdefence/whatwedo/informationmanagement/modaf/
44   See the following for information about the National Institute of Health Enterprise Architecture: https://enterprisearchitecture.nih.gov/Pages/Framework.aspx
45   See the following for information on the Open Security Architecture: http://www.opensecurityarchitecture.org/cms/
46   See the following for information on SABSA: http://www.sabsa.org/home.aspx
47   See the following for information on SOMF: http://www.modelingconcepts.com/pages/download.htm

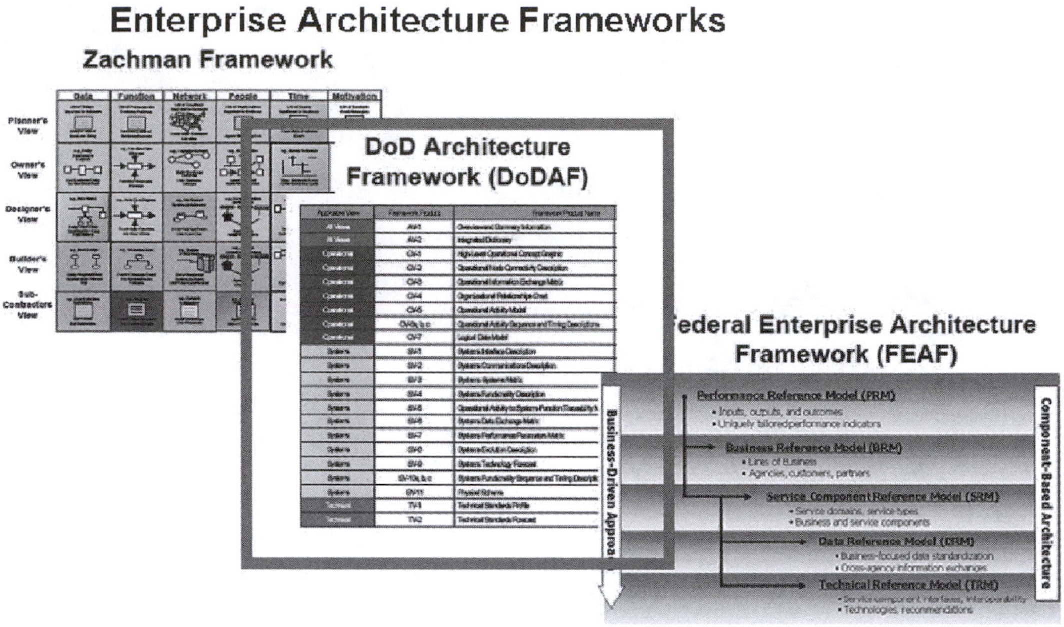

Enterprise Architecture Frameworks
Zachman Framework

Figure 4.7 - **Sample Enterprise Architecture Frameworks**

Department of Defense Architecture Framework (DoDAF)

DoDAF is the standard framework chosen by the U.S. Department of Defense to comply with the Clinger–Cohen Act and the U.S. Office of Management and Budget based on Circulars A-11 and A-130. It is administered by the Office of the DoD Deputy CIO Enterprise Architecture and Standards Directorate. Other derivative frameworks based on DoDAF include the NATO Architecture Framework (NAF) and Ministry of Defense United Kingdom Architecture Framework (MoDAF).

Similar to other enterprise architecture approaches, The Open Group Architecture Framework (ToGAF) and DoDAF are organized around a shared repository to hold work products. The repository is defined by the Core Architecture Data Model 2.0 (CADM) - (essentially a common database schema) and the DoD Architecture Repository System (DARS). A key feature of DoDAF is interoperability, which is organized as a series of levels, called Levels of Information System Interoperability (LISI). The developing system must not only meet its internal data needs but also those of the operational framework into which it is set. The current version of DoDAF 2.02 consists of 52 views organized into eight basic view sets:

- All Viewpoint (AV) - AV 1 and 2
- Capability Viewpoint (CV) - CV-1 through CV-7
- Data and Information Viewpoint (DIV) - DIV-1 through DIV-3

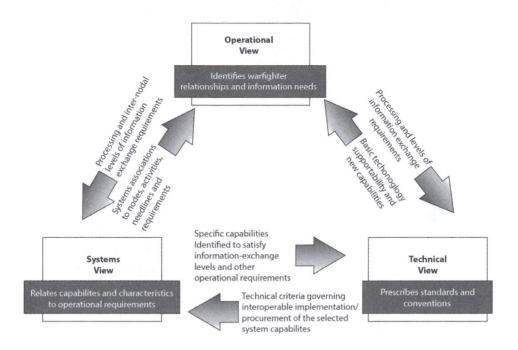

Figure 4.8 - **XYZ Inc. enterprise architecture.**

- Operational Viewpoint (OV) - OV-1 through OV-6c
- Project Viewpoint (PV) - PV-1 through PV-3
- Services Viewpoint (SvcV) - SvcV-1 through SvcV-10c
- Standards Viewpoint (StdV) - StdV-1 through StdV-2
- Systems Viewpoint (SV) - SV-1 through SV-10c

Only a subset of the full DoDAF view set is usually created for each system development. A security architect using this model should plan on developing parallel views that focus specifically on developing the security architecture. For instance, the All View should best be depicted by overlaying the high-level security services, capabilities, and function over the functional architecture view. This method would apply to the Operational View as well. By taking this approach, the security architect establishes a link between the functional system and the security functionality.

Figure 4.9 shows XYZ Inc. (XYZnet), a small LAN in the context of an Operational View 1 (OV-1). The high-level graphic shows typical network connections over the Internet through WAN or MAN connections. These connections are to the customers, suppliers, and other stakeholders over the public switched telephone networks (PSTN).

The functional OV-1 for the XYZ Inc. shows the need to communicate with internal and external organizations. Security mechanisms typically are used to ensure that these networks operate securely, and safety would be overlaid on

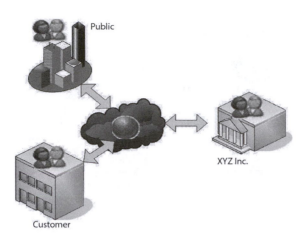

Figure 4.9 - **Systems engineering architecture and security engineering relationships**

the functional OV-1 to show where security mechanisms and services would typically be placed. These security mechanisms would include firewall or demilitarized zone (DMZ) to filter or proxy incoming and outgoing traffic, intrusion detection systems (IDS) to monitor and analyze both malicious and legitimate activities, and virus protection to ensure that the latest virus signatures are blocked. The OV-1 is a typical DoDAF artifact that shows the overall connections to various networks.

The Zachman Framework

The Zachman Framework is a logical structure for identifying and organizing the descriptive representations that are important in the management of enterprises and to the development of the system, both automated and manual, that comprise them. It is a schema that represents the intersection between two classifications. The first is the fundamentals of communication found in the interrogatives: *what, how, when, who, where, and why.* It is the integration of answers to these questions that enables the comprehensive, composite description of complex ideas. The second is derived from reification, the transformation of an abstract idea into an instantiation, that was initially postulated by ancient Greek philosophers and is labeled in the Framework: Identification, Definition, Representation, Specification, Configuration, and Instantiation.

More specifically, the Zachman Framework is an ontology - a theory of the existence of a structured set of essential components of an object for which explicit expressions is necessary and perhaps even mandatory for creating, operating, and changing the object (the object being an enterprise, a department, a value chain, a "sliver," a solution, a project, an airplane, a building, a product, and a profession of almost anything).

According to Zachman, this ontology was derived from analogous structures that are found in the older disciplines of architecture, construction, engineering, and manufacturing that classify and organize the design artifacts created in the process of designing and producing complex physical products (e.g., buildings or airplanes). It uses a two-dimensional classification model based on the six basic interrogatives (*what, how, where, who, when, and why*) intersecting six distinct perspectives, which relate to stakeholder groups (Planner, Owner, Designer, Builder, Implementer, and Worker). The intersecting cells of the framework correspond to models that, if documented, can provide a holistic view of the enterprise.

Design Process

The design process follows the systems engineering and architecture framework. These steps are discussed in the following section.

System Security Engineering Methodologies

Information System Security Engineering (ISSE) is the art and science of discovering users' information protection needs and the designing and making of information systems, with economy and elegance, so that they can safely resist attacks, malicious activities, or other threats to which they may be subjected [IATF v3.0].

There must be an alignment of the SE and the ISSE. The Security Engineering and System Engineering steps take place at the same time. While the Systems Engineers are discovering the system needs, the system requirements the Systems Security Engineers are discovering the security needs and security requirements and so on. The System Engineering Process consists of the following six steps:

1. *Discover information protection needs* - Ascertain why the system needs to be built and what information needs to be protected.
2. *Define system security requirements* - Define the system in terms of what security is needed.
3. *Define system security architecture* - Define the security functions needed to meet the specific security requirements. This process is the core of designing the security architecture.
4. *Develop detailed security design* - Based on the security architecture, design the security functions and features for the system.
5. *Implement system security* - Following the documented security design, build and implement the security functions and features for the system.
6. *Assess security effectiveness* - Assess the degree to which the system, as it is defined, designed, and implemented, meets the security needs. This assessment activity occurs during and with all the other activities in the ISSE process.

In reviewing the details of the ISSE process, systems engineering, and architecture process, the information protection needs include developing an understanding of the customer's mission or business needs. The security architect should work with the customer to determine what information management is needed to support the mission or business, and draft the Information Management Model (IMM) (shown in *Table 4.6*) and conduct a threat analysis. This will be the basis for creating an Information Protection Plan (IPP) that describes how this information will be protected. The results of these two activities should be documented in the Information Management Plan (IMP).

Information Domain	User	Rules/ Privileges	Process	Information
Data entry	Data entry personnel	Read/write	Entry	Raw
Accept	Course coordinator/ manager	Read/write	Accept	Analyzed
Distribute materials	Course coordinator	Read/write	Distribute	Releasable/ processed
Review data	Manager	Read	Review/print reports	Processed

Table 4.6 - **Information Management Tool**

These results should support Certification and Accreditation by identifying the Accreditation Authority and any security oversight bodies and identify the classes of threats, security services, and design constraints.

Some common pitfalls of not adequately determining the information protection needs are:

  a. Poor working relationships with stakeholders
  b. Inadequate coordination/support
  c. Business understanding
  d. Excessive categorization
  e. Failure to document critical information
  f. Excessive documentation

The next step is to understand the Systems Security Requirements. These requirements will drive the system development and include functional, contractual, or regulatory requirements. These requirements are most often found in Statements of Work (SOW), Statement of Requirements (SOR), Statements of Objectives (SOO), or Service Level Agreements (SLAs). A key of this model is a feedback loop, and the key stakeholders are involved in each process.

Design Validation

Design validation is done during phase 2 of the systems development life cycle. It ensures that the design meets the security requirements that were allocated to the original baseline for the development. Validation is often done in accordance with an established design specification, functional capability, security policy, customer requirements, or any combination of these.

Design validation requires the development of a test and evaluation plan. These plans are often called Security Tests and Evaluation Plans or Certification Tests and Evaluation Plans. They include test methods that identify how the test is conducted, the criteria for testing, and how the requirement is met. The test and evaluation methods include functional demonstration of the security feature, documentation that includes policies, and procedures that describe how the system, feature or capability is operated. Other methods may include electronic instrumented tests and interviews with employees, managers, and users of the system.

Step 3 activities define the system's security architecture. This design is based on a thorough understanding of the system's Security Concept of Operations (SECONOP), which discusses how the system's security mechanisms will be implemented[48]. The security functions needed to meet the specific security requirements called for in the specifications should also include the system security modes of operation. Will the system be a stand-alone, closed LAN not connected to the Internet or will it have Internet access with a variety of users with different types of need to know and user roles. Once this is established, trade-off studies should be conducted to ensure that the appropriate hardware and software are selected. Some products may require Common Criteria-evaluated products, as discussed earlier. Finally, the security architect should be involved in assessing the information protection effectiveness. These are the core processes involved in designing the security architecture.

Step 4 involves developing the detailed architecture so that security services can be allocated to architecture by selecting the appropriate security mechanisms. The architecture is then submitted for evaluation by the test and evaluation team. The architecture is revised to accommodate mission capabilities and requirements that may need adjusting in order to function properly. A risk

---

48   "A Security Concept of Operations (SECONOP) may be included in the System Security Plan. The CONOPS shall at a minimum include a description of the purpose of the system, a description of the system architecture, the system's accreditation schedule, the system's Protection Level, integrity Level-of-Concern, availability Level-of-Concern, and a description of the factors that determine the system's Protection Level, integrity Level-of-Concern, and availability Level-of-Concern. " See the following for the supporting document | DIRECTOR OF CENTRAL INTELLIGENCE DIRECTIVE 6/3PROTECTING SENSITIVE COMPARTMENTED INFORMATION WITHIN INFORMATION SYSTEMS (appendices)   http://www.fas.org/irp/offdocs/6-3_20Appendices.htm

analysis is conducted to evaluate all potential vulnerabilities that may be caused by relaxing or restraining the configuration settings. The results are provided to customers to obtain concurrence that the architecture meets their needs.

The security architect also participates in the various decisions that are taken at particular development milestone Preliminary Design Reviews, Critical Design Reviews, Systems Readiness Reviews, and Technical Interchange meetings. A variety of working groups may also be established to resolve design or program management issues that occur throughout the design process. These working group meetings and the like should include the oversight committees, accreditors, and systems certifiers in support of the Certification and Accreditation process if one is required.

Certification

Certification has been defined as the comprehensive evaluation of the security features and functions of an information system. It provides evidence that the system is configured to provide the most effective security protection based on specific security policies, standards, or industry best practices. Certification can be done based on a variety of public security policies or standards. A list of some of the certification policies include but are not limited to the following:

1. Health Insurance Portability and Accountability Act (HIPAA)
2. NIST Certification and Accreditation Process (NIST SP 800-37)
3. ISO/IEC 27002, Certification for commercial information systems
4. Sarbanes–Oxley Act of 2002
5. Payment Card Industry Data Security Standard (PCI-DSS)
6. U.S Department of Defense Information Assurance Certification and Accreditation Process (DIACAP)[49]

Peer Reviews

Peer review processes exist in many companies, particularly those that have attained CMMI for Development Maturity Level 3 or higher. They may be automated or manually implemented. If they are automated, they contain processes and procedures for inviting peers to the review, prework such as reviewing the document or code prior to meeting, recording the defects, or problems with the article under review. The chair of the peer review should assign roles to individuals supporting the review.

Peer review is a methodical examination of a work product by the author's peers to provide comments and to identify and categorize defects in the work product as efficiently and as early in the life cycle as possible (see *Figure 4.10*).

---

49   http://www.dtic.mil/whs/directives/corres/pdf/851001p.pdf

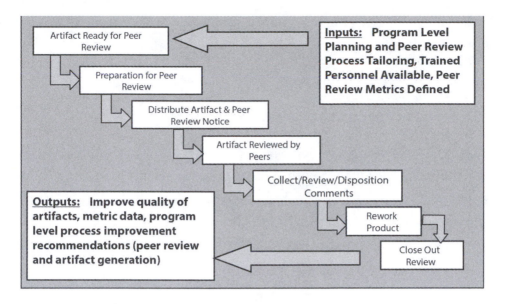

Figure 4.7 Peer review process.

The peer review process requires planning, advanced preparation, discussion, recording, measurement, rework, and follow-up. It typically reviews contract deliverable documentation for internal and external customers based primarily on materials (PDR and CDR charts). Program Planning Documents (e.g., SEP, HDP, Tailoring Matrix) include the requirements for a peer review process. Design and Development of work products (Requirements, Design description, Module Design Specifications, Board layout, S/W Code, Trade Studies, Plans and Procedures) should all be peer-reviewed.

There are several types of peer reviews:

- *Formal inspection* - Typically used for initial deliveries of contractually required products.
- *Structured walkthrough* - Typically used for complex products, where an off-line review may not be efficient. Product is reviewed in real time during a meeting.
- *Critique* - Used for simple products, small changes, or use of the product limited to internal customers.

Peer review teams can be composed of the following types of personnel:

- *Manager/team lead* - Ultimately responsible for the product; ensures that the product is ready for PR; assists author in identifying reviewers.
- *Moderator* - In a formal or walkthrough review, conducts the PR meeting; is responsible for identifying predicted defects using the Inspection Calculator and for determining if a reinspection is required.

417

- **Author** - Generates the product, schedules the PR, and incorporates comments.
- **Recorder** - In a formal or walkthrough review, records defect data during the meeting.
- **Reviewers** - Relevant stakeholders review the work product to identify defects and potential issues.
- **Reader** - In a walkthrough review, presents the item under review.
- **Quality Engineer** - Ensures the PR process is followed, and ensures compliance with standards and conventions.

The benefit of having a peer review process is to ensure that a quality product is delivered to the customer without any defects. This reduces rework and shows the customer that the organization is conducting due diligence in product delivery.

Audit reports are sometimes referred to as Security Test and Evaluation Reports or certification reports. They are assessments of the system's security mechanisms and services based on the predefined requirements that were implemented in the system during the development process. They can range from running simple risk assessment tools to full-blown penetration testing and reporting the findings or results back to the system owners or regulators. The level of the evaluations is dependent on the sensitivity of the information being processed or stored on the system.

Audit reports provide evidence to the system owners and regulators that the system has met the prescribed specifications for security assurance. The reports point out the strengths and weaknesses of the system and provide recommendations to correct any deficiencies. Sometimes, the deficiencies are so severe that the recommendation is not to allow the system to proceed to operation. When this happens, it is often because of a failure to implement a countermeasure to provide adequate protection to the system. Deficiencies are often ranked as to the severity of the vulnerability. For instance, when a technical protection mechanism does not work, a procedural one might do the trick in the short term. When deficiencies are less severe, the system may be allowed to operate as long as those deficiencies are corrected within a prescribed timeline. The ultimate goal of the audit report is to determine if the system meets a level of risk the organization deems sufficient for secure operation.

Following the documented security design, build, and implementation of the security functions and features of the system, the security architect works with the systems engineer and security engineer to ensure that all the requirements of the system have been satisfied. They support the system certification and assist in verifying the interoperability of security tools and mechanisms against the

4

security design and evaluate security components against the evaluation criteria as well as the integration and configuration of components.

Finally, the security architect supports the build, test, and evaluation strategy for the system. This may include developing test plans and procedures using the demonstration, observation, analysis, and testing methods. The security architect assesses available test and evaluation data for applicability, supports development of test and evaluation procedures and evaluation activities to ensure that the security design is implemented correctly, and conducts or updates a final risk analysis. If certification and accreditation (C&A) is required, the security architect ensures the completeness required for C&A documentation with the customer and the customer's certifiers and accreditors or regulators. Security training on the system may also be required, and the security architect may be called upon to support development of security training material.

Documentation

A variety of documents is usually required as part of the program administration. The security architect will have input into these documents and may be directly responsible for developing program documents or providing input to the list of documents being developed. Document development may be required by policy or regulation as part of the contract. The documents list includes but is not limited to the following:

- **IMM** - Information Management Model
- **MNS** - Mission Needs Statement (what is the overall mission and need for this product)
- **IPP** - Information Protection Policy
- **PNE** - Protection Needs Elicitation (appendix H of the IATF)
- **CONOPS** - Concept of Operations (user perspective and functional/ technical - sometimes on large projects the security is removed and made a different document)
- **SSP** - System Security Plans
- **Security Architecture** - Discusses the security functions, safeguards, and configurations

Some common pitfalls of this security architecture and design:

- The security architecture is not compatible with system architecture, which means the wrong mechanisms may have been selected for a particular function or provide inadequate security protections.
- The security is not integrated with non-security functionality or use of modified Commercial Off-The-Shelf (COTS) /Government Off-The-Shelf (GOTS) products.

- Occasionally, a poorly documented architecture, meant to clearly describe the costs/benefits of the security design elements or provide adequate design context or rationale, may leave the customer in doubt as to whether the system meets their specification, so it is important to ensure that the documentation is complete and is written to address the appropriate audience.

Summary

This domain covers the information essential to understanding requirements analysis and security standards/guidelines criteria and their elements. This chapter has discussed requirement analysis, current architectures, and solutions, systems engineering methodologies, methods of attack vectors, design validation, and legal and regulatory requirements.

Requirements analysis is one of the most important activities of systems security architecture and systems development. Security requirements are based on industry best practices, regulatory statutes, customer needs, and contractual obligations. Proper analysis of the requirements can prove to be critical to developing and delivering a secure system that is usable and provides customer satisfaction. The security architect begins by gathering requirements from customers who submit Statements of Work (SOW), contract documents, system specifications, Service Level Agreements (SLAs), Requests for Proposals (RFPs), legal and regulatory documents from federal, state, local, or international policy, or other documents such as security best practices and industry standards for safety and security. The security architect should be able to gather the rele-vant requirements and determine at a high level the best solutions to satisfy those requirements and the impact they may have on the system as the system development life cycle progresses.

The security architect should be intimately familiar with the most common types of attacks in order to select countermeasures that will combat these attacks. An attack vector is a path or means by which an attacker can gain access to a computer or network server in order to deliver a payload or malicious outcome. Attack vectors enable hackers to exploit system vulnerabilities, including the human element. This includes viruses, e-mail attachments, Web pages, pop-up windows, instant messages, chat rooms, and deception. All of these methods involve programming or, in a few cases, hardware, except deception, in which a human operator is fooled into removing or weakening system defenses. It is unrealistic to think that 100% protection against all possible threats, at all times, is attainable or desirable. The objective is to develop a system that allows the customer to conduct their business or mission at an acceptable level of residual risk.

There are a number of methods and techniques used by the security architect to ensure that the requirements are satisfied. These include using Common Criteria-evaluated products when required for security relevant applications and services, engaging architecture processes such as DoDAF, MoDAF, FEAF, or Zachman, and supporting the Systems Security Engineering process. The ISO/IECs and RFCs can also be helpful in providing best practice guidance. A secure information system is best achieved when the security architect practices due diligence and pays attention to details of standards, threats awareness, risks identification, and the value of the data. In all cases, the security architect should be aware of the relevant policies, procedures, and techniques needed to architect an information system using defense in depth.

Review Questions

Bradley, M., Data valuation: rethinking "one size fits all" data protection - Storage Networking, *Computer Technology Review,* Jan., 2003.

Capability Maturity Model (CMM) Key Practices Version 1.1

CMMI Product Team, (2010) *CMMI® for Development, Version 1.3 (CMMI-DEV, V1.3), Improving processes for developing better products and services, Technical Report* Software Engineering Institute Carnegie Mellon University Pittsburgh, Pennsylvania 15213 CMU/SEI-2010-TR-033 ESC-TR-2010-033.

Common Criteria (CC) for Information Technology Security Evaluation Part 1: Introduction and general model September 2006 Version 3.1, Revision 1.

Common Criteria (CC) for Information Technology Security Evaluation Part 1: Introduction and general model September 2012 Version 3.1, Revision 4.

Common Criteria (CC) for Information Technology Security Evaluation Part 2: Security Functional Component, September 2006 Version 3.1, Revision 1.

Common Criteria (CC) for Information Technology Security Evaluation Part 2: Security Functional Component, September 2012 Version 3.1, Revision 4.

Common Criteria (CC) for Information Technology Security Evaluation Part 3: Security Assurance Component, September 2006 Version 3.1 Revision 1.

Common Criteria (CC) for Information Technology Security Evaluation Part 3: Security Assurance Component, September 2012 Version 3.1 Revision 4.

Hansche, S., *The Official Guide to the CISSP-ISSEP CBK*™, Auerbach Publications, Boca Raton, FL, 2005

Happy Trails Computer Club, http://cybercoyote.org/index.shtml

Information Assurance Technical Framework IATF V.3.0

IT Law Group, http://www.itlawgroup.com/Resources/Archives.html, Accessed Nov. 2009.

Paulk, M. C., Weber, C. V., Garcia, S. M., Chrissis M. B., and Bush, M. (1993a) *Key Practices of the Capability Maturity Model*ˢᴹ*, Version 1.1,* Software Engineering Institute Carnegie Mellon University Pittsburgh, Pennsylvania 15213 CMU/SEI-93-TR-25 ESC-TR-93-178.

Paulk, M. C., Curtis, B., Chrissis M. B., Weber, C. V. (1993b), *Capability Maturity Model for Software, Version 1.1, Technical Report,* CMU/SEI-93-TR-024, ESC-TR-93-177, February 1993.

Review Questions

1. The approach in which policies, procedures, technology, and personnel are considered in the system security development process is called
  A. defense in depth.
  B. requirements analysis.
  C. risk assessment.
  D. attack vectors.

2. Software that adds hidden components to a system without end user knowledge is
  A. Virus.
  B. Spyware.
  C. Adware.
  D. Malware.

3. Risk is assessed by which of the following formulas?
  A. Risk = Vulnerability × Threat × Impact Divided by Countermeasure
  B. Risk = Annual Loss Opportunity ÷ Single Loss Expectancy
  C. Risk = Exposure Facture divided by Asset Value
  D. Risk = Vulnerability × Annual Loss Expectancy

4. Requirements definition is a process that should be completed in the following order:
  A. Document, identify, verify, and validate.
  B. Identify, verify, validate, and document.
  C. Characterize, analyze, validate, and verify.
  D. Analyze, verify, validate, and characterize.

5. A path by which a malicious actor gains access to a computer or network in order to deliver a malicious payload is a
  A. penetration test.
  B. attack vector.
  C. vulnerability assessment.
  D. risk assessment.

6. Which of the following is **BEST** as a guide for the development, evaluation, and/or procurement of IT products with security functionality?

    A. ISO/IEC 27001

    B. FIPS 140-2

    C. Common Criteria

    D. SEI-CMM

7. Which of the following **BEST** defines evaluation criteria for Protection Profile (PP) and Security Target (ST) and presents evaluation assurance levels rating assurance for the TOE?

    A. Part 3—Security assurance requirements

    B. Part 2—Security functional requirements

    C. Part 1—Introduction and general model

    D. Part 4—History and previous versions

8. The National Voluntary Laboratory Accreditation Program (NVLAP) must be in full conformance with which of the following standards?

    A. ISO/IEC 27001 and 27002

    B. ISO/IEC 17025 and Guide 58

    C. NIST SP 800-53A

    D. ANSI/ISO/IEC Standard 17024

9. A software application in combination with an operating system, a workstation, smart card integrated circuit, or cryptographic processor would be considered examples of a

    A. Functional Communications (FCO)

    B. Functional Trusted Path (FTP)

    C. Target of Evaluation (TOE)

    D. Security Target (ST)

10. A security architect requires a device with a moderate level of independently assured security, and a thorough investigation of the TOE and its development without substantial reengineering. It should be evaluated at which CC EAL?

    A. EAL6

    B. EAL5

    C. EAL4

    D. EAL3

4

11. At which Common Criteria EAL would a security architect select a device appropriate for application in extremely high-risk situations or where the high value of the assets justifies the higher costs?

    A. EAL4

    B. EAL5

    C. EAL6

    D. EAL7

12. A list of Common Criteria–evaluated products can be found on the Internet on the site at the

    A. NIAP

    B. CCEVS

    C. IASE

    D. CERIS

13. Which of the following describes the purpose of the Capability Maturity Model?

    A. Determine business practices to ensure creditability for the company's commitment to quality and excellence.

    B. Provide assurance through active investigation and evaluation of the IT product in order to determine its security properties.

    C. Establish a metric to judge in a repeatable way the maturity of an organization's software process as compared to the state of the industry practice.

    D. Provide an overview of standards related to the Information Security Management family for uniformity and consistency of fundamental terms and definitions.

14. Which one of the following describes the key practices that correspond to a range of maturity levels 1–5?

    A. Common Criteria

    B. SEI-CMM

    C. ISO/IEC 27002

    D. IATF v3

15. Which of the following CMMI levels include quantitative process management and software quality management as the capstone activity?

    A. CMMI Level 5

    B. CMMI Level 4

    C. CMMI Level 3

    D. CMMI Level 2

16. Where can the general principles of the OSI Reference Model architecture be found that describes the OSI layers and what layering means?

    A. Clause 3

    B. Clause 5

    C. Clause 7

    D. Clause 9

17. A privately held toy company processing, storing, or transmitting payment card data must be compliant with which of the following?

    A. Gramm–Leach–Bliley Act (GLBA)

    B. Health Insurance Portability and Accountability Act (HIPAA)

    C. Sarbanes–Oxley Act of 2002

    D. PCI-DSS

18. In which phase of the IATF does formal risk assessment begin?

    A. Assess effectiveness

    B. Design system security architecture

    C. Define system security requirements

    D. Discover information protection needs

19. Which of the following describes a methodical examination of a work product by the author's coworkers to comment, identify, and categorize defects in the work product?

    A. Formal inspection

    B. Structured walkthrough

    C. Critique

    D. Peer review

20. Which of the following is a critical element in the design validation phase?

    A. Develop security test and evaluation plan

    B. Develop protection needs elicitation

    C. Develop the concept of operation

    D. Requirements analysis

Architecture

Domain 5

Technology Related
Business Continuity Planning (BCP)
& Disaster Recovery Planning (DRP)

"RECENT WORLD EVENTS have challenged us to prepare to manage previously unthinkable situations that may threaten the organization's future.

The new challenge goes beyond the mere emergency response plan or disaster management activities that we previously employed. Organizations must now engage in a comprehensive process best described generically as Business Continuity.

Today's threats require the creation of an on-going, interactive process that serves to assure the continuation of an organization's core activities before, during, and most importantly, after a major crisis event ..." (*ASIS 2005*) [1]

Business continuity planning provides a quick and smooth restoration of operations after a disruptive event. Business continuity planning is a major component of risk management. Business continuity planning includes business impact analysis, business continuity plan (BCP) development, testing, awareness, training, and maintenance.

---

1   The main website for the American Society for Industrial Security (ASIS International) can be found here: http://www.asisonline.org/

A business continuity plan addresses actions to be taken before, during, and after a disaster. A BCP spells out in detail the what, who, how, and when of the plans required to be followed in the event of a disaster striking the business in order to ensure that all required resources and efforts are directed towards one common goal. It requires a continuing investment of time and resources. Interruptions to business functions can result from major natural disasters such as tornadoes, floods, and fires, or from man-made disasters such as terrorist attacks. The most frequent disruptions are less sensational — equipment failures, theft, or employee sabotage. The definition of a disaster, then, is any incident that causes an extended disruption of business functions.

Business continuity planning is the process whereby institutions ensure the maintenance or recovery of operations, including services to customers, when confronted with adverse events such as natural disasters, technological failures, human error, or terrorism. The objectives of a business continuity plan (BCP) are to minimize financial loss to the institution; continue to serve customers; and mitigate the negative effects disruptions can have on an institution's strategic plans, reputation, operations, liquidity, credit quality, market position, and ability to remain in compliance with applicable laws and regulations. Changing business processes (internally to the institution and externally among interdependent services companies) and new threat scenarios require institutions to maintain updated and viable BCPs.

Business Continuity Planning is a comprehensive and often complex discipline that delves deeply into the business as a whole. In fact, many IT departments provide a support function to the business overall, while many businesses have separate departmental systems for specific business functions. Both the overarching IT systems functions such as e-mail and telephony, as well as departmental specific systems such as employee badge creation, or benefits administration must all be assessed equally when creating a Business Continuity Plan / Disaster Recovery Plan solution for the business.

Business continuity planning (BCP) and disaster recovery planning (DRP) involve the identification of adverse events that could threaten the ability of the organization to continue normal operations. Once these events are identified, the security architect will implement countermeasures to reduce the risk of such incidents occurring. Furthermore, the security architect will play a key role in designing and developing business continuity plans that will meet the operational business requirements of the organization through planning for the provisioning of appropriate solutions. Key areas of knowledge include:

1. Evaluating recovery requirements and strategy

2. Designing and developing business continuity plans

3. Assessing the business continuity plan and disaster recovery plan

5

Technology Related
BCP and DRP

TOPICS

- Incorporate Business Impact Analysis (BIA)
  - Legal
  - Financial
  - Stakeholders)
- Determine Security Strategies for Availability and Recovery
  - Identify solutions
    - Cold
    - Warm
    - Hot
    - Insource
    - Outsource
  - Define processing agreement requirements
    - Reciprocal
    - Mutual
    - Cloud
    - Outsourcing
    - Virtualization
  - Establish recovery time objectives and recovery point objectives
- Design Continuity and Recovery Solution
  - High availability, failover and resiliency
    - Communication path diversity
    - Paired deployment
    - Pass-through network interfaces
    - Application
  - Availability of service provider/supplier support
    - Cloud
    - SLAs
  - BCP/DRP Architecture Validation
    - Test Scenarios
    - Requirements Traceability Matrix
    - Trade-Off Matrices

OBJECTIVES

The security architect needs to understand the business continuity and disaster recovery domain to ensure development of plans for the protection and recovery of the critical IT infrastructure. This Domain focuses on the technology recovery strategies in support of the overall business continuity program.

- BCP is defined as:
  - Preparation that facilitates the rapid recovery of mission-critical business operations
  - The reduction of the impact of a disaster
  - The continuation of critical business functions
- DRP is defined as:
  - A subset of BCP that emphasizes the procedures for emergency response relating to the information infrastructure of the organization
  - DRP includes:
    - Extended backup operations
    - Post-disaster recovery for data center, network, and computer resources

A business continuity plan is the tool that results from the planning and is the basis for continued life-cycle development [Waxvik 2007]. Continuity planning is a significant management issue and should include all parts or functions of the organization. Together, BCP and DRP ensure adequate preparations and procedures for the continuation of all business functions.

Planning Phases and Deliverables

Whether developing a new plan or updating an older one, the following planning phases are recommended:

1. Identify the planning team and critical staff.
2. Validate vital records.
3. Conduct risk and business impact analyses.
4. Develop recovery strategy.
5. Select alternate sites.
6. Document the plan.
7. Test, maintain, and update the plan.

Planning Team and Critical Staff - The security architect will need to identify and build contact lists for the planning team, leadership, and critical staff. The deliverable from this phase is the Emergency Notification List (ENL).

Vital Records - Validating that all the records needed to rebuild the business are stored off-site in a secure location that will be accessible following a disaster. This includes backups of your technology as well as paper records. The deliverable from this phase is a list of the vital records, where they are stored off-site, how to retrieve them, and who is authorized to retrieve them.

Risk Analysis and Business Impact Analysis - This is where decisions are made about what risks will be mitigated and which processes will be recovered and when. The deliverable from this phase of the planning is a list of risks by site and recommendations to be implemented to reduce the impact of the risk. The security architect has a responsibility to help guide the organization to focus on those risks that will be addressed through planning at some level, and to clearly identify which risks will not be mitigated because of the costs involved in doing so.

Strategy Development - In this phase, the security architect will review the different types of strategies for the recovery of business areas and technology based on the recovery time frame(s) that have been identified for each, do a cost–benefit analysis on the viable strategies to be selected, and make a proposal to leadership to implement the selected strategies. The deliverable from this phase is the recommended strategies for recovery.

Alternate Site Selection and Implementation - During this phase, the security architect selects and builds out the alternate sites to be used in the event of a recovery. The deliverable from this phase is a functional alternate site [2].

Documenting the Plan - This phase is where all the information collected up to this point is combined into a formal plan document. The deliverable from this phase is the documented recovery plan for each site.

Testing, Maintenance, and Update - During the final phase is where the security architect will validate the recovery strategies implemented through testing, establish a maintenance schedule for the plan, and an update schedule for the plan documentation. The deliverable from this phase is ongoing results from validating the plan.

Risk Analysis

As part of the planning process, the security architect will need to perform a risk analysis or assessment to determine the threats to which the organization is vulnerable and where mitigating investments should be applied to attempt to reduce the impact of a threat. To do this, security architects need to determine the risks faced by the organization. This includes risk from natural hazards, industry risks, and environmental risks.

The security architect needs to look at natural hazard risks based on the location of the organization; industry risks based on the organization's type of business or mission; crime risks based on the geographic location(s) of the organization; human-made hazards such as transportation accidents based on proximity to highways, train lines, airports, etc.; proximity risks based on other industries near where the organization is located such as chemical plants, and natural gas storage facilities; and then recommend mitigating strategies to protect the business where appropriate. Once the risk analysis is completed, the

5

---

2   It is important for the security architect to be aware of emerging trends in their areas of responsibility as well as existing standards. The integration of cloud computing solutions within the security architecture of many organizations is an ongoing process that requires attention and consideration. There are many factors that the security architect will need to consider as they ensure that cloud based solutions and platforms are fully integrated and properly secured as part of the organization security architecture. The need to address Service Level Agreements (SLA's) and hosting arrangements with regards to BCP/DRP is just one small area for the security architect to be concerned with. Several good starting points can be found here:

A. The Cloud Security Alliance main web site: https://cloudsecurityalliance.org/

B. European Network and Information Security Agency (ENISA) Cloud Computing Information Assurance Framework, 11/20/2009. :   http://www.enisa.europa.eu/activities/risk-management/files/deliverables/cloud-computing-information-assurance-framework

C. European Network and Information Security Agency (ENISA) Cloud Computing Risk Assessment, 11/20/2009. :   http://www.enisa.europa.eu/activities/risk-management/files/deliverables/cloud-computing-risk-assessment

security architect will need to document the findings. A sample risk model from the US National Institute of Standards and Technology (NIST) is below:[3]

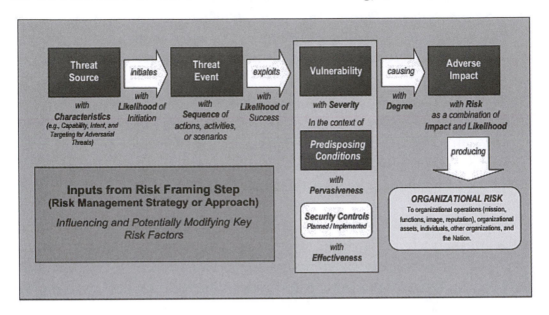

Documentation of the risk analysis is a critical success factor with regards to risk mitigation. If the risk analysis is not clearly presented to the business, allowing for key decision makers to understand the risks that are likely to occur, and those that are not very likely to occur, then risk mitigation cannot take place. The output of the risk analysis will require the security architect to create a matrix to represent the risks found, and the likelihood of their occurrence. A sample risk analysis matrix can be seen in *Figure 5.1*.

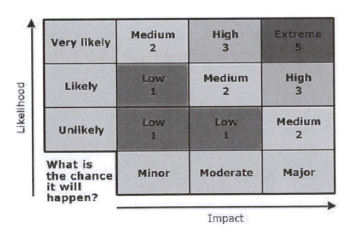

Figure 5.1 - **Risk Analysis matrix**

The security architect will also need to create a description of the rankings used in the risk analysis matrix to help explain what each rating will mean. An example of a risk level explanation can be seen in *Table 5.1*

---

3   See the following for the NIST Special Publication 800-30 Revision 1 Guide for Conducting Risk Assessments: http://csrc.nist.gov/publications/nistpubs/800-30-rev1/sp800_30_r1.pdf (page 21)

Risk Level	Risk Description
Extreme	The loss of confidentiality, integrity, or availability could be expected to have a catastrophic adverse effect on organizational operations, organizational assets or individuals.
High	The loss of confidentiality, integrity, or availability could be expected to have a severe adverse effect on organizational operations, organizational assets or individuals.
Medium	The loss of confidentiality, integrity, or availability could be expected to have a serious adverse effect on organizational operations, organizational assets or individuals.
Low	The loss of confidentiality, integrity, or availability could be expected to have a limited adverse effect on organizational operations, organizational assets or individuals.

Table 5.1 - **Risk Level explanation for a risk analysis matrix**

In addition, the security architect will also want to document any specific terms that are used to describe state or activity within the risk analysis being presented to the business. For instance, in the risk level explanation for the risk analysis matrix presented in Table 5.1, the terms Confidentiality, Integrity, and Availability are used with regard to " loss ", but are not clearly defined for the reader. In order to ensure that there is no confusion on the part of anyone who would be examining the risk analysis documentation, the security architect would also want to provide a definition table of terms for the reader, as shown in *Table 5.2*

Security Objective	Low	Medium	High	Extreme
Confidentiality Preserving authorized restrictions on information access and disclosure, including means for protection personal privacy and proprietary information [44 USC, SEC. 3542]	The unauthorized disclosure of information could be expected to have a limited adverse effect on organizational operations, organizational assets, or individuals.	The unauthorized disclosure of information could be expected to have a serious adverse effect on organizational operations, organizational assets, or individuals.	The unauthorized disclosure of information could be expected to have a severe adverse effect on organizational operations, organizational assets, or individuals.	The unauthorized disclosure of information could be expected to have a catastrophic adverse effect on organizational operations, organizational assets, or individuals.
Integrity Guarding against improper information modification or destruction, and includes ensuring information non-repudiation and authenticity. [44 USC, SEC. 3542]	The modification or destruction of information could be expected to have a limited adverse effect on organizational operations, organizational assets, or individuals.	The modification or destruction of information could be expected to have a serious adverse effect on organizational operations, organizational assets, or individuals.	The modification or destruction of information could be expected to have a severe adverse effect on organizational operations, organizational assets, or individuals.	The modification or destruction of information could be expected to have a catastrophic adverse effect on organizational operations, organizational assets, or individuals.
Availability Ensuring timely and reliable access to and use of information. [44 USC, SEC. 3542]	The disruption of access to or use of information or an information system could be expected to have a limited adverse effect on organizational operations, organizational assets, or individuals.	The disruption of access to or use of information or an information system could be expected to have a serious adverse effect on organizational operations, organizational assets, or individuals.	The disruption of access to or use of information or an information system could be expected to have a severe adverse effect on organizational operations, organizational assets, or individuals.	The disruption of access to or use of information or an information system could be expected to have a catastrophic adverse effect on organizational operations, organizational assets, or individuals.

Table 5.2 - **Confidentiality, Integrity, and Availability Defined** [4]

5

Technology Related BCP and DRP

---

4   Table 2 is found in the Centers for Disease Control and Prevention (CDC) Draft Risk Assessment Report, submitted 2007, on page 19. The full draft report can be found here: http://csrc.nist.gov/groups/SMA/fasp/areas.html

The report is listed under the Incident Response Capability section, and is titled "Business Continuity Plan Functional Test After-Action Report - (CDC)"

Finally, the security architect will also need to provide a risk level definition along with all other items already discussed in order to ensure that the business is able to clearly understand the magnitude of the risks being discussed, and the necessary level of response required to mitigate the risk, if it is deemed appropriate to do so. *Table 5.3* illustrates what the risk level definition would look like.

Magnitude of Impact	Risk Level Definition
Extreme	There is an immediate need for corrective measures. An existing system may not continue to operate unless a corrective action plan is put in place immediately, or already exists.
High	There is a strong need for corrective measures. An existing system may continue to operate, but a corrective action plan must be put in place as soon as possible.
Medium	Corrective actions are needed and a plan must be developed to incorporate these actions within a reasonable period of time.
Low	The organization's management must determine whether corrective actions are still required or decide to accept the risk.

Table 5.3 - **Risk Level Definition**

There are many samples of risk analysis templates available for download through the World Wide Web. A quick search using Google will turn up hundreds of options for the security architect to access and examine as a starting point to creating their own. Microsoft, NIST, the Virginia Information Technologies Agency (VITA), the United Nations, the US Army Core of Engineers, and the governments of Australia, Japan, Germany, France, and the United Kingdom all have sample templates available to be downloaded. [5]

In addition to sample templates, there are a number of Frameworks and Relevant Standards that the security architect should become familiar with. While most of these are focused on Corporate Governance and financial controls, the security architect will still play a part in supporting these frameworks, and will have to build and maintain systems in accordance with their guidance if the industrial verticals that the architect works in are required to use them. These include the following:

---

5 See the following for a simple template that is available for free from Microsoft's Office templates download library: http://office.microsoft.com/en-us/templates/risk-assessment-and-financial-impact-model-TC001184173.aspx

This template is designed to assist executives, risk management, and line management in analyzing the potential risks facing an organization, as well as mitigating controls that can be used to manage these risks. It allows you to weight the financial impact and probability of specified risks versus the cost of controls, in order to facilitate a cost/benefit decision analysis.

1. *The Criteria of Control(CoCo)*, a control framework issued by the Canadian Institute of Chartered Accountants (CICA) in 1995 [6].

2. *KonTrag, (Gesetz zur Kontrolle und Transparenz im Unternehmensbereich - German Act on Control and Transparency in Business)*, which is a framework that promotes corporate governance in both the public and private sectors [7].

3. *Committee of Sponsoring Organizations (COSO) Enterprise Risk Management (ERM) Framework:2004*, which consists of eight components designed to help organizations formally organize ERM responsibilities and activities, providing a comprehensive roadmap for establishing the critical processes needed for effective risk management [8].

4. *ISO 31000:2009, Risk Management – Principles and Guidelines*, which provides principles, framework and a process for managing risk [9].

5. *ISO/IEC 31010:2009, Risk Management – Risk Assessment Techniques*, which provides guidance on selection and application of systematic techniques for risk assessment [10].

6. *ISO Guide 73*, Risk management – vocabulary, which provides basic vocabulary to develop common understanding on risk management concepts and terms among organizations and functions, and across different applications and types. [11]

6　　See the following for the Canadian Institute of Chartered Accountants (CICA) website: http://www.cica.ca/index.aspx

7　　See the following for the initial announcement of the draft publication of KonTrag:

Remarks by Dr. Gerhard Cromme

Chairman of the Goverment Commission German Corporate Governance Code on the publication of the draft German Corporate Governance Code December 18, 2001 in Düsseldorf

http://www.corporate-governance-code.de/eng/news/rede-crommes.html

8　　See the following for the Committee of Sponsoring Organizations (COSO) website: http://www.coso.org/

9　　See the following for the ISO 31000 Standard:　http://www.iso.org/iso/home/standards/iso31000.htm

10　　See the following for the ISO/IEC 31010 Standard:　http://www.iso.org/iso/catalogue_detail?csnumber=51073

11　　See the following for ISO Guide 73:　http://www.pqm-online.com/assets/files/standards/iso_iec_guide_73-2009.pdf

Natural Hazard Risks [12]

There are many different types of natural hazard risks organizations and individuals may face today. The security architect needs to be able to provide guidance on known risks within the theater of operations that an organization covers. If that is localized to a small area, then the security architect's job becomes focused specifically on the risks associated with that well-defined area. Information and resources from local or municipal government agencies would be used by the security architect during the planning cycle to ensure identification and exposure of known risks. If on the other hand, the organization is regional, or national, or multi-national in its coverage, then the security architect needs to draw information in from a variety of sources in order to ensure that as many identified risks as possible are exposed in the planning cycle, and are addressed through mitigation efforts based on a cost benefit analysis[13]. Within the United States, security architects can check with the U.S. Geological Survey (USGS) for a natural hazards map of specific areas with regards to risks such as earthquakes, volcanic activity, and landslides[14].

---

12   See the following for the Global Risks 2012 Insight report prepared by the World Economic Forum: http://www3.weforum.org/docs/WEF_GlobalRisks_Report_2012.pdf

The Global Risks Insight report is a yearly series that is published by the World Economic Forum. The WEF is an independent international organization committed to improving the state of the world b y engaging business, political, academic and other leaders of society to shape global, regional and industry agendas. See their main web site here: http://www.weforum.org/

13   There are many sources for regional based analysis and information on risks and threats, both by country and internationally. A small sampling of these would include the United Nations and all of its various working bodies and committees, the World Economic Forum, the Organization for Economic Co-Operation and Development (OECD), The World Bank, and the International Monetary Fund (IMF), all of which engage in risk and threat analysis by region globally and publish their findings in a variety of formats.

14   See the following for specific hazards information by category from the USGS: http://www.usgs.gov/natural_hazards/

In 2010, the USGS realigned its organizational structure around the missions identified in the USGS Science Strategy. The Natural Hazards Mission Area includes six science programs: Coastal & Marine Geology, Earthquake Hazards, Geomagnetism, Global Seismographic Network, Landslide Hazards, and Volcano Hazards. Through these programs, the USGS provides alerts and warnings of geologic hazards and supports the warning responsibilities of the National Oceanic and Atmospheric Administration (NOAA) for geomagnetic storms and tsunamis. The Coastal and Marine Geology Program supports all the missions of the USGS, characterizing and assessing coastal and marine processes, conditions, change and vulnerability.

The Natural Hazards Mission Area is responsible for coordinating USGS response following disasters and overseeing the bureau's emergency management activities. The mission area coordinates long-term planning across the full USGS hazards science portfolio, including activities funded through many other programs across the bureau, including floods, hurricanes and severe storms, and wildfires.

For security architects outside of the United States, or those that have a multi-national focus due to the nature of the organizations they work for, there are many good starting points for risk identification and planning activities, from the United Nations Office for Disaster Risk Reduction (UNISDR)[15], to frameworks such as the Hyogo Framework for Action[16], to the many national and international research programs such as those that support the Charter On Cooperation To Achieve The Coordinated Use Of Space Facilities In The Event Of Natural Or Technological Disasters Rev.3 (25/4/2000)[17], and the PREVIEW program of the European Commission[18]. Some common natural hazards include:

- Earthquake
- Tornado
- Floods
- Hurricane
- Ice storms
- Blizzards
- Tsunami
- Cyclone
- Drought
- Dust storm
- Flash Flood
- Fog
- Heat Wave
- Lightning

15   See the following for information on the UNISDR: http://www.eird.org/index-eng.htm

16   See the following for the Hyogo Framework for Action document: http://www.eird.org/mah/hyogo-framework-for-action-english.pdf

17   The International Charter aims at providing a unified system of space data acquisition and delivery to those affected by natural or man-made disasters through Authorized Users. Each member agency has committed resources to support the provisions of the Charter and thus is helping to mitigate the effects of disasters on human life and property. The International Charter was declared formally operational on November 1, 2000. See the following for the text of the Charter On Cooperation To Achieve The Coordinated Use Of Space Facilities In The Event Of Natural Or Technological Disasters Rev.3 (25/4/2000):   http://www.disasterscharter.org/web/charter/charter

For a list of organizations that currently support the Charter, see the following: http://www.disasterscharter.org/web/charter/members

For an interactive mashup of categorized disasters from 2000 through the present, using the Charter Geographic Tool online, see the following: http://engine.mapshup.info/charterng/

18   The PREVIEW program of the European Commission is chartered with providing Geo-information services for risk management on a European level. PREVIEW is an EC-co funded research project looking for new techniques to better protect European citizens against environmental risks and to reduce their consequences.

See the following for more information on PREVIEW: http://www.preview-risk.com/site/FO/scripts/myFO_accueil.php?lang=EN&flash=1

- Rain
- Snow
- Thunder
- Tornado
- Tropical storm
- Water Spout
- Wind
- Wind Storm
- Fire Storm
- Fire - Wild, Rural or Urban

Human-Made Risks and Threats

Human-made risks may also be called "man-made" risks or anthropogenic hazards. There are many different areas where the security architect will find risks and threats as potential liabilities that will need to be addressed. The category of human-made risks and threats is a very broad one, as there are so many things that can cause a risk event to occur. There are many methodologies available to the security architect to help with the assessment and measurement of human-made risks and threats. Some examples include the approaches presented in the overview briefing paper " Development of a methodology to assess man-made risks in Germany"[19], the briefing document "Natural and man-made disaster risks of Kabul city"[20], the research work being done by universities around the world, such as the University of Cambridge Judge Business School's Centre for Risk Studies[21], the Université de Strasbourg through the REseau Alsace de Laboratoires en Ingénierie et Sciences pour l'Environnement (REALISE) network[22], the " Information Technology Sector Baseline Risk Assessment (ITSRA) " [23], and the " Risk Management Strategy

[19]   See the following for the full abstract of this paper: http://www.nat-hazards-earth-syst-sci. net/6/779/2006/nhess-6-779-2006.pdf

The citation for the paper is as follows: Nat. Hazards Earth Syst. Sci., 6, 779–802, 2006 www.nat-hazards-earth-syst-sci.net/6/779/2006/

[20]   See the following for the full briefing document: http://www.preventionweb.net/files/ section/230_KabulDRRPresentation.pdf

The paper was prepared and presented by Arch./ Urban Designer Wahid A Ahad Technical Deputy Mayor Of Kabul, June 2010.

[21]   See the following for more information on the Centre for Risk Studies Catastrophe Risk Management for Natural and Man-Made Perils research programs: http://www.risk.jbs.cam.ac.uk/ research/programmes/catastropherisk.html

[22]   See the following for information on the REALISE network: http://realise.unistra.fr/en/ the-network/

See the following for information on the research being conducted on natural and man-made risks: http://realise.unistra.fr/en/risques-naturels-et-anthropiques/

[23]   See the following for the full report: http://www.dhs.gov/xlibrary/assets/nipp_it_baseline_

– Internet Routing, Access and Connection Services"[24] reports, both produced by the Information Technology Sector Coordinating Council (ITSCC), the Information Technology Government Coordinating Council (ITGCC) and the United States Department of Homeland Security. Some common human-made risks and threats include:

- Terrorism
- Bio-Hazard
  - Biological
  - Chemical
  - Nuclear
- Epidemic/Pandemic
- Theft/Vandalism
- Work Stoppage
- Riot
- Power/HVAC Failure
- Systems Configuration Error(s)
- Security Updates for systems not kept up to date
- Communications Failure
- Hardware Failure
- Software Failure
- Security Incident
- Individual Behavior
- Mass Behavior
- Hijacking of an individual, a VIP, or a Group
- Assassination
- Torture
- Poisoning
- Wounding
- Bomb
  - Bomb Threat
  - (IED) Improvised Explosive Device
  - Car Bomb
  - Suicide Bomb
- Cyber attacks
- Espionage

risk_assessment.pdf

24   See the following for the full report: http://www.dhs.gov/xlibrary/assets/itsrm-for-inter-net-routing-report.pdf

Industry Risks[25]

Some risks are associated with the business or mission of an organization. Convenience stores face a threat of robbery. Banks may not only face robbery but also need to be concerned about money laundering. Department stores are frequent victims of shoplifting and also need to worry about identity theft. Insurance companies sometime face threats of workplace violence from claimants who are dissatisfied with the handling or a claim. Every industry will have its own specific risks associated with it, based on a variety of factors that are unique to those industries. As a result, the security architect will want to engage industry expertise to help them better assess the specific risks associated with the industry or mission in question as they engage in risk analysis and risk assessment activities. Some common industry risks are as follows:

- Robbery and theft
- Workplace violence
- Money laundering
- Identity theft
- Theft of trade secrets and Intellectual Property
- Fraud
- Supply Chains
- Loan defaults
- Market risk
- Credit risk
- Labor disputes

Do Not Forget the Neighbors!

There are many different entities that an organization may become neighbors with, depending on where the organization chooses to locate. Some of these neighbors will be fairly benign in nature and as a result, will not pose significant risks and threats to the business; as a matter of fact, they may even provide unforeseen benefits to the organizations locating near them, such as enhanced security and surveillance capabilities, upgraded infrastructure such as roads and bridges, rail and port facilities, and air terminals capable of handling large cargo

---

25   Some general overarching risk and threat themes exist regardless of industry or mission, such as the ones cited below:

   A. See the following report for an overview of risks associated with the supply chain and transportation areas common to all businesses today in some form:
      - http://www3.weforum.org/docs/WEF_SCT_RRN_NewModelsAddressingSupplyChainTransportRisk_IndustryAgenda_2012.pdf
   B. See the following report for an overview of risks associated with talent acquisition, retention and management that are common to all businesses today:
      - http://www3.weforum.org/docs/PS_WEF_GlobalTalentRisk_Report_2011.pdf

capacities and jumbo jets. Other neighbors may prove to be more of a potential source of risks and threats due to the nature of the kinds of activities carried out on site. It is the security architect's responsibility to ensure that the business is aware of all of the potential risks and threats, as well as any potential benefits arising from a choosing to locate in any particular area, as required based on circumstances. Some potential neighbors that the security architect may have to evaluate include:

- Nuclear power plants
- Civil Defense / Military installations
- Intelligence gathering installations
- Oil storage facilities
- Hazardous waste producers
- Chemical factories
- Biomedical research facilities

Some of the events are fairly localized, such as a facility fire, and others, such as a hurricane, have a more regional impact. These are important factors in the risk consideration. A regional risk can affect not just the business but the homes and families of its employees, and can cause competition for the availability of contracted alternate sites.

Once a risk has been identified and analyzed, the security architect will need to make choices about how to respond to that risk: accept it, transfer it, reduce /mitigate it, or avoid it.

Risk Acceptance
If the risk of occurrence is so small or the impact so minimal or the cost to mitigate it so substantial, the security architect can recommend to the organization that the risk be accepted.

Risk Transfer
When a risk is too costly to mitigate, but too big to just accept, the security architect can choose to recommend that the organization transfer the monetary risk by purchasing an insurance policy. Similar to car insurance, business interruption insurance is often used to transfer the monetary risk of an event that cannot be mitigated because of either cost or some other factor. The security architect should understand that while the monetary exposure of the organization may be covered as a result of the transference event, other areas of risk such as reputation and goodwill must still be considered.

Risk Reduction / Mitigation
Putting controls in place to prevent the most likely of risks from having an impact on the ability to do business leads to having fewer actual events from

which to recover. The risks that the security architect needs to address are the ones most likely to occur. A business continuity plan is one type of mitigation strategy. In fact, a business continuity plan is what is implemented when all other mitigating factors have failed.

Risk Avoidance

There are certain risks that can be dealt with by not dealing with them in the first place. The security architect can guide the business away from activities and behaviors that lead to risks that are best dealt with by not allowing them into the business in the first place. These risks may be too big to contain if realized, and too costly to mitigate, accept, or transfer based on their potential impacts on the business.

Business Impact Analysis

The Business Impact Analysis (BIA) attempts to determine the consequences of disruptions that could result from a disaster and guides the organization's decision regarding what needs to be recovered and how quickly it needs to be recovered. The BIA is the foundation of the plans that will be built for the business.

While performing the BIA, security architects should avoid using the term *critical* or *essential* in defining the processes or people during this phase of the planning. Instead, use the term *time sensitive*. Generally speaking, organizations do not hire staff to perform nonessential tasks. Every function has a purpose, but some are more time sensitive than others when there is limited time or resources available to perform them.

A bank that has suffered a building fire could easily stop its marketing campaign but would not be able to stop processing deposits and checks written by its customers. The bank's marketing campaign is very essential to the bank's growing its business in the long term but in the middle of a disaster, marketing will take a backseat, not because it is not critical but because it is not time sensitive.

All business functions and the technology that supports them need to be classified based on their recovery priority[26]. Recovery time frames for business operations are driven by the consequences of not performing the function. The consequences may be the result of business lost during the down period;

---

26   The Insurance Institute for Business & Home Safety produces a yearly commercial series of articles on a variety of topics important to security architects and businesses. See the following for their article " Recovery Priorities for Cost-Effective Business Continuity Planning: http://disastersafety. org/wp-content/uploads/03_comms-priorities.pdf

contractual commitments not met, resulting in fines or lawsuits; lost goodwill with customers, etc. Impacts generally fall into one or more of these categories: financial, regulatory, or customer.

All applications, and the business functions that they support, need to be classified as to their time sensitivity for recovery even if they do not support business functions that are time sensitive. For applications, this is commonly referred to as Recovery Time Objective (RTO). This is the amount of time the business can function without that application before significant business impact occurs.

Once the business has determined the time frame for recovery of the different business operations and identified the applications that are essential to perform those functions, the security architect can establish RTOs for each of the applications to be recovered by the technology plan. The RTO will define for the technology recovery team how much time can elapse between the time the disaster occurs and the time the application is recovered and available to the business.

The business also needs to determine the amount of work in process that can be at risk during an event. The data that is on an employee's desk when a fire occurs would be lost forever if that information was not backed up somewhere else. The information stored in file cabinets, incoming mail in the mailroom, and the backup tapes that have not yet left the building are all at risk.

Decisions need to be made about all types of data because data is what is needed to run the business. How much data is it acceptable to lose? A minute's worth? An hour's worth? A whole business day's worth? The answers to these questions are used to determine the Recovery Point Objective (RPO). This is the point in time that the security architect will recover to. The vital records program, backup policies, and procedures for electronic data and hard copy data need to comply with the RPO established by the business. An example of the RTO and RPO together can be seen in *Figure 5.2*.

The origination of the RTO concept as a formalized recovery objective is found in the BS-25999-2 standard. BS 25999-2 defines RTO as "…target time set for resumption of product, service or activity delivery after an incident". RTO is determined during the Business Impact Analysis (BIA), and the preparations are defined in the business continuity strategy. Recovery Point Objective is a totally different thing, as RPO is defined as the maximum tolerable period in which data might be lost. The RPO is crucial for determining one specific element of the business continuity strategy – the frequency of data backups. If your RPO is 4 hours, then you need to perform backups at least every 4 hours.

RTO & RPO Definitions

- The Recovery Time Objective (**RTO**) for an application is the goal for how quickly you need to have that application's information back available after downtime has occurred.
- The Recovery Point Objective (**RPO**) for an application describes the point in time to which data must be restored to successfully resume processing (often thought of as time between last backup and when an "event" occurred)

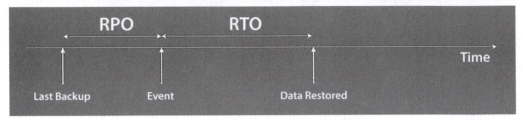

RTO & RPO Objectives should be set for each application based on:-
- the expected loss to the business with the objective
- the cost of achieving the objective

Figure 5.2 - **RTO and RPO Definitions**

The difference is in the purpose – RTO has a broader purpose because it sets the boundaries for your whole business continuity management strategy, while RPO is focused solely on the issue of backup frequency. They are not directly related, although they do support the same common goals, as they are both crucial for creating a successful Business Impact Analysis and for successfully carrying out a business continuity management strategy – for example, you could have an RTO of 12 hours and an RPO of 1 hour, or an RTO of 2 hours and an RPO of 12 hours.

BS 25999-2 was a British standard issued in 2007, which quickly became the main standard for business continuity management – although it is a British national standard, it was used in many other countries; on May 15, 2012 BS 25999-2 was replaced by international standard ISO 22301.

BS 25999-2 defined a business continuity management system which contains four management phases: planning, implementing, reviewing and monitoring, and finally improving.

The following are some of the key procedures and documents required by BS 25999-2:

- *Scope of the BCMS* – precise identification of that part of the organization to which business continuity management is applied
- *BCM policy* – defining objectives, responsibilities, etc.

- Human resource management
- Business impact analysis and risk assessment
- Defining business continuity strategy
- Business continuity plans
- Maintenance of plans and systems; improvement

In addition to BS 25999-2, BS 25999-1 is an "auxiliary" standard which provides more details on how to implement specific parts of BS 25999-2.

Other useful standards are ISO 27001, which places business continuity in a broader context of information security, and ISO 27005 which gives a detailed description of the risk assessment process.

ISO 22301 is the new de-facto standard for Business Continuity Management. The full name of this standard is ISO 22301:2012 Societal security – Business continuity management systems – Requirements. This standard is written by leading business continuity experts and provides the best framework for managing business continuity within an organization.

The standard includes these sections:

Introduction	5 Leadership	8 Operation
0.1 General	5.1 General	8.1 Operational planning and control
0.2 The Plan-Do-Check-Act (PDCA) model	5.2 Management commitment	8.2 Business impact analysis and risk assessment
0.3 Components of PDCA in this International Standard	5.3 Policy	
	5.4 Organizational roles, responsibilities and authorities	8.3 Business continuity strategy
1 Scope		8.4 Establish and implement business continuity procedures
2 Normative references	6 Planning	
3 Terms and definitions	6.1 Actions to address risks and opportunities	8.5 Exercising and testing
4 Context of the organization		9 Performance evaluation
4.1 Understanding of the organization and its context	6.2 Business continuity objectives and plans to achieve them	9.1 Monitoring, measurement, analysis and evaluation
4.2 Understanding the needs and expectations of interested parties	7 Support	9.2 Internal audit
	7.1 Resources	9.3 Management review
4.3 Determining the scope of the management system	7.2 Competence	10 Improvement
	7.3 Awareness	10.1 Nonconformity and corrective action
4.4 Business continuity management system	7.4 Communication	10.2 Continual improvement
	7.5 Documented information	Bibliography

Other standards that are helpful for the implementation of business continuity are:

- **ISO/IEC 27031** – Guidelines for information and communication technology readiness for business continuity [27]
- **PAS 200** – Crisis management – Guidance and good practice [28]
- **PD 25666** – Guidance on exercising and testing for continuity and contingency programmes [29]
- **PD 25111** – Guidance on human aspects of business continuity [30]
- **ISO/IEC 24762** – Guidelines for information and communications technology disaster recovery services [31]
- **ISO/PAS 22399** – Guideline for incident preparedness and operational continuity management [32]

---

27   See the following for an overview abstract of the ISO/IEC 27031 standard: http://www.iso.org/iso/catalogue_detail?csnumber=44374

28   See the following for an overview abstract of the PAS 200 Specification: http://shop.bsigroup.com/en/ProductDetail/?pid=000000000030252035

See the following for an overview summary of the Publically Available Specification, PAS 200, which the UK Cabinet Office and the British Standards Institute (BSI) jointly published, after a peer review process.   http://www.regesterlarkin.com/uploads/PAS_200_An_assessment_by_Regester_Larkin_2011.pdf

29   See the following for an overview abstract of the Published Document, PD 25666: http://shop.bsigroup.com/ProductDetail/?pid=000000000030203702

See the following for additional summary information on PD 25666:   http://www.continuityforum.org/content/news/press_release/126935/bsi-guidance-exercising-and-testing-pd256662010-now-available

30   See the following for an overview abstract of the Published Document, PD 25111: http://shop.bsigroup.com/en/ProductDetail/?pid=000000000030229830

31   See the following for an overview abstract of the ISO/IEC 24762 standard: http://www.iso.org/iso/catalogue_detail?csnumber=41532

See the following for a Draft Standards copy of the ISO/IEC 24762 standard as suggested for implementation by the Uganda National Bureau of Standards in 2012.   http://www.unbs.go.ug/resources/DUS%20ISO%20IEC%2024762.pdf

32   See the following for an overview abstract of the ISO/PAS 22399 standard: http://www.iso.org/iso/catalogue_detail?csnumber=50295

See the following for an overview summary of the ISO/PAS 22399 standard from the Ghana Standards Board: http://www.gsa.gov.gh/site/pdf/ISO%20PAS%2022399.pdf?phpMyAdmin=2dc4ecf5c1bt1ce2db13

- *ISO/IEC 27001* – Information security management systems – Requirements [33]
- *NIST Special Publication 800-34 Rev 1* – Contingency Planning Guide for Federal Information Systems [34]

Data Stored in Electronic Form

Backup strategies for data used to restore technology are varied and are driven by the RTO and the RPO needed to support the business requirements. Some organizations tier data based on its importance to the business and frequency of use. The more time-sensitive data is replicated off-site either synchronously or asynchronously to ensure its availability and its currency. Other data is backed up to tape and sent off-site once or a day or more frequently if required.

If the data needed to rebuild the technology environment is stored somewhere else besides the alternate site, then the time it takes to pack and transport that data must be included in the RTO. Factors such as how the data is stored, how far away it is, and how it will be delivered to the recovery facility will determine how much the recovery time could be increased. Delivery of off-site data to the recovery facility could delay the recovery by hours or even days. To reduce the recovery time, the data that will be used to recover any mission critical systems and applications should be stored in the recovery site whenever possible.

It is vital that the data that is stored off-site include not only the application data but also the application source code, hardware and software images for the servers and end user desktops, utility software, license keys, etc. Application data alone will not be sufficient to rebuild an application.

Remote Replication and Off-Site Journaling

Remote replication involves moving data over a network to secondary storage devices in another location. It can be an expensive solution to implement, but it will meet the needs of an application RPO that is immediate or near immediate. It can be done either synchronously or asynchronously.

Synchronous replication is when the data is written to the production environment disk and to the remote disk at the same time. Until both "writes"

---

33   See the following for an overview abstract of the ISO/IEC 27001 standard: http://www. iso.org/iso/catalogue_detail?csnumber=42103

See the following for the YouTube ISO/IEC27001 channel: http://www.youtube.com/channel/ HCaqgODxx3tGs

See the following for the British Standards Institute's (BSI) product guide for ISO/IEC27001: http://www.bsigroup.com/Documents/iso-27001/resources/BSI-ISOIEC27001-Product-Guide-UK-EN.pdf

34   See the following for the NIST Special Publication 800-34 Rev.1 Contingency Planning Guide for Federal Information Systems: http://csrc.nist.gov/publications/ nistpubs/800-34-rev1/sp800-34-rev1_errata-Nov11-2010.pdf

occur, the next process cannot begin. There are distance limitations on performing synchronous remote replication as well as network bandwidth requirements that can be extremely demanding. Synchronous replication has the potential to impact production, but is the best solution when time to recovery and data loss matter. This type of replication is commonly deployed in dual data center environments where applications are load-balanced between the two or more sites but can be used for other strategies when the currency of the data, not the actual time of the recovery is key.

Asynchronous replication occurs when the data is written to the production environment and then is queued to write to the backup environment at scheduled intervals depending on the RPO for the data. This can occur several times a day, several times an hour, or several times a minute, depending again on the need for data currency[35].

Asynchronous data replication's advantage is that it does not impact production performance as it takes place offline from the production environment and provides long-distance, remote data replication while still providing disaster recovery data protection.

Remote replication does not eliminate the need for point-in-time copies of the data. If data in the production environment becomes corrupt, the replicated data will also be corrupt. A point-in-time copy of the data is still required for restoration from this type of event[36].

35   See the following for an academic paper on the data currency problem with regards to how to determine the currency of data within the constraints of a system defined architecture. http://homepages.inf.ed.ac.uk/fgeerts/pdf/currency.pdf

See the following paper for research on a data currency model: http://informatique.umons.ac.be/ssi/jef/time-wijsen.pdf

36   SHARE is a volunteer-run user group for IBM mainframe computers that was founded in 1955 by Los Angeles-area IBM 701 users. It has evolved into a forum for exchanging technical information about programming languages, operating systems, database systems, and user experiences for enterprise users of small, medium, and large-scale IBM computers. The SHARE web site can be found here: http://www.share.org/p/cm/ld/fid=1

In 1992, the SHARE user group in the United States, in combination with IBM, defined a set of Disaster Recovery tier levels. The Seven Tiers of Disaster Recovery solutions offer a simple methodology for how to define the current service level, the current risk, and the target service level and target environments for a business. The 7 tiers are as follows:

> *Tier 0:* No off-site data – Possibly no recovery
> *Tier 1:* Data backup with no hot site
> *Tier 2:* Data backup with a hot site
> *Tier 3:* Electronic vaulting
> *Tier 4:* Point-in-time copies
> *Tier 5:* Transaction integrity
> *Tier 6:* Zero or near-Zero data loss
> *Tier 7:* Highly automated, business integrated solution

The original publication document that defines and discusses the 7 tiers can be found here: http://www.redbooks.ibm.com/redbooks/pdfs/sg246844.pdf

Backup Strategies

Most companies, no matter what strategy they employ for storing data off-site, start by performing full backups of all their data followed by periodic incremental backups. Incremental backups take copies of only the files that are new or have changed since the last full or incremental backup was taken, and then set the archive bit to "0." The other common option is to take a differential backup. Differential backups copy only the files that are new or have changed since the last full backup and do not change the archive bit value.

If an organization wants the backup and recovery strategy to be as simple as possible, then they should only use full backups. They take more time and hard drive space to perform, but they are the most efficient in recovery. If that option is not viable, a differential backup can be restored in just two steps. The full backup of the data is restored first, then the differential backup on top of it. Remember, the differential backs up every piece of data in file that has changed since the last full backup was taken.

An incremental backup takes the most time to restore because the system must lay down the full backup first and then every incremental backup taken since the last full backup. If daily incremental backups are performed, along with **only** monthly full backups, and recovery is attempted on the 26th day of the month, the organization will have to perform the full backup restore first and then 26 incremental backups must be laid on top in the same order that they were taken in. This example illustrates how the backup method chosen could have a significant impact on the recovery timeline.

There are several other backup methods that the security architect should consider when planning for data integrity, confidentiality, and availability within the context of a recovery strategy.

Synthetic Full Backup

A synthetic full backup is a variation of an incremental backup. Like any other incremental backup, the actual backup process involves taking a full backup, followed by a series of incremental backups. But synthetic backups take things one step further.

What makes a synthetic backup different from an incremental backup is that the backup server actually produces full backups. It does this by combining the existing full backup with the data from the incremental backups. The end result is a full backup that is indistinguishable from a full backup that has been created in the traditional way.

The primary advantage to synthetic full backups is greatly reduced restore times. Restoring a synthetic full backup does not require the backup operator to restore multiple tape or disk sets as an incremental backup does. Synthetic full backups provide all of the advantages of a true full backup, but offer the decreased backup times and decreased bandwidth usage of an incremental backup.

Incremental-Forever Backup

Incremental-forever backups are often used by disk-to-disk-to-tape backup systems. The basic idea is that like an incremental backup, the incremental-forever backup begins by taking a full backup of the data set. After that point, only incremental backups are taken.

What makes an incremental-forever backup different from a normal incremental backup is the availability of data. Restoring an incremental backup requires the tape or disk set containing the full backup, and every subsequent backup set in order up to the point in time that you want to restore to. While this is also true for an incremental-forever backup, the backup server typically stores all of the backup sets on either a large disk array or in a tape library. It automates the restoration process so that you do not have to figure out which tape sets need to be restored. In essence, the process of restoring the incremental data becomes completely transparent and mimics the process of restoring a full backup.

Mirror Backup

A mirror backup is a straight copy of the selected folders and files at a given instant in time. That is, the destination becomes a "mirror" of the source. Any mirror operation after the first will only copy new and modified files, making the operation faster. And deleted files will be removed from the set as well. Some key disadvantages to be aware of with Mirror Backups are that they consume more space than other backup types will, they are not able to be password protected to ensure confidentiality of the data they contain, and they are not capable of tracking different versions of the files that they contain.

Disk Imaging

This type of backup is often described as a "bare metal backup" because it backs up physical disks at the volume level. In other words, a true disk image is an exact copy of an entire physical disk or disk partition.

In its simplest form a disk imaging program creates a bit identical copy of a drive which is made by dumping raw data byte by byte, sector by sector from the source disk into an image file. Disk imaging programs have the ability to interpret the data being copied and remove or compress the empty blocks on a disk which leads to much smaller image files. The majority of programs also create compressed image formats that can be mounted and explored making it possible to retrieve individual files. In addition, the creation of successive incremental or differential backups is often supported, which further reduces the demands on storage. Other techniques have been developed that allow file-level operations such as file type filtering, the ability to exclude non-essential files from the image, such as pagefile.sys, and the ability to image a drive or partition while it is currently in use.

Advantages of Image Backup Systems include allowing for rapid full system restores with the operating system across similar or different hardware platforms. Speed and simplicity is unsurpassed when working with large numbers of files. Many modern image formats can be mounted and used like any other drive making accessing backed up files very user friendly.

File Synchronization

File Synchronization is a specialized adaptation of file based backup technologies. The primary design of synchronization programs are to replicate or mirror working files in two or more locations, allowing for both sets of files to be available and used in real time. The main difference between file synchronization and backup solutions is that a backup will copy files in one direction, while synchronization copies files (or changes) in two directions. With backups there is a "source" and a "destination." With synchronization there are two sources. For example, when a group of files are set to be synchronized between two systems, files which are changed on either system will be reflected on the other.

Synchronization that replicates changes in both locations is called two-way synchronization. Synchronization that only replicates the changes from one location to the second is called one-way synchronization. One-way synchronization differs from traditional backups when the propagation of deletions or renames is performed, because backups do not generally delete files, and a renamed file is usually copied again.

One-way synchronization can be used as a way to both backup and synchronize computers. A one-way synchronization may be made to a portable hard drive. The hard drive may then be used as a source to sync with another computer and new files will be transferred from the portable drive to the pc. New files on the second pc may also be backed up to the portable drive and then can be transferred to the first pc. Thus both computers will remain in sync, and the data on the drive will remain as a backup of both systems. Similar setups are often used by online storage services which may be seen as being both an online backup as well as an online synchronization solution.

Some key advantages of file synchronization systems are that files synchronized to online sources can often be easily accessed from any computer or mobile device such as a smart phone or tablet, and some programs combine real-time synchronization with a versioning system that allows for easy collaboration between individuals working on the same file, as well as usually providing for difference comparisons and merging capabilities.

Managed Backup Services

A remote, online, or managed backup service, commonly referred to as a "cloud backup" solution, is a service that provides users with a system for the backup and storage of computer files. Online backup providers are companies that provide this type of service to end users (or clients). Such backup services are considered a form of cloud computing. Online backup systems are built around a client software program that runs on a schedule, typically once a day, and usually at night while computers are not in use. This program collects, compresses, encrypts, and transfers the data to the remote backup service provider's servers or off-site hardware.

These solutions are service-based, meaning that in order to provide for the assurance, guarantee, or validation that what was backed up is recoverable whenever it is required, data stored in the service provider's cloud must undergo regular integrity validation to ensure its recoverability. Cloud services need to provide for granularity when it comes to Recovery Time Objectives (RTO's), as one size does not fit all either for the customers or the applications within a customer's environment. The customer should never have to manage the back end storage repositories in order to back up and recover data, this should be the responsibility of the service provider. Cloud backup needs to be an active process where data is collected from systems that store the original copy. This means that cloud backup will not require data to be copied into a specific appliance from where data is collected before being transmitted to and stored in the service provider's data center(s).

Cloud backup solutions offer ubiquitous access, meaning that they utilize standard networking protocols, primarily, but not exclusively IP based, to transfer data between the customer and the service provider over secured connections. Vaults or repositories need to be always available to restore data to any location connected to the service provider's cloud via private or public networks, as needed during a Disaster Recovery event or test.

Scalability and elasticity enable flexible allocation of storage capacity to customers without limit. Storage is allocated on demand and also de-allocated when customers delete backup sets as they age. The service provider can then release and reallocate that same capacity to a different customer in an automated fashion.

Metering by use allows the security architect to align the value of data with the cost of protecting it. It is procured on a per-gigabyte per month basis. Prices tend to vary based on the age of data, type of data (email, databases, files etc.), volume, number of backup copies and RTOs.

Data mobility/portability prevents service provider lock-in and allows customers to move their data from one service provider to another, or entirely back into a dedicated Private Cloud or a Hybrid Cloud, as needed. Security in the cloud is a critical factor for the security architect to consider. One customer can never have access to another's data. Additionally, even service providers must not be able to access their customer's data without the customer's permission. The security architect needs to ensure that security issues are addressed up front with the vendor in order to make sure that all risks and threats are identified and documented to the fullest extent possible.

Some advantages of managed backup services over traditional backup methods are that they are storing the backups of system data in a different location from the original data. Traditional backup requires manually taking the backup media offsite. Remote backup does not require user intervention. The user does not have to change tapes, label CDs or perform other manual steps to ensure the success of the backup. Remote backup services can be set up to work continuously, backing up files as they are changed.

Some disadvantages of managed backup services over traditional backup methods are that depending on the available network bandwidth, the restoration of data can be slow. It is possible that a remote backup service provider could go out of business or be purchased, which may affect the accessibility of one's data or the cost to continue using the service. While the data is encrypted during transit through the cloud, it is impossible for the customer to know exactly where their data is transiting, and what country, or countries, it may pass through between the customer's network and the service provider's end point for data storage. As a result, the confidentiality and integrity of the customer's data could be compromised without their knowledge. Further, privacy laws and data regulatory requirements differ by country, and depending on those laws, the customers data could potentially be exposed to regulatory compliance requirements that the customer is not prepared to comply with for a variety of reasons. The security architect must take these issues into account as they examine the various managed backup services available as part of their BCP/DRP architecture.

The RTO for a business process or for an application will determine the recovery strategy for the process or application. The more time that can elapse before the recovery needs to occur, the more recovery options are available. The more time sensitive an application or function is, the fewer options the security architect will have in selecting a recovery strategy. Also, the plan will be more detailed and require more testing and training to successfully implement.

Selecting a Recovery Strategy for Technology

Selecting a recovery strategy depends on how much downtime is acceptable before the technology recovery must be complete. The security architect should examine recovery strategies available to them, and based on weighing the recovery requirements, select the best strategy for the technology environment. The most common strategies are as follows:

- **Dual Data Center** - This strategy is employed for applications that cannot accept any downtime without unacceptably impacting the business. The applications are split between two geographically dispersed data centers and either load-balanced between the two centers or hot-swapped between them. The surviving data center must have enough capacity to carry the full production load in either case.

- **Internal Hot Site** - An internal hot site is standby ready with all the technology and equipment necessary to run the applications to be recovered there. The security architect will be able to effectively restart any application in hot site recovery without having to perform a bare metal recovery of servers. Because this is an internal solution, often the business will run non-time-sensitive processes there, such as development or test environments that can be pushed aside for recovery of production when needed. When employing this strategy, it is important that the two environments be kept as close to identical as possible to avoid problems with OS levels, hardware differences, capacity differences, etc., that could prevent or delay recovery.

- **External Hot Site** - This design has equipment on the floor waiting for recovery, but the environment must be rebuilt for the recovery. These are services contracted through a recovery service provider. Again, it is important that the two environments be kept as close to identical as possible to avoid problems with OS levels, hardware differences, capacity differences, etc., that could prevent or delay recovery. Hot site vendors tend to have the most commonly used hardware and software products to attract the largest number of customers to utilize their sites. Unique equipment or software would generally need to be provided by the organization either at the time of disaster or stored there prior to the disaster.

- **Warm Site** - A warm site is a leased or rented facility that is usually partially configured with some equipment, but not the actual computers. It will generally have all the cooling, cabling, and networks in place to accommodate the recovery, but the actual servers, mainframe, and other equipment are delivered to the site at the time of the disaster recovery event.

- **Cold Site** - A cold site is a shell or empty data center space with no technology on the floor. All technology must be purchased or acquired at the time of disaster recovery event.

- **Reciprocal Agreement** - In this strategy, the organization signs an agreement with a similar business operation to provide backup capabilities to each other in the event either experiences a disaster.
- **Mobile Unit** - A mobile unit is typically a contract with a vendor to provide a mobile trailer at the time of disaster, which contains the specified equipment necessary to support recovery.
- **Outsourcing / Cloud** - The technology environment is outsourced to a vendor who provides the disaster recovery plan for the applications that are deemed critical to the business.

Each of these recovery strategies has advantages and disadvantages.

Creating a picture of what the recovery strategy looks like for the business is important for the security architect, because it allows the business to have an understanding of what will happen, and what to expect when a disaster event occurs. The documentation of the disaster recovery strategy will have many elements, such as call trees, password and user accounts lists, system baselines, and procedure documents. In addition, there are a few things that are often overlooked, or just not thought about prior to the disaster event that the security architect should plan for.

The first item is to ensure that user awareness of the plan is up to date, especially after any changes have been adopted due to testing or compliance activities. A great way for the security architect to ensure that awareness among all users is adequate is to publish quarterly high level summaries of the plan by user role. These high level summaries can take a variety of forms from short overview documents that list the main activities and responsibilities for the user group during a disaster, to a basic work flow or picture of what the user will need to do if a disaster event occurs. *Figure 5.3* shows what a sample picture might look like for standard information workers in most businesses today with regards to network access to data in the event of a disaster event that rendered their primary office space unavailable for a period of time.

The second item is to ensure that the IP networking stack at an alternate site is ready to accept incoming traffic on demand. It needs to be sized appropriately so there are no bottlenecks when real traffic starts flowing through it. The security architect needs to work with the business's service providers to ensure that all of the public-facing websites, virtual private network gateways, Web load balancers, traffic distribution engines, firewalls, intranet access points and other critical access points are available via or at the alternate location on demand.

The third item is to avoid a single point of failure within the disaster recovery plan. Specifically, the security architect needs to ensure that the plan does not rest solely with one person for execution, or that it relies on knowledge that is

Dual Data Center

Advantages	Disadvantages
Little or no downtime	Most expensive option
Ease of maintenance	Requires redundant hardware, networks, staffing
No recovery required	Distance limitations

Internal or External Hot Site

Advantages	Disadvantages
Allows recovery to be tested	Expensive; * Terms of contract could limit usage (external site only)
Highly available	Hardware and software compatibility issues in external sites
Site can be operational within hours	Communication costs to duplicate data can be high

Warm and Cold Site

Advantages	Disadvantages
Less expensive	Not immediately available; Once up and running, delays could occur due to equipment, software, or staffing issues or mismatches
Available for longer recoveries	Not testable

Reciprocal Agreement

Advantages	Disadvantages
No cost	Technology upgrades, obsolescence, or business growth
Viable for small business operations with limited technology	Security and access by partner users; typically located in same geography as disaster, so could be of little to no practical use in the event of a large scale disaster

Mobile Unit

Advantages	Disadvantages
Self-contained unit with technology and network	Difficult and expensive to test unless you own it
Transportable to any site	Travel time to bring unit where it is needed; Access to site may be hampered or unavailable due to disaster

Outsourcing / Cloud

Advantages	Disadvantages
Transfer the ownership of recovery to vendor	Cost
May provide same recovery as dual data center but at less cost	No ownership or control over recovery program except contractually
No recovery plan to maintain or test	Security

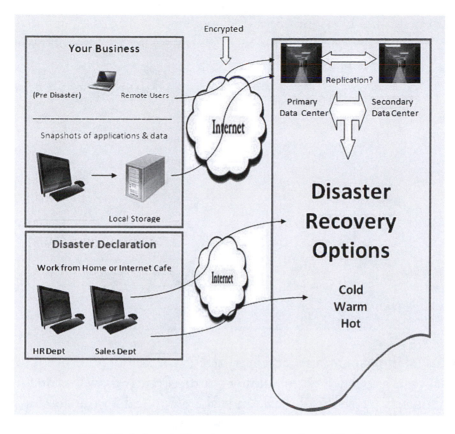

Figure 5.3 - **High level disaster recovery view of information worker activity during a disaster event**

not documented centrally and distributed to multiple members of the DR team. If the plan relies on a single person, or piece of equipment, or knowledge item, and there is no redundancy built into the plan for that element, then the plan is very likely to fail under stress.

The fourth item is to keep the plan as simple as possible. This can be achieved primarily through the use of "off the shelf" or "out of the box" solutions, as opposed to complex and highly customized solutions. The learning curve to become proficient with an out of the box solution is very small when compared to learning to master a highly customized solution. Under stress, simple systems behave better, are less prone to failures, and are easier to troubleshoot.

Cost–Benefit Analysis

Each of the foregoing strategies can be considered for the business and technology recovery. Those that are recommended need to have a Cost–Benefit Analysis (CBA) performed to determine if the costs of the strategy being recommended fits within the amount of risk or business loss the business is trying to avoid. The company would not spend $1,000,000 a year on a recovery strategy to protect

459

$100,000 of profit. Every business does not need a dual data center recovery strategy. The strategy selected must fit the business need. The following image from NIST helps visualize this tradeoff:[37]

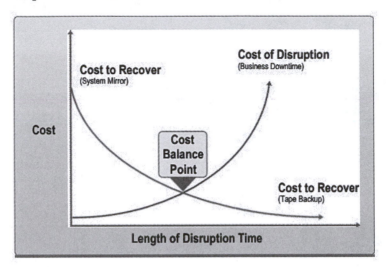

The cost of implementing the recovery strategy recommended needs to include the initial costs associated with building out the strategy as well as ongoing costs to maintain the recovery solution, and where applicable, the cost of periodic testing of the solution to ensure it remains viable.

Implementing Recovery Strategies

Once the strategy has been agreed to and funded, the next step is to implement the various strategies approved. This may involve negotiating with vendors to provide recovery services for business or technology, doing site surveys of existing sites to determine excess capacity, wiring conference rooms or cafeterias to support business functions, buying recovery technology, installing remote replication software, installing networks for voice and data recovery, assigning alternate site seats to the various business areas, and the like.

The implementation phase is a project unto itself, perhaps multiple projects, depending on the complexity of the environment and the recovery strategies selected.

Documenting the Plan

Once recovery strategies have been developed and implemented for each area, the next step is to document the plan itself. The plan includes plan activation procedures, the recovery strategies to be used, how recovery efforts will be

---

37   See the following for the NIST Special Publication 800-34 Rev.1 Contingency Planning Guide for Federal Information Systems: http://csrc.nist.gov/publications/nistpubs/800-34-rev1/sp800-34-rev1_errata-Nov11-2010.pdf (page 32).

managed, how human resource issues will be handled, how recovery costs will be documented and paid for, how recovery communications to internal and external stakeholders will be handled, and detailed action plans for each team and each team member. The plan then needs to be distributed to everyone who has a role.

The documentation for recovery of the technology environment needs to be detailed enough that a person with a similar skill set who has never executed the procedures before could use them to perform the recovery. Documentation tends to be a task that no one really likes to do; however, there is no guarantee that the people who perform this function in the production environment or the person who restored the infrastructure and application at the last test is going to be available at the time of the disaster. In addition, disasters tend to be chaotic times where many things are happening at once. Without the proper documentation, a practiced recovery strategy can fall apart and add to the chaos. Restoring an application can be challenging and restoring an entire data center just destroyed by a tornado can be overwhelming, if not impossible, without good documentation.

The documentation needs to be stored at the recovery facility, and every time the recovery is tested, the documentation should be used by the recovery participants and updated as needed. Once the level of confidence in the documentation is high, the security architect should have someone who has never performed the procedure attempt it with an expert looking over their shoulder. It may slightly delay the recovery time at that particular test, but once complete, confidence in the documentation will be strong.

The Human Factor

One common factor left out of many plans is human resource issues. Disasters are human events, and it is important that the plan document the responsibility of the firm to the employees participating in the recovery. Companies need to recognize that to respond to the company's needs in a disaster situation, it must also recognize the hardships placed on the families of its response teams. To be able to give the best to the company at the time when it is needed most, employees need to have a level of comfort that their family members are safe and the employee's absence during the recovery effort will not place undue hardship on them.

Logistics

The plan needs to document the logistics of the recovery, not just the technical documentation for recovery of the hardware and applications. The plan needs to contain answers to the following questions:

1. How the disaster will be declared and who has the authority to declare it?

2. How recovery team members will be contacted and who will contact them?

3. How recovery team members are to travel to the alternate site, and who will make any required reservations and pay for those costs?

4. Where documentation is stored and how to get it?

5. How off-site backups will be retrieved, who will do it, and how long it will take?

6. What are the address, phone number, and directions to the alternate site?

7. How necessary supplies will be provided and how more can be requested?

8. What is the command center location and phone number?

9. How problems will be reported and managed?

Plan Maintenance Strategies

As with any documentation, version control is important, particularly with detailed technical procedures. The use of version control numbers on the plan helps to ensure that everyone is using the current version of the plan documentation. The plan needs to be published to everyone who has a role and also needs to be stored in a secure off-site location that not only survives the disaster but is accessible immediately following it.

It is important that the plan be kept up to date as the business and technology environments of your company continue to change and adapt. Tying plan updates to your change management process is critical to keeping pace with significant changes in technology. The BCP must be reviewed and updated at least annually, and more often if significant business changes occur. Plan updates also frequently occur following tests of the plan, if issues or action items from the test require plan documentation changes.

Once the plan has been completed and the recovery strategies are fully implemented, it is important to test all parts of the plan to validate that it would work in a real event. The purpose of testing is to validate the readiness to recover from a real event. If we knew that it all worked, we would not need to test it in the first place. Test to find out what does not work, so that it can be fixed before it happens for real. No test is a failure as long as it provides opportunities to better the recovery process, so that if it happened for real, the organization is more likely to recover.

The first rule of conducting tests of the recovery plans is that no matter what type of test you are conducting, it is important to protect the production environment.

There are many different types of exercises that the security architect can conduct. Some will take minutes, and others hours or days. The amount of exercise planning needed is entirely dependent on the type of exercise, length of the exercise, and the scope of the exercise planned to be conducted. The most common types of exercises for technology recovery are walkthrough exercises, simulated or actual exercises, and compact exercises.

In a walkthrough or tabletop exercise, the team that would need to execute the plan holds a meeting to review the plan. When the organization has a new plan, the best type of tabletop exercise to do is a walkthrough of the actual plan document with everyone who has a role in the plan. Even the planning team is unlikely to read the entire document, and walking through the plan helps to ensure that everyone knows the whole story and everyone's role. Walking through the plan with the team will help identify gaps in the plan so that they can be addressed.

Once the security architect has conducted that type of walkthrough, the scenario-based tabletop exercises can begin. In these exercises, the security architect will gather the team in a meeting and pretend that something has happened, and the team members are supposed to respond as if it is a real event. The security architect could pretend that there is a power outage, and, based on what is backed up by alternate power sources such as generators and what is not, the team would discuss how the technology or business would be impacted and how they would exercise the portions of the plan to address that scenario.

Tabletop exercises are used to validate the plan within an actual scenario without having to actually execute the recovery procedures. The security architect will "talk through" with the team what they would do; they will not actually do it. These types of exercises are especially helpful in working through the decision processes that will have to be tackled by the leadership team when faced with an event and by other teams to talk through recovery options based on the scenario being presented for the exercise.

A simulated or actual exercise tests the actual recovery in the alternate site. The difference between a simulated and an actual exercise is that a simulated exercise operates completely independently of the production environment, whereas in an actual exercise the production environment is "moved" to the alternate site as is done with a dual data center strategy.

The purpose of this type of exercise is to validate alternate site readiness. The security architect should run this exercise as closely as possible to how it would happen if it were happening for real. Clearly, because exercises are planned events, the security architect will have an opportunity to reduce the actual timeline by pre-staging certain things that they could not do if this were an unplanned event, such as pulling backup tapes from off-site storage and having it delivered to the alternate site for use on the day of the exercise. What the security architect should not do as part of the planning is plan for success. Remember, the reason to test is to find out what does not work so that it can be fixed before it happens for real.

The final exercise is a compact exercise. This is where the security architect will begin with a call to the recovery team, assuming a scenario, and have them respond as if this were a real event and continue right through an actual exercise in the alternate site. These are sometimes done as surprise exercises, with very few people knowing in advance when they are going to happen.

After every exercise the security architect conducts, the exercise results need to be published and action items developed to address the issues uncovered by the exercise. Action items should be tracked until they have been resolved and, where appropriate, the plan updated. It is very unfortunate when an organization faces the same issue in subsequent tests simply because someone did not update the plan.

Bringing It All Together – A Sample "Walk Through" of a DR Plan

It can be very daunting to create a Disaster Recovery Plan for a business, no matter how many times you may have had to do it already, and regardless of the size of the business in question. Most security architects will only have to create some elements of a DR plan during their careers, and perhaps update an existing plan that was created by a predecessor, or colleague. It is rare that the security architect will have to take on the entire task of creating a plan from scratch by themselves, and even rarer if they have to do it more than once or twice during their careers. As a result, most security architects do not have that much experience creating DR plans, although they will have a lot of experience managing the business through them. The following outline offers a detailed guide illustrating the required steps that the security architect will need to ensure are carried out during each phase of the DR planning process to guarantee that the business has a complete and accurate DR plan to operate with should a disaster occur.

Step by Step Guide for Disaster Recovery Planning for Security Architects

I. Information Gathering

Step One - Organize the Project:

- Identify and convene planning team and sub-teams as appropriate.
- At the business and/or business unit level set:
  - ¤ Scope - the area covered by the disaster recovery plan, and objectives - what is being worked toward and the course of action that the business intends to follow.
  - ¤ Assumptions - what is being taken for granted or accepted as true without proof.
- Set project timetable.
- Draft project plan, including assignment of task responsibilities.
- Obtain senior management approval of scope, assumptions and project plan.

Forms that may be useful in organizing Step One:

1. A Project Plan template.

Step Two – Conduct Business Impact Analysis (BIA)

This step would normally be performed by the security architect in conjunction with business unit managers. In order to complete the business impact analysis, perform the following steps:

- Identify functions, processes and systems.
- Interview information systems support personnel.
- Interview business unit personnel.
- Analyze results to determine critical systems, applications and business processes.
- Prepare impact analysis of interruption on critical systems.

Forms that may be useful in organizing Step Two:

1. A Business Impact Analysis template.
2. A Critical System Ranking form.

Step Three – Conduct Risk Assessment:

The planning team will want to consult with technical and security personnel as appropriate to complete this step. The risk assessment will assist in determining the probability of a critical system becoming severely disrupted and documenting the acceptability of these risks to the business.

For each critical system, application and process as identified in Step 2 using the Critical System Ranking form:

- Review physical security.
- Review backup systems.
- Review data security.
- Review policies on personnel termination and transfer.
- Identify systems supporting mission critical functions.
- Identify vulnerabilities.
- Assess probability of system failure or disruption.
- Prepare risk and security analysis.

Forms that may be useful in organizing Step Three:

1. Security Documentation template.
2. Vulnerability Assessment template.

Step Four - Develop Strategic Outline for Recovery:

Assemble groups as Appropriate for:

- Hardware and operating systems.
- Communications.
- Applications.
- Facilities.
  - * Any / all other critical functions and business processes as identified in the Business Impact Analysis.

For each system/process above quantify the following processing requirements:

- Light, normal and heavy processing days.
- Transaction volumes.
- Dollar volume (if any)
- Estimated processing time.
- Allowable delay (days, hours, minutes, etc.)

Detail all the steps in the workflow for each critical business function (e.g., for payroll processing each step that must be complete and the order in which to complete them.):

- Identify systems and applications.
- Component name and technical id (if any)
- Type (online, batch process, script)
- Frequency.
- Run time.
- Allowable delay (days, hours, minutes, etc.)
- Identify vital records (e.g., procedures, Intellectual Property, etc.)

- Name and description.
- Type (e.g., backup, original, master, history, etc.)
- Where they are stored.
- Source of item or record.

Can the record be easily replaced from another source (e.g., reference materials):

- Backup type(s)
- Backup generation frequency.
- Number of backup generations available onsite.
- Number of backup generations available off-site.
- Location of backups.
- Media type.
- Retention period.
- Rotation cycle.

Who is Authorized to Retrieve the Backups?

Identify what would be the minimum requirements/replacement needs to perform the critical function if a severe disruption occurred.

- Type (e.g. server hardware, software, etc.)
- Item name and description.
- Quantity required.
- Location of inventory, alternative, or offsite storage.
- Vendor/supplier.

1. Identify if alternate methods of processing either exist or could be developed, quantifying where possible, impact on processing (Include manual processes.)
2. Identify person(s) who supports the system or application.
3. Identify primary person to contact if system or application cannot function as normal.
4. Identify secondary person to contact if system or application cannot function as normal.
5. Identify all vendors associated with the system or application.
6. Document business unit strategy during recovery (conceptually how will the business unit function?)
7. Quantify resources required for recovery, by time frame (e.g., 1 pc per day, 3 people per hour, etc.)

Develop and document recovery strategy, including:

- Priorities for recovering system/function components.
- Recovery schedule.

Forms that may be useful in organizing Step Four:

1. A Group Assignments spreadsheet.
2. A Critical System Processing Requirements for Recovery spreadsheet.

Step Five – Review Onsite and Offsite Backup and Recovery Procedures

- Review current records (System Instructions, documented processes, etc.) requiring protection.
- Review current offsite storage facility or arrange for one.
- Review backup and offsite storage policy or create one.

Step Six – Select Alternate Facility:

Alternate Site: A location, other than the normal facility, used to process data and/or conduct critical business functions in the event of a disaster.

Determine Resource Requirements:

- Assess platform uniqueness of business systems (e.g., Apple, Oracle database, AIX, etc.)
- Identify alternative facilities.
- Review cost/benefit.
- Evaluate and make recommendation.
- Seek approval.
- Make selection.

II. Plan Development and Testing

Step Seven – Develop Recovery Plan:

The steps for developing the Recovery Plan are listed below in outline form to demonstrate how a security architect may choose to organize their Disaster Recovery Plan.

Objective:

The objective may have been documented in the Information Gathering Step 1 Plan Organization.

Plan Assumptions:

- All assumptions that impact the plan will need to be listed.

Criteria for Invoking the Plan:

- All criteria that must be met or satisfied in order to all for the invocation of the plan need to be listed.

Document emergency response procedures to occur during and after an emergency (i.e. ensure evacuation of all individuals, call the fire department, after the emergency check the building before allowing individuals to return)

- Document procedures for assessment and declaring a state of emergency.
- Document notification procedures for alerting managers.
- Document notification procedures for alerting vendors.
- Document notification procedures for alerting staff and notifying of alternate work procedures or locations.

Roles Responsibilities and Authority:

- Identify personnel.
- Recovery team description and charge.
- Recovery team staffing.

Transportation schedules for media and teams

Procedures for operating in contingency mode:

- Process descriptions.
- Minimum processing requirements.
- Determine categories for vital records.
- Identify location of vital records.
- Identify forms requirements.
- Document critical forms.
- Establish equipment descriptions.
- Document equipment - in the recovery site.
- Document equipment - in the business.

Software Descriptions:

- Software used in recovery
- Software used in production

Produce logical drawings of communication and data networks in the business.

Produce logical drawings of communication and data networks during recovery.

Vendor List:

- Review vendor restrictions
- Miscellaneous inventory
- Communication needs - production
- Communication needs - in the recovery site
- Resource plan for operating in contingency mode
- Criteria for returning to normal operating mode
- Procedures for returning to normal operating mode
- Procedures for recovering lost or damaged data

5

Technology Related BCP and DRP

Testing and Training:
- Document Testing Dates.
- Complete disaster/disruption scenarios.
- Develop action plans for each scenario.
- Sample Testing Diagram.

Plan Maintenance:
- Document Maintenance Review Schedule (yearly, quarterly, etc.)
- Maintenance Review action plans.
- Maintenance Review recovery teams.
- Maintenance Review team activities.
- Maintenance Review/revise tasks.
- Maintenance Review/revise documentation.

Appendices for Inclusion:
- Inventory and report forms.
- Maintenance forms.
- Hardware lists and serial numbers.
- Software lists and license numbers.
- Contact list for vendors.
- Contact list for staff with home and work numbers.
- Contact list for other interfacing departments or business units.
- Network schematic diagrams.
- Equipment room floor grid diagrams.
- Contract and maintenance agreements.
- Special operating instructions for sensitive equipment.
- Cellular telephone inventory and agreements.

Step Eight - Test the Plan:
- Develop test strategy.
- Develop test plans.
- Conduct tests.
- Modify the plan as necessary.

III. Ongoing Maintenance

Step Nine - Maintain the Plan:
The security architect will be responsible for overseeing this.

- Review changes in the environment, technology, and procedures.
- Develop maintenance triggers and procedures.
- Submit changes for systems development procedures.
- Modify change management procedures.
- Produce plan updates and distribute.

Step Ten – Perform Periodic Audit:
Establish periodic review and update procedures

Summary

In summary, the security architect should have an understanding of the business continuity and disaster recovery domain to assist the organization in being prepared to recover in the event of a disaster.

The way we recover will continue to evolve. Technology recovery is moving from traditional approaches centered on a recovery strategy to a continuous operation strategy where the business never really has to "recover", but rather, simply continues to operate as if nothing, or almost nothing happened due to the fact that technology is in place that simply picks up from where the primary failed, allowing the alternate recovery site, or system, or data elements to be available in near real, or real time, depending on the needs and strategy of the business.

Cloud computing continues to change the face of the technology environment and as a result, the recovery environment.

The goal - to continue the business or mission of the organization - remains the same.

5

Technology Related BCP and DRP

References

Eric Waxvik, Risk, response, and recovery, in *Official (ISC)2 Guide to the SSCP CBK*, New York: Auerbach Publications, 2007, p. 212.

 **Review Questions**

1. Which phrase **BEST** defines a business continuity/disaster recovery plan?
    A. A set of plans for preventing a disaster.
    B. An approved set of preparations and sufficient procedures for responding to a disaster.
    C. A set of preparations and procedures for responding to a disaster without management approval.
    D. The adequate preparations and procedures for the continuation of all business functions.

2. Which of the following statements **BEST** describes the extent to which an organization should address business continuity or disaster recovery planning?
    A. Continuity planning is a significant corporate issue and should include all parts or functions of the company.
    B. Continuity planning is a significant technology issue, and the recovery of technology should be its primary focus.
    C. Continuity planning is required only where there is complexity in voice and data communications.
    D. Continuity planning is a significant management issue and should include the primary functions specified by management.

3. Risk analysis is performed to identify
    A. the impacts of a threat to the business operations.
    B. the exposures to loss of the organization.
    C. the impacts of a risk on the company.
    D. the way to eliminate threats.

4. During the risk analysis phase of the planning, which of the following actions could manage threats or mitigate the effects of an event?
    A. Modifying the exercise scenario.
    B. Developing recovery procedures.
    C. Increasing reliance on key individuals.
    D. Implementing procedural controls.

5. The reason to implement additional controls or safeguards is to
    A. deter or remove the risk.
    B. remove the risk and eliminate the threat.

C. reduce the impact of the threat.

D. identify the risk and the threat.

6. Which of the following statements **BEST** describe business impact analysis?

A. Risk analysis and business impact analysis are two different terms describing the same project effort.

B. A business impact analysis calculates the probability of disruptions to the organization.

C. A business impact analysis is critical to development of a business continuity plan.

D. A business impact analysis establishes the effect of disruptions on the organization.

7. The term *disaster recovery* commonly refers to:

A. The recovery of the business operations.

B. The recovery of the technology environment.

C. The recovery of the manufacturing environment.

D. The recovery of the business and technology environments.

8. Which of the following terms **BEST** describe the effort to determine the consequences of disruptions that could result from a disaster?

A. Business impact analysis

B. Risk analysis

C. Risk assessment

D. Project problem definition

9. The **BEST** advantage of using a cold site as a recovery option is that it

A. is a less expensive recovery option.

B. can be configured and operationalized for any business function.

C. is preconfigured for communications and can be customized for business functions.

D. is the most available option for testing server recovery and communications restorations.

10. The term RTO means:

A. Recovery time for operations

B. Return to order

C. Resumption time order

D. Recovery time objective

11. If a company wants the fastest time to restore from tape backup, it should perform their backup using the following method:

    A. Full backup

    B. Incremental backup

    C. Partial backup

    D. Differential backup

12. One of the advantages of a hot site recovery solution is

    A. Lowered expense

    B. High availability

    C. No downtime

    D. No maintenance required

13. Which of the following methods is not acceptable for exercising the business continuity plan?

    A. Tabletop exercise

    B. Call exercise

    C. Simulated exercise

    D. Halting a production application or function

14. Which of the following is the primary desired result of any well-planned business continuity exercise?

    A. Identification of plan strengths and weaknesses.

    B. Satisfaction of management requirements.

    C. Compliance with auditor's requirements.

    D. Maintenance of shareholder confidence.

15. A business continuity plan should be updated and maintained

    A. immediately following an exercise.

    B. following a major change in personnel.

    C. after installing new software.

    D. on an ongoing basis.

16. The primary reason to build a business continuity and disaster recovery plan is

    A. to continue the business.

    B. to restore the data center.

    C. to meet regulatory environments.

    D. because the customers expect it.

17. A company would chose to use synchronous remote replication for its data recovery strategy if

    A. it wanted to replace point-in-time backups.

    B. it wanted to minimize the amount of time taken to recover.

    C. time to recovery and data loss are important to the business.

    D. distance limitations existed.

18. One of the reasons asynchronous replication differs from synchronous replication is

    A. because it can impact production.

    B. because it can be done over greater distances.

    C. because it involves less loss of data.

    D. because it improves recovery time.

19. The purpose of doing a cost–benefit analysis on the different recovery strategies is

    A. to make certain the cost of protection does not exceed the cost of the risk it is protecting.

    B. to determine the cost of implementing the recovery strategy.

    C. to determine that the strategy will be effective.

    D. to analyze the cost of the different strategies.

5

Technology Related BCP and DRP

Domain 6

Physical Security Considerations

THE KEY TO A SUCCESSFUL PHYSICAL PROTECTION SYSTEM is the integration of people, process, and technology. The Physical Security domain recognizes the importance of physical security and personnel controls in a complete information system security model. The security architect is required to demonstrate understanding of the risks and tools used in providing physical security. This includes secure management, administration and deployment of physical access controls, and whether to prevent, detect, or react to suspicious activity.

TOPICS

- **Assess Requirements**
  - Policies and standards
    - Export controls
    - Escort policy
    - Liaise with law enforcement and external media
  - Integrate physical security with identity management
    - Wiring closet access
    - Badge and enterprise identity management
  - Map physical security needs against business drivers
    - Outsourcing
    - Relocations
    - Mergers and acquisitions
    - Divestitures
    - Plant closings
- **Integrate Physical Secufity Products and Systems**
  - Review common techniques, technologies and architectural principles
  - Perimeter protection and internal zoning
    -
- **Evaluate Solutions**
  - Define test scenarios
  - Evaluate test deficiencies

OBJECTIVES

Key areas of knowledge within the Physical Secuirty Considerations domain include:

- Identification and protection of restricted work areas, including traffic control, access control, and monitoring.
- Selecting the locations of and designing secure facilities.
- Addressing facility infrastructure risk and requirements, including identity management and facility protections.
- Remediation of risks associated with portable data processing and storage devices.

6

Physical Security Considerations

Physical Security Policies and Standards

There are many standards, policies, and guidelines that the security architect needs to be aware of as the totality of the security architecture is examined. There are a variety of RFC's such as 2904, AAA Authorization Framework, the draft standards for SAML2.0 and XACML 3.0, as well as ISO 27005 among many others; all of which address one or more aspects of security and secure design[1]. What is not as clear and readily apparent in all of these standards and frameworks is what structures need to look like at the next layer down in the security architecture. Specifically, as the security architect seeks to design secure systems to address the needs of the organization, what do the logical and physical design elements of the architecture look like moving from the 50,000 foot view to the 25,000 foot view and ultimately to a ground level view of the system?

The need to create defined structure that is clear and unambiguous is a key goal for the security architect, as the organization will only be able to achieve the level of security that is readily apparent and clearly defined. As a result, the security architect needs to be able to draw ever more detailed pictures for the organization to help define the who, what, when, where, why, and how of security to help guide the organization to achieve as secure a state as is required. The use of policies and standards help the security architect to provide answers to the questions that the organization has in relation to security, and therefore to create the clarity required enabling a well-defined security solution to be implemented.

The security architect will need to address a broad set of issues through the application of standards and policies to the organization. These can range from physical security issues such as facility design, location, and access control, to industry specific issues such as export control and regulatory compliance based on industry verticals. Export controls are one area where the security architect will need to either have industry specific knowledge, or seek out expertise in the areas required in order to ensure compliance activities are being carried out correctly and that the security controls required to be in place are specifically designed to address whatever levels of compliance are required based on the regime(s) that are applicable.

---

1   See the following for information:

  A. RFC 2904:http://tools.ietf.org/html/rfc2904

  B. The Version 2 Standard Draft for SAML: https://www.oasis-open.org/committees/download. php/27819/sstc-saml-tech-overview-2.0-cd-02.pdf

  C. The Version 3 Standard Draft for XACML: http://docs.oasis-open.org/xacml/3.0/xacml-3.0-core-spec-cs-01-en.pdf

  D. ISO 27000 series:http://www.iso27001security.com/

In the United States of America, Export Control regulations are federal laws that prohibit the unlicensed export of certain commodities or information for reasons of national security or protections of trade. Export controls usually arise for one or more of the following reasons:

■ The nature of the export has actual or potential military applications or economic protection issues.

■ Government concerns about the destination country, organization, or individual.

■ Government concerns about the declared or suspected end use or the end user of the export.

An export is considered to be any oral, written, electronic or visual disclosure, shipment, transfer or transmission of commodities, technology, information, technical data, assistance or software codes to anyone outside the U.S. including:

■ a U.S. citizen

■ a non-U.S. individual wherever they are (deemed export)

■ a foreign embassy or affiliate

U.S. exports are controlled for a variety of reasons, such as:

■ National Security

■ Proliferation of chemical and biological weapons

■ Nuclear Nonproliferation

■ Missile Technology

■ Anti-Terrorism (Cuba, Iran, North Korea, Libya, Sudan and Syria)

■ Crime Control

■ High Performance Computer

■ Regional Stability

■ Short Supply

■ U.N. Sanctions

Methods of Disclosure can include:

■ Fax

■ Telephone discussions

■ E-mail communications

■ Computer data disclosure

■ Face-to-face discussions

■ Training sessions

■ Tours which involve visual inspections

From the perspective of the United States, A "Foreign National" is any person who is NOT a:

- U.S. Citizen or National
- U.S. Lawful Permanent Resident
- Person Granted Asylum
- Person Granted Refugee Status
- Temporary Resident

The "Foreign National" designation includes:

- Persons in the U.S. in non-immigrant status (for example, H-1B, H-3, L-1, J-1, F-1 Practical Training, L-1)
- Persons unlawfully in the U.S.

Most exports do not require government licenses. However, licenses are required for exports that the U.S. government considers "license controlled" under:

The United States Department of Commerce's Export Administration Regulations (EAR) which covers [15 CFR 730-774]: [2]

- Dual use items
- Items designed for commercial purpose but which could have military applications (computers, civilian aircraft, pathogens)
- Both the goods and the technology
- Deemed Exports

The Commerce Control List (Short Version)[3]

- Nuclear Materials, Facilities & Equipment (and Miscellaneous Items)
- Materials, Chemicals, Microorganisms, and Toxins
- Materials Processing
- Electronics Design, Development and Production
- Computers
- Telecommunications and Information Security
- Sensors and Lasers
- Navigation and Avionics
- Marine
- Propulsion Systems, Space Vehicles and Related Equipment

---

2   See the following for complete information on The Department of Commerce's Export Administration Regulations (EAR) which covers [15 CFR 730-774]:http://www.bis.doc.gov/policiesandregulations/ear/index.htm

3   See the following for the full version of the Electronic Code of Federal Regulations, Title 15: Commerce and Foreign Trade, Part 774-The Commerce Control List: http://bit.ly/11OEjRW

See the following for the Supplement No.1 to Part 774-The Commerce Control List (Full Version) from which the Short Version is derived: http://bit.ly/12bMIxB

The Department of State's International Traffic In Arms Regulations (ITAR) (also known as the U.S. Munitions List) covers defense-related items and services [22 CFR 120-130]: [4]

- Covers military items or defense articles
- Regulates goods and technology designed to kill or defend against death in a military setting
- Includes space related technology because of application to missile technology
- Includes technical data related to defense articles and services

The United States Munitions List (Short Version) [5]

- I - Firearms, Close Assault Weapons and Combat Shotguns
- II- Guns and Armament
- III- Ammunition/Ordnance
- IV- Launch Vehicles, Guided Missiles, Ballistic Missiles, Rockets, Torpedoes, Bombs and Mines
- V- Explosives and Energetic Materials, Propellants, Incendiary Agents and Their Constituents
- VI- Vessels of War and Special Naval Equipment
- VII- Tanks and Military Vehicles
- VIII-Aircraft and Associated Equipment
- IX- Military Training Equipment
- X- Protective Personnel Equipment
- XI- Military Electronics
- XII- Fire Control, Range Finder, Optical and Guidance and Control Equipment
- XIII- Auxiliary Military Equipment
- XIV-Toxicological Agents, Including Chemical Agents, Biological Agents, and Associated Equipment
- XV- Spacecraft Systems and Associated Equipment
- XVI- Nuclear Weapons, Design and Testing Related Items
- XVII- Classified Articles, Technical Data and Defense Services Not Otherwise Enumerated
- XVIII-Directed Energy Weapons
- XIX- Reserved
- XX- Submersible Vessels, Oceanographic and Associated Equipment
- XXI- Miscellaneous Articles

---

[4]   See the following for complete information on The Department of State's International Traffic In Arms Regulations (ITAR) (also known as the U.S. Munitions List) which covers defense-related items and services [22 CFR 120-130]:http://www.pmddtc.state.gov/regulations_laws/itar.html

[5]   See the following for the ITAR document, ITAR part 121, which is the basis for the U.S. Munitions List: http://1.usa.gov/19SGps4

The Treasury Department's Office of Foreign Assets Control (OFAC) administers and enforces economic and trade sanctions that have been imposed against specific countries based on reasons of foreign policy, national security, or international agreements. OFAC covers [31 CFR §§500-599]: [6]

- Regulates the transfer of items/services of value to embargoed nations.
- Imposes trade sanctions, and trade and travel embargoes aimed at controlling terrorism, drug trafficking and other illicit activities.
- Prohibits payments/providing value to nationals of sanctioned countries and some specified entities/individuals.
- May prohibit travel and other activities with embargoed countries and individuals even when exclusions to EAR/ITAR apply.

An export license may be required before a controlled item or material may be exported. There is usually a lengthy processing time period (currently 2-3+ months). Denial is always a possibility, and approval may contain restrictive conditions. Researchers must curtail or modify activities pending license issuance by the appropriate government body. The Bureau of Industry and Security (BIS) of the U.S. Department of Commerce is responsible for regulating the export of most commercial items, often referred to as "dual-use" items which are those having both commercial and military or proliferation applications. Relatively few exports of dual-use items require obtaining an export license from BIS prior to shipment. Dual use export licenses are required in certain situations involving national security, foreign policy, short-supply, nuclear non-proliferation, missile technology, chemical and biological weapons, regional stability, crime control, or terrorist concerns. The license requirements are dependent upon an item's technical characteristics, the destination, the end-use, and the end-user, and other activities of the end-user. There are several lists that are used to determine ineligibility under the EAR/ITAR:

> *Denied Persons List* - A list of individuals and entities that have been denied export privileges. Any dealings with a party on this list that would violate the terms of its denial order are prohibited. [7]

> *Unverified List* - A list of parties where BIS has been unable to verify the end-user in prior transactions. The presence of a party on this list in a transaction is a "Red Flag" that should be resolved before proceeding with the transaction. [8]

---

6   See the following for full information on The Treasury Department's Office of Foreign Assets Control (OFAC): http://1.usa.gov/fv5LZd

7   See the following for the current Denied Persons List: http://1.usa.gov/nieNAO

8   See the following for the current Unverified List: http://1.usa.gov/TEXyfP

Entity List - A list of parties whose presence in a transaction can trigger a license requirement under the Export Administration Regulations. These end users have been determined to present an unacceptable risk of diversion to developing weapons of mass destruction or the missiles used to deliver those weapons and contrary to U.S. national security and/or foreign policy interests. Inclusion on the list may also be a result of activities sanctioned by the State Department and activities contrary to U.S. national security and/or foreign policy interests. [9]

Specially Designated Nationals List - Alphabetical master list of Specially Designated Nationals and Blocked Persons compiled by the Treasury Department, Office of Foreign Assets Control (OFAC). [10]

Debarred List - A list compiled by the State Department of parties who are barred by §127.7 of the International Traffic in Arms Regulations (ITAR) (22 CFR §127.7) from participating directly or indirectly in the export of defense articles, including technical data or in the furnishing of defense services for which a license or approval is required by the ITAR. [11]

EAR License Requirements (Dual Use/Commercial Technologies)
- "Terrorist Supporting Countries" such as Cuba, Iran, Libya, North Korea, Sudan and Syria
- "Countries of Concern" such as the former Soviet Republics, China and Vietnam
- "Friendly Countries" such as all others (Europe, Central/South America, etc.)

ITAR Licensing Policy (Military/Space Technologies) [12]
Policy of Denial:
- State Sponsors of Terrorism (Cuba, Iran, Libya, North Korea, Sudan and Syria)
- Arms Embargo (Burma, PR China, Haiti, Liberia, Somalia and Sudan)
- Others (Belarus, Iraq, Vietnam)

---

9   See the following for information on the Entity List: http://1.usa.gov/mcuO84

10   See the following for information on the Specially Designated Nationals List: http://1.usa.gov/efgDN5

11   See the following for the current Debarred List: http://1.usa.gov/nZTcy

12   See the following for Section 126 of ITAR, which lays out specific details for each of these issues: http://1.usa.gov/19jaMVK

Policy of Denial Based on Item/End-User:

- Afghanistan
- Congo
- Iraq
- Rwanda

The U.S. is a member of various multilateral nonproliferation regimes, including:

Nuclear Suppliers Group (NSG) - With 39 member states, the NSG contributes to the nonproliferation of nuclear weapons through implementation of guidelines for control of nuclear and nuclear-related exports [13].

Zangger Committee - The purpose of the 35-nation Nuclear Non-proliferation Treaty (NPT) Exporters (Zangger) Committee is to harmonize implementation of the NPT requirements to apply International Atomic Energy Agency (IAEA) safeguards to nuclear exports. The Committee maintains and updates a list of equipment and materials that may only be exported if safeguards are applied to the recipient facility (called the "Trigger List" because such exports trigger the requirement for safeguards)[14].

Missile Technology Control Regime (MTCR) - MTCR partners have committed to apply a common export policy (MTCR Guidelines) on a common list of controlled items, including all key equipment and technology needed for missile development, production, and operation. MTCR Guidelines restrict transfers of missiles - and technology related to missiles - for the delivery of WMD. The regime places particular focus on missiles capable of delivering a payload of at least 500 kg to a distance of at least 300 km -- so-called "Category 1" or "MTCR-class" missiles [15].

Australia Group (AG) – The objective of the AG is to ensure that the industries of the thirty-two participating countries do not assist, either purposefully or inadvertently, states or terrorists seeking to acquire a chemical and/or biological weapons (CBW) capability. All AG participants exercise national export control over items listed on the AG control list [16].

---

13   See the following for full information on the NSG: http://bit.ly/SwAKvM

14   See the following for full information on the Zangger Committee: http://bit.ly/11Mzc3I

15   See the following for full information on the MTCR organization: http://bit.ly/dlsSqW

16   See the following for full information on the AG organization:l http://bit.ly/16hmleh

Wassenaar Arrangement (WA) – The objective of the WA is to prevent destabilizing accumulations of arms and sensitive dual-use equipment and technologies that may contribute to the development or enhancement of military capabilities that would undermine regional security and stability, and to develop mechanisms for information sharing among the partners as a way to harmonize export control practices and policies[17] .

The Government of Japan controls sensitive goods and technologies, including relevant dual-use goods and technologies, in order to maintain both national and international peace and security. Japan bases its control regime on the Foreign Exchange and Foreign Trade Act (1949) and its relevant legislations [18]. In 1998 when the foreign exchange business was completely liberalized, the Act of 1949 was amended and was superseded by the current Foreign Exchange and Foreign Trade Act, in which the law's "control" implication was removed. As a principal economic law concerning trade and foreign exchange, the Act covers such broad areas of cross-border transactions as foreign trades, foreign payments, foreign capital transactions, and direct investments in Japan; export control is only a small part of them. Article 48-(1) of the Act stipulates that any person intending to export specific goods must obtain permission from the Ministry of Economy, Trade, and Industry (METI); Article 25-1-(1) says that those intending to transfer specific technology to a foreign person or to a foreign country must obtain permission from the ministry.

The Center for Information on Security Trade Control (CISTEC), is the Government of Japan's clearing house for information pertaining to export activities and regime compliance[19]. Under the Foreign Exchange and Foreign Trade Act, Japan implements list control and catch-all control for the purpose of preventing proliferation of weapons of mass destruction, destabilizing accumulation of conventional arms, and terrorism.

In Japan, the Ministry of Economy, Trade and Industry (METI), is the competent authority administering export controls. Placed in METI, under the Trade and Economic Cooperation Bureau, is the Trade Control Department, which has four divisions. Of the four, the Security Export Control Policy Division, the Security Export

6

Physical Security
Considerations

---

17   See the following for full information on the WA organization: http://www.wassenaar.org/

18   See the following for the full text of the Foreign Exchange and Foreign Trade Act (1949): http://www.japaneselawtranslation.go.jp/law/detail/?id=21&vm=04&re=02

19   See the following for the CISTEC website:http://www.cistec.or.jp/english/index.html

Inspection Office established under the division and the Security Export Licensing Division are the units in charge of security export control. The responsibility of each unit is as follows:

(1) The Security Export Control Policy Division

The Security Export Control Policy Division is responsible for export control policy setting, legislation, and overall administration. It joins discussions in international export control regimes.

(2) The Security Export Licensing Division

The Security Export Licensing Division is responsible for examining license applications and issuing licenses. It has some one hundred officers including those in regional offices.

(3) The Security Export Inspection Office

The Security Export Inspection Office is responsible for:

1. Enforcement activity including on-site or on-the-spot inspections.
2. Awareness promotion and enlightenment activity to prevent illegal exports.

Japan is actively taking part in international nonproliferation initiatives. It is a signatory to major treaties on nuclear, biological and chemical nonproliferation, and serves all the existing international export control regimes: the Nuclear Suppliers Group (NSG), the Australia Group (AG), the Missile Technology Control Regime (MTCR), and the Wassenaar Arrangement (WA).

The security architect needs to work with the relevant national, regional and international regimes and organizations to understand what the Export Controls that their organization may be subjected to are in order to be able to fully integrate the required compliance activities and controls into the security architecture of the organization. In order to fully communicate the required compliance activities to the organization in a timely fashion, and to ensure that all members of the organization understand their responsibilities under the compliance regime, the security architect should create the appropriate policies required to support the compliance activities, and then ensure that they are communicated broadly within the organization, at all levels. These policies could include a variety of different approaches and requirements, depending on what compliance activities are being addressed.

For example, it should be a standard practice today in almost all organizations to have visitors " check – in " in some form with either a receptionist, a guard, a sign-in log, or an automated system that can announce them to the appropriate party. While any, or all of these activities are important to ensure the security of the employees of the organization by preventing unknown and unwanted people from gaining access to the organization, they are not uniform in their application, nor are they standardized as to the details of implementation, monitoring, compliance, and reporting. The application of standards that address the key compliance requirements and activities helps the security architect to ensure that all activities surrounding compliance are undertaken with a common goal in mind, and are uniform in their application, so that the organization is able to ensure that the key requirements for successful compliance are met.

Activities within the organization that help to ensure compliance will include escort policies for non-employees, vendors, partners, and visitors, policies and controls for data access from remote locations, mobile device access policies and controls, data classification, separation of duties, the use of system baselines for deployment and monitoring, and multi-factor authentication.

In addition, the security architect should also be focused on activities such as change management, version control, incident and problem reporting, availability management, the service catalog, and release management. While some of these activities may not be thought of as " traditional " security activities, they are able to directly impact many of the compliance requirements and behaviors that the security architect needs to implement in the organization.

Physical Security Risks

Physical security is often described as the "forgotten side of security," and yet it is a key element of an overall protection strategy. Protection of restricted work areas is important to the overall functionality of the company's operation. Proprietary, sensitive, and classified material must be protected from the general population or from other employees who do not have a need to know. In the case of a company, such areas may be protected by restricting unauthorized personnel from entering the area. General traffic flow to the area must be diverted away to minimize the entry of unauthorized personnel. Personnel who are authorized to enter these restricted areas must have a badge or credential that quickly identifies them as authorized. Moreover, these authorized personnel must be on an access roster that a guard can use to verify their credentials. If the area is a large area where vehicles are used, guards at the sentry post have to verify the vehicles being used to enter the premise along with personal identification. Verification may be accomplished by using access rosters for both vehicles and personnel. By applying these preventive measures, the risk of loss or damage is reduced.

Many organizations spend thousands of dollars on IT hardware and software, only to forget about securing the actual building that houses them. Remember: Even if no one can steal or corrupt the organization's data over the network, they may still be able to walk out the front door with it.

6

Physical Security
Considerations

Unauthorized Access

Access control is the regulation of movement into, from, and within a designated building or area. The primary objective of controlling entry into a facility or area is to ensure that only authorized persons are allowed to enter. Unauthorized access in simple terms is trespassing, which is defined as making an unwarranted or uninvited incursion; to enter unlawfully the land of another. The security architect's mantra is protecting property, information, and personnel. Keeping unwanted intrusion away from the facility is paramount, and the function of the security architect is to incorporate knowledge, technology, vigilance, and professionalism into a sound security program.

Guard Force

With surveillance devices, the human element is necessary for determination of whether the event is critical and requires intervention or response. Security officers are the physical presence and the deterrence to unauthorized entry into the facility along with being the response force to an alarm activation. With all the alarm technology, it still requires human intervention to respond to an alarm, make contact with an intruder, interact with employees, and provide first-aid when necessary.

Security officers are required to conduct foot patrols of building interiors, exteriors, and parking areas. Some officers are assigned a fixed or stationary position at entrances and other designated areas in order to prevent unauthorized entrance or the introduction of prohibited items. Another security officer responsibility is to control access to the facility by checking identification badges, issuing temporary badges, and registering visitors. Officers are required to respond to fire, security, and medical emergencies, and render assistance when needed as well as submit written or oral reports regarding significant events to security management. They also escort designated visitors, usually construction and maintenance contractors, who require "after hours" access to facilities or access to areas where classified or proprietary information is accessible. They must immediately report potentially hazardous conditions and items in need of repair, including inoperative lights, leaky sprinkler heads, leaky faucets, toilet stoppages, broken or slippery floor surfaces, trip hazards, etc.

Access Control System

The primary function of an Access Control System (ACS) is to ensure that only authorized personnel are permitted inside the controlled area. This can also include the regulation and flow of materials into and out of specific areas. Persons subject to control can include employees, visitors, customers, vendors, and the public. Access control measures should be different for each application to fulfill specific security, cost, and operational objectives.

Control can begin at the facility property line to include such areas as parking lots. Exterior building entrances can then be controlled. Within the facility, any area can be controlled at the discretion of management. However, the applied control is normally consistent with identified risk, and the protective value that is desired. Protected areas can include street level entrances, lobbies, loading docks, elevators, and sensitive internal areas containing assets such as customer data, proprietary information, and classified information.

The goal of an access control program is to limit the opportunity for a crime to be committed. If the potential perpetrator of a crime cannot gain access to financial assets, data files, computer equipment, programs, documentation, forms, operating procedures, and other sensitive material, the ability to commit a crime against the institution is minimized. Thus, only identified, authorized personnel should be permitted access to restricted areas.

The basic components of an ACS include card readers, electric locks, alarms, and computer systems to monitor and control the ACS.

In order for the system to identify an authorized employee, an ACS needs to have some form of enrollment station to assign and activate an access control device. Usually, a badge is produced and issued with the employee's identifiers, with the enrollment station giving the employee specific areas that will be accessible.

In general, an ACS compares an individual's badge against a verified database. If authenticated, the ACS sends output signals that allow authorized personnel to pass through controlled areas such as a gate or door. The system has the capability of logging and archiving entry attempts (authorized and unauthorized).

A second scenario is to have an ACS reader next to a guard's desk, so that when the individual places his badge on the reader, a picture is generated from the ACS system and verifies to the guard that the person holding the badge is in fact the correct card holder and his or her card is valid. This eliminates the chance of a perpetrator stealing or finding a badge and falsely using it to gain entry.

Another safeguard is to use a card reader with a Personal Identification Number (PIN) pad. This requires the user to utilize a unique PIN number that will be needed in connection with the badge in order for the access point to open. Coded devices use a series of assigned numbers commonly referred to as a PIN. This series of numbers is entered into a keypad and is matched to the numbers stored in the ACS. This style of reader is mostly used at employee entrances that are not manned by guards and higher-security areas within the facility. This provides additional security because if a badge is lost or stolen, it will not grant entry into a controlled area without the proper PIN number, similar to an ATM bank card.

Another feature the access control system can provide is an event tracking/ event log. These are lists or logs of security events recorded by the access control system that indicate the actions performed by an individual with an access badge and monitored by the system. Each event log entry contains the time, date, and any other information specific to the event.

Card Types

- *Magnetic Stripe* (mag stripe) cards consist of a magnetically sensitive strip fused onto the surface of a PVC material, specific to a credit card. A magnetic stripe card is read by swiping it through a reader or by inserting it into a position in a slot. This style of card is old technology; it could be physically damaged by misuse and its data can be affected by magnetic fields. In terms of overall security measures, magnetic stripe cards are easy to duplicate.

- *Proximity Cards* (prox cards) use embedded antenna wires connected to a chip within the card. The chip is encoded with the unique card identification. Distances at which proximity cards can be read vary by manufacturer and installation. Readers can require the card to be placed within a fraction of an inch from the reader to six inches away. This will then authenticate the card and will release the magnetic lock on the door. Proximity cards are moderately difficult to duplicate.

- *Smart Cards* are credential cards with a microchip embedded inside. Smart cards can store data, such as access transactions, licenses held by individuals, qualifications, safety training, security access levels, and biometric templates. This card can double as an access card for doors and can be used as an authenticator for a computer. The United States government has mandated smart cards to provide Personal Identity Verification (PIV) to verify the identity of every employee and contractor in order to improve data security. The card is used for identification, as well as for facility and data access. Smart cards are hard to duplicate.

Badge Equipment

Employee badges are an excellent method of control for both identification and access. The badges need to be created and encoded by security personnel. The badges need to be maintained and accounted for, similar to key controls. These badges will allow entry into the facility, and they must be protected and controlled. The equipment necessary for a badging access control system will include:

1. Camera for capturing photographs.
2. Software for creating badge images.
3. Badge printer capable of printing a color ID template on the front and back of the badge, and capable of encoding a magnetic stripe or smart card (where applicable). There are new-technology printers that are capable of printing pseudo holograms on the clear protective laminate, which may be considered for higher-security applications.
4. Computer for retention and programming of the security credential database. This computer may be a stand-alone or client workstation that is connected to the ACS server database in a client–server architecture.

The badges that fit the needs of the operation, either magnetic, proximity, or smart, can be purchased in bulk and can be encoded and printed when needed.

The security architect should be aware of alternate mechanisms for badge management that exist. For instance, the United States government has moved to a central provisioning model for credentialing. The USAccess Program was established to provide Federal agencies with a complete solution for issuing a common federal credential (called the PIV credential) to employees and contractors. HSPD-12 requires that all federal agencies issue interoperable credentials to all federal employees and contractors [20].

The USAccess program is designed to provide a comprehensive set of services, creating a secure, standards-based enterprise identity management capability with various PIV related components implemented with high availability and disaster recovery capabilities. Credential Production, Issuance, Activation and Management are handled as follows [21]:

- Automatically batches and processes PIV credential requests, produces the credential in a central facility, and ships to designated agency locations.
- Once the applicant receives the credential, his/her identity is confirmed using biometric verification followed by credential "personalization" with the applicant's biographic information, fingerprint templates, and PIN and generates the suite of digital certificates.
- Credential management activities, such as suspensions, reprints or revocations, may be performed by authorized role holders via an intuitive user interface.

---

20   See the following for the full text of HSPD-12: http://1.usa.gov/14gWCEK

HSPD-12 mandates a federal standard for secure and reliable forms of identification.

21   See the following for a step by step breakdown of the PIV credential issuance process under the USAccess Program: http://www.fedidcard.gov/credget.aspx

- Agencies using Light Activation stations provide applicants and credential holders with more convenient locations to easily activate their credential or perform maintenance activities such as certificate updates.

The security architect will also need to ensure that all authorized users within the organization are given awareness training regarding the badge issued to them. A sample of the type of information that should be provided to users regarding their badge and its use and maintenance can be found here: http://www.fedidcard.gov/viewdoc.aspx?id=54

Access Control Head End

The application software housed in the CPU is the physical intelligent controller where all access control systems are activity monitored, recorded into history, commanded, and controlled by the operator. Current access systems allow each local security panel to hold the system logic for its associated devices. The CPU retains the system-specific programming to allow entry (access) for authorized personnel and deny access to unauthorized personnel.

Communications failure between the CPU and the local access control panel could result in new users not being permitted entry; however, the system is set so that the panel will recognize personnel already installed and will grant access to an authorized badge holder.

These systems can integrate with CCTV and provide instant visual recognition along with visual alarm activation in order to provide the security console operator visual information before dispatching a security response team.

Another feature of an access control system is it can provide event tracking/event logs, which are lists or logs of security events recorded by the access control system that indicate the actions performed by employees as they enter or attempt to enter a controlled area. Each event log entry contains the time, date, and any other information specific to the event. This is useful when identifying who has access to a specific area and verifying with management if that employee still needs access.

Physical Security Needs and Organization Drivers

The security architect needs to be able to provide guidance to the organization concerning the best ways to achieve the identified goals that the organization may have. These goals are usually represented in the form of organization drivers that have been identified at a point in time as being important catalysts for organization decisions and actions within one or more areas of the organization.

There are certain goals that almost all organizations will have in common, and as a result, the security architect should be able to easily identify these goals and plan for them. For instance, risk management is a common theme among security-related organization drivers. Therefore, risk assessment techniques are very useful in identifying and prioritizing an organization's security agenda. This enables companies to target scarce resources at the most likely and potentially damaging threats.

Among the most common organization drivers are the following:

- Governance / Compliance
  - Regulations
  - Certification
- Asset Protection
  - Authentication
  - Integrity
  - Authorization
- Personnel Protection
  - Life safety
- Business Building
  - Mergers and Acquisitions
  - New Business Models
  - Business Continuity
- Cost Control
  - Process reengineering
  - Workflow automation
- Productivity

Whether it is a common organization driver, or one that is unique to a specific organization or industry vertical, the security architect needs to be able to maintain general system capability and flexibility in the system architecture in order to enable the organization to respond quickly and appropriately to the ever-changing landscape of need and opportunity.

There are many approaches that the security architect can examine and potentially utilize. For instance, if the security architect has a need to address cloud based infrastructure and systems, then the Cloud Security Alliance's Trusted Cloud Initiative (TCI) Reference Architecture would be a good place to begin researching[22]. If the security architect is in need of basic building blocks for a security architecture to address the most common needs of organization,

---

22   See the following for an overview of the TCI Reference Architecture:http://bit.ly/olmojL

then they can examine frameworks such as COBIT and ITIL, and ISO standard 27002[23]. The security architect can also look to solutions that are emerging as new and innovative ways to address common security issues and concerns for organization, such as Physical Security Information Management (PSIM) systems [24]. If the organization is considering outsourcing some, or all of its management, monitoring and production capabilities, then the security architect will need to engage in all of the appropriate due diligence activities necessary to ensure that the vendor(s) selected will be able to perform the required activities, and provide the necessary levels of reporting, and system access necessary to allow for seamless integration with the systems that the organization still retains control over. Paying special attention to the Service Level Agreements (SLAs) negotiated, and the specifics of the coverage that they offer will be important for the security architect, as these details can negatively impact all of the remaining services that the organization still controls and manages in house if they are not understood and managed properly.

Facility Risk

It is the responsibility of the security architect to identify the facility risks and do everything possible to mitigate them. A vulnerability assessment tour of a facility is designed to gather information regarding the general layout of the facility, the location of key assets, information about facility operations and production capabilities, and locations and types of physical protection systems.

Facility risk assessments have an enormous potential to improve the safety of a facility by recognizing and eliminating potential problems. Restricted area physical security is not just about keeping bad people out with biometrics and retinal scans. It is also about keeping out the fires, floods, and hurricanes that

---

23   Control Objectives for Information and related Technology (CobiT), the International Organization for Standardization 27002:2005 (ISO/IEC 27002:2005), and the Information Technology Infrastructure Library (ITIL) have emerged worldwide as the most respected frameworks for IT governance and compliance. Other frameworks such as the United States' National Institute of Standards and Technology Risk Management Framework provide a free framework that can be tailored to any size organization.

24   While not a "new" technology, since PSIM systems have been around in some form since approximately 2005, there has been a tremendous amount of growth and change in the nature of these systems as the technology has continued to evolve. The most recent iterations of these systems are nothing like their distant cousins from the first generations of PSIM systems released in the aftermath of the 9/11 attacks on the United States and its infrastructure.

The goal of PSIM solutions is to provide a comprehensive and holistic view of a physical security environment through the integration of numerous physical security subsystems and the correlation of data from these subsystems. the ability to analyze the data from disparate, interconnected systems and then assess, based upon a range of factors including chronology, location, priority and prevailing threat, the correct response procedure which will conform to not only the regulatory requirements but also the procedural and operational needs of the enterprise.

can ravage the facility - and its data. An acceptable risk profile can only be achieved by identifying hazards and assessing the associated risks and control measures.

There are many potential risks that can take out a facility, from human error, natural disasters, to corporate espionage. The security architect needs to be aware of all types of risk and take the necessary steps to mitigate and prepare for potential hazards.

The purpose of a data security program is to ensure adherence to three basic tenets:

- **Confidentiality:** Only authorized people should be able to see the data.
- **Integrity:** Only authorized people should be able to change the data and then, only in authorized ways.
- **Availability:** Authorized persons should be able to access the data whenever they are allowed to do so.

Compromises may be necessary to provide a level of security that does a fair job of keeping out intruders but does not make the information inaccessible to authorized users. A comprehensive security program must include written policies and procedures, access control systems, user authentication technologies, auditing systems, encryption, and content security.

In order to understand how physical security dovetails with IT security, it is necessary to fully understand the basic concepts of the following:

1. **Threat** - Anything that can harm assets
2. **Vulnerability** - Anything that allows the harm to occur or a weakness that allows security breaches to occur
3. **Counter Measure** - Steps taken to reduce the risk of the occurrence or magnitude of asset loss

The following measures outline the requirements that physical security must satisfy to provide the necessary facility protections and the means to protect the personnel, information, and other assets of an organization.

Target identification involves identifying the most valuable asset that needs to be protected. Assets can be personnel, property, equipment, or information. To identify assets to be protected, it would be prudent to prioritize the assets or establish a matrix and identify the asset in conjunction with the probability of attack, along with the question: What would be the impact and consequence of the loss of the asset?

6

Physical Security Considerations

Sample of Defined Threat Matrix

Asset	Probability of Attack (Likelihood)	Consequence of Loss (Impact)
Data Center Server	Medium	Very High
Mobile Devices (critical staff)	High	High
Copy Machine	Low	Low
Mobile Devices (nonessential personnel)	High	Low
Power Control Unit (PCU)	Medium	High
Classified Containers	Low	High

Walking a team of security professionals though a facility will provide a static picture of how to protect it. However, one of the best ways to build a comprehensive approach toward protecting the facility is by doing on-site interviews. Everyone has an opinion on security, and it is amazing that often the best insight and information on what needs to be protected and how it should be protected comes from interviewing the staff. It is important for the security architect to bear in mind that any changes proposed to the security controls of the organization will need to be vetted through the standing change management processes in place. It is the responsibility of the security architect to be familiar with the change management processes that exist, and to ensure that they are followed at all times. Some questions that the security architect will want to make sure that they have answers for in this area are as follows:

1. How do changes get made to existing security controls?
2. Who authorizes changes?
3. When are users notified of the changes?
4. How are users notified of the changes?

The American Institute of Architects has established some key security questions that need to be addressed while performing a security assessment.[25]

1. What do we want to protect?
2. What are we protecting against?
3. What are the current or expected asset vulnerabilities?
4. What are the consequences of loss?
5. What specific level of protection do we wish to achieve?
6. What types of protection measures are appropriate?
7. What are our protection constraints?

---

25   See the following:*Security Planning and Design* (The American Institute of Architects. 2004)

8. What are the specific security design requirements?
9. How do the integrated systems of personnel, technologies, and procedures respond to security incidents?

Once these questions have been answered and a thorough facilities evaluation and staff interview completed, it is time to develop and outline a physical protection system for the facility.

Site Planning

The primary goal of a physical protection program is to control access to the facility. In the concept of defense in depth, barriers are arranged in layers with the level of security growing progressively higher as one comes closer to the center or the highest protective area. Defending an asset with a multiple layer posture can reduce the likelihood of a successful attack; if one layer of defense fails, another layer of defense will hopefully prevent the attack, and so on. This design requires the attacker to circumvent multiple defensive mechanisms to gain access to the targeted asset.

The single most important goal in planning a site is the protection of life, property, and operations. The security architect needs to make decisions in support of this goal, and these decisions should be based on a comprehensive security assessment of the threats and hazards so that planning and design countermeasures are appropriate and effective in the reduction of vulnerability and risk.

Technology is not the only answer to heightened security needs. It is essential to start by first looking at the way the facility is laid out and then assessing what electronic devices are needed to achieve enhanced overall security. The positioning of security personnel for presence and response capability is a key to the overall success of a comprehensive security protection program.

There is a natural conflict between making a facility as convenient and open as possible for staff and visitors and maintaining a secure facility. However, with most applications and design requirements, there needs to be cooperation between several departments. Expediency should be considered during the different phases of the design review; however, the requirement for security should not be sacrificed for convenience. Proper security controls will reduce the flow rate and ease of entry and egress into and out of a facility, but will also allow for rapid evacuation in case of emergency. These issues must be addressed in the initial planning to facilitate additional entry points or administrative requirements. Once a process has been established and there is buy-in from the employees, the acceptance of operational policy is generally embraced.

6

Physical Security Considerations

Designing a new building to mitigate threats is simpler and more cost-effective than retrofitting an existing building. Important security benefits are achieved not by hardware and electronic devices but by shrewd site selections, proper placement of the building on the site, and careful location of building occupants and functions to minimize exposure to threat. These factors also have the benefit of reducing operating expenses over the lifetime of the building, such as limiting the number of entrances to the site that must be monitored, staffed, and protected.

When there are changes to the design after the fact and personnel are used to doing something a certain way, there will be reluctance, questions, and push back. Organizations generally resist change. However, if a sound explanation is presented through an effective change management process the impact can be minimized.

To maximize safety and security, a design team should implement a holistic approach to site design that integrates security and function to achieve a balance among the various design elements and objectives. Even if resources are limited, significant value can be added to a project by integrating security considerations into the more traditional design tasks in such a way that they complement the design.

The movement of people and materials throughout a facility is determined by the design of its access, delivery, and parking systems. Such systems should be designed to maximize efficiency while minimizing conflicts between the entry and departure of vehicles and pedestrians. Designers should begin with an understanding of the organization's requirements based on an analysis of how the facility will be used. The design process of a security plan for a new facility should begin with the interior, then the exterior, and finally the outer perimeter.

When designing the data center, make sure that only durable materials are used that can exceed normal design loads. At a minimum, the facility must be capable of withstanding 200 mile per hour winds and driven rain or snow. Material such as masonry and concrete will afford the most protection to the facility, along with fire resistance. Include only necessary windows in the structure. 20-foot high ceilings provide tolerance of over-temperature conditions.

Restricted Work Areas

Sensitive Compartmental Information Facilities (SCIF) [26]

In highly restricted work areas or government SCIFs, there is a requirement to increase the security measures to ensure stricter access control to these areas. The physical security protection for a SCIF is intended to prevent as well as detect visual, acoustical, technical, and physical access by unauthorized persons. An organization may not be required to maintain government classified information; however, the organization's profitability and employment may be tied to proprietary information that requires the same level of security.

SCIF walls will consist of three layers of 5/8 inch drywall and will be from true floor to true ceiling. There will typically be only one SCIF entrance door, which will have an X-09 combination lock along with access control systems. All SCIF perimeter doors must be plumbed in their frames and the frame firmly affixed to the surrounding wall. Door frames must be of sufficient strength to preclude distortion that could cause improper alignment of door alarm sensors, improper door closure, or degradation of audio security. All SCIF primary entrance doors must be equipped with an automatic door closer.

Basic HVAC requirements are that any duct penetration into the secured area that is over 96 square inches will require bars so as to prevent an intruder from climbing through the ducts.

---

26   See the following for detailed information on SCIF/SAPF design requirements and guidelines:

A. Unified Facilities Criteria (UFC) DRAFT Sensitive Compartmented Information Facilities Planning, Design, and Construction: http://bit.ly/12dp8AM

B. Intelligence Community Standard Number 705-1: Physical and Technical Security Standards for Sensitive Compartmented Information Facilities (Effective: 17 September 2010) http://bit.ly/16j2F9S

C. Director of Central Intelligence Directive No. 6/9 Physical Security Standards for Sensitive Compartmented Information Facilities (18 November, 2002) http://bit.ly/19UVV6L

D. US Army Corps of Engineers, Engineering and Support Center, Huntsville, Engineering Guidance Design Manual, CEHNC 1110-1-1, 7th Edition, March 2008 http://1.usa.gov/1bZJW4C

E. NAVFAC Naval Facilities Engineering Command Physical Security of Sensitive Compartmented Information Facilities (SCIF) NAVFAC NORTHWEST, November 14, 2012 http://bit.ly/195ktdK

F. NISPOM.US The web resource for the National Industrial Security Program and Cyber Security Business/Law http://bit.ly/14M4ugi

G. Joint Air Force- Army- Navy JAFAN 6/9 Manual Physical Security Standards for Special Access Program Facilities 23 March 2004 http://bit.ly/flMXZl

H. National Oceanic and Atmospheric Administration (NOAA) Western Regional Center SCIF overview briefing: http://1.usa.gov/16j3Cil

White noise or sound-masking devices need to be placed over doors, in front of plenum or pointed toward windows to prevent an eavesdropper from listening to classified conversations. Some SCIFs use music or noise that sounds like a constant flow of air to mask conversation.

All access control must be controlled from within the SCIF. Intrusion detection is sent out to a central station with the requirement that a response force will respond to the perimeter of the SCIF within 15 minutes.

Data Centers

When discussing the need to secure the data center, security architects tend to immediately think of sabotage, espionage, or data theft. While the need is obvious for protection against intruders and the harm caused by intentional infiltration, the hazards from the ordinary activity of personnel working in the data center present a greater day-to-day risk for most facilities.

Personnel within the organization need to be segregated from access areas where they do not have a "need to know" for that area. The security officer will have physical access to most of the facility but has no reason to access financial or HR data. The head of computer operations might have access to computer rooms and operating systems, but not the mechanical rooms that house power and HVAC facilities. It comes down to not allowing wandering within the organization. As data centers grow, the need for physical security at the facility is every bit as great as the need for cyber security of networks. The data center is the brains of the operation and, as such, only specific people should be granted access.

The data center should have signs at the doors marking the room as "restricted access" and prohibiting consumption of food and drink, and smoking in the computer room. There should be a mandatory authentication method at the entrance to the room such as a badge reader, biometric control, or a guard station.

The Network Operations Center (NOC) is the central security control point for the data center. This is the internal gatekeeper for the data center. It must have fire, power, weather, temperature, and humidity monitoring systems in place. The NOC must have redundant methods of communication with the outside world, including telephone, cell phone, or two-way radio system. The NOC must be manned 24 hours a day.

Access to the data center should be restricted to those who need to maintain the servers or infrastructure of the room. Service engineers must go to the NOC to obtain access to the computer room.

Cleaning crews should work in groups of at least two. Cleaning crews should be restricted to offices and the NOC. If cleaning staff must access a data center for any reason, they will be escorted by NOC personnel.

The standard scenario for increased security at a data center would consist of the basic security-in-depth: progressing from the outermost (least sensitive) areas to the innermost (most sensitive) areas. Security will start with entry into the building, which will require passing a receptionist guard, and then using a proximity card to gain building entry. Access to the computer room or data center will now require the same proximity card along with a PIN and a biometric device.

Figure 6.1 - **A portal allows only one person in at a time and will only open the inner door once the outer door is closed**

Combining access control methods at an entry control point will increase the reliability of access for authorized personnel only. Using different methods for each access level significantly increases security at inner levels, because each is secured by its own methods as well as those of outer levels that must be entered first. This would also include internal door controls. For a data center, the use of an internal mantrap or portal would provide increased entry and exit control. A portal (*Figure 6.1*) allows only one person in at a time and will only open the inner door once the outer door is closed. The portal can have additional biometrics within the device that must be activated before the secured side door opens.

Protection Plans

The primary foundation of effective building security requires careful planning, design, and management of the physical protection system, in order to integrate people, procedures, and equipment into the process. Protecting a building, its occupants, and related assets can pose a complex problem, and there is no perfect defense to all of the potential threats a target may face. Optimizing building security with respect to performance, cost, and efficiency ultimately requires compromise and balance in the application and consideration of

6

Physical Security Considerations

503

people, procedures, and equipment. The fundamental aspects of building operations, however, are built upon three basic components: people, procedure, and technology. The combination of these elements contributes to overall organizational security as well as providing the basis for effective emergency preparation and response.

People are the most important consideration for any security plan. People are not considered expendable assets. Yes, people can be replaced with new personnel, but they are still an asset that must be protected to the greatest extent possible. Personnel within an organization have specific functions depending on the department in which they work and the expertise they possess. A successful plan takes into consideration which departments need to be functional in the shortest amount of time possible. It is important to understand the pattern of movement of a building's occupants. This will help to ensure the procedures outlined in the plan take into account where the highest concentration of personnel may be located. With the examination of people within an organization, it is important to determine the type of security personnel an organization will use. Contract or proprietary personnel can be utilized. The most effective and efficient methods and locations to deploy those security personnel assets must also be determined.

The other category of people is those who provide protection. In the people element of security operations, the integration of people as a layer of security in the form of security guards and other security personnel is another consideration. The architectural layout of the building can be designed to influence the movement of people for rapid evacuation, limited congregation, increased visibility, and to limit the need for a large amount of security personnel.

Security is a dynamic process, and for it to be effective, it must be procedural in nature. For example, emergency response and business continuity plans must be developed well in advance of a critical incident and must define the plan of action or steps to be taken in a logical, orderly, and procedural manner. The development of procedures involves planning for such events as evacuation, emergency response, and disaster recovery in response to fires, natural disasters, and criminal intrusions. Policies and procedures are then developed to assist with the proper response and recovery actions in the event a crisis strikes. It should be noted that policies and procedures are guides to actions that should be taken in the event of an emergency, and should not be inflexibly construed. No critical incident is the same, and it would be impossible to develop a procedure for every possible event that could occur. Procedures should be written in such a way that they can be adapted to any application.

The third element of the security operation, technology, involves hardware, electronics, and other equipment used in the security mission. In building security design, technologies can be built in or retrofitted into the existing structure to perform a variety of functions such as access control, surveillance, personnel screening, intrusion detection, and fortification. Technology has also helped to advance competitive intelligence gathering and espionage activities. Global positioning systems and high-resolution surveillance are pushing security to new levels. Using this technology, the security architect can track an item taken from a facility via GPS with a tiny sensor attached or scanned onto it.

These elements of security, people, procedures, and technology are interdependent because they rely on each other to be effective. For example, the behaviors and needs of people dictate what procedures and equipment may be deployed; procedures depend on people to be effective; and equipment requirements depend on the particular procedures to be followed in a critical incident. A cost-effective and comprehensive plan necessitates a balance of these three elements, taking into account their particular contribution to the mission; one application may be security personnel intensive, where as another may be equipment intensive.

Evacuation Drills

Every organization should have an emergency management plan developed in partnership with public safety agencies, including law enforcement, fire, and local emergency preparedness agencies. The plan should address fire, natural, and manmade disasters. An organization's plan should be tailored to address the unique circumstances and needs of the operation. For example, organizations on the east coast of the United States do not need to prepare for frequent earthquakes, but all operations in California will put this as one of their top-priority drills. The security architect needs to have a general awareness of the historical events pertinent to the geographies where the organization does business in order to be able to effectively plan and prioritize for the different kinds of events that are more or less likely to occur.

Staff training, particularly for those with specific responsibilities during an event, will include a combination of security personnel, facilities, and selected employees designated as floor fire wardens. Holding regularly scheduled practice drills, similar to the common fire drill, allows for plan testing, as well as employee and key staff rehearsal of the plan, and increases the likelihood of success in an actual event.

If the organization has a visitor management software program incorporated with access control, this will provide a system for knowing who is in a building, including customers and visitors.

In the United States, the FEMA Emergency Management Guide for Business and Industry outlines specific areas that need to be addressed and implemented during an evacuation of a facility[27]:

1. Decide in advance who has the authority to order an evacuation. Create a chain of command so that others are authorized to act in case your designated person is not available. If local officials tell you to evacuate, do so immediately.

2. Identify who will shut down critical operations and lock the doors, if possible, during an evacuation.
    - Choose employees most able to make decisions that emphasize personal safety first.
    - Train others who can serve as a backup if the designated person is unavailable.
    - Write down, distribute, and practice evacuation procedures.

3. Locate and make copies of building and site maps with critical utility and emergency routes clearly marked.
    - Identify and clearly mark entry–exit points both on the maps and throughout the building.
    - Post maps for quick reference by employees.
    - Keep copies of building and site maps with your crisis management plan and other important documents in your emergency supply kit and also at an off-site location.
    - Make copies available to first responders or other emergency personnel.

4. Plan two ways out of the building from different locations throughout your facility.

5. Consider the feasibility of installing emergency lighting or plan to use flashlights in case the power goes out.

6. Establish a warning system.
    - Test systems frequently.
    - Plan to communicate with people who are hearing impaired or have other disabilities and those who do not speak the local language.

7. Designate an assembly site.
    - Pick one location near your facility and another in the general area in case you have to move farther away.
    - Talk to your people in advance about the importance of letting someone know if you cannot get to the assembly site or if you must leave it.

---

27 See the following for the FEMA Emergency Management Guide for Business and Industry: http://www.fema.gov/pdf/business/guide/bizindst.pdf

     ¤ Ensure the assembly site is away from traffic lanes and is safe for pedestrians.

8. Try to account for all workers, visitors, and customers as people arrive at the assembly site.

     ¤ Take a head count.

     ¤ Use a prepared roster or checklist.

     ¤ Ask everyone to let others know if they are leaving the assembly site.

9. Determine who is responsible for providing an all-clear or return-to-work notification. Plan to cooperate with local authorities responding in an emergency.

10. Plan for **people with disabilities** who may need help getting out in an emergency.

11. If your organization operates out of more than one location or has more than one place where people work, establish evacuation procedures for each individual building.

12. If your company is in a high-rise building, an industrial park, or even a small strip mall, it is important to coordinate and practice with other tenants or organizations to avoid confusion and potential gridlock.

13. If the organization rents, leases, or shares space with other organizations, make sure the building owner and other companies are committed to coordinating and practicing evacuation procedures together.

There are also special requirements for high-rise buildings, which are buildings with more than seven floors:

1. Note where the closest emergency exit is.

2. Be sure personnel know another way out in case the first choice is blocked.

3. Take cover against a desk or table if objects are falling.

4. Move away from file cabinets, bookshelves, or other objects that might fall.

5. Face away from windows and glass.

6. Move away from exterior walls.

7. Listen for and follow instructions.

8. Take an emergency supply kit, unless there is reason to believe it has been contaminated.

9. Do not use elevators.

10. Stay to the side while going down stairwells to allow emergency workers to come up.

6

Physical Security Considerations

507

There may also be requirements to shelter-in-place. There may be situations when it is best to stay in the building to avoid any uncertainty outside. There are other circumstances, such as during a tornado or a chemical incident, when specifically how and where personnel take shelter is a matter of survival. The security architect should understand the different threats and plan for all possibilities. FEMA has developed a system to put into place if personnel are instructed by local authorities to take shelter.

Determine where personnel will take shelter in case of a **tornado warning:**

1. Storm cellars or basements provide the best protection.
2. If underground shelter is not available, go into an interior room or hallway on the lowest floor possible.
3. In a high-rise building, go to a small interior room or hallway on the lowest floor possible.
4. Stay away from windows, doors, and outside walls. Go to the center of the room. Stay away from corners be-cause they attract debris.
5. Stay in the shelter location until the danger has passed.

If local authorities believe the air is badly contaminated with a chemical, you may be instructed to "shelter-in-place" and seal the room (*Figure 6.2*). The process used to seal the room is considered a temporary protective measure to create a barrier between your people and potentially contaminated air outside. It is a type of sheltering that requires preplanning [28].

1. Identify a location to "seal the room" advance.
   - If feasible, choose an interior room, such as a break room or conference room, with as few windows and doors as possible.
   - If your organization is located on more than one floor or in more than one building, identify multiple shelter locations.
2. To seal the room effectively:
   - Close the organization, and bring everyone inside.
   - Lock doors, and close windows, air vents, and fireplace dampers.
   - Turn off fans, air conditioning, and forced air heating systems.
   - Take your emergency supply kit unless you have reason to believe it has been contaminated.

---

28   See the following for the Federal Emergency Management Agency (FEMA) of the United States Government's FAQ page regarding emergency preparedness: http://www.ready.gov/faq#q11

Security architects should read through the entire FAQ, as many of the questions answered will provide valuable information for planning and response purposes. In particular, the following question will prove to be very important for pre-planning activities:

- How long can a family stay in a sealed room?
- Will we run out of air to breathe?

* - DHS recommends that individuals allow ten square feet of floor space per person in order to provide sufficient air to prevent carbon dioxide build up for up to 5 hours assuming a normal breathing rate while resting.

- Go into an interior room, such as a break room or conference room, with few windows, if possible.
- Seal all windows, doors, and air vents with plastic sheeting and duct tape. Measure and cut the sheeting in advance to save time.
- Be prepared to improvise, and use what you have on hand to seal gaps so that you create a barrier between yourself and any contamination.

Local authorities may not immediately be able to provide information on what is happening and what you should do. However, you should watch TV, listen to the radio, or check the Internet often for official news and instructions as they become available.

Incident Response

An incident response plan takes its place beside business continuity and disaster-recovery plans as a key corporate document that helps guarantee that companies will survive whatever glitch, emergency, or calamity comes their way. And while a business continuity plan aims to preserve operations in the face of adversity and a disaster recovery plan details what to do in case of a disaster, an incident response plan is broader, laying out how to respond to scenarios as diverse as data security breaches and network crashes.

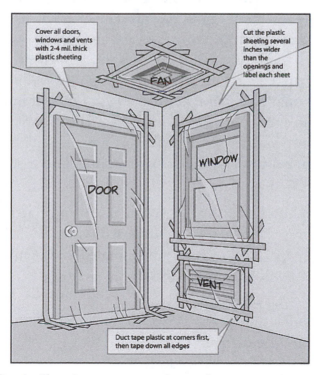

Figure 6.2 - **Shelter-in-Place is a process used to seal a room as a temporary protective measure to create a barrier between your people and potentially contaminated air outside.**

(*Source:* http://www.ready.gov/sites/default/files/shelter_in_place.jpg)

Plans and procedures, including recovery plans, emergency response, and evacuation, are deployed in response to different kinds of security and safety threats such as earthquakes, explosions, lightning damage, and fires. Once the plans and procedures have been established, policies can be deployed to show how security personnel respond to the foregoing threats and to assist in recovery from other incidents that may occur.

Technology involves where and how screening of personnel and materials will be accomplished, and what kinds of systems and equipment will be used. The technology must be suitable for the operations or mission of the facility.

There is no way to prevent a natural disaster from occurring; however, the security architect can take action to avoid the most devastating damage that the organization may face. The lack of knowledge and fear of the unknown about what to do in the case of emergency has caused organizations to fail or increased their cost due to an extended recovery time. Companies must identify the risk and hazards facing their organization, and determine what types of training are useful, and deal with and categorize the risk rationally. The goal of emergency preparedness is to be reasonably prepared and not to be swept up in the sea of confusion.

The best time to respond to a disaster is before it happens. A relatively small investment of time and money now may prevent severe damage and disruption of life and organization in the future. Every area of the world is subject to some kind of disaster. Floods, hurricanes, earthquakes, ice storms, and landslides could happen anytime. Every one responds to disasters differently; however, security architects can take advantage of typical human behavior in the aftermath of an event. Seek out those individuals who rise above the chaos, and get them trained and involved in recovery activities. This will improve the organization's chances for a shorter recovery time, and a successful recovery effort.

The security architect needs to put together a plan of action, and in doing so will identify areas that need to be addressed when an incident response is required. There are five topics that can be initiated and prepared for before an actual Incident Response becomes necessary.

1. Identify what can happen
2. Put together the team
3. A communication plan
4. Identify who does what and when
5. Test the plan

Design Validation

Penetration Tests

A penetration test is a good way to test the security operations of the organization. From an IT standpoint, the idea of a penetration test is immediately connected to testing the network defenses by attempting to access a system from the outside using "hacker" techniques. However, from the physical security aspect, there is a personal approach that needs to be addressed. There are several variations of physical penetration methods used by perpetrators, including dumpster diving, lock picking, social engineering, physical access compromise, and simulated sabotage. While these techniques may seem extreme, it is important to remember that bad guys do not follow the rules, and they do not play nice.

There are many benefits to conducting a penetration test on a facility. It will identify vulnerable areas that need to be immediately addressed. In order to determine the effectiveness of the security apparatuses in place, a penetration test is essential. It easy to say we have outstanding security personnel and a security program in place, but it is another matter to verify and confirm.

- Will the guard at the front desk actually look for a perpetrator or an individual without a badge?
- Can the guard spot a forged badge or if the picture on the badge is the same as the individual?
- Will employees stop and question someone who looks out of place inside the building? Will they contact security and notify that there is someone on their floor who does not belong?
- Will employees hold open a door for someone trying to enter through an employee-only entrance or will they make them use their access card; and does the employee-only entrance require a dual-technology badge and pin number?

Having an outside entity attempt the penetration is the best method. They look for easy accesses into the facility or they try and mingle with the crowd during morning hours when everyone is coming into work. If the facility utilizes a contract guard force, this can be done with the coordination of their upper management. There are also several companies that specialize in penetration testing.

Another perimeter area to look at: is there construction going on? Can a perpetrator put on a hard hat and walk in with the construction crew, then discard the construction gear and walk into the facility as though he belongs? How are construction, contractors, and vendors controlled?

Are secured areas truly secured? Are there layers of security within the structure? Or, is all of the security emphasis and monitoring focused externally?

6

Physical Security
Considerations

These facilities place all the emphasis on the outer security perimeter, but once you have navigated through into the building, there are virtually no security measures in place.

A penetration test can determine if security measures are enforced within the building. Are all employees required to wear identification badges in plain sight while they are inside the building? Are security awareness posters displayed?

After an intruder has entered through the perimeter, can they walk into areas within the facility and go through an employee area without being disturbed? Will anyone confront them and question their presence in the area?

The penetration test will identify vulnerabilities at the perimeter, but what about exiting the facility - are there any safeguards set up to deter the removal of classified information or property from the facility?

Other methods used in penetration testing include a social engineering scheme, in which the attacker relies on human nature to gain access to unauthorized network resources. This could be in the form of eavesdropping or "shoulder surfing" (looking over your shoulder) to obtain access information. The basic goals of social engineering are the same as hacking in general: to gain unauthorized access to systems or information in order to commit fraud, network intrusion, industrial espionage, identity theft, or simply to disrupt the system or network. The natural human willingness to accept someone at his or her word leaves many of us vulnerable to attack. The concept of "trust but verify" needs to be instilled in all staff. All employees should be trained on how to keep confidential data safe. The simple statement "I'm sorry but I do not know who you are and I will not be providing that information over the phone" will provide for a level of security.

Another of the penetration tests is the simple task of checking your trash. "Dumpster diving" is the practice of searching through the trash of an individual or organization in an attempt to obtain something useful. It can also include data aggregation by looking for passwords written on sticky notes, unwanted files, letters, memos, photographs, IDs, and other paperwork that has been found in dumpsters. This oversight is a result of many people not realizing that sensitive items such as passwords, credit card numbers, and personal information they throw in the trash could be recovered anywhere from the dumpster to the landfill.

Every organization has information that is confidential and must be disposed of properly. Carelessly discarded correspondence, financial statements, medical records, credit card statements, photocopies and computer printouts are all easily removed from the trash. Should this data get into the wrong hands, it can cause acute embarrassment, financial loss, or legal action. Loss of government data can result in a serious breach of national security[29]. The European Union may force companies operating critical infrastructure in areas such as banking, energy and stock exchanges to report major online attacks and reveal security breaches. The European Union's executive Commission presented a proposal on cybersecurity in February, 2013 once it had received feedback from the European Parliament and EU countries.

Personal information in the wrong hands can be just as damaging. Protecting personnel privacy is a vital necessity, and shredding has become standard practice in offices as well as homes. There are several methods for proper destruction of information. Organizations can contract with a licensed and bonded shredding company that will come to a site with a mobile shredding truck and dispose of classified material and sensitive information while an organization representative watches and verifies the destruction (with a photo), or organizations can shred on site depending on the volume of information that needs to be destroyed. Shredding services also have the capacity to irretrievably destroy hard drives and physical components. *Table 6.1* lists some common intrusion tactics and strategies for prevention[30].

Access Control Violation Monitoring

When doors are not physically controlled by a guard, there is a tendency for personnel to violate entry procedures. Violation of access control systems, when controlled by card reader, may occur by "tailgating" or "piggybacking," where an authorized employee with a valid entry card is accompanied by a closely spaced non-authorized perpetrator or an authorized employee who inadvertently failed to follow proper entry procedures without considering the security consequences.

If the facility has an employee entrance that does not have a mantrap or turnstile entry system and has only a single door, there are products available to announce when a tailgate has occurred. This could be a buzzer local to the door that sounds to alert a valid cardholder to challenge someone tailgating behind them.

In higher-end security systems, the alarm may be used to alert a control room operator and trigger live closed circuit television (CCTV) images allowing immediate action to be taken. When coupled with a modern integrated security

---

29 See the following for overviews of data breaches from around the world: http://www.databreaches.net/

See the following for detailed reporting on data breaches within the United States of America at all levels of government and the private sector: http://www.privacyrights.org/data-breach

See the following for the ICS-CERT Industrial Control Systems Cyber Emergency Response Team Control Systems Security Program - Incident Response Summary Report 2009–2011: http://1.usa.gov/Lx8156

30   See the following for full information on this table: S. Granger (1/9/2002) Social Engineering Fundamentals, Part II: Combat Strategies.   http://www.symantec.com/connect/articles/social-engineering-fundamentals-part-ii-combat-strategies

6

Physical Security Considerations

management system, a full alarm event history can be produced indicating the date, time, and location of the alarm, the cardholder who allowed someone to tailgate, and the digital CCTV images of the person tailgating.

This is why a defense-in-depth approach is necessary. If a perimeter door is compromised and an individual has gained entry into the facility, the area that has been entered will not be a high-value area, and a response team can cordon off the area that has been breached and make contact with the violator.

Maintaining an audit trail of improper entry attempts or entry violations (allowing tailgating) is a way to identify employees who need additional training on proper security entry requirements; more drastically, for continual violations, notify their supervisor, and if all else fails, revoke their badge and require them to be escorted all day. This is a drastic move, but they will only need to be escorted once by a fellow worker before they get the message and will adhere to proper security procedures.

Area of Risk	Penetration Test Tactic	Mitigation Strategy
Phone (help desk)	Impersonation and persuasion	Train employees/help desk to never give out passwords or other confidential information by phone
Building Entrance	Unauthorized physical access	Tight badge security, employee training, and security officers present
Office	Shoulder surfing	Do not type in passwords with anyone else present And use privacy filters on all computer and device screens
Phone (help desk)	Impersonation on help desk calls	All employees should be assigned a PIN specific to help desk support
Office	Wandering through halls looking for open offices	Require all guests to be escorted and all employees display badges
Mail Room	Insertion of forged memos	Lock and monitor mail room
Machine Room/Phone Closet	Attempting to gain access, remove equipment, or attach a protocol analyzer to grab confidential data	Keep phone closets, server rooms, etc., locked at all times and keep updated inventory on equipment
Phone and PBX	Stealing phone toll access	Control overseas and long-distance calls, trace calls, refuse transfers
Dumpsters	Dumpster diving	Keep all trash in secured, monitored areas, shred important data, erase magnetic media
Intranet–Internet	Creation and insertion of mock software on intranet or Internet to steal passwords	Continual awareness of system and network changes, training on password use
Office	Stealing sensitive documents	Mark documents as confidential and require those documents to be locked up
General–Psychological	Impersonation and persuasion	Keep employees on their toes through continued awareness and training programs

Table 6.1 - **Common intrusion tactics and strategies for prevention**

6

Physical Security Considerations

Summary

In summary, the security architect should have an understanding of the physical security domain to assist the organization in being prepared for the variety of risks that it will face through the operation of facilities and infrastructure, as well as the maintenance of data, and the safeguarding of resources.

The way facilities are planned will continue to evolve. Improvements in facility construction techniques and materials, as well as in the core infrastructure systems that are used to create the networks that drive access to organization data will continue to improve. There are some things that do not change however, such as the need for physical access control to secured areas of an organization, and the need to stay at least one-step ahead of those actors that look to gain access to system data through unregulated and unauthorized channels and means. The security architect will have to continue to be vigilant in all areas in order to ensure that the organization is always positioned to weather the many storms that will be hurled against it as new attacks and new exploits are found and tried. A strong and well-designed defense-in-depth architecture, one that takes both physical and logical security elements into account to create the strongest possible controls and overlapping areas of coverage that mutually reinforce one another is the goal, and the security architect needs to be continuously assessing and reassessing the viability of the current architecture against the latest organization drivers, need, and issues in order to make sure that the organization can continue to move forward safely and securely.

References

1. *Security Planning and Design* (The American Institute of Architects. 2004). 92.

2. J. Gompers (7/1/2004). *Security Hot Spot: Loading Docks.* SecuritySolutions.Com.

3. FEMA. Mitigate Potential Terrorist Attacks Against Buildings. 2003/426-2.6.

4. K. O'Conner. *TDR 2006.* https://engineering.purdue.edu/TDR/Papers/10_Paper.pdf.

5. http://stats.bls.gov/OCO/OCOS159.HTM.

6. *Security Planning and Design* (The American Institute of Architects. 2004).

7. M. Brunelli (6/3/2004). *Data Center Security: 10 things not to do.* SearchCIO.com. Web site: http://searchdatacenter.techtarget.com/news/article/0,289142,sid80_gci1071551_tax305172,00.html.

8. L. Fennelly. *Effective Physical Security*, 3rd edition (Butterworth-Heinemann, 2004). 195.

9. M. Desman. *Building an Information Security Awareness Program* (Auerbach Publications, 2001). 73.

10. http://www.hackingalert.com/hacking-articles/cellphone-hacking.php. Phones fall within the first-generation category.

11. M. Desman. *Building an Information Security Awareness Program* (New York: Auerbach Publications, 2001). 72.

12. NIST Special Publication 800-16. http://csrc.nist.gov/publications/nistpubs/800-50/NIST-SP800-50.pdf.

13. http://bizsecurity.about.com/od/staffingandsecurity/a/SAwarenessP.htm.

14. http://sema.dps.mo.gov/04%20Business%20plan.pdf.

15. http://www.nfpa.org.

16. http://www.fire-extinguisher101.com/.

17. Cramsession.com (2007). *Building a Defense in Depth Toolkit.* Retrieved March 1, 2007. Website: http://www.cramsession.com/articles/get-article.asp?aid=1105.

18. J. Viega and G. McGraw. *Building Secure Software: How to Avoid Security Problems the Right Way.* (Boston, MA: Addison-Wesley. 2002).

19. M. Garcia. *Vulnerability Assessment of Physical Protection Systems* (Boston, MA: Butterworth-Heinemann, 2006). 35.

20. J. Tiller. *The Ethical Hack: A Framework for Business Value Penetration Testing* (New York: Auerbach Publications, 2004).

21. H. Tipton and M. Krause. *Information Security Management Handbook* (New York: Auerbach Publications, 2006). 181.

22. S. Granger. (12/1/2001). *Social Engineering Fundamentals, Part I: Hacker Tactics.* http://www.securityfocus.com/infocus/1527.

23. S. Granger (1/9/2002) *Social Engineering Fundamentals, Part II: Combat Strategies.* http://www.securityfocus.com/infocus/1533.

6

Physical Security Considerations

 **Review Questions**

1. The primary function of a physical protection system is to
   A. determine, direct, and dispatch.
   B. deter, detection, delay, and response.
   C. display, develop, initiate, and apprehend.
   D. evaluate, dispatch, and detain.

2. The single most important goal in planning a site is
   A. protection of life, property, and operations.
   B. threat definition, conflict control, and facility characterization.
   C. risk assessment, threat identification, and incident review.
   D. threat identification, vulnerability appraisal, and access review.

3. The strategy of forming layers of protection around an asset or facility is known as
   A. secured perimeter.
   B. defense in depth.
   C. reinforced barrier deterrent.
   D. reasonable asset protection.

4. The regulation of movement into, from, and within a designated building or area is called
   A. restricted access.
   B. access control.
   C. security access.
   D. security control.

5. The key to a successful physical protection system is the integration of
   A. people, process, and technology.
   B. technology, risk assessment, and human interaction.
   C. protecting, offsetting, and transferring risk.
   D. detection, deterrence, and response.

6. What is the primary objective of controlling entry into a facility or area?

    A. Provide time management controls for all employees.

    B. Ensure that only authorized persons are allowed to enter.

    C. Keep out potential hazards and dangerous material that could be used to commit sabotage.

    D. Identification purposes.

7. The **BEST** way to test your physical security operation is by

    A. observation.

    B. penetration test.

    C. security survey.

    D. social engineering.

8. CCTV technologies make possible three distinct yet complementary functions. The first is visual assessment of an alarm or other event. What are the other two functions of CCTV?

    A. Surveillance and deterrence.

    B. Intrusion detection and response.

    C. Optical and lighting.

    D. Monitoring and inspection.

9. High-tech integrated technologies not only offer greater protection opportunities but also help minimize cost by

    A. reducing electrical costs.

    B. reducing reliance on multiple operators and guard force.

    C. providing government tax incentives for increased physical protection systems.

    D. increasing capital value of property.

10. During a vulnerability assessment tour of a facility the team should be looking to

    A. Determine where all the fire exits are located.

    B. Examine the locations of physical protection system components.

    C. Count the number of employees within the facility.

    D. Determine the structural strength of the perimeter walls.

6

Physical Security Considerations

11. Designing a new building to mitigate threats is simpler and more cost-effective than retrofitting an existing building. An obvious example of this is planning for

    A. limiting the number of entrances to the site that must be monitored, staffed, and protected.

    B. reducing the cost associated with energy needs in providing the physical protection system.

    C. giving employees easy access to the facility without their knowledge of the security components used in monitoring their activities.

    D. blast reinforcement film on all perimeter windows.

12. How must classified material and sensitive information be disposed of?

    A. Torn in half and thrown in the trash can.

    B. It should be shredded.

    C. Removed to a decontamination room.

    D. Marked declassified and thrown in a trash can.

13. Effective security solutions call for the systematic integration of

    A. design, technology, and facility operations and management.

    B. reducing vulnerability by protecting, offsetting, or transferring the risk.

    C. operational readiness, physical protection systems, standard operating processes.

    D. increase awareness, environmental design, and physical security.

14. In which order should the designing of a security plan for a new complex progress?

    A. Outer perimeter, interior, exterior

    B. Interior, outer perimeter, exterior

    C. Interior, exterior, outer perimeter

    D. Exterior, interior, outer perimeter

15. Physical security measures to prevent or minimize theft, unauthorized access, or destruction of property are applied by using

    A. layers.

    B. methods.

    C. varieties.

    D. types.

16. Two functions that employee badges serve are

    A. identify and credit.

    B. payroll and identification.

    C. identification and access.

    D. access and personal information.

17. Which security control is most effective in curtailing and preventing "piggybacking" or "tailgating" as a means of unauthorized access?

    A. Cameras

    B. Turnstiles

    C. Security guards

    D. Mantraps

Appendix A

Answers to
Review Questions

Domain 1: Access Control Systems and Methodologies

1. Which of the following represents the type of access given to a user?

    A. Permissions

    B. Subjects

    C. Objects

    D. Rights

The correct option is **A**

Permissions regulate the type of access a subject is given to an object. Common permissions include: read, write, delete, and execute.

2. The most widely adopted access control method is

    A. Discretionary access control.

    B. Mandatory access control.

    C. Rule-based access control.

    D. Role-based access control.

The correct option is **A**

Discretionary Access Control is the predominant access control technique in use today. Most commodity systems implement some form of DAC.

3. No read up and no write down are properties of

    A. Discretionary access control.

    B. Mandatory access control.

C. Rule-based access control.

D. Role-based access control.

The correct option is **B**

This is the basic functionality of Mandatory Access Control. The fundamental principles of MAC prevent a subject from reading up and writing down between classifications.

4. Access control for proprietary distributable content is best protected using

    A. Discretionary access control.

    B. Digital rights management.

    C. Distributed access control.

    D. Originator controlled.

The correct option is **B**

Among the options given, only DRM provides a means to control proprietary content.

5. When designing a system that uses least privilege, a security architect should focus on

    A. Business requirements.

    B. Organizational mission.

    C. Affected usability.

    D. Disaster recovery.

The correct option is **D**

Disasters are unlikely; therefore, least privilege should not be designed with limitations.

6. Separation of duties is **BEST** implemented using

    A. roles.

    B. permissions.

    C. rights.

    D. workflows.

The correct option is **A**

Separation of duties is best implemented with roles composed of granular rights and permissions.

7. Which of the following is the **BEST** supplemental control for weak separation of duties?

    A. Intrusion detection

    B. Biometrics

    C. Auditing

    D. Training

The correct option is **C**

Accountability becomes more important when separation of duties is weak or unachievable. Auditing is paramount. Consider implementing object-level auditing for individuals with multiple roles. Identify key areas where abuse might occur, and implement multiple methods to monitor for violations.

8. Centralized access control

    A. Is only implemented in network equipment.

    B. Implements authentication, authorization, and accounting.

    C. Is implemented closest to the resources it is designed to protect.

    D. Is designed to consider and accept business partner authentication tokens.

The correct option is **B**

Authentication, authorization, and accounting are important aspects of centralized access control.

9. Firewalls typically employ

    A. Centralized access control.

    B. Decentralized access control.

    C. Federated access control.

    D. Role-based access control.

The correct option is **A**

A firewall with an integrated authentication mechanism is an example of a centralized access control device using the gatekeeper approach. This type of approach is primarily used to control access to resources and services at particular locations within the protected network.

10. A feature that distinguishes decentralized from centralized access control is its

    A. audit logging.

    B. proxy capability.

    C. security kernel.

    D. shared database.

The correct option is **D**

Decentralized access control relies on shared databases.

11. Federated access control

    A. is implemented with RADIUS.

    B. is designed to be mutually exclusive with single sign-on.

    C. is implemented closest to the resources it is designed to protect.

    D. is designed to consider and accept business partner authentication tokens.

The correct option is **D**

Federated Access Control enables a business partner type of single sign-on.

12. Lightweight Directory Access Control is specified in

    A. X.509

    B. X.500

    C. RFC 4510

    D. RFC 4422

The correct option is **C**

RFC 4510 describes a simplified X.500 Directory Access Control protocol.

13. This technique is commonly used to collect audit logs:

    A. Polling

    B. Triggers

    C. Workflows

    D. Aggregation

The correct option is **A**

Polling by a centralized server is commonly used to query other servers to periodically collect events.

14. A word processing application, governed by Discretionary Access Control (DAC), executes in the security context of the

    A. end user.

    B. process itself.

    C. administrator.

    D. system kernel.

The correct option is **A**

In DAC, non-system processes run in the memory space owned by the end user.

15. Peer-to-peer applications are problematic primarily because they

A. are prohibited by policy.

B. may be able to access all the user's files.

C. are a new technology that is difficult to evaluate.

D. may be derived from untrustworthy open source projects.

The correct option is *B*

Vulnerabilities in the design or implementation could enable network penetration.

16. Business rules can **BEST** be enforced within a database through the use of

A. A proxy.

B. redundancy.

C. views.

D. authentication.

The correct option is *C*

Views can be used as a type of access control for designated users or database requests.

17. A well-designed demilitarized zone (DMZ) prevents

A. direct access to the DMZ from the protected network.

B. access to assets within the DMZ to unauthenticated users.

C. insiders on the protected network from conducting attacks.

D. uncontrolled access to the protected network from the DMZ.

The correct option is *D*

The goal of a DMZ is to prevent or control information flow from outside to inside.

18. Dual control is primarily implemented to

A. complement resource-constrained separation of duties.

B. distribute trust using a rigid protocol.

C. support internal workflows.

D. supplement least privilege.

The correct option is *B*

Dual control requires explicit separation of duties and protocols.

19. A well-designed security test

A. requires penetration testing.

B. is documented and repeatable.

    C. relies exclusively on automated tools.

    D. foregoes the need for analysis of the results.

The correct option is **B**

The results of a test that is not documented or repeatable are questionable.

Domain 2: Communications and Network Security

1. Compare the frequency range of a person's voice to the size of the passband in a voice communications channel obtained over the telephone. Which of the following accounts for the difference between the two?

    A. The telephone company uses Gaussian filters to remove frequencies below 300 Hz and above 3300 Hz because the primary information of a voice conversation occurs in the passband.

    B. The telephone company uses low-pass and high-pass filters to remove frequencies below 300 Hz and above 3300 Hz because the primary information of a voice conversation occurs in the passband.

    C. The telephone company uses packet filters to remove frequencies below 500 Hz and above 4400 Hz because the primary information of a voice conversation occurs in the passband.

    D. The telephone company uses low-pass and high-pass filters to remove frequencies below 500 Hz and above 4400 Hz because the primary information of a voice conversation occurs in the passband.

The correct option is **B**

The frequency range of a person's voice typically varies between 0 and 20 kHz, while a telephone channel has a passband of 3 kHz. The telephone company uses low-pass and high-pass filters to remove frequencies below 300 Hz and above 3300 Hz because the primary information of a voice conversation occurs in the passband. This allows more channels to be multiplexed onto a wideband circuit.

2. What is the data rate of a PCM-encoded voice conversation?

    A. 128 kbps

    B. 64 kbps

    C. 256 kbps

    D. 512 kbps

The correct option is **B**

The data rate of PCM-encoded voice conversation is 64 kbps.

3. How many digitized voice channels can be transported on a T1 line?

    A. Up to 48

    B. Up to 12

C. Up to 60

D. Up to 24

The correct option is *D*

There can be up to 24 digitized voice channels on a T1 line.

4. How many T1 lines can be transported on a T3 circuit?
    A. 12
    B. 18
    C. 24
    D. 36

The correct option is *C*

Up to 24 T1 lines can be transported on a T3 circuit.

5. The three advantages accruing from the use of a packet network in comparison to the use of the switched telephone network are a potential lower cost of use, a lower error rate as packet network nodes perform error checking and correction, and
    A. the ability of packet networks to automatically reserve resources.
    B. the greater security of packet networks.
    C. the ability of packet networks to automatically reroute data calls.
    D. packet networks establish a direct link between sender and receiver.

The correct option is *C*

Three advantages associated with the use of packet networks in comparison to the use of the public switched telephone network include a potential lower cost of use, a lower error rate as packet network nodes perform error checking and correction, and the ability of packet networks to automatically reroute data calls.

6. Five VoIP architecture concerns include
    A. the end-to-end delay associated with packets carrying digitized voice, jitter, the method of voice digitization used, the packet loss rate, and security.
    B. the end-to-end delay associated with packets carrying digitized voice, jitter, attenuation, the packet loss rate, and security.
    C. the end-to-end delay associated with packets carrying digitized voice, jitter, the amount of fiber in the network, the packet loss rate, and security.
    D. the end-to-end delay associated with packets carrying digitized voice, jitter, the method of voice digitization used, attenuation, and security.

The correct option is *A*

Five VoIP architecture concerns include the end-to-end delay associated with packets carrying digitized voice, jitter, the method of voice digitization used, the packet loss rate, and security.

7. What is the major difference between encrypting analog and digitized voice conversations?
    A. Analog voice is encrypted by shifting portions of frequency, making the conversation unintelligible.
    B. Digitized voice is generated by the matrix addition of a fixed key to each digitized bit of the voice conversation.
    C. Analog voice is encrypted by shifting portions of amplitude to make the conversation unintelligible.
    D. Digitized voice is encrypted by the modulo-2 addition of a fixed key to each digitized bit of the voice conversation.

The correct option is **A**

Analog voice is encrypted by shifting portions of frequency to make the conversation unintelligible. In comparison, the encryption of digitized voice occurs by the modulo-2 addition of a random key to each digitized bit of the voice conversation.

8. In communications, what is the purpose of authentication?
    A. Establishing a link between parties in a conversation or transaction.
    B. Ensuring that data received has not been altered.
    C. Securing wireless transmission.
    D. Verifying the other party in a conversation or transaction.

The correct option is **D**

Authentication is the process of verifying the other party in a conversation or transaction.

9. What is the purpose of integrity?
    A. Integrity is a process that ensures data received has not been altered.
    B. Integrity is a process that ensures a person stands by his beliefs.
    C. Integrity is a process that ensures that the amount of data sent equals the amount of data received.
    D. Integrity is a process that ensures data received has been encrypted.

The correct option is **A**

Integrity is a process that ensures data received has not been altered.

10. The key purpose of the Session Initiation Protocol (SIP) is to
    A. define the protocol required to establish and tear down communications, including voice and video calls flowing over a packet network.
    B. define the signaling required to establish and tear down communications, including voice and video calls flowing over a PSTN.

    C. define the protocol required to establish and tear down communications, including voice and video calls flowing over a circuit-switched network.

    D. define the signaling required to establish and tear down communications, including voice and video calls flowing over a packet network.

The correct option is **D**

SIP defines the signaling required to establish and tear down communications to include voice and video calls flowing over a packet network.

11. Briefly describe the H.323 protocol.

    A. It represents an umbrella recommendation from the ITU that covers a variety of standards for audio, video, and data communications across circuit-switched networks.

    B. It provides port-based authentication, requiring a wireless device to be authenticated prior to its gaining access to a LAN and its resources.

    C. It defines the protocol required to establish and tear down communications, including voice and video calls flowing over a packet network.

    D. It represents an umbrella recommendation from the ITU that covers a variety of standards for audio, video, and data communications across packet-based networks and, more specifically, IP-based networks.

The correct option is **D**

The H.323 standard can be considered to represent an umbrella recommendation from the International Telecommunications Union (ITU) that covers a variety of standards for audio, video, and data communications across packet-based networks and, more specifically, IP-based networks such as the Internet and corporate Intranets.

12. What is the difference between RTP and RTCP?

    A. RTP defines a standardized port for delivering audio and video over the Internet, while the RTCP provides out-of-band control information for an RTP port.

    B. RTP defines the protocol required to establish and tear down communications, including voice and video calls flowing over a packet network, while the RTCP provides out-of-band control information for an RTP port.

    C. RTP defines a standardized packet format for delivering audio and video over the Internet, while the RTCP provides out-of-band control information for an RTP flow.

    D. RTP defines a standardized port for delivering audio and video over the Internet, while the RTCP defines the protocol required to establish and tear down communications, including voice and video calls flowing over a packet network.

The correct option is **C**

The Real Time Protocol (RTP) defines a standardized packet format for delivering audio and video over the Internet, while the Real Time Control Protocol (RTCP) provides out-of-band control information for an RTP flow.

13. List the components defined by the H.323 standard.

    A. Terminal, gateway, gatekeeper, multipoint control unit (MCU), multipoint controller, multipoint processor, and H.323 proxy

    B. Path, gateway, gatekeeper, multipoint control unit (MCU), multipoint controller, multipoint processor, and H.323 proxy

    C. Terminal, gateway, gatekeeper, multipoint control unit (MCU), multipoint transmitter, multipoint receiver, and H.323 proxy

    D. Protocol, terminal, gatekeeper, multipoint control unit (MCU), multipoint controller, multipoint processor, and H.323 proxy

The correct option is **A**

The H.323 standard defines the following components: Terminal, Gateway, Gatekeeper, MCU (Multipoint Control Unit), Multipoint Controller, Multipoint Processor, and H.323 Proxy.

14. What are some of the major functions performed by a security modem?

    A. Allows remote access to occur from trusted locations, may encrypt data, and may support Caller ID to verify the calling telephone number.

    B. Allows remote access to occur from any location, may encrypt data, and may support Caller ID to verify the calling telephone number.

    C. Allows remote access to occur from a mobile location, may encrypt data, and may support Caller ID to verify the calling telephone number.

    D. Allows remote access to occur from trusted locations, may encrypt data, and may identify the calling telephone number.

The correct option is **A**

A security modem represents a special type of modem that allows remote access to occur from trusted locations, may encrypt data, and may support caller ID to verify the calling telephone number.

15. The major difference between a router and firewall lies in three areas:

    A. The transfer of packets based on routing tables, the degree of packet inspection, and ensuring that the header data is correct.

    B. The transfer of packets based on absolute addresses, the degree of packet inspection, and acting as an intermediate device by hiding the address of clients from users on the Internet.

C. The transfer of packets based on routing tables, the degree of packet inspection, and acting as an intermediate device by hiding the address of clients from users on the Internet.

D. The transfer of packets based on routing tables, the degree of packet inspection, and creating a DMZ behind Internet-facing applications.

The correct option is **C**

The major difference between a router and firewall lies in three areas: the transfer of packets based on routing tables, the degree of packet inspection, and acting as an intermediate device by hiding the address of clients from users on the Internet, a technique referred to as acting as a proxy.

16. What is the purpose of an intrusion detection system (IDS)?

A. To hide the address of clients from users on the Internet.

B. To detect unwanted attempts to access, manipulate, and even disable networking hardware and computers connected to a network.

C. To detect and respond to predefined events.

D. To prevent unauthorized access to controlled areas within a site or a building.

The correct option is **B**

An IDS represents hardware or software that is specifically designed to detect unwanted attempts at accessing, manipulating, and even disabling networking hardware and computers connected to a network. In comparison, an IPS represents an active system that detects and responds to predefined events. Thus, the IPS represents technology built on an IDS system. This means that the ability of the IPS to prevent intrusions from occurring is highly dependent on the underlying IDS.

17. What are the two methods that can be used for wireless LAN communications?

A. Peer-to-peer and infrastructure

B. Peer-to-peer and cloud

C. Cloud and infrastructure

D. Peer-to-peer and remote

The correct option is **A**

Wireless LANs can communicate is two different ways referred to as peer-to-peer and infrastructure.

18. What is the benefit of WPA over WEP for enhancing wireless LAN security?

A. WPA permits the equivalent of wired network privacy and includes the use of TKIP to enhance data encryption.

B. WPA implements a large portion of the IEEE 802.11i and includes the use of TKIP to enhance data encryption.

C. WPA implements a large portion of the IEEE 802.11i and includes the use of IKE to enhance data encryption.

D. WPA implements IEEE 802.11a and g and includes the use of IKE to enhance data encryption.

The correct option is **B**

The original security for wireless LANs, referred to as Wired Equivalent Privacy (WEP), permits the equivalent of wired network privacy and nothing more. WEP was broken by several persons many years ago. WPA represents a security protocol created by the Wi-Fi Alliance to secure wireless transmission and was created in response to the security weakness of WEP. This protocol implements a large portion of the IEEE wireless security standard referred to as 802.11i and WPA included the use of the Temporal Key Integrity Protocol (TKIP) to enhance data encryption.

19. What is the purpose of the IEEE 802.1X standard?

A. To provide port-based authentication.

B. To provide port-based authorization.

C. To detect and respond to predefined events.

D. To secure wireless transmission.

The correct option is **A**

The IEEE 802.1X standard provides port-based authentication, requiring a wireless device to be authenticated prior to its gaining access to a LAN and its resources. Under this standard, the client node is referred to as a supplicant while the authenticator is usually an access point or a wired Ethernet switch.

Domain 3: Cryptography

1. What cryptographic hash function would be the acceptable replacement for MD4?

A. MD5

B. RIPEMD

C. RIPEMD-160

D. SHA-1

The correct option is **C**

This strengthened version of RIPEMD was successfully developed as a collision-resistant replacement for other hash functions including MD4, MD5

(Option *a*), and RIPEMD (Option *b*) [Collisions]. Because collisions were also announced in SHA-1 (Option *d*) [SHA-1 Collisions], RIPEMD-160 would be the acceptable replacement [RIPEMD-160].

2. An IPSec Security Association (SA) is a relationship between two or more entities that describes how they will use security services to communicate. Which values can be used in an SA to provide greater security through confidentiality protection of the data payload?

    A. Use of AES within AH

    B. SHA-1 combined with HMAC

    C. Using ESP

    D. AH and ESP together

The correct option is **C**

Encapsulating Security Protocol (ESP) also provides data origin authentication and data integrity, and also offers confidentiality for the IP payload it protects.

3. Suppose a secure extranet connection is required to allow an application in an external trusted entity's network to securely access server resources in a corporate DMZ. Assuming IPSec is being configured to use ESP in tunnel mode, which of the following is the most accurate?

    A. Encryption of data packets and data origin authentication for the packets sent over the tunnel can both be provided.

    B. ESP must be used in transport mode in order to encrypt both the packets sent as well as encrypt source and destination IP Addresses of the external entity's network and of the corporate DMZ network.

    C. Use of AH is necessary in order to provide data origin authentication for the packets sent over the tunnel.

    D. Source and destination IP Addresses of the external entity's network and of the corporate DMZ network are not encrypted.

The correct option is **A**

ESP optionally provides a means of data origin authentication, and while it can be nested within AH, ESP does not require AH for this (Option *c*) [RFC 2406]. With ESP operating in transport mode (Option *b*), the original IP headers are not encapsulated within the ESP header, and the original IP addresses (source and destination IP addresses of the external entity's network and of the corporate DMZ network) are in fact not encrypted. With ESP operating in tunnel mode, the original IP addresses are actually encrypted (Option *d*).

    [*ESP*: Encapsulating Security Protocol provides data origin authentication and data integrity, and also offers confidentiality for the IP payload it protects.] .

4. What is the **BEST** reason a network device manufacturer might include the RC4 encryption algorithm within an IEEE 802.11 wireless component?

    A. They would like to use AES, but they require compatibility with IEEE 802.11i.

    B. Their product must support the encryption algorithm WPA2 uses.

    C. RC4 is a stream cipher with an improved key-scheduling algorithm that provides stronger protection than other ciphers.

    D. Their release strategy planning includes maintaining some degree of backward compatibility with earlier protocols.

The correct option is **D**

RC4 is widely used, and the manufacturer wants to make its product compatible with WPA or even WEP, which use RC4. This does not mean they do not include AES; in fact, they would likely do so in the case of a new product, because IEEE 802.11i does in fact use AES for encryption (Option *a*). Option *b* is incorrect because WPA2, which is based on IEEE 802.11i, uses AES. Option *c* is incorrect because while RC4 is a stream cipher, it has a weak key-scheduling algorithm and offers less protection than other ciphers such as AES [WPA].

5. What is true about the Diffie–Hellman (DH) key agreement protocol?

    A. The protocol requires initial exchange of a shared secret.

    B. The protocol depends on a secure communication channel for key exchange.

    C. The protocol needs other mechanisms such as digital signatures to provide authentication of the communicating parties.

    D. The protocol is based on a symmetric cryptosystem.

The correct option is **C**

It is true that the original Diffie–Hellman key exchange protocol does not provide authentication of the sender and receiver. Other protocols such as digital signatures or HMAC must be used for this [RFC4650]. The Diffie–Hellman (DH) protocol involves computing a shared secret based on exchange of a public key (Option *a*), and is intended to be performed over insecure channels (Option *b*). DH is based on public-key cryptography because it involves deriving a shared secret based on the sender and receiver each having private keys and sharing public keys, and the property of the discrete logarithm problem, which makes it computationally infeasible to derive the private key from the public key [SCHNEIER].

6. What is the main security service a cryptographic hash function provides, and what is the main security property a cryptographic hash function must exhibit?

    A. Integrity and ease of computation
    B. Integrity and collision resistance
    C. Message authenticity and collision resistance
    D. Integrity and computational infeasibility

The correct option is **B**

Message authentication codes and digital signatures provide message authenticity (Option *c*). While ease of computation is important (Option *a*), cryptographic hash algorithms are build on one-way functions, and their primary function is to produce a unique message digest. Computational infeasibility may be important in general, but collision resistance is the more specific property of hash algorithms, thus excluding Option

    7. What is necessary on the receiving side in order to verify a digital signature?
        A. The message, message digest, and the sender's private key
        B. The message, message digest, and the sender's public key
        C. The message, the MAC, and the sender's public key
        D. The message, the MAC, and the sender's private key

The correct option is **B**

Verifying a digital signature is performed by decrypting the message digest using the sender's public key. Exposing the private key would mean that anyone with the private key could now forge the signature (Option *a*). Message authentication codes (MACs) do not use public key encryption, but produce a hash of the combined message input and a secret key (Options *c* and *d*).

    8. What is a known plaintext attack used against DES to show that encrypting plaintext with one DES key followed by encrypting it with a second DES key is no more secure than using a single DES key?
        A. Meet-in-the-middle attack
        B. Man-in-the-middle attack
        C. Replay attack
        D. Related-key attack

The correct option is **A**

This attack applies to double encryption schemes such as 2DES by encrypting known plaintext using each possible key and comparing results obtained "in the middle" from decrypting the corresponding ciphertext using each possible key. Option *b* is a network-based cryptanalytic attack involving intercepting and forwarding a modified version of a transmission between two parties. Option *c* is also a network-based attack involving capturing and retransmitting a legitimate transmission between two parties. Option *d*, a related-keys attack, is often employed against stream ciphers and involves the relationships between keys that become known or are chosen while observing differences in plaintext and ciphertext when a different key is used.

9. What is among the most important factors in validating the cryptographic key design in a public key cryptosystem?
    A. Ability of a random number generator to introduce entropy during key generation
    B. Preimage resistance
    C. Confidentiality of key exchange protocol
    D. Crypto period

The correct option is *A*

The purpose of randomness in the key or keystream is to make it less likely that cryptanalysts will be able to guess or deduce the key. A random number generator that does not exhibit the property of randomness or entropy in its output will produce weak keys. Option *b* applies to cryptographic hash functions and is known as the "one-way" property of hash functions. Because the question asks about public-key cryptosystems, Option *c* is less valid because public keys can be exchanged without loss of the private key. Option *d* applies more to the operation and management of keys, because the crypto period is the time span during which an actual key can remain valid for use.

10. What factor would be most important in the design of a solution that is required to provide at-rest encryption in order to protect financial data in a restricted-access file sharing server?
    A. Encryption algorithm used
    B. Cryptographic key length
    C. Ability to encrypt the entire storage array or file system versus ability to encrypt individual files
    D. Individual user access and file-level authorization controls

The correct option is *D*

The encryption algorithm, key length, and scope of encryption provided (Options *a*, *b*, and *c*) are generally less important than the access controls that the at-rest encryption solution will require. Storage encryption is typically performed in order to ensure confidentiality, and is tied to an access control mechanism because those individuals or entities who must be able to decrypt the data will need authorized access to do so.

11. A large bank with a more than one million customer base implements PKI to support authentication and encryption for online Internet transactions. What is the best method to validate certificates in a timely manner?

    A. CRL over LDAP

    B. CRLDP over LDAP

    C. OCSP over HTTP

    D. CRLDP over ODBC

The correct option is **C**

Options *a*, *b*, and *d* are CRL-based methods that require significant network traffic between the verifying party and the LDAP or DB server where the CRL is published. It is most significant with a large base of subscribers whose certificates may point to different CRLDP and require pulling many different CRL fragments from the points of publication.

12. A car rental company is planning to implement wireless communication between the cars and rental support centers. Customers will be able to use these centers as concierge services, and rental centers will be able to check the car's status if necessary. PKI certificates will be used to support authentication, non-repudiation, and confidentiality of transactions. Which asymmetric cryptography is a better fit?

    A. RSA 1024

    B. AES 256

    C. RSA 4096

    D. ECC 160

The correct option is **D**

Option *b* refers to a symmetric algorithm that does not support non-repudiation. The algorithms in Options *a* and *c* have significantly longer keys than the algorithm in Option d, which has equivalent strength. For wireless communication, a smaller key length is an important factor.

13. A key management system of a government agency's PKI includes a backup and recovery (BR) module. PKI issues and manages separate certificates for encryption and verification. What is the right BR strategy?

    A. Back up all certificates and private keys

    B. Back up all private keys and verification certificates

    C. Back up decryption keys and all certificates

    D. Back up signing keys and all certificates

The correct option is **C**

Options *a* and *b* assume backing up signing keys, which is wrong. Option *d* assumes signing keys, which is wrong, and does not include decryption keys, which is wrong, too.

14. A company needs to comply with FIPS 140-2 level 3, and decided to use split knowledge for managing storage encryption keys. What is the right method for storing and using the key?

    A. Store the key components on the encrypted media.

    B. Create a master key and store it on external media owned by the first security officer.

    C. Store key components on separate external media owned by a different security officer.

    D. Publish key components on an LDAP server and protect them by officers' asymmetric keys encryption.

The correct option is **C**

Storing key components on the same media (Option *a*) will expose them to one administrator or officer. One officer is in possession of all components (Option *b*) and can recreate the whole key. Storing secret keys on intermediate storage (Option *d*) is not acceptable.

15. An agency is using symmetric AES 128 cryptography for distributing confidential data. Because of its growth and key distribution problems, the agency decided to move to asymmetric cryptography and X.509 certificates. Which of the following is the **BEST** strength asymmetric cryptography to match the strength of the current symmetric cryptography?

    A. RSA 2048

    B. ECC 160

    C. ECC 256

    D. RSA 7680

The correct option is **C**

According to NISTSP800-57, ECC 256 cryptographic strength is equivalent to AES 128. Options *a* and *b* are wrong because they are weaker than AES 128; Option *d* is stronger than required and comes with impractically long keys.

16. One very large company created a business partnership with another, much smaller company. Both companies have their own PKI in-house. Employees need to use secure messaging and secure file transfer for their business transactions. What is the **BEST** strategy to implement this?

    A. The larger company creates a PKI hierarchical branch for the smaller company, so all parties have a common root of trust.

    B. The larger company enrolls all employees of the smaller company and issues their certificates, so all parties have a common root of trust.

  C. Companies should review each other's CP and CPS, cross-certify each other, and let each other access each other's search database.

  D. Employ an external third-party CA and have both company's employees register and use their new certificates for secure transactions.

The correct option is **C**

Options *a*, *b*, and *d* either partially or completely disregard existing PKI infrastructure and require significant expenses for restructuring PKI or hiring an outside service.

17. When applications of cross-certified PKI subscribers validate each other's digitally signed messages, they have to perform the following steps:

  A. The signature is cryptographically correct, and sender's validation certificate and sender's CA cross-certificate are valid.

  B. Validate CRL and ARL.

  C. Validate sender's encryption certificate, ARL, and CRL.

  D. The signature is cryptographically correct, and sender's CA certificate is valid.

The correct option is **A**

Option *b* is incorrect because CRL and ARL just verify revocation status without crypto and validity period validation; Option *c* is incorrect because signature verification requires verification certificate validation rather than encryption; Option *d* is incorrect because verification of signature verification certificate is missing.

18. A company implements three-tier PKI, which will include a root CA, several sub-CAs, and a number of regional issuing CAs under each sub-CA. How should the life span of the CA's certificates be related?

  A. Root CA = 10 years; sub-CA = 5 years; issuing CA = 1 year

  B. Root CA = sub-CA = issuing CAs = 5 years

  C. Root CA = 1 year; sub-CA = 5 years; issuing CA = 10 years

  D. Root CA = 5 years; sub-CA = 10 years; issuing CA = 1 year

The correct option is **A**

In a hierarchical PKI, the upper CA should issue certificates to the subordinate CAs with a longer life span than those subordinates issue certificates to their subordinates. Otherwise, the chain will be expiring before the intermediate CA and entity certificates expire.

19. Management and storage of symmetric data encryption keys most importantly must provide
    A. Integrity, confidentiality, and archiving for the time period from key generation through the life span of the data they protect or the duration of the crypto period, whichever is longer.
    B. Confidentiality for the time period from key generation through the life span of the data they protect or duration of crypto period, whichever is longer.
    C. Integrity, confidentiality, and archiving for the duration of the key's crypto period.
    D. Integrity, confidentiality, non-repudiation and archiving for the time period from key generation through the life span of the data they protect or duration of crypto period, whichever is longer.

The correct option is *A*

 Option *b* is incorrect because without an integrity requirement a key may be tampered with. Option *c* is incorrect because if an encryption key crypto period expires before the encrypted data life span, the key destruction may leave data that is never possible to decrypt. Option *d* is incorrect because non-repudiation is not relevant to symmetric cryptography.

20. Management and storage of public signature verification keys most importantly must provide
    A. Integrity, confidentiality, and archiving for the time period from key generation until no protected data needs to be verified.
    B. Integrity and archiving for the time period from key generation until no protected data needs to be verified.
    C. Integrity, confidentiality and archiving for the time period from key generation through the life span of the data they protect or the duration of crypto period, whichever is longer.
    D. Integrity and confidentiality for the time period from key generation until no protected data needs to be verified.

The correct option is *B*

Options *a*, *c*, and *d* are incorrect because confidentiality is not required for public keys.

Domain 4: Security Architecture Analysis

1. The approach in which policies, procedures, technology, and personnel are considered in the system security development process is called
    A. defense in depth.
    B. requirements analysis.

    C. risk assessment.

    D. attack vectors.

The correct option is *A*

Best security practices should include an architecture that provides defense in depth where layers of technology are designed and implemented to provide data protection. These layers include people, technology, and operations (including processes and procedures). Defense in depth includes

    Protect—preventative controls and mechanisms

    Detect—identify attacks, expect attacks

    React—respond to attacks, recover

2. Software that adds hidden components to a system without end user knowledge is

    A. Virus.

    B. Spyware.

    C. Adware.

    D. Malware.

The correct option is *B*

Spyware is software that adds hidden components to your system on the sly.

3. Risk is assessed by which of the following formulas?

    A. Risk = Vulnerability × Threat × Impact Divided by Countermeasure

    B. Risk = Annual Loss Opportunity ÷ Single Loss Expectancy

    C. Risk = Exposure Facture divided by Asset Value

    D. Risk = Vulnerability × Annual Loss Expectancy

The correct option is *A*

Option *a* is correct the others are mixed-up derivatives of risk management.

4. Requirements definition is a process that should be completed in the following order:

    A. Document, identify, verify, and validate.

    B. Identify, verify, validate, and document.

    C. Characterize, analyze, validate, and verify.

    D. Analyze, verify, validate, and characterize.

The correct option is *B*

The proper order for completing the Requirements Definition phase is OptionDocumentation would not be done first, thus eliminating Option"Characterize" in Options *c* or *d* is not correct.

5. A path by which a malicious actor gains access to a computer or network in order to deliver a malicious payload is a

    A. penetration test.

    B. attack vector.

    C. vulnerability assessment.

    D. risk assessment.

The correct option is **B**

Option *b* is the definition of an attack vector. Risk and vulnerability assessments and penetration testing deal with ways of analyzing and protecting the system.

6. Which of the following is **BEST** as a guide for the development, evaluation, and/or procurement of IT products with security functionality?

    A. ISO/IEC 27001

    B. FIPS 140-2

    C. Common Criteria

    D. SEI-CMM

The correct option is **C**

FIPS 140-2 deals with assessing type 2 encryption, SEI-CMM is the capability maturity model, and ISO/IEC 27001 deals with the overall system security posture based on best practice implementation.

7. Which of the following **BEST** defines evaluation criteria for Protection Profile (PP) and Security Target (ST) and presents evaluation assurance levels rating assurance for the TOE?

    A. Part 3—Security assurance requirements

    B. Part 2—Security functional requirements

    C. Part 1—Introduction and general model

    D. Part 4—History and previous versions

The correct option is **A**

Parts 2 and 1 deal with other security requirements and general CC model and part 4 does not exist.

8. The National Voluntary Laboratory Accreditation Program (NVLAP) must be in full conformance with which of the following standards?

    A. ISO/IEC 27001 and 27002

    B. ISO/IEC 17025 and Guide 58

    C. NIST SP 800-53A

    D. ANSI/ISO/IEC Standard 17024

The correct option is **B**

Option *a* deals with best practice implementation on the system. Option *c* provides IA controls for federal government systems, and Option *d* is the standard for certifications such as the CISSP˚.

9. A software application in combination with an operating system, a workstation, smart card integrated circuit, or cryptographic processor would be considered examples of a

    A. Functional Communications (FCO)

    B. Functional Trusted Path (FTP)

    C. Target of Evaluation (TOE)

    D. Security Target (ST)

The correct option is **C**

Options *a* and *b* refer to families of security functions, and Option *d* refers to the evaluation criteria that TOE (Option *c*) will be assessed by.

10. A security architect requires a device with a moderate level of independently assured security, and a thorough investigation of the TOE and its development without substantial reengineering. It should be evaluated at which CC EAL?

    A. EAL6

    B. EAL5

    C. EAL4

    D. EAL3

The correct option is **D**

Option *d* refers to the criteria for EAL3 evaluation by definition. EAL6 is semiformally verified design and tested, EAL5 is semiformally designed but not verified, and EAL4 is methodically designed, tested, and reviewed.

11. At which Common Criteria EAL would a security architect select a device appropriate for application in extremely high-risk situations or where the high value of the assets justifies the higher costs?

    A. EAL4

    B. EAL5

    C. EAL6

    D. EAL7

The correct option is **D**

Again, Option *d* refers to the criteria for EAL 7 evaluation by definition. EAL6 is semiformally verified design and tested, EAL 5 is semiformally designed but not verified, and EAL 4 is methodically designed, tested, and reviewed. Options *a*, *b*, or *c* would not be appropriate for extremely high-risk situations.

12. A list of Common Criteria–evaluated products can be found on the Internet on the site at the
    - A. NIAP
    - B. CCEVS
    - C. IASE
    - D. CERIS

The correct option is *B*

NIAP is the partnership between NIST and NSA for the evaluation of products, and IASE is the site run by DISA to promote best security practices. CERIS is a consortium run by the University of Notre Dame Computer Science and Information Security department. CCEVS is the site that lists all evaluated products, those in the evaluation process, and those that have been removed or superseded.

13. Which of the following describes the purpose of the Capability Maturity Model?
    - A. Determine business practices to ensure creditability for the company's commitment to quality and excellence.
    - B. Provide assurance through active investigation and evaluation of the IT product in order to determine its security properties.
    - C. Establish a metric to judge in a repeatable way the maturity of an organization's software process as compared to the state of the industry practice.
    - D. Provide an overview of standards related to the Information Security Management family for uniformity and consistency of fundamental terms and definitions.

The correct option is *C*

Options *a* and *d* are from ISO/IEC 27001, and Option *b* is from the Common Criteria.

14. Which one of the following describes the key practices that correspond to a range of maturity levels 1–5?
    - A. Common Criteria
    - B. SEI-CMM
    - C. ISO/IEC 27002
    - D. IATF v3

The correct option is *B*

It is the only option that discusses maturity levels. Options *a, c,* and *d* are standards and processes.

15. Which of the following CMMI levels include quantitative process management and software quality management as the capstone activity?
> A. CMMI Level 5
> B. CMMI Level 4
> C. CMMI Level 3
> D. CMMI Level 2

The correct option is **B**

CMMI Level 4 includes quantitative process management and software quality management as the capstone activity.

16. Where can the general principles of the OSI Reference Model architecture be found that describes the OSI layers and what layering means?
> A. Clause 3
> B. Clause 5
> C. Clause 7
> D. Clause 9

The correct option is **B**

ISO 7498 discusses the OSI model. Within the model are clauses that describe the basis reference model. Clause 7 provides the description of the specific layers, and Clause 9 specifies compliance and consistency with the OSI reference model. Clause 3 does not exist.

17. A privately held toy company processing, storing, or transmitting payment card data must be compliant with which of the following?
> A. Gramm–Leach–Bliley Act (GLBA)
> B. Health Insurance Portability and Accountability Act (HIPAA)
> C. Sarbanes–Oxley Act of 2002
> D. PCI-DSS

The correct option is **D**

Options *a, b* and *c* do not have anything to do with card payment or credit card data.

18. In which phase of the IATF does formal risk assessment begin?
> A. Assess effectiveness
> B. Design system security architecture

    C. Define system security requirements

    D. Discover information protection needs

The correct option is **B**

Although risk assessment occurs during the assess effectiveness process after each stage, a formal risk assessment is conducted at the end of the Design System Security Architecture phase.

19. Which of the following describes a methodical examination of a work product by the author's coworkers to comment, identify, and categorize defects in the work product?

    A. Formal inspection

    B. Structured walkthrough

    C. Critique

    D. Peer review

The correct option is **D**

The overall methodical examination of the work is called the peer review. The others are specific types of peer review.

20. Which of the following is a critical element in the design validation phase?

    A. Develop security test and evaluation plan

    B. Develop protection needs elicitation

    C. Develop the concept of operation

    D. Requirements analysis

The correct option is **A**

Design validation culminates with the development of test and evaluation plans. It requires elicitation, requirements analysis, and concept of operations to be done in the early stages before the design is developed.

Domain 5: Technology-Related Business Continuity Planning (BCP) & Disaster Recovery Planning (DRP)

1. Which phrase **BEST** defines a business continuity/disaster recovery plan?

    A. A set of plans for preventing a disaster.

    B. An approved set of preparations and sufficient procedures for responding to a disaster.

    C. A set of preparations and procedures for responding to a disaster without management approval.

    D. The adequate preparations and procedures for the continuation of all business functions.

The correct option is *D*

The plan needs to be written for the recovery of all business operations and the technology that supports them.

2. Which of the following statements **BEST** describes the extent to which an organization should address business continuity or disaster recovery planning?

    A. Continuity planning is a significant corporate issue and should include all parts or functions of the company.

    B. Continuity planning is a significant technology issue, and the recovery of technology should be its primary focus.

    C. Continuity planning is required only where there is complexity in voice and data communications.

    D. Continuity planning is a significant management issue and should include the primary functions specified by management.

The correct option is *A*

Recovering from an expected disruption to normal operations requires a plan addressing all parts of the organization.

3. Risk analysis is performed to identify

    A. the impacts of a threat to the business operations.

    B. the exposures to loss of the organization.

    C. the impacts of a risk on the company.

    D. the way to eliminate threats.

The correct option is *B*

Risk Analysis identifies the different risk exposures a company has so that mitigation plans can be identified and agreed on, including a Business Continuity Plan.

4. During the risk analysis phase of the planning, which of the following actions could manage threats or mitigate the effects of an event?

    A. Modifying the exercise scenario.

    B. Developing recovery procedures.

    C. Increasing reliance on key individuals.

    D. Implementing procedural controls.

The correct option is *D*

Implementing procedural controls is one method of managing an identified risk.

5. The reason to implement additional controls or safeguards is to

A. deter or remove the risk.

B. remove the risk and eliminate the threat.

C. reduce the impact of the threat.

D. identify the risk and the threat.

The correct option is **C**

You cannot eliminate a threat; you can only reduce the impact a threat can have on your organization.

6. Which of the following statements **BEST** describe business impact analysis?

A. Risk analysis and business impact analysis are two different terms describing the same project effort.

B. A business impact analysis calculates the probability of disruptions to the organization.

C. A business impact analysis is critical to development of a business continuity plan.

D. A business impact analysis establishes the effect of disruptions on the organization.

The correct option is **D**

A business impact analysis identifies what would happen to the organization if a risk occurred, despite whatever controls were in place.

7. The term *disaster recovery* commonly refers to:

A. The recovery of the business operations.

B. The recovery of the technology environment.

C. The recovery of the manufacturing environment.

D. The recovery of the business and technology environments.

The correct option is **B**

Disaster recovery has been commonly used to define the process and procedures used to recover the technology supporting the business operations.

8. Which of the following terms **BEST** describe the effort to determine the consequences of disruptions that could result from a disaster?

A. Business impact analysis

B. Risk analysis

C. Risk assessment

D. Project problem definition

The correct option is **A**

A business impact analysis identifies what would happen to the organization if a risk occurred, despite whatever controls were in place.

9. The **BEST** advantage of using a cold site as a recovery option is that it
   A. is a less expensive recovery option.
   B. can be configured and operationalized for any business function.
   C. is preconfigured for communications and can be customized for business functions.
   D. is the most available option for testing server recovery and communications restorations.

The correct option is *A*

A cold site is less expensive because it is commonly a space to house recovery but without any infrastructure in place. Everything is recovered at the time of disaster.

10. The term RTO means:
    A. Recovery time for operations
    B. Return to order
    C. Resumption time order
    D. Recovery time objective

The correct option is *D*

RTO refers to the time the technology or business operation is planned to be operational following a disruption.

11. If a company wants the fastest time to restore from tape backup, it should perform their backup using the following method:
    A. Full backup
    B. Incremental backup
    C. Partial backup
    D. Differential backup

The correct option is *A*

A full backup copies all of the data each time it is run. When you recover from a full backup, no other backups are needed. In contrast, when an incremental backup is used in recovery, the full backup must be restored first, and then each incremental backup since the last full backup was made of the data must be sequentially restored before the data can be used.

12. One of the advantages of a hot site recovery solution is
    A. Lowered expense
    B. High availability

C. No downtime

D. No maintenance required

The correct option is **B**

A hot site has all the technology in place for recovery, so the time from the point where the disaster is declared and the time when the recovery is complete is much shorter.

13. Which of the following methods is not acceptable for exercising the business continuity plan?

A. Tabletop exercise

B. Call exercise

C. Simulated exercise

D. Halting a production application or function

The correct option is **D**

It is important not to create a disaster in the business when testing for the recovery from one.

14. Which of the following is the primary desired result of any well-planned business continuity exercise?

A. Identification of plan strengths and weaknesses.

B. Satisfaction of management requirements.

C. Compliance with auditor's requirements.

D. Maintenance of shareholder confidence.

The correct option is **A**

The purpose of conducting any exercise is to find out what works and what does not so that any weaknesses can be addressed before an actual event.

15. A business continuity plan should be updated and maintained

A. immediately following an exercise.

B. following a major change in personnel.

C. after installing new software.

D. on an ongoing basis.

The correct option is **D**

The plan needs to be updated regularly in order to maintain its viability to recover the business in a real event.

16. The primary reason to build a business continuity and disaster recovery plan is

A. to continue the business.

B. to restore the data center.

C. to meet regulatory environments.

D. because the customers expect it.

The correct option is **A**

The primary purpose of business continuity and disaster recovery is to make sure the business survives.

17. A company would chose to use synchronous remote replication for its data recovery strategy if

A. it wanted to replace point-in-time backups.

B. it wanted to minimize the amount of time taken to recover.

C. time to recovery and data loss are important to the business.

D. distance limitations existed.

The correct option is **C**

Synchronous remote replication is used to support business operations when the loss incurred by downtime is so substantial that it justifies the expense of implementing this solution.

18. One of the reasons asynchronous replication differs from synchronous replication is

A. because it can impact production.

B. because it can be done over greater distances.

C. because it involves less loss of data.

D. because it improves recovery time.

The correct option is **B**

Because asynchronous replication does not require that the data be written at the remote site at the same time as the production site, network latency is not as critical as it is in synchronous replication. It can therefore occur over greater distances.

19. The purpose of doing a cost–benefit analysis on the different recovery strategies is

A. to make certain the cost of protection does not exceed the cost of the risk it is protecting.

B. to determine the cost of implementing the recovery strategy.

C. to determine that the strategy will be effective.

D. to analyze the cost of the different strategies.

The correct option is **A**

The recovery strategies implemented should match the business being protected.

Domain 6: Physical Security Considerations

1. The primary function of a physical protection system is to

      A. determine, direct, and dispatch.

      B. deter, detection, delay, and response.

      C. display, develop, initiate, and apprehend.

      D. evaluate, dispatch, and detain.

The correct option is **B**

A physical protection system typically has a number of elements that fall into the pattern of deter–detect–delay–respond.

2. The single most important goal in planning a site is

      A. protection of life, property, and operations.

      B. threat definition, conflict control, and facility characterization.

      C. risk assessment, threat identification, and incident review.

      D. threat identification, vulnerability appraisal, and access review.

The correct option is **A**

The single most important goal in planning a site is the protection of life, property, and operations.

3. The strategy of forming layers of protection around an asset or facility is known as

      A. secured perimeter.

      B. defense in depth.

      C. reinforced barrier deterrent.

      D. reasonable asset protection.

The correct option is **B**

With defense in depth, barriers are arranged in layers with the level of security growing progressively higher as one comes closer to the center or the highest protective area.

4. The regulation of movement into, from, and within a designated building or area is called

      A. restricted access.

      B. access control.

      C. security access.

      D. security control.

The correct option is **B**

Access control is the regulation of movement into, from, and within a designated building or area. The primary objective of controlling entry into a facility or area is to ensure that only authorized persons are allowed to enter.

5. The key to a successful physical protection system is the integration of
>   A. people, process, and technology.
>   B. technology, risk assessment, and human interaction.
>   C. protecting, offsetting, and transferring risk.
>   D. detection, deterrence, and response.

The correct option is *A*

The key to a successful physical protection system is the integration of people, process, and technology.

6. What is the primary objective of controlling entry into a facility or area?
>   A. Provide time management controls for all employees.
>   B. Ensure that only authorized persons are allowed to enter.
>   C. Keep out potential hazards and dangerous material that could be used to commit sabotage.
>   D. Identification purposes.

The correct option is *B*

The primary objective of controlling entry into a facility or area is to ensure that only authorized persons are allowed to enter.

7. The **BEST** way to test your physical security operation is by
>   A. observation.
>   B. penetration test.
>   C. security survey.
>   D. social engineering.

The correct option is *B*

A penetration test is the best way to test your security operation.

8. CCTV technologies make possible three distinct yet complementary functions. The first is visual assessment of an alarm or other event. What are the other two functions of CCTV?
>   A. Surveillance and deterrence.
>   B. Intrusion detection and response.
>   C. Optical and lighting.
>   D. Monitoring and inspection.

The correct option is **A**

CCTV provides a highly flexible method of monitoring surveillance and deterrence.

9. High-tech integrated technologies not only offer greater protection opportunities but also help minimize cost by
   A. reducing electrical costs.
   B. reducing reliance on multiple operators and guard force.
   C. providing government tax incentives for increased physical protection systems.
   D. increasing capital value of property.

The correct option is **B**

The correct option isThe ability to leverage integrated technology allows a business to "do more with less", typically enabling a reduction in staffing as a result, which lowers costs.

10. During a vulnerability assessment tour of a facility the team should be looking to
    A. Determine where all the fire exits are located.
    B. Examine the locations of physical protection system components.
    C. Count the number of employees within the facility.
    D. Determine the structural strength of the perimeter walls.

The correct option is **B**

A vulnerability assessment tour of a facility is designed to gather information regarding the general layout of the facility, the location of key assets, information about facility operations and production capabilities, and locations and types of physical protection systems.

11. Designing a new building to mitigate threats is simpler and more cost-effective than retrofitting an existing building. An obvious example of this is planning for
    A. limiting the number of entrances to the site that must be monitored, staffed, and protected.
    B. reducing the cost associated with energy needs in providing the physical protection system.
    C. giving employees easy access to the facility without their knowledge of the security components used in monitoring their activities.
    D. blast reinforcement film on all perimeter windows.

The correct option is **A**

Planning to create a limited number of entrances to a building **PRIOR** to construction is always more cost effective then having to retrofit the building after construction. Limiting the number of entrances that have to be monitored and protected will mitigate multiple threats, whereas option b is only a cost savings measure. Option c does not serve to reduce costs, and may or may not be effective in mitigating threats. Option d would mitigate a specific threat, that of damage due to a close proximity blast, but It would not mitigate a variety of threats.

12. How must classified material and sensitive information be disposed of?

    A. Torn in half and thrown in the trash can.

    B. It should be shredded.

    C. Removed to a decontamination room.

    D. Marked declassified and thrown in a trash can.

The correct option is **B**

There are several methods for proper destruction of information. An organization can contract with a licensed and bonded shredding company, which will come to the site with a mobile shredding truck and dispose of classified material and sensitive information. One can watch the process and verify the destruction, or the documents can be shredded on site, depending on the volume of information that needs to be destroyed. Shredding services can also destroy hard drives and physical components.

13. Effective security solutions call for the systematic integration of

    A. design, technology, and facility operations and management.

    B. reducing vulnerability by protecting, offsetting, or transferring the risk.

    C. operational readiness, physical protection systems, standard operating processes.

    D. increase awareness, environmental design, and physical security.

The correct option is **A**

Effective building security requires careful planning, design, and management of the physical protection system, integrating people, procedures, and equipment; the foundation of all facility security operations.

14. In which order should the designing of a security plan for a new complex progress?

    A. Outer perimeter, interior, exterior

    B. Interior, outer perimeter, exterior

    C. Interior, exterior, outer perimeter

    D. Exterior, interior, outer perimeter

The correct option is **C**

The design process of a security plan for a new facility should begin with the interior, then the exterior, and finally the outer perimeter.

15. Physical security measures to prevent or minimize theft, unauthorized access, or destruction of property are applied by using
   A. layers.
   B. methods.
   C. varieties.
   D. types.

The correct option is **A**

In the concept of defense in depth, barriers are arraigned in layers, with the level of security growing progressively higher as one comes closer to the center or the highest protective area. Defending an asset with a multiple posture can reduce the likelihood of a successful attack; if one layer of defense fails, another layer of defense will hopefully prevent the attack, and so on. This design requires the attacker to circumvent multiple defensive mechanisms to gain access to the targeted asset.

16. Two functions that employee badges serve are
   A. identify and credit.
   B. payroll and identification.
   C. identification and access.
   D. access and personal information.

The correct option is **C**

Employee badges are an excellent method of control for both identification and access.

17. Which security control is most effective in curtailing and preventing "piggybacking" or "tailgating" as a means of unauthorized access?
   A. Cameras
   B. Turnstiles
   C. Security guards
   D. Mantraps

The correct option is **D**

A common and frustrating loophole in an otherwise secure access control system can be the ability of an unauthorized person to follow through a checkpoint behind an authorized person; this is called "piggybacking" or "tailgating." The traditional solution is an airlock-style arrangement called a mantrap.

Index

I

Index

I

Index

I

Index

I

Index

Index